The International Library of Sociology

THEORY OF
COLLECTIVE BEHAVIOUR

Founded by KARL MANNHEIM

The International Library of Sociology

THE SOCIOLOGY OF BEHAVIOUR AND PSYCHOLOGY
In 18 Volumes

I	The Development of Conscience	*Stephenson*
II	Disaster	*Wolfenstein*
III	The Framework of Human Behaviour	*Blackburn*
IV	Frustration and Aggression	*Dollard et al*
V	Handbook of Social Psychology	*Young*
VI	Human Behaviour and Social Processes	*Rose*
VII	The Human Group	*Homans*
VIII	Learning Through Group Experience	*Ottaway*
IX	Personality and Problems of Adjustment	*Young*
X	Psychology and the Social Pattern	*Blackburn*
XI	The Sane Society	*Fromm*
XII	Sigmund Freud - An Introduction	*Hollitscher*
XIII	Social Learning and Imitation	*Miller et al*
XIV	Society and Nature	*Kelsen*
XV	Solitude and Privacy	*Halmos*
XVI	The Study of Groups	*Klein*
XVII	Theory of Collective Behaviour	*Smelser*
XVIII	Towards a Measure of Man	*Halmos*

THEORY OF
COLLECTIVE BEHAVIOUR

by
NEIL J. SMELSER

First published in 1962 by
Routledge

Reprinted in 1998 by
Routledge
2 Park Square, Milton Park, Abingdon, Oxon, OX14 4RN
or
270 Madison Avenue, New York, NY 10016

First issued in paperback 2010

© 1962 Neil J. Smelser

All rights reserved. No part of this book may be reprinted or reproduced or utilized in any form or by any electronic, mechanical, or other means, now known or hereafter invented, including photocopying and recording, or in any information storage or retrieval system, without permission in writing from the publishers.

The publishers have made every effort to contact authors/copyright holders of the works reprinted in *The International Library of Sociology*. This has not been possible in every case, however, and we would welcome correspondence from those individuals/companies we have been unable to trace.

British Library Cataloguing in Publication Data
A CIP catalogue record for this book
is available from the British Library

Theory of Collective Behaviour
ISBN 978-0-415-17799-3 (hbk)
ISBN 978-0-415-60738-4 (pbk)
The Sociology of Behaviour and Psychology: 18 Volumes
ISBN 978-0-415-17834-1
The International Library of Sociology: 274 Volumes
ISBN 978-0-415-17838-9

Publisher's Note
The publisher has gone to great lengths to ensure the quality of this reprint but points out that some imperfections in the original may be apparent

FOR HELEN

who has taught me
that both conflict and stability
are essential for growth

CONTENTS

	PREFACE	page ix
I	ANALYZING COLLECTIVE BEHAVIOR	1
II	BASIC CONCEPTS: THE COMPONENTS OF SOCIAL ACTION	23
III	STRUCTURAL STRAIN UNDERLYING COLLECTIVE BEHAVIOR	47
IV	THE NATURE OF COLLECTIVE BEHAVIOR	67
V	THE CREATION OF GENERALIZED BELIEFS	79
VI	THE PANIC	131
VII	THE CRAZE	170
VIII	THE HOSTILE OUTBURST	222
IX	THE NORM-ORIENTED MOVEMENT	270
X	THE VALUE-ORIENTED MOVEMENT	313
XI	CONCLUDING REMARKS	382
	BIBLIOGRAPHY	388
	INDEX	428

TABLES

1	Levels of Specificity of Values	page 38
2	Levels of Specificity of Norms	39
3	Levels of Specificity of Mobilization	41
4	Levels of Specificity of Situational Facilities	43
5	Levels of Specificity of the Components of Social Action	44
6	Levels of Specificity of the Components of Social Action	50
7	Foci of Strain for the Components of Action	65
8	Levels of Specificity of Situational Facilities; Foci of Strain for the Components of Action	92–93
9	The Distribution of Incidents over the Eight-Week Life-Cycle of the Swastika Epidemic	259
10	Jewish and Non-Jewish Targets According to Time of Incident	259
11	Types of Organizations Involved in Norm-Oriented Movements	276

FIGURES

1	Value-Added in the Creation of Hysterical Beliefs	93
2	Value-Added in the Creation of Wish-Fulfillment Beliefs	95
3	Value-Added in the Creation of Hostile Beliefs	102
4	Value-Added in the Creation of Norm-Oriented Beliefs	113
5	Value-Added in the Creation of Value-Oriented Beliefs	124
6	Value-Added Process for Panic	134
7	Records of Telephone Calls to Mattoon, Illinois, Police, August–October, 1944	157

PREFACE

Gordon W. Allport of Harvard first introduced me to the study of collective behavior. When I was a freshman in 1948, his introductory course in Social Relations set my mind working. Later, when I was a graduate student in 1955, he reactivated and deepened these workings. During the years after studying with him his words have returned to haunt me. So far as I know, he is unaware of my intellectual debt; I should like to record it now.

In working on my doctoral dissertation[1] I delved into the collective protests of the British working classes in the late eighteenth and early nineteenth centuries. In trying to decipher the content and timing of these eruptions, I came to be deeply impressed with the explanatory potential of a distinctively sociological approach. The idea of attempting a theoretical synthesis of collective behavior came to me in the summer of 1958. Since then I have worked continually on this volume.

Between 1959 and 1961 I was a member of the Center for Integrated Social Science Theory at the University of California, Berkeley. Known familiarly as the Theory Center, this group consisted of six or seven scholars from various departments. Each member was relieved of academic duties for one semester in each of his two years in the Center. At meetings we discussed theoretical issues arising from the work of one or more members. We had no office for meetings; we wandered peripatetically from one member's study to another. We had no secretary, no research assistants, no stationery with letterhead. Simple as it was, the Theory Center had unparalleled value. With the advance of academic specialization in the mid-twentieth century, few things can be more salutary than to have scholars take temporary leave from the confines of their research projects to discover the minds of others in an unhurried atmosphere.

In the Theory Center we read one another's work with great care and did not fear to fire broadsides when the occasion demanded. My work on collective behavior received and gained immensely from merciless criticism. I should like to thank the following men, members whose tenure overlapped with mine: Frederick E. Balderston (Business Administration); Jack Block (Psychology); Julian

[1] Published in 1959 as *Social Change in the Industrial Revolution* by Routledge and Kegan Paul and the University of Chicago Press.

Preface

Feldman (Business Administration); Erving Goffman (Sociology); Austin C. Hoggatt (Business Administration); Leo Lowenthal (Sociology and Speech); Richard S. Lazarus (Psychology); William Petersen (Sociology); Theodore R. Sarbin (Psychology); and David M. Schneider (Anthropology, now at the University of Chicago). In addition, I profited from informal explorations with Professors Lazarus, Petersen, Block, and Sarbin.

Herbert Blumer of the University of California, Berkeley, deserves a special word. His own pioneering work on collective behavior is well known; reading it stimulated me to new lines of thought. More directly, he gave me his extraordinarily painstaking criticism of an earlier draft of Chapters I–IV. I would hesitate to estimate the time and energy he devoted to writing long, detailed memoranda and to conversing with me after I had responded to these memoranda. It is only candid to report that on points of principle we were frequently at loggerheads. But his thoroughness and his keen ability to locate weaknesses in reasoning led me to revise the early chapters extensively. Several other colleagues at Berkeley offered helpful comments on the manuscript—Reinhard Bendix, William Kornhauser, Seymour M. Lipset, and Hanan C. Selvin.

The influence of Talcott Parsons of Harvard on my intellectual development—influence which can be seen in these pages—began more than a decade ago. Even though we now stand at opposite ends of the nation, we have managed to continue periodic discussions during the past several years. His comments were especially helpful for Chapters II and III. Finally, Guy E. Swanson of the University of Michigan and Jan Hajda of Johns Hopkins wrote critical comments on the manuscript. Responsibility for all the ideas in this book is of course mine; but in the formation of these ideas all these men had an important place.

Before the final draft was prepared, Marvin B. Scott, my research assistant, combed the manuscript with unusual care. His criticisms added substance and above all clarity to the presentation. He also prepared the index and assisted with proof-reading. The inevitable but important chores of typing and writing for permissions were handled capably by Mrs. Carroll H. Harrington, Mrs. Helen Larue, Mrs. Pauline Ward, Miss Aura Cuevas, and by the staff of the Institute of Industrial Relations at Berkeley.

My wife, Helen, who is a sort of Frenchwoman at heart, conducted much independent research for me on the social and political turbulences that have appeared in France since the middle of the eighteenth century. Later she read almost the whole manuscript in draft. She is the most intelligent layman I know; she has a

Preface

disquieting ability to detect a loose argument, a subtle inconsistency, an unintended meaning, and a meaningless expression. Even more, she has a way of phrasing criticisms that makes it very difficult to rest before doing something about them. These qualities, infuriating at the moment, proved in the end to be a source of value for the manuscript, humility for the author, and charm for her husband.

NEIL SMELSER

*Berkeley, California,
February, 1962*

CHAPTER I

ANALYZING COLLECTIVE BEHAVIOR

INTRODUCTION

The Problem. In all civilizations men have thrown themselves into episodes of dramatic behavior, such as the craze, the riot, and the revolution. Often we react emotionally to these episodes. We stand, for instance, amused by the foibles of the craze, aghast at the cruelties of the riot, and inspired by the fervor of the revolution.

The nature of these episodes has long excited the curiosity of speculative thinkers. In recent times this curiosity has evolved into a loosely defined field of sociology and social psychology known as collective behavior. Even though many thinkers in this field attempt to be objective, they frequently describe collective episodes as if they were the work of mysterious forces. Crowds, for instance, are "fickle," "irrational," or "spontaneous," and their behavior is "unanticipated" or "surprising." For all their graphic quality, such terms are unsatisfactory. They imply that collective behavior flows from sources beyond empirical explanation. The language of the field, in short, shrouds its very subject in indeterminacy.

Our aim in this study is to reduce this residue of indeterminacy which lingers in explanations of collective outbursts. Although wild rumors, crazes, panics, riots, and revolutions are surprising, they occur with regularity. They cluster in time; they cluster in certain cultural areas; they occur with greater frequency among certain social groupings—the unemployed, the recent migrant, the adolescent. This skewing in time and in social space invites explanation: Why do collective episodes occur *where* they do, *when* they do, and *in the ways* they do?

In this introductory chapter we shall merely raise some questions posed by such an inquiry. What is collective behavior? What are its types? How is it to be distinguished from related behavior such as ceremonials? What are the determinants of collective behavior? Are the determinants related to one another in any systematic way? What can a sociological approach contribute to an understanding of collective behavior? Having raised the questions, we shall devote the remainder of the volume to searching for their answers.

Analyzing Collective Behavior

An Initial Clarification of Terminology. Our inquiry will cover the following types of events: (1) the panic response; (2) the craze response, including the fashion-cycle, the fad, the financial boom, the bandwagon, and the religious revival; (3) the hostile outburst; (4) the norm-oriented movement, including the social reform movement; (5) the value-oriented movement, including the political and religious revolution, the formation of sects, the nationalist movement, etc. The justification for choosing these particular types will become clear only after detailed theoretical arguments in Chapters II–V. At present we must ask: By what name shall we label these kinds of behavior?

As might be expected of a field which is underdeveloped scientifically, even its name is not standardized. Perhaps the most common general term is "collective behavior."[1] Different analysts who use this term, however, do not refer to a uniform, clearly defined class of phenomena.[2] In addition, Brown, a psychologist, has used the term "mass phenomena" to refer to roughly the same range of data which is encompassed by "collective behavior."[3] Other terms used to characterize this body of data are "mass behavior" and "collective dynamics." Both are found wanting. Because of the ideological polemics which "mass" has accumulated, this term is misleading.[4] A more neutral, but equally misleading, term has been coined recently by Lang and Lang—"collective dynamics."[5] Although collective behavior bears an intimate relation to social change,[6] it seems wise to reserve the term "dynamics" for a field more inclusive than collective behavior alone. Words like "outburst," "movement,"

---

[1] This term was given wide currency in the 1920's and 1930's by Robert E. Park at the University of Chicago. Those who follow in his general tradition have continued to use the term. Cf. H. Blumer, "Collective Behavior," in J. B. Gittler (ed.), *Review of Sociology: Analysis of a Decade* (New York, 1957), p. 127. Also R. H. Turner and L. M. Killian, *Collective Behavior* (Englewood Cliffs, N.J., 1957).

[2] Blumer, for instance, excluded R. T. LaPiere from his general survey of collective behavior—even though his major work is entitled *Collective Behavior* (New York, 1938)—on the grounds that LaPiere's treatment "represents a markedly different conception of the field." "Collective Behavior," in Gittler (ed.), *op. cit.*, p. 127.

[3] R. Brown, "Mass Phenomena," in G. Lindzey (ed.), *Handbook of Social Psychology* (Cambridge, Mass., 1954), Vol. II, pp. 833–876.

[4] Representative classics in the literature on mass society are J. Ortega y Gasset, *The Revolt of the Masses* (New York, 1932); E. Lederer, *State of the Masses* (New York, 1940); K. Mannheim, *Man and Society in an Age of Reconstruction* (London, 1940), and H. Arendt, *The Origins of Totalitarianism* (New York, 1958). For a recent attempt to eliminate some of the ambiguities of this literature and to synthesize the material theoretically, cf. W. Kornhauser, *The Politics of Mass Society* (Glencoe, Ill., 1959).

[5] K. Lang and G. E. Lang, *Collective Dynamics* (New York, 1961).

[6] Below, pp. 72–73.

and "seizure" also indicate the attempts to delineate the scope of the field. In the face of this plethora of words and meanings, we must decide early on conventions of usage.

The most accurate term for encompassing the relevant classes of events would be an awkward one: "collective outbursts and collective movements." "Collective outbursts" would refer to panics, crazes, and hostile outbursts, which frequently (but not always) are explosive; "collective movements" would refer to collective efforts to modify norms and values, which frequently (but not always) develop over longer periods. For brevity we shall condense this awkward term into the conventional one, "collective behavior." The reader should remember that this chosen term is being used as a specific kind of shorthand, and that it has its own shortcomings. In certain respects the term is too general. "In its broad sense [it] refers to the behavior of two or more individuals who are acting together, or collectively. . . . To conceive of collective behavior in this way would be to make it embrace all of group life."[1] The business firm, for instance, which responds to heightened demand by increasing its production, is engaging in "collective behavior" (because persons are acting in concert), but we would not classify this response as an instance of collective behavior. Despite such shortcomings, we shall continue to use the term, partly from a desire to avoid neologisms, and partly from a lack of suitable alternatives.

An Advantage of Studying Collective Behavior. Under conditions of stable interaction, many social elements—myths, ideologies, the potential for violence, etc.—are either controlled or taken for granted and hence are not readily observable. During episodes of collective behavior, these elements come into the open; we can observe them "in the raw." Collective behavior, then, like deviance, affords a peculiar kind of laboratory in which we are able to study directly certain components of behavior which usually lie dormant.

The State of Research on Collective Behavior. In almost every division of sociology, a general analysis must be prefaced by a commentary on the sad state of available research. Collective behavior is no exception:

> The paucity of investigation is seen easily by surveying the literature on forms of collective behavior. Examples of "forms" are: panic, fad, fashion, rumor, social epidemic, rushes, reform movements, religious movements, etc. If one examines the literature concerned with each of these forms, he can see easily both the crude descriptive level of knowledge and the relative lack of theory in this area. Most investigation is in the nature of reporting:

[1] Blumer, "Collective Behavior," in Gittler (ed.), *op. cit.*, p. 128.

either by persons fortuitously on the scene or by historians who describe, after their occurrence, certain collective behavior events.[1]

The indictment is sound for several reasons. First, because collective behavior is viewed as spontaneous and fickle, few points are available to begin a coherent analysis. Points of reference melt before one's eyes as a crowd develops into a mob, a mob into a panicky flight, and a flight into a seizure of scapegoating. Second, because many forms of collective behavior excite strong emotional reactions, they resist objective analysis.[2] Third, episodes of collective behavior, with few exceptions,[3] cannot be controlled experimentally. Even direct observation is difficult, since the time and place of collective eruptions cannot be predicted exactly. Finally, it is virtually impossible to "sample" the occurrence of collective episodes from a large population of events. The analyst of collective behavior must often settle for inaccurate and overdramatized accounts. For such reasons the field of collective behavior "has not been charted effectively."[4]

THE NATURE OF COLLECTIVE BEHAVIOR

Having chosen a term—collective behavior—we must now ask: To what kinds of phenomena does this term refer? This question breaks into two parts: (1) By what criterion or criteria do we exclude

---

[1] A. Strauss, "Research in Collective Behavior: Neglect and Need," *American Sociological Review*, Vol. 12 (1947), p. 352.

[2] For a sketch of the varying emotional attitudes toward the crowd in Western history, cf. G. W. Allport, "The Historical Background of Modern Social Psychology," in G. Lindzey (ed.), *Handbook of Social Psychology*, Vol. I, pp. 29–31.

[3] For example, G. W. Allport and L. Postman, *The Psychology of Rumor* (New York, 1947); L. Festinger, A. Pepitone, and T. Newcomb, "Some Consequences of De-Individuation in a Group," *Journal of Abnormal and Social Psychology*, Vol. 47 (1952), pp. 382–389; J. R. P. French, "The Disruption and Cohesion of Groups," *Journal of Abnormal and Social Psychology*, Vol. 36 (1941), pp. 361–377; French, "Organized and Unorganized Groups under Fear and Frustration," in *Authority and Frustration*, University of Iowa Studies: Studies in Child Welfare, Vol. XX (Iowa City, 1944), pp. 231–308; D. Grosser, N. Polansky, and R. Lippitt, "A Laboratory Study of Behavioral Contagion," *Human Relations*, Vol. 4 (1951), pp. 115–142; N. C. Meier, G. H. Mennenga, and H. Z. Stoltz, "An Experimental Approach to the Study of Mob Behavior," *Journal of Abnormal and Social Psychology*, Vol. 36 (1941), pp. 506–524; A. Mintz, "Non-Adaptive Group Behavior," *Journal of Abnormal and Social Psychology*, Vol. 46 (1951), pp. 150–159; A. Pepitone, J. C. Diggory, and W. H. Wallace, "Some Reactions to a Hypothetical Disaster," *Journal of Abnormal and Social Psychology*, Vol. 51 (1955), pp. 706–708; N. Polansky, R. Lippitt, and F. Redl, "An Investigation of Behavioral Contagion in Groups," *Human Relations*, Vol. 3 (1950), pp. 319–348; G. E. Swanson, "A Preliminary Laboratory Study of the Acting Crowd," *American Sociological Review*, Vol. 18 (1953), pp. 180–185.

[4] H. Blumer, "Collective Behavior," in Gittler (ed.), *op. cit.*, p. 127.

Analyzing Collective Behavior

and include instances as appropriate objects of study? Do we include the rumor? the riot? the mass migration? Are conventionalized festivals, demonstrations, and heroes' welcomes a part of the field? How do we classify semi-institutionalized forms like the lynching mob? In posing such questions we attempt to establish *outside limits* for the field. (2) What are the major types of collective behavior? By what principles do we derive these types? What, for instance, is the relation among the boom, the bandwagon, and the fad? Should we consider them separately, or are they special cases of a larger type? These questions demand that we establish the *internal divisions* of the field. Although the demarcation of lines is not an end in itself, and is not so intriguing as the inquiry into causes and consequences of collective behavior, it is of prime importance. Before we can pose questions of explanation, we must be aware of the character of the phenomena we wish to explain.

In delimiting and classifying the field of collective behavior, we may proceed with varying degrees of formality. By a common-sense method we would simply list those kinds of behavior that traditional conceptions of "collective" or "mass" denote and connote. The boundaries of such a common-sense classification are usually vague. By an analytic method, at the other extreme, we would specify in advance the formal rules for exclusion and inclusion and classify instances according to these rules. For purposes of scientific analysis it is always desirable to move as close as possible to the analytic extreme. Let us consider two recent attempts to demarcate the field of collective behavior, then indicate the lines along which we shall move in this volume.

Roger Brown has advanced a number of dimensions for classifying collectivities: (*a*) size—it is important to know whether a group will fit into a room, a hall, or whether it is too large to congregate; (*b*) the frequency of congregation; (*c*) the frequency of polarization of group attention; (*d*) the degree of permanence of the psychological identification of the members. Using such dimensions, Brown distinguishes collective behavior (which he calls mass phenomena) from other forms of behavior.[1] Brown, then, circumscribes the field largely on the basis of *physical, temporal,* and *psychological* criteria. Within the field, Brown first mentions crowds, which he divides into two types —mobs and audiences. Mobs are subdivided into the aggressive (lynching, rioting, terrorizing), the escape (panic), the acquisitive (looting) and the expressive. Audiences may be intentional (recreational, information-seeking) or casual. Here the criterion for

---

[1] Brown, "Mass Phenomena," in Lindzey (ed.), *op. cit.*, pp. 833-840.

sub-division seems to lie in the different *goals* of collectivities. In addition, Brown mentions certain kinds of mass contagion, mass polarization (audiences of radio or television broadcasts), the social movement, and finally "the mass as an unorganized collectivity."[1] The last four types receive little systematic treatment. Nevertheless, on the whole Brown has attempted to set off a distinctive field according to explicit criteria.

Herbert Blumer, in his attempt to circumscribe the field of collective behavior, contrasts it with (*a*) small group behavior, and (*b*) established or culturally defined behavior. In the first instance, then, the criteria for inclusion are *physical* (size), and *cultural* (relation of the behavior to rules, definitions, or norms).

The contrast between collective behavior and small group behavior reveals several criteria other than physical size alone. The first criterion is *psychological*. In the small group, the individual has a "sense of personal control or a . . . sense of command over the scene of operation." In collective behavior, or large group behavior in general, the group conveys a sense of "transcending power" which "serves to support, reinforce, influence, inhibit, or suppress the individual participant in his activity." The second criterion refers to the mode of *communication* and *interaction*. In small groups these processes "[rest] on personal confrontation and [follow] the pattern of a dialogue, with controlled interpretation by each participant of the action of the other." In large groups new forms of communication and interaction arise, such as the uncontrolled circular reaction of the psychological crowd, or the one-way communication of the mass media. The third criterion refers to the way in which participants are *mobilized for action*. "A small group uses confined, simple, and direct machinery." In larger groups new devices such as "incitation, agitation, gaining attention, the development of morale, the manipulation of discontent, the overcoming of apathy and resistance, the fashioning of group images, and the development of strategy" gain precedence.[2]

With respect to the *cultural* basis of contrast, Blumer states simply that "most large group activity and structure in human societies is an expression of [established rules, definitions or norms]." Collective behavior, by contrast, "lies outside this area of cultural prescription." It is behavior which develops new forms of interaction to meet "undefined or unstructured situations."[3] In order to decide whether an instance of behavior qualifies as collective behavior, then,

[1] *Ibid.*, pp. 840–873.
[2] Blumer, "Collective Behavior," in Gittler (ed.), *op. cit.*, pp. 129–130.
[3] *Ibid.*, p. 130.

Analyzing Collective Behavior

an analyst would apply these criteria. Although Blumer has not explored many of the logical relations among the criteria, he gives a number of relatively explicit bases for defining a relevant range of phenomena for study.

Within the field of collective behavior, Blumer notices two major foci of interest: (*a*) the study of "elementary forms of collective behavior," such as the excited mob, or the war hysteria; (*b*) the study of the ways in which these elementary forms develop into set and organized behavior.[1] The defining characteristic of elementary collective behavior is restlessness which is communicated by a process of circular reaction, "wherein the response of one individual reproduces the stimulation that has come from another individual and in being reflected back to this individual reinforces the stimulation."[2] Several mechanisms characterize the development of such a state of unrest—milling, collective excitement, and social contagion.

Blumer identifies four basic elementary collective groupings: the acting crowd, the expressive crowd, the mass, and the public. The first two differ in that the acting crowd (a mob, for instance) has a goal or objective, whereas the expressive crowd (the dancing crowd of a religious sect, for instance) expends its impulses and feelings in "mere expressive actions." The mass differs from both in that it is more heterogeneous, more anonymous, less organized, and less intimately engaged in interaction; mass behavior is, in fact, a convergence of a large number of individual selections made on the basis of "vague impulses and feelings." The public, finally, is a group of people who focus on some issue, disagree as to how to meet the issue, engage in discussion, and move toward a decision. The public differs from the crowd in that disagreement (rather than unanimity) and rational consideration (rather than spectacular suggestion) occupy a prominent place in the development of a public.[3] Even this brief summary shows that a number of disparate criteria—character of the group objective, nature of interaction, degree of organization, degree of rationality—are used to distinguish among these elementary groupings. On the whole, the relations among these criteria remain unclear in Blumer's work.

Blumer illustrates the transition from elementary collective behavior to organized behavior in discussing the social movement. During its development, the social movement "acquires organization and form, a body of customs and traditions, established leadership, an

---

[1] H. Blumer, "Collective Behavior," in A. M. Lee (ed.), *New Outline of the Principles of Sociology* (New York, 1951), p. 168.
[2] *Ibid.*, p. 170. For a critique of this and related concepts, below, pp. 154–156.
[3] *Ibid.*, pp. 178–191.

Analyzing Collective Behavior

enduring division of labor, social rules and social values—in short, a culture, a social organization, and a new scheme of life."[1] The major types of social movements are the general (for instance, the women's movement), the specific (for instance, a movement to reduce the tax on alcoholic beverages), and the expressive (for instance, a fashion movement). The difference between the general and the specific lies in the breadth of objectives involved in the attempt to reconstitute the social order. The expressive movement differs from both in that it "[does] not seek to change the institutions of the social order or its objective character."[2] Later we shall modify some of these distinctions. At present we wish merely to illustrate some of the existing principles of division in the field of collective behavior.

In this study we shall attempt a delineation of the field of collective behavior which differs considerably from those just reviewed. As a first approximation, we define collective behavior as *mobilization on the basis of a belief which redefines social action*. Blumer's definition of a social movement—"[a] collective [enterprise] to establish a new order of life"[3]—implies such a redefinition. Our conception, however, extends to elementary forms of collective behavior as well, such as the panic and the hostile outburst. Such a definition calls for clarification of such terms as "redefines" and "social action." We shall take up these tasks in Chapters II and IV.

Collective behavior must be qualified by two further defining characteristics. As the definition indicates, collective behavior is guided by various kinds of beliefs—assessments of the situation, wishes, and expectations. These beliefs differ, however, from those which guide many other types of behavior. They involve a belief in the existence of extraordinary forces—threats, conspiracies, etc.—which are at work in the universe. They also involve an assessment of the extraordinary consequences which will follow if the collective attempt to reconstitute social action is successful. The beliefs on which collective behavior is based (we shall call them *generalized beliefs*) are thus akin to magical beliefs. We shall define and explore the nature of these generalized beliefs in Chapters IV and V.

The third defining characteristic of collective behavior is similar to Blumer's contrast between collective and culturally prescribed behavior. Collective behavior, as we shall study it, is not institutionalized behavior. According to the degree to which it becomes institutionalized, it loses its distinctive character. It is behavior

[1] *Ibid.*, p. 199.
[2] *Ibid.*, p. 214.
[3] *Ibid.*, p. 199.

"formed or forged to meet undefined or unstructured situations."[1] In Chapter III, when we discuss structural strain, we shall attempt to outline how situations may lose their definition or their structure.

Such are the criteria by which we shall establish the outside limits of collective behavior. What, next, are the internal divisions of the field? Or, to put the question in terms of the definition, what are the components of social action that people attempt to reconstitute? In Chapter II we shall outline the basic components of social action. These components are: (*a*) values, or general sources of legitimacy; (*b*) norms, or regulatory standards for interaction; (*c*) mobilization of individual motivation for organized action in roles and collectivities; (*d*) situational facilities, or information, skills, tools, and obstacles in the pursuit of concrete goals. We shall derive our typology of collective behavior from these components. The basic principle is that each type of collective behavior is oriented toward a distinct component of social action. Thus (*a*) the value-oriented movement is collective action mobilized in the name of a generalized belief envisioning a reconstitution of values; (*b*) the norm-oriented movement is action mobilized in the name of a generalized belief envisioning a reconstitution of norms; (*c*) the hostile outburst is action mobilized on the basis of a generalized belief assigning responsibility for an undesirable state of affairs to some agent; (*d*) the craze and the panic are forms of behavior based on a generalized redefinition of situational facilities. In Chapter V we shall derive these types in full detail, and show their complex relations to one another.

Our definition and classification of the field differs from many previous versions in the following ways:

(1) The defining characteristics of collective behavior are not *physical* or *temporal*. Both Brown and Blumer use such criteria to set collective behavior off from other fields. On a more commonsense level, explanations of types of collective behavior are frequently guided by a sort of pictorial model. The word "panic," for instance, connotes the surge toward a theater exit when a fire breaks out, the crowd leaping from a sinking liner, the rout of troops on a battlefield, or the pile-up of traffic under threat of invasion. Although all these instances are *bona fide* cases of panic—and cases we must explain—we hope to go beyond these particular pictures.

We shall characterize panic in terms of the kind of belief which gives rise to flight. What aspects of the environment does this belief define as threatening? What is the nature of the threat? How does it

---

[1] Blumer, "Collective Behavior," in Gittler (ed.), *op. cit.*, p. 130.

operate? What are the perceived opportunities for escape? By asking such questions we shall be able to discuss, within the same conceptual framework, the dramatic incidents just mentioned as well as other forms of panic, such as the run on the bank, the speculative bust, and the desertion of a political candidate by his former supporters. All these forms possess similarities which transcend the particular physical setting in which they occur. Both small and large groups may become involved in a panic; the affected individuals may be in physical proximity or they may be dispersed; the actual panic may be completed in a matter of minutes, or it may take days or weeks to run its course.

To move beyond the particular physical and temporal setting of an episode is not to deny that physical and temporal factors affect collective behavior. The number and nature of exits, for instance, are important in determining whether a panic will materialize.[1] The sheer physical presence of other individuals makes the spread of rumor easier than if these individuals were forced to rely on modes of communication other than face-to-face interaction. The seriousness of reactions to disasters depends on the character of the catastrophe and the extent to which it destroys communications in the community.[2] These kinds of factors affect the timing, form, and extent of episodes of collective behavior. They are not, however, essential defining characteristics.

(2) The defining characteristics of collective behavior do not lie in any particular kind of *communication* or *interaction*. In Blumer's analysis concepts such as circular reaction, agitation, and incitation occupy a prominent place among the defining criteria of collective behavior. Other investigators have been even more specific in associating a type of communication with a type of collective behavior. Allport and Postman, for instance, have advanced a "law of social

---

[1] Below, p. 136–139.

[2] Carr, for instance, distinguishes among disasters on the basis of "(1) the character of the precipitating event, or catastrophe, and (2) the scope of the resulting cultural collapse. On this basis there are at least four types of disaster: (*a*) an *instantaneous-diffused type* such as the Halifax explosion which was over before anyone could do anything about it and wreaked its effects on the entire community; (*b*) an *instantaneous-focalized type* such as the Bath, Michigan, schoolhouse explosion of May, 1927, which killed or injured more than a hundred children and teachers in the village school, yet left the rest of the community physically intact; (*c*) a *progressive-diffused type* such as the Galveston hurricane of 1900 or the Mississippi floods of 1927, one of which lasted several hours and the other several weeks, and both of which affected whole communities; and (*d*) a *progressive-focalized type* such as the Cherry Mine fire or the wreck of the 'Titanic'." L. J. Carr, "Disaster and the Sequence-Pattern Concept of Social Change," *American Journal of Sociology*, Vol. 38 (1932–33), pp. 209–210. These different types of physical events have different implications for the form, timing, and seriousness of collective reactions.

Analyzing Collective Behavior

psychology" that "no riot ever occurs without rumors to incite, accompany and intensify the violence."[1] Others emphasize the interaction between the demagogue and his followers as crucial in the mobilization of collective action.

Our position on the relation between communication and interaction and the definition of collective behavior is as follows. As mentioned, the central defining characteristic of an episode of collective behavior is a belief envisioning the reconstitution of some component of social action. In order for behavior to become collective, of course, *some* mode of communicating this belief and *some* mode of bringing people to action must be available. No *single* form of communication or interaction, however, constitutes a defining characteristic of collective behavior. The belief may be communicated by gesture or sign, by face-to-face rumor, by the mass media, or by the buildup of an ideology. The form of communication may be a dialogue, an uncontrolled circular reaction, or a one-way communication. Similarly, the mode of mobilizing people for action is variable. An episode may be triggered by an actor who simply "sets an example" and who does not intend to lead the group into action; it may be initiated by a leader who has arisen spontaneously; or it may be "rigged" by a subversive organization which has moved in to capitalize on unrest. As in the case of the physical and temporal setting, the form of communication and interaction is very important in determining the timing, content, and extent of an episode of collective behavior. We shall consider their importance when we discuss the determinants of collective behavior. No particular type of communication or interaction, however, is a central defining characteristic of collective behavior.

(3) The defining characteristics of collective behavior are not *psychological*. The definition we have presented does not, by itself, involve any assumptions that the persons involved in an episode are irrational, that they lose their critical faculties, that they experience psychological regression, that they revert to some animal state, or whatever. The definition asks simply: During an episode of collective behavior, what happens to the components of social action? Any episode is to be described, in the first instance, in these terms.

We shall rely, however, on many psychological assumptions as we attempt to build determinate explanations of collective behavior. We shall assume, for instance, that perceived structural strain at the social level excites feelings of anxiety, fantasy, hostility, etc. We shall assume that people in certain kinds of social situations are more

[1] *The Psychology of Rumor*, pp. 193–196. Italicized in original.

receptive to suggestion than in others. We shall assume that individuals who hold a generalized belief respond more readily to leaders than those who do not. We shall refer to some psychological research to justify these assumptions. The reader should remember, however, that the *definition* of collective behavior is social, not psychological. In Chapters II–IV we shall attempt to say, in great detail, what we mean by the social level.

THE DETERMINANTS OF COLLECTIVE BEHAVIOR

The Organization of Determinants. So far we have attempted to establish outside limits and internal divisions for the field of collective behavior. Explanation raises a different set of issues: What determines whether an episode of collective behavior *of any sort* will occur? What determines whether one type *rather than another* will occur? Many of the existing answers to these questions are unsatisfactory scientifically. As Strauss has observed, many students of panic have failed to distinguish any specific and determinate set of conditions for the occurrence of panic above and beyond a simple list of possibly operative factors:

> The conditions of panic can be roughly classified into three categories: physiological, psychological, and sociological. Physiological factors are fatigue, under-nourishment, lack of sleep, toxic conditions of the body, and the like. Psychological factors are surprise, uncertainty, anxiety, feeling of isolation, consciousness or powerlessness before the inevitable expectancy of danger. Sociological factors include lack of group solidarity, crowd conditions, lack of regimental leadership in the group. An effective statement of the mechanics of panic causation cannot be made by merely listing the factors entering into that causation when these factors are as diverse in character as they seem to be. A student seeking a genuinely effective statement of panic causation would attempt to find what is essential to these diverse conditions and tie these essential conditions into a dynamic statement of the development and outbreak of the panic occurrence.[1]

These determinants must be organized. Each must be assigned to its appropriate contributory role in the genesis of panic. A mere list will not suffice.

Even more, we must organize the determinants precisely enough so that panic is the *only* possible outcome; we must rule out related outbursts. To quote Strauss again,

> ... the conditions of panic which have been noted, because they are not genuine causative conditions, are conditions for more than panic. That is

---

[1] A. Strauss, "The Literature on Panic," *Journal of Abnormal and Social Psychology*, Vol. 39 (1944), p. 324.

to say, the conditions for panic which are listed in the literature are not conditions for panic specifically; they are also conditions for other kinds of closely related phenomena.... The thin line between the occurrence of panic and the occurrence of... other types of nonrational behavior is attested to by the rapid shifts from one of these forms to another in battle—from collective exaltation to panic, from panic to collective fascination, and the like.

In a genuine sense, then, the causes for panic are not specific causes. They are also conditions for other types of collective behavior.[1]

We need, then, a *unique* combination of determinants which yields a *unique* outcome, panic. We must systematize the determinants, and note the changes in the combinations of determinants which produce different outcomes.

Similar problems of explanation arise in connection with social movements. In examining the anthropological literature on messianic movements, Barber concludes that there exists a "positive correlation of the messianic movement and deprivation [of various types]."[2] The first difficulty in attempting to assess this correlation—assuming that it exists—is that "deprivation" is a vague term. A statement of the kinds of deprivation is necessary. In addition, there are many types of messianic movements; some are associated with a positive sense of regeneration of society, others with passive resignation. Finally, as Barber notes, messianism is not the only reponse to deprivation; among "several alternative responses" he mentions "armed rebellion and physical violence" and "depopulation." Thus, in spite of Barber's correlation, there remain several kinds and levels of deprivation and several responses besides messianism. This is what we mean when we say that there exists a residue of indeterminacy in the connections between determinants and outcomes in the field of collective behavior. To reduce this residue is one of the major tasks of this study.

The Logic of Value-added. The scheme we shall use to organize the determinants of collective behavior resembles the conception of "value-added" in the field of economics.[3] An example of the use of this term is the conversion of iron ore into finished automobiles by a number of stages of processing. Relevant stages would be mining, smelting, tempering, shaping, and combining the steel with other parts, painting, delivering to retailer, and selling. Each stage "adds

[1] *Ibid*, pp. 324–325.
[2] B. Barber, "Acculturation and Messianic Movements," *American Sociological Review*, Vol. 6 (1941), pp. 663–669.
[3] For an elementary account of the nature of value-added, cf. P. A. Samuelson, *Economics: An Introductory Analysis* (fourth edition) (New York, 1958), pp. 187–188.

its value" to the final cost of the finished product. The key element in this example is that the earlier stages must combine *according to a certain pattern* before the next stage can contribute its particular value to the finished product. It is impossible to paint iron ore and hope that the painting will thereby contribute to the desired final product, an automobile. Painting, in order to be effective as a "determinant" in shaping the product, has to "wait" for the completion of the earlier processes. Every stage in the value-added process, therefore, is a necessary condition for the appropriate and effective addition of value in the next stage. The sufficient condition for final production, moreover, is the combination of *every* necessary condition, according to a definite pattern.

As the value-added process moves forward, it narrows progressively the range of possibilities of what the final product might become. Iron ore, for instance, is a very general resource, and can be converted into thousands of different kinds of products. After it is smelted and tempered into a certain quality of steel, the range of possible products into which it might enter is narrowed considerably. After it is pressed into automotive parts, it can be used for very few products other than automobiles. If we were to view the finished automobile as the "outcome" to be explained and the stages of value-added as "determinants," we would say that as each new stage adds its value, the "explanation" of the outcome becomes increasingly determinate or specific. As the value-added process develops, it allows for progressively fewer outcomes other than the one we wish to explain.

This logic of value-added can be applied to episodes of collective behavior, such as the panic or the reform movement. Many determinants, or necessary conditions, must be present for any kind of collective episode to occur. These determinants must combine, however, in a definite pattern. Furthermore, as they combine, the determination of the type of episode in question becomes increasingly specific, and alternative behaviors are ruled out as possibilities.[1]

---

[1] This methodological position has been developed by Meyer and Conrad with reference to explanation in economic history. "If [the economic historian's] intention is indeed to know about and explain specific, historical events, then it is our contention that he must follow the rules of scientific explanation. To explain an event one must be able to estimate a range of admissible possibilities, given a set of initial conditions and a causal or statistical law. . . . Like other economists and other scientists, it must be [the economic historians'] aim to narrow the range of possibilities, to explain why the particular realized development did in fact occur." J. R. Meyer and A. H. Conrad, "Economic Theory, Statistical Inference, and Economic History," *Journal of Economic History*, Vol. 17 (1957), p. 532. For a mathematical formalization of such logic, cf. M. E. Turner and C. D. Stevens, "The Regression Analysis of Causal Paths," *Biometrics*, Vol. 15 (1959), pp. 236–258. Our approach also seems consistent with two general remarks made

Analyzing Collective Behavior

The following are the important determinants of collective behavior:

(1) *Structural conduciveness.* We read that financial booms and panics, fashion cycles and crazes do not plague simple, traditional societies; we also read that America as a civilization is prone to such seizures, and that, within America, places like Los Angeles and Detroit are especially productive of bizarre movements.[1] Are such statements true, and if so, why? Do certain structural characteristics, more than others, permit or encourage episodes of collective behavior? To illustrate this condition of structural conduciveness with respect to the occurrence of financial panic, let us assume that property is closely tied to kinship and can be transferred only to first-born sons at the time of the death of the father. Panic under such conditions is ruled out, simply because the holders of property do not have sufficient maneuverability to dispose of their assets upon short notice. Under conditions of economic pressure, certain responses are possible—for instance, a movement to change the customs of property transfer—but not panic. The structure of the social situation does not permit it. At the other extreme lies the money market, in which assets can be exchanged freely and rapidly.

Conduciveness is, at most, permissive of a given type of collective behavior. A money market, for instance, even though its structure is conducive to panic, may function for long periods without producing a crisis. Within the scope of a conducive structure, many possible kinds of behavior other than panic remain. We must narrow the range of possibilities. In order to do so, we add several more determinants. In this way we make more probable the occurrence of that event (e.g., panic) which is merely possible within the scope of conduciveness.

(2) *Structural strain.* Financial panics develop when loss or annihilation threatens the holders of assets.[2] Real or anticipated economic deprivation, in fact, occupies an important place in the initiation of hostile outbursts, reform movements, revolutionary

---

recently by Morris Ginsberg on the problem of social change. The search for social causation (or explanation), he maintains, involves a search for "an assemblage of factors which, in interaction with each other, undergo a change of character and are continued into the effect." Such processes of social causation, moreover, often have a "cumulative and frequently circular character." "Social Change," *British Journal of Sociology*, Vol. 9 (1958), pp. 220–223; see also R. M. MacIver, *Social Causation* (Boston, 1942), pp. 251–265. Thus it may be possible to treat many types of social change other than collective behavior by this value-added conception. Cf. N. J. Smelser, *Social Change in the Industrial Revolution* (Chicago, 1959), pp. 60–62.

[1] Below, pp. 175–188, and 345.
[2] Below, pp. 149–150.

movements, and new sects as well.[1] Extreme religious movements seem to cluster among deprived groups such as colonial populations, the disinherited members of a society, and recent migrants.[2] Race riots follow population invasions and new kinds of cultural contacts.[3] In Chapter III we shall outline the major types of structural strain—ambiguities, deprivations, conflicts, and discrepancies—and show how these give rise to episodes of collective behavior.

In explaining any case of collective behavior (a panic, for instance), we must consider the structural strain (the threat of economic deprivation, for instance) as falling *within the scope established by the condition of conduciveness*. Otherwise this strain cannot be a determinant of panic, however important it may be as a determinant of some other kind of behavior. It is the *combination* of conduciveness and strain, not the separate existence of either, that radically reduces the range of possibilities of behavior other than panic.

(3) Growth and spread of a generalized belief. Before collective action can be taken to reconstitute the situation brought on by structural strain, this situation must be made meaningful to the potential actors. This meaning is supplied in a generalized belief, which identifies the source of strain, attributes certain characteristics to this source, and specifies certain responses to the strain as possible or appropriate. In Chapter V we shall examine the anatomy of several beliefs—hysterical, wish-fulfillment, hostile, norm-oriented, and value-oriented. The growth and spread of such beliefs are one of the necessary conditions for the occurrence of an episode of collective behavior.

Many generalized beliefs, however, enjoy a long existence without ever becoming determinants of a collective outburst. Throughout history, for instance, men have harbored superstitions about creatures from other planets, their powers, and their potential danger. Only on very specific occasions, however, do such beliefs rise to significance as determinants of panicky flights. These occasions arise when the generalized beliefs combine with the other necessary conditions of panic.

(4) Precipitating factors. Conduciveness, strain, and a generalized belief—even when combined—do not by themselves produce an episode of collective behavior in a specific time and place. In the case of panic, for instance, these general determinants establish a predisposition to flight, but it is usually a specific event which sets the flight in motion. Under conditions of racial tension, it is nearly always a dramatic event which precipitates the outburst of violence —a clash between two persons of different race, a Negro family

[1] Below, pp. 54–59, 245–246, 287–288 and 339–340.
[2] Below, pp. 324–330.   [3] Below, pp. 241–245.

Analyzing Collective Behavior

moving into a white neighborhood, or a Negro being promoted to a traditionally white job.[1] These events may confirm or justify the fears or hatreds in a generalized belief; they may initiate or exaggerate a condition of strain; or they may redefine sharply the conditions of conduciveness. In any case, these precipitating factors give the generalized beliefs concrete, immediate substance. In this way they provide a concrete setting toward which collective action can be directed.

Again, a precipitating factor by itself is not necessarily a determinant of anything in particular. It must occur in the context of the other determinants. A fistfight, for instance, will not touch off a race riot unless it occurs in the midst of—or is interpreted in the light of—a general situation established by conduciveness, strain, and a generalized belief.

(5) Mobilization of participants for action. Once the determinants just reviewed have been established, the only necessary condition that remains is to bring the affected group into action. This point marks the onset of panic, the outbreak of hostility, or the beginning of agitation for reform or revolution. In this process of mobilization the behavior of leaders is extremely important.

(6) The operation of social control. In certain respects this final determinant arches over all the others. Stated in the simplest way, the study of social control is the study of those counter-determinants which prevent, interrupt, deflect, or inhibit the accumulation of the determinants just reviewed. For purposes of analysis it is convenient to divide social controls into two broad types: (*a*) Those social controls which minimize conduciveness and strain. In a broad sense these controls *prevent* the occurrence of an episode of collective behavior, because they attack very nonspecific determinants. (*b*) Those social controls which are mobilized only *after* a collective episode has begun to materialize. These determine how fast, how far, and in what directions the episode will develop. To assess the effectiveness of the second kind of controls, we shall ask how the appropriate agencies of control—the police, the courts, the press, the religious authorities, the community leaders, etc.—behave in the face of a potential or actual outburst of collective behavior. Do they adopt a rigid, uncompromising attitude? Do they vacillate? Do they themselves take sides in the disturbance? In later chapters we shall examine how these responses of the agencies of social control affect the development of the different kinds of collective behavior.

By studying the different combinations of these six determinants,

[1] Below, pp. 249–250.

Analyzing Collective Behavior

we hope to provide the best possible answer to the explanatory questions posed at the beginning of this section: What determines whether an episode of collective behavior *of any sort* will occur? What determines whether one type *rather than another* will occur? By utilizing these analytically distinct determinants, moreover, we shall be better equipped to untangle those complex empirical situations (e.g., wars, depressions) in which many different types of collective behavior unfold simultaneously.[1]

Value-added and Natural History. According to the logic of the value-added approach, any event or situation, in order to become a determinant of a collective episode, must operate within the limits established by other determinants. At first glance this approach is very similar to the widespread "natural history" approach to collective behavior. In its simplest form, this approach involves the claim that there exist certain empirical uniformities of sequence in the unfolding of an episode of collective behavior. A classic model of the stages of a social movement is the sequence developed by Dawson and Gettys—the sequence beginning with a "preliminary stage of social unrest," passing through a "popular stage of collective excitement" and a "stage of formal organization," and finally reaching a kind of terminal point of "institutionalization." The entire sequence introduces some new institutional form—a sect, a law, a new kind of family structure, or a political reform.[2] A comparable model for revolutions is Crane Brinton's suggestive sequence involving first economic and political weakness of the old regime in the midst of general prosperity; disaffection of specific groups, especially the intellectuals; transfer of power; rule of the moderates; accession of the extremists and the reign of terror and virtue; and finally, a period of relaxation of some of the revolution's excesses, institutionalization of some elements of its program, and a return to many of society's old ways.[3] Many investigators, following the pioneer work of Prince,

---

[1] For an account of the parade of outbursts during the early part of World War I in England, cf. W. Trotter, *Instincts of the Herd in Peace and War* (London, 1922), pp. 140–141. For other characterizations of the clustering of collective behavior, cf. L. Whiteman and S. L. Lewis, *Glory Roads: The Psychological State of California* (New York, 1936), pp. 4–5; K. G. J. C. Knowles, " 'Strike-Proneness' and its Determinants," *American Journal of Sociology*, Vol. 60 (1954–55), p. 213; J. W. Thompson, "The Aftermath of the Black Death and the Aftermath of the Great War," *American Journal of Sociology*, Vol. 32 (1920–21), p. 565. At the level of social movements, "it is rare for a mass movement to be wholly of one character. Usually it displays some facets of other types of movement, and sometimes it is two or three movements in one." E. Hoffer, *The True Believer* (New York, 1958), p. 26.

[2] C. A. Dawson and W. E. Gettys, *An Introduction to Sociology* (New York, 1929), pp. 787–803.

[3] *The Anatomy of Revolution* (New York, 1958). See also P. A. Sorokin, *The*

have used the logic of natural sequence to account for the events during and after disasters.[1] Dahlke has suggested a typical sequence of events leading to a race riot.[2] Recently Meyersohn and Katz have attempted to outline the natural history of the adoption of fads[3]. In most of these accounts it is not stated whether the temporally prior stages are necessary conditions for the later stages.

To appreciate the difference between the value-added and the natural history approaches, let us return to the analogy of the production of an automobile. In one respect the stages of value-added can be described as a natural history. The ore is smelted before the steel is shaped; the steel is shaped before the paint is applied, and so on. It is possible, however, that the paint itself has been *manufactured* prior to the shaping of the steel. This circumstance complicates the simple account of a natural history. Now we must consider the paint to have been in existence—dormant, as it were, as a determinant—*before* the preceding determinant. The paint can be activated as a determinant, however, only after the steel has been shaped and readied for painting. In the value-added process, then, we must distinguish between the *occurrence* or *existence* of an event or situation, and the *activation* of this event or situation as a determinant. The value-added logic implies a temporal sequence of activation of determinants, but any or all of these determinants may have existed for an indefinite period before activation.

The same logic governs the explanation of an episode of collective behavior. A simple natural history approach to panic would involve an account of one event or situation (for example, the closing off of exits) followed by a second (the growth of fear), followed by a third (a shout or loud noise), followed by yet another (someone starting to run), and so on. Under the value-added approach, these events or situations would become activated as determinants in a certain temporal order, but any of them might have been in existence already. The fear of entrapment, for instance, is a near-universal fear which has endured through the ages. It is activated as a determinant of

---

Sociology of Revolution (Philadelphia, 1925); L. P. Edwards, *The Natural History of Revolution* (Chicago, 1927); R. D. Hopper, "The Revolutionary Process: A Frame of Reference for the Study of Revolutionary Movements," *Social Forces*, Vol. 28 (1950), pp. 270–279.

[1] S. H. Prince, *Catastrophe and Social Change* (New York, 1920); for more recent use of the concept, cf. W. H. Form and S. Nosow, with G. P. Stone and C. M. Westie, *Community in Disaster* (New York, 1958), and Carr, "Disaster and the Sequence-Pattern Concept of Social Change," *op. cit.*

[2] H. O. Dahlke, "Race and Minority Riots—A Study in the Typology of Violence," *Social Forces*, Vol. 30 (1951–52), pp. 419–425.

[3] R. Meyersohn and E. Katz, "Notes on a Natural History of Fads," *American Journal of Sociology*, Vol. 62 (1956–57), pp. 594–601.

panic, however, only after conditions of conduciveness and strain (danger) have been established. Even precipitating factors need not occur at a specific moment in time. A loud explosion may have occurred some time in the past without causing any particular alarm. Once certain determinants of panic have accumulated, however, this explosion may be remembered and reinterpreted (i.e., activated as a determinant) in the light of the new situation. The logic of value-added, in short, does posit a definite sequence for the activation of determinants but does not posit a definite sequence for the empirical establishment of events and situations.

Finally, certain *single* empirical events or situations may be significant as *several* determinants of collective behavior. A severe financial crisis, for instance, may create widespread economic deprivation (structural strain) and at the same time may touch off one or more outbursts (precipitating factor). A long-standing religious cleavage, such as that between Protestants and Catholics, may be frustrating for each group (structural strain); the same cleavage may harbor hostile sentiments within each group toward the other (generalized beliefs). Under the appropriate conditions these latent determinants may be activated to contribute to a collective outburst. We must always distinguish clearly, therefore, between the empirical occurrence or existence of an event or situation, and its significance as one or more determinants in the value-added process.

Psychological Variables and the Determination of Collective Behavior. Our outline of determinants departs radically from the social psychological tradition of the analysis of crowds and other collective behavior—the tradition of Tarde, Le Bon, Ross, Freud, Martin, F. A. Allport, MacDougall and others. These men and their followers have based their explanations primarily on psychological variables, whether of the "superficial" types such as imitation, sympathy, contagion, and suggestion or the "deeper" types such as projection, regression, and transfer of libidinal ties.

Although recognizing the importance of such psychological variables in crowd behavior,[1] we must introduce determinants at the social level for an adequate explanation of collective behavior. With psychological variables alone we cannot discriminate between the occasions on which these variables will manifest themselves and the occasions on which they will lie dormant. Let us illustrate this point with reference to fashion. Nystrom, in attempting to explain some of the vagaries of fashion behavior, has claimed that

---

[1] These variables have been questioned on psychological grounds. Cf. Brown's criticism of terms like "circular reaction," "rapport," "contagion," and "social facilitation." "Mass Phenomena," in Lindzey (ed.), *op. cit.*, p. 843.

Analyzing Collective Behavior

... The specific motive or factors for fashion interest and fashion changes, in addition to the physical reasons for change such as occur at the end of each season, are the boredom and fatigue with current fashion, curiosity, desire to be different, or self-assertion, rebellion against convention, companionship and imitation....[1]

To this primarily psychological explanation Bell responds:

This is no doubt true enough as far as it goes; we have here a sufficient catalogue of human motives, but obviously it leaves a great deal unexplained. Why, for instance, should these human motives have expired among men and yet persisted among women at the beginning of the nineteenth century, and why should they have been absent in China until our own times? We may here have an accurate account of states of mind, but we do not have the reasons which produce them, the motor of fashion itself. We can only conclude that human nature is itself subject to fashion.[2]

Like the episodes of collective behavior itself psychological variables, such as suggestion, projection, displacement and fetishism, are products in part of social determinants. In using the sociological approach, we shall be asking: Under what social conditions do these psychological variables come into play as parts of collective behavior?[3]

PLAN OF THE VOLUME

Two main theses underlie the argument of this volume: (*a*) Collective behavior can be classified and analyzed under the same conceptual framework as all social behavior. (*b*) The forms of collective behavior constitute a series ranging from the simple to the complex. The more complex forms, moreover, include *as components* the elements found in the simpler forms, but not vice-versa.

To implement these propositions, we shall first outline, in Chapter II, the basic components of social action. Although abstract and distant from the concrete details of collective behavior, this chapter must come first in the volume, since it constitutes the foundation on which we shall build a definition of collective behavior, a classification of types of collective behavior, a classification of types of structural strain, and a discussion of the operation of social controls.

Chapters III and IV also are general. In Chapter III we shall classify and discuss the many foci of structural strain which are important in the genesis of collective behavior. In Chapter IV we shall define collective behavior in a way which distinguishes it from other types of behavior.

[1] Quoted in Q. Bell, *On Human Finery* (London, 1947), p. 50.
[2] *Ibid.* For similar remarks on the use of psychoanalytic variables as explanatory concepts, cf. p. 52.
[3] Below, pp. 152–153.

Analyzing Collective Behavior

After establishing this theoretical groundwork, we shall turn in Chapter V to the analysis of beliefs on the basis of which action is mobilized for collective behavior. We shall arrange these beliefs in a series from the simple to the complex. From this typology of beliefs we shall derive the major types of collective behavior.

In the chapters which follow—Chapters VI through X—we shall analyze each type of collective behavior in detail: the panic, the craze, the hostile outburst, the norm-oriented movement, and the value-oriented movement. We shall recapitulate each in terms of the six basic determinants of the value-added scheme: structural conduciveness, structural strain, growth of a generalized belief, precipitating factors, mobilization for action, and social control. In Chapter XI we shall set forth some concluding remarks.

CHAPTER II

BASIC CONCEPTS:
THE COMPONENTS OF SOCIAL ACTION

INTRODUCTION

Collective behavior is analyzable by the same categories as conventional behavior. The two differ, to be sure. At one hypothetical extreme, collective behavior involves a collective redefinition of an unstructured situation; at the other extreme, conventional behavior is the working-out of established expectations. In spite of this difference, the two have an essential similarity. Both face exigencies imposed by social life. In many cases, for example, both must be legitimized by values; both involve an assessment of the situation in which they occur, and so on. Because of these common characteristics it is possible to use the same theoretical framework to analyze both conventional and collective behavior.

Given this position, it is important to assemble a number of categories to describe the components of action at the social level. This is our task in this chapter. The result will be a kind of "map" or "flow chart" of paths along which social action moves. In the chapters which follow we shall investigate what happens to these components of action when established ways of acting fail in the face of unstructured situations. One major set of reactions to this failure constitutes the major types of collective behavior. Such behavior is an attempt to reconstruct a disturbed social order, or at least a part of it.

In discussing the principal components of action, we shall rely on the accumulated sociological thought in Europe and America during the last century or so. In a more direct sense, we shall refer most to the work of Talcott Parsons, Edward Shils, R. F. Bales, and their associates.[1] In this study we shall not attempt any direct application of this body of thought. Rather we shall borrow generously from its logic and substance.[2]

[1] T. Parsons and E. A. Shils (eds.), *Toward a General Theory of Action* (Cambridge, Mass., 1951); Parsons, *The Social System* (Glencoe, Ill., 1951); Parsons, R. F. Bales, and Shils, *Working Papers in the Theory of Action* (Glencoe, Ill., 1953); Parsons, Bales, *et al., Family, Socialization and Interaction Process* (Glencoe, Ill., 1955); Parsons and N. J. Smelser, *Economy and Society* (London and Glencoe, Ill., 1956).

[2] In certain respects the theory to be developed in this volume marks an

Basic Concepts: The Components of Social Action

THE COMPONENTS OF SOCIAL ACTION

Parsons and Shils have defined action in the following way:

[The theory of action] conceives of [the behavior of living organisms] as oriented to the attainment of ends in situations, by means of the normatively regulated expenditure of energy. There are four points to be noted in this conceptualization of behavior: (1) Behavior is oriented to the attainment of ends or goals or other anticipated states of affairs. (2) It takes place in situations. (3) It is normatively regulated. (4) It involves expenditure of energy or effort in "motivation" (which may be more or less organized independently of its involvement in action).[1]

According to this formulation, a number of things must be known before we can describe action: the valued ends, the environmental setting, the norms governing the behavior, and the ways in which motivation is mobilized.

Parsons and Shils define action from the actor's point of view. It is possible, however, to apply the same definition to a system of action composed of the *interaction* of two or more actors. At this level of abstraction we no longer treat individual personalities as the principal systems; we move to the analysis of the *relations* among actors. At this, the social-system level, the units of analysis are not need-dispositions or motives, but roles (e.g., husband, church-member, citizen) and organizations (e.g., political parties, business firms, families).[2] A social system may be constituted by an informal, even casual interaction among two persons, or it may be constituted by a large-scale, enduring institutional complex such as a church, a market system, or even a society. In this chapter we shall deal with action at the social system level.

The four basic components of social action, then, are: (1) the generalized ends, or *values*, which provide the broadest guides to purposive social behavior; (2) the regulatory rules governing the pursuit of these goals, rules which are to be found in *norms*; (3) the mobilization of individual energy to achieve the defined ends within the normative framework. If we consider the individual person as actor, we ask how he is *motivated*; if we move to the social-system level, we ask how motivated individuals are *organized* into roles and organizations; (4) the available *situational facilities* which the actor utilizes as means; these include knowledge of the environment,

---

extension of the thought begun in my study of social change in the North of England during the Industrial Revolution. *Social Change in the Industrial Revolution*, especially Chapters VII–XI.

[1] *Toward a General Theory of Action*, p. 53.
[2] *Ibid.*, pp. 23, 190–197.

Basic Concepts: The Components of Social Action

predictability of consequences of action, and tools and skills. Let us now define these components more thoroughly and illustrate them with political and economic examples.

Values. The most general component of social action resides in a value system. Values state in general terms the desirable end states which act as a guide to human endeavor; they are so general in their reference that they do not specify kinds of norms, kinds of organization, or kinds of facilities which are required to realize these ends.

To illustrate this *general* character of values, let us first examine "democracy." This value, as it has evolved in the liberal traditions of the eighteenth and nineteenth centuries, forms the core of legitimacy for the political systems of Great Britain, the United States, and the French Republics. Although common elements are present in the definition of democracy for all these nations—the principles of representation, elective systems, majority rule, etc.—these do not specify the exact institutional arrangements. In fact, the systems of representation, election, courts, legislation, and administration differ widely among these three political systems. But these differences do not lie at the value level; they are differences in regulative norms, in social organization, and in means of attaining concrete political goals.

The economic value of "free enterprise," like the political value of democracy, is extremely general. One of the apparent paradoxes of free enterprise is that it has been the basis for legitimizing *many* types of economic organization. The two most conspicuous forms have been the owner-managed enterprise of the late nineteenth century and the manager-dominated corporate enterprise which has come to dominate in the twentieth century. The structural characteristics of these two forms vary considerably,[1] yet both came to be institutionalized under the label of free enterprise.

Values, then, are the most general statements of legitimate ends which guide social action. According to Kluckhohn, they involve "generalized and organized conception[s], influencing behavior, of nature, of man's place in it, of man's relation to man, and of the desirable and nondesirable as they may relate to man-environment and interhuman relations."[2] Kluckhohn's choice of the words "nature, man's place in it, and man's relation to man," implicitly restricts his definition to very comprehensive kinds of values, usually

---

[1] A. A. Berle and G. C. Means, *The Modern Corporation and Private Property* (New York, 1935).
[2] C. Kluckhohn, "Values and Value-Orientations," in Parsons and Shils, *Toward a General Theory of Action,* p. 411. Actually, Kluckhohn's definition applies to "value-orientations" which include not only notions of the desirable and nondesirable but also existential claims.

those found in religious belief-systems. Values such as "democracy" and "free enterprise" show, however, that general values may refer only to sectors of society, such as the political or economic. Later in the chapter we shall show how values may vary in their specificity of reference.

Two clarifying remarks on the study of values are in order: (*a*) Like all the components of social action, the concept of value is a construct; it refers to an aspect of social action which is not physically and temporally isolable. Therefore the social scientist cannot simply identify values as things which are given in nature; rather he must impute values to social systems. To assess the correctness of this imputation, two kinds of evidence are available. The first is direct; the investigator uses a number of indices, such as written documents, verbal statements, institutional patterns, ritual expressions of devotion to the sacred, and so on. No one index is valid. To unravel the different kinds of evidence given by the different indices, moreover, poses many difficult methodological problems. The second kind of evidence is indirect, but very important; the social scientist must incorporate his version of values into definite empirical propositions. If he has erred in his imputation of values, his error will be revealed by his inability to explain the behavior he wishes to explain. (*b*) At any given instant in history, a given society is characterized by some values which are accepted more or less universally, some values which are in conflict with dominant values, some values toward which the populace is ambivalent, and so on. Our definition of values does not imply any perfectly integrated system of values for any society. In fact, we shall devote much of this volume to studying those occasions on which the legitimacy of values is challenged, and the ways in which people collectively attempt to change values.

Norms. If values only are present, no action is possible. The value of "democracy," for instance, provides only criteria for judging the legitimacy or illegitimacy of whole classes of behavior. Various rules must be established which indicate how democracy (or any other system of values) may be realized—rules of election, office-holding, rights and privileges of the state and the citizens. These rules represent, in certain respects, a narrowing of the possible applications of the general values.

Again, "free enterprise," as a value, defines the general relationships of man to the economy, and of men to one another in the economy. This value, however, does not define any detailed mutual rights and privileges of actors, or norms for expected behavior. Such norms are found in the institutional structure of the economy, par-

Basic Concepts: The Components of Social Action

ticularly in the legal institutions of contract, property, and employment, as well as in more informal customs governing economic behavior, such as understandings among producers concerning the share of the market which should go to each.

Norms, then, are more *specific* than general values, for they specify certain regulatory principles which are necessary if these values are to be realized. They are the "ways in which the value patterns of the common culture of a social system are integrated in the concrete action of its units in their interaction with each other."[1] Norms range from formal, explicit regulations found, for instance, in legal systems to informal, sometimes unconscious understandings found, for instance, in neighborhood cliques. One purpose of this study is to examine the conditions under which new norms arise and become established through a norm-oriented movement.

Mobilization of Motivation into Organized Action. By themselves values and norms do not determine the *form of organization* of human action. They supply certain general ends and general rules; they do not specify, however, who will be the agents in the pursuit of valued ends, how the actions of these agents will be structured into concrete roles and organizations, and how they will be rewarded for responsible participation in these roles and organizations. In fact, norms allow considerable variability at the organizational level. Property law (which is a system of norms) specifies rights and obligations which cut across organizational forms of individual enterprise, partnerships, and corporations.[2] So while norms regulate organizations, they do not define the precise structure and system of rewards for these organizations.

We have to specify, therefore, in addition to values and norms, a third component which gives more detail to social action, and which cannot be reduced to either of the other two components. In dealing with this third component, we ask questions such as the following: Will economic processes be carried on by individual merchants and artisans, by small firms, or by gigantic corporations? Will political processes be carried on by small, informal political cliques, by pressure groups, by political parties, or by a structure involving the interaction of all of these types?

Most of what sociologists call "social organization" or "social structure"—families, churches, hospitals, government agencies, business firms, associations, political parties—is specified by this

[1] Parsons and Smelser, *Economy and Society*, p. 102.
[2] Some branches of law, e.g., corporation law or partnership law, define rights and obligations appropriate for specific kinds of organizations. Even these kinds of law do not specify, however, all the characteristics—e.g., size, internal power relations—of such organizations.

Basic Concepts: The Components of Social Action

third component of "mobilization of motivation into organized action." Furthermore, around this component we find the operative play of rewards, such as wealth, power, and prestige, which accrue as a result of effective performance in roles and organizations.

Situational Facilities. The final component of social action involves the means and obstacles which facilitate or hinder the attainment of concrete goals in the role or organizational context. We call this component "situational facilities." It refers to the actor's knowledge of the opportunities and limitations of the environment and, in some cases, his knowledge of his own ability to influence the environment. In both cases this knowledge is relative to the possibility of realizing a goal which is part of his role or organizational membership.

To illustrate this fourth component in the economic example which we have used throughout the discussion, the term "situational facilities" refers to the various means for making a decision in the market. How thorough is the producer's knowledge of market conditions? How much capital is available for the investment, and how well is the businessman able to finance his projected enterprise? How thoroughly can the businessman rely on the behavior of those who work for him? In sum, the businessman acts on his knowledge of the means and obstacles to attain his goals of producing and profit-making.[1] This characterization does not imply that his knowledge is always complete; it does imply, however, that his assessment of the situation is one of the components that enters his action.

For any instance of action which we wish to analyze, then, we have to pose four basic questions: What are the values that legitimize this action at the most general level? By what kinds of norms is this action coordinated and kept relatively free from conflict? In what ways is the action structured into roles and organizations? What kinds of situational facilities are available? As we shall see, when strain is exerted on one or more of these components, *and* when established ways of relieving the strain are not available, various kinds of collective outbursts and movements tend to arise. We shall interpret these episodes as attempts to reconstitute the component or components under strain.

---

[1] Max Weber's famous list of the conditions for the maximum realization of the goals of economic rationality can be viewed as a specification of two of the components of action, norms and situational facilities. (1) Norms: the institutional arrangements required for maximum rationality, such as segregation of the enterprise from the workers' appropriation, ownership of the means of production, etc.; (2) Situational facilities: calculability of the technical conditions of production, including labor discipline, etc. *The Theory of Social and Economic Organization* (Glencoe, Ill., 1947), pp. 275-276.

Basic Concepts: The Components of Social Action

INDIVIDUAL ATTITUDES TOWARD THE COMPONENTS OF SOCIAL ACTION

In ordinary language we often distinguish—implicitly and vaguely—among these four components of social action by using different words to characterize the relevant individual attitude toward each. In connection with values, for instance, the relevant attitude is *belief in*, or *commitment to*, or *faith in* the value in question. This commitment often takes an "either-or" form. This is not to claim as an empirical generalization that people do not "compromise their values" from time to time. All we are attempting to do at this time is to outline the conventions of usage of words like "faith" and "commitment."

With respect to norms, the appropriate individual attitude is *conformity* or *deviation*. Does the individual observe the rule or not? In general a person "conforms" to norms rather than "believes" in them. When we say we believe in property law, we do not mean that we conform to its specific regulations; we mean rather that we are committed to the value of regulating property by law. When we say we conform to the laws of private property, however, we mean that we are obeying the particular laws; whether or not we believe in the value of property is irrelevant. To say we conform to a value—such as free enterprise—is senseless, for such a value is too general to prescribe ways of conforming. We can conform only to the more specific laws of private property by which the free enterprise system is institutionalized.

One appropriate attitude toward the component of organization is the individual's *responsibility* or *lack of responsibility* in a role—whether this role be in a business firm, a postal agency, a hospital, a school, a church, or a family. We also refer to the individual's *loyalty* to these organizations by referring to him as a faithful employee, a faithful husband, or a faithful churchgoer. It is meaningless to say that an individual is "committed" to an organization; rather he is "committed" to the overall values of the organization. Nor can we say properly that he "conforms" to the organization; rather he "conforms" to the norms which regulate the organization.

Finally, with respect to situational facilities, one appropriate attitude is one of *confidence* or *lack of confidence* in our ability to predict and control the environment. If uncertainty is high, we have little confidence; as uncertainty diminishes, confidence grows.

The loose conventions for using the words "values," "norms," "role or organization," and "facilities" parallel the conventions for using words like "commitment," "conformity," "responsibility," and "confidence" in the following way:

Component of social action	Definition of individual attitude toward component	Economic example
Values	Commitment, belief in, faith in	Free enterprise
Norms	Conformity	Contract, property, etc.
Role or organization	Responsibility, loyalty	Business firm
Situational facilities	Trust, confidence	Confidence in skills, knowledge, availability of capital, etc.

This is not to claim that people always have these attitudes toward the components of action. Opportunists, for instance, may feign commitment to values in order to maximize power or prestige. Yet the very fact that we use the word "opportunist" illustrates the conventions for using the above terms; this word implies that the actor is, by adopting an expedient attitude toward value-commitments, "using" them illegitimately for purposes other than personal belief. In the chapters that follow we shall show how these connections between individual attitudes and the components of action help us to identify the kinds of strains that give rise to collective behavior, as well as to identify the episodes of collective behavior itself.

FURTHER ILLUSTRATIONS OF THE FOUR COMPONENTS

In illustrating the components of social action we have relied on economic and political examples. In other spheres the same components are equally applicable:

(1) Religion. The *value-component* is found in the theology and cosmology of the religion. In Christianity, for instance, the most general values include the belief in God, the mission of Christ, the implications of sin, grace, and salvation, and the eschatological notions found in the Bible. Religious *norms* are the general prescriptions and prohibitions believed to emanate from the general values. Examples of such norms are the Ten Commandments, various dietary regulations, and rules regarding the observation of holidays. At the *organizational* level is some set of roles or organizations—monasteries, churches, sects, or individual ascetic roles—which constitute the organized social medium for pursuing the religious life. Finally, with respect to *facilities*, we would identify the liturgy, techniques of prayer and communion, rituals, confession, and so on,

Basic Concepts: The Components of Social Action

which constitute the means for worshipping and attaining the desired religious state.

(2) Education. In America we are committed to a *value* of free public education. To implement this value at a *normative* level, we establish rules guaranteeing children of certain ages an opportunity to go to school, specify qualifications for entering and leaving school, enact property laws and float bonds to construct schools, and so on. At the *organizational* level we mobilize human motivation and talent into roles of administrators, teachers and pupils to realize the goals of education in a concrete social setting. And finally, with regard to *facilities*, we use techniques of instruction, books, musical instruments, etc., to implement the goals of education.

(3) Family. Normally the nuclear family is *valued* as an organization which perpetuates the central values of a culture through the socialization of children.[1] As *norms* to implement these values, we have marriage and divorce laws which specify how families are formed and broken, customs regulating the rights and obligations of family members to one another, and so on. Many norms are found in domestic law; many persist in less formal traditions. At the *organizational* level we have the kinship system, which is variable in its structure and residential patterns. Finally, we might specify several *facilities* for the family, such as the techniques of socialization, a minimum level of wealth, power, and prestige (to maintain a style of life for the family), and so on.

THE COMPONENTS OF SOCIAL ACTION AND CONCRETE SOCIAL ACTION

No concrete instance of action is identical to any one of the components of action. In fact, because the components are analytic aspects of action, any concrete instance of action includes all the components, whether this action be designed to maximize wealth, to implement territorial claims through war, to promote social stability, or to attain a state of religious bliss.

Some institutional clusterings of concrete action, however, seem to bear an especially close connection with one or more components of action. To illustrate this connection, we may consider values, norms, organized motivation, and facilities as "resources" which enter the "production" of action.[2] We may classify various institutional clusters of a society in terms of their "specialization" in supplying these resources. On the whole, the religious, philosophical, literary

---

[1] Families also may transmit wealth, perpetuate lineages, link clans, and so on.
[2] For an exposition of this concept of social resources, cf. Smelser, *Social Change in the Industrial Revolution*, Chs. III, VIII.

Basic Concepts: The Components of Social Action

and esthetic complex creates and defines general *values*. Legislatures, courts, police forces, social welfare agencies, schools, families, and informal groups specialize in varying degrees in creating *norms* and bringing deviant individuals and groups "back into line" through processes of social control. Governments, political parties, advertisers and the press are among the agencies responsible for *mobilizing* motivation. Finally, scientific research and education specialize in creating and transmitting *facilities* required for attacking a wide range of problems which arise in the pursuit of individual and social goals.

THE HIERARCHICAL RELATIONS AMONG THE COMPONENTS OF SOCIAL ACTION

How are the four components related to one another? To state it most simply, they stand in a *hierarchy* which reads as follows:

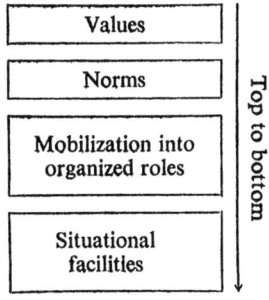

Values stand highest, situational facilities lowest. Several dimensions characterize this hierarchy:

(1) As we move from top to bottom, the concrete details of action receive increasingly more specific definition. Values provide only general notions of desirable end states, and hence are the most general guides to action. At the level of norms certain general rules define the broad rights and duties of human agents in interaction. This transition from values to norms *restricts the possible situational applications* of values as such. Property law, for instance, although it might favor the producer at the expense of other economic agents, limits the broadest interpretation of the value of "free enterprise." Broadly interpreted, the value could include piracy, use of duress, neglect of the interests of third parties, etc., in the pursuit of profits.[1] Property norms allow certain kinds of interactions and rule

---

[1] These normative restrictions of law received classic definition in E. Durkheim, *The Division of Labor in Society* (Glencoe, Ill., 1949), especially Ch. 7.

Basic Concepts: The Components of Social Action

out others. At the organizational level even more detailed characteristics are specified—the structure of roles and organizations, the nature of their situational goals, and the kinds of sanctions that facilitate the interaction of roles and organizations. Finally, at the level of situational facilities, the specification of knowledge, skills and tools leads us to the most detailed aspects of action.

(2) As we move from top to bottom, we approach components which are progressively less central to the integration of the social order. A change in the basic definition of values—for instance, from free enterprise to socialism—perforce implies a revamping of the laws of property, employment, and contract. Further, such a change would alter radically the organization of authority and control of economic organizations.[1] Finally, the acquisition of the facilities for production—technological knowledge, capital funds, etc.— would cease to be a matter of private financing and would pass to public control over capital resources.

Reading back up the hierarchy, however, the same logic does not apply. It is possible to modify the techniques of production without *necessarily* modifying the business firm's organization, much less the laws of property and contract or the general value of free enterprise. Furthermore, the firm may introduce structural changes—changes in the sales department, its personnel department, or in the relations between them, for instance—without modifying the economic laws and customs that regulate the general behavior of the firm. Finally, economic norms such as property and contract may undergo considerable modification without necessarily changing the definition of free enterprise.

To put the matter formally: any redefinition of a component of social action necessarily makes for a readjustment in those components below it, but not necessarily in those above it. It should be kept in mind that this is a statement of the *logical* or *theoretical* relations among the components of action. It is a statement of what changes follow, necessarily and by definition, from modifications of one or another of the components. Changes in the basic values entail changes in the definition of norms, organization and facilities. Changes in norms entail changes in the definition of organization and facilities, but not values. Changes in organization entail changes

---

[1] This is not to say that the entire structure of business enterprise would be modified. Both free enterprise and socialist systems are characterized by remarkably similar bureaucratic forms. The important modification which alteration in economic values would foist on business enterprise would be to discard "private profit-making" and to impose "service of the public interest" as the guiding philosophy of economic production. This would change the entire significance of sanctions and controls within economic organizations.

in the definition of facilities, but not norms or values. Changes in facilities, finally, do not necessarily impose any changes on the other components. This is not to say that *empirical* modifications at the lower levels do not ever constitute conditions of structural strain which initiate higher-level changes.[1] This last problem, however, constitutes a set of issues separate from the simple logical relations among the components.

THE INTERNAL ORGANIZATION OF EACH COMPONENT

Although the four components of action are systematically related to one another in a hierarchy, this is not sufficient for a detailed analysis of the structure of social action. *Each* of the components possesses an internal organization which also involves various levels of specification. Mere commitment to free enterprise, for instance, is insufficient as a guide to appropriate behavior in particular social contexts. The general value of free enterprise must be translated, by a number of specifications, into terms appropriate for more operative levels of social action. Similarly, with respect to facilities, possessing technology to produce goods and services does not guarantee their production. "Know-how" must be linked, in a series of specifications, to various other kinds of facilities—capital, tools, skills, etc.—to become operative as means at the "plant" level. Thus, to produce concrete social action, every component must be progressively "narrowed" in definition so that it can be "consummated" in some sort of operative social act.

We must deal, then, with a second type of specification. The first type, discussed in the section above, concerns specification *among* the components. This means that norms, organization and facilities add qualitatively new elements which give more detailed definition to action. The second type, which we take up now, concerns specification *within* each component. This involves a restriction of the meaning of the component itself which makes it more nearly applicable to concrete action. The first type of hierarchy deals with the addition of *different* components; the second restricts the applicability of the *same* component.

Let us now outline the internal structure of each of the four components of action, showing how each is subject to progressively finer definition.

[1] In fact, because many adjustments may occur at the lower levels without presupposing higher-level adjustments, the lower levels usually possess greater flexibility and adaptability. Therefore it is likely that structural imbalances accumulate easily at these lower levels.

Basic Concepts: The Components of Social Action

The Seven Levels of Specificity of Values: Free Enterprise. Values are the major premises of the social order; they set the bearings of society toward general kinds of ends and legitimize these ends by a particular view of man, nature, and society. The most general version of these values is found in the religion of the society, whether or not this religion is rooted in the supernatural.[1] But for these general values to be meaningful in the context of action, they must be defined in terms of the institutional sectors of society. To illustrate, let us posit that "freedom" is a basic and general American value. "Freedom" is the subject of profound individual commitment; it is frequently appealed to as a source of legitimacy in public controversy.[2] In order to give the value social meaning, however, we must place restrictions on it. In the economic sector freedom becomes "free enterprise" or perhaps even "laissez-faire"; in the political sector it concerns civil and political liberties; in the educational sector it becomes the separation (i.e., the freedom each from each) of federal government, church, and school; in the religious sector it becomes the separation of church and state, the freedom to choose any or no religion, and the philosophy of denominational pluralism. Each specific value is *a part of* freedom as a general value; what is added is a qualification as to freedom's definition in the various institutional sectors of society.[3]

The most general level of values, then, is the societal. The second level involves the specification of the value with reference to different institutional sectors of society. The third level specifies what kinds of activities and rewards are legitimately to be pursued. For the American "free-enterprise" system, we would expect to find at this third level some version of the "profit system," or a value legitimizing production and sales for monetary reward in the market. The value of "profit-making" adds a new, more specific element to the

---

[1] This most general basis for the establishment of civilization is not far from Sorokin's notion of "culture mentality." P. A. Sorokin, *Social and Cultural Dynamics* (New York, 1937), Vol. I, Chs. 2–3. The logic of general values is not far, either, from A. L. Kroeber's conception of the "culture pattern" or the "basic idea-system" of a civilization or one of its parts. *Configurations of Culture Growth* (Berkeley, 1944), pp. 763, 772. Cf. also Parsons' conceptualization of a society's "paramount value pattern" in "A Revised Analytical Approach to the Theory of Social Stratification," *Essays in Sociological Theory* (Revised Edition: Glencoe, Ill., 1954), pp. 398 ff.

[2] For instance, the statement, "This is a free country," can be used to justify (i.e., make legitimate) a whole variety of public and private actions.

[3] Note that this kind of specification of a general value differs from the stipulation of norms, organization, and facilities as discussed above. The move from "freedom" to "free enterprise" is a specification of the *scope of application* of the value. "Free enterprise" is, however, still a value; it still leaves open the working-out of the details of norms, organization, and facilities for realizing the implications of this value.

value of "free enterprise." To legitimize the values of "profit-making," however, we return to the higher-level versions of the value; we feel that "profit-making" is legitimate *because* we are committed to the system of free enterprise, or even more, freedom in general. Reading from less specific to more specific in the hierarchy of values, therefore, we learn more and more *how the value applies* to definite social contexts; reading from more specific to less specific in the hierarchy, we find the *bases of legitimacy* for the lower-level specifications.

The fourth level specifies the appropriate kind of commitment for the individual actor at the role level. In the business sphere the value of "personal success"—defined within the context of the higher-level values—constitutes this level of specification.

At these four levels the commitment to values are very general. In addition, therefore, three further levels of values must be specified—levels which redefine or restrict the meaning of values within the context of business and marketing operations.

The fifth level of specification, then, limits the scope of business activity by citing other, competing values which must be respected in business practice. These other values are respect for an individual's political freedom, the "humane" treatment of workers and their families, and so on. Such restrictions on business practice constitute part of the "ethics of business." A "good businessman" is committed to respect these other values, whereas the opportunist or fly-by-night pirate in the market evades them.[1]

The sixth level of specification involves a commitment to the values of efficiency—keeping the firm in the black, meeting payrolls, keeping accurate accounts, and so on. These values specify the sorts of commitments that are necessary at the operative organizational level if the higher-level value of profit-making is to be realized.

Finally, at the seventh level, we find the commitment to implement —by personal effort and expenditure of energy—the higher-level values of the organization. We might call this level the commitment to values of personal responsibility.

Table 1 summarizes this discussion of values. Column (1) numbers the levels of specificity; Column (2) states the transition from level to level in abstract terms; Column (3) states the transition from level to level in economic terms; and finally, Column (4), by way of even more concrete illustration, states the transition from level to level in terms of the value-system of American business. The higher levels define the general nature of values; the lower levels define the

---

[1] Empirically the definition of the "ethics of business" are never entirely unambiguous.

Basic Concepts: The Components of Social Action

commitments necessary at operative levels of action if these general values are to be realized. As we read down the levels, moreover, the values become increasingly short-term and detailed in their reference to action.[1]

The Seven Levels of Specificity of Norms: the Regulation of Economic Activity. Norms are primarily integrative in their significance for social action; they regulate social conduct. Like values, norms have a number of levels of specificity. We shall outline these levels, with illustrations again from the economic sector.

At the first level, the definition of normative regulation involves general conformity to social norms, no matter what the content. This provides the broadest kind of predisposition to engage in cooperative activity. Just as "freedom" lacks specific reference, so "conformity" refers to no specific social settings. Hence we have to use very nonspecific words like "conformity," "cooperation," and perhaps "altruistic attitude" to define this kind of normative regulation. It is difficult, furthermore, to produce specifically economic examples at this level because of the extremely general nature of conformity.

At the second level of specificity we begin to read some content into conformity. Various institutional sectors—familial, economic, political, administrative, etc.—are differentiated with regard to the types of conformity appropriate to each. The law is the most visible source of norms at this level—property law, domestic law, civil law, and so on. Less formalized traditions also carry much of the normative regulations of a society. The peculiarly economic norms at this second level are property and contract law, as well as the customs and traditions covering "fair" economic practices.

Level 3 restricts normative principles according to the types of organization to which they apply. Thus, the *general* features of property and contract law characterize Level 2; those features of law dealing with particular agents—corporations, partnerships, labor unions, widows, minors, etc.—characterize Level 3. They take account of the type of role or organization to which the more general norms must be tailored.

At Level 4 are found the requirements for individual adherence to norms—for example, honesty, reliability, trustworthiness, cooperative attitudes, etc., with regard to the law and other norms.

---

[1] Levels 2, 3, and 4 parallel Levels 5, 6, and 7, respectively. Level 2 specifies the general conditions of free enterprise; Level 5 specifies certain operative restrictions on its uninhibited realization. Level 3 specifies the general nature of rewards as defined by the profit system; Level 6 specifies the day-by-day conditions at the organizational level for guaranteeing the successful pursuit of these rewards. Level 4 involves personal commitment to success; Level 7 involves the commitment to day-by-day efforts to implement this commitment.

Basic Concepts: The Components of Social Action

Level 5 refers to the normative rights and obligations toward others in connection with the pursuit of a given type of activity. In the economic example, this would involve those rules that businessmen have to observe outside the strict normative regulation of economic activity itself.

TABLE 1
LEVELS OF SPECIFICITY OF VALUES

(1) Level	(2) General character of specification	(3) Specification of economic values	(4) Example from "free enterprise"
1	Societal values	Societal values	Commitment to "freedom"
2	Legitimization of values for institutional sectors	Economic definition of societal value	Commitment to "free enterprise"
3	Legitimization of rewards	Definition of rewards for economic activity	Commitment to "profit-making"
4	Legitimization of individual commitment	Definition of values for individual actor in economic world	Commitment to "personal success"
5	Legitimization of competing values	Definition of values which compete with economic values	Commitment to "ethics of business"
6	Legitimization of values for realizing organizational goals	Definition of values for running business firm	Commitment to "efficiency"
7	Legitimization of values for expenditure of effort	Definition of values of "work" and "the job"	Commitment to "personal responsibility"

(Less specific ↑ → More specific ↓)

Level 6 concerns the coordination of activity within an organization. In the business firm the executive is the specialist in this kind of coordination; he coordinates departmental activities, enforces company rules, smooths over conflicts among departments, adjusts competing claims, and so on.

Finally, at Level 7 we find detailed rules for operation. These involve such matters as timing of production schedules, hours of work, definition of tasks on the job, and so on. Table 2 summarizes the levels of specificity of normative regulation.[1]

---

[1] The transitions between levels of the Normative Series parallel those of the Values Series. The move from Level 1 to Level 2, for instance, involves a specification of a general category according to institutional sectors; the move from Level 2 to Level 3 specifies kinds of activities and rewards; and so on.

Basic Concepts: The Components of Social Action

The Seven Levels of Specificity of Mobilization of Motivation. How is individual motivation generated, allocated to roles and organizations, and finally expended in organized activity?

Level 1, the most general level, involves the formation of an individual's basic character. The most general set of predispositions to

TABLE 2
LEVELS OF SPECIFICITY OF NORMS

(1) Level	(2) General character of specification	(3) Economic example
1	General conformity	Conformity to all institutionalized economic activity
2	Specification of norms according to institutional sectors	Laws and customs of contract and property
3	Specification of norms with special reference to types of roles and organizations	Corporation, labor law, and related customs
4	Specification of requirements for individual observation of norms	Definition of business honesty, decency, etc.
5	Specification of norms of competing institutional sectors	Coordinating business activity with competing norms
6	Specification of rules of cooperation and coordination within organization	Executive coordination
7	Specification of schedules and programs to regulate activity	Code of operations

(Less specific ↑ ... More specific ↓)

motivational commitment is generated at a very early age in the family setting.[1] In this first stage of socialization the individual learns to curb his most blatant anti-social impulses and to acquire the basic capacity to enter roles of various sorts.

At Level 2, the individual acquires a generalized performance capacity. This capacity carries the individual beyond the mere ability to assume membership in a role or collectivity; it gives him the capacity to contribute individual talents to it. In the case of

[1] Parsons, Bales, *et al.*, *Family, Socialization and Interaction Process*, Ch. II.

economic motivation this second stage of socialization might be called the generation of a degree of "ambition."

At Level 3 simple generalized capacity to perform leads to trained capacity. This involves the acquisition of attitudes and skills geared to specialized roles, whether these roles be economic, political, familial, or associational. We refer to this level as training, which must always supplement simple ambition.

The first three levels are critical stages of socialization. By the time these stages are completed, the period of formation nears its end, and the period of allocation and utilization of the individual's talents begins. Level 4, then, corresponds roughly to adolescence in the individual's life, when he moves into the adult realm of more responsible motivational commitment to role. He is confirmed into a religious community; he enters the labor force; he is enfranchised with the vote; he marries and forms his own family. All these transitions mark the movement into the world of adult roles.

Level 5 involves greater specialization within the context of these adult roles. In the economic sector this means choosing one's line of work. The individual may make this commitment actively, or he may "float" into some line of work. In any case, some such commitment must be made before he can expend his energy in a concrete economic setting.

At Level 6, the individual's talents and skills are allocated to specific organizations. He takes a job, which means more than merely being available for employment. And finally, at Level 7, the transition to roles and tasks within the organization appears. The individual is now in the position to do the job.

Table 3 summarizes the levels of specificity of motivational mobilization. The distinguishing characteristic of this series is that it prepares motivation for role behavior in progressively more specific ways. From the point of view of the individual actor, the series constitutes successive degrees of *narrowing* his motivational energy into concrete channels; from that of the social system the series involves the *mobilization* of motivated activity into roles and organizations. Each level provides a more detailed definition of the conditions for motivated behavior; hence each level is a kind of added "insurance" that energy will be expended in an appropriate organizational context.

The Seven Levels of Specificity of Situational Facilities. In general, situational facilities refer to the actor's power over the environment. This power may be passive—a simple ability to predict the course of events and act accordingly—or active—the ability to manipulate environmental elements.

Basic Concepts: The Components of Social Action

At Level 1, the most general level, situational facilities include a general set of assumptions concerning means-end behavior or causality. These preconceptions need not be scientific or objective;

TABLE 3
LEVELS OF SPECIFICITY OF MOBILIZATION

(1) Level	(2) Nature of motivational commitment	(3) Economic example
1	Socialized motivation	Formation of basic character
2	Generalized performance capacity	Ambition
3	Trained capacity	Training
4	Transition to adult role-assumption	Getting out into the world
5	Allocation to sector of society	Choosing your line of work
6	Allocation to specific organization	Taking a job
7	Allocation to roles and tasks within organization	Doing the job

(↑ Less specific / More specific ↓)

indeed, they may rest on magical bases. Whatever the case they provide the broadest kinds of facilities for the solution of problems which arise in the course of social action. The American pragmatic world view is an example of such a set of preconceptions concerning efficacy, causality, and the relations between means and ends.

Specific problems are not solved, however, merely by having preconceptions about causality. This view must be made more specific. At Level 2 these preconceptions are organized into codified empirical claims and generalizations. The most formal kind of codified empirical knowledge is found in systems of scientific thought. Level 2 also consists of proto-science, folklore, and principles of knowledge derived from a supernatural view of the universe. With respect to business activity, codification usually involves several different kinds of knowledge. For a businessman, the grasp of business principles represents the possession of a semi-codified knowledge about the workings of production and the market. A part of this may be scientific, but much of it may rest on crude empirical generalizations from experience and hunches about human nature.

At Level 3 general knowledge is tailored to specific situations, and the result is technology, or the definition of codified knowledge in practical terms. An example of the transition from Level 2 to Level 3 is found in the transition from the principles of classical

Basic Concepts: The Components of Social Action

mechanics to the application of these principles in mechanical engineering.

Technological knowledge alone is not sufficient as facilities for social action. Other specifications must be added to make this knowledge useful. For economic production, for instance, we must tie the technological know-how to capital investment in order that it be incorporated into the industrial structure. The attachment of capital funds to knowledge authorizes this knowledge to be incorporated as part of the productive process. This activation of knowledge, by giving it the backing of wealth (or power or prestige, depending on the social context) constitutes Level 4 of the specification of situational facilities.

At Level 5 the technology is allocated to appropriate sectors of society. Economic technology may be turned to the production of consumers' goods (of many different kinds), investment goods, weapons of war, cathedrals, monuments to the past, schools, or hospitals. Political know-how may be used to regulate enterprise, to distribute wealth, to conduct war, or to enforce moral or religious decrees.

At Level 6 the facilities are allocated to particular organizations or roles within the appropriate sectors. With respect to economic production, the relevant decisions to be made at this level is which firms within an industry will receive investment funds.

Finally, at Level 7, the facilities are converted to operative use by allocating them to specific roles and tasks within organizations and roles. Funds must be used to hire laborers, buy machines, acquire working capital, and so on. Table 4 summarizes the levels of specificity of situational facilities.

SUMMARY: THE STRUCTURE OF THE COMPONENTS OF SOCIAL ACTION

Table 5 consolidates this lengthy discussion of the components of action by combining the first four tables. Before stating how we plan to use this scheme of components to analyze collective behavior, let us note a few formal characteristics of Table 5 as a whole.[1]

The table is a kind of map of social action; it indicates the principal transition points as human resources move from their general, undefined states to their more specific, operative states. Reading *across each row* (e.g., across Levels 1, 2, 3, etc.), we see how each

---

[1] For other, less thoroughly developed versions of this resource table, cf. Parsons and Smelser, *Economy and Society*, Ch. III, and Smelser, *Social Change in the Industrial Revolution*, Chs. III, VIII.

Basic Concepts: The Components of Social Action

transition adds a qualitatively new component of action to values—first norms, then form of mobilization, and finally facilities. Reading *down each column* (e.g., down the Facilities Series), at each transition a single component is prepared for implementation by the addition of some new restricting condition. For instance, Level 5 settles which sector of society (e.g., the political, the economic, the religious) will utilize available facilities; Level 6 settles the decision as to what roles or organizations will utilize these facilities. Each transition across a row to the right and each transition down a column, then, adds more specific meaning to the process of producing concrete

TABLE 4
LEVELS OF SPECIFICITY OF SITUATIONAL FACILITIES

(1) Level	(2) General nature of specification	(3) Economic example
1	Preconceptions concerning causality	Pragmatic view of world
2	Codification of knowledge	Grasp of business principles
3	Technology, or specification of knowledge in situational terms	Know-how
4	Procurement of wealth, power or prestige to activate Level 3	Financing
5	Allocation of effective technology to sector of society	Investing
6	Allocation of effective technology to roles and organizations	Procurement of funds for firm
7	Allocation of facilities within organization to attain concrete goals	Operative utilization of funds

(Less specific ↑ / More specific ↓)

social action. For social action to occur, moreover, every transition must be given some sort of meaning.

From any given point in Table 5, any redefinition of the component at this point *necessarily* requires a corresponding redefinition of all points *below and to the right*. This redefinition, however, does not *necessarily* require any redefinition of the points *either above or to the left* of the point in question. To illustrate, a reallocation of trained personnel to a certain industrial sector (Mobilization Level 5) necessarily involves a reallocation to specific organizations (Mobilization Level 6) and a reallocation of roles and tasks within

Basic Concepts: The Components of Social Action

these organizations (Mobilization Level 7). Furthermore, the initial reallocation, by definition, redefines the allocation of technological know-how (Facilities Level 5), and this in turn is reflected in the

TABLE 5
LEVELS OF SPECIFICITY OF THE COMPONENTS OF SOCIAL ACTION

Level	Values	Norms	Mobilization of motivation for organized action	Situational facilities
1	Societal values	General conformity	Socialized motivation	Preconceptions concerning causality
2	Legitimization of values for institutionalized sectors	Specification of norms according to institutional sectors	Generalized performance capacity	Codification of knowledge
3	Legitimization of rewards	Specification of norms according to types of roles and organizations	Trained capacity	Technology, or specification of knowledge in situational terms
4	Legitimization of individual commitment	Specification of requirements for individual observation of norms	Transition to adult-role assumption	Procurement of wealth, power, or prestige to activate Level 3
5	Legitimization of competing values	Specification of norms of competing institutional sectors	Allocation to sector of society	Allocation of effective technology to sector of society
6	Legitimization of values for realizing organizational roles	Specification of rules of cooperation and coordination within organization	Allocation to specific roles or organizations	Allocation of effective technology to roles or organization
7	Legitimization of values for expenditure of effort	Specification of schedules and programs to regulate activity	Allocation to roles and tasks within organization	Allocation of facilities within organization to attain concrete goals

More specific ↓
More specific →

reallocation of know-how to organizations (Facilities Level 6) and within organizations (Facilities Level 7). If these redefinitions of Levels 6 and 7 of the Mobilization Series and Levels 5, 6, and 7 of the Facilities Series did not occur, moreover, it would not be possible

Basic Concepts: The Components of Social Action

to produce effective changes in production by means of the original reallocation at Level 5 of the Mobilization Series. The initial reallocation, however, does not necessarily involve a redefinition of either the normative structure or the value system *at any level*; nor does it necessarily involve a redefinition of the Mobilization and Facilities Series above Level 5.[1] *Empirically* the resulting redefinitions at Levels 5-7 of the Mobilization and Facilities Series (if we stay with the same example) *may* set up structural imbalances in the system which may eventually give rise to widespread redefinitions in the normative structure and the value system, as well as the higher levels of the Mobilization and Facilities Series. Whether or not these latter changes occur, however, is an open, empirical matter, not a matter which follows from the definition of and logical relations among the components. Therefore, as we move either upward or to the left in Table 5, any reorganization of a component necessarily implies a corresponding reorganization of a greater proportion of the entire table. These logical relations will prove to be very important when we examine the character of beliefs which envision changes in the components of action, and when we outline the relations among such beliefs.

THE USES OF THESE BASIC CONCEPTS IN THE STUDY OF COLLECTIVE BEHAVIOR

Table 5 by itself yields no dynamic propositions concerning the course of behavior during an episode of collective behavior. How, then, is this extended discussion of the components of action related to the analysis of collective behavior? How are we going to use these basic concepts?

Basically, the components of social action provide a common theoretical framework with which to attack several of the elusive issues of collective behavior noted in Chapter I:

(1) What kinds of structural strain give rise to the different types of collective behavior? In Chapter III we shall outline the points of strain in terms of the theoretical framework developed in this chapter.

(2) Along what lines do collective behavioral responses to this structural strain flow: In Chapter IV we shall define collective behavior technically in terms of what happens to the components of action. By using the same conceptual framework as in Chapter III, we shall build a more substantial link between the strains which give

---

[1] For further illustration of these logical relations among the components, above, pp. 32-34.

rise to episodes of collective behavior and the character of these episodes themselves.

(3) What are the major types of collective behavior and how are they related to one another? In Chapter V we shall classify the various kinds of collective behavior in terms of the component of action that each attempts to reconstitute. Some types of collective behavior will be value-oriented, some norm-oriented, and so on.

(4) How does social control affect the development of episodes of collective behavior? We shall analyze the operation of social control in terms of which component of social action it affects.

In short, we shall discuss most of the major issues of collective behavior in the same theoretical terms. By employing identical concepts our aims are (*a*) to raise the theory of collective behavior to a more coherent, more systematic level, and (*b*) to build a framework for explaining the empirical occurrence of collective behavior more adequately.

CHAPTER III

STRUCTURAL STRAIN UNDERLYING COLLECTIVE BEHAVIOR

INTRODUCTION

Writers on collective behavior assume almost universally that people enter episodes of such behavior because something is wrong in their social environment. People panic, for instance, because they face some extreme danger. They take up fads or crazes because they are bored with their surroundings. They riot because they have experienced a sharp deprivation such as an inflationary price rise. They join reform and revolutionary movements because they suffer from the injustices of existing social arrangements. Such assumptions isolate an important set of determinants in the genesis of collective behavior. In this study we group such determinants under the heading of "structural strain."

Most formulations of strain are unsystematic. We do not possess, for instance, an exact classification of types of strain. Nor do we know the relations among the major types of strain. Perhaps most important, we have no adequate theory of how strain combines with other determinants—conduciveness, growth of beliefs, operation of social controls, for instance—in the rise of an episode of collective behavior. In this volume we hope to lessen these deficiencies. In this chapter we shall define strain as an impairment of the relations among and consequently inadequate functioning of the components of action. To give technical meaning to this definition we shall develop and illustrate a classification of types of strain on the basis of the categories developed in the last chapter. In later chapters we shall discuss the complex interaction among strain and the remaining determinants.

The literature on strain has produced an abundance of words and a poverty of consistent meanings. Among the existing concepts designed to encompass the relevant body of data are "strain," "pressure," "malintegration," "disequilibrium," "disintegration," "imbalance," "disorganization," "inconsistency," "conflict," "deprivation," and "anomie."[1] From this array of overlapping terms we

---

[1] For samples of the ways in which such terms are used, cf. A. R. Lindesmith

Structural Strain Underlying Collective Behavior

shall choose "strain," though both "pressure" and "malintegration" would suffice. The terms "disintegration" and "disorganization" are too strong; we shall find instances of strain underlying collective episodes which are too mild to warrant the use of such words. "Disequilibrium" and "imbalance" also are unsatisfactory, for they imply, or have been taken to imply, a model of stable equilibrium as the "normal state" of society. We wish to avoid such an implication. "Disequilibrium" also seems to imply that the system is on the verge of major change. We do not wish to build this connotation into a concept used to describe strain, for strain can persist for long periods without necessarily leading to social change. Terms like "inconsistency," "conflict," and "deprivation" all can be instances of strain, but each is too specific to cover all types of strain. Finally, "anomie," as defined classically by Durkheim,[1] is too narrow for our purposes; moreover, in recent times the word has been used in so many different ways that it has lost much of its original meaning. The term "strain" seems to avoid many of these difficulties.

Strain and Collective Behavior. Some form of strain must be present if an episode of collective behavior is to occur. The more severe the strain, moreover, the more likely is such an episode to appear. No direct causal link exists, however, between a *particular* kind of strain and a *particular* kind of collective episode. In the case of hostile outbursts, for instance, Bernard observes:

> Mobs develop with special ease under social conditions in which conflicting interests, ideals and controls are prevalent. The presence in close proximity of two or more races with fairly distinct customs, traditions and standards; of distinct social classes, such as capitalist and labor, rich and poor; of radically distinct religious alignments, each sect or religion holding firmly to its own tenets; of two rival gangs, each intent upon dominating the situation; or of two or more political parties, each with its patronage and graft to protect and candidates to elect, is especially conducive to the appearance of the mob spirit and mob action. Such conditions easily evoke race, class, religious or partisan animosities and hatreds, which become chronic prejudices.[2]

Hostile outbursts may develop from conflicts of interest, normative malintegration, and differences in values, as well as other kinds of

---

and A. L. Strauss, *Social Psychology* (Revised Edition) (New York, 1957), pp. 615–627, and M. Sherif, "The Concept of Reference Groups in Human Relations," in M. Sherif and M. O. Wilson (eds.), *Group Relations at the Crossroads* (New York, 1953), pp. 219–229. For an excellent discussion of the concept of disequilibrium, cf. G. Wilson and M. Wilson, *The Analysis of Social Change* (Cambridge, 1954), Ch. V.

[1] E. Durkheim, *Suicide* (Glencoe, Ill., 1951), pp. 241–276.
[2] L. L. Bernard, "Mob," *Encyclopaedia of the Social Sciences*, Vol. 10, p. 553.

Structural Strain Underlying Collective Behavior

strain. Therefore we should not search for specific causal laws such as "economic deprivation gives rise to hostile outbursts."

In addition, those same strains which contribute to the development of hostile outbursts may also help to generate other types of collective behavior. In Chapter IX, for instance, we shall see that the same cultural and normative strains, competition for rewards, and so on, provide the background for many norm-oriented movements. In Chapter X we shall note that behind a vast array of religious and political value-oriented movements lie the same kinds of strain.

These observations lead to the proposition: *Any kind of strain may be a determinant of any kind of collective behavior*. The foci of structural strain constitute a *class* of determinants which may produce a *class* of collective episodes. Some structural strain must be present for one or more types of collective behavior to appear. Which type or types depend on the progressive accumulation of the other determinants in the value-added process. We should not attempt to establish particular causal connections between a single kind of strain and a single kind of collective behavior.

Strain and the Components of Social Action. The components of social action form two hierarchies—one among the components and one within each component—which define social action in progressively more detailed ways. The levels of specificity of each component can be grouped into larger segments. The top three levels (Levels 1–3 of Table 5) generate resources, or "prepare" them for utilization in concrete action. Level 4 marks a transition between preparation and utilization. Finally, the lower levels (Levels 5–7 of Table 5) utilize the resources in concrete action. These lower levels constitute short-term operations which take the higher levels "for granted." Therefore the concrete allocation, use, and manipulation of the components transpires at the lower levels of Table 5. This is true even though the social product of these lower levels may generate simultaneously some component at a higher level. For instance, a family engaged in rearing children, maintaining a standard of life, etc., is a concrete organization in operation. Therefore Levels 5–7 of Table 5 have been specified for it, even though one of the family's "products" is the creation of motivational resources at the higher levels of the Mobilization Series.

It follows that strain at any level of any component will "show up" first at the lower, more operative levels. For instance, if an individual's personality structure is inadequately formed at Levels 1–3 of the Mobilization Series, this failing will appear concretely in his inability to hold jobs, obey the law, perform tasks, participate in family life, and so on (Levels 5–7). These are the points of operative

Structural Strain Underlying Collective Behavior

failure. Similarly, the immediate impact of calamities such as floods, storms, and explosions is in the daily affairs of life; offices cease to function, trains do not run, families are separated, and schools burn. *Whatever the source of strain* in Table 5, therefore, this strain appears first, and dissatisfactions accumulate first, at the operative levels, which we represent as Levels 5–7. Only as the dissatisfaction spreads and attention turns to a search for the source of operative failures are the higher levels of the components activated. In fact, in Chapter IV, we shall consider collective behavior as a search at the higher levels for ways to reduce the effects of strain. In this chapter we shall simply classify the foci of strain at Levels 5–7 of Table 5. At each

TABLE 6
LEVELS OF SPECIFICITY OF THE COMPONENTS OF SOCIAL ACTION

Level	Values	Norms	Mobilization of motivation for organized action	Situational facilities
5	Legitimization of competing values	Specification of norms of competing institutional sectors	Allocation to sector of society	Allocation of effective technology to sector of society
6	Legitimization of values for realizing organizational goals	Specification of rules of cooperation and coordination within organization	Allocation to specific roles or organizations	Allocation of effective technology to roles or organizations
7	Legitimization of values for expenditure of effort	Specification of schedules and programs to regulate activity	Allocation to roles and tasks within organization	Allocation of facilities within organization to attain concrete goals

level of each component we shall identify a focus of strain. For convenience of reference we reproduce these levels in Table 6.

Two qualifying remarks on this procedure of classifying strain are in order:

(1) The procedure translates the effects of complex empirical events into analytic terms. A single type of concrete phenomenon (for instance,[1] an increase in immigration, a business crisis, a flood,

---

[1] For a list of the kinds of events and situations which contribute to strain, cf. J. O. Hertzler, *Social Institutions* (Lincoln, Nebr., 1946), pp. 261–266. See also H. Blumer, "Social Disorganization and Individual Disorganization," *American Journal of Sociology*, Vol. 42 (1936–37), pp. 873–874; Turner and Killian, *Collective Behavior*, pp. 519–522. For another statement on the multiplicity of sources of strain, cf. L. Wirth, "Ideological Aspects of Social Disorganization," *American Sociological Review*, Vol. 5 (1940), pp. 474–475.

Structural Strain Underlying Collective Behavior

a technological innovation) may be significant at many points in the table of components. A financial crash, for instance, may mean both widespread economic losses and a collapse of norms that govern transactions in the money market. The table of components, therefore, provides a means for unraveling the complex effects of concrete events and situations.

(2) Before we can classify any event or situation as a source of strain, we must assess this event or situation with reference to cultural standards and personal expectations. For instance, the inequalities between the white and black races is a source of strain in the United States because of the cultural values of civil liberty and equality of opportunity. In a society with different cultural standards —classical India, for instance—such caste-like inequalities were not a source of strain. At the psychological level, some persons are more sensitive to possibly threatening situations than others. One worker, for instance, may face unemployment as a temporary hardship to be endured calmly until business improves. Another may see unemployment as a threat to his whole personal identity. Strain, then, always expresses a relation between an event or situation and certain cultural and individual standards.[1]

STRAIN AND SITUATIONAL FACILITIES

The principal kind of strain on situational facilities involves a condition of *ambiguity* as to the adequacy of means for a given goal. This ambiguity may stem from many sources: It may be that certain risks cannot be foreseen; it may be that knowledge or skills are insufficient to avoid misfortune or attain a goal; it may be that several different kinds of means conflict with one another.[2] Some types of ambiguity result from the unpredictability of the natural elements. Other types are built into social situations—e.g., the ambiguity inherent in forecasting the state of the market six months from now.

---

[1] For development of the logic of reference groups and relative deprivation, cf. R. K. Merton, *Social Theory and Social Structure* (Glencoe, Ill., 1957), Chs. VIII–IX. Sometimes reference standards are established by episodes of collective behavior itself. Cf. Heberle's discussion of the "political generation," an age group sharing certain "decisive politically relevant experiences," which shape the standards by which they assess social and political events. R. Heberle, *Social Movements* (New York, 1951), pp. 119–123.

[2] For an account of these kinds of ambiguity at the psychological level, cf. M. Deutsch, "The Directions of Behavior: A Field-Theoretical Approach to the Understanding of Inconsistencies," in I. Chein, M. Deutsch, H. Hyman and M. Jahoda (eds.), "Consistency and Inconsistency in Intergroup Relations," *Journal of Social Issues*, Vol. V (1949), pp. 44–51. For a discussion of the relations among logical, psychological, and sociological inconsistencies, cf. M. Jahoda, "The Problem" in the same issue, pp. 4–11.

At the psychological level the corresponding term for ambiguity is "uncertainty."

Strain may appear at the following levels of situational facilities:

Facilities Level 7: Ambiguity in Allocating Facilities to Attain Operative Goals. At this level ambiguity centers around the completion of concrete tasks. The question of the adequacy of means is always present, whether the task at hand involves producing economic goods, killing of an animal, enforcing a political order, performing a circumcision, disciplining a child, or warding off an environmental threat. The ambiguity involved in controlling the effects of floods, earthquakes, fires, and "other convulsions of nature" is usually very high. In some simple societies, precarious occupations such as "hunting, fishing, gardening . . . , cattle breeding, and the art of sailing" are filled with uncertainty, whereas "such homely occupations as food collecting, fire making, the manufacture of utensils, and house building" are more nearly "within human capacity."[1] The ability of the postal service to deliver a letter is normally not a matter of uncertainty; the ability of the merchant marine to deliver a cargo shipment to Great Britain during World War II was a matter of great uncertainty.

Facilities Level 6: Ambiguity in Allocating Facilities to Organizations. As a rule the realization of organizational goals requires the successful performance of many tasks (Level 7). In addition, certain policy decisions must be made at the organizational level itself (Level 6). These decisions allocate facilities to the goals of the organization as a whole. Consider the following examples: (*a*) The managers of a business firm must decide on several possible lines of investment. How certain can they be that one line rather than another will produce profits for the firm over the next three years? How great is the residue of uncertainty that stems from market conditions, levels of the rate of interest, etc., which lie outside their control? (*b*) Is a political leader certain that his party's stand on a particular issue will guarantee the support of a large number of voters? How much of the political situation remains outside his control? (*c*) Can the football coach guarantee a winning team by recruiting athletes, adopting a split-T, and engaging in a spring practice secretively? Or do other factors, such as the tactics of competing teams, introduce a factor of uncertainty? Ambiguity at Level 6 involves the allocation of facilities to the goals of the organization in question; for this reason it is more general than the ambiguities associated with task-performance which implement these organizational goals.

---

[1] H. Webster, *Magic: A Sociological Study* (Stanford, 1948), pp. 306, 497.

Structural Strain Underlying Collective Behavior

Facilities Level 5: Ambiguity in Allocating Facilities to Sectors of Society. Ambiguity at this level concerns the problem of allocating wealth, political support, information, skills, etc. to the various sectors of society. To take a contemporary political issue as an instance, let us ask how best to compete with the communist world. Assuming such competition to be a desired goal, how should we allocate our financial, political, and intellectual resources? To the continuation of the high-production, high-consumption economy we now have? To organizations engaged in basic research? To primary and secondary education? To the project of stirring national morale from its alleged doldrums? Such issues are fraught with uncertainty. We do not know, and cannot know, that any one pursuit will be most effective (indeed, effective at all) in guaranteeing success in international competition. These and other kinds of ambiguity may give rise to a vast array of collective episodes, which we shall trace in later chapters.

The three kinds of ambiguity concerning facilities stand in a hierarchy that parallels the hierarchy among the corresponding components of action.[1] Ambiguity of facilities for any sector of society necessarily creates ambiguity of the facilities available for organizational purposes within this sector (Level 6) and ambiguity of the facilities available for task-performance (Level 7). For example, congressional allocation of the budget to various branches of the government each year (Level 5) casts a shadow of uncertainty over the governmental agencies which face the possibility of being "axed" or "cut" (Level 6); this uncertainty, moreover, endangers the capacity of the threatened agencies to continue their operations at a concrete level (Level 7). Similarly, uncertainty as to the business firm's policy (Level 6), although it may not cast any uncertainty on the overall societal allocation of resources (Level 5), does create uncertainty in the day-to-day task activities of the firm (Level 7). For instance, if management wavers over whether to emphasize sales or personnel policy in a firm (Level 6), this brings the supply of facilities for each department into doubt, and creates an atmosphere of uncertainty within both departments (Level 7).

Accumulation of ambiguity at the lower levels does not necessarily mean ambiguity at the higher levels. Even though a surgeon may face great risks when he is forced, in an emergency, to operate without adequate equipment (Level 7), this does not necessarily generate uncertainty as to the supply of facilities for the whole hospital (Level 6), much less the medical profession as a whole (Level 5). Similarly, the precariousness of any one firm's capital position in the market

---

[1] Above, pp. 42–45.

(Level 6) does not necessarily create a capital crisis for the whole industry (Level 5).

To put the matter formally: Ambiguity at a higher level is a sufficient but not a necessary condition for ambiguity at all lower levels; ambiguity at a lower level is neither necessary nor sufficient for ambiguity at higher levels. We shall illustrate this same type of hierarchy for mobilization, norms, and values.

STRAIN AND THE MOBILIZATION OF MOTIVATION

The Mobilization Series characterizes the generation of human motivation and its channeling into organizations and roles. This series is also the seat of rewards—wealth, power, prestige, esteem—for responsible fulfillment of role behavior into which motivation is channeled. Strain, therefore, involves a relation between responsible performance in roles and the rewards which accrue thereby. We shall examine the strains which appear at the operative levels (5-7), even though the source of the strains may lie elsewhere. As in the case of facilities, we shall proceed from the lower to the higher levels of strain.

Mobilization Level 7: Actual or Potential Deprivation in Role Performance. The focus of strain is on the rewards for individual performance in a role within an organization.[1] Any discontinuity between roles and performance at this level constitutes strain. A clear instance of this kind of strain can be found in the process of draining responsibility and rewards from an unwanted executive in order to force him to resign. The continually "unavailable" superior, the "gradual freeze-out" whereby responsibility is shunted to others, and the "by-pass" create conditions of reduced prestige and power for the executive.[2] The opposite kind of strain arises when an executive, political, or administrative position is overloaded with responsibility. In either kind of strain the important element is the relation between expected performance and rewards.

Another example of the disjunction between responsibility and rewards is found in the woman's role in the contemporary American family. With the advent of labor-saving devices and the partial opening of masculine spheres of achievement to women, there has arisen

[1] The individual role which is not part of an organization—for example, the individual artisan, the unattached general practitioner, the free-lance artist or writer—is subject to the same kinds of strain. We select roles within organizations for illustration because they are characteristic of contemporary society and because such examples maintain clearly the distinction between strain at Level 7 and that at Level 6.

[2] P. Stryker, "How to Fire Executives," in Editors of Fortune, *The Executive Life* (Garden City, N.Y., 1956), pp. 185-187.

a confusion in the definition of their responsibilities in the home, and the kinds and amount of prestige which should accrue to them.[1]

Mobilization Level 6: Actual or Potential Deprivation Related to Organizational Membership. The critical issue at this level is a person's membership in an organization. A person joins a business firm primarily for economic remuneration; a political party for political interest; a church for religious salvation; an association for affiliative or status reasons.[2] Loyalty, affection, or labor given to the organization is matched by some kind of social reward, such as wealth, power, or prestige.

Strain at Level 6 involves a derangement of the expected balance between participation and recompense. The most obvious kind of strain results when membership (and rewards) are severed altogether, as in unemployment, disenfranchisement, expulsion, or excommunication. Thus events such as economic depressions, natural disasters, or political purges—all of which sever individuals' membership ties or reduce the rewards of membership—are sources of strain.[3] Runaway inflation, which reduces the value of workers' wages, may have the same effect.[4] Furthermore, tampering with contracted or

---

[1] This confusion of responsibilities and rewards is closely related to the concept of role-conflict, which we shall examine presently. For comment on these strains within the family, cf. W. Waller, *The Family: A Dynamic Interpretation* (Revised by Reuben Hill) (New York, 1951), pp. 282–286; M. Mead, *Male and Female* (New York, 1949), Ch. XV; Parsons, "Age and Sex in the Social Structure of the United States," in *Essays in Sociological Theory*, especially pp. 95–99.

[2] These manifest reasons for assuming membership in organizations may cross over in practice. A person may join a church or political association for reasons of prestige, for instance.

[3] For discussion of the effects of economic depression on collective behavior, cf. S. M. Lipset, *Agrarian Socialism* (Berkeley, 1950), pp. 89 ff., 174–178; R. E. L. Faris, *Social Disorganization* (New York, 1948), pp. 75–81; W. W. Rostow, *British Economy of the Nineteenth Century* (Oxford, 1949), Ch. V; E. J. Hobsbawn, "Economic Fluctuations and Some Social Movements since 1800," *Economic History Review*, Second Series, V (1952), pp. 1–25. Changes in precipitation, bad harvests, food shortages, etc., have tipped off numerous kinds of disturbances, as seen, for instance, in R. Marshall, "Precipitation and Presidents," *The Nation*, Vol. 124 (1927), pp. 315–316; J. D. Barnhart, "Rainfall and the Populist Party in Nebraska," *American Political Science Review*, Vol. 19 (1925), pp. 527–540. M. L. Starkey, *The Devil in Massachusetts* (New York, 1949), p. 13, for the climatic influences on the outburts of witchcraft in 1692. Cf. also the hard economic conditions which immediately preceded the major Western revolutions as noted in Brinton, *The Anatomy of Revolution*, p. 33.

[4] Cf., for instance, the price riots in Brazil in 1946, which sprang immediately from the outrage at inflationary price increases. Faris, *Social Disorganization*, p. 404. For an account of the German, Russian and other European inflations—all of which generated much unrest in these countries in the years after World War I—cf. W. A. Lewis, *Economic Survey 1919–1939* (London, 1949), Ch. II. On the psychological aspects of inflation, cf. G. Katona, *Psychological Analysis of Economic Behavior* (New York, 1951), pp. 257–262.

implicitly accepted patterns of rewards creates similar strains; examples are wage-reductions, unanticipated demotions, and political ostracism of a faction.[1]

Mobilization Level 5: Actual or Potential Deprivation of Major Social Sectors. At Levels 6 and 7 we have dealt with threats to two types of interests accruing from organizational and role involvement: (*a*) a person's interest in rewards associated with *attaching* himself to an organization; (*b*) his interest in rewards *within* an organization.[2] The junior executive, for instance, is interested both in his general terms of employment (Level 6), and in his position in the working organization once his employment has been settled (Level 7); the political office-seeker is interested both in receiving some appointment (Level 6) and in his day-to-day situation within the office once this political reward has been paid (Level 7).

At Level 5 we must consider a third category of interests as a potential focus of structural strain. These interests concern relevant sectors of society—labor, business, religion, education, the family, and (as a kind of combination category) the "public." Strain at this level usually involves a perceived misallocation of rewards whereby too much of the "cake" goes to one interested sector and too little to another.

An example from the field of labor relations will illustrate the difference between Levels 5 and 6. Many industrial strikes are concerned with local, short-term wage conditions. If we take the wage demands at their face value—i.e., assume that the strike is really about wages—we would say that these strikes have their origin in strains accumulating at Level 6.[3] Other more general disturbances are found in labor-wide agitations for minimum wages, price control, or tax measures. In such cases the interests of labor as a whole are ranged against the interests of business or government. A more extreme example is the general strike, which pits the interests of

---

[1] The Great Riots of 1877 were tipped off by a ten per cent reduction in pay of the employees of the Baltimore and Ohio Railroad. E. W. Martin, *The History of the Great Riots* (Philadelphia, 1877), p. 17. Many of the strikes in the British textile industries in the early nineteenth century stemmed from wage-manipulations resulting from new types of machinery. Smelser, *Social Change in the Industrial Revolution*, pp. 231–236.

[2] This second type of rewards usually involve respect for position, power within the organization, prestige, symbolized by the paraphernalia of office, etc. Many bureaucratic rewards and symbols are described in C. I. Barnard, "The Functions and Pathology of Status Systems in Formal Organizations," in W. F. Whyte (ed.), *Industry and Society* (New York, 1946), pp. 47–52. Cf. pp. 71–83 for some of the detrimental consequences of these reward systems.

[3] Many strikes are concerned with the "conditions of work," especially authority relationships, rights of management to fire workers, and so on. These conditions refer to Levels 6 and 7 of the Normative Series. Below, pp. 59–60.

labor against the rest of society.¹ In many cases, however, the general strike means more than a protest on behalf of the economic interests of labor; it may be used as a technique for the revolutionary overthrow of government.²

Another example of strain at Level 5 is indicated in A. M. Schlesinger's observations on a rough fifteen-year "cyclical" alternation of liberalism and conservatism in American history. Periods of liberalism have emphasized "human welfare" issues on the whole, whereas periods of conservatism have encouraged the "welfare of property" primarily.³ From these observations we might suggest that politics in America has vacillated between periods of emphasizing business values and periods of mitigating the effects of strains which unrestricted business practices create. Such strains concern labor's share of increasing prosperity, unemployment compensation, consumers' rights, needs for social security that stem from the growing isolation of the aged, and so on. These "human welfare" aspects of life are slighted under conditions of business dominance. After a season of emphasis on business values, the accumulated strains in other sectors of society are righted by a period of liberal dominance. In modern times the political role of conservatism has fallen, in a rough way, to the Republicans, that of liberalism to the Democrats.⁴

Similar types of strain might be found in social systems—such as the Soviet or Communist Chinese—which place a premium on the political control of resources and the subordination of other interests to those of the state.⁵ Under such systems we would expect many political problems to center on balancing the demands for all-out political mobilization against the demands of groups placed under strain by the maximization of political interests.⁶

[1] A. Plummer, "The General Strike During One Hundred Years," *Economic Journal* (*Economic History Supplement*), Vol. I (1926-29), pp. 184-204.

[2] E.g., J. G. Brooks, *American Syndicalism: The I.W.W.* (New York, 1913), Ch. X; G. Sorel, *Reflections on Violence* (Glencoe, Ill., 1950); W. H. Crook, *Communism and the General Strike* (Hamden, Conn., 1960), pp. 320-328.

[3] A. M. Schlesinger, "Tides of American Politics," *Yale Review*, Vol. 29 (Winter, 1940), pp. 217-230.

[4] For a theoretical rationale for such political oscillations, cf. T. Parsons, "'Voting' and the Equilibrium of the American Political System," in E. Burdick and A. Brodbeck (eds.), *American Voting Behavior* (Glencoe, Ill., 1959), pp. 99-107. It is interesting to note that *both* the swings from conservatism to liberalism and back again have been triggered by short-term deprivations, usually business fluctuations (Level 6). L. Bean, *How to Predict Elections* (New York, 1948), Ch. 6.

[5] A brief characterization of the importance of political values in the Soviet Union may be found in R. A. Bauer, A. Inkeles and C. Kluckhohn, *How the Soviet System Works* (Cambridge, Mass., 1957), pp. 2-28. The authors note also some popular dissatisfactions which accumulate from these policies. Perhaps the most conspicuous example is the peasants' chronic dissatisfaction with forced collectivization.

[6] For an interpretation of the fall of Malenkov, Molotov and Kaganovich, the

Structural Strain Underlying Collective Behavior

Within the Mobilization Series, the levels of strain stand in a hierarchy. Furthermore, the strains of the Mobilization Series stand above those of the Facilities Series. We may illustrate these two hierarchical principles[1] in the following ways:

Strains at Level 5 of the Mobilization Series imply strains at the lower levels; strains at Level 6 imply strains at Level 7; these implications do not, however, work back up the line. For example, a complaint that organized labor—as a part of the social order—is not receiving its just share of the national income (Level 5) clearly implies strains at the level of particular contracts with particular firms (Level 6). Finally, since the contract of labor is unsatisfactory, this necessarily casts a shadow of dissatisfaction on the conditions of work themselves (Level 7).

The same relations do not work in the other direction. Difficulties in plant conditions may give rise to dissatisfaction with the labor contract, but this is not necessarily the case. Dissatisfaction with particular labor contracts may, by a process of generalization, give rise to the complaint that labor in general is being wronged, but again this is not necessarily the case.

Strain within the Mobilization Series necessarily generates strain within the Facilities Series. For instance, if economic depression threatens to wipe out a businessman (Mobilization Level 6), this creates uncertainty as to the appropriate kinds of investments he should make to safeguard his market position (Facilities Level 6). If a sect's membership is endangered by the advent of a competing sect (Mobilization Level 6), the question of the means to be used to maintain the adherence of the congregation becomes a concern (Facilities Level 6). This process does not necessarily work in the opposite direction, however. A degree of uncertainty as to the appropriate channels of investment (Facilities Level 6) does not imply loss of profits for the firm (Mobilization Level 6); doubt as to the means of increasing the flock (Facilities Level 6) does not necessarily mean failure in the earthly strivings of the church (Mobilization Level 6).

Looking at Table 6, we can extend strain at any single focus (for instance, Level 6 of the Mobilization Series) to all foci to the right and below this focus (in this case to Level 7 of the Mobilization

---

driving forces behind the "Khrushchev Theses" of 1957, and other political events as a struggle between the political and the economic interests in the Soviet Union, cf. E. Crankshaw, "Big Business in Russia," *Atlantic*, Vol. 202, No. 5 (Dec., 1958), pp. 35–41. Apparently the recent easing of the commune program in Communist China is related in part to the tremendous opposition from family and community interests which were being sacrificed in the headlong rush to communization.

[1] Above, pp. 32–34 and 39–40.

STRAIN AND NORMS

Normative strain is discussed frequently under headings such as "role strain,"[1] "role conflict,"[2] and "cross-pressure."[3] These terms imply competing demands of different roles for the expenditure of limited time and energy, or for qualitatively different actions on the part of an individual.[4] The severity of role strain may be reduced by socially acceptable mechanisms such as timing, the institutionalization of priorities, compromise,[5] or even more subtle mechanisms such as the expression of embarrassment.[6] Another term used in connection with role strain is "role ambiguity," which concerns "how far the expectations of conformity are or are not specified and detailed."[7] Technically this term refers to the availability of information, and should be treated under situational facilities.[8]

Norms Level 7: Conflict of Operative Rules. Students of bureaucracy have described role strains which develop because of conflicting directives from authority, ossification, and red tape.[9] Within the

---

[1] W. J. Goode, "A Theory of Role Strain," *American Sociological Review*, Vol. 25 (1960), pp. 483–496.

[2] For a definition of role conflict, cf. Parsons, *The Social System*, p. 280. See also S. A. Stouffer, "An Analysis of Conflicting Social Norms," *American Sociological Review*, Vol. 14 (1949), pp. 707–717; S. A. Stouffer and J. Toby, "Role Conflict and Personality," in Parsons and Shils (eds.), *op. cit.*, pp. 481–496. Particular studies of role conflicts for the foreman may be found in D. E. Wray, "Marginal Men of Industry: The Foremen," *American Journal of Sociology*, Vol. 54 (1948–49), pp. 298–301; F. J. Roethlisberger, "The Foreman: Master and Victim of Double Talk," *Harvard Business Review*, Vol. XXIII (1945), pp. 282–298; W. F. Whyte and B. Gardner, "The Position and Problems of the Foreman," *Applied Anthropology*, Vol. IV (1945), pp. 17–28.

[3] Cf. P. F. Lazarsfeld, B. Berelson, and H. Gaudet, *The People's Choice* (New York, 1952), especially pp. 56–64; S. M. Lipset, P. F. Lazarsfeld, A. H. Barton, and J. Linz, "The Psychology of Voting: An Analysis of Political Behavior," in Lindzey (ed.), *Handbook of Social Psychology*, Vol. II, pp. 1133–1134, 1155–1156. A particular case study may be found in M. Kriesberg, "Cross-Pressures and Attitudes: A Study of Conflicting Propaganda on Opinions Regarding American-Soviet Relations," *Public Opinion Quarterly*, Vol. 13 (1949), pp. 5–16.

[4] Goode, "A Theory of Role Strain," *op. cit.*, pp. 484–486.

[5] *Ibid.*, pp. 486–490; see also R. K. Merton, "The Role Set: Problems in Sociological Theory," *British Journal of Sociology*, Vol. 8 (1957), pp. 113 ff.

[6] E. Goffman, "Embarrassment and Social Organization," *American Journal of Sociology*, Vol. 62 (1956–57), especially p. 270: "By showing embarrassment when he can be neither of two people, the individual leaves open the possibility that in the future he may effectively be either."

[7] Parsons, *The Social System*, p. 269. For an experimental investigation of the effects of role ambiguity on small-group behavior, cf. French, "The Disruption and Cohesion of Groups," *op. cit.*

[8] Above, pp. 52–54.

[9] Cf. the following articles in R. K. Merton, A. P. Gray, B. Hockey, and H. C.

contemporary American family the married woman is likely to be faced with competing demands from her many roles—wife, mother, career-seeker, contributor to community affairs, and so on.

Norms Level 6: Strain on Integration of Organization. Within a bureaucracy, some of those very strains which make for individual role strain—red tape, failure of authority, etc.—also create strains for the organization as a whole, since they constitute obstacles to the attainment of organization goals. In addition, the norms of informal organization—small cliques, coalitions, etc.—sometimes undermine the formally defined goals of organization.[1]

With respect to the family as an organization, its functions may also be impaired by sources of strain such as destructive personality characteristics of one or more of its members, the tensions occasioned by assimilating to a new cultural milieu, and so on. Such strain may lead to the development of personality disturbances among children, the breakup of the family by divorce or desertion, and other kinds of family instability.[2] The difference between these effects of strain at Level 6 and those mentioned under Level 7 is that the former lead to disruption of the family as a unit, whereas the latter lead to strains on the roles of the individual members.

Norms Level 5: Strain in the Relations among Major Social Sectors. At this level we consider the normative regulation of the relations among the various sectors in society. We may illustrate first from the area of labor relations. Many industrial disputes deal with the legality of union practices, such as wildcat strikes, featherbedding, sit-down strikes, and political activity; others deal with the legality of management practices such as black-listing and inciting violence

---

Selvin (eds.), *Reader in Bureaucracy* (Glencoe, Ill., 1952): S. A. Stouffer *et al.*, "Barriers to Understanding between Officers and Enlisted Men," pp. 265–272; The Hoover Commission, "Duplication of Functions: A Case Study in Bureaucratic Conflict," pp. 291–297; W. R. Sharp, "Procedural Vices: *La Paperasserie*," pp. 407–410; R. K. Merton, "Bureaucratic Structure and Personality," pp. 361–371. Cf. also B. Gardner and D. G. Moore, *Human Relations in Industry* (Homewood, Ill., 1955), pp. 67–70. For a discussion of a number of such strains which in fact led to a sort of "social movement" within a company, cf. G. C. Homans, *The Human Group* (New York, 1950), Ch. 15.

[1] A sample of sociological research on the relationship between formal and informal organization may be found in F. Roethlisberger and W. F. Dickson, *Management and the Worker* (Cambridge, Mass., 1953), Chs. VI–IX; P. Selznick, *Leadership in Administration* (Evanston, Ill., 1957), pp. 7–10; D. Roy, "Efficiency and 'The Fix': Informal Intergroup Relations in a Piecework Machine Shop," *American Journal of Sociology*, Vol. 60 (1954–55), pp. 255–266.

[2] Examples of such malintegration may be found in E. Vogel, "The Marital Relationship of Parents and the Emotionally Disturbed Child," Unpublished Ph.D. Dissertation, Harvard University, 1958. Cf. also the remarks of F. L. Strodtbeck, "The Family as a Three-Person Group," *American Sociological Review*, Vol. 19 (1954), especially, pp. 27–28. Also Parsons, Bales, *et al.*, *Family, Socialization and Interaction Process*, Chs. II, III.

during strikes. The point at issue in all these disputes is the rights and obligations of labor and management toward one another and toward the public at large.[1] A recent issue involving the normative regulations of labor unions is racketeering, which concerns the relation of labor to the public.

Another instance of normative strain at Level 5 may be found in Tocqueville's characterization of the relations among the peasants and the aristocracy before the French Revolution. Tocqueville noted the *persistence* of many taxes, duties, and other traditional obligations of the peasants and the simultaneous *decline* of the feudal responsibilities among the nobles who benefited from these obligations. Then, with characteristic acumen, he observed:

> The feudal system, though stripped of its political attributes, was still the greatest of our civil institutions; but its very curtailment was the source of its unpopularity. It may be said, with perfect truth, that the destruction of a part of that system rendered the remainder a hundred-fold more odious than the whole had ever appeared.[2]

To the strain created by this half-obsolete system, Tocqueville attributed the greatest revolutionary fervor; in areas where feudal institutions were "in full vitality" the spirit of the revolution was relatively weak.[3]

We might distinguish between strain at Norms Level 5 and Mobilization Level 5 with a hypothetical example concerning the profits of American business. A possible complaint at Mobilization Level 5 is that business profits are too high in relation to the income of other groups—laborers, professionals, white-collar workers, and so on. The corresponding complaint at Norms Level 5 would be, however, that businessmen fail to observe an appropriate code of

---

[1] For discussion of conflicts on these issues of legality, cf. K. G. J. C. Knowles, *Strikes—A Study in Industrial Conflict* (Oxford, 1952), Ch. III; see also L. G. Reynolds, *Labor Economics and Labor Relations* (New York, 1954), Ch. 12.

[2] A. de Tocqueville, *The Old Regime and the Revolution* (New York, 1856), p. 49.

[3] *Ibid.*, pp. 38–41. The strain imposed by the partial decay of the normative order has been observed in connection with many periods of revolutionary and related movements. For remarks on the state of feudal society on the eve of the Reformation, cf. E. B. Bax, *German Society at the Close of the Middle Ages* (London, 1894), pp. 2–4; for the disorganization of governmental and other institutions in Reconstruction and post-Reconstruction South, cf. E. M. Coulter, *The South During Reconstruction 1865–1877* (Baton Rouge, La., 1947), and S. F. Horn, *Invisible Empire* (Boston, 1939), pp. 30–31; for the structural background of peasant religious and political movements in Norway during the nineteenth century, cf. P. A. Munch, "The Peasant Movement in Norway," *British Journal of Sociology*, Vol. 5 (1954), pp. 63–77; and finally, for an application of the logic of structural disorganization to the rise of German fascism and to Western society in general, cf. Parsons, "Some Sociological Aspects of Fascist Movements," *Essays in Sociological Theory*, pp. 124–141.

ethics—in pricing, advertising, labor policy, and fair practices—in accumulating such profits. The first strain concerns the balance of rewards and performance alone; the second concerns the legal and moral restrictions violated in reaping the rewards.

Among the levels of the Normative Series, strain at Level 5 poses threats to the normative integration of organizations (Level 6) and activities (Level 7). Furthermore, various normative strains that endanger the realization of organizational goals (Level 6) also carry disruptive implications for role-incumbents within the organization (Level 7). This logic does not work in reverse, however; simple role strain or disruption of organizational integration does not necessarily imply strain at the higher levels of the Normative Series.

Normative strain stands higher in the hierarchy than strain relative to the Mobilization and Facilities Series. Uncertainty about the efficacy of facilities and threatened deprivation do not necessarily endanger a normative structure. In a political campaign, for instance, politicians may be very uncertain as to the best techniques (facilities) to appeal to the voters; they may also fear a loss of political power, which would occur in the event of a victory for the opposing party. Both these types of strain may exist, however, without necessarily placing any strain on the rules, regulations, and customs by which parties assume office. On the other hand, if one party consistently violates the political norms by the widespread use of coercion to obtain votes, this threatens not only the normative structure of the political system, but also the attainment of political goals by the other parties and the efficacy of traditionally employed means for attaining these goals. Normative strain, therefore, is a sufficient, but not a necessary, condition for strain at the lower levels. Although strain at these lower levels may lead to normative strain empirically, it does not constitute either a sufficient or a necessary condition for this effect.

STRAIN AND VALUES

What are the sources of strain in systems of values? In many cases such strain results from the spread of other types of strain in society. For instance, in the heat of conflicts of interest, arguments begin to generalize, and attacks begin to be directed more and more at the values, or the basis of legitimacy of opposing groups.[1] In such cases strain on values is an extension of other kinds of strain.

Other sources of value strain may be found in cultural contacts between two groups with divergent value systems (e.g., in the mass migration of ethnic or religious groups into societies unlike their

---

[1] J. S. Coleman, *Community Conflict* (Glencoe, Ill., 1957), pp. 10–11.

Structural Strain Underlying Collective Behavior

own, or in proselytization by missionaries).[1] The waves of immigration into the United States during the nineteenth and twentieth centuries[2] fired religious conflicts between Catholics and Protestants, between Americans of Anglo-Saxon stock and Southern or Eastern Europeans, and so on. Sometimes these conflicts dwelt on particular subjects such as public education, but in many cases the strains between the antagonists were diffuse. The high points of foreign immigration are closely related in time to outbursts of fervent native Americanism.[3] We should not, however, attribute such nativistic movements to value strains alone. Both Know-Nothingism and the A. P. A. Movements flourished in part because of the moribund character of the major political parties of the day.[4] Economic competition also fanned the flames of nativism.[5]

Let us now mention the levels at which value strains appear:

Values Level 7: Strain on Commitment to Personal Values. Values at Level 7 refer to personal commitments at the role level. By strain on these personal values we refer to attempts to convince those committed to them—by exhortation, by example, by coercion, or other means, that these values are wrong or immoral. A clear example of such strain might be found in the formation of an industrial labor force in the early stages of economic development. The industrial changes create pressure to change the definition of a "devoted individual" *from* a person who devotes much labor to reciprocal aid to kinsmen *to* a person who devotes his time and energy to work for money wages. This pressure calls for more than a change in contractual norms; it also implies a change in the personal commitments of the worker, a change in his definition of man's relation to other men.[6] Any pressure on traditional values implies,

---

[1] For the effects of combined political domination and religious proselytizing, below, pp. 326–329.

[2] Summarized by Mecklin as occurring from "1831 to 1861, reaching a peak in 1855. During these three decades some four millions of foreigners were added to our population. The second wave extended from 1862 to 1877, reaching its peak in 1873. From 1831 to 1877 the immigrants came principally from the British Isles and Germany. The third great immigrant wave extended from 1878 to 1897, reaching its peak in 1882. This wave added something like nine millions to our population, German and British subjects still predominating though immigrant tides from Italy, Austria-Hungary, and Russia were getting under way.... The fourth and last immigrant wave extended from 1898 to the outbreak of the war and was marked by two peak years ... 1907 [and] 1914." J. M. Mecklin, *The Ku Klux Klan* (New York, 1924), pp. 128–129.

[3] *Ibid.*, pp. 130–132.

[4] Cf. H. J. Desmond, *The A.P.A. Movement* (Washington, 1912), pp. 11–13; L. F. Schmeckebier, *History of the Know Nothing Party in Maryland* (Baltimore, 1899), p. 69.

[5] For a variety of the complaints associated with early nativism, cf. G. Myers, *History of Bigotry in the United States* (New York, 1942), pp. 166 ff.

[6] For an account of the complex character of commitment to an industrial

however, a modification of particular norms, motivation, and facilities; this is true because values stand at the highest level of the hierarchy of components.

Values Level 6: Strain on Commitment to Organizational Goals. This level involves commitment to the purposes of organized collectivities. In business it means a commitment to efficiency; in politics it means a commitment to the political undertakings of the state; in religion it means commitment to the organizational purposes of the church; in voluntary associations it means commitment to the goals of the group. All these commitments stand above Level 7 commitments to faithfulness in discharging role obligations in these organizations. Value strains at Level 6 involve pressures to weaken or destroy individual commitments to the organizational values.

Values Level 5: Strain on the Principles of Integration of Values. At this level we find many of the "isms" that constitute the principles of integration of the social order—capitalism, socialism, feudalism, totalitarianism. In one version of the capitalist system, for instance, governmental activities are legitimate only on condition that they interfere minimally with the pursuits of business enterprise.

Value strains at this level bring the legitimacy of this patterning of values into question, not merely particular loyalties to organizations or roles. To illustrate the levels of value strain, let us take the social reactions to a hypothetical government scandal. If public indignation centers on the morality of the public servant himself, the strain is defined at Level 7. If the same scandal is felt to reflect badly on the efficiency of organized government operations as a whole, the strain is defined at Level 6. If, however, criticism turns to the *kind of social system* that would permit such scandals, we then move to the issue of the social integration of values (Level 5).

CONCLUSION

Table 7 summarizes the foci of strain for the components of social action. Value strain poses the issue of commitment; normative strain concerns the integration of human interaction; strain on mobilization

---

labor force, cf. A. S. Feldman and W. E. Moore, "Commitment of the Industrial Labor Force," in Moore and Feldman (eds.), *Labor Commitment and Social Change in Developing Areas* (New York, 1960), pp. 1–12. Much of the confusion in the discussion of whether values change during periods of rapid development is perhaps a confusion of levels. As the above example shows, the change from a traditionalized economic role to membership in a formally free labor force does in fact involve a change in the values of role commitment. Furthermore, this change may occur and may be legitimized by higher level values (e.g., a religious definition of the universe) which themselves remain unaltered. Any discussion of value change, therefore, must begin by specifying the several levels at which values are structured.

Structural Strain Underlying Collective Behavior

concerns the balance between motivated activity and its rewards; strain on facilities concerns the adequacy of knowledge and skills. In Table 7 strain at any point is a sufficient but not a necessary condition for strain at all points downward and to the right, but is neither necessary nor sufficient for strain at points upward or to the left. Table 7 also includes an example of each type of strain discussed in the body of the text. For purposes of continuity we have selected economic and political examples; the presence of many other illustrations in the text should correct for any apparent bias in this selection.

TABLE 7

FOCI OF STRAIN FOR THE COMPONENTS OF ACTION

Level	Values	Norms	Mobilization of motivation for organized action	Situational facilities
5	Strain on the principles of integration of values (Ex: attack on capitalism)	Strain in relations among major social sectors (Ex: the "legality" of labor practices)	Actual or potential deprivation of major social sectors (Ex: squeeze on salaried employees because of high profits and wages)	Ambiguity in allocating facilities to sectors of society (Ex: how to allocate resources to meet communist challenge)
6	Strain on commitment to organizational goals (Ex: attack on "profits")	Strain on integration of organization (Ex: interference of "informal organization" on production)	Actual or potential deprivation related to organizational membership (Ex: loss of income through unemployment)	Ambiguity in allocating facilities to organizations (Ex: how to invest wisely in business firm)
7	Strain on commitment to personal values (Ex: challenge to value of personal honesty)	Strain at level of operative rules (Ex: conflicting directives from a bureaucratic superior)	Actual or potential deprivation in role performance (Ex: "freezing out" the business executive)	Ambiguity in allocating facilities to attain operative goals (Ex: how to guarantee a good planting for a crop)

For any episode of collective behavior, we shall always find some kind of structural strain in the background. One or more forms of strain underlie, for instance, the riot and the norm-oriented movement, which differ in aim and method. Knowing only the structural strain, however, we cannot predict whether one or the other, or neither, will occur. Only by exploring the world of precipitating factors, structural conduciveness, and social controls can we chart the path of behavior and show why one rather than another form of collective behavior makes its appearance. This approach enables us to reach a more determinate statement of conditions that give rise to collective behavior and at the same time to observe the cautions advanced at the beginning of this chapter. These cautions are: (*a*) Structural strain is a necessary, but not sufficient, condition for an episode of collective behavior; (*b*) Any type of structural strain may give rise to any type of collective behavior. We wish, therefore, to explain collective behavior not in extremely refined statements of the direct relations between specific strains and specific collective episodes, but in an investigation of how these inherently indeterminate strains combine with other factors.

The connection, then, between foci of structural strain and collective behavior is indirect. In two other ways, however, they link more directly. The first link lies in the theoretical continuity between a statement of the conditions of strain and the collective responses to these conditions. We analyzed the foci of strain in terms of values, norms, mobilization, and facilities. We shall, in turn, analyze the aims and methods of the various kinds of collective behavior by using the identical theoretical terms.

Second, in analyzing the symbolism of collective behavior, we must return to the specific strains which give rise to the episode in question. Every form of collective behavior attempts to "solve" certain problems—e.g., the riot is aimed at destroying some noxious object, the norm-oriented movement at affecting the normative order, and so on. Collective behavior is also embellished with symbols to explain and justify the participants' actions. To determine why certain objects and symbols are chosen, we must refer to the specific strains. Again, we shall discuss these objects and symbols in the same theoretical framework as strain itself.

CHAPTER IV

THE NATURE OF COLLECTIVE BEHAVIOR

INTRODUCTION

Having identified several components of action and sources of strain, we now ask: What is the nature of collective behavior in general? How does it differ from conventional behavior? Our answers will be framed in terms of the components of social action.

THE GENERAL NATURE OF STRUCTURAL REORGANIZATION

When strain exists, we might say that the components of social action are out of order and require fixing. How, *in general*, is strain overcome? How is social action repaired? By outlining the general character of the process of reorganizing the components of action, we shall be able to specify the nature of collective behavior. To facilitate our discussion we have reproduced Table 5—the components of social action in full detail—on p. 68.

The general principle for reconstituting social action is this: when strain exists attention shifts to the higher levels of the components to seek resources to overcome this strain. We may characterize this process in the language of Table 5 by saying that, in the search for solutions to conditions of strain, people turn their attention either *upward* or *to the left*, or *both*.

To illustrate the *upward* movement we shall consider a situation of strain in American society which was particularly acute during the first two years or so following the launching of the first Russian Sputnik in the fall of 1957. Because Americans judged that progress in the conquest of space was important for our international prestige, the pressure to produce successful space vehicles was great. Yet we could not assemble the facilities to put even a modest capsule into orbit. We were uncertain whether a military or civilian agency was better suited to develop a space program, and how resources should be allocated to develop the best space equipment in the shortest time. Thus serious strains began to build up at the operative levels of the Facilities Series (Levels 5–7 of Table 5).

TABLE 5
LEVELS OF SPECIFICITY OF THE COMPONENTS OF SOCIAL ACTION

Level	Values	Norms	Mobilization of motivation for organized action	Situational facilities
1	Societal values	General conformity	Socialized motivation	Preconceptions concerning causality
2	Legitimization of values for institutionalized sectors	Specification of norms according to institutional sectors	Generalized performance capacity	Codification of knowledge
3	Legitimization of rewards	Specification of norms according to types of roles and organizations	Trained capacity	Technology, or specification of knowledge in situational terms
4	Legitimization of individual commitment	Specification of requirements for individual observation of norms	Transition to adult role-assumption	Procurement of wealth, power, or prestige to activate Level 3
5	Legitimization of competing values	Specification of norms of competing institutional sectors	Allocation to sector of society	Allocation of effective technology to sector of society
6	Legitimization of values for realizing organizational goals	Specification of rules of co-operation and coordination within organization	Allocation to specific roles or organizations	Allocation of effective technology to roles or organizations
7	Legitimization of values for expenditure of effort	Specification of schedules and programs to regulate activity	Allocation to roles and tasks within organization	Allocation of facilities within organization to attain concrete goals

← More specific

More specific →

How might these strains have been overcome? We could have encouraged the space program by increasing its budget and by giving political authorization to various space agencies to move ahead quickly. Such action would have invested greater financial and political resources in the space effort. Formally, this kind of action can be described as a movement *up* the Facilities Scale to Level 4 in order to overcome the strains at the lower levels.

This movement to Level 4, however, would have been satisfactory

The Nature of Collective Behavior

only if we had already possessed an adequate technology for producing the appropriate kinds of space vehicles. In fact, we did not. Merely to allocate more funds and greater authority to space agencies would not have been enough. It was necessary to move higher in the Facilities Scale in an attempt to improve our technology (Level 3).

Yet technology alone might not have been enough. Some persons felt that without "basic research" we were inherently limited in our ability to develop an effective space program. What is basic research? It is the production of *scientific knowledge itself*, on which new technology can be built. Formally, basic research means activity at Level 2 of the Facilities Series; this activity is more generalized than the production of technology. The principle of moving up the levels of generality, then, is that when any given level (e.g., technology) reaches a limit and becomes inadequate to deal with the condition of strain, it is necessary to move to the next higher level (e.g., basic research) in order to broaden the facilities for attacking the strain.

One more level of generality goes beyond Level 2. In the flurry of excitement, dismay, and self-criticism after the Russians launched their first Sputnik, some persons felt that American society has the wrong "approach" to scientific endeavor. American society, it was felt, is too pragmatic. Historically we have had to rely on European scientists for high-level theory in mathematics and physics; we, as technicians, have applied this theory, not created it. To develop a really advanced space program it is necessary to *go beyond* the basic research possible in our system; it is necessary to create a new outlook, perhaps even a new philosophy (Level 1). Only then would we generate fundamental scientific knowledge (Level 2) and apply it down the line through technology (Level 3) and investment (Level 4) to the world of operations (Levels 5–7).

The reduction of strains such as the unfulfilled demand for an adequate space program frequently lies in the *generalization* of facilities. If facilities at one level are inadequate, attention turns to the next higher level. After reconstitution occurs at the higher level, moreover, the new higher-level facilities must be reapplied back down the line to the lower levels. New basic research must be converted into new technology; new investment and authorization must be given this new technology; new agencies must be set up or old ones modified, and so on. For any given empirical case of strain, the exact level of generality which must be reconstituted to overcome the strain depends on two things: (*a*) the seriousness of the initial conditions of strain, and (*b*) the adequacy of the existing facilities at each level to meet the conditions of strain.

The Nature of Collective Behavior

To illustrate the process of generalization *to the left* in Table 5, we shall consider the strains occasioned by a major financial crisis and business depression. Many persons lose their jobs, others their fortunes. Strain concentrates on the deprivation of rewards (Mobilization Series) and on the disorganization of norms governing market behavior (Normative Series).[1] How can such conditions of strain be attacked? The first line of attack would be to punish those individuals—e.g., financiers or government officials—who behaved irresponsibly. This reaction concentrates on the Mobilization Series. It is not too drastic from the standpoint of the total system, for it merely withholds rewards from *particular* agents who presumably behaved imprudently or dishonestly enough to bring on an economic crisis.

A more general solution would be to pass laws and regulations which affect not only those who behaved irresponsibly in the past, but also all others who might do so in the future. An example would be to place restrictions on those speculative practices that were to blame for the financial collapse. Thus the slogan "there ought to be a law" is more drastic than the slogan "throw the rascals out" because it is more general in its applicability. The former deals with the Normative Series rather than with particular agents.

Even more general is a solution that brings the values of the economic system itself into question. The most drastic attack on the system that produces economic crises and business depressions would be to do away with the system itself and bring some sort of socialistic values to bear. This solution is more far-reaching than merely passing laws and regulations, for it means reorganizing the values by which the laws and regulations are legitimized.

What happens, then, to social action when strain exists? Attempts are made to move to higher-level components, reconstitute them, then incorporate the new principles back into the more concrete, operative levels of social action. In the event of failure at one level of generality, moreover, the tendency is to "appeal to an even higher court" in an attempt to understand and control the action that is under strain at the lower levels. This process of generalization moves toward the higher levels of each individual component, toward the higher-level components (norms, values), or both. Having generalized to higher levels, attempts are then made to work "back down the line." Attempts are made to generalize, then respecify; the components of action are first *de*structured, then *re*structured.[2] Many

---

[1] Above, pp. 54–62.
[2] This principle of generalization followed by re-specification has been identified in studying the organism's reaction to stress, learning processes, personality

The Nature of Collective Behavior

instances of social change can be interpreted according to this scheme.[1]

COLLECTIVE BEHAVIOR AS GENERALIZED BEHAVIOR

Collective behavior involves a generalization to a high-level component of action. Like many other kinds of behavior, it is a search for solutions to conditions of strain by moving to a more generalized level of resources. Once the generalization has taken place, attempts are made to reconstitute the meaning of the high-level component. At this point, however, the critical feature of collective behavior appears. Having redefined the high-level component, people do not proceed to respecify, step by step, down the line to reconstitute social action. Rather, they develop a belief which "short-circuits" from a very generalized component *directly* to the focus of strain. The accompanying expectation is that the strain can be relieved by a direct application of a generalized component. From a slightly different perspective, collective behavior is a *compressed* way of attacking problems created by strain. It compresses several levels of the components of action into a single belief, from which *specific operative solutions* are expected to flow. An episode of collective behavior itself occurs when people are mobilized for action on the basis of such a belief. Thus our formal characterization of collective behavior is this: *an uninstitutionalized*[2] *mobilization for action in order to modify one or more kinds of strain on the basis of a generalized reconstitution of a component of action.*

In the following chapter we shall discuss hysterical and wish-fulfillment beliefs. Both beliefs arise in a situation of strain (for example, danger to life, threat of loss of funds). Both beliefs also constitute redefinitions of the situation of strain. In these redefinitions some aspect of the situation is selected and attributed a *power* or *force* (Facilities Level 1)[3] that is sufficiently generalized to *guarantee the outcome* of the situation at hand. This outcome may be a catastrophe (produced by the negative forces envisioned in a

---

development, and problem-solving processes in small groups. Cf. H. Selye, *The Story of the Adaptation Syndrome* (Montreal, 1952), pp. 15–71, 203–225; Parsons, Bales, *et al.*, *Family, Socialization and Interaction Process*, Chs. IV, VII; R. F. Bales, "How People Interact in Conferences," *Scientific American*, Vol. 192 (1955), pp. 31–35.

[1] For an attempt to apply this logic to historical sequences during the Industrial Revolution in Great Britain, cf. Smelser, *Social Change in the Industrial Revolution*.

[2] Above, pp. 8–9 for an initial contrast between established behavior and collective behavior. The "uninstitutionalized" character of collective behavior is also implied by the fact that the high level component is *re*defined or *re*constituted.

[3] Above, p. 41.

The Nature of Collective Behavior

hysterical belief) or a blessing (produced by the positive forces envisioned in a wish-fulfillment belief). The force may be felt to reside in any object, event, action, or verbal formula. The defining characteristic of such a force is that it will guarantee the outcome of an ambiguous situation of strain. Such a force operates, moreover, without reference to the many steps of respecification that must intervene between generalized force and concrete situation to make the force genuinely operative.

Take the space example again. We would consider it a wish-fulfillment belief if a body of persons subscribed to the following: *If only we concerned ourselves with purifying and reaffirming the American way of life, we would not be experiencing frustrations in the development of operative space vehicles.* This assumes that generalized facilities—"the American way"—will guarantee a specific solution and that the intervening steps of scientific codification, technological specification, investment, and so on, will follow. In reality each of these steps contributes in transforming the American way into particular successes. The hypothetical faith in the American way alone, however, short-circuits many of these necessary steps, and thus constitutes a compressed solution to the problem of facilities.

We shall find this "if only" mentality in the beliefs associated with all forms of collective behavior. For instance, in the norm-oriented movement, we shall find extraordinary results promised if only certain reforms are adopted, and (on the negative side) gloomy predictions of decay and collapse if the sources of strain are not attacked quickly and vigorously. Adherents to such movements exaggerate reality because their action is based on beliefs which are both *generalized and short-circuited.*

In the detailed expositions that comprise the rest of the volume we shall expand and document our characterization of collective behavior. We can suggest already, however, why collective behavior displays some of the crudeness, excess, and eccentricity that it does. By short-circuiting from high-level to low-level components of social action, collective episodes by-pass many of the specifications, contingencies, and controls that are required to make the generalized components operative. This gives collective behavior its clumsy or primitive character. Furthermore, "solutions" to situations of strain that are produced by the riot and craze are sometimes "irresponsible" because the headlong attempt to apply generalized beliefs to specific situations disregards many existing moral and legal restrictions and violates the interests and integrity of many individuals and groups.

Collective behavior, then, is the action of the impatient. It con-

The Nature of Collective Behavior

trasts with the processes of social readjustment that do not short-circuit the journey from generalized belief to specific situations. Historically, collective behavior is closely associated with processes of structural reorganization of the components of action. In fact, episodes of collective behavior often constitute an early stage of social change;[1] they occur when conditions of strain have arisen, but before social resources have been mobilized for a specific and possibly effective attack on the sources of strain.[2] This is one reason for defining collective behavior as uninstitutionalized; it occurs when structured social action is under strain and when institutionalized means of overcoming the strain are inadequate. We might note that certain types of social control operate as an intermediary between these short-circuited collective episodes and orderly social change. Social control blocks the headlong attempts of collective episodes to bring quick results; if social control is effective, moreover, it channels the energy of collective outbursts into more modest kinds of behavior.

EXCLUSION OF OTHER PHENOMENA FROM THE FIELD OF COLLECTIVE BEHAVIOR

According to our definition, any instance of collective behavior must contain the following: (*a*) uninstitutionalized (*b*) collective action, (*c*) taken to modify a condition of strain (*d*) on the basis of a generalized reconstitution of a component of action. The term "collective behavior" has in the past been applied to many types of behavior which have one or several, but not all, of these characteristics. For this and other reasons, "collective behavior ... is obviously a catchall for various phenomena that do not readily fit into conceptions of institutional order."[3] We shall now mention several types of behavior—some of which have been called collective behavior—which we do not intend to encompass by our technical definition:

(1) Collective reaffirmations of values, rituals, festivals, ceremonials, and rites of passage. By these we mean, for example, the homecoming, the alumni rally, the salute to the flag, the patriotic demonstration on holidays, the ritual rebellion, and the revelry which

---

[1] For statements of this sort of relationship between collective behavior and social change, cf. Blumer, "Collective Behavior," in Lee (ed.), *op. cit.*, p. 169; H. Gerth and C. W. Mills, *Character and Social Structure* (New York, 1953), p. 429; E. B. Reuter and C. W. Hart, *Introduction to Sociology* (New York, 1933), p. 527.
[2] For an account of the timing of collective outbursts in these terms, cf. Smelser, *Social Change in the Industrial Revolution*, Chs. II, III, XV, especially pp. 29–32.
[3] Gerth and Mills, *Character and Social Structure*, p. 455.

The Nature of Collective Behavior

frequently accompanies such occasions.[1] Even though these celebrations may provide the setting for genuine collective outbursts—e.g., the patriotic demonstration that turns into a riot—they are not in themselves examples of collective behavior. True, they are based often on generalized values such as the divine, the nation, the monarchy, or the *alma mater*. True, they are collective. True, they may release tensions generated by conditions of structural strain. The basic difference between such ceremonials and collective behavior—and the reason for excluding them—is that the former are institutionalized in form and context. The index of their institutionalization is that such events are often scheduled for definite times, places, and occasions,[2] and are shrouded in formal rituals such as chants, or semi-formal "ways of celebrating," such as drinking, whooping, marching, and so on. Such celebrative activities are well described by the phrase "conventionalization of the crowd."[3] The beliefs on which they are based are not assembled as quick solutions for problems arising out of structural strain. Ceremonial activities are occasions for periodic reaffirmation of existing generalized components of action rather than the creation of new components.

We may illustrate the difference between ceremonial behavior and collective behavior further by reference to two aspects of the same episode of behavior. The worker-socialist movements that have developed in the history of American labor are episodes of collective behavior, since they involve unprecedented and uninstitutionalized mobilization of action to abolish many institutional norms (and even values) of industrial capitalism, and to establish corresponding social forms envisioned in the socialist ideology. We must exclude from our definition, however, their collective songs, pledges to solidarity, initiation rites, and so on, because they are significant primarily as regularized reaffirmations of the established values and

[1] E.g., E. Shils and M. Young, "The Meaning of the Coronation," *Sociological Review*, New Series, Vol. 1 (1953), pp. 63–81. For a brief discussion of the "demonstration" as mass behavior, cf. Dawson and Gettys, *An Introduction to Sociology*, p. 775. For descriptions of festive holiday celebrations, cf. F. T. Tinker and E. L. Tinker, *Old New Orleans: Mardi Gras Masks* (New York, 1931), pp. 66–69; W. W. Fowler, *The Roman Festivals of the Period of the Republic* (London, 1899), pp. 270–272; A. Munthe, *The Story of San Michele* (London, 1930), pp. 470–477. For an account of the ritual rebellion, cf. M. Gluckman, *Rituals of Rebellion in South-east Africa* (Manchester, 1954), pp. 20–31. Further examples of collective celebrations are found in LaPiere, *Collective Behavior*, pp. 464–481.

[2] For example, military or athletic victories are celebrated in this way. As LaPiere notes, much revelrous behavior involves "carrying out socially designated formulas." Even that revelry which "does not occur at socially designated times," such as honoring the chieftain or religious leader, picnics, etc., is heavily burdened with stylized and ritual elements. *Collective Behavior*, pp. 465–466.

[3] Turner and Killian, *Collective Behavior*, pp. 143–161.

The Nature of Collective Behavior

symbols of the movement itself. Thus, even though we include such social movements as instances of collective behavior, we do not include the ceremonies that build up within movements.

Empirically some types of behavior are on the borderline between collective behavior and ceremonial behavior. Let us examine lynching, for instance. In some cases it is a genuine hostile outburst, closely related to economic and status deprivation.[1] As such it would fit the definition of collective behavior. Lynching also has been, both in the West and the South, a quasi-institutionalized form of justice to replace weak civil regulations or general conditions of political disorganization.[2] Furthermore, some evidence indicates that lynching was in part a ritual to reaffirm old Southern values and to defy the North during Reconstruction and post-Reconstruction times.[3] Finally, as the term "lynching bee" connotes, it is possible that lynching was a kind of periodic, partially organized entertainment or release of tension for people who "crave some excitement, some interest, some passionate outburst."[4] The multiple significance of lynching should remind us that in many cases history does not always produce instances that fit neatly into our analytic definition of collective behavior. We must examine carefully the context of the event in question before we decide upon its relevance for study.

(2) *The audience.* Let us consider both the casual and the intentional audiences. An example of the first is a gathering of passers-by to watch construction crews at work, the second an audience at a symphony. We would exclude the "watchers" as an instance of collective behavior on several grounds: (*a*) The common object on which they focus is not generalized in a technical sense. It is simply men and machinery at work. (*b*) In all likelihood structural strain does not underlie the gathering. (*c*) No modification of any component of action is envisioned. In the case of the symphony audience, they may gather on the basis of generalized esthetic symbols; in addition, the music may have certain tension-release functions. Still, the audience is an institutionalized form. Persons gather at fixed

---

[1] For such background conditions, cf. H. Cantril, *The Psychology of Social Movements* (New York, 1941), pp. 110–113; Commission on Interracial Cooperation, *The Mob Still Rides* (Atlanta, 1935), p. 5. Also C. I. Hovland and R. R. Sears, "Minor Studies of Aggression: VI. Correlation of Lynchings with Economic Indices," *The Journal of Psychology*, Vol. 9 (1940), pp. 301–310. For a convincing critique of Hovland and Sears' statistical methods, cf. A. Mintz, "A Re-examination of Correlations between Lynchings and Economic Indices," *Journal of Abnormal and Social Psychology*, Vol. 41 (1946), pp. 154–160.

[2] J. E. Cutler, *Lynch Law* (New York, 1905), pp. 82, 137 ff; W. Cash, *The Mind of the South* (Garden City, N.Y., n.d.), pp. 124–126.

[3] Cash, *The Mind of the South*, p. 128.

[4] F. Tannenbaum, quoted in K. Young, *Source Book for Social Psychology*, (New York, 1927), pp. 524–525.

times and places, even evoke enthusiastic "bravos" at selected moments. Both the street throng and the audience provide common settings for genuine collective episodes such as the panic or the riot.[1] This is true, however, not because the audience itself is an instance of collective behavior, but rather because the audience situation provides geographical proximity and ease of communication and mobilization (as contrasted with other more dispersed situations).

(3) Public opinion. In general the term "public opinion" refers to a body of significant ideas and sentiments about controversial issues.[2] This kind of opinion is related to our definition of collective behavior in two ways: (*a*) Collective episodes may constitute a part of total "public opinion." In the 1880's and 1890's, for instance, a significant part of American public opinion was a product of collective movements—the Farmers' Alliance, the Grange, and the Populists—which gripped many parts of the agricultural population. (*b*) Public discussion of an issue may contribute to the rise of episodes of collective behavior. For instance, the spread and discussion of information on the danger of radioactive fall-out may produce widespread fears and perhaps a number of movements to prevent testing. Despite these links between public opinion and our definition of collective behavior, we do not treat public opinion as a type of collective behavior; it lies on a different conceptual level.[3]

(4) Propaganda is the "expression of opinion or action . . . deliberately designed to influence opinions or actions of . . . individuals or groups with reference to predetermined ends."[4] Propaganda is related to collective behavior in several ways: (*a*) It may be an attempt to create attitudes that will inspire collective outbursts. An example is the broadcasts to enemy populations in wartime with the intention of aggravating the dissatisfactions and discomforts from which they are suffering already. (*b*) Propaganda may attempt to prevent the rise of beliefs which could produce collective outbursts. Government propaganda that exaggerates the prosperous condition of a starving population is an example. (*c*) Reform and revolutionary movements themselves may use propaganda to gain adherents. Thus, propaganda may be a discouragement to, an encouragement to, or an adjunct of collective behavior. Propaganda

---

[1] For a discussion of some of the ways of changing an audience into a crowd, cf. W. D. Scott, *The Psychology of Public Speaking* (New York, 1926), pp. 180–182.

[2] Cf. Blumer, "Collective Behavior," in Lee (ed.), *op. cit.*, pp. 191–193.

[3] For discussion of the relations between public opinion and norm-oriented movements, below, pp. 273–274.

[4] Definition from the Institute for Propaganda Analysis quoted in A. M. Lee and E. B. Lee, *The Fine Art of Propaganda* (New York, 1939), p. 15; cf. also L. W. Doob, *Propaganda* (New York, 1935), p. 89.

The Nature of Collective Behavior

does not, however, qualify as a type of collective behavior as we define the term. Often it is institutionalized—as in advertizing, political campaigning, or political control—even though its aim may be to stir uninstitutionalized behavior. Even when it is the adjunct of a reform or revolutionary movement, propaganda is not the act of collective mobilization; it is one instrument by which participants in the movement hope to convince others and mobilize them for action.

(5) Crime. Individual crime poses no problems for classification, since it is not collective. What about organized crime? In many cases it flatly violates institutionalized property and personal rights.[1] In addition, crime often springs from conditions of social strain such as poverty and broken families.

Why, then, is organized crime not a form of collective behavior? In criminal activity no attempt is made to *reconstitute* a component of action on the basis of a generalized belief. Organized robbery, for instance, differs from a reform movement to change property laws in two senses: (*a*) In one sense criminals *accept* the existing social arrangements more than do adherents of the reform movement. They do not attempt to redefine or modify the general definition of property. Rather, crime feeds on existing property arrangements by stealing, pilfering, extorting, and blackmailing. Criminals attempt to subvert or avoid authority rather than change its form. Furthermore, a band of criminals offers no institutional "solutions" for the social problems created by the conditions of strain underlying criminal activity. (*b*) In another sense, criminals *reject* the social order more than adherents of the reform movement. The former wish to break the law as such. Reformers are not interested in illegality for its own sake; they desire to reject *but also to substitute* new institutional definitions. Participants in collective episodes may break the law—as in the riot or revolutionary outburst—but the aim of the outburst is not simply to profit from defiance. In collective behavior, law-breaking is generally a concomitant of a headlong attempt to modify some component of social action. Criminal activity, then, may be an aspect of collective behavior, but crime alone does not constitute collective behavior. The criminal act of robbery, for instance, differs radically from the prison riot of convicted criminals. The latter is generally a protest against the conditions of prison life with the implication that these conditions should be modified.[2]

[1] Quasi-institutionalized forms of crime such as protection rackets, dope or gambling rings, etc., that are organized with full knowledge and cooperation of political authorities are not by any criteria instances of collective behavior.

[2] Cf. F. E. Hartung and M. Floch, "A Socio-psychological Analysis of Prison Riots: An Hypothesis," *Journal of Criminal Law, Criminology, and Police Science*, Vol. 47 (1956–57), pp. 51–57.

The Nature of Collective Behavior

(6) Individual deviance such as hoboism, addiction, or alcoholism. Although such behavior has social and psychological origins similar to those of collective behavior, much deviance poses no problem of classification because it is individual, not collective. Furthermore, such behavior—like crime—does not involve any envisioned change in the components of social action. On occasion the use of drugs is an aspect of a collective movement—as in the Peyote cults among the American Indians—but it is not the use of the drug which makes the movement an instance of collective behavior. Rather it is the belief in the regeneration of a social order that gives the movement its distinctive character as a collective episode.

CHAPTER V

THE CREATION OF GENERALIZED BELIEFS

INTRODUCTION

Present in all collective behavior is some kind of belief that prepares the participants for action. Le Bon, for example, writes:

... It now remains for us to study the ... immediate factors of the opinions of crowds ... Images, Words and Formulas ... Illusions. ...

... To bring home conviction to crowds it is necessary first of all to comprehend thoroughly the sentiments by which they are animated, to pretend to share these sentiments, then to endeavour to modify them by calling up, by means of rudimentary associations, *certain eminently suggestive notions*, to be capable, if need be, of going back to the point of view from which a start was made, and, above all, to divine from instant to instant the sentiments to which one's discourse is giving birth.[1]

And Meerloo comments:

... The constant repetition of an emotional symbol makes the masses ripe for government by catchword. The catchword can precipitate the discharge of a specific collective explosion.[2]

Again, Brinton notes:

No ideas, no revolution. This does not mean that ideas cause revolutions, or that the best way to prevent revolutions is to censor ideas. It merely means that ideas form a part of the mutually dependent variables we are studying.[3]

Beliefs associated with collective behavior differ, however, from many of those which characterize everyday action. Observe, for instance, Le Bon's effort to grasp the essence of the crowd's "reasoning" power:

Whatever be the ideas suggested to crowds they can only exercise effective influence on condition that they assume a very absolute, uncompromising, and simple shape. ...

[1] G. Le Bon, *The Crowd* (London, 1952), pp. 101–113. Italics added.
[2] A. M. Meerloo, *Delusion and Mass-delusion* (New York, 1949), p. 59.
[3] *The Anatomy of Revolution*, p. 52. Cf. also Turner and Killian, *Collective Behavior*, p. 120.

The Creation of Generalized Beliefs

It cannot be said absolutely that crowds do not reason and are not to be influenced by reasoning.

However, the arguments they employ and those which are capable of influencing them are, from a logical point of view, of such an inferior kind that it is only by way of analogy that they can be described as reasoning.

The inferior reasoning of crowds is based, just as is reasoning of a higher order, on the association of ideas, but between the ideas associated by crowds there are only apparent bonds of analogy or succession.... The characteristics of reasoning of crowds are the association of dissimilar things possessing a merely apparent connection between each other, and the immediate generalization of particular cases....

Whatever strikes the imagination of crowds presents itself under the shape of a startling and very clear image, freed from all accessory explanation, or merely having as accompaniment a few marvellous or mysterious facts; examples in point are a great victory, a great miracle, a great crime, or a great hope....[1]

We shall now investigate the peculiarities of those beliefs that activate people for participation in episodes of collective behavior. We refer to such beliefs as *generalized beliefs*. We hope to give more precise theoretical meaning to the insights of Le Bon and others who have attempted to fathom the mysteries of these kinds of beliefs.

Generalized beliefs constitute one stage in the total value-added process by which we account for the occurrence of episodes of collective behavior.[2] Such beliefs become significant as determinants in the value-added process only when conditions of structural conduciveness and strain are present; these beliefs are necessary, however, to mobilize people for collective action. In this chapter we shall examine only the build-up of generalized beliefs themselves; in the following chapters we shall examine the place of these beliefs in the total value-added process.

A study of rumor, ideology, and superstition will illuminate the character of generalized beliefs. We shall examine rumors—those "proposition[s] . . . of topical reference . . . [intended] for belief . . . [and] disseminated without official verification."[3] Rumors frequently precede short-term outbursts, such as panics, crazes, and riots; they play a part in long-term disturbances, such as revolutionary movements and religious secessions. We shall also study the ideologies

---

[1] *The Crowd*, pp. 61–72.
[2] Above, pp. 15–17. This is not to claim as an empirical generalization that all persons who become involved in episodes of collective behavior "adhere" to the generalized beliefs associated with these episodes. As we shall see in connection with the "derived" or "speculative" stage of such behavior, many participants capitalize on the *momentum of the episode itself.*
[3] R. H. Knapp, "A Psychology of Rumor," *Public Opinion Quarterly*, Vol. 8 (1944), p. 22.

The Creation of Generalized Beliefs

which often draw people into movements directed toward normative change and revolutionary overthrow. In addition, we shall learn much about the structure of generalized beliefs from the study of superstition and institutionalized magic.

Generalized Beliefs and Strain. We assume that when generalized beliefs arise, some sort of strain is present. Most of the literature on rumor, for instance, reports that rumors arise in situations which are "ambiguous," "uncertain," "uncommon," "unfamiliar," "unknown," "unverifiable," or "uncontrollable."[1] These characteristics emphasize cognitive elements of ambiguity—elements which we discussed under the Facilities component.[2] It should be pointed out, however, that strain other than simple situational ambiguity (Facilities Series) may give rise to rumors and related beliefs. Deprivations (Mobilization Series), normative misalignments (Normative Series) and value dissonance (Value Series) are also appropriate settings. Because of the hierarchical relations among the components of social action,[3] all these other kinds of strain *necessarily* imply a degree of ambiguity for Facilities. Words like "ambiguity" and "uncertainty," which describe the initiating conditions for generalized beliefs, serve as a shorthand for all kinds of structural strain. The general principle is this: Rumor and related beliefs arise when structural strain is not manageable within the existing framework of action.

Generalized Beliefs and the Reduction of Ambiguity. Generalized beliefs reduce the ambiguity created by conditions of structural strain. The Detroit race riots of 1943, for example, were a source of uncertainty. Many responded to these disturbing events by spreading rumors that gave some meaning to the outbursts:

> Because spontaneous combustion is mysterious, weird rumors have been widely circulated that the Detroit riot was Nazi inspired, that the Ku Klux Klan was at the root of it. The FBI, the attorney general of Michigan, the prosecuting attorney of Wayne County, and other investigating officials unanimously repudiate these rumors. They have found no evidence to

---

[1] J. Prasad, "The Psychology of Rumour: A Study Relating to the Great Indian Earthquake of 1934," *British Journal of Psychology*, Vol. 26 (1935), pp. 5, 15; T. Shibutani, "The Circulation of Rumors as a Form of Collective Behavior" (Chicago, 1948), pp. 157–195; L. Festinger *et al.*, "A Study of Rumor: Its Origin and Spread," *Human Relations*, Vol. 1 (1948), pp. 483–484; W. Peterson and N. Gist, "Rumor and Public Opinion," *American Journal of Sociology*, Vol. 57 (1951–52), p. 160; Allport and Postman, *The Psychology of Rumor*, p. 33. Allport and Postman mention "importance" of the situation as a second factor in rumor transmission. In the discussion which follows we assume that the structural strain which gives rise to "ambiguous" situations is also important for the actors in question.
[2] Above, pp. 51–54.
[3] Above, pp. 32–34.

The Creation of Generalized Beliefs

substantiate them. . . . Nor is there a shred of evidence to implicate the Negro leadership here.[1]

Rumor and related beliefs restructure an ambiguous situation by explaining what has happened, by reporting what is happening, and by predicting what will happen.

Generalized Beliefs and the Short-circuiting Process. Generalized beliefs restructure an ambiguous situation in a short-circuited way. In fact, this process of short-circuiting constitutes the central defining characteristic of a generalized belief as opposed to other kinds of beliefs. Short-circuiting involves the jump from extremely high levels of generality to specific, concrete situations.[2] Later in the chapter we shall illustrate this process for each major type of generalized belief.

Generalized Beliefs and Preparation for Action. Generalized beliefs prepare individuals for collective action. They create a "common culture" within which leadership, mobilization, and concerted action can take place. This principle, readily observable in the ideological indoctrination of political and religious movements, is operative in rumor as well:

> . . . the situation [which generates rumour] must be of group interest. This makes rumour fundamentally a social phenomenon. . . . Unless a situation is of group of "public" interest, no rumours about it will arise, because the members of the group are not called upon to respond to it in a "collective" way. The moment a rumour spreads about a matter of even private and personal importance, such as the rumours about the marriage of a person or of one's tour programme, one's health, one's appointment to a job, etc., the matter is at once converted into a social situation which is of interest and importance to the group, and is no longer a merely private affair.[3]

This "preparing" function is implicit in our view of generalized beliefs as determinants that add their value in the process that builds up to an episode of collective behavior. We should not, however, conceive of generalized beliefs simply in terms of whether they

---

[1] W. J. Norton, "The Detroit Riots—and After," *Survey Graphic*, Vol. 32 (Aug., 1943), p. 317.
[2] Above, pp. 71–73.
[3] Prasad, "The Psychology of Rumour," *op. cit.*, pp. 8–9. Turner and Killian also emphasize this collective aspect. *Collective Behavior*, p. 68. On the basis of such reasoning the authors criticize Allport and Postman for their "psychological" view of rumor as a mere series of distortions. Thus rumor has a social or collective aspect, and is not merely the adaptation of information to individual needs and attitudes. Cf. also Festinger *et al.*, "A Study of Rumor," *op. cit.*, p. 484, and Shibutani, "The Circulation of Rumors as a Form of Collective Behavior," pp. 195–199.

The Creation of Generalized Beliefs

"cause" such behavior.[1] To ask whether rumor compares strongly or weakly with other "causes" creates an inappropriate logic for assessing its influence. Rumor and other generalized beliefs are better understood as necessary conditions that become effective when structural conduciveness and strain are present. These generalized beliefs, furthermore, culminate in episodes of collective behavior only if other determinants—specifically mobilization for action and the response of agencies of control—appear.

In this chapter we shall outline the major types of generalized beliefs: (a) *hysteria*, which transforms an ambiguous situation into an absolutely potent, generalized threat; (b) *wish-fulfillment*, which reduces ambiguity by positing absolutely efficacious, generalized facilities; (c) *hostility*, which involves removing some agent or object perceived as a generalized threat or obstacle; (d) *norm-oriented beliefs*, which envision the reconstitution of a threatened normative structure; (e) *value-oriented beliefs*, which envision the reconstitution of a threatened value system. These types of belief stand in a hierarchy which parallels the hierarchy governing the components of social action in general.

From these beliefs we may look in two directions in the value-added process as a whole. First, we may look "backward" to the particular component under strain which each generalized belief restructures. Thus hysteria and wish-fulfillment restructure the Facilities Series; hostility restructures the Mobilization Series; the norm-oriented belief restructures the Normative Series, and the value-oriented belief restructures the Values Series. This formal connection between strain and types of beliefs is not a causal connection. Many different kinds of strain may give rise to one type of belief, and one kind of strain may give rise to many different types of belief. Which type of generalized belief, if any, arises is a function of both the character of strain and the character of other determinants (e.g., conduciveness and the response of agencies of social control).

Second, we may look "forward" to the kind of collective behavior each type of belief produces—*if* other determinants permit action to flow. Hysterical beliefs, if and when they give rise to action, lead to panic; wish-fulfillment beliefs to the "craze" (e.g., the boom, the bandwagon, the fad, and certain types of revivalism); hostile beliefs, to scapegoating and in extreme cases, mob violence; norm-oriented beliefs, to reform movements and counter-movements; and

---

[1] This logic of "causality" seemed to guide A. M. Rose unduly in his research reported in "Rumor in the Stock Market," *Public Opinion Quarterly*, Vol. 15 (1951), pp. 461–486. Cf. also J. Mindell, *The Stock Market: Basic Guide for Investors* (New York, 1948), p. 79.

The Creation of Generalized Beliefs

value-oriented beliefs, to political and religious revolution, nationalist movements, secessions, and formation of cults. In this chapter we shall consider only the generalized beliefs themselves. In later chapters we shall examine the conditions which encourage their spread and expression in action.

Concerning these conditions of spread and expression, Penrose has maintained that the transmissibility of beliefs depends on three things: "(1) the quality [i.e., the content] of the idea itself, (2) the available means of transmission, and (3) the condition [i.e., the circumstances] of the recipient."[1] We might add that the operation of social controls also influences transmissibility.[2] In this chapter we shall study only the first factor. Later we will discuss the modes of transmission, such as milling, collective excitement, social contagion, and suggestion; we also postpone discussing what kinds of people accept such beliefs and why they accept them; and the obstacles to acceptance, which are found in the operation of individual and social controls.

In this chapter, then, we shall analyze the development of generalized beliefs which redefine an unstructured situation and which precede collective outbursts. For the purposes of this analysis, we shall ignore certain of their additional functions, such as their use for personal advancement of an ambitious person who wishes to defame the reputation of another, their use as "feelers" to test public reactions to an idea, etc.[3] However important these functions are in the genesis of generalized beliefs, they are not immediately relevant to the incorporation of these beliefs into a value-added process which produces an episode of collective behavior.

THE SIMPLEST FORM OF GENERALIZED BELIEF: HYSTERIA

We define a hysterical belief as a belief empowering an ambiguous element in the environment with a generalized power to threaten or destroy. Examples of hysterical beliefs are premonitions of disaster and bogey rumors, both of which frequently build up as a prelude to panic. Other hysterical beliefs may be found in institutionalized

---

[1] L. S. Penrose, *On the Objective Study of Crowd Behaviour* (London, 1952), p. 56.

[2] For discussion of the influence of social controls on the spread of rumor, cf. Peterson and Gist, "Rumor and Public Opinion," *op. cit.*, p. 160, and A. Chorus, "The Basic Law of Rumor," *Journal of Abnormal and Social Psychology*, Vol. 48 (1953), pp. 313–314.

[3] For discussion of these other functions cf. Festinger, *et al.*, "A Study of Rumor," *op. cit.*, pp. 473–474; R. Firth, "Rumor in a Primitive Society," *Journal of Abnormal and Social Psychology*, Vol. 53 (1956), pp. 130–132.

The Creation of Generalized Beliefs

beliefs, such as superstitions, fears of witchcraft, demons, spirits, and the like.

The three components of a hysterical belief are (*a*) an ambiguous situation, (*b*) anxiety, and (*c*) redefinition of the situation. Each component is a necessary condition for the next. Thus they stand in value-added relation to one another.[1] The value-added process unfolds in the following way at the psychological level:

... The stability of [a person's] ego, hence the consistency of his reactions, is built up in relation to physical and social anchorages. As the physical and social anchorages become more unstable, more uncertain, the individual's personal bearings become more unstable, more uncertain. . . . [Anxiety or insecurity involves a] state of ego tension produced by actual or perceived uncertainty of one's physical or social grounds in the present or in the future.

The psychological sequences of the actual or experienced loss of physical and social bearings are at least *initially* increased fluctuations, variations in reactions, floundering around in search of something to hold on to, strivings to reestablish some level of stability through available anchorages.[2]

In these "flounderings around" for meaning *one* result is the rise of a hysterical belief. How does a hysterical belief "reestablish some level of stability"? It eliminates the ambiguity which gives rise to anxiety by positing a threat that is generalized and absolute. Thus the threat, originally only ambiguous or precarious, becomes *certain to harm or destroy*. In this way a hysterical belief structures the situation and makes it more predictable, even though the structuring process results in deep pessimism or terrible fears. In an ambiguous setting, a person is anxious because he does not know what to fear; holding a hysterical belief, a person at least believes he knows what he fears.

The growth of a hysterical belief is not the only response to ambiguity and anxiety.[3] Sometimes generalized beliefs other than hysteria —e.g., wish-fulfillment or hostility—appear. If an uncertain situation is properly controlled, it need not give rise to *any* generalized belief. In later chapters we shall look into the problem of predicting the development of the different forms of generalized beliefs. Here we maintain only that hysteria presupposes conditions of ambiguity and anxiety. These conditions are necessary but not sufficient for the appearance of a hysterical belief.

---

[1] The logic of the value-added process is outlined above, pp. 13–20.

[2] M. Sherif and O. J. Harvey, "A Study in Ego Functioning: Elimination of Stable Anchorages in Individual and Group Situations," *Sociometry*, Vol. 15 (1952), p. 302.

[3] The diversity of responses to uncertainty is suggested in F. Knight, *Risk, Uncertainty and Profit* (Boston, 1921), p. 235.

The Creation of Generalized Beliefs

Of all the generalized beliefs accompanying collective episodes, hysteria is the simplest. In ways which we shall examine, all other generalized beliefs have an implied hysteria as *one component*. Hysteria, on the other hand, does not include these other kinds of beliefs as elements of itself. Hysteria, then, is simplest because it stands at the bottom of a hierarchy which increases in complexity and inclusiveness.

Ambiguity. We may speak of unstructured and structured ambiguity. The first—an irregular or abnormal event, unanticipated information, or dangers of unknown proportions—occurs fortuitously and beyond the realm of institutionalized expectations. Structured ambiguity, on the other hand, is part of the definition of the social situation.

The clearest instances of unstructured ambiguity are found in situations of "totally incomprehensible disaster"[1]—sudden explosions, unexpected storms or floods, unanticipated enemy attacks, etc. Dramatic items of information also may give rise to unstructured ambiguity; news about atomic tests and a number of scare headlines regarding these tests apparently underlay a postwar hysterical outburst in Seattle.[2] In wartime situations it is of great advantage if one belligerent is able to keep the situation unstructured:

> It is the secret of the war of nerves that the initiative is retained by one side, that while tension mounts the world is kept guessing. In each phase of the war of nerves Hitler's next step was an unknown danger. A situation of this kind, where activity cannot be directed toward any one goal, creates a feeling of mental paralysis and helplessness. . . .[3]

The difference between unstructured and structured ambiguity may be illustrated in the economic sphere. The businessman faces two types of risks: (*a*) General risks not tied specifically to his market situation—risks stemming from natural calamities, sickness, accidents, carelessness, variations in weather, dangers from criminal activity, etc. All such risks are unstructured in the sense that they are not an aspect of the institutionalization of business itself; the businessman would face them whether in business or some other kind of activity. (*b*) Some risks fall under the heading of "market risks" which are structured aspects of his specific situations:

[1] P. B. Foreman, "Panic Theory," *Sociology and Social Research*, Vol. 37 (1952–53), p. 302.
[2] N. Z. Medalia and O. N. Larsen, "Diffusion and Belief in a Collective Delusion: The Seattle Windshield Pitting Epidemic," *American Sociological Review*, Vol. 23 (1958), pp. 185–186.
[3] E. Kris, "Danger and Morale," *American Journal of Orthopsychiatry*, Vol. 14 (1944), p. 153.

The Creation of Generalized Beliefs

By market risks we mean the unavoidable uncertainties due to the fact that *time* elapses between the purchase and the sale of commodities, during which time unpredictable changes often occur in the prices and other market conditions surrounding the commodities dealt in.[1]

Market risks, in turn, are of two types: (*a*) Some are manageable through aggregation. An insurance company, for instance, always faces a residue of uncertainty in predicting any given person's death. By treating this individual as part of an aggregate population that possesses an average life expectancy, the company protects itself against the possibility of his premature death (and resulting loss of funds by the company). In this case uncertainty is managed by pooling the individual into an aggregation with known average characteristics. (*b*) As Frank Knight has shown, many market risks cannot be managed by methods of aggregation:

... Business decisions embody an effort to predict and control the course of events in a particular case, and the liability to error in foresight and in action differs in principle from the ideal of a probability situation. Not only is it impossible to group such decisions into classes approximately alike from the probability standpoint, but they are subject to a complicated and vital "moral hazard." In large scale business organizations the decisions of the ultimate managers relate chiefly to the selection of persons who shall make more concrete decisions of policy and to the definition of their powers and duties. The motivations involved in making commitments on the basis of an exercise of one's own judgment are very different from those involved in gambling on a mechanical probability. Actual gambling may of course be connected with an exercise of judgment, real or supposed, as when one picks the winner of a horse race; but the motives are still very different when the better himself is the runner. Similar considerations apply when personal relations are involved, as when one "bets" on his judgment of collaborators in an enterprise, selected and directed by himself. It becomes therefore quite impossible in the case of business risks to assert on any objective ground that there is even approximately a certain fractional "chance" of any particular result; an assertion in this form merely expresses a certain degree of confidence or belief on the part of the person who makes it and rather accidentally resembles a statement of a certain quantitative probability.[2]

This kind of ambiguity abounds outside the market as well, as the following examples show:

(1) High executives in government face many risks which are not

---

[1] C. O. Hardy, *Risk and Risk-bearing* (Chicago, 1923), p. 3. For a similar dichotomization of risks into "static" and "dynamic" cf. J. Haynes, "Risk as an Economic Factor," *Quarterly Journal of Economics*, Vol. 9 (1895), pp. 412–414.

[2] F. H. Knight, "Risk," *Encyclopaedia of the Social Sciences*, Vol. 13, p. 394. For fuller developments of this theme, cf. *Risk, Uncertainty and Profit*, pp. 216–234. Also Hardy, *Risk and Risk-bearing*, p. 1.

reducible by conventional means of aggregation. The number of potentially relevant determinants of the success of, say, a foreign-policy decision is enormous. More important, the ambiguity is increased because many of these determinants lie outside the control of those officials who must make the decisions.

(2) Structured ambiguity is great in contemporary courtship and marriage arrangements. Presumably, those ready to take the vows share the desire for permanent, happy, and fruitful marriage. Yet it is, indeed, uncertain at the time of deciding to marry that the marriage *will be* permanent, happy, and fruitful. How are the spouses to know that this once-and-for-all decision is the right one? No matter how rationally the potential spouse tries to predict his future happiness, he simply does not command the knowledge to guarantee that he is making the correct choice.

(3) The football coach commands *some* of the means to win—the power to substitute players, the power to call special training sessions, the power to whip up his team's morale by pep talks. On the other hand, many of the means to win lie outside his control. He cannot control the strength of the opposing team; he cannot direct the movements of his players on the field once the ball has been snapped; he cannot dictate recruitment policy for athletes unequivocally to administration and faculty—these are some of the kinds of uncertainty which are built into his situation.

Unstructured and structured ambiguity both involve the actor's limited capacity to overcome some unknown or unpredictable element in the situation, whether this element be an unanticipated interruption of the flow of life or an ingrained part of an organized social role.

Ambiguity, if controlled, does not give rise to anxiety and hysteria. For *unstructured* ambiguity the following kinds of control are available: (*a*) supplying information—authentic or "magical"—which defines a surprising event as non-threatening; (*b*) guaranteeing firm and effective leadership in the face of unanticipated crises; (*c*) regimenting a group in advance by creating norms to follow in the event of unanticipated occurrences—e.g., civil defense procedures, fire-drills, air-raid alerts; (*d*) discounting uncertainty by appeal to values; e.g., remaining firm in the conviction that "having faith" in the face of crises will make everything turn out satisfactorily.[1] For *structured*

[1] For examples of the importance of such controls, cf. J. Rickman, "Panic and Air-raid Precautions," *The Lancet*, Vol. 234 (1938), p. 1293; H. Brucker, "Press Communication in Relation to Morale and Panic," and J. A. M. Meerloo, "Peoples' Reaction to Danger," in *Panic and Morale* (New York, 1958), pp. 67–68 and 174–175. Formally, these four means of control correspond to Facilities, Mobilization, Norms, and Values, respectively.

The Creation of Generalized Beliefs

ambiguity the same classes of controls reduce the probability of anxiety; (*a*) increasing the supply of information (e.g., giving "hot tips" in the stock market); (*b*) organizing and controlling the ambiguity through authoritative leadership (e.g., following the "insiders" in the stock market); (*c*) creating norms which act as cushions against the possible risks of social life (e.g., social security reduces the risks of old age by establishing procedures for saving and repayment); (*d*) maintaining faith in a set of values (e.g., having faith in "free enterprise" is one way to mollify the potentially disturbing features of market life).[1] In later chapters we shall see how such controls determine in part *which kind* of collective response, if any, arises from situations of strain and ambiguity. In order to trace the development of hysterical beliefs, however, we now assume that such controls do not operate successfully.

Anxiety. Anxiety is such a diffuse state that it is difficult to characterize it in other than negative terms. Quarantelli, for instance, observes that anxiety "is marked by an inability to designate any object in the environment to account for the diffuse sense of foreboding or even dread the individual is experiencing."[2] Anxiety, rooted in situations of ambiguity,[3] is a generalized response not tied to precisely definable objects. It is a vague and incomprehensible uneasiness about unknown threats. Because these threats are undefined, *they contain potentially enormous power of destruction.*

We may characterize anxiety formally in terms of the components of social action. Anxiety involves a *negative generalization.* It is negative because it is limited to the disturbing, harmful, or threatening possibilities of an ambiguous situation. It is generalized because these negative possibilities are envisioned as boundless powers, forces, or causes at work. This generalization involves a move, moreover, to Level 1 of the Facilities Scale.[4]

[1] For discussion of such means of reducing anxiety and insecurity, cf. Knight, *Risk, Uncertainty and Profit*, pp. 238–257, 347–349; Hardy, *Risk and Risk-bearing*, p. 9; J. K. Galbraith, *The Affluent Society* (Boston, 1958), Ch. VIII. For a study of attitudinal adaptations on the part of medical students in the face of uncertainty, cf. R. Fox, "Training for Uncertainty," in R. K. Merton, G. C. Reader, and P. L. Kendall (eds.), *The Student Physician* (Cambridge, Mass., 1957), pp. 207–241.

[2] E. L. Quarantelli, "The Nature and Conditions of Panic," *American Journal of Sociology*, Vol. 60 (1954–55), p. 271, fn. For similar views of anxiety, cf. R. May, *The Meaning of Anxiety* (New York, 1950), pp. 190–193; and H. Basowitz, H. Persky, S. J. Korchin, and R. R. Grinker, *Anxiety and Stress* (New York, 1955), pp. 1–5.

[3] For reviews of the literature on the genesis of anxiety, cf. B. B. Hudson, "Anxiety in Response to the Unfamiliar," *Journal of Social Issues*, Vol. 10 (1954), pp. 53–60; and Basowitz, Persky, Korchin, and Grinker, *Anxiety and Stress*, Ch. II.

[4] Above, pp. 71–72.

The Creation of Generalized Beliefs

Anxiety is the generalized component of a hysterical belief. Like all beliefs that underlie episodes of collective behavior, however, hysteria includes both this generalized component and a short-circuited return to the world of concrete events and situations. We shall now inquire into this process of short-circuiting.

The Structuring of Anxiety. A hysterical belief purports to explain a past event or situation, report a present one, or predict a future one. In any case, it marks a focusing of the generalized powers and forces inherent in anxiety—a focusing toward concrete negative outcomes. In this way hysteria reduces the ambiguity inherent in a situation; it posits completely omnipotent forces and explains, reports, or predicts events as manifestations of the operation of these forces.

Consider the following examples: (*a*) Predictions of the end of the world frequently cluster upon the heels of the appearance of comets, pestilences, calamities and other sources of possible danger.[1] (*b*) Recently, anxieties over the potentialities of atomic warfare have led not only to predictions of world destruction, but also to many apparent misperceptions and hallucinations of "flying saucers" believed to be omens of destruction.[2] (*c*) It has been observed that early in World War II British authorities vastly overestimated the severity of panic that would grip the population if bombing raids were to commence on a large scale.[3] In all these examples a threatening situation of unknown proportions was structured by predicting specific negative outcomes.

The anxiety rumor—or "bogey rumor"[4]—which frequently circulates on the eve of panic reactions also structures an ambiguous situation. Such rumors transform generalized anxiety into fear. As Quarantelli notes:

> Fear, rather than anxiety, is the affective component of the panic reaction.... The fear-stricken individual perceives some highly ego-

[1] C. Mackay, *Extraordinary Popular Delusions and the Madness of Crowds* (Boston, 1932), pp. 258–259.

[2] D. H. Menzel, *Flying Saucers* (Cambridge, Mass., 1953), pp. 144–145. Cf. also the interesting case study of a small movement which incorporated this theme in L. Festinger, H. W. Riecken, and S. Schachter, *When Prophesy Fails* (Minneapolis, 1956).

[3] R. M. Titmuss, *Problems of Social Policy* (London, 1950), pp. 16–21, 327.

[4] Allport and Postman, *The Psychology of Rumor*, pp. 6–7; D. J. Jacobson, *The Affairs of Dame Rumor* (New York, 1948), pp. 6–14, 562–563; Knapp, "A Psychology of Rumor," *op. cit.*, pp. 23–24. Perhaps the most thorough documentation of anxiety rumors may be found in the study of the circulation of rumors among German troops shortly after the invasion of Belgium in World War I. These rumors concern supposed acts of atrocity committed by Belgian citizens and inspired by the Catholic clergy. F. van Langenhove, *The Growth of a Legend* (New York, 1916), especially pp. 5–6, 17, 125–126, 147, 155–156, 205–206.

The Creation of Generalized Beliefs

involved value greatly endangered. The threat is something that can be labeled, localized in space, and therefore potentially can be escaped from. The threat is specific. . . . Not only do panic participants know what they are immediately afraid *for* (which is their own physical safety), but they also are aware of what they are afraid *of*. The fear that is experienced in panic is of something specific, of something which can be designated. The covert reaction of the individual in panic is never in regard to the unknown or the incomprehensible as such. It is always of a specific threat, the particularization of which may be arrived at individually or through social interaction.[1]

Sometimes anxiety rumors concerning an imminent crisis (e.g., the collapse of stock market prices) are started in unstructured situations by persons interested in their own gain (e.g., persons wishing to profit speculatively on panic selling of stocks).[2] Such rumors are not initiated spontaneously. Even in such cases ambiguity, anxiety, and the need to structure the ambiguous situation must be present if the rumor is to spread and be accepted.

Frequently hysterical beliefs find their way into the lore of a culture. One of the universal characteristics of religion, for instance, is the presence of "evil geniuses . . . which [enable] men to explain the permanent evils that they have to suffer, their nightmares and illnesses, whirlwinds and tempests, etc."[3] In popular folklore we observe the traditionalized fears of hobgoblins, spooks, ghosts, witches, and—more recently—gremlins.[4] One function of all these beliefs is to structure anxiety. They have other functions as well, however; they may be used as techniques to socialize children through fright, as instruments of social control, and so on.[5]

Summary and Conclusions. To facilitate the following summary, Table 8 reproduces two versions of the components of social action:

---

[1] Quarantelli, "The Nature and Conditions of Panic," *op. cit.*, p. 271. See also Bull's characterization of fear: "[Fear] occupies a unique position in the sequence between the primary state of surprise and eventual specific adaptive behavior for which it is a kind of fumbling in the dark before a satisfactory appraisal of the danger has been made. It means that fear is primarily bound up with the feeling of *uncertainty* as to (*a*) the exact nature of the danger stimulus, and, therefore, (*b*) how to act with reference to it." N. Bull, "The Dual Character of Fear," *Journal of Psychology*, Vol. V (1938), p. 212. For experimental evidence on the process of structuring anxiety, cf. Sherif and Harvey, "A Study in Ego Functioning," *op. cit.*, pp. 273-274.

[2] C. Duguid, *The Story of the Stock Exchange* (London, 1901), pp. 27-28; Mindell, *The Stock Market*, p. 73.

[3] E. Durkheim, *The Elementary Forms of the Religious Life* (Glencoe, Ill., 1954), p. 281.

[4] For a brief account of modern magical survivals, cf. W. J. J. Cornelius, *Science, Religion and Man* (London, 1934), pp. 209-213.

[5] For the functions of witchcraft for social control, cf. C. Kluckhohn, *Navaho Witchcraft* (Cambridge, Mass., 1944), pp. 63-64. We shall discuss the multiple functions of magical beliefs at greater length below, pp. 95-96.

The Creation of Generalized Beliefs

(*a*) the seven levels of specificity of the Facilities Series; (*b*) the foci of strain underlying all episodes of collective behavior.

We may represent the growth of hysterical beliefs as a value-added process. Shown graphically in Figure 1, this process has three stages:

(1) Ambiguity. This may result from any kind of strain (Levels 5–7 of any component of action).[1] The essence of an ambiguous situation is this: The situation may frustrate, harm, or destroy; but the kind and degree (if any) of the resulting frustration, harm, or destruction is unknown.

(2) Anxiety. The initial response to ambiguity is a selection of the

TABLE 8A

LEVELS OF SPECIFICITY OF SITUATIONAL FACILITIES

1	Preconceptions concerning causality
2	Codification of knowledge
3	Technology, or specification of knowledge in situational terms
4	Procurement of wealth, power or prestige to activate Level 3
5	Allocation of effective technology to sector of society
6	Allocation of effective technology to roles and organizations
7	Allocation of facilities within organization to attain concrete goals

negative possibilities of the situation and a generalization of these possibilities into unlimited forces. In formal terms it is a movement to Level 1 of the Facilities Series. Anxiety, in this sense, involves the creation of or appeal to a new view of causality by converting ambiguity into an absolute threat.

(2*a*)[2] Restructuring. Finally, anxiety short-circuits from the world of generalized forces directly to specific outcomes. In formal terms this third phase by-passes Levels 2–4 of the Facilities Series. No attempt is made to delimit consistently the logical boundaries of the generalized forces; they are undifferentiated sources of power that

[1] Above, p. 81.
[2] We use (2a) rather than (3) to facilitate comparison with the Figures for wish-fulfillment beliefs, hostile beliefs, etc.

The Creation of Generalized Beliefs

are unlimited (Facilities Level 2). No attempt is made to specify determinate rules as to how these forces "work" in situations (Facilities Level 3). No attempt is made to specify the conditions under

TABLE 8B
FOCI OF STRAIN FOR THE COMPONENTS OF ACTION

Level	Values	Norms	Mobilization of motivation for organized action	Situational facilities
5	Strain on the principles of integration of values	Strain in relations among major social sectors	Actual or potential deprivation of major social sectors	Ambiguity in allocating facilities to sectors of society
6	Strain on commitment to organizational goals	Strain on integration of organization	Actual or potential deprivation related to organizational membership	Ambiguity in allocating facilities to organizations
7	Strain on commitment to personal values	Strain at level of operative rules	Actual or potential deprivation in role performance	Ambiguity in allocating facilities to attain operative goals

which situational impetus is supplied to the generalized forces (Facilities Level 4).

We may now suggest some reasons why hysterical beliefs (like all generalized beliefs) are likely to be exaggerated: (*a*) Because Stage 2 selects unfavorable possibilities from an ambiguous situation—

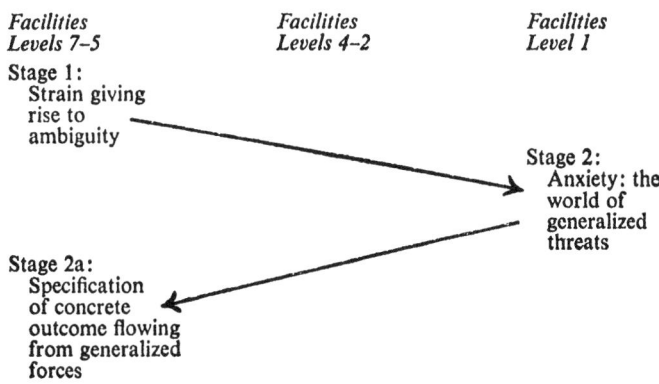

FIGURE 1
VALUE-ADDED IN THE CREATION OF HYSTERICAL BELIEFS

The Creation of Generalized Beliefs

which, by definition, has many possible outcomes—hysterical beliefs are unduly pessimistic. (*b*) Because Stage 2 also involves a leap to a world of unlimited powers and forces, it exaggerates the efficacy of these forces. (*c*) Because Stage 2*a* involves a leap back to the concrete situation, it is likely to exaggerate the outcomes to be expected from the initially ambiguous situation. (*d*) Because Stage 2*a* by-passes many logical and empirical contingencies in Levels 2–4 of the Facilities Scale, this stage is likely to involve still more distortions.

Because of these exaggerations, it is unlikely that the account of affairs contained in a hysterical belief is a true account. Because the initial situation is itself realistically ambiguous, it is logically possible —though seldom empirically the case—that the actual course of events will be the same as that given in the hysterical belief. It is more nearly accurate, then, to say that hysterical beliefs are "unverified" rather than "untrue." The lack of verification stems from the dynamics of the value-added process itself—the leap from situational ambiguity to diffuse anxiety, then back to specific situational outcomes. These leaps by-pass many logical and empirical contingencies.

WISH-FULFILLMENT BELIEFS

We have treated the hysterical belief as a *negative* generalization up the Facilities Series and a short-circuited return to the concrete situation. Now we shall consider the corresponding *positive* generalization up the same series. Such a response—which we call the creation of a wish-fulfillment belief—guarantees a positive outcome in an uncertain situation by empowering some force with generalized potency to overcome the possibly frustrating, harmful or destructive possibilities.

As examples of wish-fulfillment beliefs, we shall examine first "pipe-dream" rumors, which explain, report, or predict some favorable event. Such rumors frequently precede the boom, the bandwagon, and related forms of craze behavior. In addition, we shall examine various forms of magic—especially the magic of protection, production, and conservation—from which we may learn much about wish-fulfillment beliefs in general.[1]

What are the characteristics of a wish-fulfillment belief? Like hysteria, it is rooted in ambiguity stemming from situations of strain. This constitutes Stage 1 in the value-added process (see Figure 2).

[1] For a brief discussion of these types of magic, cf. R. Firth, *Primitive Polynesian Economy* (London, 1939), pp. 170–171; and "The Sociology of 'Magic' in Tikopia," *Sociologus*, Vol. 4 (1954), pp. 100 ff. The fourth type of magic, the magic of destruction, will be discussed in connection with the development of hostile beliefs.

The Creation of Generalized Beliefs

Stage 2 consists of anxiety, which may be short-circuited to fears about specific events, objects, and situations (Stage 2a). Thus far the stages of value-added for the wish-fulfillment belief are identical to those of the hysterical belief. To complete the formation of the wish-fulfillment belief, Stage 3 involves the positing of generalized forces to counter the potential threats of the ambiguous situation. These generalized forces are then short-circuited to the concrete situation (Stage 3a). A belief in positive outcomes for the ambiguous situation is thus completed. As Figure 2 shows, this generalized belief has the same stages of value-added as the hysterical belief, *plus two addi-*

FIGURE 2
VALUE-ADDED IN THE CREATION OF WISH-FULFILLMENT BELIEFS

	−Facilities	+Facilities
Stage 1:	Stage 2:	Stage 3:
Strain giving rise to ambiguity	Anxiety: the world of generalized threats	Generalized forces to counter potential threats
	↓ (Short-circuit)	↓ (Short-circuit)
	Stage 2a: Possible negative outcomes	Stage 3a: Positive outcomes

tional ones. Hysteria, then, is a part, sometimes explicit and sometimes implicit, of a wish-fulfillment belief.

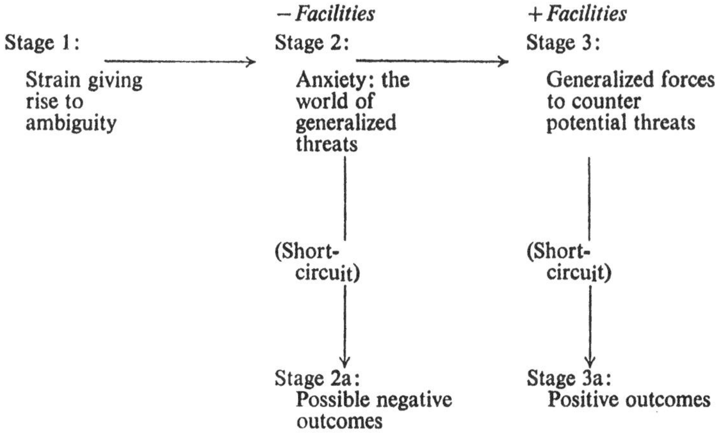

The paradigm in Figure 2 refers to a value-added process involved in creating or assembling a wish-fulfillment belief. The major function of such beliefs is to give structure to ambiguous situations. Sometimes we shall illustrate the stages of value-added by referring to beliefs that exist as parts of institutionalized magic. In so doing, we do not wish to support the view that the only function of magic is to give structure to, or indeed reduce, ambiguity. As part of ritual, institutionalized magical beliefs *may* reduce uncertainty, allay anxiety, and explain unfortunate events. The research of Malinowski and others has demonstrated this function amply.[1] On the other

[1] B. Malinowski, *Magic, Science and Religion and Other Essays* (Garden City, N.Y., 1955), esp. pp. 30–31; Parsons, *The Social System*, pp. 468–469. For other examples, cf. E. E. Evans-Pritchard, "The Morphology and Function of Magic:

hand, an equally convincing array of evidence shows that magic, once institutionalized, may serve a great variety of sustaining and controlling functions—the maintenance of prestige and power of a ruling group; the maintenance of integration through social control; the protection of property and other rights; the perpetuation of tradition; and finally, diversion and entertainment through ceremonial and ritual.[1] We should distinguish, then, between the conditions that *encourage the growth* of magical beliefs and the conditions that *sustain* magical beliefs once established. We are interested only in the former in this study.

Let us now discuss each of the stages in the value-added process of the wish-fulfillment belief.

Ambiguity. Like hysteria, the wish-fulfillment belief arises in ambiguous situations. Our remarks on ambiguity and rumor above apply to the pipe-dream as well as the bogey rumor.[2] Many panaceas that persist through the ages also have roots in inherently ambiguous aspects of the human condition. As Mackay noted:

> Three causes especially have excited the discontent of mankind; and, by impelling us to seek for remedies for the irremediable, have bewildered us in a maze of madness and error. These are death, toil, and ignorance of the

---

A Comparative Study of Trobriand and Zande Ritual and Spells," *American Anthropologist*, Vol. 31 (1929), pp. 621–622; Webster, *Magic*, p. 497; A. C. Haddon, *Magic and Fetishism* (London, 1906), pp. 62–63; R. Allier, *The Mind of the Savage* (New York, 1930), pp. 92–101; E. Z. Vogt and R. Hyman, *Water Witching, U.S.A.* (Chicago, 1959); also J. A. Roth, "Ritual and Magic in the Control of Contagion," *American Sociological Review*, Vol. 22 (1957), pp. 310–314.

[1] A. I. Hallowell, *The Role of Conjuring in Saulteaux Society* (Philadelphia, 1942), pp. 85–87; Evans-Pritchard, "The Morphology and Function of Magic," *op. cit.*, pp. 635–636; S. F. Nadel, "Witchcraft in Four African Societies: An Essay in Comparison," *American Anthropologist*, Vol. 54 (1952), pp. 28–29; Webster, *Magic*, pp. 180, 237, 279, 498–499; Sir J. G. Frazer, *The New Golden Bough* (New York, 1959), pp. 54–65; J. D. Krige, "The Social Function of Witchcraft," *Theoria*, Vol. I (1947), pp. 8–21; reprinted in Lessa and Vogt, *Reader in Comparative Religion*, esp, p. 290; V. Rydberg, *The Magic of the Middle Ages* (New York, 1879), pp. 55–56. Even Malinowski on occasion treats magic as "integrative" in the scheduling of work activities, thereby going beyond the narrow "uncertainty" theory which has been attributed to him. B. Malinowski, *Coral Gardens and Their Magic* (New York, 1935), pp. 444–451. Many of the critiques of Malinowski's classical theory of the functions of magic (developed in *Magic, Science and Religion*) seem to revolve around this problem of the "multiple functions" of magic. Some investigators point out first that magic serves other functions; others point out that "uncertainty-reduction" *must not* be the *only* function of magic, since many magical practices persist in the face of non-dangerous situations and since many dangerous situations do not give rise to magical practices. Cf. A. L. Kroeber, *Anthropology* (New York, 1948), pp. 308–310, 603–604; Firth, *Primitive Polynesian Economy*, pp. 184–186; R. Benedict, "Magic," *Encyclopaedia of the Social Sciences*, Vol. 10, p. 42.

[2] Pp. 84–91. For another example of the assignment of rumor to uncertainty, cf. Rose, "Rumor in the Stock Market," *op. cit.*, pp. 485–486.

The Creation of Generalized Beliefs

future—the doom of man upon this sphere, and for which he shews his antipathy by his love of life, his longing for abundance, and his craving curiosity to pierce the secrets of the days to come. The first has led many to imagine that they might find means to avoid death, or, failing in this, that they might, nevertheless, so prolong existence as to reckon it by centuries instead of units. From this sprang the search, so long continued and still pursued, for the *elixir vitae*, or *water of life*, which has led thousands to pretend to it and millions to believe in it. From the second sprang the search for the philosopher's stone, which was to create plenty by changing all metals into gold; and from the third, the false sciences of astrology, divination, and their divisions of necromancy, chiromancy, augury, with all their train of signs, portents, and omens.[1]

Anxiety. Anxiety is one of the universal—if not always explicit—elements in the growth of positive magic. Various writers have noted the importance of anxiety in ritual.[2] Malinowski, in fact, in one place defined magic as "the institutionalized expression of human optimism, of constructive hopes overcoming doubt and pessimism."[3]

Generalized Wish-fulfillment. The wish-fulfillment fantasy involves the creation of a world of positive generalized powers—a system of causality, as it were—which counteracts or overcomes the negative forces implicit in anxiety.[4] In the study of magic, many writers have noticed the universal presence of generalized forces. Loomis, for instance, writes:

Magic suggests aid from sources lying in the unseen and in the unknown. Magic is knowledge beyond the average man's comprehension; it is a secret mastering influence which inspires wonder or fear....[5]

Thus, the "man [who] desires his child to grow ... chews the sprouts of the salmon berry and spits it over the child's body that it may grow as rapidly as the salmon berry" transfers the *powers* of growth of the plant to the child.[6] In such magical acts a generalized force,

---

[1] Mackay, *Extraordinary Popular Delusions and the Madness of Crowds*, p. 99.
[2] G. C. Homans, "Anxiety and Ritual," *American Anthropologist*, Vol. 43 (1941), pp. 164–172; reprinted in Lessa and Vogt (eds), *Reader in Comparative Religion*, pp. 112–118. For a psychological account of the relationship between anxiety and magical thinking, cf. C. Odier, *Anxiety and Magic Thinking* (New York, 1956), pp. 60–66.
[3] *Coral Gardens and Their Magic*, p. 239.
[4] For a brief discussion of positive and negative magical forces, cf. E. E. Burris, *Taboo, Magic, Spirits: A Study of Primitive Elements in Roman Religion* (New York, 1931), pp. 9–14.
[5] C. G. Loomis, *White Magic: An Introduction to the Folklore of Christian Legend* (Cambridge, Mass., 1948), p. 3. For similar statements, see E. Clodd, *Magic in Names and in Other Things* (London, 1930), p. 10; Rydberg, *The Magic of the Middle Ages*, pp. 52–53; G. Storms, *Anglo-Saxon Magic* (The Hague, 1948), p. 49; Webster, *Magic*, p. 55.
[6] Example from Benedict, "Magic," *op. cit.*, p. 39.

The Creation of Generalized Beliefs

or means, always operates to guarantee an outcome in a specific situation. This outcome may be to avoid unfortunate events (protective or conservative magic) or to attain a problematical goal (productive magic). In both cases a generalized force intervenes. This force may emanate from an impersonal force, such as *mana*, from a personalized spirit, or from a semi-personal agency.[1]

Wish-fulfillment in magical thought, then, involves the operation of a generalized power which can, in its most extreme form, make any wish come true. This force is most explicit in magical and religious cosmologies. In rumors, which are often truncated and fleeting, the generalized forces are frequently implicit.[2] In later sections of this chapter we shall observe the operation of generalized forces in the ideologies of norm-oriented and value-oriented beliefs.

The Structuring of Generalized Wish-fulfillment. The value-added process is completed by the short-circuiting back to the world of specific outcomes. Generalized wish-fulfillment is not enough. Besides an "idea of [a] ... power or force," magical systems contain an "insensorial transmission of this power to the place where it must operate."[3] Such a transmission makes the generalized forces operative in concrete situations. To illustrate the structuring of generalized wish-fulfillment, let us consider the following examples of rumor and magic:

(1) To reduce the ambiguity inherent in economic endeavor,

---

[1] G. E. Swanson, *The Birth of the Gods* (Ann Arbor, 1960), pp. 6–8. Certain writers have extended the particular Melanesian concept of *mana*—an "anonymous and impersonal force"—to cover the generalized power implicit in all magic and, indeed, to make it, as Durkheim attempted to do, the basis from which a vast body of religious ideas is derived. For discussion of the logic of *mana* and related concepts, cf. R. H. Marett, "Mana," *Encyclopaedia of Religion and Ethics*, Vol. VIII, pp. 375–380; R. Firth, "The Analysis of *Mana*: An Empirical Approach," *The Journal of the Polynesian Society*, Vol. 49 (1940), pp. 483–510; Malinowski, *Magic, Science and Religion*, pp. 19–20; Durkheim, *Elementary Forms of the Religious Life*, pp. 121–122, 188–190, 201–202, 221, 266–267; Firth, "The Sociology of 'Magic' in Tikopia," *op. cit.*, pp. 102–103; Webster, *Magic*, p. vii. We might object to this extension, since magical forces are not always anonymous and impersonal; the existence of animism alone defies the attempt to generalize the "impersonality" of magical forces to all systems of magic. Nevertheless, it is possible to speak of generalized forces as always present in magical systems. As Marett observed, "[there] is no reason why, for the general purposes of comparative science, *mana* should not be taken to cover all cases of magico-religious efficacy, whether the efficacy be conceived as automatic or derived, i.e., as proceeding immediately from the nature of the sacred person or thing in question." "Mana," *op. cit.*, p. 377.

[2] For instance, in two "wishful rumors" just before the outbreak of the World War II—i.e., that there would be no war, and that Germany was on the verge of revolution—the only explicit element is the final prediction. Whatever generalized forces were going to bring this about are absent from the rumor itself, which contains only the result. Cf. Knapp, "A Psychology of Rumor," *op. cit.*, p. 32.

[3] Storms, *Anglo-Saxon Magic*, p. 49.

The Creation of Generalized Beliefs

people sometimes dream of exaggerated success and some "sure-fire system" to realize these dreams. Such dreams abound on the eve of attempts to exploit sources of unknown wealth. For instance, in the early eighteenth century, "France had been deluged with books, pamphlets, engravings, and all kinds of advertisements and prospectuses descriptive of the extent and wealth of Louisiana."[1] Shortly thereafter Frenchmen embarked on a gigantic enterprise to exploit the wealth of the New World—an enterprise which failed disastrously and thereafter received the name "Mississippi Bubble." Visions of infinite wealth have accompanied land booms, gold and silver rushes, and so on.[2] In the stock market, where uncertainty is great, "gimmicks" for beating the market proliferate: relying on astrology or sunspots; relying on "personal intuition"; endowing "big names" or "insiders" with extraordinary shrewdness or intelligence; relying on "hot tips"; relying on "odd lots," or the assumption that the public is always wrong, etc.[3] The workability of these systems varies greatly; all resemble one another, however, in the sense that they promise tremendous success in the market.

(2) Throughout history the uncertainties of health have promoted the appearance of miracle cures, panaceas, fads, crazes, as well as faith-healing cults.[4]

(3) In contemporary courtship it is impossible to determine, on objective grounds, whether a particular choice of spouse will fulfill the desire for future family happiness.[5] In one sense the feeling of being "in love" is a kind of magical solution to this otherwise insoluble problem. The declaration, "As long as we're in love, nothing else matters," illustrates the essentially magical element. Often, of course, this feeling, genuinely experienced, may contribute greatly

---

[1] A. W. Wiston-Glynn, *John Law of Lauriston* (Edinburgh, 1907), p. 16; for similar developments in the South Sea Bubble in England about the same time, cf. L. Melville, *The South Sea Bubble* (London, 1921), p. 34.

[2] H. H. Bancroft, *History of California* (San Francisco, 1888), Vol. VI, pp. 54–57; T. H. Weigall, *Boom in Paradise* (New York, 1932), pp. xi–xii; B. Taylor, *Eldorado* (New York, 1871), pp. 91–92.

[3] Benedict, "Magic," *op. cit.*, pp. 40–41; Rose, "Rumor in the Stock Market," *op. cit.*, p. 464; Mindell, *The Stock Market*, pp. 10–23.

[4] For discussion of the natural sequence of a health craze, cf. Penrose, *On the Objective Study of Crowd Behaviour*, pp. 20–22; cf. also C. S. Braden, *These Also Believe* (New York, 1956), for the "health" elements in the I Am Movement, the Unity School of Christianity, the New Thought movement, Psychiana, Theosophy, etc. Also G. B. Cutten, *Three Thousand Years of Mental Healing* (New York, 1911), and Bryan Wilson's discussion of the Gnostic-type sect in "An Analysis of Sect Development," *American Sociological Review*, Vol. 24 (1959), pp. 3–15. For general discussion of the medical role, cf. T. Parsons, *The Social System*, Ch. X.

[5] Above, p. 88.

The Creation of Generalized Beliefs

to future marital stability and happiness. The feeling alone, however, does not erase all other realistic factors which affect the marriage.

(4) The outcome of an athletic event is uncertain. Otherwise it would be boring. As argued above,[1] the football coach is assigned great responsibility for guiding his team to victory, but he does not have absolute control over the means to guarantee victory. Under such conditions magical beliefs flourish. Fans tend to worship the successful coach, to endow him with a variety of generalized powers (great intelligence, extraordinary shrewdness, "the touch," and so on). Such powers presumably operate through the coach's hunches, intuitions, and decisions. The hero-worship of coaches—and the scapegoating which results when the coach's powers fail—stem from the process of assigning certainty to an uncertain situation.[2]

Conclusion. Hysterical and wish-fulfillment beliefs display the following similarities: (*a*) Both are generalized responses that select potentialities of ambiguous situations. Formally we characterize this generalization as a movement to Level 1 of the Facilities Series. (*b*) Each, in its own way, restructures the situation and thereby reduces the ambiguity. (*c*) Both are likely to be distorted because they involve leaps up and down the Facilities Series.[3] The two beliefs differ in the following ways: (*a*) Hysterical beliefs select the negative possibilities of an ambiguous situation, wish-fulfillment beliefs the positive. (*b*) Wish-fulfillment beliefs are more complex than hysterical beliefs because they involve additional stages in the value-added process.

---

[1] P. 88.

[2] Football and baseball fans tend to deify coaches. In these sports the outcome depends in large part on the coaches' strategy. This is not true in swimming and track. Thus these sports are devoid of a folklore such as that surrounding a Knute Rockne or a Casey Stengel.

[3] Festinger, *et al.* summarize the distortions of rumor under what they call the "principle of integrative explanation." This principle is that "once the central theme of a rumor is accepted, there will be a tendency to reorganize and to distort items so as to be consistent with the central theme." "A Study of Rumor," *op. cit.*, p. 485. The "central theme" of a rumor often involves some generalized force. In the rumor which Festinger and his associates investigated the force was the operation of "communist influence"—a vague, threatening and diffuse power—which was used to explain a difficult social situation in a housing project. Once this theme of communist influence was available, many specific events were interpreted (through a process of short-circuiting) as verifying its operation—"so that [these events] fitted the conception people had of what communists are like and what sorts of things communists do." *Ibid.* For a discussion of rumor's "syncretic" elements which emerge in the search for meaning, cf. Knapp, "A Psychology of Rumor," *op. cit.*, p. 33. For discussion of three principles of distortion—levelling, sharpening, and assimilation—cf. Allport and Postman, *The Psychology of Rumor*, pp. 134–136.

The Creation of Generalized Beliefs

THE HOSTILE BELIEF

Hysterical and wish-fulfillment beliefs have two salient characteristics: (*a*) They are necessary conditions for the development of the panic and the craze, respectively. (*b*) They reconstitute the Facilities Series in the table of components. Each posits generalized forces that are extraordinarily efficacious, whether for evil or for good.

The corresponding characteristics of hostile beliefs are as follows: (*a*) Hostile beliefs are necessary conditions for outbursts of scapegoating and rioting. Turner and Surace have concluded "that a necessary condition for both the uniform group action and the unrestricted hostile behavior of the crowd is a symbol which arouses uniformly and exclusively unfavorable feelings toward the object under attack."[1] (*b*) Hostile beliefs are more complex than either hysteria or wish-fulfillment; in fact, hostility contains hysterical and wishful elements as parts of itself. In what sense is this so? Like the hysterical and wish-fulfillment beliefs, the hostile belief is a compressed belief resulting from the processes of generalization and short-circuiting. Hostility extends beyond the Facilities Series alone, however. It marks a qualitatively new type of compression; it compresses not only many levels of the same component (Facilities) into a belief, but also two separate components—Facilities and Mobilization.[2] Hostility involves not only a redefinition of generalized forces in an ambiguous situation, but also an identification and modification of *persons* thought to be agencies of these forces. The modification is to be effected by *destroying, injuring, removing, or restricting a person or class of persons considered responsible for the evils at hand.* In this way hostility modifies two components, Facilities and Mobilization.

To understand the hostile belief, we shall investigate the hostile rumor, commonly called the "wedge-driving" rumor.[3] In addition, we shall refer to social psychologists' and psychoanalytic writers' observations on the "mob mentality" of the hostile crowd. Finally, we shall examine institutionalized forms of hostility such as "destructive magic" and prejudice.

Value-added in the Creation of Hostile Beliefs. As Figure 3 shows, the initial stages (Stages 1, 2) are identical to those of the hysterical belief. Hostility passes through the stages of ambiguity and anxiety. At this point, however, the development of hostility diverges from

---

[1] R. H. Turner and S. J. Surace, "Zoot-Suiters and Mexicans: Symbols in Crowd Behavior," *American Journal of Sociology*, Vol. 62 (1956–57), pp. 15, 16; also Allport and Postman, *The Psychology of Rumor*, pp. 193–196.
[2] Above, pp. 39–41, for a characterization of the Mobilization Series.
[3] Allport and Postman, *The Psychology of Rumor*, pp. 10–11.

The Creation of Generalized Beliefs

that of both hysteria and wish-fulfillment, even though ultimately the hostile belief includes both of these as components. What are these additional stages in the development of the hostile belief?

Stage 3 involves a fusion of anxiety (the negative generalization of Facilities) with the Mobilization Series. This results in a generalized belief that some agent or agents are *responsible* for the anxiety-producing state of affairs. This fusion marks an extension from the attribution of evils to forces (which would be hysteria) to an identification of agents of these forces of evil.[1]

This generalized suspicion of agents is then short-circuited (Stage 3a) in the selection of a particular kind of agent—Wall Street, labor

FIGURE 3
VALUE-ADDED IN THE CREATION OF HOSTILE BELIEFS

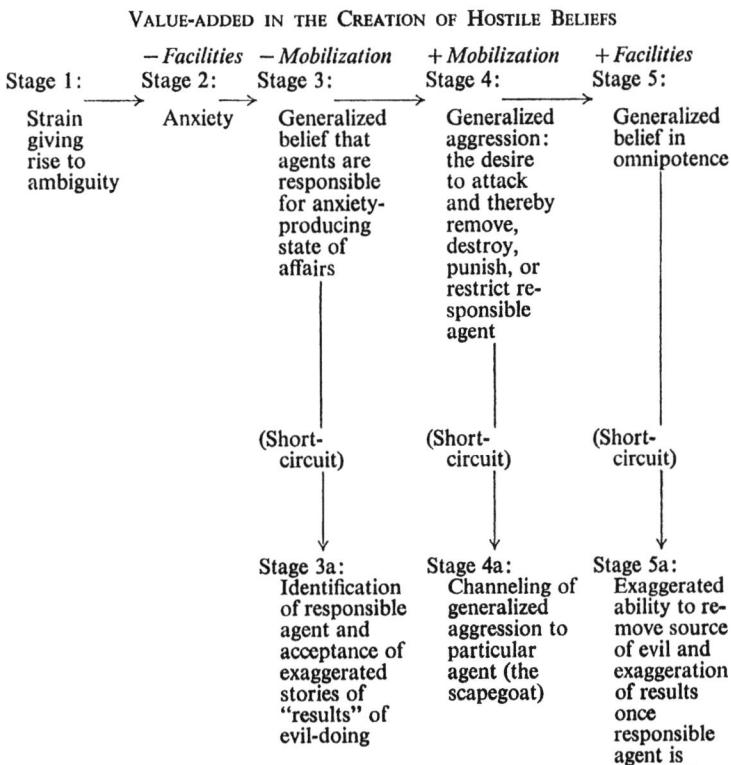

Stage 1:	Stage 2: −Facilities	Stage 3: −Mobilization	Stage 4: +Mobilization	Stage 5: +Facilities
Strain giving rise to ambiguity	Anxiety	Generalized belief that agents are responsible for anxiety-producing state of affairs	Generalized aggression: the desire to attack and thereby remove, destroy, punish, or restrict responsible agent	Generalized belief in omnipotence
		(Short-circuit)	(Short-circuit)	(Short-circuit)
		Stage 3a: Identification of responsible agent and acceptance of exaggerated stories of "results" of evil-doing	Stage 4a: Channeling of generalized aggression to particular agent (the scapegoat)	Stage 5a: Exaggerated ability to remove source of evil and exaggeration of results once responsible agent is punished

[1] How does this fusion relate to the Mobilization Series? The theme in this series is the mobilization of individuals into roles and collectivities, and the attempt to guarantee that these individuals will perform responsibly in these positions. Above, pp. 27–30.

The Creation of Generalized Beliefs

unions, communists, Catholics, Jews, Negroes, or whatever. Usually the generalized forces are felt to reside in these agents. Having identified the source of evil, those who hold hostile beliefs are prepared to accept exaggerated stories about the agents, and attribute all kinds of unfortunate events to their insidious activity.

Stage 4 involves a desire to punish, remove, damage, or restrict the responsible agent. This is literally the desire to *move against* or mobilize (we designate this by the symbol +Mobilization). This desire to mobilize for an attack on an agent has a generalized and a specific component. The generalized component is aggression, or the diffuse desire to punish or harm. By a process of short-circuiting (Stage 4a), aggression focuses on a specific object. Usually this object is the same as—or symbolically related to—the agent selected as the object of hysterical fear. This focusing of aggression on a particular object is referred to commonly as scapegoating.

Stage 5 in the hostile belief involves wish-fulfillment (+Facilities) of two sorts: (*a*) an exaggerated ability of the attackers to punish or harm the agent of evil, and (*b*) an exaggerated ability, therefore, to remove the evils which have been ascribed to this agent. This stage involves a generalized sense of omnipotence, which is short-circuited (Stage 5a) to specific results.

Before examining each stage of the value-added process, we must set two limitations on the applicability of the scheme: (*a*) We are not attempting to explain the mechanisms which sustain institutionalized antagonisms such as race prejudice or witchcraft;[1] we wish to account only for the value-added processes by which hostile beliefs arise under conditions of strain. (*b*) We are not attempting to account for the development of anxiety, fantasy, or aggression as *personality* variables;[2] we wish to explore only how these kinds of variables are assembled into a belief under conditions of strain. The variables may have existed in the personalities of those who subscribe to the hostile belief long before the onset of strain. For instance, persons holding a prejudice against Negroes tend, under conditions of strain, to attribute all sorts of unfortunate states of affairs to the insidious influence of Negroes.[3] In the value-added process it does not matter

---

[1] In interpreting the extensive findings of *The Authoritarian Personality* (New York, 1950), by T. W. Adorno *et al.*, we might say that "families under strain" produce the anxieties and rigidities that help to sustain prejudice in society. See also Parsons, "Certain Primary Sources and Patterns of Aggression in the Social Structure of the Western World," in *Essays in Sociological Theory*, pp. 302–314.

[2] It may be that the model of value-added is relevant to the formation of these personality variables; to assess this relevance, however, we would have to make an independent theoretical statement.

[3] This resembles the process of "assimilation" in the development of rumors. Allport and Postman, *The Psychology of Rumor*, pp. 99–115.

The Creation of Generalized Beliefs

whether the anxiety or hostility is created directly in response to strain or is "brought" to the strain.[1]

Let us now discuss each stage of the value-added process that results in a hostile belief:

Ambiguity. The more ambiguous the situation (importance remaining constant), the greater the magnitude of rumor-spreading.[2] This formula holds for the hostile rumor as well as other types.[3] The connection between ambiguity and hostility appears in studies of witchcraft. In general, the incidence of the practice of witchcraft has been found to be positively correlated with situations of structured strain and conflict.[4] In addition, witchcraft, witch persecution, and related forms of scapegoating appear to rise markedly in periods of famine, internal social disorder, and so on.[5] Finally, on those occasions when a hostile belief gives rise to actual mob violence, we find conditions of deprivation, normative malintegration, conflicts of values, and so on, in the background.[6]

Anxiety. Lowenthal and Guterman discovered a consistent theme of anxiety in the hate literature spread by anti-Semitic agitators in the United States during the 1930's:

> This [fear] complex manifests itself in a general premonition of disasters to come, a prominent part of which seems to be the middle-class fear of a dislocation of its life by revolutionary action, and its suspicion that the moral mainstays of social life are being undermined. The agitator speaks of "the darkest hour in American history" and graphically describes a pervasive sense of fear and insecurity. . . .[7]

The association between anxiety and hostility in crowd behavior was observed in 1915 by Christensen, who maintained, first, that *"fear is near akin to self-assertion in essence and practice,"* and, second, that "a factor which often accompanies self-assertion or fear in

---

[1] Above, p. 16.
[2] Allport and Postman, *The Psychology of Rumor*, pp. 33-45.
[3] Knapp, "A Psychology of Rumor," *op. cit.*, p. 33.
[4] Swanson, *The Birth of the Gods*, pp. 151-152; M. H. Wilson, "Witch Beliefs and Social Structure," *American Journal of Sociology*, Vol. 56 (1951), pp. 307-313; Krige, "The Social Function of Witchcraft," *op. cit.*; J. J. Honigmann, "Witch-Fear in Post-Contact Kaska Society," *American Anthropologist*, Vol. 49 (1947), pp. 222-243; S. F. Nadel, "Witchcraft in Four African Societies: An Essay in Comparison," *op. cit.*, pp. 18-29; E. E. Evans-Pritchard, *Witchcraft, Oracles and Magic among the Azande* (Oxford, 1958), pp. 62-63.
[5] Kluckhohn, *Navaho Witchcraft*, pp. 64-65; R. T. Davies, *Four Centuries of Witchcraft* (London, 1947), pp. 147, 200-202; R. D. Loewenberg, "Rumors of Mass Poisoning in Times of Crisis," *Journal of Criminal Psychopathology*, Vol. V (1943), pp. 131-142.
[6] Above, pp. 48-49.
[7] L. Lowenthal and N. Guterman, *Prophets of Deceit* (New York, 1949), p. 14.

The Creation of Generalized Beliefs

crowds is *cruelty*, the cheerful enjoyment of the sorrows of others."[1] Psychoanalytic writers have noted that anxiety is an underlying component of hostile feelings.[2] And finally, destructive magic such as witchcraft frequently serves as an institutionalized medium for expressing "fear reactions."[3]

Assignment of Responsibility to Agents. The growth of suspicion and stereotyping is illustrated in Turner and Surace's study of the changing image of the Mexicans in selected Los Angeles newspapers during the weeks before the outbreak of the zoot suit riots in 1943. Before this period the public image of Mexicans in Southern California included a positive stereotype of the romantic Spanish heritage as well as a negative stereotype of licentiousness, crime, and violence. During the weeks preceding the riots this complex set of stereotypes became more simplified; the negative aspects began to be emphasized almost exclusively. In this way a hysterical belief emerged and the Mexicans became agents responsible for a multitude of ills:

The symbol "Zoot-suiter" evoked none of the imagery of the romantic past. It evoked only the picture of a breed of persons outside the normative order, devoid of morals themselves, and consequently not entitled to fair play and due process. Indeed, the zoot-suiter came to be regarded as such an exclusively fearful threat to the community that at the height of rioting the Los Angeles City Council seriously debated an ordinance making the wearing of zoot suits a prison offense.

The "zooter" symbol had a crisis character which mere unfavorable versions of the familiar "Mexican" symbol never approximated. And the "zooter" symbol was an omnibus, drawing together the most reprehensible elements in the old unfavorable themes, namely sex crimes, delinquency, gang attacks, draft-dodgers, and the like and was, in consequence, widely applicable.

The "zooter" symbol also supplied a tag identifying the object of attack. It could be used, when the old attitudes toward Mexicans were evoked, to differentiate Mexicans along both moral and physical lines. While the active minority were attacking Mexicans indiscriminately, and frequently including Negroes, the great sanctioning majority heard only of attacks on zoot suiters.

Once established, the zooter theme assured its own magnification. What previously would have been reported as an adolescent gang attack would now be presented as a zoot-suit attack. Weapons found on apprehended

---

[1] A. Christensen, *Politics and Crowd-Morality* (London, 1915), pp. 28, 30; see also F. K. Notch, *King Mob* (New York, 1930), pp. 10–11.

[2] May, *The Meaning of Anxiety*, pp. 222–232; L. J. Saul, *The Hostile Mind* (New York, 1956), pp. 42–44, 50–53. Cf. also Freud's discussion of panic and hostility in *Group Psychology and the Analysis of the Ego* (London, 1955), pp. 95–99.

[3] Benedict, "Magic," *op. cit.*, p. 43; Kluckhohn, *Navaho Witchcraft*, p. 62.

youths were now interpreted as the building-up of arms collections in preparation for zoot-suit violence. In short, the "zooter" symbol was a recasting of many of the elements formerly present and sometimes associated with Mexicans in a new and instantly recognizable guise.[1]

All the elements of hysteria were present: (*a*) positing a generalized force which manifested itself in the form of the zoot-suiter; (*b*) attributing to this force an extraordinary power to undermine community life; (*c*) short-circuiting, or assigning a whole variety of events—weakness of the war effort, falling sexual standards, etc.— to the operation of this force. Furthermore, this hysteria focused on a particular subclass of individuals in the community—Mexican adolescents.

Anti-Semitic propaganda before World War II displays the same characteristics. In the first place, the "enemy"—always directly or indirectly identified with the symbol of Jewishness—constituted a threat to the economic welfare of the nation, to the freedom of the media of communication, and, more generally, to the moral fiber of the nation.[2] Moreover, this enemy was pictured as extremely shrewd and powerful:

> The enemy is conceived of not as a group that stands in the way of achieving a certain objective, but as a super-oppressor, a quasi-biological archdevil of absolute evil and destructiveness. He is irreconcilable, an alien body in society which has no useful productive function. Not even in theory is he amenable to persuasion. There is no bridge which the enemy can cross for repentance. He is there—forever, evil for the sake of evil.[3]

The world was pictured as frustrating, hostile, and conspiratorial. All this was traced, furthermore, to the insidious influence of the "pseudo-reality reference," the Jew.

Finally, identical characteristics appear in instances of violence against the Negro. One regularity of mob lynchings is that members of the mob

> ... tended to accept unqualifiedly any and all reports which fitted into certain preconceived notions about Negroes and the kinds of crimes which warrant lynching ... though informed physicians refuted many of the bloody stories which motivated the mob, once the excitement was aroused, facts made no difference.[4]

Facts are assimilated to an image of the Negro as the incarnation of generalized and threatening forces.[5]

---

[1] Turner and Surace, "Zoot-Suiters and Mexicans," *op. cit.*, p. 20.
[2] Lowenthal and Guterman, *Prophets of Deceit*, pp. 12–13.
[3] *Ibid.*, p. 38.
[4] A. F. Raper, *The Tragedy of Lynching* (Chapel Hill, 1933), p. 8.
[5] This tendency to "jump at oversimplified explanations offered him" is one

The Creation of Generalized Beliefs

Hostility. Generalized aggression is the tendency to punish someone or something felt to be responsible for an unwanted state of affairs.[1] In the hostile belief this generalized aggression is short-circuited to particular objects when these objects are thought to be agents of evil.[2] This process of scapegoating occupies, as Galbraith has argued, a notable place in our own political tradition. The scapegoat is a "generalized symbol of evil," a "wrongdoer whose wrongdoing will be taken by the public to be the secret propensity of a whole community or class."[3] In many societies scapegoating has been formally institutionalized, *with the recognition* that the object attacked or sacrificed is only a symbol of more generalized evils:

A scapegoat ... is an animal or human being used in public ceremonies to remove the taint or impairment consequent upon sin which, for one reason or other, cannot be saddled upon a particular individual. Such a scapegoat is a means of "cleansing" a community of a collective stain which cannot be wiped out by the normal procedure of individual penitence, restitution, or reform.... Its purpose is ... to remove from the body politic any pollution or disaster responsibility for which cannot be precised....[4]

Such ceremonies render explicit the short-circuiting from generalized

---

of the characteristics of the "mentality" of the mob member listed by Cantril. *The Psychology of Social Movements,* p. 118.

[1] A formal definition of aggression appears in J. Dollard *et al., Frustration and Aggression* (New Haven, 1939), p. 9. The nonspecific character of aggression is discussed in N. R. F. Maier, "The Role of Frustration in Social Movements," *Psychological Review,* Vol. 49 (1942), pp. 586-587. F. H. Allport considered aggression to rest on a diffuse desire to "restore ... thwarted responses to their normal operation." *Social Psychology* (Boston, 1924), p. 294. Allport recognized the "reconstitutive" character of aggression in this statement, and refused to subscribe to the simpler belief that "the mob members ... demand a victim merely in order to shed blood."

[2] Bucher notes the following conditions which must be present for the occasions when mere assignment of responsibility turns into outright blame. "First, those who blame the agents of responsibility are convinced that the agents will not of their own volition take action which will remedy the situation.... The second condition that must be met before blame occurs is that the responsible must be perceived as violating moral standards, as standing in opposition to basic values." R. Bucher, "Blame and Hostility in Disaster," *American Journal of Sociology,* Vol. 62 (1956-57), pp. 472-473. Bucher's remarks are limited to the occurrence of disasters, but they apply generally. These conditions for the conversion of responsibility into scapegoating are implicit in the image of zoot-suiters, Jews and Negroes in the examples above.

[3] J. K. Galbraith, *The Great Crash* (Boston, 1955), p. 159. Galbraith analyzed the scapegoating of certain Wall Street figures after the crash of 1929, and compared it with more recent political events like the trial of Alger Hiss. Pp. 159-169. For an example of the scapegoating of William Miller, the millenarian prophet, after the failure of his prophecies, cf. C. E. Sears, *Days of Delusion* (Boston, 1924), p. 249.

[4] Gaster, in a comment on Frazer's theory of scapegoating in *The New Golden Bough,* p. 554.

evil to particular object manifesting the evil which is only implicit in other forms of hostile beliefs.

Wish-fulfillment. Wish-fulfillment endows those feeling hostility with an immense power to destroy the forces responsible for anxiety, and thereby to "set the world right." Many lynchings of Negroes are preceded by a build-up of righteous feelings among the white citizens of a community:

> Rumors spread . . . among the whites of the community to the effect that they must play an active part as hero. To see that the officials do their duty, men . . . drift down to the courthouse and there provide an audience for anyone who feels most inclined to speak. This may be the father of the girl, a political opponent of the local sheriff, or someone else with a bone to pick. He harangues the group, usually upon the need for keeping "niggers in their place," and may deliberately direct his efforts to the formation of a lynching party.[1]

Themes of omnipotence appeared in the literature distributed by anti-Semitic agitators in the 1930's. The agitator portrayed himself as the representative of true Americanism who alone could thwart the insidious Jewish threat. In addition to this heroic theme, Lowenthal and Guterman located the theme of the "Bullet-Proof Martyr," who, despite attacks from the enemy, would lead Americans in the battle to stamp out the forces of evil. In the end, then, the agitators presented the world as two gigantic forces locked in combat. Correspondingly, anti-Semitic agitators emphasized the themes of awareness and alertness:

> For all their strength, the Simple Americans are apathetic and lethargic, they are like a "slow, muscular, sleeping giant." This fact fills the agitator with a kind of despair; he argues, implores, cajoles, shouts himself hoarse to arouse them to awareness of their danger. . . .[2]

Psychoanalytic writers have observed the similarity between the symbolism of the angry crowd and that of certain types of patients, particularly the paranoid. They speak of the mob as "narcissistic, megalomaniacal, and hostile," of the "self-adulation of crowds," and of the "delusions of grandeur."[3]

[1] R. T. LaPiere and P. R. Farnsworth, *Social Psychology* (New York, 1936), p. 469.
[2] Lowenthal and Guterman, *Prophets of Deceit*, p. 111.
[3] E. A. Strecker, *Beyond the Clinical Frontiers* (New York, 1940), pp. 56–57, 59–60, 76, 83–84, 90–91, 93–94, 100, 106–108; E. D. Martin, *The Behavior of Crowds* (New York, 1920), pp. 44, 77, 163; Martin, "Some Mechanisms which Distinguish the Crowd from Other Forms of Social Behavior," *Journal of Abnormal and Social Psychology*, Vol. 18 (1923), pp. 195–197; Martin, *The Conflict of the Individual and the Mass in the Modern World* (New York, 1932), pp. 179–192.

The Creation of Generalized Beliefs

Conclusion. Rooted in situations of strain and ambiguity, the hostile belief assembles various elements which redefine the Facilities and Mobilization Series. The elements of a hostile belief are anxiety (−Facilities); the identification of this anxiety with some responsible agent (−Mobilization); hostility, or the desire to mobilize to attack this agent (+Mobilization); and wish-fulfillment, or the exaggeration of the power to remove the source of evil (+Facilities).

Thus the hostile belief is more complex than either hysteria or wish-fulfillment. It includes both of these as parts of itself, but it also involves a redefinition of the component of Mobilization. The three beliefs stand in the following hierarchy:

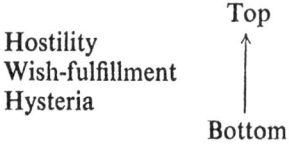

Hostility includes hysteria and wish-fulfillment, but the latter do not have hostility as a component. Wish-fulfillment includes hysteria, but hysteria includes neither wish-fulfillment nor hostility. As we read up the hierarchy, then, each new belief differs from the lower one *only in limited respects.* Hostility, for instance, redefines everything that wish-fulfillment redefines, plus one new component. Soon we shall see that the norm-oriented and value-oriented beliefs stand even higher in the hierarchy.

NORM-ORIENTED BELIEFS

Persons who subscribe to a norm-oriented belief envision the restoration, protection, modification, or creation of social norms. More particularly, they may demand a rule, a law, a regulatory agency, designed to control the inadequate, ineffective, or irresponsible behavior of individuals. Formally, a norm-oriented belief involves a reconstitution of the Normative Series of the table of components of social action.

Many agitations commonly designated as "social movements" or "reform movements" are undertaken in the name of a norm-oriented belief—an agitation to establish harsh laws against sexual psychopaths (or to repeal such laws); a movement to integrate schools racially (or to keep them segregated); a movement for government subsidy of school buses (or against such a subsidy); a movement to restrict immigration (or the corresponding movement to relax quotas); the movement to disenfranchise (or enfranchise) Negroes; a prohibition movement (or the movement for repeal); a movement to increase (or decrease) taxes; a movement for (or against) a working-day of a given length. Examples of specific historical movements include the Townsend movement of the 1930's, whose objective was to provide a very large subsidy for the aged; the Farmers' Alliance of the 1880's, designed in part to control middlemen by the establishment of buying and selling systems for farm produce; Technocracy, a movement of the 1920's and 1930's, designed to replace the capitalistic price and production methods with a new system of management by engineers and a new basis for calculating cost and production; the Dixiecrat movement of the late 1940's, which advocated "the retention of present southern customs, especially segregation, by obtaining control of the Federal policy, or failing that, by strictly limiting the powers of the Federal government;"[1] Henry George's single tax movement of the 1880's, which proposed that the entire federal revenue be gained by a tax on land values; Greenbackism, a movement of the 1870's among farmers and workers, who felt that governmental reissue of greenback currency would relieve an apparent lack of capital, particularly in the Western states.[2] Such a list could be expanded almost indefinitely.[3]

A norm-oriented movement, then, involves mobilization for action in the name of a belief envisioning the reconstitution of the Normative Series. Our conception of a norm-oriented movement thus differs from Heberle's conception of a social movement: the "direct orientation toward a change in the social order, that is, in the patterns of human relations, in social institutions and social norms."[4]

The major differences are: (*a*) We shall use the term "norm-oriented movement" rather than the term "social movement," since the latter has been applied (by Heberle and others) to phenomena such as revolutionary movements which we wish to separate analytically from attempts to reconstitute the normative order. (*b*) We substitute for Heberle's word "change" the words "restoration," "protection," "modification," or "creation." Norm-oriented movements do not always envision a *change* in the normative order; in the case of the segregationist movement (and many other movements which resist

[1] S. M. Lemmon, "The Ideology of the 'Dixiecrat' Movement," *Social Forces*, Vol. 30 (1951–52), p. 171.
[2] Cf. F. E. Haynes, *Third Party Movements Since the Civil War with Special Reference to Iowa* (Iowa City, 1916), pp. 91–92.
[3] Cf. H. D. Lasswell, R. D. Casey, and B. L. Smith, *Propaganda and Promotional Activities: An Annotated Bibliography* (Minneapolis, 1935).
[4] R. Heberle, "Observations on the Sociology of Social Movements," *American Sociological Review*, Vol. 14 (1949), p. 349.

The Creation of Generalized Beliefs

reform) the object is to protect existing norms from threatened change.

Unlike the panic, the craze, and the hostile outburst, the norm-oriented movement, if successful, leaves an observable mark—a norm or an organization—in its wake. The successful agitation against child labor creates laws, customs, and practices concerning the employment of children; these endure long after the movement has run its course. Other kinds of social units deposited in the social structure by a movement such as that for restricting child labor are a governmental agency to enforce the new set of laws, as well as a pressure group, an association, or some segment of a political party which "safeguards" the new norm or perhaps initiates new movements along the same lines.[1]

In this chapter we shall inquire only into the beliefs that guide norm-oriented movements. We shall postpone until Chapter IX the treatment of several topics: the differences between norm-oriented movements and other phenomena, such as trends or tendencies, public opinion, parties, pressure groups, and associations; the conditions of structural conduciveness which permit norm-oriented movements to develop; the internal organization of norm-oriented movements; the place of agencies of social control in shaping the development of movements, and so on.

Value-added in the Creation of Norm-oriented Beliefs. The norm-oriented belief includes, *as elements of itself*, a reconstitution (sometimes implicit) of the lower-level Mobilization and Facilities Series. The total value-added process, then, has the following stages. Stage 1 involves a condition of ambiguity arising from structural strain; Stage 2 involves anxiety (−Facilities); Stages 3 and 3a attach this anxiety to some agent, and exaggerate, correspondingly, the threatening character of this agent (−Mobilization). Thus far the value-added process is identical to that which results in the hostile belief. At this point, however, a new, higher level belief arises (Stage 4)—a generalized belief that the *normative* regulation or control of these agents is inadequate (−Norms). This belief is short-circuited (Stage 4a) to a particular set of laws, rules or customs. By this process the original unsatisfactory state of affairs is traced to normative regulation.

Stage 5 involves a belief that the trouble—now pinned to normative malfunctioning—can be "cured" by reorganizing the normative

[1] For the "society-forming" function of social movements, cf. Turner and Killian, *Collective Behavior*, p. 199; Blumer, "Collective Behavior," in Lee (ed.), *op. cit.*, p. 214. We should not exaggerate, however, the complete transience of shorter-term outbursts such as the craze. These may become institutionalized as rituals, parts of religion and folklore, and so on.

The Creation of Generalized Beliefs

structure itself (+Norms). This generalized belief is short-circuited (Stage 5a) to a particular kind of normative change (passing a law, redefining role responsibilities and obligations, establishing a regulatory agency to enforce norms, etc.). This envisioned normative change presumably will immobilize, damage, remove, or destroy those agents deemed responsible for the unwanted situation (Stage 6, +Mobilization), and will have the power thereby to erase the original source of strain (Stage 7,+Facilities). Figure 4 represents these stages of the value-added process graphically.

Let us now illustrate these ingredients of a norm-oriented belief.

Ambiguity Arising from Strain. In theory, any kind of strain outlined in Chapter III can give rise to a norm-oriented belief. Consider the following examples: (*a*) The strains giving rise to agitations for reform of laws concerning sexual psychopaths have been summarized as follows: "a state of fear developed, to some extent, by a general, nationwide popular literature and made explicit by a few spectacular sex crimes."[1] (*b*) Many norm-oriented movements are set off by other movements which threaten to change the existing order—the opposition to socialized medicine, the opposition to the prohibition of alcoholic sales, and so on.[2] (*c*) Crises such as economic depression may trigger a wide variety of movements.[3] (*d*) The Social Gospel movement of the late nineteenth and early twentieth centuries within the Protestant churches seemed to arise from a great variety of social discontinuities which were accumulating as a result of rapid industrialization, urbanization, and immigration.[4] (*e*) Social movements of many types apparently appeal to persons who have been dislodged from traditional social ties by structural change but who have not been integrated into a new social order.[5]

Whether a norm-oriented movement, some other kind of collective behavior, some other response, or no response at all, occurs in the face of these kinds of strain depends on the other determinants in the value-added process—e.g., structural conduciveness, social control—with which strain combines. We shall investigate the relations among strain and the other determinants of norm-oriented movements in Chapter IX.

Anxiety and Identification of Responsible Agents. One of the

[1] E. H. Sutherland, "The Diffusion of Sexual Psychopath Laws," *American ournal of Sociology,* Vol. 56 (1950–51), pp. 146–147.
[2] Turner and Killian, *Collective Behavior,* pp. 383–384.
[3] Above, pp. 55–56.
[4] C. H. Hopkins, *The Rise of the Social Gospel in American Protestantism 1865–1915* (New Haven, 1940), pp. 318 ff.; A. I. Abell, *The Urban Impact on American Protestantism 1865–1900* (Cambridge, Mass., 1943), p. 57.
[5] Kornhauser, *The Politics of Mass Society,* Parts II and III; S. M. Lipset, *Political Man: The Social Bases of Politics* (Garden City, N.Y., 1960), Ch. II.

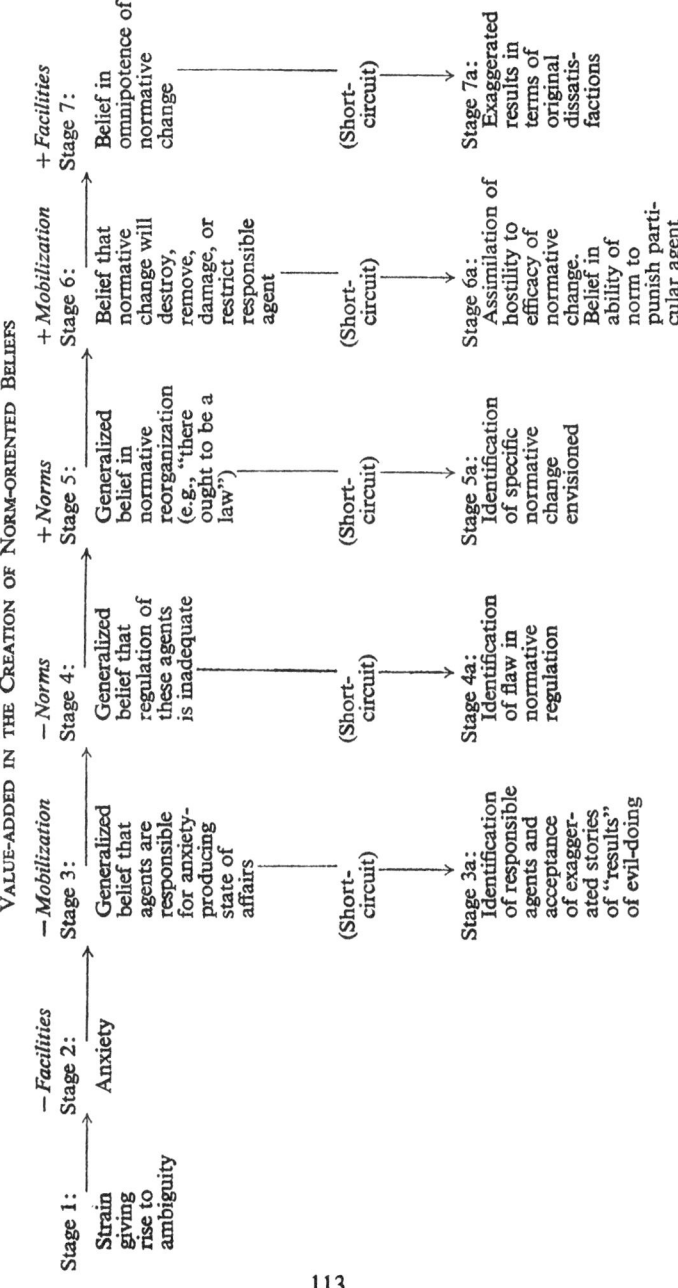

FIGURE 4
VALUE-ADDED IN THE CREATION OF NORM-ORIENTED BELIEFS

The Creation of Generalized Beliefs

ingredients of movements to reform laws concerning sexual psychopaths is hysteria and finger-pointing:

> The attention of the community is focused on sex crimes, and people in the most varied situations envisage dangers and see the need of and possibility for their control. . . . The mother of the murdered girl [in the Stroble case] demanded punishment for the daughter of Stroble, who had harbored him without notifying the parents of girls in the neighborhood that he was a dangerous criminal. A woman spoke in condemnation of striptease and other lewd shows as stimulating sex fiends. . . .[1]

Supporters of the Townsend Plan found generalized economic threats in a system which left the aged isolated and poor, and generalized moral threats in tobacco, liquor, petting, and the laziness of the young.[2] Adherents of the movement also singled out political authorities (especially Roosevelt and the Supreme Court) whom they viewed as obstacles to the realization of their design to eradicate these evils.[3]

The Dixicrat rebels feared not only the abolition of segregation, but also the trend toward a centralized state which "would further limit and control the entrepreneurs, the corporations, and the profit system."[4] The Southern adherents of this movement also tended to personify these trends in the Supreme Court and in Truman.

Technocrats of the 1930's saw the nation staggering under the wastefulness of profit, the misdirection of investment, the massive unemployment of the day, and the outrageous size of the national debt.[5] In addition, the Technocrats, by their theory of production, tied the responsibility to the captains of industry:

> The captains of industry are, as it were, defying the laws of physics. They know a good deal about the manipulation of money, credit and high finance, but they do not know a turbine from a bus bar. They think these machines are toys to play with. But the machines are not toys; they are the means, the overwhelming means, by which the people of a continent are fed, housed and clothed; and they operate only by virtue of certain physical laws of energy and dynamics which have a sequence, an integration and a rhythm that cannot be indefinitely outraged.[6]

In the prohibition movement which culminated in the Eighteenth Amendment, liquor became a symbol for a whole variety of forces—the city, the "foreign element," Catholics, and so on—which were

---

[1] Sutherland, "The Diffusion of Sexual Psychopath Laws," *op. cit.*, p. 144.
[2] R. L. Neuberger and K. Loe, "The Old People's Crusade," *Harper's Magazine* (Mar., 1936), pp. 434–435.
[3] Whiteman and Lewis, *Glory Roads*, pp. 101–102.
[4] Lemmon, "The Ideology of the 'Dixiecrat' Movement," *op. cit.*, p. 171.
[5] F. Arkwright, *The ABC of Technocracy* (New York, 1933), pp. 51–54.
[6] S. Chase, *Technocracy: An Interpretation* (New York, 1933), pp. 5–6.

The Creation of Generalized Beliefs

felt to be undermining traditional rural values of American Protestantism. These forces were, in a rather mysterious combination with liquor, causing "disease, destitution and depravity," and were, as "the Great Destroyer of the Temple of the Soul,"[1] working against organized religion.

The growth of the American Protective Association in the 1890's marked the apex of a nativistic, primarily anti-Catholic movement during the last part of the nineteenth century. At the height of the movement, many Catholic "bogey" stories were spread; for instance, the report of a famous Papal bull calling for the massacre of the Protestants "on or about the feast of St. Ignatius in the year of our Lord, 1893."[2] Such stories circulated widely despite the attempt of Protestant leaders to deny them publicly. Furthermore, when the day for the "massacre" passed without incident, the *failure* of the event to occur was taken as evidence of Catholics' trickery; the Catholics "were still biding their time, waiting to find their Protestant neighbors off guard."[3] Such is the assessment of "evidence" under a generalized belief-system. Even if predictions are apparently refuted, the evil is defined as so *generalized* that its operations can be reinterpreted handily without apparent explanatory loss. If the prediction does materialize, it is because the evil forces are unfolding according to plan; if it fails to materialize, it is because the evil forces have, in the interests of trickery, changed their plan of attack.[4]

The Vision of a "Cure" Through Normative Reconstitution. Let us now sketch the rejection (sometimes implicit) of one normative situation (−Norms), and the advocacy of another (+Norms), which gives the norm-oriented movement its distinctive character.

Between 1890 and 1908, after the South was emerging from the relative anarchy of the Reconstruction period, there arose a number of social movements to exclude the Negro from the vote by means of one legislative device or another.[5] The objective of such movements was to exclude a significant class of voters by redefining the rules of voting. As norm-oriented movements, they stood in contrast to

[1] P. H. Odegard, *Pressure Politics: The Story of the Anti-Saloon League* (New York, 1928), pp. 29–34; A. M. Lee, "Techniques of Social Reform: An Analysis of the New Prohibition Drive," *American Sociological Review*, Vol. 9 (1944), pp. 66–68; also C. Darrow and V. S. Yarros, *The Prohibition Mania* (New York, 1927), p. 172.
[2] Desmond, *The A.P.A. Movement*, p. 12.
[3] *Ibid.*, p. 24. In addition to these specific stories, the A.P.A. harbored various "theories regarding the insidious corruption of the American school system by 'foreign ecclesiastical sources.'" *Ibid.*, p. 39.
[4] Formally, this kind of reasoning "skips steps" in the specification of components which is required to give an adequate account of events. Above, pp. 94–94.
[5] Described in P. Lewinson, *Race, Class & Party: A History of Negro Suffrage and White Politics in the South* (London, 1932), pp. 79 ff.

simple exclusion of Negroes by coercion each time one tried to vote. The latter solution was a lower-level solution (Mobilization Series). The movements culminating in legislation had the same effect, but constituted a broader solution, because the law covered every situation rather than handled each situation as it arose.

The aim of Technocracy was to replace existing price and production arrangements with a new system of management by engineers and a new system of calculating productivity on the basis of expenditure of energy rather than by price. A corollary was that engineers would take over industrial management from the captains of industry.[1] The core objective of Technocracy, therefore, was to revise the economic system of production, and to impose a new set of norms for production, distribution and exchange.

Native Americanism has produced a number of distinct movements: "Nativistic movements of the 1830's, the Know-Nothing movement of the 1850's, the Loyalty League, the original Ku Klux Klan and allied movements of the post-Civil war period, the American Protective Association of the 1890's, the revived Ku Klux Klan after the World War [I] and anti-Semitism in the 1930's."[2] Although many of these movements contained much more than norm-oriented beliefs, most envisioned some kind of legislation aimed either at restricting foreigners or at bringing them more in line with traditional American ways. For instance: (*a*) The A. P. A., in its statement of principles in 1894, called for prohibiting employment of "the subjects of any un-American ecclesiastical power" in public schools; supporting or exempting from taxation of any sectarian school; excluding persons not actually American citizens from military service; the strengthening and tightening of the naturalization laws, and so on.[3] (*b*) About the turn of the century a movement arose to restrict the immigration of various nationalities; this culminated in the laws limiting immigration of 1917, 1921, and 1924.[4] (*c*) Simultaneously with the movement to curtail immigration arose a movement to establish language schools and other devices to facilitate the assimilation of foreigners into American culture.[5]

In 1864 Ira Steward launched his reform program for an eight-hour day. In 1866 the National Labor Union[6] endorsed the eight-hour day

---

[1] Arkwright, *The ABC of Technocracy*, pp. 72–73; J. G. Frederick (ed.), *For and Against Technocracy: A Symposium* (New York, 1933), pp. 96–97.
[2] E. R. Clinchy, *All in the Name of God* (New York, 1934), p. 144.
[3] Desmond, *The A.P.A. Movement*, pp. 38–43.
[4] O. Handlin, *The Uprooted* (New York, 1951), pp. 286–291.
[5] R. Lewis, "Americanization," *Encyclopaedia of the Social Sciences*, Vol. 2, p. 33.
[6] "A loosely built federation of national trade unions, city trades' assemblies,

The Creation of Generalized Beliefs

as a means of relieving unemployment stemming from Civil War demobilization and the closing of war industries. Between 1867 and 1873 many organizations were formed to agitate for eight-hour legislation.[1]

The depression of the 1930's witnessed a number of plans to maximize wealth by establishing new systems of production and exchange: (*a*) The E.P.I.C. plan (End Poverty in California), associated with the name of Upton Sinclair, advocated a large-scale system of cooperative state-land colonies to provide for the unemployed which the capitalist system could not support.[2] (*b*) Harold Loeb's Plan of Plenty called for a general moratorium, a general registration of the population for vocational choice, and temporary governmental supply of all necessities of life to the population.[3] (*c*) The Tradex movement in Southern California aimed to set up a new money system for listed commodities. According to this system, people would bring commodities to a distribution center and receive Tradex coupons for them. The aim of the scheme was to create "an honest medium of exchange with which business may be transacted."[4]

Magic and Omnipotence in Normative Beliefs. Those who adhere to normative beliefs endow themselves and the envisioned reconstitution of norms with enormous power, conceived as the ability to overcome that array of threats and obstacles which constitute the negative side of the adherents' world-picture. The proposed reform will render opponents helpless, and will be effective immediately (+Mobilization and +Facilities). Because of this exaggerated potency, adherents often see unlimited bliss in the future if only the reforms are adopted. For if they are adopted, they argue, the basis for threat, frustration, and discomfort will disappear. Let us trace these themes of unlimited potency and happiness in a number of movements.

The Townsend Plan's promise is revealed in their chant:

> Two hundred dollars a month.
> Youth for work, age for leisure,
> Two hundred for the oldsters,
> To be spent in ceaseless pleasure.[5]

---

local trade unions, and reform organizations of various descriptions," S. Perlman, *A History of Trade Unionism in the United States* (New York, 1937), p. 45.

[1] *Ibid.*, pp. 45–51; also N. J. Ware, *The Labor Movement in the United States, 1860–1895* (New York, 1929), p. 5.

[2] Summarized in Whiteman and Lewis, *Glory Roads*, pp. 243–244.

[3] *Ibid.*, p. 11.

[4] *Ibid.*, pp. 188 ff. This little scheme is similar to the Equitable Labour Exchange, established briefly and unsuccessfully under the aegis of Robert Owen in London in 1834. Cf. F. Podmore, *Robert Owen* (London, 1906), pp. 402–23.

[5] Whiteman and Lewis, *Glory Roads*, p. 75.

The Creation of Generalized Beliefs

The Townsend planners not only planned to save capitalism, but also to engulf competing plans; the movement would "swallow the EPICS and Utopians . . . would gather the Technates and Continentals under its wings. Humanity marches on."[1]

Symbols of omnipotence also appeared:

> Nothing can stop us! (cheers and more cheers). Not even President Roosevelt and the Supreme Court can stop us (tremendous cheers—no one is afraid of that big bad wolf, the Supreme Court). The speaker can hardly go on. Higher and higher he lifts his voice in exultation—"No, not even Almighty God can stop us!"[2]

Thus normative movements frequently display the world-view of conflicting forces of good and evil which characterize many types of generalized beliefs—two omnipotent forces locked in combat.

Technocrats also envisioned an almost instantaneous reorganization of society:

> . . . the engineers—who could bring the whole economic system to complete quiescence in a few days' time—disallow the dams and barricades of the captains of industry, and proceed to vindicate their integrity, and justify their technical training, by taking over the industrial system and operating it on the principles of the laws of physics and of the balanced load; the latter meaning smooth operation at capacity, where the cost per unit of output is at a minimum.[3]

This wholesale transformation promised to bring a state of affairs in which "citizens, down to the last family, would enjoy a standard of living hitherto undreamed of."[4]

Like the Townsend Plan, furthermore, Technocracy promised to by-pass competing programs:

> What of the philosophy which [the Technocrats] represent? It is described as being something totally new. It abolishes politics and economics. It will have no traffic with such outworn ideas as those, not only of the standard economists and social theorists, but of economic planning, socialism, communism, or fascism.[5]

Just as the threats depicted in the norm-oriented belief are generalized, so the program promises to sweep away these threats, whether by outright destruction or by absorption.[6]

---

[1] *Ibid.*, pp. 101–102.
[2] *Ibid.*
[3] Chase, *Technocracy*, p. 6.
[4] *Ibid.*
[5] Frederick (ed.), *For and Against Technocracy*, p. 97.
[6] For a study of the contrasting themes of destruction and absorption in two early-nineteenth century English social movements, cf. Smelser, *Social Change in the Industrial Revolution*, pp. 250–261.

The Creation of Generalized Beliefs

A final example of the promises held out in normative beliefs is seen in the Greenback movement of the 1870's. Actually the two groups that supported this movement most ardently—the farmers and the workers—interpreted its promises differently. The Western farmers perceived their basic problem to be a shortage of funds for investment and repayment of debts. For these farmers Greenbacks meant inflation and easy money, which would end the depression.[1] For the workers—in the 1860's at any rate—Greenbackism held out the promise of escape from the status of wage-earner. Because of credit and easy money for producers, adherents argued, wage earners "would be placed on a competitive level with the middleman and the wage-earner would be assisted to escape the wage system into self-employment."[2] So strong was this belief that workers attempted frequently—especially after unsuccessful strikes—to establish producers' cooperatives between 1866 and 1869. Later, in the 1870's, Greenbackism came to mean for the workers "primarily currency inflation and a rise of prices and, consequently, industrial prosperity."[3]

Conclusion. Norm-oriented beliefs involve the attempt to reconstitute—by creating, modifying, preserving, or restoring—one or more norms. Because of the hierarchy governing the components of action, these beliefs also affect the Mobilization and Facilities Series.[4] On the other hand, norm-oriented beliefs do not necessarily involve a reconstitution of the Values Series. In fact, adherents to norm-oriented movements *justify* their program in terms of the higher values of a society. Dixiecrats, for instance, referred continually to the sanctity of the founding fathers and the Constitution.[5] In the 1890's the statement of principles of the nativist American Protective Association made their claim to legitimacy in terms of traditional American values:

... the first clause makes "loyalty to true Americanism, which knows neither birthplace, race, creed nor party ... the first requisite for membership in the American Protective Association." ... The second disclaims political partisanship. ... The third holds that support of any ecclesiastical power of non-American character, and which claims higher sovereignty than that of the United States, is irreconcilable with American citizenship....[6]

Finally, although the Technocrats unleashed attacks on the capitalist system, they justified their program in terms of economic

---
[1] Haynes, *Third Party Movements Since the Civil War*, pp. 91–92.
[2] Perlman, *A History of Trade Unionism in the United States*, p. 52.
[3] *Ibid.*, p. 58.
[4] Above, pp. 32–34.
[5] Lemmon, "The Ideology of the 'Dixiecrat' Movement," *op. cit.*
[6] Desmond, *The A.P.A. Movement*, pp. 38–39.

The Creation of Generalized Beliefs

productivity, another core American value. The Technocrats, maintaining that the price system under capitalism had failed, argued that the only way to save American society was to reorganize the system of production and distribution.

Norm-oriented beliefs, however, may have revolutionary implications. Opponents of Technocracy, for instance, argued that such complete control of the productive system as it advocated would mean that "dictatorship is its inexorable accompaniment, indeed its first step."[1] Or, again, if adherents to a norm-oriented belief have a different definition of legitimacy than the constitutional authorities have, the movement may be revolutionary in fact but not in name. Furthermore, during the course of its development, a norm-oriented movement may be taken over by revolutionary forces, or turn into a revolutionary movement on its own. As beliefs alone, however, norm-oriented beliefs contrast with value-oriented beliefs, which envision a more sweeping reorganization of the bases of social life.

VALUE-ORIENTED BELIEFS

Introduction. A value-oriented belief envisions a modification of those conceptions concerning "nature, man's place in it, man's relation to man, and the desirable and nondesirable as they may relate to man-environment and inter-human relations."[2] This kind of belief involves a basic reconstitution of self and society. Thus our conception of the value-oriented belief resembles Wallace's conception of revitalization: "a deliberate, organized, conscious effort by members of a society to construct a more satisfying culture."[3]

Examples of value-oriented beliefs are classic religious doctrines (such as early Christianity or early Mohammedanism); classic revolutionary doctrines (such as the ideals of the Enlightenment, Marxism-Leninism, or Naziism); religious and secular beliefs associated with cults of withdrawal (such as the communitarian experiments in nineteenth-century America); beliefs associated with "nativistic movements" (such as the Ghost Dance of the American Indians, or the Melanesian Cargo Cult);[4] beliefs associated with movements of religious secession (with which the history of Protestantism is filled); nationalist beliefs (such as those which now grip many societies in Asia, the Middle East, Africa, and Latin America);

---

[1] Frederick (ed.), *For and Against Technocracy*, p. 204.
[2] Above, pp. 25–26.
[3] A. F. C. Wallace, "Revitalization Movements," *American Anthropologist*, Vol. 58 (1956), p. 265.
[4] Cf. R. Linton, "Nativistic Movements," *American Anthropologist*, Vol. 45 (1943), pp. 230–240.

The Creation of Generalized Beliefs

miscellaneous beliefs which give rise to bizarre cults (such as the scattered millenarian cults which sprang up during the flying-saucer scare).[1]

What kinds of movements do these beliefs typically accompany? In answering this question it is important to distinguish clearly between the *structure of a belief* and the *kind of action or social movement* into which the belief ultimately is incorporated. In this chapter we shall analyze only the former. Value-oriented beliefs *may* be associated with cult formation, secession from a parent political or religious body, withdrawal into isolation, or internal political or religious revolution. We shall inquire into several types of outcome in detail in Chapter X.

In this section we shall ask what *all* value-oriented beliefs have in common. We shall by-pass, for the moment, several issues and distinctions which commonly arise in studying such beliefs: (*a*) We shall not distinguish between religious and secular beliefs; at present we ask only if such beliefs—either religious or secular—envision a regeneration of self and society. (*b*) We shall not inquire into the intellectual origins of the beliefs, however important these may be for certain purposes. We shall not ask, for instance, what parts of Hitlerism came from Nietzsche and what parts from the anti-Semitic traditions of nineteenth-century Austria; we shall ask only what place such elements occupy in the internal structure of Nazi beliefs. Indeed, we shall even ignore the issue of whether a value-oriented belief is a revival of past cultural patterns, the invention of new ones, or the importation of foreign ones.[2] (*c*) We shall not be interested in the particular content of value-oriented beliefs. For certain purposes, of course, it is very important to know whether a belief is reactionary or radical; it is also important to know why a particular symbol rather than another is incorporated into a belief. For the moment, however, we shall interpret value-oriented beliefs within a single, abstract framework; by using very general categories we shall emphasize the similarities rather than the differences among value-added beliefs. What, then, are these similarities?

Value-added in the Creation of Value-oriented Beliefs. The value-oriented beliefs differs from lower-level beliefs in that it envisions a direct reconstitution of the Values Series. Because values stand at the top of the hierarchy of components, however, this belief necessarily implies a reconstitution of the lower-level components as well.

Thus the value-added sequence includes the following stages. As in

---

[1] B. Reeve and H. Reeve, *Flying Saucer Pilgrimage* (Amherst, Wisc., 1957); Festinger, Riecken and Schachter, *When Prophesy Fails.*
[2] Wallace, "Revitalization Movements," *op. cit.*, pp. 275-276.

The Creation of Generalized Beliefs

the case of all generalized beliefs, Stage 1 involves a condition of ambiguity rising from conditions of strain. Stage 2 involves anxiety (−Facilities). This is focused, furthermore, on specific agents of evil, such as demons, minority groups, or capitalists (Stage 3, −Mobilization). For instance, the ideological outlook of millenarianism, according to Shils, is

> ... preoccupied with the evil of the world as it exists; it believes in the immissibility of good and evil. It distinguishes sharply between the children of light and the children of darkness. It believes that no earthly action can ameliorate or attenuate evil. ....[1]

In addition, society is believed to be in a state of chaos, instability, disharmony, or conflict (Stage 4, −Norms). And finally, the pervading sense of evil is extended to include a threat to the values of the civilization as a whole (Stage 5,−Values).[2]

In addition, the value-oriented belief promises a vast regeneration of values (Stage 6,+Values). To quote Shils again,

> The ideological outlook expressed by millenarism asserts ... that the reign of evil on earth is of finite duration. There will come a moment when time and history as we know them shall come to an end. The present period of history will be undone by a cosmic act of judgment which will do justice to the wronged and virtuous by elevating them to eternal bliss, and equal justice to the powerful and wicked by degrading and destroying them for all time to come.[3]

This regeneration of values is the identifying characteristic of a value-oriented belief. Adherents see a new world, not merely an improvement of individuals or a reform of institutions—even though the latter are aspects of regeneration. The potential for regeneration may rest in a personal savior, in impersonal values such as liberty or communism, in national destiny, or in a combination of these. In any case the value-oriented belief involves a preoccupation with the highest moral bases of social life.

---

[1] E. A. Shils, "Ideology and Civility: On the Politics of the Intellectual," *The Sewanee Review*, Vol. LXVI (1958), p. 460.

[2] Nowhere is this total generalization of anxiety seen more clearly than in the rise of nationalist movements. In the developing society, for instance, "whenever competing nationalist movements developed within any one society, they became usually totally opposed to one another in terms of differences over policies." S. N. Eisenstadt, "Sociological Aspects of Political Development in Underdeveloped Countries," *Economic Development and Cultural Change*, Vol. V (1957), p. 296. Even in countries with a single dominant nationalistic movement, the rejection of the West had this character of the "total opposition" between value-systems. M. Matossian, "Ideologies of Delayed Industrialization," *Economic Development and Cultural Change*, Vol. VI (1958), pp. 218 ff.

[3] "Ideology and Civility," *op. cit.*, p. 260.

The Creation of Generalized Beliefs

Value-oriented beliefs contain a vision of future harmony and stability (Stage 7, + Norms) which is in direct contrast to the here-now decay and instability. A major function of messiahs, Barber has argued, is "to proclaim a *stable order*."[1] Nationalistic movements as well focus on symbols of solidarity and social stability.[2]

Finally, adherents of value-oriented beliefs hold that through regeneration of values the agents of evil (infidels, whites, capitalists, etc.) will be smitten (Stage 8, + Mobilization), and that a condition of human happiness will be ushered in forthwith (Stage 9, + Facilities). Figure 5 summarizes these stages of the value-added process in graphic form.

Illustration of Themes in Value-oriented Movements. In this section we shall select examples from value-oriented beliefs which have eventuated in a variety of outcomes—religious cults, nativistic movements, nationalist movements, and revolutionary movements. We shall postpone the problem of strain giving rise to value-oriented beliefs until Chapter X.

(1) A religious cult—the Father Divine Peace Mission. Though an abundant supply of value-oriented beliefs can be found in the history of Christianity,[3] we shall restrict our analysis to a single Negro cult which flourished—especially in Harlem—during the depression of the 1930's.[4] The doctrines of this movement display all the characteristics of a value-oriented belief.

According to the theology of this group, God, having tired of prophets, has himself made an appearance on earth in the person of Father Divine. Heaven also is here and now, and immortality is given to the faithful. Neither Father Divine nor his true followers can die; illness means that one has strayed from the fold. Adherents never mention the passing of time, since immortality and timelessness mark the condition of the faithful. Finally, the spirit of God, as manifested in Father Divine, is available to anyone who will believe. The Negroes, however, have been chosen because of their lowly status.[5] The faithful are promised regeneration and the obliteration of "all vestiges of the past ... family, race, habit, and even name."[6]

What are the consequences of regeneration? It will erase all those

---

[1] "Acculturation and Messianic Movements," *op. cit.*, p. 665.
[2] Eisenstadt, "Sociological Aspects of Political Development in Underdeveloped Countries," *op. cit.*, p. 296.
[3] For an analysis of these kinds of movements, cf. N. Cohn, *The Pursuit of the Millenium* (New York, 1961), and R. A. Knox, *Enthusiasm: A Chapter in the History of Religion* (New York, 1950).
[4] Other Negro cults might have been chosen. Cf. A. H. Fauset, *Black Gods of the Metropolis* (Philadelphia, 1944).
[5] *Ibid.*, pp. 62–64.
[6] R. A. Parker, *The Incredible Messiah* (Boston, 1937), p. 157.

FIGURE 5
VALUE-ADDED IN THE CREATION OF VALUE-ORIENTED BELIEFS

	−Facilities	−Mobilization	−Norms	−Values	+Values	+Norms	+Mobilization	+Facilities
Stage 1: Strain giving rise to ambiguity →	**Stage 2:** Anxiety →	**Stage 3:** Generalized belief that agents are responsible for anxiety-producing state of affairs	**Stage 4:** Generalized sense of social disharmony, failure of institutional life	**Stage 5:** Generalized belief in degeneration of values	**Stage 6:** Generalized belief in regeneration of values	**Stage 7:** Belief in restoration of harmony and stability	**Stage 8:** Belief that value change will destroy, remove, damage or restrict the responsible agents	**Stage 9:** Belief in omnipotence of regeneration
		(Short-circuit) →	(Short-circuit) →	(Short-circuit) →	(Short-circuit) →	(Short-circuit) →	(Short-circuit) →	(Short-circuit) →
		Stage 3a: Identification of responsible agent and acceptance of exaggerated stories of "results" of evil-doing	**Stage 4a:** Identification of salient points of normative failure	**Stage 5a:** Identification of points of decay of values (sin, heresy, etc.)	**Stage 6a:** Specification of "savior," ideals, etc.	**Stage 7a:** Characterization of social life in the perfect society	**Stage 8a:** Assimilation of hostility to the effectiveness of value-regeneration	**Stage 9a:** Exaggerated ability of change to remove evil and bring bliss

The Creation of Generalized Beliefs

distasteful elements of the contemporary social order and bring about a condition of social harmony—"Americanism, Democracy, and Christianity—the Amalgamation of all Races, Creeds, Colors."[1] Almost half of Father Divine's Righteous Government platform in the 1930's concerns the abolition of racial iniquities—lynching, unfair employment, racial slang or abuse, segregation, etc.[2] The establishment of Righteous Government, moreover, will obliterate all such bases for conflict (Normative Component).

In the Father Divine Movement, the theme of the elect is quite explicit, but the theme of the non-elect is more subtle; the latter will be assimilated into the vast regeneration of humanity and swept before the tide. Related Negro movements envision the outright destruction of the whites, or the inversion of the traditional relations among the races[3] (Mobilization Component).

Finally, the themes of magically attained and unlimited gratification dominate the Father Divine doctrines. Faith-healing occupies a prominent place in the cult.[4] Father Divine's apparently inexhaustible sources of funds, as well as the feasting symbolism in the services, suggest the disappearance of economic deprivation.[5] In addition, Father Divine promises sexual bliss through abstinence; he also predicts an end to racial handicaps.[6] Finally, the movement envisions the establishment of a "Promised Land" on a piece of land in upstate New York; this would be a kind of heaven on earth based on cooperative principles (Facilities Component).

As in most cults, the Father Divine Peace Mission developed an elaborate set of taboos, practices and rituals. The taboos included stealing, refusing to pay debts, drinking, smoking, using obscene language, gambling, playing numbers, showing lust for the opposite sex, displaying racial bigotry, and using terms such as "Negro" and "white." When man and wife become members of the Kingdom, they separate immediately and remain brother and sister thereafter. All these practices and beliefs are simultaneously requirements for and signs of membership in the Kingdom of Heaven on Earth.[7]

(2) A nativistic movement—the Ghost Dance. The term "Ghost Dance" signifies especially the activities of American Indian prophets and their followings in 1870-71 in California and the early 1890's in

[1] *Ibid.*, p. 18.
[2] Braden, *These Also Believe*, pp. 17-24.
[3] Fauset, *Black Gods of the Metropolis*, pp. 35, 47.
[4] Braden, *These Also Believe*, pp. 17-24.
[5] Parker, *The Incredible Messiah*, pp. 125-126, 284 ff.; J. Hoshor, *God in a Rolls Royce* (New York, 1936), pp. 92 ff.
[6] Hoshor, *God in a Rolls Royce*, pp. 105-113.
[7] Summarized in Fauset, *Black Gods of the Metropolis*, pp. 62-67.

The Creation of Generalized Beliefs

the plains. Although tribal variations are enormous,¹ the various doctrines display all the ingredients of regeneration, re-establishment of social order, bliss, exclusion of enemies, and so on. Mooney's summary of the Ghost Dance runs as follows:

> The great underlying principle of the Ghost Dance doctrine is that the time will come when the whole Indian race, living and dead, will be reunited upon a regenerated earth [+Values], to live a life of aboriginal happiness, forever free from death, disease, and misery [+Norms, + Facilities].² On this foundation each tribe has built a structure from its own mythology, and each apostle and believer has filled in the details according to his own mental capacity or ideas of happiness, with such additions as come to him from the trance. Some changes, also, have undoubtedly resulted from the transmission of the doctrine through the imperfect medium of the sign language. The differences of interpretation are precisely such as we find in Christianity, with its hundreds of sects and innumberable shades of individual opinion.³ The white race, being alien and secondary and hardly real, has no part in this scheme of aboriginal regeneration, and will be left behind with the other things of earth that have served their temporary purpose, or else will cease entirely to exist [−and +Mobilization].
>
> All this needs to be brought about by an overruling spiritual power that needs no assistance from human creatures [+Facilities]; and though certain medicine-men were disposed to anticipate the Indian millennium by preaching resistance to the further encroachments of the whites, such teachings form no part of the true doctrine, and it was only where chronic dissatisfaction was aggravated by recent grievances, as among the Sioux, that the movement assumed a hostile expression. On the contrary, all believers were exhorted to make themselves worthy of the predicted happiness by discarding all things warlike and practicing honesty, peace, and good will, not only among themselves, but also toward the whites so long as they were together.⁴

Parallel themes could be found in a myriad of examples from the history of Christianity and of colonialism.⁵

---

¹ These are discussed in detail in J. Mooney, "The Ghost-Dance Religion and the Sioux Outbreak of 1890," *Fourteenth Annual Report of the Bureau of Ethnology* (Washington, 1896), and C. Du Bois, *The 1870 Ghost Dance* (Berkeley, 1939).

² Barber emphasizes a "happy return to a golden age" and thus suggests a more concrete kind of "happiness" for each individual tribe. "Acculturation and Messianic Movements," *op. cit.*, p. 663.

³ Mooney here recognizes implicitly the kind of objective we have in mind in this chapter; he is trying to rise above the individual and tribal differences and thereby extract the central distinguishing and common characteristics of the cults.

⁴ "The Ghost-Dance Religion and the Sioux Outbreak of 1890," *op. cit.*, p. 777; for a discussion of the different kinds of movements into which this and related beliefs developed, cf., below, pp. 365–366.

⁵ Mooney himself listed a large number of parallels to the Ghost Dance religion. *Ibid.*, pp. 928–947. Worsley, whose main interest was the Cargo Cult in Melanesia, mentions a large number of parallel kinds of beliefs in different

The Creation of Generalized Beliefs

(3) Contemporary nationalist movements in underdeveloped countries. The modern world is characterized by a vast number of industrially backward "new nations" with the following characteristics:

(1) [they have] been in contact with the industrial West for at least fifty years; (2) in [them] there has emerged a native intelligentsia composed of individuals with at least some Western education; and (3) large-scale industrialization is currently being contemplated or has been in progress for no more than twenty-five years.[1]

A common feature of these nations is the presence of one or more aggressive nationalist movements.

Most of these movements envision the establishment or re-establishment of basic values. According to Eisenstadt's summary,

the common bond which [nationalist movements] tried to create with the masses was almost entirely couched in modern solidarity-political terms and did not emphasize the solution of immediate economic and administrative problems. The political symbols used were intended to develop new, ultimate, common values and basic loyalties, rather than relate to current policy issues within the colonial society. . . .

A somewhat similar attitude can be observed in respect to economic, administrative and instrumental problems. Most nationalist movements did develop an economic ideology either stressing romantically the maintenance of the old village community or the necessity of state planning. All decried the injustices of the economic policies and discrimination of the colonial powers. But the nationalist leaders did not deal concretely with current economic problems or problems of daily administration.[2]

As these nationalist ideologies become the legitimate basis for independent national governments, more specific policies may develop; in their early stages, however, such ideologies are dominated by generalized symbols.

With regard to the specific content of the values to be realized, the kind of social integration to be achieved (Normative Component), the fate of agents responsible for social ills (Mobilization Component), and the means of realizing national purpose (Facilities Component), these nationalist movements display a kind of ambivalence toward absolutes. Ardent nationalists alternate between xenophobia and xenophilia; they predict that they will "out-modernize" the West in the future and simultaneously "restore" the true values of the ancient civilization; they argue for egalitarian and

---

historical contexts. P. M. Worsley, "Millenarian Movements in Melanesia," *The Rhodes-Livingstone Journal*, No. XXI (1957), pp. 18–19.

[1] Matossian, "Ideologies of Delayed Industrialization," *op. cit.*, p. 217.

[2] "Sociological Aspects of Political Development in Underdeveloped Countries," *op. cit.*, pp. 294–295.

The Creation of Generalized Beliefs

hierarchical principles of social organization at the same time.[1] Whatever the content of the ideologies, they envision a more or less absolute reorganization of all the components of the social order; thus they conform to the pattern of value-oriented beliefs.

(4) *An ideology of internal revolution—Naziism.* Because nationalist doctrines frequently accompany revolutions, and because many revolutions have a strong nationalist flavor, this section overlaps considerably with the last. In particular, Naziism—because of its anti-foreign and nationalist overtones, and because it occurred little more than a half-century after German industrialization began to move ahead in earnest—is a close relative of the ideologies of underdeveloped nations. Its differences are sufficiently great, however, to bear separate examination as a final example of a value-oriented belief.[2]

A core defining element of the Nazi ideology was the vision of thorough regeneration of German society and citizenry:

> The leitmotif of the Hitler movement is contained in the slogan, "*Gemeinnutz vor Egennutz*" (common good before personal advancement).
>
> At the core of the concept is the idea of *Gemeinschaft*, an untranslatable term which combines the meaning of "unity," "devotion to the community," mutual aid, brotherly love, and the family, in which these social values are most easily realized because of the ties of kinship and mutual interest. But the National Socialists were not concerned with the family; they talked about the nation as a *Gemeinschaft*. They were thus expressing a desire for a social order, in which the organization of national life would follow the family pattern....
>
> The concept of the nation as a *Gemeinschaft* is, in the last analysis, utopian. Accordingly, those who advocated it insisted upon a "change of heart" and even the need of breeding a new species of human being to make its realization possible.[3]

Under this umbrella (+Values) all institutions were to be subordinated—the arts, the press, the army, the family, the economy, and so on (+Norms).[4] Each was to maintain a separate existence,

---

[1] Matossian, "Ideologies of Delayed Industrialization," *op. cit.*

[2] Other possible examples of revolutionary ideology might be the Fascism of early twentieth-century Italy, the Marxism-Leninism of many Russian intellectuals early in the twentieth century, the doctrines of the Protestant Reformation (which combined both political and religious revolution), the ideology of the Enlightenment in France, and so on.

[3] T. Abel, *Why Hitler Came to Power* (New York, 1938), p. 137, 146-147. For the "Blood and Soil" theory of the German people, cf. S. H. Roberts, *The House that Hitler Built* (London, 1939), pp. 45-57.

[4] For brief analyses of the normative changes which the Nazi ideology envisioned, cf. the original twenty-five points of the Nazi party in 1920 as analyzed by K. Heiden, *A History of National Socialism* (New York, 1935), pp. 14-20; C. B. Hoover, *Germany Enters the Third Reich* (New York, 1933), pp. 187-199.

The Creation of Generalized Beliefs

but because all were to be engulfed in unity and national purpose, all bases of conflict were to disappear; correspondingly a state of social stability would ensue.[1] As for the means (+Facilities) of attaining this broad national regeneration, Naziism laid particular stress on the principle of leadership under Hitler himself.[2] Finally, millenarian visions—such as the Thousand-Year Reich—completed the utopian picture of the national socialist ideology.

Corresponding to these positive visions were the gloom and despair about contemporary Germany—the decay of the Aryan race, the feebleness of social and political life (−Values, −Norms) and so on. These themes of pessimism were traced to a number of threats—communism, urbanism, industrialization, the Treaty of Versailles, the foreign powers—but in the end all of these rested on an international Jewish conspiracy (−Mobilization) with enormous power and insidiousness (−Facilities).[3] One of the major objectives, moreover, of the gigantic national regeneration prophesied by the Nazis was to obliterate the Jews and thus remove the multi-sided threat to German national life (+Mobilization).

SUMMARY

We may summarize briefly the basic themes of this complicated analysis of generalized beliefs. Essentially, all the beliefs dissected in this chapter have a kinship to one another. All are generalized attempts to reconstitute the components of social action. Their major differences stem from the particular components which each attempts to reconstitute. Hysteria and wish-fulfillment focus in different ways on facilities; hostile beliefs on mobilization; norm-oriented beliefs on norms; and value-oriented beliefs on values.

The several beliefs stand in a hierarchy of increasing complexity and inclusiveness:

Top
↑

Value-oriented beliefs
Norm-oriented beliefs
Hostile beliefs
Wish-fulfillment beliefs
Hysterial beliefs

Bottom

---

[1] Neumann has suggested that demagoguery in general rests on a "promise of stability" during periods in which institutional action has failed. S. Neumann, "The Rule of the Demagogue," *American Sociological Review*, Vol. 13 (1948), pp. 488–489.
[2] Abel, *Why Hitler Came to Power*, p. 147.
[3] *Ibid.*, pp. 154–155.

The Creation of Generalized Beliefs

This hierarchy, derived from the general relations among the components of action, reveals the components that any one belief reconstitutes. The belief in question includes all the components of the beliefs below it in the hierarchy, plus one new ingredient which gives this belief its distinctive character. Thus we identify a norm-oriented movement because of its focus on norms, but it also includes hostility, wish-fulfillment, and hysteria as elements of itself. Hostility, although containing those beliefs below it as elements, does not involve a reconstitution of either norms or values. Such are the relations among the several generalized beliefs.

The objective of this chapter has been anatomical—to analyze in theoretical terms the structure of the beliefs which accompany collective behavior of every sort. The major questions which remain are (*a*) Why does one, rather than another type of belief arise under conditions of strain? (*b*) How does each kind of belief, once having arisen, work its way into definite episodes of collective behavior? To these questions we devote the remainder of the volume.

CHAPTER VI

THE PANIC

INTRODUCTION

We have analyzed strain and generalized beliefs. Now we shall assign these determinants to their place in the total value-added process by considering each type of collective episode in its entirety. We begin with panic.

Definition of Panic. Precise referents of "panic" are not consistently identifiable. "Almost every kind of socially disorganizing or personally disrupting type of activity has been characterized as panic. The range includes everything from psychiatric to economic phenomena (e.g., the 'panics' involved in bank runs, stock-market crashes, depressions, etc.)."[1] In addition, different *aspects* of these diverse events are treated as the essence of panic. Sometimes panic is defined in behavioristic terms—"an animal-like stampede in which wildly excited people crush each other to death"; or it may refer to an internal feeling of intense terror "with or without justification"; or to non-adaptive or useless behavior in general; or to the contagion of fear.[2] Thus the literature yields few coherent definitions of "panic."[3]

We define panic as *a collective flight based on a hysterical belief.* Having accepted a belief about some generalized threat, people flee from established patterns of social interaction in order to preserve life, property, or power from that threat.[4] This definition covers many concrete settings in which panic occurs—the battlefield, the

---

[1] Quarantelli, "The Nature and Conditions of Panic," *op. cit.*, fn., p. 268; D. Robinson, *The Face of Disaster* (Garden City, N.Y., 1959), p. 166.

[2] These and other meanings of the term are discussed in M. Wolfenstein, *Disaster* (Glencoe, Ill., 1957), pp. 85–86. See also Quarantelli, "The Nature and Conditions of Panic," *op. cit.*, p. 267.

[3] Quarantelli, "The Nature and Conditions of Panic," *op. cit.*, p. 267; in a remark concerning the related field of disaster research, Killian complained of the "fanciful and inaccurate ... accounts of disaster found in most non-scientific writings." L. M. Killian, "Some Accomplishments and Some Needs in Disaster Study," *Journal of Social Issues*, Vol. 10, No. 3 (1954), p. 66.

[4] Thus our definition of panic meets all the criteria for classifying an episode as collective behavior. It is collective; it is uninstitutionalized; it arises under conditions of strain; and it is based on a generalized belief. Above, pp. 8–9, 71–73, and 84–94.

The Panic

sinking ship, the burning building, the money market, and so on.

How is our definition of panic related to other meanings which have been assigned to the term? By viewing panic as a value-added process, we shall include many of its aspects—threat, anxiety, suggestion, contagion, flight—in a model pattern of determinants. Our definition excludes related kinds of behavior. We shall not discuss orderly withdrawal, since it is not based on a hysterical belief.[1] Furthermore, we shall not investigate the enduring psychiatric complications of persons that arise from intense fear-producing situations—complications such as sustained depressions, psychoses, traumatic neuroses, and psychosomatic disorders.[2] In addition, our definition does not include that large group of miscellaneous phenomena that investigators (*viz.*, Meerloo and LaPiere) have discussed under "panic"—lynching mobs, plundering troops, social unrest, war, confused voting behavior, orgiastic feasts, collective self-sacrifice, rapacity, or group tensions generally.[3]

The Value-added Process. The logic of explanation under the value-added scheme is to start with the most indeterminate necessary conditions for panic, then, *within the confines of these conditions*, to inquire how other, progressively more determinate conditions come to bear on panic. Together all these necessary conditions constitute the sufficient condition for panic. In arranging the necessary conditions in a series of increasing determinacy, we rule out consequences other than panic. By using the value-added scheme, then, we attempt to organize that set of conditions which give rise to panic and not to something else.[4] Variation of a single condition or variation of a

[1] C. E. Fritz and H. B. Williams, "The Human Being in Disasters: A Research Perspective," *The Annals of the American Academy of Political and Social Science*, Vol. 309 (Jan., 1957), p. 44; Robinson, *The Face of Disaster*, p. 116.

[2] For summary indications of some of these kinds of complications, cf. I. L. Janis, *Air War and Emotional Distress* (New York, 1951), pp. 64–66, 96–97, 177–179; A. Kardiner, "The Traumatic Neuroses of War," *Psychosomatic Medicine Monograph II-III* (Washington, D.C., 1941), pp. 198–202; J. A. M. Meerloo, *Aftermath of Peace* (New York, 1946), p. 70.

[3] J. A. M. Meerloo, *Patterns of Panic* (New York, 1950), pp. 72–104; LaPiere, *Collective Behavior*, pp. 447–451.

[4] For a fuller statement of the logic of the value-added process, above, pp. 13–20. Our aims are implied in Wallace's questions: "What are the determinants and conditions of panic and other forms of mass hysteria? Granted the same impact, under what conditions does panic *not* occur?" A. F. C. Wallace, *Human Behavior in Extreme Situations* (Washington, D.C., 1956), p. 27. Note that Wallace's questions parallel those we asked of collective behavior in general, above, pp. 12–13. For a statement of the great variety of behaviors which may arise in a danger situation, cf. Quarantelli, "The Nature and Conditions of Panic," *op. cit.*, p. 275. MacCurdy, following Rivers, mentions the following reactions which occur involuntarily in the presence of danger: flight, aggression, manipulative activity, collapse, and immobility. J. T. MacCurdy, *The Structure of Morale* (Cambridge, 1943), pp. 31–35.

The Panic

combination of similar conditions will give rise to behavior other than panic.[1]

The first and most determinate condition for panic is *structural conduciveness*. To assess this condition in any situation we ask: What are the opportunities for communication among persons? What are the opportunities for escape? Are the major social rewards —such as wealth, power, or prestige—freely disposable, or are they "locked" into the social structure in a way that prevents rapid and panicky withdrawal? The condition of conduciveness makes panic possible, but also allows for a wide range of other consequences. This is what we mean when we say it is an indeterminate condition. This indeterminacy is represented graphically in Figure 6. In addition to conduciveness, then, we have to inquire into other conditions that come into play within the scope established by conduciveness.

The second condition for panic is some kind of *strain*. To assess this condition, we ask: What kinds of threats give rise to panic? Conduciveness and strain, however, even in combination, do not necessarily produce panic; they may, as Figure 6 shows, give rise to other consequences such as hostility, immobility, or resignation. Further conditions are necessary to rule out these other possibilities.

A particular kind of *belief* must be present in order for panic to occur. This is the hysterical belief.[2] This belief has a generalized component (anxiety) and a specific or short-circuited component (fear). In the conversion of generalized anxiety into specific fear, we shall examine the place of events which act as *precipitating factors*. Such events constitute "evidence" for anxious persons that the terrible and unknown forces implicit in anxiety are manifesting themselves in concrete ways. A final necessary condition for panic is the actual *mobilization for flight*. What is the pattern of rout? What is the place of leadership in triggering the flight? If all these conditions combine, panic occurs.

Also relevant to the determination of panic is a series of counterdeterminants, which we group under the heading of *social control*. Social control operates to minimize the influence of all the conditions

---

[1] Above, pp. 12ff. Thus our position differs from the position of "indeterminacy" maintained by LaPiere: "Panic behavior is fortuitous; that is to say, it is the consequence of the coming together of a great many factors in entirely unpredictable ways. About the only thing which can be said with certainty is that the behavior of the individuals in a panic situation will not be a direct consequence of their inborn natures. It will be a fortuitous synthesis of their acquired patterns of response." *Collective Behavior*, p. 443. Although we agree that many of the conditions for panic exist prior to the panic, these conditions must come to play at definite and appropriate times in the value-added process.

[2] Above, pp. 84–94.

The Panic

just reviewed, and thus prevent the occurrence of panic. Toward the end of the chapter we shall discuss the control of panic.

The various necessary conditions for panic may accumulate in a temporal sequence that parallels the value-added stages. For instance, the perception of a limited number of exits (structural conduciveness) may occur before the onset of a dangerous situation (strain). On the other hand, the necessary conditions may build up simultaneously. Or, finally, the perception of danger may precede a rumor which reports only limited opportunities for escape. The important point, however, is this: *unless* the condition of conduciveness is established (at what point in time is irrelevant), the threat *cannot* rise

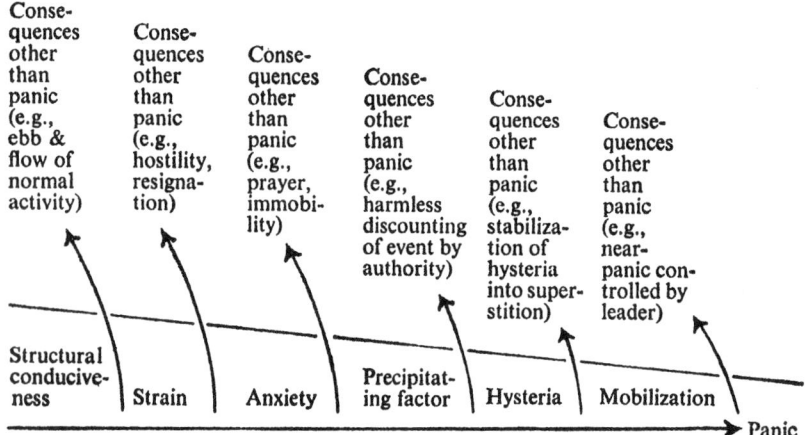

FIGURE 6
VALUE-ADDED PROCESS FOR PANIC

to significance as a determinant of panic. The threat may determine other things, but not panic. The same logic holds for precipitating factors. Unless they occur, or are interpreted within a context of structural conduciveness, strain, and anxiety, they cannot give rise to panic, even though they may give rise to other kinds of behavior. This is what we mean when we say that the indeterminate conditions in the value-added process are logically, but not necessarily temporally prior to the determinate conditions.[1]

Three Further Clarifications. Before treating in detail each condition in the value-added process, let us mention three further restrictions on the scope of our analysis:

(1) Much of the available literature on panic is found in studies of

---

[1] Above, pp. 18–20.

The Panic

disaster. Our purpose is to select only the material specifically related to panic. We shall not be concerned with rescue techniques, orderly evacuation, remedies for disaster dislocations, or recovery from disaster conditions.

(2) One of the most instructive findings in recent disaster research is that outright panic occurs rarely during air raids, earthquakes, tornadoes, and so on.[1] In other kinds of situations—battlefields and stock exchanges, e.g.—the incidence of panics is very high. One of our problems is to account for the different incidence of panics.

(3) Though many statements in this exposition will be obvious—e.g., situations of danger may give rise to panics—our purpose is not simply to gather established propositions about panic. Instead we wish to *organize* both the obvious and not-so-obvious characteristics of panic into a single coherent explanatory scheme.

STRUCTURAL CONDUCIVENESS

We shall discuss structural conduciveness under three headings: (*a*) the possibility of strain; (*b*) the possibility of withdrawal from danger, and (*c*) the possibility of communication.

The Possibility of Strain. Some kinds of strain lie at least partially beyond human control. These include the ravages of storms, floods, and earthquakes. Besides these threats of nature, man faces dangers and uncertainties that vary according to the mode of institutionalization.[2] If property, for instance, can be transferred only to first-born sons upon the death of the father, it is closely regulated. Dangers which arise from lack of knowledge of the market, fluctuating prices, and so on, are ruled out because property is linked to ascribed bases. In the money market and the stock exchange, on the other hand, vulnerability to these kinds of dangers is an institutionalized aspect of exchange.[3] To choose another example, recent institutional changes—such as monopolistic control of the market by business firms, unemployment insurance, old age and survivors' pensions,

---

[1] Quarantelli, "The Nature and Conditions of Panic," *op. cit.*, p. 275; Janis, *Air War and Emotional Stress*, p. 43; F. C. Iklé and H. V. Kincaid, *Social Aspects of Wartime Evacuation of American Cities* (Washington, D.C., 1956), pp. 7–8.

[2] This distinction between "natural" and "institutionalized" possibilities for threat or danger, which is only relative and changes with the accumulation of knowledge and technology, parallels our distinction between unstructured and structured uncertainty, above, pp. 86–89.

[3] For a statement of some of the sources of instability in stock and money markets, as well as some of the modes of reducing this instability, cf. C. A. Dice, *The Stock Market* (New York, 1926), pp. 415–433; E. D. Jones, *Economic Crises* (New York, 1900), pp. 56–57, 103–104; Hardy, *Risk and Risk Bearing*, p. 9; Parsons and Smelser, *Economy and Society*, pp. 58–64, 123–139, 162–173, 211–213.

farm supports, trade union regulation of employment, and so on—have reduced the threats created by economic fluctuations.[1] When the structural possibility of threat is thus minimized, the probability of strain, hysteria, and panic is reduced correspondingly.

The Possibility of Withdrawal from Danger. Panic is not possible if the routes for escape are—or are conceived to be—completely open. According to Iklé and Kincaid:

> ... one fact is borne out by various data of past disasters: the freedom to escape from threat of death or injury has a calming effect on the population.... [One] of the most ill-advised civil defense measures in this country was the placing of signs on outgoing-highways from the large cities, indicating that these escape routes would be closed to the public in case of enemy attack. Fortunately, they will now be removed in most cities. Exactly the opposite is to be recommended, namely, well marked exit routes and instructions concerning how to leave in case of emergency.[2]

Nor can panic occur if routes are conceived to be completely blocked, e.g., in submarine or mine disasters.[3] Reactions such as terror or infantile regression can occur in such settings, but not panic. Marshall notes that in amphibious attacks during World War II immobility in the face of enemy fire was a common response: "... the sea was at [the troops'] back; there was no place to run even had they been capable of movement. They sat there dumbly in the line of fire, their minds blanked out, their fingers too nerveless to hold a weapon."[4] But panic proper—collective flight based on a hysterical belief—did not occur.

What kinds of escape possibilities, then, permit panic?

> The important aspect is the belief or feeling of *possible* entrapment. This is reiterated again and again in the remarks of panic participants. It is not that affected individuals believe or feel they are definitely trapped. In such instances panic does not follow.... The flight of panic arises only when being trapped is sense or thought of as a possibility rather than as an actuality....[5]

In addition, people who panic sense that this "limited number of escape routes" is "closing (not closed) so that escape must be made quickly."[6]

[1] Galbraith, *The Affluent Society*, Ch. VII.
[2] *Social Aspects of Wartime Evacuation of American Cities*, p. 8.
[3] Mintz, "Non-Adaptive Group Behavior," *op. cit.*, pp. 157–158.
[4] S. L. A. Marshall, *Men Against Fire* (Washington, 1947), p. 148.
[5] Quarantelli, "The Nature and Conditions of Panic," *op. cit.*, p. 273. Also Foreman, "Panic Theory," *op. cit.*, p. 303; Robinson, *The Face of Disaster*, p. 167; C. E. Fritz and E. S. Marks, "The NORC Studies of Human Behavior in Disaster," *Journal of Social Issues*, Vol. 10 (1954), pp. 30–31.
[6] Fritz and Williams, "The Human Being in Disasters," *op. cit.*, p. 44. For a discussion of the ways in which the feeling of being possibly trapped may arise—

The Panic

Limited (and possibly closing) access to exit characterizes certain "classic" panic situations. Consider the following examples: (*a*) People pile up at doorways in theater, night club and school fires when it appears that these escape routes are closing.[1] (*b*) Miners trapped in a mine explosion charge toward a shaft that might possibly lead them from entrapment.[2] (*c*) Passengers leap into lifeboats or into the water when it appears that their possibility of escape from the ship lessens as the ship begins to list or sink.[3] (*d*) People begin to hoard food and other scarce items as a rumored shortage threatens to close off their access to these items. (*e*) People panic more readily in response to a rumor of an approaching flood (which threatens to seal off escape routes) than in response to an actual flood condition (which seals off these routes altogether).[4] (*f*) Limited and closing

---

from physical obstacles, from personal interaction, from individual inference—cf. Quarantelli, "The Nature and Conditions of Panic," *op. cit.*, p. 274. The relationship between partial blocking of exits and panic is suggested in Mintz' experiments on non-adaptive group behavior. In an effort to simulate the escape situation, Mintz asked subjects to draw cones from a narrow-necked bottle (i.e., to "make them escape" through the neck) under a number of different experimental conditions: "The subjects had to take cones out of a bottle; only one cone could be taken out at a time and the bottle neck was easily blocked by too many cones arriving simultaneously, so that the cones came out only if the subjects cooperated with each other. The situation was represented to some of the groups of subjects as a game in which one could win or lose small sums of money; to other groups the experiment was described as a measure of their ability to cooperate.... In the majority of cases, serious 'traffic jams' resulted when individual rewards and fines were offered, preventing the taking of any or most of the cones. No similar disturbances were observed in the 'measure of cooperativeness' experiment." "Non-Adaptive Group Behavior," *op. cit.*, p. 158. Mintz describes the reward-and-fine conditions as an "unstable reward situation." In our terminology, these competitive conditions represent the partially blocked exit. Exits were available, but always in danger of being closed off by a competitor. In the "cooperativeness" situation, the optimum exit situation became one of lining up together and filing out. "Panicky" behavior occurred, in short, more frequently when the exits were defined as available, but possibly closing off. Mintz also tried to rule out the effects of mutual emotional facilitation among the subjects by varying their ability to communicate with one another, and by arranging excited screaming at intervals during the experiments. These factors seemed to have little effect on the subjects' performances. For an attempt to apply this theory of unstable reward situations to a non-experimental setting, cf. A. Mintz, "The Failure of a Propaganda Campaign Attempting to Influence the Behavior of Consumers in the National Interest by Predominantly Selfish Appeals," *Journal of Social Psychology*, Vol. 38 (1953), pp. 49–62.

[1] For example, E. Foy and A. F. Harlow, *Clowning Through Life* (New York, 1928), pp. 280–282; B. Kartman and L. Brown (eds.), *Disaster!* (New York, 1948), p. 278.

[2] Cf. the account of panic in the Cherry, Ill., mine disaster of 1909 in Kartman and Brown (eds.), *Disaster!*, p. 134.

[3] *Ibid.*, p. 116.

[4] For an example of the Port Jervis, N.J., flood threat, which was interpreted as offering avenues of escape (and which caused flight), cf. E. R. Danzig, P. W. Thayer and L. R. Galanter, *The Effects of a Threatening Rumor on a Disaster-Stricken Community* (Washington, D.C., 1958); summarized briefly in Robinson,

The Panic

exits characterized the famous Orson Welles broadcast on the invasion from Mars in October, 1938. The broadcast dramatically depicted the advance of the Martians on New York in terms of *partial* encirclement. A possible escape from the invasion lay to the north of the city, but this, too, was likely to be closed off by a further advance by the Martians.[1]

In institutionalized settings the possibility of being "closed off" also arises. Some banks maintain a limited level of reserves in the expectation that only a small proportion of depositors will withdraw their funds in any given period. If everybody decides to withdraw at once, however, many will discover that they are unable to acquire their deposits; their access to funds will be closed off. Walter Bagehot, writing on the money market almost a century ago, remarked:

> Of the many millions in Lombard Street, infinitely the greater proportion is held by bankers or others on short notice or on demand; that is to say, the owners could ask for it all any day they please: in a panic some of them do ask for some of it. If any large fraction of that money really was demanded, our banking system and our industrial system too would be in great danger.[2]

Under other institutional arrangements, e.g., the federal deposit insurance system, the possibility of being closed off from deposits is ruled out by guaranteeing access completely through insuring the funds. Such measures reduce the possibility of panic. Only if people lose faith in the insurance system itself—i.e., interpret the situation as really closing off—can a panic occur.

What are the implications for panic, then, of this possibility of withdrawal? The possibility of panic is ruled out under two conditions: (*a*) if access to exits is defined as completely open; (*b*) if access

---

The Face of Disaster, pp. 172–173. In the Holland floods of 1953 the incidence of panic was very low, possibly because of the particularly dramatic and sudden character of the torrent, which rendered avenues of escape completely closed. Below, p. 139. Finally, in the flood of Kimbark, England, in 1953, behavior varied according to individuals' assessment of the possibilities of escape. "When one finally realized that the water was rising very rapidly outside, and could be seen rising within the house as well, a rapid decision had to be made. What to do? Should one try to get out the front door, or try to get up higher in the house? But these were bungalows without second stories, so where was one to go? Those who made the correct decision saved their lives. The correct decision was to get up through the ceiling onto the roof or up onto the porch if there was a high porch railing. Fortunately, most people did make the correct assessment. Those who did not and who tried to open the door and get out [i.e., those who looked upon the escape routes as possible but closing] either let in a mountain of water which trapped them in the house, or they were swept away." J. P. Spiegel, "The English Flood of 1953," *Human Organization*, Vol. 16 (Summer, 1957), p. 4.

[1] H. Cantril, *The Invasion from Mars* (Princeton, 1947), pp. 29–31.
[2] W. Bagehot, *Lombard Street: A Description of the Money Market* (London, 1931), p. 16.

The Panic

to exits is defined as completely closed. Panic is possible only when exits are defined as limited and possibly closing.

The Possibility of Communication. Panic can occur only if information, opinions, and emotional states can be communicated from one potential participant to another.[1] Confusion and individual terror may arise in the face of danger, but not collective panic as we have defined it.

The importance of communication is seen in the observation that allowing troops to cluster on the battlefield is potentially dangerous. As Marshall notes, "They will always bunch unless they are insistently told by voice to stop bunching. They will always run if they see others running and do not understand why. In these natural tendencies lie the chief dangers to battlefield control and the chief causes of battlefield panic."[2] In natural disasters, when telephone and radio service—as well as face-to-face contact—are restricted, panic may be reduced. In the Dutch floods of 1953, for instance,

People were amazed to observe that in spite of [the shock and suddenness of the disaster] ... no panic had broken out. Almost everyone had been in bed. Those who were struck simply had no time to contact others; everyone was confronted with the water in his own house, individually, or as a family ... many people did not hear the siren, owing to the gale. ...[3]

On the other hand, when communication is possible, rumors can flow, crowds can form, and hysterical beliefs can develop.[4] Such

---

[1] Such a condition, of course, is necessary for the occurrence of any kind of collective behavior, which by definition rests on a generalized *and shared* belief. Hence this condition is not useful in discriminating between panic and other types of response.

[2] Marshall, *Men Against Fire*, p. 145. Etlinge also refers to the connection between the tendency to panic and "troops in the peculiar crowded state brought into being by ... combat." L. Etlinge, *Psychology of War* (Fort Leavenworth, 1917), p. 52.

[3] M. J. van Doorn-Janssen, "A Study of Social Disorganization in a Community," in *Community Studies. Studies in Holland Flood Disaster 1953*. Volume III (Amsterdam and Washington, D.C., 1955), p. 183; in the Waco Tornado, as analyzed by Moore, "the failure of radio and telephone service was attributed to [heavy rain], possibly preventing some panic as well as greater congestion of streets and highways." H. E. Moore, *Tornadoes over Texas* (Austin, 1958), p. 182. For the disruption of almost every form of communication in the Halifax explosion, cf. Prince, *Catastrophe and Social Change*, p. 31.

[4] Cf. the graphic representation of the communication patterns in the Port Jervis flight following the spread of a threatening rumor in Danzig, Thayer, and Galanter, *The Effects of a Threatening Rumor on a Disaster-Stricken Community*, p. 13. For further study of communication patterns in hysteria, cf. Cantril, *The Invasion from Mars*, pp. 68 ff., and D. M. Johnson, "The 'Phantom Anesthetist' of Mattoon: A Field Study of Mass Hysteria," *Journal of Abnormal and Social Psychology*, Vol. 40 (1945), pp. 175-186: reprinted in T. M. Newcomb and E. L. Hartley (eds.), *Readings in Social Psychology* (New York, 1947), pp. 650-654. Festinger and his associates found data to support the hypothesis that "the

The Panic

communication need not be face-to-face; in financial panics, for instance, the ticker-tape is an anonymous but effective mode of conveying relevant information. The possibility of rapid interaction in face-to-face situations, however, does make for an acceleration of the communication process.[1]

The difficulty of communication accounts in part for the fact that panic is uncommon in disasters, such as air raids, explosions and floods. As Killian has noted, most of the research on disasters "has been concentrated chiefly on disasters characterized by sudden, physically violent impact, with a brief period of warning or no warning at all."[2] Such disasters minimize the possibilities of communication. Although sudden catastrophes may produce much extreme behavior, the inability to communicate with others reduces the possibility of defining the situation in such a way as to produce a collective panic.[3]

STRAIN

By itself conduciveness does not cause panic; it permits it to occur only if the other conditions of the value-added process are present. Within the limits set by conduciveness, some threat must be present if panic is to appear. "Panic participants invariably define the situation as highly and personally dangerous."[4] What are the characteristics of threats that give rise to panic?

The threat is perceived as immediate, not distant.[5] In addition, the threat is perceived as ambiguous; its exact dimensions are not known. LaPiere speaks of "any *unusual* event which is defined by the members of the situation as a source of danger" as a condition for panic.[6] Demerath holds that social disorganization and stress are "the greater as . . . the disaster agent [is] less well known and less clearly

---

number and nature of the channels of communication" are important in determining the spread of a rumor. Festinger *et al.*, "A Study of Rumor," *op. cit.*, pp. 481–482. For some of the physical features of the audience situation which facilitate effective communication, cf. H. L. Hollingworth, *The Psychology of the Audience* (New York, 1935), pp. 170–171.

[1] For a broad analysis of communication as the basis of formation of both face-to-face and dispersed crowds, cf. R. H. Gault, *Social Psychology* (New York, 1923), pp. 158–159.

[2] "Some Accomplishments and Some Needs in Disaster Study," *op. cit.*, pp. 67–68.

[3] This aspect of the importance of communication is emphasized, in a slightly different context, by H. B. Williams in "Some Functions of Communication in Crisis Behavior," *Human Organization*, Vol. 16 (Summer, 1957), p. 17.

[4] Quarantelli, "The Nature and Conditions of Panic," *op. cit.*, p. 271; also Strauss, "The Literature on Panic," *op. cit.*, p. 319; LaPiere, *Collective Behavior*, pp. 437–438.

[5] Quarantelli, "The Nature and Conditions of Panic," *op. cit.*, p. 271.

[6] *Collective Behavior*, pp. 437–438.

The Panic

perceived."[1] Foreman stresses the importance of "a totally incomprehensible disaster" that dwarfs other background conditions of panic.[2] Finally, Meerloo writes of "mystery, unexpected danger, and unknown threat, [which] always prepare for collective fear."[3]

In most military panics, lack of information about enemy attacks and enemy weapons are important prior conditions.[4] The phenomenon of unpredictability may also explain why ground weapons such as the German 88 mm. created such extraordinary fears among Allied troops in World War II.[5] Linebarger has reported many panics in military history that have been caused by unusual and unexpected events on the battlefield.[6] Some military manuals advise commanders that "troops should not only cover themselves in all directions from which the enemy may approach, but they should also, if possible, be warned in advance of the probable incidents of the combat."[7]

Studies of civilian reactions to enemy air attack indicate that the greater the degree of ambiguity, the greater the fear reaction. A long period of mild bombing attacks experienced by the British early in World War II apparently had the effect of familiarizing them with some of the features of bombing raids and thus lowering their anxiety about them.[8] In air raids themselves, anxiety seems to be augmented by variable and long intervals between attacks (i.e., greater unpredictability) rather than regular, short intervals. Night raids (which are more mysterious) produce more acute fright than day raids. High explosives (which have a suddenness and drama) are the source of more anxiety than incendiaries.[9]

Other examples of the anxiety-provoking effect of an ambiguous environment can be found in specific instances of panic behavior. For Americans in 1938—the year of the "Invasion from Mars" panic—domestic and international events had created an exceptionally uncertain atmosphere, within which any number of unusual events could have been interpreted as omens of disaster.[10] Two panics—fear

---

[1] N. J. Demerath, "Some General Propositions: An Interpretative Summary," *Human Organization*, Vol. 16 (Summer, 1957), p. 28.
[2] "Panic Theory," *op. cit.*, p. 302.
[3] *Patterns of Panic*, p. 48.
[4] Foreman, "Panic Theory," *op. cit.*, pp. 297–298. For a discussion of the ambiguity of battle conditions in general, cf. Marshall, *Men Against Fire*, p. 47.
[5] S. A. Stouffer, *et al.*, *Studies in Social Psychology in World War II. Volume II: The American Soldier: Combat and Its Aftermath* (Princeton, 1949), pp. 234–240.
[6] P. M. A. Linebarger, *Psychological Warfare* (Washington, D.C., 1954), pp. 3–7.
[7] Etlinge, *Psychology of War*, p. 74.
[8] D. Denny-Brown, "Effects of Modern Warfare on Civil Population," *Journal of Laboratory and Clinical Medicine*, Vol. 28 (1942–43), p. 641.
[9] Janis, *Air War and Emotional Distress*, pp. 124–125.
[10] Cantril, *The Invasion from Mars*, pp. 154–155, 195.

The Panic

of the "dreadnought" and fear of the "airship"—gripped the people of Great Britain immediately before World War I.[1] Postwar Germany and Japan provided many examples of collective hysteria.[2]

Threats which give rise to panic are typically perceived as uncontrollable. Psychologically this involves a feeling of helplessness. Welles' broadcast on the Martian invasion accentuated this element of uncontrollability:

> ... the extreme behavior evoked by the broadcast was due to the enormous ... ego-involvement the situation created and to the complete inability of the individual to alleviate or control the consequences of the invasion. The coming of the Martians did not present a situation where the individual could preserve one value if he sacrificed another. It was not a matter of saving one's country by giving one's life, of helping to usher in a new religion by self-denial, of risking the thief's bullet to save the family silver. In this situation the individual stood to lose *all* his values at once. Nothing could be done to save *any* of them.[3]

Air crews in World War II tended to fear enemy flak more than enemy fighter planes. "Enemy planes are objects that can be fought against.... Flak ... is nothing that can be dealt with—a greasy black smudge in the sky until the burst is close."[4]

Not all immediate, ambiguous and uncontrollable dangers give rise to outright panic. In the flying saucer scare after World War II, virtually no cases of panic were reported—terror, bodily symptoms of fright, anxiety, fantastic beliefs, perhaps, but not panic.[5] During a scare in Seattle, in which many citizens "saw" mysterious marks on the windshields of their automobiles, people displayed anxiety, defense against anxiety, and hysteria, but they did not panic.[6] Many hysterical seizures involving sobbing, dancing, twitching, or paralysis are attributed to the operation of unusual agents or unknown forces, but no collective panic occurs.[7] Why not?

---

[1] F. W. Hirst, *The Six Panics and Other Essays* (London, 1913), pp. 59–118.
[2] Sherif, *An Outline of Social Psychology*, pp. 405–406.
[3] Cantril, *The Invasion from Mars*, pp. 200–201. Similar statements of uncontrollability are found in G. M. Gilbert, "Social Causes Contributing to Panic," in *Panic and Morale* (New York, 1958), pp. 152–153; J. E. Ellemers, *General Conclusions. Studies in Holland Flood Disaster*, Vol. IV (Amsterdam and Washington, D.C., 1955), p. 10; E. P. Torrance, "The Behavior of Small Groups under the Stress Conditions of 'Survival,'" *American Sociological Review*, Vol. 19 (1954), p. 752; Rickman, "Panic and Air-Raid Precautions," *op. cit.*, p. 1293.
[4] R. F. Grinker and J. P. Spiegel, *Men Under Stress* (Philadelphia, 1945), p. 34.
[5] E. J. Ruppelt, *The Report on Unidentified Flying Objects* (Garden City, N.Y., 1956), pp. 284–285.
[6] Medalia and Larsen, "Diffusion and Belief in a Collective Delusion," *op. cit.*, pp. 185–186.
[7] For studies of cases of such hysteria which finds its way into "contagious" bodily manifestations, cf. R. E. Park and E. W. Burgess, *Introduction to the*

The Panic

Why does panic arise in some situations of uncontrollable danger of unknown proportions and not others? (*a*) Conditions of structural conduciveness may not be present. In the examples above, for instance, most of the unusual agents are perceived as present, but *not* in the context of limited and closing possibilities of escape. (*b*) Even if conditions of conduciveness combine with an unknown threat, a number of other conditions—anxiety, hysteria, mobilization for flight—must be present. To be able to separate those dangerous situations which produce panic from those which do not, we have to discuss several more determinants. First, however, let us clarify the conditions of conduciveness and strain further.

CULTURAL AND INDIVIDUAL DIFFERENCES IN THE DEFINITION OF THE PANIC SITUATION

The conditions of conduciveness and strain—numbers and kinds of exits, opportunities for communication, threats, etc.—are determined in part by situations in the external environment of the people affected by these conditions. The external environment, however, does not tell the whole story. As Rickman observes:

... since panic occurs (though infrequently) apart from external dangers and may occur when the external dangers are diminishing, we cannot regard external dangers as "the" cause of panic; though of course external dangers contribute very much indeed to the release of panic.[1]

People differ greatly in their susceptibility to danger, anxiety, threatening rumors, and therefore panic.[2] What are some of the factors that contribute to this differential susceptibility?

(1) Beliefs. All religions, in some degree, characterize the world as capricious, uncertain, and threatening:

... terror holds sway over large domains. True, the demons have now assumed the anthropomorphic lineaments of a personal godhead; they

---

Science of Sociology (Chicago, 1924), pp. 878–879, and E. A. Schuler and V. J. Parenton, "A Recent Epidemic of Hysteria in a Louisiana High School," *Journal of Social Psychology*, Vol. 17 (1943), pp. 221–235. In the first case one of the "explanations" of such behavior was that a plague was being introduced by cotton, which had recently become the basis of factory manufacture. In the second case the curious behavior on the part of girls who twitched and trembled was attributed, in some cases, to something wrong with the water supply. In both cases the disturbed behavior was attributed to some unusual, uncontrollable, and dangerous agent, but no panic occurred.

[1] Rickman, "Panic and Air-raid Precautions," *op. cit.*, p. 1291.
[2] For a general statement of this differential susceptibility, cf. Cantril, *The Invasion from Mars*, pp. 88 ff. For a study of differential interpretations of a single incident in Houston, Texas, cf. L. M. Killian, *A Study of Response to the Houston, Texas, Fireworks Explosion* (Washington, D.C., 1956), especially pp. 15–21.

have divested themselves of the beast's hide and horns, of the dragon's tail and the wolf's ravening maw; they no longer roar and bellow, but speak with the human voice: yet these gods in human form remain incalculable, malicious, bloodthirsty; and mortals' attitude toward them is one of blind, perplexed, despairing uncertainty.[1]

Persons who hold such beliefs, and who also believe in omens, signs, etc., are more susceptible to hysterical interpretations of unanticipated events.[2] In Cantril's follow-up study of those who panicked after Welles' broadcast in 1938, he found that those who tended to accept the program literally were characterized more by "fatalism," "religiosity," and "frequency of church attendance" than those who did not.[3] The fact that the program occurred on Halloween probably means that it tapped a reservoir of lingering superstitions about ghosts, spooks, and mysterious happenings.[4]

Other beliefs encourage the definition of situations as "those that are likely to eventuate in panic flight," e.g., the belief that fires in crowded theaters are causes of panic, the belief that good market conditions can't last, the belief that a person's luck is bound to run out, the belief that a person's number will come up sooner or later, and so on.[5] Individuals and cultures vary greatly with regard to these predisposing beliefs.[6] Insofar as individuals adhere to them, they may convert all sorts of situations into feelings of "being trapped" and all sorts of events into "dangers"—situations and events which would not excite such interpretations if not assessed in the context of these beliefs.

(2) *Other personality variables.* The Freudian variables of guilt, anxiety, hostility, and especially the tendency to project these outward, are important determinants of a person's susceptibility to possibly dangerous situations. During the air raid drills in New York City during World War II, for instance, most people remained calm,

---

[1] R. Fülöp-Miller, *Leaders, Dreamers, and Rebels* (New York, 1935), pp. 11–12.
[2] For a discussion of the framework of superstition which has surrounded past sightings of unfamiliar objects in the skies, cf. Menzel, *Flying Saucers*, pp. 106, 124.
[3] *The Invasion From Mars*, p. 131, also p. 197.
[4] *Ibid.*, p. 3. For discussion of such beliefs as the universal fear of suffocation, cf. Meerloo, *Patterns of Panic*, pp. 60–61.
[5] Quarantelli, "The Nature and Conditions of Panic," *op. cit.*, p. 275. Sometimes such beliefs are augmented by recent personal experiences. For instance, "one of the most common reactions of people who have undergone a disaster is the fear that it will happen again." Wolfenstein, *Disaster*, p. 151. The importance of near-misses in bombing raids in provoking fear reactions is a similar phenomenon. *Ibid.*, p. 67, and MacCurdy, *The Structure of Morale*, pp. 12–13.
[6] I. L. Janis, "Problems of Theory in the Analysis of Stress Behavior," *Journal of Social Issues*, Vol. 10 (1954), p. 21; D. M. Schneider, "Typhoons on Yap," *Human Organization*, Vol. 16 (Summer, 1957), p. 14.

The Panic

but a small proportion of the participants—both adults and children—experienced seizures of acute anxiety. Clinical analysis of persons who showed this reaction revealed that they

... were individuals who in their family relations experienced intense hostility together with great fear of retaliation if they expressed it. They felt that they would be precipitated into great danger if the hostility which they inhibited precariously and with great effort were to break through. This, then, was the explosion which they dreaded, the image of which became projected on the outer world. The danger of bombs exploding thus seemed imminent to them though it did not to others in the same external circumstances.[1]

Such personality characteristics determine in part a person's assessment of dangers, possibilities of escape, and so on, in potentially threatening situations.

Many investigators mention "morale" as contributing to panic and related reactions.[2] Morale is largely a function of the personality variables just reviewed, of leadership, of the kinds of interaction and communication in a group under stress, and so on.

(3) Physical condition. "Fatigue, undernourishment, lack of sleep, toxic conditions of the body, and the like" frequently appear among the listed causes of panic, especially on the battlefront.[3] Such factors presumably increase the tendency to define situations as dangerous by increasing irritability, by reducing the ability to control the situation, by lowering resistance to anxiety, and so on.

(4) Miscellaneous factors. Women, it has been maintained, are more susceptible to hysteria than men;[4] less educated persons are

---

[1] Wolfenstein, *Disaster*, pp. 7-8; also pp. 37-38; Cantril, *The Invasion from Mars*, pp. 130 ff.; Janis, "Problems of Theory in the Analysis of Stress Behavior," *op. cit.*, p. 21.

[2] Strauss, "The Literature on Panic," *op. cit.*, p. 319; Etlinge, *Psychology of War*, p. 65; C. T. Lanham, "Panic," in J. I. Greene (ed.), *The Infantry Journal Reader* (Garden City, N.Y., 1943), pp. 279-281. For an experimental study of the relationship between social organization and the tendency to panic, cf. French, "Organized and Unorganized Groups under Fear and Frustration," *op. cit.*, especially pp. 270-273, 301-303.

[3] Strauss, "The Literature on Panic," *op. cit.*, pp. 324, 319. See also Foreman, "Panic Theory," *op. cit.*, pp. 297-298; Etlinge, *Psychology of War*, p. 65; F. Aveling, "Notes on the Emotion of Fear as Observed in Conditions of Warfare," *British Journal of Psychology*, Vol. XX (1929), p. 139.

[4] This belief has an ancient heritage in Western civilization. Recent research relevant to such a relationship may be found in Johnson, "The 'Phantom Anesthetist' of Mattoon," *op. cit.*, p. 648; Cantril, *The Invasion from Mars*, p. 148. Ruppelt reported that in the overall sightings of "flying saucers" women made two reports for every one for men. *The Report on Unidentified Flying Objects*, pp. 277-278. On the other hand, in those sightings which were never really "explained" in the official investigations, "the men beat out the women ten to one." *Ibid.*, p. 278. Medalia and Larsen have also criticized the Johnson-Cantril findings on the basis of their study of the windshield-pitting epidemic in Seattle, in which

The Panic

more susceptible to anxiety in threatening situations than more educated; persons from lower economic levels are more susceptible to anxiety than persons from higher economic levels.[1] In the Waco, Texas, disaster, the tornado apparently induced greater fear of unusual weather among Negroes than among whites; also "Negroes reacted to the disaster more sharply in changes in their religious practices than did [whites]."[2] Although each of these relationships seems to have some validity of its own, the data are so poor that it is difficult to relate the variables systematically to the formation of personal beliefs about threatening situations.

The cultural, psychological, physical, and other variables are not necessary conditions for panic in the same sense as structural conduciveness, strain, anxiety, and so on. They lie outside the value-added process itself. They are determinants, however, insofar as they contribute to the strength of conduciveness, strain, anxiety, etc. At one extreme—for instance, in a catastrophic explosion—these background factors are subordinated to external threats.[3] At the other extreme, an anxiety-ridden and projecting person brings his expectations of disaster to all kinds of situations which are not objectively threatening. In any case, the seriousness of a potentially threatening situation is a function of both the external environment of the persons affected and predispositions they bring to this environment.

ANXIETY—THE GENERALIZED ELEMENT OF A HYSTERICAL BELIEF

In Chapter V we outlined the general character of anxiety and established the universal connection between strain and anxiety.[4] At this time we shall place anxiety in the total value-added process that results in panic.

Most panics are preceded by a build-up of what some observers have called a "tense psychological state of mind."[5] This is most

---

men seemed to be more susceptible to the belief in the operation of some "unusual agent." "Diffusion and Belief in a Collective Delusion: The Seattle Windshield Pitting Epidemic," *op. cit.*, p. 184.

[1] Cantril, *The Invasion from Mars*, pp. 113, 157. The correlations on the education and socio-economic level continued to hold even when the other was held constant. Also Johnson, "The 'Phantom Anesthetist' of Mattoon," *op. cit.*, p. 648. Again, Medalia and Larsen have disputed these relationships with their findings on the diffusion of the rumors and hysteria concerning the windshield-pitting epidemic in Seattle. "Diffusion and Belief in a Collective Delusion," p. 184.

[2] Moore, *Tornadoes Over Texas*, pp. 150–151.

[3] Foreman, "Panic Theory," *op. cit.*, p. 302.

[4] Above, pp. 85–86.

[5] Lanham, "Panic," *op. cit.*, p. 287; also A. Argent, "Characteristics of Panic Behavior," in W. E. Daughtery (in collaboration with M. Janowitz), *A Psycho-*

The Panic

evident in situations of immediate physical danger—the battlefield, the community stricken by natural disaster, etc. Anxiety also precedes panic reactions in less obviously threatening situations. Even in the later phases of speculative booms—which stereotypically are periods of euphoria, enthusiasm, and dreams of unlimited riches—an undercurrent of anxiety begins to develop. Before the panic of 1847 in this country, for instance,

> The resources of the States were so great, so varied, so extraordinary, their extent almost boundless; and with such room for development and the employment of capital. There was not a suggestion of trouble in the commercial horizon that in any way indicated a possible financial storm, although the seasons were backward, the Mexican War was on, and an air of uncertainty pervaded the country.[1]

In a study of the behavior of prices of stocks before the panics of 1837, 1857, 1884, 1893, and 1903, Gibson found that "in the majority of instances, highest prices for stocks were reached long before business troubles were openly apparent. This action represents to a certain extent the selling of stocks by men who were wise enough to foresee trouble."[2] As financial panic breaks, this anxiety focuses on more specific threats of loss of capital.

THE PRECIPITATING FACTOR—THAT WHICH TRANSFORMS ANXIETY INTO FEAR

The place of a precipitating factor in the value-added process is that it "confirms" the generalized suspicions and uneasiness of anxious people. In this way it provides an occasion for structuring an ambiguous situation, by rumors, "explanations," and predictions. This structuring by a dramatic event—an explosion, a governmental collapse, a bank failure—is essential in the determination of panic. Anxiety alone does not produce panic; it must be transformed into a fear of a specific threatening agent.[3]

---

logical Warfare Casebook (Baltimore, 1958), p. 669. For a statement of the view of this state of mind as developed in Nazi literature, cf. L. Farago (ed.), *German Psychological Warfare* (New York, 1942), pp. 122–123; for specific instances of the growth of this state of mind under battle conditions, cf. Lanham, "Panic," *op. cit.*, pp. 276–278, 278–279, and 281–282; also Lagenhove, *The Growth of a Legend*, pp. 183–184.

[1] D. W. Perkins, *Wall Street Panics 1813–1930* (Waterville, N.Y., 1931), p. 44. For a similar example, cf. the developing uneasiness of the frame of mind of the country in 1797 in England, before the suspension of specie payments (Duguid, *The Story of the Stock Exchange*, p. 69), and on the growing caution toward the end of the Florida Land Boom (A. M. Sakolski, *The Great American Land Bubble*, [New York, 1932], pp. 341–343).

[2] T. Gibson, *The Cycles of Speculation* (New York, 1917), pp. 28–29.

[3] Cf. Quarantelli: "The flight behavior is always oriented with reference to a threatening situation; that is, people in panic flee from a general locale, such as a

The Panic

Analytically, then, the precipitating factor "adds its value" to the anxiety created by an unknown and uncontrollable threat. In this analytic sense, anxiety must precede the precipitating event if this event is to be a determinant in the value-added process that results in panic. Temporally, however, the dramatic event and the actual arousal of anxiety may occur in any order. Let me illustrate this from a personal experience. The first time I heard a sonic boom, I found the event to be disturbing. It was a loud and unfamiliar sound. Immediately I began to interpret the explosion in terms of anxieties about atomic attack. Had I been in a place that was structurally conducive to panic (e.g., a crowded street with limited access to shelter entrances), and had a large number of others experienced the same fears as I, the possibility of panic would have arisen. In this case, the precipitating factor occurred temporally before the arousal of latent anxieties. Only after the explosion occurred did I interpret it in terms of these anxieties. If I had *not* assembled these latent feelings, however, the precipitating factor would have passed less noticed. In fact, now that I recognize sonic booms, and expect them to occur from time to time, I experience only mild irritation at the Air Force for allowing pilots to behave irresponsibly around metropolitan centers. Moreover, sonic booms can now no longer be significant as determinants in a process which results in panic, because I no longer interpret them as the same kind of anxiety-provoking events as before.

The following temporal relations between anxiety and precipitating factors may hold: (*a*) The precipitating factor may "confirm" a culturally conditioned anxiety that has existed for generations or centuries. If sailors believe in superstitions concerning sea monsters, for instance, any number of dramatic events may be taken as "signs" of danger from the monsters. (*b*) The precipitating event may occur after the build-up of anxiety. In the panic of the Austria X Corps in 1866, an officer had informed the men that the Prussians had assumed a position from which they would be able to cut off the Austrians from the rear. In response to this information the men became extremely uneasy and anxious. The mere sound of a few shots and the cry "We're cut off from the corps!" led to a spread of fear and a panic.[1] (*c*) The precipitating factor and the arousal of anxiety may occur simultaneously, e.g., when fire breaks out in a building. (*d*) The

---
collapsing building or a gas-filled house." "The Nature and Conditions of Panic," *op. cit.*, p. 269.

[1] Example taken from Lanham, "Panic," *op. cit.*, p. 276. For an example of the uneasiness connected with the Revolutionary and Napoleonic Wars in England, and the oversensitivity which this generated in the stock exchange to various dramatic events, cf. Duguid, *The Story of the Stock Exchange*, p. 82.

The Panic

precipitating event may occur before it is interpreted as a source of anxiety. An unknown explosion, an anomalous political event such as an assassination are examples of incidents that may be defined as progressively more perilous after they have occurred. Then, after this build-up of anxiety has occurred, the events are "reinterpreted" as precipitating factors.[1] No matter what the temporal order of the arousal of anxiety and the occurrence of a precipitating event, the analytic significance of the precipitating event remains unchanged: Unless the event in question is interpreted as occurring in a structurally conducive context (e.g., limited opportunity to escape), as an appropriately threatening stimulus (e.g., an unknown, uncontrollable danger), and in a context of anxiety, it cannot be a precipitating factor for panic.

Because of the importance of the context of precipitating events, their content is enormously variable. The important thing is not their objective characteristics (except in the case of obviously threatening events such as a fire) so much as the meaning which they are assigned in terms of anxious expectations. For this reason we find a most extraordinary variety of events which have precipitated the panic reaction. On the battlefield, for instance, the immediate occasion for panicky behavior may be a cry, a gesture, a shout, a shadow, a false report, a herd of frightened pigs, the appearance of a horse, the appearance of unexpected weapons, etc.[2] If anxiety is sufficiently strong or widespread, any of these—or even more trivial incidents—may tip the balance and set off collective flight.

The triggering of financial panics is equally varied. In the history of panics precipitating factors have been a natural event such as a hurricane;[3] a bad harvest;[4] a readjustment in a bank rate;[5] the suspension of payments by banks;[6] the failure of a bank;[7] the failure

---

[1] For a discussion of this kind of feedback, cf. Williams, "Some Functions of Communication in Crisis Behavior," *op. cit.*, p. 17.

[2] These examples mentioned in Etlinge, *Psychology of War*, p. 49; Lanham, "Panic," *op. cit.*, pp. 282-283, 284-285, 289; Farago (ed.), *German Psychological Warfare*, p. 123; P. M. A. Linebarger, *Psychological Warfare* (Washington, 1954), pp. 3-7. In the period following the collision between the *Andrea Doria* and the *Stockholm*, the captain of the former hesitated to sound the ship's alarm sirens because he feared that the noise would precipitate a panic. A. Moscow, *Collision Course: The Andrea Doria and The Stockholm* (New York, 1959), p. 105.

[3] For the significance of a hurricane in operating to dampen the Florida land boom, cf. Sakolski, *The Great American Land Bubble*, p. 346.

[4] Jones, *Economic Crises*, p. 40; crop failures played a part in the American crisis of 1837. R. H. Mottram, *A History of Financial Speculation* (London, 1929), p. 184.

[5] Jones, *Economic Crises*, pp. 108-109; for a specific instance in the panic of 1919 in the United States, cf. Perkins, *Wall Street Panics 1813-1930*, pp. 176-177.

[6] Gibson, *The Cycles of Speculation*, pp. 24-27; Perkins, *Wall Street Panics 1813-1930*, pp. 33 ff., 47, 49 ff.; Melville, *The South Sea Bubble*, p. 138.

[7] Perkins, *Wall Street Panics 1813-1930*, p. 43, for the initiation of the panic of

of a business concern;[1] a political event such as an assassination, the outbreak of war, an election, etc.;[2] sometimes the changing behavior of a leader on the stock market will stimulate panicky selling;[3] indeed the mere prediction of an imminent collapse—such as the famous prognostication of Roger Babson before the Annual National Business Conference in September, 1929—may have the same effect.[4] In all cases these events provide "evidence" that the worst which has been feared is now manifesting itself.

All the above examples have been taken from situations which actually have given rise to panics. Sometimes, startling events produce hysterical beliefs but not panic. For instance, during the prolonged flying saucer scare of the late 1940's and early 1950's, all kinds of objects were interpreted in the context of anxieties concerning Russia, secret weapons, atomic war, etc.[5] Why does outright panic not occur in such instances? Usually conditions that are structurally conducive to panic are not present. The objects were often seen when the observer was alone (e.g., in an airplane, in open country) or when he was unable to communicate his excitement immediately. Furthermore, the sighted objects were characterized as moving high in the sky and hence not closing in on the observers. Under such conditions hysterical interpretations may well arise, since the objects are unknown and thus anxiety-producing. Because the situation was not structurally conducive, however, collective panic was not one of the reactions to the flying saucers.

FEAR—THE SPECIFIC ELEMENT OF A HYSTERICAL BELIEF

The role of the precipitating factor is to focus generalized anxiety on a specific event or situation. This leads to the formation of fears of immediate objects, and thus creates something definite from

---

1841. Also E. Vaught, "The Release and Heightening of Individual Reactions in Crowds," *Journal of Abnormal and Social Psychology*, Vol. 22 (1928), p. 404.

[1] Jones, *Economic Crises*, p. 40; such failures tripped off the panics of 1864, 1884, 1890, and 1893. Perkins, *Wall Street Panics 1813–1930*, pp. 71–72, 99 ff., 115 ff.; Duguid, *The Story of the Stock Exchange*, pp. 322–323.

[2] Panics of 1814, 1857, 1861, 1865, 1914, and even during the early part of the Korean War, are instances of the influence of such political events on financial crises. Duguid, *The Story of the Stock Exchange*, pp. 107–108, 185–186, 198; Perkins, *Wall Street Panics 1813–1930*, pp. 19 ff., 61–62, 169 ff.; also Gilbert, "Social Causes Contributing to Panic," *op. cit.*, pp, 158–159.

[3] Perkins, *Wall Street Panics 1813–1930*, pp. 81 ff., 90 ff., and 161 ff., for an account of these factors in the panics of 1869, 1873, and 1907.

[4] Galbraith, *The Great Crash*, p. 89.

[5] For a report on the official governmental breakdown of sighted objects which led to such fantasies, cf. Ruppelt, *The Report on Unidentified Flying Objects*, pp. 276–277; also Menzel, *Flying Saucers*, pp. vii–viii, 83.

The Panic

which to flee. This transformation of generalized anxieties into hysterical fears must occur if panic is to appear.[1]

The hysterical belief is communicated among the persons involved in the threatening situation, becoming a shared belief.[2] We should not exaggerate the "individualistic" and "heterogeneous" character of the panic reaction.[3] True, much fumbling, confusion, and random behavior follow events such as explosions or sudden earthquakes. Foreman has characterized the immediate response to such events as follows:

Shock is quickly followed by confusion, that is, by individual and random efforts to interpret events in terms of reasonable experiences or relatable antecedent situations... shock and confusion are phases of "indecisive inactivity occasioned by an emergency." When interpretations of the stimulus are so acutely pressing that instantaneous action is demanded, the sensing of this acuteness frequently blocks logical definition of the crisis and induces terror. Initial terror responses include shouts, screams, and excited physical movements. This is not a lull phase; it is a period of din. These indecisive acts of initial terror, if not immediately controlled by an overwhelming order-producing stimulus, compound into bedlam.[4]

But if panic is to occur, there must be a common definition of the situation. In panics that take several days or longer to develop—e.g., some stock market panics—the development of a collective definition of the situation is readily observable. News comes over the ticker, passes around, and can be traced. For some collective panics which develop in response to threats like floods, investigators have traced patterns of communication which structure the threatening situation

---

[1] Above, pp. 16–17. In many cases these fears are extremely explicit; persons who panic generally know what they fear, and can report later on these fears. E. Boring, *Psychology for the Armed Forces* (Washington, D.C., 1945), pp. 443–453.

[2] Information may stimulate persons to panic, but it also may control their behavior by restructuring the situation along less threatening lines. Cf. O. N. Larsen, "Rumors in a Disaster," *Journal of Communication*, Vol. IV (1954), p. 118; Janis, "Problems of Theory in the Analysis of Stress Behavior," *op. cit.*, p. 21. For a discussion of the controlling and diverting aspects of information, below, pp. 158–161.

[3] LaPiere, for instance, maintains that in a panic, "the members of the situation [!] behave, not as the members of a group, but as isolated individuals. Each individual fumbles by himself to find a way to respond to the crisis.... The immediate origin of panic behavior is, thus, seen to lie in the individual heterogeneous reactions of a group to a crisis." *Collective Behavior*, pp. 440–441.

[4] "Panic Theory," *op. cit.*, p. 298. Also Wolfenstein, *Disaster*, pp. 28–29, 51–52, 77 ff.; Strauss, "The Literature on Panic," *op. cit.*, p. 317; J. S. Tyhurst, "Individual Reactions to Community Disaster: The Natural History of Psychiatric Phenomena," *American Journal of Psychiatry*, Vol. 107 (1951), pp. 766–767; LaPiere, *Collective Behavior*, pp. 445 ff.; Meerloo, *Patterns of Panic*, pp. 175–176; A. F. C. Wallace, "Mazeway Disintegration: The Individual's Perception of Socio-Cultural Disintegration," *Human Organization*, Vol. 16 (Summer, 1957), pp. 23–24.

The Panic

and prepare the way for flight.[1] Even in telescoped and dramatic panics—as on the battlefield—communication, through either word or gesture, of a common assessment of the situation is apparent. Sometimes the fact that someone starts to run in a certain direction constitutes an effective definition of the situation. As Foreman observes,

> [Terror reactions] ... serve as reinforcing stimuli for the terror of others and may be reflected back, circularwise, to reinforce the frenzy of the original actor. Linked in these ways, the terror of interacting individuals is heightened. Occasionally, participant observers record the fact that these augmented terror responses serve to reduce confidence in whatever, if any, organizing interpretations of the crisis had been effected and to establish convictions of doom. Terror movements, among whatever else they may suggest, may channel attention and direct activity to flight. Actors who offer such suggestions are in this context flight models. Panic is activated when interacting terrorized individuals surge away in flight.[2]

Finally, even when the precipitating factor "contains" obvious information as to its danger—e.g., fire in a specific location[3]—a prior common definition concerning the danger of fire leads to the convergence of individual reactions to the fire.

The importance of communicating a common definition of a situation, even under critical conditions, should remind us that panic is structured collective action.[4] Moreover, panic is action based on a hysterical belief that arises from strain in a structurally conducive context. Thus it fits our general definition of collective behavior.[5]

The concept of suggestion arises in connection with the communication of a common definition of the situation. "Suggestion" has long been used as an explanatory concept for crowd behavior, as well as human conduct in general.[6] McDougall defined suggestion as "a process of communication resulting in the acceptance with

---

[1] E.g., Danzig et al., *The Effects of a Threatening Rumor on a Disaster-Stricken Community*; Robinson, *The Face of Disaster*, pp. 169–174; Meerloo, *Patterns of Panic*, pp. 38–42; also Larsen, "Rumors in a Disaster," *op. cit.*, pp. 114–115, 118; Williams, "Some Functions of Communication in Crisis Behavior," *op. cit.*, p. 17.
[2] "Panic Theory," *op. cit.*, pp. 298–299.
[3] Penrose, *On the Objective Study of Crowd Behavior*, pp. 28–29.
[4] Specifically, what gives panic its "common character" is (1) "circular and chain suggestions presented during flight," and (2) "the identity or similarity in escape opportunities afforded by the setting in which rout proceeds." Foreman, "Panic Theory," *op. cit.*, p. 299. Those elements, then, which give the identifiable structure to the panic are the initial conditions of structural conduciveness and the structure of the hysterical belief-system which develops out of a threatening situation.
[5] Above, pp. 71–72.
[6] Allport, "The Historical Background of Modern Social Psychology," *op. cit.*, pp. 24–29; Brown, "Mass Phenomena," *op. cit.*, pp. 842–843.

conviction of the communicated proposition in the absence of logically adequate grounds for its acceptance."[1] Such a concept is useful in characterizing many kinds of behavior,[2] including panic. During the transformation of anxiety into fear, various "propositions" regarding the threatening situation are passed by rumor or gesture; they are uncritically incorporated as beliefs by the participants. Suggestion operates in such situations.[3] It should be stressed, however, that as an explanatory concept in collective behavior, suggestion should be limited to its appropriate place in the value-added process.[4]

MOBILIZATION FOR FLIGHT

The final necessary condition for the occurrence of a panic is mobilization for flight. Empirically this process is sometimes indistinguishable from the process of communicating a hysterical belief among participants in a panic. Since, however, a hysterical belief does not always give rise to pell-mell flight,[5] it is necessary to consider the process of mobilization separately.

Usually a primitive form of leadership arises to touch off a panic. Someone (a "flight model") starts running, and others join.[6] On the basis of seven incidents of panic in World War II, Marshall ventured the following generalization:

I think it can be laid down as a rule that nothing is more likely to collapse a line of infantry in combat than the sight of a few of its number in full and unexplained flight to the rear. Precipitate motion in the wrong direction is an open invitation to disaster. That was how each of these seven incidents got its start. One or two or more men made a sudden run to the rear which others in the vicinity did not understand. But it was the lack of information rather than the sight of running men which was the crux of

[1] W. McDougall, *Introduction to Social Psychology* (London, 1908), p. 100.
[2] Allport, "The Historical Background of Modern Social Psychology," *op. cit.*, pp. 28-29.
[3] Cf. Kilpatrick: "In the absence of reliable guides from past experience for perceiving or acting, suggestibility is high." F. P. Kilpatrick, "Problems of Perception in Extreme Situations," *Human Organization*, Vol. 16 (Summer, 1957), p. 21.
[4] Technically, "suggestion" refers to the influence of one actor on another in the movement from a generalized component (Level 1) to a lower-level component. Above, pp. 71-73.
[5] Put another way, panic can be brought under control even though all the determinants except mobilization are present. Above, p. 134 and below, pp. 161-163.
[6] The reason why one individual rather than another is the first to flee lies beyond the scope of our investigation. Perhaps it lies in differing individual predispositions to turn fear into actual flight; perhaps it depends on the position of a given person with regard to the perceived threat; or perhaps it depends on a combination of these factors.

The Panic

the danger. For in every case the testimony of all witnesses clearly developed the fact that those who started the run, and thereby spread the fear which started the panic, had a legitimate or at least a reasonable excuse for the action. It was not the sudden motion which of itself did the damage but the fact that the others present were not kept informed.[1]

This pattern of mobilization reveals two distinct phases of the actual rout—a "real" and a "derived" phase.[2] The first phase often consists of flight as a response to the original threatening situation. This threatening situation is made up of appropriate conditions of conduciveness, strain, anxiety, and so on. *But then the initial flight itself creates*—as the remarks of Marshall show—*a new set of necessary conditions for panic.* To see someone running wildly is *prima facie* evidence that he is seeking to escape through limited exits (structural conduciveness), that he is fleeing from an unknown threat (strain), and that he is anxious. Furthermore, this observed flight is a precipitating event for the observer, and gives rise to a belief that something frightening is present, even though this "something" may not be identical to that which caused the original flight.

Thus, even for those persons not immediately affected by the original threat, precipitate flight creates a new set of determinants for panic. In this way panic compounds from a real into a derived phase. The second phase is so-named because people develop a hysterical belief when they observe others in flight. The determination of *their* behavior can be accounted for in terms of the same conditions as the behavior of those who joined the panic because of the original threat. In this way panic, created by one set of conditions, constitutes another set of conditions for further panic.

This compounding of two analytically distinguishable phases into a single empirical phenomenon we call "panic" lies behind many of the common characteristics of the panic response. Panic has been defined as a "fear which feeds upon itself,"[3] and as a "*highly emotional behavior* which is excited by the presence of an immediate severe threat, and which *results in increasing the danger for oneself and for others* rather than in reducing the danger."[4] In addition, this

---

[1] Marshall, *Men Against Fire*, pp. 145-146. Examples illustrating this general position are to be found on pp. 146 ff.

[2] For a characterization of these phases in other forms of collective behavior, below, pp. 212-215, 257-261, 298-301, and 356-358.

[3] H. S. Holland, quoted in Lanham, "Panic," *op. cit.*, p. 283.

[4] Definition of the Disaster Research Group of the National Academy of Sciences, quoted in Robinson, *The Face of Disaster*, p. 166. Thus the logic of the development of the panic is a special case of the logic of vicious circles, or those "morbid [processes] in which a primary disorder provokes a reaction which perpetuates and aggravates the said disorder." J. B. Hurry, *Vicious Circles in Sociology and Their Treatment* (London, 1915), p. 1. For a description of a

The Panic

compounding effect is reflected in many terms—imitation, rapport, and social facilitation—used to describe interaction patterns in panic and other kinds of collective behavior.[1] An example of contagion is found in the following account of a woman's reactions during a run on a bank:

> Having once adopted the idea of getting her money, the stimulations received from others in great numbers on all sides apparently trying to do the same thing and expressing the same common purpose augmented her desire to respond to such an extent that everything was excluded from the field. Attention was focused on the one suggested act. Any reasoning about the matter was inhibited. As she said, she didn't *think* when she saw *all the crowd* trying to get their money out.[2]

On the basis of our account of panic, we may give a more determinate account of contagion and related phenomena than has been possible up to now.[3] *The "contagious" or "imitative" aspects of panic are simply repetitions of the same value-added process which gave rise to the initial panic reaction.* Thus to introduce a new emotional state or special type of interaction to account for panic behavior is unnecessary. Both the initial flight and the panic derived from the flight itself can be explained in terms of the same set of determinants.

The combination of the real and derived phases of panic gives a distinctive "curve" to the panic response. A number of individuals begin to flee on the basis of the conditions we have reviewed. Then this flight is compounded to give an extraordinarily rapid rise in flight behavior. The enormous bulge of flight behavior, then, occurs after the initial stages of panic.

The shape of this curve is difficult to measure for two reasons: (*a*) In most situations panic reactions are not recorded. In battlefield panics, for instance, data on the internal dynamics of flight are

---

business panic as a vicious circle, cf. I. Fisher, *Booms and Depressions: Some First Principles* (New York, 1932), pp. 25–27.

[1] These several terms, some of which describe the emotional and cognitive side of interaction (and hence are close cousins of the concept of suggestion), and some of which describe the action side of the interaction, are reviewed in Brown, "Mass Phenomena," *op. cit.*, pp. 842–843.

[2] Vaught, "The Release and Heightening of Individual Reactions in Crowds," *op. cit.*, p. 405. In the Martian panic, people who listened in public places and saw more frightened people were more violently seized by panic than others. Cantril, *Invasion from Mars*, p. 146.

[3] Brown considers terms like contagion and imitation to be unsatisfactory because they do not answer two kinds of questions: "We should like, first of all, to know why this kind of behavior 'contages,' rather than reasonable, cooperative action. In the second place, it is clear that even irrational and emotional behavior does not always diffuse through a collectivity. Under what conditions will it do so? The answer to this has too often been that contagion of emotion will occur in the mob, with the mob defined as a collectivity manifesting contagion. Something better than this must be found." "Mass Phenomena," *op. cit.*, p. 843.

unavailable. It is plausible, however, to infer from several qualitative descriptions a sort of curve. (*b*) Many so-called "panics" are in fact several sub-panics rolled into one:

> Milling and canalization of milling responses into flight by effective models continue to appear when rout is in process. Milling is accentuated wherever flight is blocked; flight proceeds when a participant hits upon some newly evident means of escape. If many avenues of escape are apparent, the terrorizing pressure of the perceived crisis is lessened; if few or no avenues of escape are evident or if available avenues are blocked, terror-accentuating pressure is augmented.[1]

Financial panics are also subject to fits and starts, and to the development of sub-panics.[2]

In one case of hysteria, the curve of recorded fear reactions followed a modest beginning, then a terrific bulge shortly after the news of the fear reactions began to circulate. After the "Phantom Anesthetist" of Mattoon, Illinois, was first reported in September, 1944, the calls to the police reporting a gassing "started from zero, reached a peak rapidly, and rapidly returned to the baseline."[3] Moreover, general calls reporting prowlers showed a parallel increase, as Figure 7 shows. This distinctive pattern seems to result from the introduction of an initially disturbing event, a series of fear reactions to it, then a series of derived reactions based on the perception of the initial reactions. This pattern resulted in the rapid acceleration of the calls to a high point.[4]

Termination and Aftermath of Panic. How does a panic end, and what follows a panic? These matters are subject to wide variation:

> The tensions of rout are acute and tend to be short-lived. People in panic may attain safety; they may strive until death, strain, fatigue, and despair ends their participation; or, given sufficient suggestions, they may shift to some other form of collective behavior—perhaps that of a mob or an orgiastic crowd.... The usual ending of panic clearly is not a group process; panic ends as selective influences eliminate individuals from rout. But panic behavior is not necessarily complete when flight terminates. There are common sequelae to panic—fatigue and stupor, extreme anxiety, excitability and aggression, perhaps persistent terror, and, not infrequently, secondary panics.[5]

[1] Foreman, "Panic Theory," *op. cit.*, p. 299.
[2] Galbraith, *The Great Crash*, pp. 88 ff.; Melville, *The South Sea Bubble*, pp. 111 ff.
[3] Johnson, "The 'Phantom Anesthetist' of Mattoon," *op. cit.*, p. 642.
[4] We shall observe this kind of curve even more clearly in connection with other kinds of collective behavior.
[5] Foreman, "Panic Theory," *op. cit.*, p. 299; also Strauss, "The Literature on Panic," *op. cit.*, p. 325. Wolfenstein (*Disaster*, pp. 189 ff.) speaks of the rise and fall of post-disaster euphoria.

The Panic

A panic is frequently a source of strain, and is thus a condition for other kinds of collective behavior, such as the hostile outburst and the norm-oriented movement. We shall inquire into these post-panic reactions in later chapters; we shall ask particularly why one, rather than another kind of reaction arises.

FIGURE 7[1]
RECORDS OF TELEPHONE CALLS TO MATTOON, ILLINOIS, POLICE, AUGUST–OCTOBER, 1944

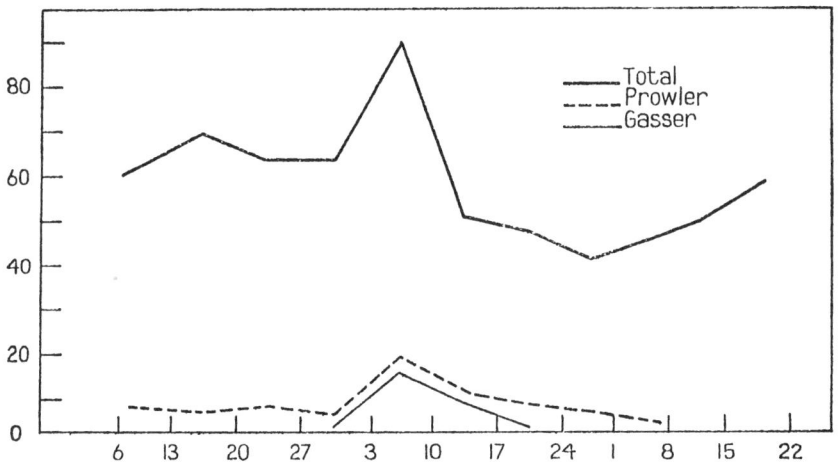

THE PREVENTION AND CONTROL OF PANIC

Thus far we have asked what conditions are necessary if panic is to occur, and what relations obtain among the several necessary conditions. Each condition operates within the limits established by the previous stage of value-added. Each condition narrows the range of possible kinds of behavior, and makes the occurrence of panic more likely than it is in the prior stages. When the value-added process reaches the stage of mobilization, panic has been "determined."

The transition from one stage to the next is not automatic. Anxiety, for instance, predisposes a person to react to precipitating factors and to accept a hysterical belief; but anxiety alone does not guarantee the transition to these stages. To put it formally, each stage of the value-added process is necessary if the next stage is to become significant as a condition, but the first is not sufficient for the next.

[1] Johnson, "The 'Phantom Anesthetist' of Mattoon," *op. cit.*, p. 643.

The Panic

Whether the value-added process is completed depends in large part on counter-influences that we discuss under the heading of control. These influences may prevent one necessary condition from giving rise to the next; in this way they may prevent the occurrence of panic.

The variety of possible controls over panic is enormous, as Nazi ideas on the handling of panic illustrate:

> How is panic avoided, alleviated, controlled and exploited?
>
> Discipline, education, indoctrination, habituation to danger, and outstanding leader-personalities among field officers are held to be the best antidotes to panic. Education and training are of particular importance. To aid the field officer in handling panic situations, in detecting disturbing factors and eliminating the possible causes of panic, official Army regulations contain exhaustive and minute instructions. Officers, moreover, receive special training on how to act in panic. . . .
>
> Education and indoctrination strive to mold "men with never-failing nerves" . . . automatically decreasing their susceptibility to fear and doubt. Habituation to danger includes extended night drills . . . and prolonged maneuvers in thickly wooded country and in terrain where vision is naturally obstructed. If panic breaks out despite all precautionary measures, the officers' duty is to "suppress it at once, by force of arms if necessary. . . ."[1]

We shall organize our analysis of control in two ways: (*a*) We shall classify controls in terms of the components of action—facilities (especially information), organization (especially leadership), norms, and values. We shall ask how each can act as a control over panic. (*b*) We shall ask at what stages in the value-added process each kind of control operates. Any one concrete act—such as a fire department's denial of a scare rumor in a community threatened by disaster—may affect more than one component of action. In the example given, the denial controls the growth of anxiety by providing information (facilities) and authority (organization). Furthermore, a single act may be significant at several stages of the value-added process. The denial of the scare rumor, again, may be primarily operative in preventing anxiety from turning into a fear of immediate threats. At the same time, the denial may reduce anxiety itself by defining the entire situation as non-threatening (thus assuming significance at a prior stage in the value-added process).

Facilities and Control of Panic. Facilities can be used to reduce the possibility of dangerous situations by destroying an enemy, by constructing fire-proof buildings, by improving fire-fighting equipment.[2]

---

[1] Farago, *German Psychological Warfare*, pp. 123–124; also Strauss, "The Literature on Panic," *op. cit.*, pp. 319–320.

[2] Rickman ("Panic and Air-raid Precautions," *op. cit.*, p. 1293) lists the removal of the cause of danger as an obvious preventative for panic.

The Panic

Information can also be used to diminish superstitions, reduce fears based on ignorance, and so on. More precisely, information may be effective in controlling panic at the following stages of the value-added process:

(1) Structural conduciveness. To circulate information either that danger cannot arise or that escape is easy reduces the tendency to panic. Walter Bagehot's advice to banks faced with a panic shows the importance of such information:

> In opposition to what might at first sight be supposed, the best way for the bank or banks who have the custody of the bank reserve to deal with a drain arising from internal discredit, is to lend freely. The first instinct of every one is the contrary. There being a large demand on a fund which you want to preserve, the most obvious way to preserve it is to hoard it—to get in as much as you can, and to let nothing go out which you can help. But every banker knows that this is not the way to diminish discredit. This discredit means "an opinion that you have not got any money," and to dissipate that opinion, you must, if possible, show that you have money: you must employ it for the public benefit in order that the public may know that you have it. The time for economy and accumulation is before. A good banker will have accumulated in ordinary times the reserve he is to make use of in extraordinary times....
>
> A panic, in a word, is a species of neuralgia, and according to the rules of science you must not starve it.[1]

The same kind of control is exercised by the military commander who convinces his troops that they are not being cut off, and by the stage manager who assures an audience that there is time to evacuate a burning theater by filing out.

(2) Strain. To define a situation as unambiguous and non-threatening reduces the tendency to panic. One reason fear rumors continued during the flying saucer scare, for instance, is that the government delayed issuing reports on the unidentified flying objects:

> The mysterious character of the phenomena appeared to demand secrecy. But the restrictions and red tape of military classification, however necessary, have long delayed the solution of the problem. Scientists who might easily have provided the key that would unlock the secrets of the saucers did not receive detailed information—information necessary for a serious study of the whole problem. Second, the restrictions placed on the saucer projects served only to deepen the fear of an already frightened public. Rumors flew like the saucers.[2]

---

[1] *Lombard Street*, pp. 48–51; also pp. 38, 44.
[2] Menzel, *Flying Saucers*, p. 2. For further evidence on the importance of authoritative information in the control of fear and rumors, cf. Danzig, *et al.*, *The Effects of a Threatening Rumor on a Disaster-Stricken Community*, pp. 20–21,

The Panic

In the "Invasion from Mars" panic of 1938, those who tuned in late to Welles' broadcast (i.e., did not possess information that the broadcast was only a radio play) were more likely to experience fright than those who had listened from the beginning.[1] On the battlefield fear of the enemy is closely associated with the degree of unfamiliarity with battle conditions and specific weapons.[2] Military writers emphasize the importance of information to reduce surprise and to acquaint soldiers with the actual possibilities of danger.[3] Writers on disaster insist on the importance of providing "(1) an educational program designed to acquaint the public with the nature of potential disaster and the requisite actions for survival, and (2) prompt reduction of ambiguity concerning the range of destruction while the disaster is in progress."[4]

(3) Precipitating factors. To define a precipitating factor as harmless reduces the tendency to panic by preventing the conversion of anxiety into hysteria. For instance, to interpret a sonic boom in terms of jet airplanes and the speed of sound removes the fears that are excited if the explosion is interpreted in terms of atomic warfare. On the battlefield, one of the rules for controlling events that might precipitate panics is given by Marshall: "When a retrograde movement becomes necessary in combat, it is an invitation to disaster to move before men are told why they are moving."[5] A final example: Once the federal government undertook to investigate the flying saucer scare, its final report (the report of Project Grudge) had the effect of discounting virtually all the "anxious" interpretations of the objects—interpretations that assigned the objects to the workings of secret weapons, enemy reconnaissance, interplanetary messages, and so on. The report attributed most of the sightings to "war nerves,"

78–79; Williams, "Some Functions of Communication in Crisis Behavior," *op. cit.*, p. 19; Rickman, "Panic and Air-raid Precautions," *op. cit.*, p. 1294; Ruppelt, *The Report on Unidentified Flying Objects*, pp. 94–97; Medalia and Larsen, "Diffusion and Belief in a Collective Delusion," *op. cit.*, pp. 182 ff.

[1] Cantril, *The Invasion from Mars*, pp. 78 ff. In a newspaper strike in Butte, Montana, the absence of news contributed to the spread of rumors of terrible murders, the destruction of the White House, and the assassination of President Hoover. H. Brucker, "Press Communication in Relation to Morale and Panic," *op. cit.*, p. 67.

[2] Stouffer *et al.*, *Combat and Its Aftermath*, pp. 220–241. For similar findings with regard to atomic maneuvers, cf. S. Schwartz and B. Winograd, "Preparation of Soldiers for Atomic Maneuvers," *Journal of Social Issues*, Vol. 10 (1954), pp. 42–52.

[3] Marshall, *Men Against Fire*, pp. 88–91; National Research Council, "Fear: Ally or Traitor," in Greene (ed.), *The Infantry Journal Reader*, pp. 268–269.

[4] Danzig, *et al.*, *The Effects of a Threatening Rumor on a Disaster-Stricken Community*, p. 80.

[5] *Men Against Fire*, p. 140; also pp. 145–147.

The Panic

misidentification of conventional objects, or the antics of frauds and psychopaths.[1]

Organization and Control of Panic. Here "organization" refers to a structure of roles that enables a group to resist the conditions that build up toward panic.

Military observers stress that one of the general ways to lessen the probability of panic is to minimize the heterogeneity among troops:

... troops that are composed of individuals who are all of the same race, same class of society, same language, same political and religious faith, and who are uniformly educated and instructed till they have confidence in their officers, their comrades and themselves, will be little subject to panic; but even these will sometimes have panics among them.[2]

More specifically, the role structure of a group should be clearly defined. In a combat unit, for instance, panic is less likely if "each individual has been given, or has taken over, certain functions."[3] Troops "must fight in the organization they are used to in time of peace, each man in his habitual place and with his proper unit."[4] Similarly, in disaster situations, the more adequately defined are the purposes of formal organizations involved (the army, the Red Cross, the police department, and the fire department), the less likely is social disorganization to appear.[5] Finally, in the financial sphere, the presence of poorly defined and badly coordinated banking facilities increases the likelihood of the overextension of credit, which is among the major determinants of a financial panic.[6]

Leadership is extremely important in the control of panic. Most writers on panic list divided authority, distrust of leaders, and so on,

---

[1] Ruppelt, *The Report on Unidentified Flying Objects*, p. 97. For similar attempts to "explain" phenomena which were not understood and became the subject of a hysterical outburst, cf. Medalia and Larsen, "Diffusion and Belief in a Collective Delusion," *op. cit.*, pp. 183–184; Park and Burgess, *Introduction to the Science of Sociology*, pp. 878–879.

[2] Etlinge, *Psychology of War*, p. 49; Lanham cited heterogeneity of composition as one of the causal factors in the panic of Italian troops in Abyssinia in 1896. "Panic," *op. cit.*, pp. 278–279.

[3] Torrance, "The Behavior of Small Groups under the Stress Conditions of 'Survival,'" *op. cit.*, p. 752.

[4] Etlinge, *Psychology of War*, p. 72.

[5] Form and Nosow, *Community in Disaster*, pp. 123–124, 137–138, 168; Prince, *Catastrophe and Social Change*, pp. 59–60; for a comparative study of the role of formal organizations in a Texas and Mexican community during a flood disaster, cf. R. A. Clifford, *The Rio Grande Flood: A Comparative Study of Border Communities in Disaster* (Washington, D.C., 1956), especially pp. 131–134.

[6] The "wildcat banking" period of the early nineteenth century in the United States is the most conspicuous illustration of the connection between poorly-organized banks and financial panic. Perkins, *Wall Street Panics 1813–1930*, pp. 25 ff. For a discussion of the importance of the banking structure in the British crisis of 1878, cf. Mottram, *A History of Financial Speculation*, pp. 200–201.

The Panic

high among the conditions that facilitate panic.[1] Some have emphasized the importance of leaders in debunking superstitions and fears.[2] Others of a more psychoanalytic bent have framed the problem of leadership in terms of the presence of a father figure.[3]

Leadership is especially critical in those last few moments before panic breaks. Events have proceeded too far for mere information or existing norms to be workable; what is needed is definitive regimentation on the spot by leaders. As Marshall observes,

> Unity of action is restored by the prompt decision of a few volunteers who stand squarely in the path of the flight, command the man to turn back, and do not hesitate to manhandle such of the men as come within reach or to threaten the others with weapons.[4]

Leaders can also reduce the panic reaction by removing "panicking" individuals from the sight of other men.[5] Finally, examples of fearlessness by leaders in crisis conditions may set the same pattern for followers.[6]

The importance of authority appears in financial crises. On the eve of the crash of the depression of 1929, for instance, the actions of various authorities postponed, at least for a brief time, the downward plunge of prices. Hoover's inauguration, by itself, strengthened the market for a few weeks. After this time, however, news trickled back to Wall Street that the Federal Reserve Board was meeting daily in

---

[1] Strauss, "The Literature on Panic," *op. cit.*, p. 319; Meerloo, "Peoples' Reaction to Danger," *op. cit.*, pp. 174–175; Rickman, "Panic and Air-raid Precautions," *op. cit.*, p. 1293. For specific historical examples of the importance of leadership in the early stages of panic, cf. Lanham, "Panic," *op. cit.*, pp. 282–283, 285–287. Also, W. N. Maxwell, *A Psychological Retrospect of the Great War* (London, 1923), pp. 174–175.

[2] Cf. the role of Thomas Edison in debunking the objects-in-air hysteria of 1896–1897 as described in Ruppelt, *The Report on Unidentified Flying Objects*, pp. 280–282, and Menzel, *Flying Saucers*, pp. 63 ff.

[3] Rickman, "Panic and Air-raid Precautions," *op. cit.*, p. 1294; H. X. Spiegel, "Psychiatric Observations in the Tunisian Campaign," *American Journal of Orthopsychiatry*, Vol. 14 (1944), p. 382; W. Schmideberg, "The Treatment of Panic in Casualty Area and Clearing Station," *Life and Letters Today*, Vol. 23 (1939), p. 163. Meerloo, *Patterns of Panic*, pp. 65–67.

[4] *Men Against Fire*, p. 147. For Marshall's general thoughts on leadership, cf. pp. 100–107. See also Meerloo, *Patterns of Panic*, pp. 110–112.

[5] National Research Council, "Fear: Ally or Traitor," *op. cit.*, p. 269.

[6] L. A. Pennington, R. B. Hough, Jr., and H. W. Case, *The Psychology of Military Leadership* (New York, 1943), pp. 235–238. General findings based on interviews about critical situations in World War II yield valuable information on the importance of the status of the aircraft commander. "Considerable evidence has been found to substantiate the findings of Polansky, Lippitt, and Redl that individuals with high group prestige more frequently initiate behavioral contagion." Torrance, "The Behavior of Small Groups under the Stress Conditions of 'Survival,'" *op. cit.*, p. 753. For specific instances of this effect of leadership, cf. Foy and Harlow, *Clowning Through Life*, p. 279, and Kartmann and Brown (eds.), *Disaster!*, p. 278.

The Panic

Washington. This created nervousness among the investors once again, even though (or perhaps because) the Board was silent and took no action one way or the other. After two weeks of this uncertainty, selling began to get out of control. After two bad days (March 25 and 26, 1929), Charles Mitchell, director of the New York Federal Reserve Bank, gave a number of assurances, among them the promise to lend money to prevent complete liquidation.

Mitchell's words were like magic. By the end of trading on the 26th money rates had eased, and the market had rallied. The Federal Reserve remained silent, but now its silence was reassuring. It meant that it conceded Mitchell's mastery. The next day the National City regularized its commitment to the boom; it announced that it would insure reasonable interest rates by putting $25 million into the call market....[1]

During the worst of the panic in September and October, 1929, the roles of leadership were equally instructive. Through September and into October the trend of the market was down, though there were both good and bad days. There continued to be much talk of "organized support," i.e., numbers of powerful people banding together to keep stock prices at a reasonable level. Monday, October 21, was a very bad day in the market. Thursday, October 24, was Black Thursday, with 12,894,650 shares trading hands. By 11 o'clock in the morning of that day a real panic had developed.

What did the leaders of Wall Street do to stem the tide? By noon on Black Thursday, a number of big bankers met and decided to pool their resources to support the market. With this news, the prices firmed, and started to rise; in fact, when Black Thursday was over, the average industrials had fallen only 12 points. Prices were steady, and there were even evidences of optimism on the following Friday and Saturday.

On Monday, October 28, panic selling commenced again. By that day *Times* industrials were down 49 points. The bankers met again that afternoon, but on this occasion decided that "it was no part of the bankers' purpose . . . to maintain any particular level of prices or to protect anyone's profit." Now prices were to be allowed freely to go their way. The following day, prices plummeted again, with the *Times* industrials falling 43 points. There were two further meetings of the bankers on this day, the 29th, but indications are that their purposes were now different. There had been earlier rumors that the bankers were, far from mobilizing support, selling stocks. At any rate, the bankers' failure to take immediate, firm and decisive action killed all talk of organized support, and the panic was by now clearly out of hand.[2]

[1] Galbraith, *The Great Crash*, pp. 40–43.
[2] *Ibid.*, pp. 99–119.

The Panic

Such was the fate of the bankers. For the next decade they were fair game for congressional committees, courts, the press, and the comedians. The great pretensions and the great failures of these days were a cause. A banker need not be popular; indeed, a good banker in a healthy capitalist society should probably be much disliked. People do not wish to trust their money to a hail-fellow-well-met but to a misanthrope who can say no. However, a banker must not seem futile, ineffective, or vaguely foolish. In contrast with the stern power of Morgan in 1907, that was precisely how his successors seemed, or were made to seem, in 1929.[1]

Examples of the roles of leaders—both successful and unsuccessful in stemming prices—could be multiplied from the history of financial crises.[2]

Norms and Control of Panic. Norms overlap with organization, because the presence of organized roles implies certain norms by which these roles are regulated. We may distinguish, however, between an individual acting in a specific role to control panic (e.g., a schoolteacher directing children toward fire exits) and norms that persist without organized roles to implement them (e.g., a well-rehearsed fire drill). LaPiere notes the importance of this distinction.

[The origins of panic lie in part in] the lack of regimental leadership for ... crisis—the result *either* of lack of regimentation for the particular kind of crisis, *or,* when such regimentation does exist, lack of a person who can exercise regimental leadership.[3]

Norms deal with general regimentation for crisis; leadership (or organization in general) deals with the creation or implementation of such norms.

Norms are significant in two ways for the prevention or control of panic:

(1) Certain norms provide specific directives for behavior in the face of definite threats. Examples of such directives are fire drills, police training, training for battle, training for fire-fighting, and so on. All these have been shown to reduce the potentiality for anxiety, fear, and social disorganization under threatening conditions.[4]

---

[1] *Ibid.,* p. 120.
[2] On the control of the British crisis of 1890, in which the Bank of England and many financial houses formed a syndicate to guarantee the liabilities of the Baring firm, cf. Mottram, *A History of Financial Speculation,* pp. 204-205; for the role of the bank in the crises of 1825 and 1866, cf. Bagehot, *Lombard Street,* pp. 35-36, 190; for discussion of the limited effectiveness of authorities in the Tulip Mania of the 1630's in Holland, the Mississippi Bubble and the South Sea Bubble, cf. N.W. Posthumus, "The Tulip Mania in Holland in the Years 1636 and 1637," *Journal of Economic and Business History,* Vol. 1 (1928-1929), pp. 444-448; and Mackay, *Extraordinary Popular Delusions and the Madness of Crowds,* pp. 32-33, 65-70.
[3] *Collective Behavior,* p. 438. Italics added.
[4] Foy and Harlow, *Clowning through Life,* p. 277; Form and Nosow, *Community*

The Panic

(2) Certain norms, although they do not provide directives as to how to contend with threats, direct behavior toward some other kind of activity—e.g., saving loved ones—and thus minimize panicky flight from the dangerous situation.

Military writers emphasize that the tendency to panic is reduced by encouraging troops to concentrate on norms and activities that distract from threatening stimuli. Hocking, for instance, suggests the following "natural aids" to officers in managing combat fear:

1. Turning the mind deliberately to something in the region of habit,—i.e., to something in which your control is certain and easy. . . .
2. Turning the mind to the troubles of the other men. . . .
3. Turning the mind to what you are going to do to the enemy, rather than what he is going to do to you. . . .
4. Recollection of first principles.[1]

Frequently in disaster situations persons turn to loved ones and others rather than flee from the threat itself. This attention to competing norms reduces the tendency to panic. According to Form and Nosow

. . . The type of behavior that may be predicted for given types of persons [in a disaster situation] depends on the following variables: (1) *where* the individual is when the destructive force has hit *with respect to family* and *with respect to home and neighborhood*; (2) the *knowledge* the individual has about the fate or extent of safety or injury to persons *significant* to him, especially immediate family members; (3) the extent of *injury* to *himself* and to *significant others*; (4) the degree of *identification* of the individual with his community, friends, and neighbors; (5) his *training* (occupational, professional, technical) relevant to emergency situation; (6) his *membership* in emergency-oriented organizations, and (7) others peculiar to the type of destructive agents involved.[2]

---

in Disaster, pp. 137–138, 168; Stouffer *et al.*, *Combat and Its Aftermath*, pp. 228–231; Schwartz and Winograd, "Preparation of Soldiers for Atomic Maneuvers," *op. cit.*; Wallace, "Mazeway Disintegration: The Individual's Perception of Socio-Cultural Disorganization," *op. cit.*, p. 26.

[1] W. E. Hocking, *Morale and Its Enemies* (New Haven, 1918), pp. 161–162. Also National Research Council, "Fear: Ally or Traitor," *op. cit.*, pp. 268–269.

[2] Form and Nosow, *Community in Disaster*, pp. 26–27. Also pp. 23, 28–29, 62, 67, 70, 81–82, 90. For other research on this subject, cf. L. M. Killian, "The Significance of Multiple-Group Membership in Disaster," *American Journal of Sociology*, Vol. 57 (1951–52), pp. 309–314; M. Young, "The Role of the Extended Family in a Disaster," *Human Relations*, Vol. VII, No. 3 (1954), pp. 383–391; Wolfenstein, *Disaster*, pp. 91 ff.; Clifford, *The Rio Grande Flood*, pp. 127–131; Ellemers, *General Conclusions. Studies in Holland Flood Disaster*, Vol. IV, p. 18; Prince, *Catastrophe and Social Change*, pp. 36 ff.; Moore, *Tornadoes over Texas*, p. 255; W. H. Form, C. P. Loomis, *et al.*, "The Persistence and Emergence of Social and Cultural Systems in Disasters," *American Sociological Review*, Vol. 21 (1956), pp. 180–185; M. Sherif, *An Outline of Social Psychology* (New York, 1948), pp. 107 ff.; Fritz and Williams, "The Human Being in Disasters," *op. cit.*,

The Panic

In the panic to leave metropolitan New York during the "Invasion from Mars" broadcast, most who fled *either* were unattached to families *or* fled after family members had been united for joint flight.[1]

These norms which take precedence over flight itself provide further explanation of why so little panic occurs in community disasters wrought by bombings, earthquakes, fires, floods, and storms.[2] Family and community life involves a multiplicity of loyalties and desires for the individual. If he follows these, he will be less likely to panic. In fact, most "disorganized" behavior in disasters—i.e., most panic-like behavior—occurs under conditions of role conflict or inaccessability to loved ones:

> Dysfunctional behavior may be expected from persons physically removed from the disaster scene, but who are at the same time uncertain about the welfare and safety of their families. Such behavior may also arise when a person arrives at an impact area and is either unable to locate his family or finds that his family has been injured and that others have removed them from the area.

. . . .

The data on panic and shock showed that most people in conflict did not undergo panic or shock, but most people in panic or shock did evidence some conflict in their behavior. In both cases, the existence of some functioning social organization in which the person could assume a significant role was the crucial variable in minimizing dysfunctional behavior.[3]

In some disasters panic behavior turns out to be a scramble to save loved ones.[4] These are instances of panic, to be sure, but panic of a

---

pp. 48–49; D. N. Michael, "Civilian Behavior under Atomic Bombardment," *Bulletin of the Atomic Scientists*, Vol. XI (1955), p. 174; J. E. Ellemers and H. M. in 't Veld-Langeveld, "A Study of the Destruction of a Community," in *Community Studies. Studies in Holland Flood Disaster 1953*, Vol. III (Amsterdam and Washington D.C., 1955), pp. 101–109. For evidence of the strength of such bonds in connection with wartime evacuation, cf. E. H. Bernert and F. C. Iklé, "Evacuation and the Cohesion of Urban Groups," *American Journal of Sociology*, Vol. 58 (1952), pp. 133–138. In an experimental test of a hypothetical disaster, Pepitone, Diggory and Wallace found that in both low-threat and high-threat situations many of the respondents indicated that they either would help friends, neighbors, and strangers, or would go after money and belongings. Such responses, while stimulated by the danger, obviously operate as preventatives of responses to the threat itself. Pepitone, Diggory and Wallace, "Some Reactions to a Hypothetical Disaster," *op. cit.*, pp. 706–708. See also R. H. Blum and B. Klass, *A Study of Public Response to Disaster Warnings* (Menlo Park, Calif., 1956), pp. 37, 41.

[1] Cantril, *The Invasion from Mars*, pp. 144–146.
[2] See above, pp. 135 and 139–140.
[3] Form and Nosow, *Community in Disaster*, pp. 85, 109–110; also p. 90. Also Killian, "The Significance of Multiple-Group Membership in Disaster," *op. cit.*, pp. 311–313; Killian, "Some Accomplishments and Some Needs in Disaster Study," *op. cit.*, p. 69; Fritz and Marks, "The NORC Studies in Human Behavior in Disaster," *op. cit.*, pp. 38–40; C. E. Fritz, "Disasters Compared in Six American Communities," *Human Organization*, Vol. 16 (1957), p. 7.
[4] Cf. the description of the fire on the General Slocum in East River, N.Y.,

The Panic

special kind. They stem from a derived threat of loss of loved ones, not the immediate danger of loss of life from fire or flood. Panic occurs because people fear that their access to loved ones is limited and closing.

In settings where norms to protect or rescue others do not operate with equal strength, the tendency to panic is greater. For example: (*a*) Norms of mutual aid are weak in a money market or stock exchange. Considering that in these settings self-interest is institutionalized, we expect mutual aid in conditions of panic to be an inappropriate response. (*b*) On the battlefield immediate family members and other loved ones are absent. To the extent that the unit is a face-to-face, loyal unit, however, competing norms to panic are present, and we would expect more heroic rescue behavior and less panic in dangerous situations.

Values and Control of Panic. Walter Bagehot, in commenting on Englishmen's attitudes toward the Bank of England, remarked:

> The English world at least believes that it [the Bank] will not, almost that it *cannot* fail. Three times since 1844 the Banking Department has received assistance, and would have failed without it. In 1825 the entire concern almost suspended payment; in 1797 it actually did so. But still there is a faith in the Bank, contrary to experience, and despising evidence ... no one in London ever dreams of questioning the credit of the Bank, and the Bank never dreams that its own credit is in danger. Somehow everybody feels the Bank is sure to come right.[1]

Such faith offers a general sense of invulnerability, and thus cushions believers against becoming alarmed at possibly threatening events and situations.

Thus values are as significant as controls at the very general stages of the process of value-added. Once a situation has been perceived as genuinely threatening, however, faith ceases to serve the same general protective function. Having accepted a hysterical belief, the individual feels that he is not only vulnerable but doomed unless some quick escape can be made.[2] At this stage the general protective function of values is irrelevant.

The general protective function of values operates under battle conditions. Prayer on the battlefield apparently was often a source of support to many American soldiers during World War II.[3] Others

---

in 1904: "The passengers looked at one another in horror, then broke in a wild stampede to find their children. In the first moments of that awful scramble, dozens were trampled to insensibility." Kartman and Brown (eds.), *Disaster!*, p. 115.

[1] *Lombard Street*, pp. 40–41.
[2] Cf. Cantril, *The Invasion from Mars*, pp. 199–200.
[3] Stouffer *et al.*, *Combat and Its Aftermath*, pp. 172–189.

The Panic

have pointed to the protective features of another kind of faith—faith in the fighting unit to which one belongs.[1]

As with any team, the center of activity shifts from one crew-mate to another in accordance with the combat situation. At one time it may be the waist gunner, at another, the tail gunner, upon whose skill and courage depend the lives of all the others. The combined efforts of all the crew may be wasted if the bombardier is incompetent or anxious and fails to line-up correctly on the target. All members of the crew are dependent upon each other to an unusual degree. Day after day, on mission after mission, this mutual dependence is made to pay dividends in safety and effectiveness of the combat crew. It is no wonder then that the emotional relationships among these fliers assume a special character. The men and their plane become identified with each other with an intensity that in civil life is found only within the family circle. Crew members habitually refer to each other as "my pilot," "my bombardier," "my gunner," and so on, and their feeling for their plane is equally strong, since its strength and reliability are as important as those of any human members of the crew.[2]

Perhaps this faith in the fighting unit accounts for some of the differences in combat ability during World War II. Individual stragglers placed in new units tended under battle conditions to quit their positions and move toward the rear; gun crews, squad groups or platoons that had been separated from their parent units fought as effectively as before.[3] Two factors account for this: the clarity of organization that the unit had accumulated through training and combat,[4] and the faith in the fighting unit as a whole.

SUMMARY AND CONCLUSIONS

In this chapter we have organized the conditions of panic into a scheme of value-added. We have listed the most indeterminate conditions first, and have proceeded to the conditions which operate with progressively greater determinacy. The first condition is structural conduciveness, which refers to the degree to which danger, communication of danger, and restricted egress can arise at all. Within the limits established by conduciveness, the next necessary condition is strain, or the presence of some danger of unknown and uncontrollable proportions. The next condition is the growth of

[1] Some writers consider this faith in the effective primary unit to override the faith in larger cultural symbols. Marshall, *Men Against Fire*, pp. 152-153; E. A. Shils and M. Janowitz, "Cohesion and Disintegration in the Wehrmacht," in D. Lerner (ed.), *Propaganda in War and Crisis* (New York, 1951), pp. 371-382.
[2] Grinker and Spiegel, *Men Under Stress*, pp. 23-24; also Spiegel, "Psychiatric Observations in the Tunisian Campaign," *op. cit.*, p. 382.
[3] Marshall, *Men Against Fire*, pp. 151 ff.
[4] Above, p. 161.

The Panic

anxiety, which is converted into hysteria by the appearance of a significant event (precipitating factor). This fixes the threat on some specific destructive agent, from which it is possible to flee in certain directions. Finally, on the basis of this hysterical belief, action is mobilized, usually under a primitive form of leadership—the "flight model"—and collective flight occurs.

It is important to emphasize that this order of conditions—from indeterminate to determinate—is a logical, not a temporal order. A single event—e.g., approaching troops—may be significant in establishing the conditions of conduciveness (e.g., the belief that the avenues for escape are closing), in creating strain (e.g., the unknown strength of the approaching troops), and in precipitating the formation of a hysterical belief on the basis of which flight occurs. In this instance the analytically distinguishable necessary conditions are telescoped temporally into a single event. But unless this event is interpreted in a context of conduciveness and strain, panic cannot arise. If the approaching troops were interpreted as dangerous but as *already* having cut off access to escape completely, other reactions —resignation, apathy, desire to fight, etc.—might arise, but not panic. If the approaching troops were interpreted as neither dangerous nor cutting off escape routes, the event might precipitate curiosity or relief, but not panic.

In addition to the analytic order of determinants which eventuates in panic, we have asked also how panic may be prevented, deflected, or controlled. In doing so, we created a model of panic as a series of equilibrium states. At any given stage of the value-added process it is possible to assess the operation of those forces making for panic and those making for control. Given the balance of these forces, it is further possible to estimate the probabilities of whether the process will continue toward the panic reaction, halt in its path, take another path, or return to the state which existed before the necessary conditions began to combine. For any given panic, then, it should be possible to recapitulate the events and states leading to collective flight in terms of the general categories of conduciveness, strain, beliefs, precipitating factors, mobilization, and controls.

CHAPTER VII

THE CRAZE

INTRODUCTION

When people rush with sound and fury *toward* something they believe to be gratifying—*viz.*, in manias, booms, bandwagons, "fashion races" and fads—we characterize their behavior as crazelike. Such behavior, at first glance, appears to contrast with the panic, which involves a headlong rush *away* from something. We should not, however, push the contrast between the craze and the panic too far. *Formally* it is possible to analyze crazes in the same framework used for panic—conduciveness, strain, generalized beliefs, precipitating factors, and so on. *Substantively* as well, many conditions that result in the craze are similar, if not identical to the conditions that result in the panic. Further, the panic often accompanies the craze. At the end of the chapter we shall elucidate the similarities and differences between the craze and the panic.

Definition of Craze. As in the case of panic, the terms used by various writers to define the craze suffer from a lack of consistent meaning. LaPiere, for instance, characterizes crazelike behavior as "fanatical behavior," of which he identifies three types: the boom, or "any fanatical behavior which is based upon the idea that there has been discovered a new and infallible way to material wealth"; the mass movement, or "a 'spontaneous' uprooting of a considerable proportion of the social population in a movement to a new promised land"; and the messianic movement, or "a collective flight from reality by following a new form of leadership which will bring health, wealth, or happiness."[1] For LaPiere the identifying characteristic of the craze is the type of *goal*, though quality of leadership also is important in setting the messianic movement off from the other two forms. Various writers have attempted to distinguish among fad, fashion, boom, and craze in terms of their differing degrees of *superficiality, duration, intensity,* and *social acceptability.*[2] Turner and Killian differentiate between the fad and the craze, which

[1] *Collective Behavior*, pp. 502–510; also pp. 488–497.
[2] LaPiere and Farnsworth, *Social Psychology*, pp. 443–44; J. Davis and H. E. Barnes, *An Introduction to Sociology* (Boston, 1927), pp. 478–479; E. Sapir, "Fashion," *Encyclopaedia of the Social Sciences*, Vol. 6, p. 139.

170

The Craze

occur in "diffuse crowds," and other forms of collective behavior which occur in "compact crowds."[1] E. A. Ross, a pioneer theorist on collective behavior, has included under the heading of "craze" early Christianity, the crusades, prophecies of world destruction, the prohibition movement, and financial stampedes.[2] Bogardus discusses panic under the headings of "manias" and "crazes."[3] To add to this confusion, the literature yields no consistent difference between the terms "boom" and "bubble," though the latter suggests the giddier aspects of speculative movements.[4]

We define the "craze" as *mobilization for action based on a positive wish-fulfillment belief*.[5] So defined, the term encompasses many institutional spheres of society (e.g., economic, political, religious). It refers to behavior ranging from the most superficial (e.g., teenage fads in jewelry) to the most serious (e.g., the nomination of a presidential candidate). It refers to behavior which occurs in groups in close physical proximity (e.g., in the stock exchange or on the floor of a political convention) and widely dispersed groups (e.g., a nationwide speculative boom in stocks). The definition excludes collective behavior which is oriented toward norms and values (e.g., the prohibition movement and early Christianity, respectively).

The Occurrence of Crazes. In theory crazelike behavior can occur anywhere in society. It is possible to speak of fads, for instance, in literary taste.[6] Most of our analysis, however, focuses on four spheres of society:

(1) The economic sphere, in which we study the speculative boom in securities, land, and miscellaneous items, such as tulips, mulberry trees, etc. Among all types of crazes, the speculative boom has been most thoroughly studied.

(2) The political sphere, in which we study the bandwagon effect in the selection of a candidate for succession to high executive office. The political bandwagon at an American convention has been described as follows:

Approximately eleven hundred delegates from forty-eight states and six territories constitute each of these gatherings. Intense in spirit, ruthless in

[1] *Collective Behavior*, pp. 207–208.
[2] E. A. Ross, *Social Psychology* (New York, 1916), pp. 65–76.
[3] E. A. Bogardus, *Fundamentals of Social Psychology* (New York, 1942), p. 399.
[4] W. L. Thorp, "Speculative Bubbles," *Encyclopaedia of the Social Sciences*, Vol. 3, pp. 24–27.
[5] For a characterization of the wish-fulfillment belief, above, pp. 94–100. Thus the belief under which mobilization takes place distinguishes the craze from the panic. Panic flows from a generalized projection of the negative possibilities of an ambiguous situation, craze from a generalized projection of its positive possibilities.
[6] Cf. E. E. Kellett, *Fashion in Literature: A Study in Changing Taste* (London, 1939), pp. 64, 67.

The Craze

action, tumultuous, and often gripped in contentions lasting through several days and nights—exhausted—the delegates frequently put aside their own favorite candidates, and a new name—a "dark horse"—comes to the front to bear the banner of the party in the November struggle at the polls. That rush for the band wagon is popularly called a "stampede." It is here that the state or city boss proves his mettle. If he gets a front seat on the band wagon by picking the right moment to deliver his delegates to the winner he has the prospect of four years of national patronage.[1]

Though many aspects of a political convention are arranged in advance, examples of unanticipated bandwagon surges for a candidate have been documented. Thus we can analyze this kind of behavior and show its analytic kinship to the boom and other forms of the craze.

(3) The expressive sphere, in which we shall discuss fashion and fad. Fashion and fad extend to all aspects of life—"clothes, architecture, vehicles, conversation, . . . the arts and . . . popular philosophy."[2] Common to all these aspects, however, is the use of fads and items of fashion as expressive symbols of differential prestige in ranking systems.[3] In this study we concentrate on the fashion cycle, or yearly and seasonal changes especially in clothing styles,[4] and the diffusion of fads, especially among adolescents.

There is some argument for omitting the fashion cycle in clothing from study because it is so highly institutionalized. Patterns of leadership are fairly definite, and the timing of fashions is governed mainly by "season"[5] Despite these regularized features, the fashion

---

[1] H. L. Stoddard, *Presidential Sweepstakes: The Story of Political Conventions and Campaigns* (New York, 1948), pp. 20–21. Cf. also M. Conway, *The Crowd in Peace and War* (New York, 1915), p. 13, and for an attack on the "crowd" basis of politics, cf. J. L. Tayler, *Social Life and the Crowd* (Boston, 1907), p. 125. Gault also described the political campaign (as well as the convention) in terms of mob behavior. *Social Psychology*, p. 170.

[2] K. Young, *Social Psychology* (New York, 1945), p. 441. Also E. B. Hurlock, *The Psychology of Dress* (New York, 1929), p. 213.

[3] For the discussion of prestige symbolization as the basis of fashion, cf. G. Simmel, "Fashion," *International Quarterly*, Vol. 10 (1904–1905), p. 134; Sapir, "Fashion," *op. cit.*, p. 142; Bell, *On Human Finery*, p. 126–217; H. Spencer, *The Principles of Sociology* (New York, 1897), Vol. II-1, pp. 210–211. For the role of sex-role symbolization, cf. Sapir, p. 142, and Bell, pp. 88–89.

[4] In considering fashion we shall not discuss the general social and psychological significance of fashion, as analyzed, for instance, in J. C. Flugel, *The Psychology of Clothes* (London, 1930), and E. Bergler, *Fashion and the Unconscious* (New York, 1953). Nor shall we consider the very long-term (e.g., half-century) fluctuations of style as analyzed, for instance, by J. Richardson and A. L. Kroeber, "Three Centuries of Women's Dress Fashions: A Quantitative Analysis," *Anthropological Records*, Vol. 5 (1947), pp. 111–153; A. L. Kroeber, "On the Principle of Order in Civilization as Exemplified by Changes of Fashion," *American Anthropologist*, Vol. 21 (1919), pp. 235–263; A. B. Young, *Recurring Cycles of Fashion 1760–1937* (New York, 1937).

[5] For these and related features of fashion, cf. Blumer, "Collective Behavior,"

The Craze

cycle displays a sufficient number of features of a fully developed craze—a clear division into a "real" and "derived" phase, for instance—to justify inclusion.

Fads have been characterized as involving a more "unimportant matter or detail" than fashion,[1] as being less widespread than fashion,[2] and as being generally less "harmful" than other kinds of collective behavior.[3] Finally, even though a small organized segment of the population is likely to initiate a fad,[4] the propagation of fad behavior—especially among adolescents[5]—is likely to be less structured than that of fashion behavior.[6]

(4) The religious sphere, in which we study the phenomenon of revivalism. A revival, as we use the term, involves an enthusiastic redefinition of religious methods, but not a challenge to basic religious values. Thus a revival stands in contrast to value-oriented movements— movements to form sects, to form ideal religious communities, to make a revolution, etc.—which we shall consider in Chapter X. Our purpose in this chapter is to elucidate the unique conditions that underlie revivalism.

The term "revivalism" has been used to refer to religious enthusiasm in general (such as the crusades, or behavior on festive religious occasions), and to periodic general awakenings of religion (e.g., pietism in the seventeenth and eighteenth centuries). We shall restrict the meaning of the term to that given by Schneider:

---

in Lee (ed.), *op. cit.*, pp. 216–218; Bogardus, *Social Psychology*, pp. 299–301; LaPiere and Farnsworth, *Social Psychology*, p. 452; P. H. Nystrom, *The Economics of Fashion* (New York, 1928), pp. 36–37.

[1] Nystrom, *The Economics of Fashion*, p. 5. Nystrom gives the following list of fads: "Deauville scarves, flopping galoshes, Russian boots, Helen Wills tennis caps, kewpies, Mary Pickford curls, Chaplin moustaches, Ford jokes, rose-enameled finger-nails, finale hoppers, rolled stockings, grotesque spider-like dolls, King Tut designs, women's handbags shaped like dogs, rag flowers, etc. Fads, like fashions, invade every field—sports, literature, religion, medicine, politics and education. For a brief period we have great interest in the sport of dog racing. Then we rush to telepathy, psychoanalysis, wearing sandals, fortune-telling, ukelele playing, ping-pong, mah jong, crossword puzzles, and ask-me-another fads." Also Bogardus, *Social Psychology*, pp. 306–308.

[2] Hurlock, *The Psychology of Dress*, p. 11.

[3] Mackay, *Extraordinary Popular Delusions and the Madness of Crowds*, p. 630; Meyersohn and Katz, "Notes on a Natural History of Fads," *op. cit.*, p. 594; also L. W. Doob, *Social Psychology* (New York, 1952), p. 386.

[4] Meyersohn and Katz, "Notes on a Natural History of Fads," *op. cit.*, p. 598. See also Hurlock, *The Psychology of Dress*, pp. 9–10.

[5] Hurlock, *The Psychology of Dress*, pp. 182–183. H. A. Bloch and A. Niederhoffer, *The Gang* (New York, 1958), pp. 95 ff.

[6] Turner and Killian, *Collective Behavior*, p. 216. See also J. E. Janney, "Fad and Fashion Leadership among Undergraduate Women," *Journal of Abnormal and Social Psychology*, Vol. 36 (1941), pp. 275–278; J. Johnstone and E. Katz, "Youth and Popular Music: A Study in the Sociology of Taste," *American Journal of Sociology*, Vol. 62 (1956–57), pp. 563–568.

The Craze

[Revivalism] signifies the phenomenon and methods of modern evangelism ... directed as a rule to the founding of evangelistic churches or societies. The characteristic features of such evangelism are itinerant preaching and camp meetings; extreme emotional appeals and religious demagogy; public confession, conversion and reform of personal conduct; fixed seasons for revival meetings when whole congregations or communities are organized for a period of intense emotional stimulation and of concerted appeals to the "unregenerate."[1]

The large waves of revivalism in the United States—on which we shall concentrate—have clustered in distinct periods; McLoughlin restricts the really "great awakenings" to four—from 1725 to 1750, from 1795 to 1835, from 1875 to 1915, and from 1945 to, perhaps, 1970.[2] These as well as the American, Irish and Welsh Revivals of 1857–59, the Welsh Revival of 1905–06, and other minor revivals constitute the empirical basis for our analysis of revivals.[3]

Three qualifications on our study of revivals are in order; (a) In considering only the "craze" aspects of revivalism, we deliberately by-pass the fact that revivals have coincided with other types of religious movements— for instance, major reformulations of theology, formation of sects, and social movements within the church.[4] Some of these phenomena are determinants of revivalism itself; others are consequences of revivalism; and still others are the products of separate sets of determinants. (b) We shall not discuss the long-term evolution of revivalism toward secularization, routinization, and public acceptability.[5] (c) We shall depart from the social

---

[1] H. W. Schneider, "Religious Revivals," *Encyclopaedia of the Social Sciences*, Vol. 13, p. 364. As Schneider points out (p. 365) there is considerable variability in the kind of preaching, church organization, etc.

[2] W. G. McLoughlin, Jr., *Modern Revivalism* (New York, 1959), p. 8.

[3] G. B. Cutten, *The Psychological Phenomena of Christianity* (New York, 1908), p. 186; G. C. Loud, *Evangelized America* (New York, 1928), pp. 5 ff.; for some of the predecessors of revivalism, cf. Cutten, pp. 175–176. The breaking of revivalism into "waves" seems essentially correct, though McLoughlin's groupings, for instance, obscure major movements within each wave. His period from 1795 to 1835 includes both the Kentucky revivals which began at the very end of the eighteenth century, and the revivals headed by Charles Grandison Finney, which began about 1825; also the period from 1875 to 1915 includes the work of both Dwight L. Moody and Billy Sunday. For some purposes we shall isolate these shorter waves for discussion.

[4] McLoughlin, *Modern Revivalism*, pp. 7–10. For its relation to sect formation and divisiveness, cf. W. W. Sweet, *Revivalism in America* (New York, 1944), pp. 140–143, 174–176; for a general clustering of incidence of revivalism, frontier utopias, Mormonism, and other movements in the late eighteenth and early nineteenth centuries, cf. W. W. Sweet, *Religion in the Development of American Culture 1765–1840* (New York, 1952), pp. 203–311.

[5] McLoughlin, *Modern Revivalism*, pp. 122–123, 126, 160–161, 400, 523. Some churches, as a matter of routine, lay emphasis on the employment of revivalistic methods. Schneider, "Religious Revivals," *op. cit.*, p. 365. For an analysis of the changing themes of popular inspirational literature over the past 75 years, cf. L.

The Craze

psychological tradition which has fixed primarily on the bizarre elements of revivalism, such as "speaking with tongues" (glossolalia), seizures, howling, falling, twitching, jerking, and barking.[1] Rather we shall emphasize the structural setting for revivals in which such behavior occurs.

The Value-added Process for the Craze. We shall organize the determinants of the craze in the same way as we did for the panic, using the value-added process. Toward the end of the chapter we shall discuss social control, or the ways in which crazes are prevented, stopped, or deflected. As we shall see, many controls are institutionalized —in expectation, as it were, of the potential explosiveness of crazes. For this reason crazes seldom display the violence of panics. In addition, because of the presence of so many controls, we shall have to be content with analyzing many "partial" crazes (such as the fashion cycle) in which even the most immediate determinants are triggered, guided or controlled by institutionalized mechanisms.

STRUCTURAL CONDUCIVENESS

Previously we have shown that conditions of structural conduciveness for panic include the possibility of danger, withdrawal, and communication. Sometimes these conditions arise unexpectedly (e.g., in the case of encirclement on a battlefield); sometimes, however, conduciveness is institutionalized (e.g., in the case of the definition of exchange in the money market).[2] In the latter case conduciveness is part of the normal definition of the social situation. In the study of crazes we can observe these conducive institutional conditions very clearly.

General Conditions of Conduciveness. Four structural conditions are necessary if any craze is to appear:

(1) A structurally differentiated setting for social action. Structural differentiation refers to the level of specialization of a given kind of action (e.g., economic), and the degree to which specialized sanctions (money, in this case) are allowed to operate without intervention of other kinds of sanctions (e.g., political controls, kinship and other particularistic demands, etc.). An example of a highly differentiated economic structure is the market structure of the capitalist economies

---

Schneider and S. M. Dornbusch, *Popular Religion: Inspirational Books in America* (Chicago, 1958).

[1] Cf. F. M. Davenport, *Primitive Traits in Religious Revivals* (New York, 1910), pp. 73-83; G. B. Cutten, *Speaking with Tongues* (New Haven, 1927), p. 120; J. F. K. Hecker, *The Dancing Mania of the Middle Ages* (London, 1833), pp. 42-43; J. B. Pratt, *The Religious Consciousness* (New York, 1920), pp. 173-176; Loud, *Evangelized America*, pp. 95-102.

[2] Above, pp. 135-136.

of Great Britain and the United States in the nineteenth century, in which the norm was the pursuit of economic activity free from political interference and free from traditional loyalties to family and community. An example of an economic structure with a low degree of differentiation is the nuclear family, in which the allocation of economic resources is subordinated to the demands of the family as a unit (e.g., the demand that parents support children).

(2) A relatively well-defined "rationality" which governs the differentiated social action. People should be prepared to respond to specialized sanctions (e.g., money), and to make calculations in terms of maximizing their rewards. An example of this kind of rationality is the hypothetical "economic rationality" of classical economics, in which economic actors ignore all kinds of rewards except economic ones. An example of low economic rationality is the attitude of a person who refuses to maximize his income because in so doing he might hurt his family or friends.

(3) A possibility of committing, recommitting, and withdrawing resources with flexibility. In the economic sphere this involves a certain level of fluidity of capital.

(4) A "medium" which can be stored, exchanged, and extended to future commitments. Again in the economic sphere, money would be such a medium, perishable vegetables would not.

Let us illustrate these four general conditions of conduciveness in more detail in the economic, political, expressive, and religious spheres.

Conditions of Conduciveness in the Economic Sphere. The first structural condition for the occurrence of a speculative boom is a relatively differentiated market structure. Perhaps we can illustrate first by negative examples. Certain types of economic exchange are functions *not* of independent market mechanisms, but are tied to other kinds of sanctions; hence they are not *differentiated* structurally from these other sanctions. The following three examples show how non-economic elements constrict the free play of economic calculation and maneuverability which is essential for speculation:[1]

(*a*) In reciprocative exchange, the parties are segmentary units—usually families, neighborhoods, communities, clans, etc.; exchange of goods and services follows from an implied reciprocative balance between the units.[2] In order to modify the resulting flow of

---

[1] The following argument is based on reasoning incorporated into my review article of K. Polanyi, C. M. Arensberg and H. W. Pearson (eds.), *Trade and Market in the Early Empires* (Glencoe, Ill., 1957). The article appeared as "A Comparative View of Exchange Systems," *Economic Development and Cultural Change*, Vol. VII (1959), pp. 173-182.

[2] A thorough comparative analysis of these kinds of exchange is to be found in M. Mauss, *The Gift* (Glencoe, Ill., 1954).

The Craze

commodities, there must be a structural alteration of the exchanging units—families, clans, etc.—themselves. Of course, this alteration has little or nothing to do with any *market* conditions of supply and demand, but rather with the dynamics of kinship, clanship, tribalism, neighborhood, and demography. Because reciprocative exchange is, therefore, normally a function of an *ascribed base* (frequently kinship), a peculiar inflexibility governs such exchange. Since the sources of change lie in the modification of ascribed roles, moreover, this change is likely to be gradual.

(*b*) In *redistributive* systems of exchange, the flow of goods and services is tied closely to stratification in societies. The redistribution of wealth through charity or progressive taxation is an example of exchange which is a function of non-market considerations. Rapid changes in these exchanges of goods and services rest not so much on economic conditions of supply and demand as in the changes in the ideologies governing the relations among various classes in society.

(*c*) In still other cases the flow of goods and services is subordinated to *political* considerations. Examples are eminent domain, taxation, direct appropriation, and selective service. Modification of these kinds of exchange arises not so much from direct market influences as from changes in the authority in question and its capacity to mobilize resources.

These types of exchange systems—constricted by noneconomic imperatives—impair flexibility in the commitment and recommitment of resources in the face of *economic* sanctions. By contrast, a differentiated market system operates relatively independently of kinship, political or class affiliations, and relies on economic mechanisms of price and credit. Where we find speculation and speculative outbursts, moreover, we find also a differentiated market system. Regarding the development of land speculation, Gray observes:

> Land speculation has constituted in the main a comparatively recent phase of the development of capitalism. So long as property in land was tribal, corporate or public, there was lacking the freedom of transfer essential to speculative activity. Under the manorial system in Europe land tenure was rigidly governed by custom, and even after that system was replaced by more modern forms of tenure and long after the development of a money economy—a *sine qua non* of land speculation—property in agricultural land was subject to numerous customary or legal incidents that restrained the freedom of transfer essential to speculation. Traditional attachments of families, whether of peasants or of landlords, to particular holdings; long leases; the embryonic character of the land market and of facilities for mortgage credit; and the crude and costly methods of effecting

The Craze

transfer of land titles exerted a severely restraining influence on the sale of land, particularly of agricultural land.[1]

In money markets and stock exchanges, too, maneuverability and flexibility depends on the ability of people to save, borrow, and dispose of funds easily. Bagehot attributed the existence of the Lombard Street money market partially to the presence of the diversion of savings to a centralized source, through which they were lent freely through elaborate credit machinery.[2] The existence of such a centralized market system lay behind the proclivity for speculative crazes in Great Britain—as contrasted with France—during the nineteenth century. Mottram commented that

In France... during seventy years the material organisation of the State suffered changes between the empires, a kingdom, and three republics. Now, although the sort of convulsion caused by war is favourable to speculation, that which results from political theorising makes merely for uncertainty of authority and hence of credit, which is the necessary basis for Speculation on any large scale. Moreover, a large portion of the soil of France had passed by this time into the possession of small cultivators. So that, while on paper still a very rich country whose wealth is very well distributed, actually France is much less aptly organised for Financial Speculation.

Thus arises the contrast, that while the handling of credit instruments and speculative machinery is more widely developed in Great Britain, yet the financial history of the kingdom contains far more frequent and serious commotions... that of France has been marked by greater stability and far less general consequences arising from credit upheavals, and the habitual use of speculation remains more in the hands of a small specialised class.[3]

Of all exchangeable commodities, stocks and money are the most storable, services are the most perishable, and various kinds of goods lie somewhere in between. For this reason it is impossible to speculate in services which are consumed at the moment of transaction. Also for this reason various semi-durable goods such as agricultural

---

[1] L. C. Gray, "Land Speculation," *Encyclopaedia of the Social Sciences*, Vol. 9, p. 66. Of course other characteristics of land such as its immobility, its division into small holdings, etc., restrict easy transfer. *Ibid.*, p. 65. For brief discussion of the process whereby "complete and final freedom, in principle as well as practice, in the transfer of real estate" was established in the early history of the American nation, cf. P. J. Davies, *Real Estate in American History* (Washington, D.C., 1958), pp. 2–3.

[2] *Lombard Street*, pp. 3–9, 124–132. Cf. also C. O. Hardy, "Speculation," *Encyclopaedia of the Social Sciences*, Vol. 9, p. 289.

[3] *A History of Financial Speculation* pp. 172–173; for a study of the "private" (i.e. differentiated) character of American and British as opposed to continental exchanges, cf. H. C. Emery, *Speculation, on the Stock and Produce Exchanges of the United States* (New York, 1896), pp. 13–18.

The Craze

commodities must have a shorter-term speculative cycle; completely storable goods (money, securities, land) are subject to all lengths of speculative cycle.

If the storability, flexibility, or maneuverability of resources is restricted, the situation becomes less conducive for a craze. An example of such restriction would be ownership of securities by trusts, institutions, and corporations; in this case buying and selling, if they occur at all, proceed according to relatively fixed rules—or at least deliberate policy decisions—and not necessarily in response to short-run market conditions.[1]

A final condition conducive to speculation is the institutionalization of the values of economic rationality—the predilection to react to market conditions in terms of economic self-interest rather than "irrational" considerations. Thus Handman lists as one major prerequisite for a boom:

[the society's members] must be animated primarily by pecuniary motives and constantly on the alert for the possibility of making money. It is obvious that a society which is interested in living according to the standards handed down for generations, and in which large monetary incomes are not accompanied by corresponding social prestige, will not be interested in any explosive speeding up of its economic output in order to make money which it does not need.[2]

Historically speculation and speculative booms have been associated with the rise of these structurally conducive conditions: a differentiated market structure, maneuverability, flexibility, and economic rationality. Gray points out, for instance, that land speculation

first acquired economic significance as a concomitant of urban development [especially in continental European cities in the nineteenth century]...

Speculation in agricultural and mineral land has accompanied the opening to settlement of new areas in all parts of the world throughout the nineteenth and twentieth centuries.[3]

Public speculation began in Holland in the late sixteenth century and spread thereafter as appropriate political and economic conditions were established.[4] Further evidence of the historical association

[1] Mindell, *The Stock Market*, p. 40.
[2] M. Handman, "Boom," *Encyclopaedia of the Social Sciences*, Vol. 2, p. 638. It is important to realize that this institutionalization of economic rationality is structurally variable and is not a universal psychological "given." Parsons and Smelser, *Economy and Society*, pp. 175–184.
[3] "Land Speculation," *op. cit.*, p. 68.
[4] Emery, *Speculation on the Stock and Produce Exchanges of the United States*,

The Craze

between speculation and the appropriate conditions of conduciveness is shown in the fact that many controversies on "the problem of speculation" deal with the degree of maneuverability and flexibility that is desirable in exchange and credit markets.[1]

Structural conduciveness does not, of course, explain the occurrence of any single speculative boom. As a determinant it merely indicates what kind of social structure must be present if a boom is to occur at all. Hence the historical correlation between conducive conditions and the occurrence of booms is very rough; not all conditions of conduciveness produce booms. We shall make our account of speculative booms more determinate as we take up additional determinants throughout the chapter. Meantime, let us examine the parallel conditions of conduciveness in the political, expressive, and religious spheres.

Conditions of Conduciveness in the Political Sphere. The following conditions are conducive to the development of the political bandwagon: (1) a highly differentiated political structure; (2) an institutionalized "political rationality," whereby decisions are relatively unencumbered by non-political considerations;[2] (3) the possibility of committing and withdrawing political support; (4) a generalized medium of exchange—in this case power—which can be exchanged, bargained with, and stored (i.e., promised for future delivery). In discussing these characteristics we shall limit our concern to the transmission of power from one leader to another.[3]

Let us begin with Max Weber's classic discussion of the transmission of charismatic authority. Weber characterizes this type of authority as resting on "devotion to the specific and exceptional sanctity, heroism or exemplary character of an individual person,

---

pp. 32–41; W. F. Hickernell, *Financial and Business Forecasting* (1928), Vol. 1, pp. 57–69.

[1] For a discussion of Max Weber's study of the German stock exchanges in the late nineteenth century, cf. R. Bendix, *Max Weber: An Intellectual Portrait* (Garden City, N.Y., 1959), pp. 47–52. For a brief sketch of restrictions on French credit and speculation following the Mississippi Bubble, cf. C. A. Conant, *A History of Modern Banks of Issue* (New York, 1915), pp. 40–41. For a brief sketch of American legislation and court decisions relating to this problem of speculation, cf. Emery, *Speculation on the Stock and Produce Exchanges of the United States*, pp. 194 ff.

[2] This parallels economic rationality in the sense that decisions are presumably made on a calculation of the political consequences of a decision. For a formal attempt to deal with political rationality, cf. A. Downs, *An Economic Theory of Democracy* (New York, 1957).

[3] This choice of a single point of interest does not exhaust all possible foci of political crazes. In the area of budgetary allocation, spending crazes have occurred. For instance, the "dreadnought panic" in Great Britain just before World War I led to an extraordinary assignment of government funds to naval preparations. F. W. Hirst, *The Six Panics and Other Essays* (London, 1913), pp. 100–102.

The Craze

and of the normative patterns or order revealed or ordained by him."[1] Charismatic authority is frequently generated during a political or religious revolution. In its early stages it is without fixed rules for transmitting power from a leader to his successor. As charismatic authority becomes routinized, however, one of several methods of transferring power to future leaders may evolve. Possible methods are, according to Weber,

... (a) The search for a new charismatic leader on the basis of criteria of the qualities which will fit him for the position of authority. (b) By revelation manifested in oracles, lots, divine judgments, or other techniques of selection. (c) By the designation on the part of the original charismatic leader of his own successor and his recognition on the part of the followers ... (d) Designation of a successor by the charismatically qualified administrative staff and his recognition by the community ... (e) By the conception that charisma is a quality transmitted by heredity; thus that it is participated in by the kinsmen of its bearer, particularly by his closest relatives. This is the case of hereditary charisma.... (f) The concept that charisma may be transmitted by ritual means from one bearer to another or may be created in a new person.[2]

For each method the emphasis is on the way the extraordinary quality of charisma is passed from individual to individual.

When a political group "undergoes a process of rationalization,"[3] Weber points out that

instead of recognition being treated as a consequence of legitimacy, it is treated as the basis of legitimacy. Legitimacy, that is, becomes "democratic." Thus, for instance, designation of a successor by an administrative staff may be treated as "election" in advance; while designation by the predecessor is "nomination"; whereas the recognition by the group becomes the true "election." The leader whose legitimacy rested on his personal charisma then becomes leader by the grace of those who follow him since the latter are formally free to elect and elevate to power as they please and even to depose. For the loss of charisma and its proof involves the loss of genuine legitimacy. The chief now becomes the freely elected leader.[4]

Under such an arrangement the mechanism of political succession becomes more differentiated. Recognition of authority is no longer a duty which is incumbent upon the follower because the leader possesses—or is said by some oracle to possess—charisma. The

---
[1] *Theory of Social and Economic Organization*, p. 328.
[2] *Ibid.*, pp. 364–366.
[3] Rationalization as used here is roughly equivalent to the concept of differentiation as I have been employing it; both refer to the growth of specialized and autonomous structures for carrying out certain social functions.
[4] *Ibid.*, pp. 386–387.

The Craze

power to "elect and depose" is now separated from any specific charismatic quality. Power is more generalized; it can be given and taken more freely from a given individual by supporters. This condition, combined with others to be examined presently, is conducive to phenomena like the political bandwagon, which is by definition a headlong rush to support a given candidate for leadership.

Historically the growth of the American nominating convention conforms to Weber's conception of the "democratization" of the political process. Bishop's summary runs as follows:

> The nominating convention is a purely American invention and a natural outgrowth of popular government. It came into being with the enlargement of the suffrage through the gradual removal of restriction upon it and with the steadily increasing demand of the people to have a voice in the selection of candidates for office. Before the [American] Revolution, and for many years afterwards, political action was controlled by unofficial and voluntary associations or coteries of persons [caucuses] who were drawn together by kindred opinions and whose prominence in the affairs of the community made them its natural leaders.[1]

These caucuses—constituted by wealthy and clerical citizens in the main—nominated presidential candidates at the Congressional level and state candidates in local legislative caucuses. This system continued with few modifications until 1824. Because of its limited popular base, however, dissatisfaction began to mount; this dissatisfaction was augmented by the growth of population, the extension of suffrage, and a growing democratic spirit. In 1824 the first state convention met in Utica, New York, and thereafter spread to other states. The first national convention for nominating candidates was that of a minor group, the Anti-Masonic Party, in 1830. This was followed in short order by conventions in the major national parties.[2] Although the early conventions produced few genuine contests on the convention floor,[3] popular maneuvering at the conventions

[1] J. B. Bishop, *Our Political Drama: Conventions, Campaigns, Candidates* (New York, 1904), p. 17.

[2] For a historical sketch of the caucus system and the rise of the convention system, cf. P. T. David, R. M. Goldman, and R. C. Bain, *The Politics of National Party Conventions* (Washington, D.C., 1960), pp. 10–23, and Bishop, *Our Political Drama*, pp. 17–42.

[3] In the Democratic party, Jackson, the incumbent President, was nominated without a contest in 1832; in 1836 he was able to name his successor, Martin Van Buren, who also received the nomination without a contest; in 1840 Van Buren was able to be renominated despite some dissatisfaction, but he was not able to dictate the vice-presidential nomination. A contest among Henry Clay, General Winfield Scott, and General Henry Harrison developed at the first Whig convention in 1840, but it was resolved quickly by the maneuverings of Thurlow

The Craze

became a possibility. The first stampede for a dark horse occurred as early as 1844, in the defeat of Van Buren and the nomination of James K. Polk at the Democratic Convention.[1]

To stress the role of structural conduciveness, let us contrast on four counts the American political convention system with the transmission of charisma by heredity in a hypothetical version of the Divine Right of Kings:

(1) The level of political differentiation. In the heredity transmission of the throne, three elements fuse in the same political transaction—charisma, or the possession of divinity; power, or the right to command on the basis of this quality; and kinship, or the determination of succession by a blood line. Under the rules of a political convention, a higher level of political differentiation results. Access to power is not contingent on a revealed quality such as divinity, but rather on the political support of a body of delegates. Furthermore, support for a candidate is removed formally from any kinship ties of the candidate.[2] The process of political selection is more differentiated because it rests primarily on grounds of political support; it is not considered to be a function of divinity or kinship.

(2) Power as a generalized medium. Because power under the convention system is relatively free from ascribed bases, it is more negotiable. Under the Divine Right system the issues of support, succession, and office are solved automatically by heredity and divinity. If a subject wishes to challenge the heir's right to the throne, he must challenge his *legitimacy*. In the American political convention, power is not tied to these automatic criteria; it is possible to promise, withdraw, and trade power. Empirically the contrast between the two systems is not perfect. Kings, even if divinely chosen, engaged historically in "dealing" with supporters. In the American political system some political commitments are relatively rigid and non-negotiable (e.g., those of the Deep South).

(3) Political rationality. Because the transmission in the system of Divine Right manifests the divinity of kinship and the blood tie to the king, loyalty and support presumably follow without calculation. In an American nominating convention, a supporter deliberately decides, on political grounds, whether to give his loyalty to his chosen

---

Weed, the New York politician. R. C. Bain, *Convention Decisions and Voting Records* (Washington, D.C., 1960), pp. 17–28.

[1] *Ibid.*, pp. 31–35; Bishop, *Our Political Drama*, pp. 37–42. Jackson's introduction in 1832 of the rule that the votes of two-thirds of the delegates be required for nomination gave rise to the greater possibility of deadlock and the appearance of dark horses and stampedes. Below, pp. 193–195.

[2] Informally, of course, kinship is not irrelevant to political success, as the recurring names of Roosevelt, Taft, Lodge, Stevenson, and more recently Kennedy, show.

candidate in the hope that he may receive a maximum of political benefits in return. The institutionalization of political rationality is greater in the latter system.

(4) The maneuverability of supporters. Because the issue of succession is formally "closed" under the Divine Right system, maneuverability in supporting the heir is held to a minimum. Under the system of nominating conventions, delegates may change their loyalties. This freedom to dispose of political support is often restricted in advance by commitments of blocs of votes, by the presence of "favorite sons," by the unit rule, and so on. Even these commitments may be broken sometimes, especially on later ballots.

The arrangements of a political convention, then, permit a rapid transfer of political support in a short time. This does not *guarantee* that a political bandwagon will develop in every nominating convention; as a matter of fact, genuine bandwagons are sporadic in the history of American conventions. The arrangements of a political convention do *permit* bandwagons to occur. For this reason we consider the political convention to possess the conditions of structural conduciveness.

Conditions of Conduciveness in the Symbolization of Status. The contemporary status systems of Western Europe and the United States are very conducive to fashion cycles. These status systems are characterized by: (1) a highly differentiated system of status-symbolization; (2) rapid maneuverability in the symbolization of status; (3) a "status rationality"; and (4) a generalized "medium" for the representation of status.

As a result of a number of historical trends in Western society, contemporary stratification systems possess the following two salient characteristics. First, relative to traditional stratification systems, differential ranking depends largely on achievement, wealth, influence, etc., not on membership in ascribed kinship, ethnic, and religious groupings.[1] Second, relative to traditional systems, contemporary Western stratification emphasizes individual mobility from level to level within the stratification system.[2]

What are the implications for status symbolization of these broad characteristics of contemporary systems of stratification? Most generally, contemporary stratification is relatively free from those restrictions which inhibit persons from adopting and using status

[1] For a study of the cross-cultural similarity in the ranking of industrial occupations in advanced countries, cf. A. Inkeles and P. H. Rossi, "National Comparisons of Occupational Prestige," *American Journal of Sociology*, Vol. 61 (1956), pp. 329–339.
[2] S. M. Lipset and R. Bendix, *Social Mobility in Industrial Society* (Los Angeles and Berkeley, 1959), pp. 13 ff.

The Craze

symbols freely. This feature has been produced by a number of related historical processes:

First, symbols (ceremonies, modes of dress, etc.) symbolizing the relatively fixed relationships among "estates" have declined in significance.[1]

Second, an emphasis on individual mobility continuously supplies a large number of individuals with facilities to imitate the styles of the groups into which, or near which they are moving. As Flugel observes:

So long as the system of "fixed" costume prevails, each social grade is content to wear the costume with which it is associated. But when the barriers between one grade and another become less insuperable, when, in psychological terms, one class begins seriously to aspire to the position of that above it, it is natural that the distinctive outward signs and symbols of the grades in question should become imperilled . . . it is a fundamental human trait to imitate those who are admired or envied. At the stage of social development in question, those who are above them; they therefore tend to imitate them; and what more natural, and, at the same time, more symbolic, than to start the process of imitation by copying their clothes, the very insignia of the admired and envied qualities?[2]

Third, contemporary stratification systems emphasize geographical and social mobility, as well as mass education. These features have lessened traditional differences in education and speech, which are among the more inflexible of status symbols. In addition, distinctive regional, ethnic, and national styles have diminished in the past several centuries, even though vestiges of these remain.[3]

Fourth, with the general decline of sumptuary legislation, status symbolization has become relatively free from political control.[4]

Fifth, increasing productive efficiency, new techniques of manufacturing, and improved communication and transportation have led to the production of cheap imitations of valuable objects on a mass scale.[5]

All of these historical developments have augmented the structural

---

[1] Spencer, *Principles of Sociology*, Vol. II-1, pp. 214–215. See also Bell, *On Human Finery*, pp. 21–22, 40, 117; T. Veblen, *The Theory of the Leisure Class* (New York, 1934), pp. 175–176.

[2] Flugel, *The Psychology of Clothes*, p. 138. Cf. also Ross: "In immobile caste societies the inferior does not think of aping the superior, and hence the superior is not obliged to devise new styles. . . ." *Social Psychology*, p. 102; also, p. 80. Also E. Goffman, "Symbols of Class Status," *British Journal of Sociology*, Vol. 2 (1951), pp. 302–303.

[3] Hurlock, *The Psychology of Dress*, pp. 71 ff.

[4] Simmel, "Fashion," *op. cit.*, p. 137; Hurlock, *The Psychology of Dress*, pp. 68–70.

[5] Flugel, *The Psychology of Clothes*, pp. 151–152; Simmel, "Fashion," *op. cit.*, pp. 151–152; Hurlock, *The Psychology of Dress*, pp. 82–83.

The Craze

conduciveness for "crazes" in fashion. Status symbolization has become relatively free from the restrictions of political control, ascribed status, inflexible barriers such as language and cultivation, and so on. Such structural arrangements are relatively conducive to phenomena which have been described as the fashion cycle, the "downward and upward circulation of symbols," the "trickle effect," etc.[1]

With these changes a distinctive "rationality" of status symbolization has arisen—we might call it the rationality of social conformity or of "being in fashion."[2] In the absence of legal, religious, moral and other controls over the symbolization of status, a person no longer risks legal punishment or religious censure for changing his style. A distinct set of "social" sanctions—snobbishness, ridicule, "not being in the swim," etc.—become the basis for calculating a person's choice of symbols.[3]

What, finally, is the generalized medium of exchange which has emerged in status symbolization? "Prestige" is the most appropriate term. A person can gain prestige by appropriate symbolization, lose it by being out of step, waste it by purchasing items which are out of fashion, and conserve it by refusing to fling himself at an item which is not likely to come into fashion.[4]

Our discussion of status symbolization has concentrated on community-wide or society-wide status systems. The same line of reasoning can be applied to other kinds of symbolization, for instance, the symbolization of age grades. American society, by contrast with others, displays a characteristic "looseness" in the definition of *rites*

---

[1] P. Clerget, "The Economic and Social Role of Fashion," *Annual Report of the Smithsonian Institution, 1913* (Washington, D.C., 1914), p. 755; Goffman, "Symbols of Class Status," *op. cit.*, pp. 303–304; B. Barber and L. S. Lobel, " 'Fashion' in Women's Clothes and the American Social System," *Social Forces*, Vol. 31 (1952), pp. 124–131; L. A. Fallers, "A Note on the 'Trickle Effect,' " *Public Opinion Quarterly*, Vol. 18 (1954), pp. 314–321. The total "freedom" of fashion choices should not, however, be exaggerated; custom, modesty, and economy continue to operate as restrictive factors. Nystrom, *The Economics of Fashion*, p. 124; Sapir, "Fashion," *op. cit.*, p. 143; Hurlock, *The Psychology of Dress*, pp. 49–50, 211.

[2] The use of the term "conformity" is not identical with the more general use above, pp. 29–30.

[3] For discussion of the strength of these social sanctions, cf. Hurlock, *The Psychology of Dress*, p. 7; Bell, *On Human Finery*, pp. 14–15. Because this rationale is one of appropriate adornment in the service of status, it has frequently brought down the censure of observers because it is not "vital," "useful," or "important." Cf. Bell, *On Human Finery*, p. 13; Veblen, *The Theory of the Leisure Class*, pp. 173–174; Ross, *Social Psychology*, p. 94; Simmel, "Fashion," *op. cit.*, p. 135.

[4] Frequently this rationality seems to enter consciously into decisions to spend on status symbols. E. B. Hurlock, "Motivation in Fashion," *Archives of Psychology*, Vol. 17, No. 111 (1929–30), p. 69; W. G. Cobliner, "Feminine Fashion as an Aspect of Group Psychology: Analysis of Written Replies Received by Means of a Questionnaire," *Journal of Social Psychology*, Vol. 31 (1950), p. 289.

The Craze

de passage which mark the transition from one age level to another. This is particularly pronounced in the transition from childhood to adult responsibilities in adolescence.[1] The looseness in the definition of specific symbols for age grading is conducive to extensive experimentation and faddism in this period of transition.[2]

Conditions of Conduciveness in the Religious Sphere. Revivalism is a phenomenon primarily of the United States and Great Britain—countries with Anglo-Saxon, Protestant traditions. What kinds of religious settings characterize these countries, and how are these settings conducive to the occurrence of religious revivals?

(1) Differentiation of religious commitment. One of the major consequences of the Protestant Reformation was a redefinition of the basis of authority in society. The Protestants—with much variation among them—turned from the authority of a hierarchically ordered church to the reliance on an individual's relationship with God, with the Bible rather than the Church serving as the important intermediary.[3] Structurally this brought differentiation—a split between the *religious* and the *political* authority of the church. For some time this split was not completed; many Protestant churches maintained a political fusion with the nation-state rather than the Papacy —Lutheranism in the German provinces and Scandinavia, Anglicanism in England, and Presbyterianism in Scotland.[4]

Later the fusion of Protestantism with political units began to give way to even more differentiated religious arrangements. The features of this development were the growth of Nonconformity in England and the separation of church and state in the American Constitution.[5] In modern times a system of "denominational pluralism" has emerged, especially in the United States.[6]

The religious outlook of some Protestant churches—especially Presbyterian, Congregationalist, Methodist, Baptist, and more recently, the Holiness branches—has developed in a way parallel to

---

[1] On the character of this transition, cf. R. Benedict, "Continuities and Discontinuities in Cultural Conditioning," *Psychiatry*, Vol. I (1938), pp. 161–167. Also Block and Niederhoffer, *The Gang*, pp. 11, 17, 95–112.

[2] Janney, "Fad and Fashion Leadership among Undergraduate Women," *op. cit.*, pp. 275–278.

[3] G. G. Atkins, *Modern Religious Cults and Movements* (New York, 1923), pp. 29–35.

[4] H. R. Niebuhr, *The Social Sources of Denominationalism* (Hamden, Conn., 1954), pp. 124–134.

[5] For discussion of the segregation of religion from politics in early America, cf. Myers, *History of Bigotry in the United States*, pp. 100 ff.; H. P. Douglass, and E. deS. Brunner, *The Protestant Church as a Social Institution* (New York, 1935), pp. 22–23.

[6] T. Parsons, *Structure and Process in Modern Societies* (Glencoe, Ill., 1960), Ch. 10.

The Craze

these lines of differentiation of religion from other spheres of society. Religious commitment, many within these churches have argued, should be a matter of voluntary choice based on faith, not a matter of being born into a church, being a citizen of a political unit, and so on.[1] The voluntaristic position of these Protestant churches has been most conspicuous in their formative periods.[2]

(2) *Flexibility of religious commitment.* Because of the voluntaristic definition of religious commitment in some branches of Protestantism, flexibility is increased. Church members can move from one denomination to another; they can, by emotional experience or personal choice, be "reborn" or "regenerated" without affecting their political citizenship, ascribed membership in a church, ethnic origin, etc. Hence evangelical Protestantism makes for a great fluidity of religious commitment.

(3) *Commitment as "generalized medium."* Religious belief thus becomes something that one can gain, lose, save and spend, according to the quality of one's personal conduct and faith. Other religions than evangelical Protestantism make such demands as well, but they impose these demands on top of an ascribed or semi-ascribed basis of inclusion.

(4) *Religious rationality.* In the evangelical branches of Protestantism, churches can be in the "business of saving souls" alone,[1] and not concern themselves with political, economic, and social goals with which less differentiated churches invariably become entangled. Religious salvation, regeneration, and backsliding become more and more exclusively based on religious experience alone.

From a structural standpoint, then, the definition of the religious situation in the evangelical Protestant churches parallels that of a free market system, a system of open nomination of political candidates by convention, and an open stratification system. Within these churches we observe those features of differentiation, flexibility, and maneuverability that are conducive for crazelike behavior in general.

STRAIN

Given the conditions of structural conduciveness just outlined, the following kinds of strain operate to produce craze phenomena: (*a*) Ambiguity as to the level of rewards to be expected from an existing

[1] Atkins, *Modern Religious Cults and Movements*, pp. 41–42.
[2] Any given sect, as it evolves towards a denomination, continues to define its membership in terms of voluntary choice, but informal restrictions—such as common socio-economic background—discriminate against free admission. Wilson, "An Analysis of Sect Development," *op. cit.*, pp. 4–6.
[3] Many revivalists defined their own purposes in precisely these terms. Below, pp. 208–210.

The Craze

allocation of resources (e.g., in the economic sphere, ambiguity concerning the profitability of current patterns of investment); (*b*) Ambiguity as to the level of rewards to be expected from alternative modes of allocation (e.g., in the economic sphere, ambiguity concerning the profitability of new investments); (*c*) Ready availability of facilities which permits *some* line of reallocation to be pursued (e.g., in the economic sphere, the availability of capital). From the available descriptions of crazes, it appears that all three conditions must be present for a craze to occur; one or two are not sufficient.

What form to these general conditions of strain take in the economic, political, expressive, and religious spheres?

Conditions of Strain Underlying the Speculative Boom. The first element of strain is a state of uncertainty concerning the returns on existing investment. This appears in several guises:

(*a*) An absolute need for income. Examples are the desperate state of the finances of the French government in 1715 on the death of Louis XIV;[1] the debts of the government of Great Britain at the same time;[2] the burdens of the original states of the United States which had accumulated from financing the Revolutionary War.[3] In each case the government was faced with a revenue crisis.

(*b*) A relative decline in returns on existing investments. This condition is illustrated in several sectors of American agriculture before the agricultural crazes of the early nineteenth century:

... as transportation facilities improved, especially transportation facilities which opened up new areas of the western states, the farmers of the East were incited or compelled to look around for crops that they could raise profitably in the face of new competition from Ohio and Indiana. Possibly, too, the decline of household manufacture which accompanied the growing dominance of industrial factory production set labor free in the rural districts—labor that would look with particular favor upon the cultivation of articles such as Berkshire hogs, broom corn, or hens, which would bring cash into the farming communities.[4]

In 1924 and 1925, just before a great period of speculation in Florida land, low yields on high-grade investments tempted investors to purchase the eight per cent bonds available on Florida real estate.[5]

---

[1] Mackay, *Extraordinary Popular Delusions and the Madness of Crowds*, pp. 6–7; Wiston-Glynn, *John Law of Lauriston*, pp. 34–35; Hickernell, *Financial and Business Forecasting*, Vol. II, pp. 73–74.
[2] Melville, *The South Sea Bubble*, p. 1; Hickernell, *Financial and Business Forecasting*, Vol. I, p. 87.
[3] Sakolski, *The Great American Land Bubble*, pp. 31–32.
[4] A. H. Cole, "Agricultural Crazes: A Neglected Chapter in American Economic History," *American Economic Review*, Vol. 16 (1926), p. 638.
[5] H. B. Vanderblue, "The Florida Land Boom," *The Journal of Land & Public Utility Economics*, Vol. III (1927), pp. 116.

The Craze

Before the gold rush of 1849, "the hard times of the Forties had blanketed the East with mortgages. Many sober communities were ready, deliberately and without excitement, to send their young men westward in the hope of finding a way out of their financial difficulties."[1] Perhaps, finally, the relative uncertainty about returns accounts for the fact that speculative booms cluster "when the business cycle reaches its peak, in an excessively rapid development of certain industries."[2] Capital is available, but there is a growing uneasiness as to the status of returns.

(c) The perception—correct or incorrect—that no or few investment opportunities are available. Shortly after the American Revolution, for instance,

> [the thoughts of colonists freed from the British] turned again to gainful ventures. Trade and shipping projects had almost ceased during the hostilities. Aside from privateering, little profit and much risk were involved in overseas trading. Accordingly new fields for material gain must be opened up. Before the Revolution, the colonists had been kept free from the unsavory stock-jobbing schemes that beset England in the early part of the eighteenth century. Corporations, as a form of business enterprise, were practically unknown on American soil, and joint stock associations were few, and usually frowned upon. There were no securities in America, except possibly the state and federal debts—which for the most part were not interest bearing and were of little present or prospective value. The bulk of permanent wealth was in ships and land. Due to the ravages of war, ships were relatively few. Land there was in plenty.[3]

The great speculative schemes of the early eighteenth century also were preceded by a period of perceived dearth in profitable investment outlets.[4]

Closely related to this perceived lack of opportunity is an uncertainty as to how *new* lines of investment can be made to yield profits.[5] This uncertainty may result from the repeated failure of recent ventures—for example, the abortive legal and financial mea-

---

[1] S. E. White, *The Forty-Niners* (New Haven, 1921), p. 55. Allen and Avery suggest that the revolutions of 1848 and the consequent political instability in Europe also gave a "push" to some Europeans to come to California in the gold rush. W. W. Allen and R. B. Avery, *California Gold Book* (San Francisco, 1893), p. 44.
[2] Handman, "Boom," *op. cit.*, p. 638.
[3] Sakolski, *The Great American Land Bubble*, p. 29.
[4] Galbraith, *The Great Crash*, pp. 175-176, quoting Macaulay and Bagehot, and implying the same about the 1928-29 boom in America. For the same conditions which preceded the railway mania of the 1840's in England, cf. Duguid, *The Story of the Stock Exchange*, pp. 146-147.
[5] All investment has an element of uncertainty, of course. G. Haberler, *Prosperity and Depression* (Lake Success, N.Y., 1946), p. 145. The important feature here is that this uncertainty be *combined* with the other conditions.

The Craze

sures tried by the French government on the eve of the Mississippi Bubble.[1] On the other hand, the uncertainty may result from a simple lack of knowledge of investment possibilities. Asking why the agricultural crazes of the early nineteenth century occurred in the United States and not elsewhere, Cole argues that

> account must be taken of the newness and shifting character of American agriculture. Domestic farmers were by no means so well apprised as to the potentialities of the American soil, climate, and markets as, for example, the farmers of an older country such as England or France. Who could say with surety that the physical and commercial conditions would not be favorable to the cultivation of merino wool, Rohan potatoes or silk? Cotton had grown from an insignificant crop to one of outstanding importance within a few decades, and progress had been made with the growing and marketing of wheat. Why would success not crown the propagation of these other cultures?[2]

A final instance of this uncertainty concerning appropriate lines of investment occurs when considerable idle capital lies in the hands of persons inexperienced in investment.[3]

A final aspect of strains that underlie the boom is the presence of resources for *some* experimentation in investment. Gayer, Rostow, and Schwartz list "easy money conditions in the short- and long-term capital markets" as one of the necessary conditions for an investment boom.[4] Galbraith, while arguing that booms can occur under tight money conditions, does note the need for an accumulation of savings on the part of the participating populace.[5] This availability of capital funds has been mentioned as preceding the Florida land bubble, the tulip mania in Holland, the railway mania in Britain in the 1840's, the speculation in German industrial development in the late nineteenth century, and the stock market speculation in the late 1920's before the great depression.[6] In addition, the

---

[1] Mackay, *Extraordinary Popular Delusions and the Madness of Crowds*, pp. 6–7; Wiston-Glynn, *John Law of Lauriston*, pp. 34–35.
[2] "Agricultural Crazes," *op. cit.*, pp. 637–638.
[3] *Ibid.* Posthumus writes of the "speculation of non-professional people of small means" in the Dutch tulip boom of the early seventeenth century. "The Tulip Mania in Holland in the Years 1636 and 1637," *op. cit.*, pp. 438, 449. Both the South Sea Bubble and the American speculation of 1928–29 displayed this "popular" participation as well.
[4] A. D. Gayer, W. W. Rostow, and A. J. Schwartz, *The Growth and Fluctuation of the British Economy 1790–1850* (Oxford, 1953), Vol. II, p. 559.
[5] *The Great Crash*, pp. 174–175.
[6] Sakolski, *The Great American Land Bubble*, p. 237; Weigall, *Boom in Paradise*, pp. 38–39; Posthumus, "The Tulip Mania in Holland in the Years 1636 and 1637," *op. cit.*, pp. 114 ff.; Duguid, *The Story of the Stock Exchange*, p. 146; Hickernell, *Financial and Business Forecasting*, Vol. II, pp. 394–395; Galbraith, *The Great Crash*, pp. 174–176.

The Craze

timing of agricultural crazes in the early nineteenth century shows the peculiar importance of the availability of capital:

> ... the crazes ... appeared in the United States at times which have been identified as periods of general upswings in business. The merino mania came when domestic industry was stimulated by the dislocated commercial conditions of the Embargo and Non-Intercourse acts, and the Saxony craze when business was moving to a minor crisis in 1835. Then, the sundry speculations of the thirties were synchronous with the upward movement of prices and trade which for business reached a culmination in 1837 and more particularly for agriculture reached a final turning point in 1839. These manias for morus multicaulis, Berkshire hogs, and the like may be viewed as the agricultural aspect of that broad speculative development which involved public lands, canals, railroads, and banks.... And, finally, the "hen fever" raged when, after the gold discoveries in 1849, prices and the volume of business moved upward to a crisis in 1857. Even if the correlation is not complete between these agricultural manias and the general business situation, it is significant that the decades of the twenties and the forties, which on the whole were periods of quiet growth in American business, were also periods when agricultural manias were few or wholly lacking.[1]

The availability of capital may be a matter of future *expectation* rather than present reality, as the following examples show: (*a*) In 1896, the general expectation was that the election of McKinley and the adoption of the gold standard would give rise to a season of prosperity; this expectation provided a sense of opportunity for investment and availability of resources.[2] (*b*) In the period preceding the Mississippi Bubble, John Law introduced a number of banking reforms. Though these measures did not solve all of France's financial problems, they breathed confidence into such methods of bringing the desperate government into solvency.[3]

The necessity for available funds accounts in part for the fact that speculative booms usually cluster *after* substantial periods of prosperity. In the wake of depressions persons are still paying off on unwise investments, and this is reinforced by "the decline in commercial and industrial profits, the fall in the value of new investments, by bankruptcies, and other phenomena of severe depression."[4] All of these sap sources of funds which might flow into speculative booms.

Conditions of Strain Underlying the Political Bandwagon. Many

---

[1] Cole, "Agricultural Crazes," *op. cit.*, p. 638.
[2] Hickernell, *Financial and Business Forecasting*, Vol. II, p. 403.
[3] A. Thiers, *The Mississippi Bubble* (New York, 1859), Ch. II.
[4] Gayer, Rostow, and Schwartz, *The Growth and Fluctuation of the British Economy 1790–1850*, Vol. II, p. 559. See also Galbraith, *The Great Crash*, p. 176.

The Craze

conditions of strain are "built into" the procedures of the American nominating convention, and hence are "forced upon" the major political parties every four years. What are these conditions of strain?

First, because national elections for the executive must occur by law every four years, this creates an automatic period of ambiguity for both parties—ambiguity concerning their best plan of attack to retain or gain office. How effective has party leadership been for the past four years? How successful have the leaders been in pursuing party policy in government or in developing an opposition to the administration? Parties must ask these questions of their leadership, but they do not have completely unambiguous criteria with which to arrive at answers.[1]

A related kind of ambiguity concerns the pattern of leadership which will be most successful in winning the election and governing the country in years to come.[2] More specifically, who should be selected as presidential and vice-presidential candidates?[3] In many cases this ambiguity is reduced by political maneuvering prior to the nominating convention. In the case of self-succession of a popular leader (Grant in 1872, McKinley in 1900, Theodore Roosevelt in 1904, Franklin D. Roosevelt in 1936, 1940, and 1944, and Eisenhower in 1956), there is little ambiguity concerning the nomination.[4] The same is true when a leader is able to hand-pick his successor (e.g., Van Buren chosen by Jackson in 1835, Taft chosen by Theodore Roosevelt in 1908).[5] Furthermore, if large numbers of delegates can

[1] This parallels the economic problem of ambiguity as to the returns from an existing pattern of investment.

[2] For a discussion of the uncertainties the parties face in predicting their own fate at the coming election, cf. David, Goldman, and Bain, *The Politics of National Party Conventions*, pp. 442–477. This political ambiguity parallels the economic ambiguity as to the payoff expected from alternative investments.

[3] By a kind of averaging procedure, David, Goldman, and Bain have isolated certain common characteristics of nominees and candidates for the nomination. They found that important limiting factors on choices were geography, age, education and educational background, governmental experience and position, and previous electoral success. It is important to note, however, that these are only limiting factors, and that "there is no single pattern of characteristics for presidential nominees that the conventions will invariably choose." *Ibid.*, pp. 128–163.

[4] David, Goldman, and Bain have calculated that "in 17 of the 63 major-party nominations since the beginnings of the convention system [1832 to 1956], the party conventions confirmed an existing leadership by renominating an incumbent President; eight of the cases were Democratic, and nine Republican. In addition, titular leaders have been renominated by the Democrats four times and by the Republicans once, producing a total of 22 cases of leadership confirmation." *Ibid.*, p. 427.

[5] Bain, *Convention Decisions and Voting Records*, pp. 20–23, 171–174. David, Goldman, and Bain have calculated that inheritance of leadership has characterized six nominations between 1832 and 1956. *The Politics of National Party Conventions*, pp. 427, 432.

The Craze

be lined up in advance of the convention (as in the case of both presidential candidates in the 1960 conventions), ambiguity is reduced, and the chances of a bandwagon lessen correspondingly.[1]

Sometimes prior commitments of delegates are not sufficient to guarantee early nomination.[2] This occurs when various factions are unable to come to agreement before the convention itself.[3] In such cases a tremendous residue of uncertainty remains as to the choice of nominees. Stoddard has described this uncertainty as follows:

> "What is there to fear?" asked a hopeful supporter of Blaine just before the 1880 Republican convention.
> "The Great Unknown!" replied the Maine statesman.
> Blaine had been overwhelmed in the 1876 convention by Governor Rutherford B. Hayes of Ohio, who was not regarded as a probable nominee when the roll call began. In the convention just about to meet, the unexpected nomination of Garfield was to justify the Blaine prophecy.
> Nor is that example unique [examples of Wendell Willkie in 1940, Grover Cleveland in 1884, William Jennings Bryan in 1896, Woodrow Wilson in 1912, all of whom were unanticipated winners]. . . .
> Truly, no one can say of a convention, "It can't happen here." The established fact is that no one can foretell what may happen when eleven hundred delegates from all sections of our country and with opinions often as far apart as our national boundaries, undertake to agree upon the candidate for President having surest promise of election.[4]

Such uncertainty becomes critical in the face of an impasse on the convention floor—the presence of two or more candidates who have solid (sometimes rigid) support, but none of whom has the necessary majority or the immediate hope of swinging one.[5] The ambiguity is

---

[1] David, Goldman, and Bain have calculated that conventions have accepted "inner group selection" in 10 of the 63 major-party conventions between 1832 and 1956. *The Politics of National Party Conventions*, p. 432.

[2] The Democratic two-thirds rule, instigated by Jackson in 1832 and not abrogated until 1936, made the mustering of prior commitments by any one faction or candidate very difficult. For a brief history of the two-thirds rule, *ibid.*, pp. 208–213.

[3] David, Goldman, and Bain have calculated that seven conventions have been characterized by "compromise at the end of a factional struggle," and that 18 have been "factional victories in situations of insurgent or coordinate factionalism." *Ibid.*, pp. 432–433.

[4] *Presidential Sweepstakes*, pp. 26–29. For further discussion of ambiguity in the nominating process, cf. Bain, *Convention Decisions and Voting Records*, pp. 1–2.

[5] The degree of ambiguity that conventions face may be subject to long-term changes. Moos and Hess have maintained that "it . . . takes fewer ballots to reach agreement now because much of the real struggle for the nomination goes on during the preconvention period. As the scene of battle shifts, the convention outcome is becoming more of a foregone conclusion." M. Moos and S. Hess, *Hats in the Ring* (New York, 1960), p. 136.

The Craze

this: a goal (nomination) must be achieved, but there is strong disagreement (therefore uncertainty) as to how it is best to be achieved. On a few occasions in American political history this disagreement has been sufficiently intense that the party split and gave birth to a third party.[1] In most cases, however, the need for party unity to ensure any chance of electoral victory has led to a break in the impasse at the convention itself. This frequently takes the form of the development of a bandwagon for one candidate—sometimes a "dark horse"—who, in the situation of ambiguity and conflict, is swept in by stampede. Later in the chapter we shall examine the mechanisms of this stampede. Let us now merely list a few of the occasions in which deadlock gave rise to a political craze: the nomination of Polk in 1844 after a prolonged deadlock between Van Buren and Lewis Cass; the nomination of General Winfield Scott in 1852 after a long deadlock between him and Fillmore; the nomination of Franklin Pierce, a dark horse, after a deadlock among Cass, William L. Marcy, and James Buchanan; the nomination of Buchanan in 1856 after a deadlock among him, Pierce, and Stephen A. Douglas; the nomination of Horatio Seymour in 1868 after unsuccessful attempts to nominate George H. Pendleton, Andrew Johnson, and Thomas Hendricks; the nomination of Hayes in 1876 after a deadlock among him, Roscoe Conkling, Oliver P. Morton, James G. Blaine, and Benjamin H. Bristow; the nomination of Garfield, a dark horse, in 1880, after a deadlock among Blaine, Grant, and John Sherman; the nomination of Harrison in 1888 after a deadlock among numerous candidates; the nomination of Wilson in 1912 after a deadlock among him, Champ Clark, Oscar W. Underwood and Judson Harmon; the nomination of Harding in 1920 after a deadlock among Leonard Wood, Frank Lowden, and Hiram Johnson; the nomination of James Cox in 1920 after a deadlock among him, William McAdoo, A. Mitchell Palmer, and Alfred E. Smith; the nomination of James Davis in 1924 after a deadlock among him, McAdoo, and Smith.[2]

A further condition for a political bandwagon is the availability of "facilities." In the political arena these take the form of the political support that a party can lend a candidate during the subsequent electoral campaign. Under our two-party system, both parties have the *possibility* of gaining access to power. Though many one-sided

---

[1] Examples are the Democratic convention of 1860, the Republican convention of 1912, and the Democratic convention of 1948. Bain, *Convention Decisions and Voting Records*, pp. 61–67, 72–76, 178–184, 272–277. See also Bishop, *Our Political Drama*, pp. 68–72.

[2] Bain, *Convention Decisions and Voting Records*, pp. 31–35, 44–47, 47–51, 56–60, 88–92, 99–105, 109–116, 136–141, 184–192, 200–208, 208–214, 218–226.

The Craze

elections have occurred in our history, and though parties have sometimes become very demoralized,[1] the institutionalization of two parties virtually guarantees the opposition a chance of access to office if the party in power bungles sufficiently or if enough grievances accumulate between elections. In this way the two-party system provides facilities, in the form of meaningful support, for both major parties. If it were a foregone conclusion that a party had no hope whatsoever of winning in the coming election, no bandwagon would occur at its convention, for the party would have no power to invest in the candidate.

Given this complex of strains—some of which reside in the institutional structure of the party system, and some of which rise from the ebbs and flows of the political process—the stage for the bandwagon is set. Later in the chapter we shall trace the development of the bandwagon.

Conditions of Strain Underlying the Fashion Cycle. As in the political case, many of the strains that give rise to the fashion cycle are institutionalized; by examining the typical course of this cycle, however, we can see how these institutionalized strains periodically create conditions of ambiguity.

The first condition of ambiguity concerns the lessening appropriateness of a given item of fashion to symbolize status. Many observers have noted the tendency for the upper classes to desert an item of fashion as soon as it ceases to differentiate the holder from others who have adopted it.[2] In this way, "as fashion spreads, it gradually goes to its doom."[3] The effect of such behavior is the constant re-creation of the "trickle-effect," by which there is gradual passage of fashions from, say, Paris, which are imitated in America in "limited editions" of varying degrees of exclusiveness, and which may drift down to the lower-priced retail brackets. But as soon as everyone has adopted a pattern, or a cheaper version of it,[4] this means that it has lost its distinctively "fashionable" character of being used "at one time only by a portion of the given group, the great majority being merely on the road to adopting it."[5] This effect is shown in the contrasting advertisements in various class-level

---

[1] For example, the Democratic Party between 1900 and 1908, *Ibid.*, pp. 161–163, 167–170, 174–177.
[2] Simmel, "Fashion," *op. cit.*, pp. 133, 135–136, 138–139; Flugel, *The Psychology of Clothes*, p. 139; Goffman, "Symbols of Class Status," *op. cit.*, pp. 302–303.
[3] Simmel, "Fashion," *op. cit.*, pp. 138–139.
[4] On modes of vulgarization, cf. Goffman, "Symbols of Class Status," *op. cit.*, pp. 303–304.
[5] Simmel, "Fashion," *op. cit.*, p. 138. This process parallels the "drying-up" of investment opportunities in the economic sphere, and the uncertainty as to the effectiveness of existing political leadership in the political sphere.

magazines. At the "high-fashion" levels the emphasis is on the daring and the unusual patterns, and on the theme of "the elite are wearing it." In contrast, the middle or lower-middle class advertisements shun the experimental and emphasize the theme of "everybody's wearing it."[1] This pattern of initiating and "filling-up" is highly institutionalized by year and season.[2] For our purposes it is important to note only that this pattern continuously re-creates the conditions of diminishing returns on any given fashion pattern.[3]

The same "filling-up" principle applies to fads as well. Meyersohn and Katz outline the phases of "dissemination, eventual loss of exclusiveness and uniqueness, and death by displacement" in the natural history of fads.[4] In her study of fad patterns over a two-year period among undergraduate women, Janney noted a small class of clique-leaders who initiated fads of various sorts; a group of conforming faddists (by far the largest group) who followed, after some delay, the fads initiated by the leaders; and a small group of "egregious faddists," or compulsive conformists, none of whom were clique leaders and whose adoption of an item was generally "the quickest way to kill a fad."[5] Such evidence, though limited, indicates that the same "trickle" effect exists for fads as well as fashions, and generally creates the conditions for terminating one fad and initiating another.[6]

The second element of strain is a corresponding uncertainty as to the appropriate *new* item which will be adopted in the next cycle of fashion. Certain conditions limit the freedom to innovate in fashion. The item in question must symbolize *roughly* some kind of role of the user—such as business, entertainment, or leisure—and cannot overstep the limits set by conventional dress in these roles.[7] In

[1] Barber and Lobel, " 'Fashion' in Women's Clothes and the American Social System," *op. cit.*, pp. 128–129.
[2] Young, *Recurring Cycles of Fashion, 1760–1937*, pp. 204–205.
[3] Longer-term instabilities in fashion occur in periods during which entire systems of stratification are disrupted as in revolutions and other periods of rapid social change. Cf. Richardson and Kroeber, "Three Centuries of Women's Dress Fashions: A Quantitative Analysis," *op. cit.*, pp. 149–150; Bell, *On Human Finery*, p. 84. Though this erratic behaviour on the part of fashions in such periods could be interpreted according to the conceptual scheme we have developed, we shall restrict our interest to recurrent, institutionalized cycles.
[4] "Notes on a Natural History of Fads," *op. cit.*, p. 594. Quoted from abstract of article.
[5] "Fad and Fashion Leadership among Undergraduate Women," *op. cit.*, pp. 275–276.
[6] Unstructured situations generally and periods of "social stress and strain" make for instability in the adoption of fads. Turner and Killian, *Collective Behavior*, p. 211; D. Katz and R. L. Schank, *Social Psychology* (New York, 1938), pp. 29–30. Such instability parallels the fluctuations of fashion in periods of social turmoil.
[7] Doob, *Social Psychology*, pp. 396–397; Janney noted that "the types of fads

addition, modesty restricts extreme deviations.[1] Nevertheless, there is not, and cannot be, exact predictability—even on the part of designers of fashions—as to the precise item which will be adopted in the coming season:

> ... the producers of fashion as a group are not so all-powerful as the writers of the theological literature of fashion, in their more inspired utterances, would lead us to suppose.
> ... fashions cannot be entirely accounted for in terms of individuals, either on the side of the producers or the wearers. For a new style of dress to become fashionable, it must in some way appeal to a large number of people. The mysterious dictates of Paris are, as a matter of fact, by no means always obeyed.[2]

As in the choice of a particular line of economic investment and the choice of a political candidate, there is always an element of uncertainty in predicting the success of any particular item of fashion.

The third element underlying a fashion cycle lies in the availability of facilities for investment in new styles. For these we refer back to the conditions of structural conduciveness which make for a more flexible system of status-symbolization—decline of barriers to imitation, cheapening of products, enhanced mobility, etc.[3] All these create a greater ability to maneuver, to imitate, to "be in fashion." This supply of "facilities" for fashion behavior, though variable, continues through prosperity and depression. Only in periods of social tumult is the question of style and display *in general* brought into question, and this usually accompanies a larger conflict or revolution in class relations.[4]

Conditions of Strain Underlying the Religious Revival. The structural strains underlying the revival are perhaps most elusive, because data are lacking and because so many of the operative factors— "hidden" in the institutionalized features of the churches—do not appear so clearly as in other forms of the craze. A further difficulty lies in the fact that the strains which initiate the religious revival are very similar to those which set off other kinds of collective outbursts —messianic and nativistic cults, reform movements, revolutionary movements, and so on. Finally, we must be wary of oversimplified

---

bore certain resemblances to the types of social activities engaged in by the cliques in question." "Fad and Fashion Leadership among Undergraduate Women," *op. cit.*, p. 275; Barber and Lobel, " 'Fashion' in Women's Clothes and the American Social System," *op. cit.*, p. 130.

[1] N. K. Jack and B. Schiffer, "The Limits of Fashion Control," *American Sociological Review*, Vol. 13 (1948), pp. 730–738.
[2] Flugel, *The Psychology of Clothes*, pp. 146–147.
[3] Above, pp. 184–186.
[4] Bell, *On Human Finery*, p. 84.

The Craze

correlations between revivalism on the one hand and economic or political crisis, important elections, personalities of revivalists, etc.[1] Nevertheless, a common pattern of strain seems to make its appearance before revivals, and to conform to the general picture of structural strain underlying crazes in general.

The first common element seems to be that far-reaching social changes in the recent past have reduced the churches' access to large bodies of potentially faithful who, it is felt, need the spiritual services of the church. This may result from a tremendous expansion of the frontier, as in the periods preceding the Great Awakening of the early eighteenth century and that which spanned the end of the eighteenth and the beginning of the nineteenth.[2] Or it may be associated with the rise of cities, and, with them, new classes of unattached persons who flood into urban centers, as seemed to be the case especially in the late nineteenth and mid-twentieth centuries.[3] Or, indeed, it may be associated with the complaints of a "pinched" group within the church. For instance, rural and village Protestants who had been put under pressure by industrialization and urbanization, and who had also been "neglected" by the churches during the Social Gospel period seemed to constitute the backbone of support for Billy Sunday's success in the second decade of the twentieth century.[4] Under such conditions clergymen and others interested in the church begin to express dissatisfaction; they sense that the clergy is isolated from the flock, apathetic, even decaying, and that people in general have fallen into a low moral and religious state.[5] The

[1] McLoughlin, *Modern Revivalism*, pp. 6–7, 454–463, for a criticism of such oversimplifications.
[2] For discussion of the frontier in the genesis of American revivalism, cf. Douglass and Brunner, *The Protestant Church as a Social Institution*, p. 22; S. Persons, "Christian Communitarianism in America," in D. D. Egbert and Persons (eds.), *Socialism and American Life* (Princeton, 1952), pp. 128–130. C. C. Cleveland, *The Great Revival in the West 1797–1805* (Chicago, 1916), pp. 34–35; W. M. Gewehr, *The Great Awakening in Virginia, 1740–1790* (Durham, 1930), pp. 19, 103–104; C. A. Beard and M. R. Beard, *The Rise of American Civilization*, Vol. I, pp. 524–529; Sweet, *Religion in the Development of American Culture, 1765–1840*, pp. 134–153.
[3] McLoughlin, *Modern Revivalism*, pp. 219–267, 415 ff., 430, 474; C. F. Williams, "The Welsh Religious Revival, 1904–05," *British Journal of Sociology*, Vol. 3 (1952), pp. 244, 246; for a classification of the ways in which churches meet urban change, cf. H. P. Douglass, *The Church in the Changing City* (New York, 1927), pp. xvii–xxii; also J. F. Cuber, "The Measurement and Significance of Institutional Disorganization," *American Journal of Sociology*, Vol. 44 (1938–39), p. 411.
[4] McLoughlin, *Modern Revivalism*, pp. 168–169, 397, 432.
[5] B. A. Weisberger, *They Gathered at the River* (Boston, 1958), pp. 5–6; W. W. Sweet, *The Rise of Methodism in the West* (Nashville, 1920), pp. 62–63; Cleveland, *The Great Revival in the West 1797–1805*, pp. 7 ff., 29 ff.; Davenport, *Primitive Traits in Religious Revivals*, pp. 133 ff.; Gewehr, *The Great Awakening in Virginia, 1740–1790*, pp. 36–37, 71; McLoughlin, *Modern Revivalism*, p. 241.

common theme emerging from these dissatisfactions is the feeling that the church is unable or unwilling to deal with social changes that have, in certain senses, by-passed it.[1]

Meantime, the period before a revival is one of intense exploration —sometimes at high theological levels—regarding the church, the character of religious experience, and the best means to attack the growing problems of decaying religious commitment. These debates and controversies reveal an uncertainty as to how to draw the church from its apparent doldrums. Examples of such turmoil are the battle between Calvinism and Arminianism in the late eighteenth and early nineteenth centuries, the debate over liberal Protestantism in the late nineteenth and early twentieth centuries, and the debate over the new orthodoxy in the mid-twentieth century.[2] We should not reduce all aspects of these controversies—which sometimes lead to a major theological reorientation within Protestantism—to the social conditions at hand; nevertheless, they do occur frequently during periods of uncertainty and despair which pervade the church before religious revivals.

Finally, general "facilities" for reinvigorating the church are to be found in the evangelical—or as Wilson calls them, the conversionist —branches of Protestantism:

> The Conversionist sect is one whose teaching and activity centers on evangelism; in contemporary Christianity it is typically the orthodox fundamentalist or pentacostal sect.[3] It is typified by extreme bibliolatry: the Bible is taken as the only guide to salvation, and is accepted as literally true. Conversion experience and the acceptance of Jesus as a personal saviour is the test of admission to the fellowship; extreme emphasis is given to individual guilt for sin and the need to obtain redemption through Christ. Despite the theoretical limit on the number who can gain salvation, the sect precludes no one and revivalist techniques are employed in evangelism.[4]

In the ideologies of these churches lies the conviction that with effort sinners can be saved and the mission of the church realized through

---

[1] To use the economic analogy, the church is not receiving "returns" from its organizational "investment."

[2] McLoughlin, *Modern Revivalism*, pp. 9, 168–169, 397, 399, 474; J. Tracy, *The Great Awakening* (Boston, 1842), pp. 60–61; Sweet, *The Rise of Methodism in the West*, pp. 14–15, 49 ff.; Davenport, *Primitive Traits in Religious Revivals*, pp. 180 ff.; Williams, "The Welsh Religious Revival, 1904–05," *op. cit.*, pp. 246, 251–252. See also C. R. Keller, *The Second Great Awakening in Connecticut* (New Haven, 1942), pp. 13–35.

[3] At an earlier period of development, the Methodist and Baptist sects would have met this definition more closely than they do at present. Cf. E. D. C. Brewer, "Sect and Church in Methodism," *Social Forces*, Vol. 30 (1951–52), pp. 400–408.

[4] Wilson, "An Analysis of Sect Development," *op. cit.*, pp. 5–6.

The Craze

conversion and individual regeneration. This active interest in saving souls contrasts with churches having more rigorous and exclusive tests for admission.[1]

In addition to the general "spiritual facilities" which reside in the ideology of evangelical churches, there must be available as well certain "methods" whereby the gospel may be spread widely and effectively. One of the unique contributions of the revivalist leaders has been to shape the methods of revivalism to the needs of the social environment:

As American home missionary activity began to shift the emphasis from the frontier to the city, [Dwight L.] Moody's methods seemed to offer a quick and easy system to meet the new need. The religious climate and facilities of the 1870's made possible revivalistic endeavors far beyond [Charles G.] Finney's dreams. Growing interdenominational unity, the general acceptance of modern revivalism, the rise of lay influence, improved methods of communication and transportation, the multiplication of inexpensive newspapers and magazines, and the increased literacy provided the general means for promoting and coordinating urban mass evangelism on a large scale.[2]

Despite radical differences among institutional contexts, then, a common pattern of strain emerges before crazes develop; this pattern involves a sense of uncertainty about existing commitments of resources and about possible future lines of commitment, but at the same time an availability of resources to facilitate an attack on the unsettling conditions of uncertainty.

THE GROWTH OF A GENERALIZED WISH-FULFILLMENT FANTASY

For three reasons we shall devote little space to this element of the belief accompanying a craze. First, we have dealt extensively with the nature of the wish-fulfillment belief in Chapter V; at present we wish merely to locate it in the total value-added process that results in the craze. Second, this generalized element is frequently implicit because it is an enduring element of culture. The "get-rich-quick" mentality, for instance, is an established cultural belief that does not have to be "created" for every new speculative outburst. It is always present, and needs only to be excited by the presence of other conditions. Third, we have already covered the sense of wish-fulfillment in our discussion of the availability of facilities.

[1] *Ibid.*, for a contrast among the Conversionist sect on the one hand and the Adventist, Pietist, and Gnostic sects on the other. Cf. also Sweet, *The Rise of Methodism in the West*, pp. 14–15.
[2] McLoughlin, *Modern Revivalism*, pp. 220–221.

The Craze

Let us review the ingredients of a wish-fulfillment belief:

Fanatical behavior [i.e., the craze] is simply a collectively provided outlet for the feeling of discontent. On the covert side, such behavior consists of hope, faith, anticipation, or the like, which has arisen from a belief in a specific way of escape from the causes of discontent. On the overt side, such behavior consists in acting directly upon that belief.

Some who participate in a fanatical pattern may experience mild doubts.[1]

The components—sometimes implicit—of such a belief are (*a*) uncertainty stemming from structural strain; (*b*) anxiety; (*c*) a generalized wish-fulfillment fantasy designed to reduce uncertainty and anxiety; (*d*) the attachment of this fantasy to some specific "gimmick."[2] At present we shall discuss only the generalized elements—anxiety and generalized wish-fulfillment.

Generalized Belief Underlying the Speculative Boom. Anxiety arises from the uncertainty about returns on current investment of economic resources and uncertainty about the ways to improve this investment. Such uncertainty does not, however, lead to panic, because of an available supply of capital with which to attack the problem. This unique combination of uncertainty *plus* a supply of capital makes for a generalized belief that the uncertainties may be overcome by the proper use of resources.[3]

Generalized Belief Underlying the Political Bandwagon. Anxiety stems from the possibility that the coming election will be lost, and from the incomplete knowledge of strategies and tactics which will most nearly guarantee victory. Subdued anxiety thus underlies the convention gathered to nominate candidates and prepare a platform. At the same time, however, the prospect of success is always present, if only right support is cultivated and right means used. The result is a fantasy of success in the coming fight for access to power. This fantasy is sometimes reflected in the universal predictions of victory by recently nominated candidates.

Generalized Belief Underlying the Fashion-cycle. In the world of fashion, the anxieties about being "passé" or "outmoded" are counterbalanced by the hopes of being "in fashion," "in the swim," "à la mode," "with it," and so on. These generalized elements are not created with each new fashion item that appears on the market; usually they are stable attitudes which people share.

Generalized Belief Underlying the Religious Revival. Anxiety in this belief stems from the uneasy feeling that the church is out of

---

[1] LaPiere, *Collective Behavior*, pp. 499–500.
[2] Above, pp. 94–96.
[3] For a discussion of the ways in which this generalized element is incorporated into institutionalized magic and folklore, above, pp. 97–98.

The Craze

step with the times. Sometimes religious leaders and others attribute their anxiety to specific evils, such as sinning, drinking, gambling, lax church attendance, or the apathy of the clergy. Because of the peculiar ideology of the evangelical branches of Protestantism, however, or because of the development of an unusual sense of anticipation before an awakening,[1] religious leaders also have a generalized hope for coming regeneration.

THE PRECIPITATING FACTOR—THAT WHICH TRANSFORMS GENERALIZED FAITH INTO SPECIFIC BELIEF

The study of precipitating factors illustrates the fact that empirically a *single* person or set of events may contain *many* of the analytical determinants of the craze. A leader, by a series of planned actions, may deliberately "arrange" for the occurrence of a precipitating event, may formulate a belief and disseminate it, and may actually mobilize people for the craze. Speculative booms, for instance, have been triggered by promoters who systematically spread information and give "cues" as to when to buy by manipulating the market.[2] The fashion cycle is advertised, initiated, and in certain respects guided by fashion designers and merchandisers.[3] Revivals of religion are sometimes initiated by the preaching of a single man—a man, moreover, who formulates the beliefs which guide the revival and who mobilizes both pastors and their flocks to join the revival.[4] Despite this empirical fusion of determinants, it is possible to isolate the specific significance of persons and events as precipitating factors in the craze.

Precipitating Factors for Speculative Booms. What does the precipitating factor contribute to the build-up of a craze? Earlier we outlined several types of broad preconditions for the craze—structural conduciveness (e.g., maneuverability in the market) and structural strain (e.g., uncertainty as to returns on investment, uncertainty as to new lines of investment, etc.). What the precipitating factor does is to give "evidence" that a single line of investment will provide a "way out" of the imbalance created by these conditions.

---

[1] For a commentary on the sense of anticipation which built up before the arrival of Whitefield in New England in 1740, cf. Tracy, *The Great Awakening*, pp. 83-84.

[2] Sakolski, *The Great American Land Bubble*, pp. 32-53, 219-231, 232-254, 334-352; Davies, *Real Estate in American History*, pp. 17-18; R. C. McGrane. *The Panic of 1837* (Chicago, 1924), pp. 43-65.

[3] Bogardus, *Social Psychology*, p. 300; Nystrom, *The Economics of Fashion* pp. 36-37; Hurlock, *The Psychology of Dress*, pp. 102-103; LaPiere and Farnsworth, *Social Psychology*, p. 452.

[4] McLoughlin, *Modern Revivalism*, Chs. 1, 2.

The Craze

The most obvious kind of precipitating factor is the appearance of a source of returns—the discovery of a mineral, the opening of new lands, a political crisis that promises to stimulate demand for armaments, etc.[1] The appearance of a wealthy few who presumably have capitalized on this opportunity confirms and exaggerates the expectations of great returns.[2] In fact, a mere rumor of extraordinary gain—often propagated for speculative purposes—can precipitate a rash of investment.[3] All such events focus attention on a single opportunity for investment.

From another angle, the appearance of a supply of capital—e.g., in the form of an influx of foreign capital or gold, or the political backing of credit—may set off a wave of speculation.[4] Direct intervention of a government on behalf of a speculative enterprise may serve the same stimulating function.[5]

Precipitating Factors in a Political Bandwagon. In a political convention the precipitating factor for a bandwagon is the appearance of a candidate or an event that promises to mobilize political support behind a single nominee. Thus it shows a "way out" of an ambiguous and frustrating political deadlock. This precipitating factor most often appears in the form of a significant political figure or a sizeable state delegation which, at a critical moment, shifts support to one of the parties of the deadlock or to a "dark horse."[6] Though such events are frequently arranged behind the scenes and in caucus,[7] they nevertheless have the effect of endowing the prospective successful candidate with extraordinary promise. A less frequent precipitating event is the appearance of spontaneous support in demonstrations,

---

[1] Handman, "Boom," *op. cit.*, p. 639; White, *The Forty-Niners*, p. 58; Duguid, *The Story of the Stock Exchange*, pp. 141–142; Gilbert, "Social Causes Contributing to Panic," *op. cit.*, pp. 158–159.

[2] Mackay, *Extraordinary Popular Delusions and the Madness of Crowds*.

[3] Cf. the references to Sakolski, *The Great American Land Bubble*, in fn. above, p. 203; Galbraith, *The Great Crash*, pp. 71 ff.

[4] Hickernell, *Financial and Business Forecasting*, Vol. II, pp. 394–395, 403.

[5] Governmental action precipitated the South Sea Bubble, the Mississippi Bubble, and some of the post-Revolutionary land speculation in the United States. Above, p. 189. For further comment on the role of political leadership, cf. below, pp. 218–219.

[6] For examples, cf. Bain, *Convention Decisions and Voting Records*, pp. 34, 45–47, 50, 91, 104, 115. Also Bishop, *Our Political Drama*, p. 68; Stoddard, *Presidential Sweepstakes*, pp. 83, 94, 163, 182. For an account of one of the few bandwagon situations for vice-presidential nomination in convention history—the contest between Estes Kefauver and John F. Kennedy for the Democratic nomination in 1956—cf. Bain, *Convention Decisions and Voting Records*, pp. 297–298, and J. M. Burns, *John Kennedy: A Political Profile* (New York, 1960), pp. 185–190.

[7] For brief discussion of the famous "smoke-filled room" nomination of Warren Harding, cf. Bain, *Convention Decisions and Voting Records*, pp. 200–208.

The Craze

which may have played a role in the selection of Lincoln in 1860 and Wendell Willkie in 1940.¹ Most demonstrations are now routine methods or affirming existing political loyalties.

Precipitating Factors in the Fashion Cycle. The occurrence of precipitating events is highly routinized in the fashion world; "this season's" fashions appear at scheduled intervals in prearranged exhibits in New York or Paris, and this signals the beginning of the fashion cycle.² The exhibits are followed by advertising, "shows," window displays, and informal communication about fashion.³ The initiation of fads is less institutionalized; the adoption of an item by an informal clique leader, by a "popular girl," by a movie star, etc., frequently precipitates the fad cycle.⁴

Precipitating Factors in Religious Revivals. The events that "trigger" a religious revival are closely related to the activities of a leading evangelist. In fact, most revivals are initiated by evidence of success on the part of a revivalist—for instance, the conversions by Jonathan Edwards in Northampton in December of 1734, the revivals of James G. Finney in upstate New York between 1825 and 1827, the successes of Dwight Moody in England and Scotland before his American tours began in 1875, and the preaching of Evan Roberts in Wales in 1905.⁵

THE CRYSTALLIZATION AND SPREAD OF A SPECIFIC BELIEF

The role of the specific belief is to attach a general wish-fulfillment fantasy to definite goals and kinds of behavior. In so doing it prepares the way for a craze; indeed, without a specific belief action

[1] Bishop, *Our Political Drama*, pp. 63–65; Stoddard, *Presidential Sweepstakes*, p. 190. For such a demonstration which did not precipitate anything in terms of changing lines of support, cf. the demonstration for Adlai Stevenson in the Democratic convention of 1960.
[2] Nystrom, *The Economics of Fashion*, pp. 36–67; Bogardus, *Social Psychology*, p. 300.
[3] Though the propagation of fashion is highly institutionalized, the sources of fashion ideas are diversified and complex. The choice of particular fashion items is influenced, for instance, by "(a) outstanding or dominating events; (b) dominating ideals which mold the thought and action of large numbers of people; and (c) dominating social groups that rule or lead and influence the rest of society." Nystrom, *The Economics of Fashion*, p. 83. For historical changes in the source of ideas for fashion, cf. Hurlock, *The Psychology of Dress*, pp. 102–103, and Clerget, "The Economic and Social Role of Fashion," *op. cit.*, pp. 756–757.
[4] Janney, "Fad and Fashion Leadership among Undergraduate Women," *op. cit.*; Johnstone and Katz, "Youth and Popular Music: A Study in the Sociology of Taste," *op. cit.*
[5] Tracy, *The Great Awakening*, pp. 13 ff.; O. A. Winslow, *Jonathan Edwards, 1703–1758* (New York, 1940), pp. 160–171; McLoughlin, *Modern Revivalism*, pp. 26–27, 216; Cutten, *The Psychological Phenomenon of Christianity*, pp. 184–185.

could not be sufficiently directed to generate such purposive activity.

Sometimes these specific beliefs exist in men's minds long before the appearance of conditions of conduciveness and strain. Indeed, Eldorados that become the focus of booms may have existed as legend for generations. In this discussion we are not interested in the historical origins of specific beliefs so much as in the occasions upon which such beliefs are considered seriously by a body of persons as the basis for immediate action. This is what the terms "crystallization" and "spread" of beliefs connote.

Economic Beliefs. Before booms people characteristically come to believe that some line of endeavor will yield enormous gains. Sometimes these beliefs have an "indispensable element of substance" which may be confirmed, moreover, by the appearance of a few great fortunes. Realistic promise is soon overshadowed, however, by wild stories of unlimited riches. Of Florida in the early 1920's, for instance, it was believed "that the whole peninsula would soon be populated by the holiday-makers and the sun-worshippers of a new and remarkably indolent era. So great would be the crush that beaches, bogs, swamps, and common scrubland would all have value."[1] Before the English railway mania of the 1840's, "newspapers teemed with the advertisements of schemes offering profits of eight to ten per cent and over, for no scheme promising less received the slightest attention, and it was easy enough to promise."[2] During the South Sea Bubble, "the public mind was in a state of unwholesome fermentation. Men were no longer satisfied with the slow but sure profits of cautious industry. The hope of boundless wealth for the morrow made them heedless and extravagant for to-day."[3] Examples could be multiplied.[4] Depending on the economic setting, market concentration, the media of communication, etc., the beliefs may be disseminated by intense face-to-face rumors, by letter, by advertising, and by other means.

Political Beliefs. The sort of belief which builds up as a prelude to a stampede for a candidate in a deadlocked convention is that he will be a sure winner, that he will command wide support, that he will be best for party and country, etc.[5] In this connection the

[1] Galbraith, *The Great Crash*, p. 9; also Sakolski, *The Great American Land Bubble*, pp. 337, 339–341, 344–345.
[2] Duguid, *The Story of the Stock Exchange*, pp. 146–147.
[3] Mackay, *Extraordinary Popular Delusions and the Madness of Crowds*, pp. 71–72; also pp. 93–94; Melville, *The South Sea Bubble*, p. 34.
[4] Above, pp. 98–100. Posthumus, "The Tulip Mania in Holland in the Years 1636 and 1637," *op. cit.*, pp. 448–449; N. C. Wilson, *Silver Stampede* (New York, 1937), pp. 88–89.
[5] For an example of the spread of such a belief-system through convention

The Craze

symbolism of the convention demonstrations is instructive. Many demonstrations are no more than a routine expression of loyalties to a favorite son or homage to a past political leader (e.g., the perennial demonstrations for Herbert Hoover at the Republican National Conventions or for Eleanor Roosevelt at the Democratic Conventions). On the few occasions when demonstrations may have had a noticeable effect, the symbolic significance is that the apparently extraordinary support and enthusiasm is evidence that the candidate "can't lose" with such universal backing. Even in demonstrations which merely display affection or enthusiasm for a candidate who has the nomination "in the bag," the mob scene gives both supporters and the outside public the impression of overwhelming, enthusiastic, uncontrollable support, with which the candidate cannot fail to win for the party. This symbolic significance of the convention demonstration has contributed to its persistence in our political system, even though its manifest aim of helping the candidate to achieve nomination is almost never realized.

Fashion Beliefs. The spread of a belief that a given item is "in fashion" is highly institutionalized. Its propagation proceeds by two more or less distinct stages: spread from community to community, and spread within the community.[1] The first involves mainly international and national advertising in the mass media.[2] The second involves the influence of local fashion leaders who are familiar with the cosmopolitan sources which advertise the latest fashions. On the basis of their leadership position and command of knowledge, these leaders influence other persons in the community in their ideas on fashion and their decisions to buy. Katz and Lazarsfeld have summarized this process as follows:

Fashion leaders are concentrated among young women, and among young women of high gregariousness. Status level plays some part, too, in giving women a head start for leadership in this arena, but it is not a major factor. There is some indication that fashion influence travels down the status ladder to a modest extent and there is very slight evidence for an upward flow between age groups. The overall picture in the case of fashion is of women influencing other women very much like themselves, with particularly heavy traffic within the group of younger, gregarious women who do not belong to the lowest status level.[3]

---

ranks in the Republican convention of 1860, cf. Bishop, *Our Political Drama*, p. 65.

[1] Nystrom, *The Economics of Fashion*, pp. 36–37. This is what Katz and Lazarsfeld call the "two-step flow of communication." E. Katz and P. F. Lazarsfeld, *Personal Influence* (Glencoe, Ill., 1955), pp. 32–42.

[2] Hurlock, *The Psychology of Dress*, p. 127; Young, "Fashion," p. 73; J. B. Swinney, *Merchandising of Fashions* (New York, 1942), pp. 52–53.

[3] Katz and Lazarsfeld, *Personal Influence*, pp. 331, 314.

The Craze

Some fads follow the same pattern; local "fad leaders" in informal cliques pick up their leads from movie stars, disc jockeys, magazines, and other distant sources.

Revivalistic Beliefs. Revivalistic endeavors have been undertaken in the name of a wide variety of beliefs. The revivalists have been associated with different Protestant sects—Congregational, Presbyterian, Methodist, Baptist, and Holiness. They have differed in their theological interpretations—some have stressed God's justice, others His love; some have been optimistic premillenarian, others pessimistic premillenarian.[1] Again, there is enormous variation in the specific social evils attacked by these men—some have emphasized the evils of the city; others the threats emanating from Mormons, Odd Fellows, or Catholics; others the evils of liquor; the most modern theme—that of Billy Graham—is the threat of communism.[2] Historical differences also abound in the mode of propagating these beliefs. The early itinerant preachers gave way to the camp meeting of the late eighteenth century, and in modern times revivalists have been deliberate, organized, advertised, and professional.[3] Finally, there has been considerable historical variation in the degree of emotionality "expected" to accompany personal conversion.

Despite these historical differences, the revivalism of evangelical Protestantism has been dominated by one central theme: religion can be restored and revitalized through the personal conversion and regeneration of souls. "To [the] one end . . . [of] bringing of people to repentance and to a conversion experience . . . all their preaching was pointed."[4] Furthermore, most of the major revivalists have

---

[1] Sweet, *Revivalism in America*, p. 44; McLoughlin, *Modern Revivalism*, pp. 67–68, 101, 106, 167, 249–255, 257, 280.

[2] McLoughlin, *Modern Revivalism*, pp. 188–189, 138–140, 285–286, 314, 339, 411–413, 437, 510–511.

[3] For evidence on the changing methods of organizing revivals, cf. P. Cartwright, *The Autobiography of Peter Cartwright* (New York, 1856), pp. 45–46; Cleveland, *The Great Revival in the West 1797–1805*, pp. 52 ff.; McLoughlin, *Modern Revivalism*, pp. 12–13, 57, 88 ff., 221–230, 244–245, 304–305, 407–408, 420–426, 488 ff.

[4] Sweet, *Revivalism in America*, p. 14. For Jonathan Edwards' and George Whitefield's ideas on personal regeneration, cf. S. P. Hayes, "An Historical Study of the Edwardean Revivals," *American Journal of Psychology*, Vol. 13 (1902), p. 558; Tracy, *The Great Awakening*, pp. 3–8; Loud, *Evangelized America*, pp. 11–37; McLoughlin, *Modern Revivalism*, pp. 8–9. For parallel doctrines among the Freewill Baptists, an evangelical group which grew out of the eighteenth-century revivals, cf. Persons, "Christian Communitarianism in America," *op. cit.*, pp. 130–131. For the "gospel of repentance [for] the common man" which characterized the early Methodists and Baptists, cf. Sweet, *Revivalism in America*, p. 128; Cleveland, *The Great Revival in the West 1797–1805*, pp. 47 ff. For discussion of Finney's "heart religion," cf. McLoughlin, pp. 67, 76, 106–107, 131. For discussion of Moody's "repenting and turning from sin," *ibid*, pp. 247–252, 169–170. For Sam Jones' reaction against "heart religion" but continuing emphasis on

The Craze

insisted that conversion and religious regeneration will by themselves guarantee, albeit in vague ways, the disappearance of the evils confronting church and humanity. For example,

Whether [Finney] was discussing relations among businessmen, between businessmen and employees, and between businessmen and the public, [he] offered only the same solution for the ethical problems of the system of *laissez faire* capitalism arising in the United States that he did for the evils of slavery: i.e., the personal reformation of the individual malefactor.[1]

Sam Jones in the late nineteenth century admonished the debt-ridden farmers who were protesting against capitalism that "it was a matter of character and not of economics."[2] J. Wilbur Chapman, a revivalist of the transition period between Moody and Billy Sunday, said, "Talk about the difficulties between capital and labor—I believe there would be no such things if the spirit of Jesus controlled both sides."[3] And Billy Graham, finally "preferred to make all social reforms an appendage of revivalism and to subordinate all other activities to soul-winning. He, too [like Finney], held out the promise of utopia through supernatural eradication of personal sin."[4] Such attitudes have won for revivalists the epithet that they are socially, economically, and politically conservative. In the sense that they define the problems of social evils in terms of individual moral commitment, this characterization is deserved.

Thus the explicit or implicit belief underlying evangelical revivalism is that by saving *individuals* the church can be saved and some of the major problems of humanity can be erased. In a certain sense, such a belief is revolutionary, for it envisions a new commitment to fundamental religious values, and through this, the remaking of many undesirable features of the social order. Because of the peculiar ideology and social structure of evangelical Protestantism, however, this revolution is to be accomplished by massive regeneration of

---

personal salvation and repentance, *ibid.*, pp. 290 ff.; even though the revivalists of the social gospel period interested themselves in social evils, their efforts were pale by comparison with other revivalists. *Ibid.*, pp. 283-284, 358. For discussion of the fundamentalist character of Billy Sunday's "theology," *ibid.*, p. 409.

[1] McLoughlin, *Modern Revivalism*, p. 115.
[2] *Ibid.*, p. 308.
[3] *Ibid.*, p. 384. Chapman and a host of others of this period "shared [the] conviction that national solidarity and future national greatness depended entirely upon the progress of revivalistic religion." *Ibid.*, pp. 365 ff.
[4] *Ibid.*, pp. 504-505. The one exception to this complete subordination of social evils to personal regeneration occurred in the work of revivalists like Sam Jones and B. Fay Mills, who, under the influence of the social gospel movement, called for enacting laws to "restrict the evil tendencies of monopolies, political machines, and fraudulent business practices," p. 346. As Jones' opinion on the farmers' woes quoted above indicates, however, he was at best ambivalent on the question of the basic reform of capitalism.

The Craze

individuals. The result is a religious "craze." If religious commitment were defined as less flexible, and if the source of social problems were defined differently, the "revolution" in religion would be more likely to flow into other channels, such as secession, withdrawal, or outright political revolution. In this sense, then, revivalism is an alternative to other forms of protest. When we turn to the analysis of these other forms in Chapter X, we shall elucidate the conditions which give rise to the several different types of value-oriented movements.

MOBILIZATION FOR ACTION

Once a concrete belief is crystallized, the stage is set for action. Penrose has compared the unfolding of behavior in a craze to the epidemiology of a disease.

The course of any craze is marked by certain phases, which sometimes can be very clearly distinguished and which follow closely the pattern shown in an epidemic physical disease. First there is a latent period, during which the idea, though present in the minds of a few, shows little sign of spreading. Next comes the phase during which time the idea spreads rapidly. The number of people who accept the idea mounts with an increasing velocity which may develop an almost explosive character. As the market of susceptible minds becomes saturated, the velocity of the wave—as shows by the number of articles bought in any given time, for instance—begins to slacken. This is the third phase. The fourth phase is marked by the development of mental resistance against the idea which resembles immunity to infection in the sphere of physical disease. During this period, the mental infection wanes; in those already infected, the enthusiasm becomes weaker and there are few new cases. In the fifth or final phase, if the idea still persists, it remains stagnant; either it is incorporated into the occasional habits of many or kept alive in the minds of a few enthusiasts. In favourable circumstances, it may remain to blossom again at some future time, when the immunity has disappeared.[1]

We shall examine three selected aspects of this process: (1) leadership in the craze; (2) the speculative phase of the craze; (3) the turning point of the craze.

Leadership in the Craze. As Young pointed out, a leader in a collective outburst has many functions:

(1) He gives a focus to a crowd which might otherwise become diffused in space and attention. That is, he aids in polarizing and thus unifying the crowd. (2) He verbalizes people's vague attitudes and feelings and gives

---

[1] *On the Objective Study of Crowd Behaviour*, p. 19. For similar characterizations, cf. B. Sidis, *The Psychology of Suggestion* (New York, 1916), pp. 349, 353; Nystrom, *The Economics of Fashion*, p. 18.

The Craze

them communicative symbols, which, repeated and spread, serve later as stimulators to action. (3) He uses myths, legends, and a rehearsal of recent events to arouse emotion and instigate action. . . . (4) He points out the direction in which the mass action shall take place. . . . (5) He may lead the action, although in some instances the verbal agitator gives the overt leadership to another.[1]

We have considered the first three functions of leadership in the sections on precipitating factors and beliefs. In this section we shall concentrate on the last two functions. Frequently leadership in the realm of ideas is not clearly differentiated from leadership in the realm of action, particularly in telescoped sequences such as the boom; the speculator or revivalist who formulates the belief is also the leader who convinces people to commit their capital or their souls. In the fashion cycle, on the other hand, there is often a differentiation between the "style planner" [i.e., the designer] and the "style leader" [i.e., the prestigious user and the merchandiser].[2] In a political convention three determinants—the precipitating factor, the belief, and leadership—converge when a powerful political figure throws his support to a candidate.

(1) Economic leadership. Handman has maintained that in most booms "the major portion of . . . success . . . should be ascribed to the skill and energy of the promoter and manipulator."[3] Standard methods of manipulation—on the stock market, for instance—are "wash sales," or fictitious transactions in which no real change of ownership takes place, but a sale is reported at high prices; "matched order," or buying and selling simultaneously to different brokers or to drive the price up, then sell when it is high; to spread rumors and tips about stock dividends, what people are doing, of impending splits, of successes of new enterprises, of mergers, etc.[4] Some booms, such as gold or silver rushes, are less organized, but even these may fall into the hands of manipulators.

(2) Political leadership. As mentioned, the most frequent precipitating factor in a convention bandwagon is a change in support by a political leader or important delegation, which initiates a pattern of switching toward the new favorite.

(3) Fashion leadership. Nationally and internationally leadership in fashion is institutionalized formally in exhibitions, advertising, and merchandising. At the local community level, leadership through personal influence is less formal.[5]

[1] *Social Psychology*, pp. 394–395.
[2] Turner and Killian, *Collective Behavior*, pp. 215–216.
[3] "Boom," *op. cit.*, p. 639.
[4] Dice, *The Stock Market*, pp. 421–427.
[5] Above, pp. 207–208.

The Craze

(4) Leadership in revivals. Few revivals arise without revivalists—Jonathan Edwards, John Wesley, and George Whitefield in the Great Awakening; Benjamin Randall in the Freewill Baptist movement of the eighteenth century; James McGready and others in the great revival at the very end of the eighteenth century; James G. Finney and a number of followers and imitators in the revival in the second quarter of the nineteenth century; Dwight Moody and a number of lesser revivalists during the last quarter of the century; Billy Sunday in the early twentieth century; Evan Roberts in the Welsh Revival of 1905–06; and Billy Graham during the contemporary revival. This prominent role of leaders in the revival is probably due to the fact that a revival, which extends over a long period of time, must be coordinated and sustained through leadership to a greater degree than a briefer collective outburst.[1] In the few historical instances of "leaderless" revivals—such as the bursts of religious enthusiasm after the financial panics of 1857–58 and 1907—the duration was brief, and the impact on the churches' theology and activities negligible.[2]

The Speculative Phase. In the last chapter we distinguished between two phases of the mobilization for panic: (*a*) a flight reaction to initial threatening conditions; (*b*) a "derived" flight reaction based on the first flight, which creates, on its own, the necessary conditions for further panic.[3] This derived phase gives an accelerated upward sweep to the panic curve. The derived element is even more clearly observable in the speculative phase of the craze, as the following instances show:

(1) Economic speculation. Many writers have noticed the dual character of booms. Bagehot, for instance, perceived that

> The fact is, that the owners of savings not finding, in adequate quantities, their usual kind of investments, rush into anything that promises speciously, and when they find that these specious investments can be disposed of at a high profit, they rush into them more and more. The first taste is for high interest, but that taste soon becomes secondary. There is a second appetite for large gains to be made by selling the principal which is to yield the interest. So long as such sales can be effected the mania continues; when it ceases to be possible to effect them ruin begins.[4]

---

[1] For the exigencies which lead to more structured forms of leadership in reform and revolutionary movements, below, pp. 297–298 and 355–356.
[2] McLoughlin, *Modern Revivalism*, p. 163.
[3] Above, pp. 154–156.
[4] *Lombard Street*, pp. 131–132. For essentially identical distinctions, cf. Hardy, "Speculation," *op. cit.*, pp. 288–289; Gray, "Land Speculation," *op. cit.*, p. 64; Handman, "Boom," *op. cit.*, p. 638; Thorp, "Speculative Bubbles," *op. cit.*, p. 27.

The Craze

An inital promise of profits from returns on investment gives rise to heated investment activity; this drives up the price of land, securities, or whatever. Thus a *new* source of profits arises—capitalizing on rising prices and profiting by time rather than real returns. This constitutes the derived or speculative phase of the boom. Seekers of profit are not interested in real returns, but are reacting to the fact that others are buying and selling rapidly.

It is this speculative phase that gives the boom its rapid upward sweep.[1] Speculation is frequently accelerated by credit mechanisms which facilitate rapid buying and selling; Galbraith, in fact, maintains that "the volume of brokers' loans—of loans collateraled by the securities purchased on margin—is a good index of the volume of speculation."[2] Finally, speculation is frequently compounded by the appearance of *new* investment projects—the "bubble companies" in England in 1720, for instance, or the "island boom" in Florida during the general land speculation in the 1920's.[3] Occasionally booms initiate secondary crazes in banks and other agencies of credit, which are greatly stimulated by the demand for credit.[4]

(2) Political speculation. The political bandwagon also displays real and derived phases. The real phase of support for a given candidate is bestowed by political leaders and others who "place their bets" early on the candidate. As support begins to flow toward a chosen candidate time assumes a new significance. Early support means the possibility of later rewards; withholding support too long is likely to be remembered when the candidate, if successful, comes to the allocation of patronage. It is of tremendous symbolic (and sometimes real) significance to be able to "push the candidate over the top." Once it becomes clear, moreover, that one candidate is going to be the winner, the stampede begins, and political supporters flock to the winner in order to profit from being among the first to throw their support.[5] In this connection the custom of making

---

[1] For qualitative descriptions of this upward sweep, as well as the quantitative analysis of price- and volume-series, cf. Thiers, *The Mississippi Bubble*, pp. 107–108; Vanderblue, "The Florida Land Boom," *op. cit.*, pp. 128–131; Galbraith, *The Great Crash*, pp. 12–23; Posthumus, "The Tulip Mania in Holland in the Years 1636 and 1637," *op. cit.*, pp. 442–443.

[2] *The Great Crash*, p. 25; further discussion of these methods on pp. 23–25; also Weigall, *The Boom in Paradise*, pp. 224–225.

[3] Melville, *The South Sea Bubble*, pp. 75–76; Weigall, *The Boom in Paradise*, pp. 207 ff., for similar developments in the speculation of 1928 and 1929, cf. Galbraith, *The Great Crash*, pp. 51–70.

[4] I. Ryner, "On the Crises of 1837, 1847, and 1857, in England, France, and the United States," *University Studies* (published by the University of Nebraska), Vol. V (1905), pp. 143 ff.

[5] For descriptions of such scenes, cf. Bishop, *Our Political Drama*, pp. 37–42; Stoddard, *Presidential Sweepstakes*, pp. 77–83, 88–95, 170.

The Craze

nominations "unanimous" once a clear winner has been named is instructive. It is the symbolic completion of the bandwagon forces which have been accumulating to carry him to nomination. Another function of unanimous nomination is, of course, to prepare a front of party unity for the coming election.

Limited evidence indicates that something of a bandwagon operates in elections as well as nominations; some tend to vote for the candidates they expect to win.[1] The structure of the election situation is such, however, that the voter's potential political gain by supporting a man merely because he is expected to be a winner is miniscule by comparison with the politician's gain by supporting a nominee at the right moment; for such reasons the "speculative" aspects of the bandwagon effect at elections are much less pronounced than in the convention setting.

(3) "Speculation" in fashion. Faris has noted two distinctive patterns of motivation in fashion-spending:

It is important to [style leaders] to be among the first, in order to reap the psychological rewards of being in the forefront of fashion, and it is almost as important to flee from a new style when it is assumed by the masses. Farther back in the procession, among the followers, the motivation is more purely sociable—persons adapt to styles to avoid being conspicuously traditional, rather than to be conspicuously original.[2]

The first motive is a real commitment in the sense that the buyer is interested in establishing an appropriate symbolic differentiation in his status level. The stimulus to early buying, then, is an instance of what Simmel calls the essence of fashion—the desire to include one's particular kind, and to exclude those not of one's kind.[3]

The second phase of fashion-buying, however, stems from the desire to capitalize on *that which is currently coming into style*. Timing is of the greatest importance in this phase. Most studies indicate that the major motive in fashion-buying is either conformity explicitly stated or the decision to buy only when one is certain that the item is in fashion.[4] Sometimes this decision to purchase at the right time is made at the expense of the desire for economy.[5] This speculative phase of fashion-buying capitalizes on the time element in the sequence of adopting a given fashion item.

(4) "Speculation" in revivalism. The data on the development of

---

[1] Lazarsfeld, Berelson, and Gaudet, *The People's Choice*, pp. 107–109.
[2] *Social Disorganization*, p. 380. Also S. H. Britt, *Social Psychology of Modern Life* (New York, 1950), p. 306.
[3] "Fashion," *op. cit.*, p. 133.
[4] Cobliner, "Feminine Fashion as an Aspect of Group Psychology," *op. cit.*, p. 289; Hurlock, "Motivation in Fashion," *op. cit.*, p. 69. Above, pp. 196–198.
[5] Hurlock, "Motivation in Fashion," *op. cit.*, p. 68.

The Craze

revivals is too sparse to establish a definite "speculative phase" of the revival which follows its initial successes. Two kinds of evidence, however, suggest such a phase: (*a*) In the revivals of the eighteenth and early nineteenth centuries, the revival began first in the "higher-status" churches of the Presbyterians and Congregationalists, and spread shortly thereafter—with greater vigor and numerical success—to the Methodist and Baptist churches.[1] (*b*) A host of minor revivalists generally follow in the wake of a major one, and in a sense "capitalize" on the spiritual awakening which he has stimulated.[2]

The Turning-point of the Craze. Crazes always reach a point at which activity slows, or even turns into panicky withdrawal. While crazes in different institutional contexts display differences in precipitiousness, the mechanisms are identical in all cases.

(1) *Economic turning-point.* If a boom is not overburdened with speculation, it generally levels off slowly:

> Gradually the possibilities of making large and rapid profits vanish and individuals attracted by such an economic incentive begin to leave a boom locality. The price of land settles down to a reasonable relationship between cost and income. In cases where the boom is due to the exploitation of minerals, the fall in the productivity of wells or mines causes a shrinking of the population and the petering out of the boom into a moderate economic activity which continues as long as the mineral is there to be exploited.[3]

When speculation is rampant, the turning-point is sharper. People begin to suspect that speculation has carried investment beyond its income-generating capacities; in other words, they suspect a discrepancy between the real and speculative aspects of a boom. This suspicion begins to create many of the necessary conditions for panic. The broad conditions of structural conduciveness are, of course, already present. As the threat of loss begins to appear, however, the other determinants switch suddenly from those which underlie a boom to those which underlie a panic.[4] In fact, the events which mark the turning-point of a boom frequently constitute the strains and precipitating factors for panic.[5] The following are the most common origins of the turning-point and panic:

[1] For descriptions of this typical sequence, cf. Gewehr, *The Great Awakening in Virginia, 1740–1790,* pp. 101–102, 106, 165, 185–186; Cleveland, *The Great Revival in the West 1797–1805,* pp. 84–85; Persons, "Christian Communitarianism in America," *op. cit.,* p. 131; McLoughlin, *Modern Revivalism,* p. 136.
[2] This phenomenon seems clear after the revival headed by Finney and somewhat less clear in the successes of Jones and Mills after Moody. McLoughlin, *Modern Revivalism,* pp. 144, 282–283.
[3] Handman, "Boom," *op. cit.,* p. 640.
[4] Above, pp. 132–134.
[5] Above, pp. 149–150.

215

The Craze

(*a*) The participants in the boom simply become more and more apprehensive as the price of the investment spirals. It becomes increasingly evident that prices bear "little relation to . . . income yield." Thus in the Tulip Mania in Holland Mackay reports that

> At last . . . the more prudent began to see that this folly could not last forever. Rich people no longer bought the flowers in their gardens, but to sell them again at per cent profit. It was seen that somebody must lose fearfully in the end. As this conviction spread, prices fell, and never rose again. Confidence was destroyed, and a universal panic seized upon the dealers.[1]

The resultant stagnation of volume and prices leads first to uneasiness and then to precipitous flight from the market.

(*b*) Some event may illustrate the clear discrepancy between the real and speculative aspects of the boom. In the Mississippi scheme, for instance, the initial incident which gave the lie to John Law's speculative bubble was the mass purchase of estates and luxuries by those who had profited from speculation; those who did so "thus obtained the real for the imaginary."[2] This drove up the price of luxuries, created widespread anxiety and precipitated the first decline in the Mississippi shares.[3] Manipulations by Law and the French government stayed the decline for a time, but a growing demand to convert the inflated shares into specie punctured the bubble altogether.[4] In the case of the Florida land boom, a number of factors broke the spell of speculation. The Florida railroads, under great pressure from the boom, placed an embargo on freight traffic, thus constricting construction activity. Perhaps more important, "the rush of newcomers who were to buy lots [the real value] in the newly planned paper cities failed to materialize in November and December [of 1925],"[5] thus giving rise to the realization that the land had skyrocketed far beyond any possibility for real profit through use.

(*c*) Sometimes loss of confidence in the boom results from the desertion—or rumor of desertion—of the boom by the very leaders who stimulated it. Examples are the rumors that the holders of the South Sea Company deserted the company at the peak of the boom,

---

[1] Mackay, *Extraordinary Popular Delusions and the Madness of Crowds*, p. 95; also Posthumus, "The Tulip Mania in Holland in the Years 1636 and 1637," *op. cit.*, pp. 444–448. A similar desire on the part of many, including a number of noblemen who were accompanying the king to Hanover, to sell out, led to the turning point of the South Sea Bubble. Mackay, pp. 64–65.
[2] Thiers, *The Mississippi Bubble*, p. 127.
[3] *Ibid.*, p. 128.
[4] Wiston-Glynn, *John Law of Lauriston*, pp. 154–155.
[5] Vanderblue, "The Florida Land Boom," *op. cit.*, p. 258.

The Craze

that the Wall Street Bankers were planning to desert the market shortly after its first plummet in 1929, and so on.[1]

These incidents illustrate how the value-added processes of the boom and the panic intermesh empirically. Both rest on the same conditions of structural conduciveness; both begin in periods of uncertainty in the market; and, finally, the speculative phase of the boom constitutes many of the strains and precipitating factors for subsequent panic.

(2) *Termination of the political bandwagon.* The end of the political stampede is regulated by the institutionalized mechanisms of the political convention and the subsequent election. The bandwagon ends automatically with the nomination of the candidate; the convention adjourns, and the candidate is the party's committed choice for the election campaign. At this time it is impossible to desert him. In formal terms, the commitment of party support to a candidate at the time of nomination erases the flexibility and maneuverability of the holders of political support; hence it removes the condition of structural conduciveness for either a new boom or a panic. Of course, a "delayed panic" may occur if the candidate fails to win the election. He may be "dumped" as a possible future candidate. The widespread suspicion of a loser, and especially a two-time loser—e.g., Dewey, Stevenson—reflects this delayed panic, which occurs only when the opportunity for "uncommitting" one's support arises after the election campaign is over.

(3) *Termination of the fashion cycle.* As the majority of buyers begin to purchase a fashion-item for reasons of conformity—to "be in the swing"—the power of the item to symbolize differentially the status of the earlier class of users is deflated. This initiates the very conditions for a new attempt to symbolize status, and hence a new fashion cycle.[2]

(4) *Termination of the revival.* The sparse literature on the reasons for the ending of revivals permits no satisfactory generalization. Perhaps the churches and the flocks weary of the techniques and message of the revivalist; perhaps revivalism is cheapened by the would-be revivalists who flock in after the leading revivalist. Whatever the case, the revival usually gives way to a period of religious lull, disillusionment, or even conflict and scapegoating of the revivalist.[3]

---

[1] Melville, *The South Sea Bubble*, pp. 111-120; above, pp. 163-164.
[2] Above, pp. 196-198.
[3] For discussion of these aftermaths of revivals, cf. Hayes, "An Historical Study of the Edwardean Revivals," *op. cit.*, p. 573; Weisberger, *They Gathered at the River*, p. 266; McLoughlin, *Modern Revivalism*, pp. 144-145, 452-455; Winslow, *Jonathan Edwards*, pp. 194-205.

The Craze

SOCIAL CONTROL AND THE CRAZE

Because panic usually involves such a complete breakdown of social interaction, almost every kind of control—values, norms, organization, and facilities—has potential utility in preventing, deflecting, or halting the panic.[1] In most crazes, the situation seldom gets completely out of hand because so many "built-in" controls operate continuously. We shall illustrate these controls in detail for the economic boom, then mention similar kinds of control for the political, expressive, and religious spheres.

Control of the Boom. Normative regulation and the active intervention of leaders constitute the two most effective controls over financial speculation.

(1) Normative regulation. As a rule, laws and other norms prevent or mitigate conditions of structural conduciveness in the market. Galbraith argues as follows:

> Since [the great crash of] 1929 we have enacted numerous laws designed to make securities speculation more honest and, it is hoped, more readily restrained. None of these is a perfect safeguard. The signal feature of the mass escape from reality that occurred in 1929 and before—and which has characterized every previous speculative outburst from the South Sea Bubble to the Florida land boom—was that it carried Authority with it. Governments were either bemused as were the speculators or they deemed it unwise to be sane at a time when sanity exposed one to ridicule, condemnation for spoiling the game, or the threat of severe political retribution.[2]

Laws typically regulate the exchange of securities, credit margins, banking policy, etc.[3]—in short, anything which restricts maneuverability in the transfer of wealth. Frequently a disastrous bubble experience itself will call forth restrictive legislation; both the Mississippi Scheme and the South Sea Bubble were followed by legislation which delayed the rise of banks of issue and joint stock companies in France and England, respectively.[4]

(2) Control through leadership. Once the speculative boom has commenced another kind of control is available—direct action by

---

[1] Above, pp. 157–168.
[2] *The Great Crash*, pp. 4–5.
[3] Contrast, for instance, the wildcat banking period of the early nineteenth century with the regulatory influence of agencies such as the Federal Reserve and the Securities Exchange Commission. Cf. D. W. Dewey, "Wildcat Banks," *Encyclopaedia of the Social Sciences*, Vol. 2, p. 455; Hickernell, *Financial and Business Forecasting*, Vol. II, pp. 139–140; Beard, *The Rise of American Civilization*, Vol. I, pp. 570–571.
[4] Conant, *A History of Modern Banks of Issue*, pp. 40–41; Gayer, Rostow, and Schwartz, *The Growth and Fluctuation of the British Economy, 1790–1850*, Vol. I, pp. 410–411.

The Craze

leaders. Examples of this are activities of the government during booms, such as public pronouncements discouraging speculation or manipulation of interest rates. However, because the collapse of a boom is so frequently followed by scapegoating of leaders considered responsible for the collapse, authorities hesitate to control speculative movements:

> A bubble can easily be punctured. But to incise it with a needle so that it subsides gradually is a task of no small delicacy. Among those who sensed what was happening in early 1929, there was some hope but no confidence that the boom could be made to subside. The real choice was between an immediate and deliberately engineered collapse and a more serious disaster later on. Someone would certainly be blamed for the ultimate collapse when it came. There was no question whatsoever as to who would be blamed should the boom be deliberately deflated. (For nearly a decade the Federal Reserve authorities had been denying their responsibility for the deflation of 1920-21.)[1]

Historically the only action which governments have taken during booms is to give occasional warnings (e.g., by tightening credit), which in fact may serve to precipitate panic.[2] Once panic has broken, governments may engage in the attempt to stay the collapse.[3] More frequently, the control of boom-panic cycles occurs after the fact in the form of scapegoating business leaders, reforming the market apparatus, etc.

(3) We should mention, as a third focus of control, the importance of information in preventing and diminishing the intensity of booms. Laws against fraud, misrepresentation in advertising, as well as regulations which require minimum information to accompany sales, are examples of the ways in which information can be brought to bear on the control of speculative developments.

Control in Other Kinds of Crazes. In the political convention, the world of fashion, and to a lesser extent the religious revival, automatic mechanisms of self-termination reduce the need for independent controls. Party conventions, for instance, cannot "lose their heads" to the extent of trying to stampede their nominee into the Presidency itself in their enthusiasm. A separate set of mechanisms guarantees that the political bandwagon will terminate at the end of the nominating convention and that a new set of political rules—the rules of national election—will henceforth control the problem of succession to high executive office. Similarly, the evident institutionalization of fashion "seasons"—as well as more general restrictions

---
[1] Galbraith, *The Great Crash*, p. 30.
[2] Above, pp. 149-150.
[3] Above, pp. 162-164.

on fashion[1]—automatically terminate the fashion cycle, so that no extraordinary controls are necessary. Finally, at least three kinds of controls operate to keep the religious revival from getting out of hand. First, leaders within the church can bring the revivalist into line; in periods of wilder revivalism, the churches themselves have instituted sanctions such as licensing and ejection of errant revivalists.[2] Second, the revivalist usually works in coordination with hundreds of pastors, churches, and agencies, all of which control his behavior materially. Third, over the years revivalism itself has become more instiutionalized, and traditions concerning a revivalist's conduct have evolved.[3]

CONCLUSION

To conclude, we shall comment on the analytic similarities and differences between the panic and boom—both of which reconstitute the Facilities Series[4]—according to the various stages in the value-added process.

(*a*) Structural conduciveness. Many conditions of conduciveness are identical for the panic and the boom—the ability to commit, recommit, and withdraw resources freely. We have discussed these conditions under the concepts of maneuverability, fluidity, disposability, etc.

(*b*) Strain. Both the boom and panic rest on uncertainty about the current allocation of facilities, and uncertainty as how best to re-allocate these facilities. In panic, the threatening situation is defined in terms of inability to control the threat, and closing exits; hence the problem is defined in terms of *withdrawal*. In the boom, however, the situation is defined in terms of how best to overcome the threat with a supply of facilities; hence the problem of adjustment to ambiguity is defined in terms of *recommitment* of resources.

(*c*) Beliefs. The panic rests on a negative generalization (hysteria); the boom on a positive generalization (wish-fulfillment). The wish-fulfillment belief has a component of anxiety, whereas hysteria does not include positive wish-fulfillment as an ingredient.[5]

(*d*) Precipitating factor. In both cases the precipitating factor plays the same role. It accentuates one of the prior conditions—for example it "confirms" the existence of a threat, or gives "evidence" of

---

[1] Turner and Killian, *Collective Behavior*, p. 217. Above, pp. 197–198.
[2] McLoughlin, *Modern Revivalism*, Chs. 1, 2; especially p. 132 for a discussion of how revivalism was tamed between 1827 and 1845.
[3] Above, p. 208.
[4] Above, pp. 84–100.
[5] Above, p. 100.

The Craze

tremendous rewards—and in this way converts the generalized anxiety or wish into a specific hysterical or wishful belief.

(e) Mobilization. Both the panic and the boom have a real phase based on the accumulation of initial conditions and a derived stage which arises "on top of" the initial flight or plunge. The major empirical difference between the panic and the craze concerns leadership; in the panic the "flight model" tends merely to tip a balance of fear and throw the group into rout, whereas in the craze—particularly in those which cover long periods of time—the leaders actually mobilize and even manipulate the headlong rush for rewards.

(f) Social control. In theory the kinds of controls appropriate for the panic are the same as those appropriate for the boom. Empirically, however, certain differences emerge. With the possible exception of the speculative boom, "built in" controls more frequently keep the craze from getting out of hand. In panic the situation is frequently so disorganized that controls, if they are to be effective, have to be assembled "on the spot." This probably accounts for the salient role of leadership in the control of panics.

CHAPTER VIII

THE HOSTILE OUTBURST

INTRODUCTION

The Craze, the Panic, and the Hostile Outburst. To set forth the issues involved in analyzing the hostile outburst, let us consider two common sequences: craze followed by panic, and panic followed by hostility.

As we have seen, the speculative phase of the craze frequently constitutes a sufficient condition for the occurrence of a panic.[1] For instance, as prices spiral giddily in a boom, apprehension increases among stock holders. A critical event, perhaps a rumor that a big holder is selling out, crystallizes this anxiety and triggers a dash for funds. In many cases the leaders of the boom try to stem the collapse; but once a panic has started, stabilizing the market is difficult.[2]

Panics and hostile outbursts also occur in sequence frequently. In panic after panic, the collapse of organized behavior has been followed by attacks on persons and agencies perceived to be responsible for the debacle. In 1720, for example, when the stock of the South Sea Company plummeted

> The outcry was terrible. It is almost impossible to-day to realize the wave of anger which then overwhelmed almost the entire upper and middle classes throughout the country. The demand for vengeance, for ... punishment of the offenders, was universal. Petitions to Parliament were prepared in every part of the country, from the City of London to a borough so inconsiderable as Chipping Wycombe.[3]

Cartoons of ridicule, angry petitions, scathing pamphlets, and threats of rioting converged on government officials and directors of the South Sea Company.[4] Similarly, in France, as the Mississippi Scheme staggered to its ignominious end, "a storm of opposition amongst the public towards [John] Law" burst out. Mobs threatened his life; he fled to Belgium; the French government revoked his

[1] Above, pp. 215–217.
[2] Above, pp. 218–219.
[3] Melville, *The South Sea Bubble*, p. 138.
[4] *Ibid.*, pp. 140–141; Mackay, *Extraordinary Popular Delusions and the Madness of Crowds.*, pp. 87–88.

The Hostile Outburst

citizenship, and "for several generations after the downfall . . ., [John] Law was held in deep and bitter hatred by the people of France."[1] We could adduce many more examples of cries for retribution after financial panics.[2]

Outside the financial sphere the same pattern of panic followed by scapegoating holds. On the day after the "Invasion from Mars" broadcast of 1938,

> explanations for the strange events were rampant. . . . Dorothy Thompson, columnist, blamed the "incredible stupidity" of the victims; a prominent psychologist said that no "intelligent" person would be taken in; another claimed that the disturbed people were all neurotic.[3]

In Quito, Ecuador, a similar broadcast in 1949 created a panic. When the people learned that the invasion was fictional, they set fire to the radio station.[4]

After the Cocoanut Grove fire in Boston during World War II, the public fixed on a succession of scapegoats—the busboy who actually started the fire while replacing a light bulb, the prankster who had removed the bulb, public officials who apparently had been lax in certifying the safety of the club building, and the owners of the club. Each accusation marked an attempt to assign *personal responsibility* for the tragedy:

> Many of the accusations made by the papers and the public were no doubt well founded; some of the persons involved in the case seem to be actually guilty of violation of safety ordinances. Yet whether these violations were the cause of the fire and of the terrific death toll is far from established. From the beginning, however, the papers and the public assumed that such violations, if not actually deliberate, were certainly among the *causes* of the catastrophe. The people felt some person or persons must be held responsible; attaching responsibility to mere laws or to the *panic* provided neither sufficient outlet for their emotions nor opportunity for punishment. . . . This personalization is the rule in scapegoating.[5]

---

[1] Wiston-Glynn, *John Law of Lauriston*, pp. 159–200.
[2] For the after-effects of the Tulip Mania in the Netherlands, cf. Posthumus, "The Tulip Mania in Holland in the Years 1636 and 1637," *op. cit.*, pp. 435–436; Mackay, *Extraordinary Popular Delusions and the Madness of Crowds*; for the demands for retribution following the Washington Land Boom and the California Gold Rush, cf. Sakolski, *The Great American Land Bubble*, pp. 164–168, 272–274; for the reactions to the crash of 1873, cf. C. A. Collman, *Our Mysterious Panics* (New York, 1931), pp. 64–65; for the scapegoating of businessmen, bankers, and government officials after the crash of 1929, above, p. 164; Galbraith, *The Great Crash*, pp. 159–172.
[3] Cantril, *The Invasion from Mars*, p. 127.
[4] S. H. Britt (ed.), *Selected Readings in Social Psychology* (New York, 1950), pp. 304–307. For the reasons why the mob was able to wreak such damage, cf. the discussion of social control below, p. 263.
[5] H. R. Veltford and S. E. Lee, "The Cocoanut Grove Fire: A Study in

The Hostile Outburst

Outbursts of hostility also follow those disasters in which a failure of responsibility is indicated. For instance, two factors that increased "aggressive attitudes and resentment ... against the home authorities or toward fellow citizens" during periods of aerial bombing in World War II were "failure to retaliate" and "visible lack of defensive preparation."[1] Disaster research teams have reported many instances of hostility and scapegoating during and after community catastrophes.[2] Frequently this hostility is directed against external agencies—e.g., the Red Cross, the National Guard, the Salvation Army, civil defense agencies—which have moved into the community during the disaster and come into conflict with local norms and authorities. More generally,

> when ... disaster cannot be assimilated to a conventional frame of reference, the cause of it becomes a prolonged and serious issue. People continue to puzzle over what kind of disaster it was, why it happened, and under what conditions it may happen again. In our data blame arose out of this process of inquiry which followed when conventional explanations failed.[3]

Panics produce many consequences other than hostility,[4] and disasters may give rise to rationalization, magical thinking, regression, withdrawal, constructive activity, and social reform as well as scapegoating.[5] The question thus becomes: what unique conditions give rise to the hostile outburst rather than some other response?

Salient Issues in the Study of Hostile Outbursts. For what immediate reasons are people likely to become hostile after a panic or disaster? Have they suffered deprivation? Have norms been broken? Has there been a failure of responsibility? More generally, what kinds of threats and tensions are likely to arouse aggression? These questions involve the issue of *strain.*

If hostility is to arise from conditions of strain, these conditions must exist in a *structurally conducive* setting—a setting which is either

---

Scapegoating," *Journal of Abnormal and Social Psychology,* Vol. 38 (1943), Clinical Supplement, p. 141.

[1] Janis, *Air War and Emotional Stress,* p. 150.

[2] Moore, *Tornadoes over Texas,* pp. 314–315; Form and Nosow, *Community in Disaster,* pp. 17–21; van Doorn-Janssen, "A Study of Social Disorganization in a Community," *op. cit.,* pp. 190–203.

[3] R. Bucher, "Blame and Hostility in Disaster," *American Journal of Sociology,* Vol. 62 (1956-1957), p. 468. The "data" Bucher refers to are materials on a number of disasters gathered by the Disaster Team of the National Opinion Research Center.

[4] Above, pp. 156–157.

[5] Moore, *Tornadoes over Texas,* p. 316; Wolfenstein, *Disaster,* pp. 199 ff.; Prince, *Catastrophe and Social Change,* pp. 16, 18–21, 34, 69, 145; Form and Nosow, *Community in Disaster,* pp. 17–21; Foy and Harlow, *Clowning Through Life,* pp. 291–293.

The Hostile Outburst

permissive of hostility or prohibitive of other responses, or both. To specify this setting, we ask a series of more detailed questions: (*a*) Is responsibility clearly institutionalized, so that all failures are automatically and legitimately blamed on responsible agents? (*b*) Is the community characterized by established hostilities among various ethnic, religious, political, or other groupings? In such cases we would expect responsibility for unsettling states of affairs to be assigned more or less instinctively to the hated group. (*c*) Are authorities in the community able to control hostile outbursts? Do political leaders and other important figures actively encourage such outbursts? (*d*) What *alternative* means for expressing dissatisfaction are available? Are peaceful demonstration, petition, and political influence permanently closed to the group under strain? Have such channels recently been closed? (*e*) What are the opportunities for communication among the group under strain? Can people interact to form a "common culture" on the basis of which they can take action?

Given these conditions of conduciveness and strain, we then inquire into the dynamics of hostility itself. How is aggression crystallized on specific situations through the passage of rumor, information, and emotion? What is the role of critical events in this crystallization? How are people mobilized for attack? What role does leadership play in this mobilization? These questions focus our interest on *beliefs*, *precipitating factors*, and *mobilization*.

At every stage in the development of a hostile outburst, counter-influences—*viz.*, *social control*—may be at work to diminish the force of the above conditions.

By discussing hostility in terms of these issues, we shall illuminate two vexing problems which continuously arise in the study of aggression—the intensity of hostility and the organization of hostility: (*a*) How can we account for variations in the intensity of hostility? Hostility ranges all the way from mild irritation to violent, illegal attack.[1] The degree of intensity depends on the degree of strain, on how effectively leaders can mobilize an aggrieved group, and on the effectiveness of counteracting social controls. In this chapter we shall observe the interaction of these variables. (*b*) How can we account for different levels of organization of hostility? At one extreme is an uncoordinated brawl; at the other a highly organized, even conspiratorial attack.[2] The level of organization

---
[1] For the wide variation in the expression of hostility among the Russian workers before and during the Bolskevik Revolution, cf. L. Trotsky, *History of the Russian Revolution*, Vol. I (Ann Arbor, 1957), pp. 38–39.

[2] For examples of the varying structure of hostility, cf. LaPiere and Farnsworth, *Social Psychology*, p. 470 ff.; LaPiere, *Collective Behavior*, pp. 529–542;

The Hostile Outburst

depends on the character of the belief underlying the outburst, the kind of mobilization, and the influence of social control.

In these introductory remarks we have framed hostility in the same general set of concepts with which we analyze all forms of collective behavior—the concepts of conduciveness, strain, generalized beliefs, precipitating factors, mobilization for action, and social controls. Before examining each condition in detail, let us comment further on the hostile outburst and its social context.

Formally defined, a hostile outburst is simply *mobilization for action under a hostile belief*.[1] The criterion for identifying such an outburst is its objective as revealed in its belief. Hence our definition is both broader and narrower than legal or political definitions of hostile outbursts such as riots; broader, because it includes scapegoating which is not necessarily illegal (e.g., the Red Scare after World War I); narrower, because it does not include mere disturbances of the peace, revelrous displays of crowds, etc.[2] To fit our definition the participants in an outburst must be bent on attacking someone considered responsible for a disturbing state of affairs.

What the "responsible" party may be to blame for is as variable as the disturbing conditions themselves. A mob, in burning the home of a local official, may wish to punish him for an unpopular political decision; another mob may wish to prevent the introduction of labor-saving machinery; strikers may riot because of the importation of scabs. All these examples involve specific dissatisfactions. Other outbursts of hostility may flow from standing cleavages along class, economic, ethnic, or religious lines.[3] We shall illustrate this variability in social context of hostile outbursts especially under the headings of conduciveness and strain.

Another important point: hostile outbursts are frequently ad-

---

Barnard, "Mob," *op. cit.*, pp. 552–553; L. von Wiese, *Systematic Sociology* (adapted and amplified by Howard Becker) (New York, 1932), pp. 453–454. For discussion of different kinds of organization of anti-Semitic activity in the Middle Ages, cf. L. J. Levinger, *Anti-Semitism Yesterday and Tomorrow* (New York, 1936), pp. 40–41; for discussion of different kinds of organization of mob violence in South Asia, cf. M. Weiner, "The Politics of South Asia," in G. A. Almond and J. S. Coleman (eds.), *The Politics of the Developing Areas* (Princeton, 1960), pp. 215–218.

[1] For the formal characterization of the hostile belief, and its relation to the hysterical and wish-fulfillment beliefs, above, pp. 101–109.

[2] Bargar, for instance, states that "if . . . a party assembles at midnight, in a city, and marches through the streets [blowing horns, shooting guns and yelling 'fire' and other alarming words], few judges would hesitate to pronounce it a riot." B. L. Bargar, *The Law and Customs of Riot Duty* (Columbus, O., 1907), p. 47.

[3] For a sample of the various contexts of hostility, cf. K. Smellie, "Riot," *Encyclopaedia of the Social Sciences*, Vol. 13, pp. 386–388, and D. Katz, "The Psychology of the Crowd," in J. P. Guilford (eds.), *Fields of Psychology* (New York, 1940), pp. 146–147, 159.

The Hostile Outburst

juncts of larger-scale social movements. On certain occasions reform movements like feminism or prohibitionism, normally peaceful, may erupt into violence. Revolutionary movements as well, because they challenge the legitimacy of the power wielders, are frequently accompanied by violence. The primary differences among terms such as "riot," "revolt," "rebellion," "insurrection," and "revolution"[1]—all of which involve hostile outbursts—stem from the scope of their associated social movement. That outbursts of hostility should frequently accompany social movements[2] is to be expected, for, as we have seen, hostility is a component of the beliefs that guide such movements.[3] When such hostile outbursts occur in the development of these movements depends, however, on other factors, especially conduciveness, strain, and social control. In this chapter we are primarily interested in the question of when hostility of *any* sort is likely to occur. Later we shall analyze social movements themselves, and inquire further into the relations among hostility, reform, and revolution.

Much of the language in the literature on hostility is value-laden. Many writers consider overt hostility to be an unwanted source of social instability, and concern themselves largely with its prevention and control. We do not venture judgment as to the desirability of overt hostility. Sometimes violence is necessary to smash a brittle social order; sometimes it merely adds to social chaos.[4] Our aim is not to consider these matters, but to explain, as objectively as possible, the content and timing of hostile outbursts. We shall study the consequences of such outbursts only if they lead to the development of other collective behavior.

STRUCTURAL CONDUCIVENESS

We shall examine three aspects of structural conduciveness: (*a*) the structure of responsibility in situations of strain; (*b*) the presence of channels for expressing grievances; (*c*) the possibility of communication among the aggrieved.

---

[1] For such distinctions, cf. Smellie, "Riot," *op. cit.*, p. 386; E. D. Martin, *Farewell to Revolution* (New York, 1935), pp. 26–27; S. A. Reeve, *The Natural Laws of Social Convulsion* (New York, 1933), pp. 33–34; C. W. Gwynn, *Imperial Policing* (London, 1934), pp. 10–14. Bargar distinguishes a rebellious mob from a common mob in that "the first is in treason and the latter a riot. The mob wants the universality of purpose to make it a rebellious mob or treason." *The Law and Customs of Riot Duty*, p. 47.

[2] Cf. Hook: "Practically all movements of social revolt which have been proved to be successful have been compelled to use violence at some point in acquiring power." S. Hook, "Violence," *Encyclopaedia of the Social Sciences*, Vol. 15, p. 265.

[3] Above, pp. 112–115 and 121–123.

[4] Bernard, "Mob," *op. cit.*, pp. 553–554.

The Hostile Outburst

The Structure of Responsibility. The structure of responsibility in a situation of strain and the growth of hostile outbursts are closely associated. This association can be seen clearly when the definition of responsibility is diffuse—e.g., in high executive positions in business, government, and the military. Under conditions of strain, those perceived to be responsible are expected to take remedial steps. In post-disaster situations, for instance,

> The assessment for the disasters proceeded directly from what people thought should be done about them. Responsibility was laid where people thought the power resided to alleviate the conditions underlying the [airplane] crashes.... Responsibility thus tended to shift upward in a hierarchy of authority.[1]

The officer is court-martialled for allowing his unit to panic, even though uncontrollable factors precipitated the panic; the coach is fired from a losing team, even though the causes of team failure may lie only remotely in his hands; the home government is blamed for bomb damage "almost more than the enemy";[2] prison wardens and political officials apparently are tremendously concerned with justifying themselves to the public because of their fears that they will be scapegoated for negligence after prison disturbances;[3] specific figures in responsible positions (e.g., Wall Street bankers, Herbert Hoover) become the focus of public anger after business crises; government officials and other leaders of the community are attacked in times of famine and drought.[4]

In certain respects such outbursts of hostility are unrealistic because they oversimplify the causes of unsatisfactory states of affairs.[5] On the other hand, we should not dismiss scapegoating of responsible figures simply as "relatively sudden and uncontrolled outbursts of hostility." They are the culmination of a build-up of a belief in which responsibility is assigned to some figure or agency.[6]

In the examples above responsibility is defined in terms of the *failure* to act under conditions of strain. Another kind of assessment commonly made under such conditions is to assign responsibility to

---

[1] Bucher, "Blame and Hostility in Disaster," *op. cit.*, p. 471.
[2] J. Hirshleifer, "Some Thoughts on the Social Structure after a Bombing Disaster," *World Politics*, Vol. VIII (1956), p. 212; Janis, *Air War and Emotional Distress*, pp. 124–152.
[3] V. Fox, *Violence Behind Bars* (New York, 1956), pp. 43–53.
[4] C. L. Guthrie, "Riots in Seventeenth Century Mexico City" (Berkeley, 1937), p. 214; J. W. Heaton, "Mob Violence in the Late Roman Republic," *Illinois University Studies in the Social Sciences*, Vol. 23 (1938–39), p. 90.
[5] Above, pp. 105–106.
[6] Bucher, "Blame and Hostility in Disaster," *op. cit.*, p. 467. Also Fritz and Williams, "The Human Being in Disasters," *op. cit.*, pp. 49–50.

The Hostile Outburst

some person or group for causing the trouble in the first place. This assignment is frequently found in generalized stereotypes which stem from religious, economic, class, racial, and other cleavages.

Historically outbursts of violence and other kinds of hostility have followed the lines set down by these cleavages. The types of cleavages are as numerous as the possible bases of identification or role-differentiation in society. To mention only a few: (*a*) religious divisions, which have underlay violence in antiquity, medieval and modern times, in East and West;[1] (*b*) ethnic, tribal, national, regional, and racial divisions;[2] (*c*) cleavages based on the unequal allocation of wealth, power, and prestige. Slave insurrections, labor-capitalist riots, feudal revolts, riots of prison inmates, etc., are disturbances which flow from such cleavages.[3]

Besides these established cleavages, hostility can emerge from temporary cleavages created by social movements which divide society into opposing camps—each of which defines the other as responsible for a variety of evils. Examples are the hostility flowing from nationalist movements in colonial countries; from movements like anticlericalism, royalism, anarchism, and syndicalism in

---

[1] For examples of Protestant-Catholic divisions which lay the foundation for violence, cf. C. Hibbert, *King Mob: The Story of Lord George Gordon and the London Riots of 1780* (Cleveland, 1958); C. Beals, *Brass-Knuckle Crusade* (New York, 1960), pp. 23-34, 32-44, 84-90; H. M. Stephens, *The History of the French Revolution* (New York, 1886), Vol. I, p. 486; Clinchy, *All in the Name of God*, pp. 62-63. For a sample of anti-Semitic violence, cf. J. F. K. Hecker, *The Black Death in the Fourteenth Century* (London, 1833), pp. 102 ff. For a brief discussion of religious rioting in the Orient, cf. Smellie, "Riots," *op. cit.*, p. 388. For discussion of the hatred between Jews and Arabs which gave rise to the Palestine Riots in 1929, cf. Gwynn, *Imperial Policing*, pp. 221-223. For discussion of the Hindu-Muslim division which has underlain much violence in South Asia, cf. R. D. Lambert, "Religion, Economics, and Violence in Bengal," *Middle East Journal*, Vol. IV (1950), pp. 308-320.

[2] For a sketch of the ethnic bases of much violence in American history, cf. L. Adamic, *Dynamite: The Story of Class Violence in America* (New York, 1934), pp. 3-4; H. Asbury, *The Gangs of New York* (Garden City, N.Y., 1928), pp. 118-120; W. H. Lofton, "Northern Labor and the Negro During the Civil War," *The Journal of Negro History*, Vol. 34 (1949), pp. 262 ff.; and Smellie, "Riot," *op. cit.*, p. 387. On the Negro-white cleavage in the United States, cf. Coulter, *The South During Reconstruction*, pp. 163-164. For evidence of the importance of the Japanese-Korean problem in Japan at the time of the earthquake of 1923, cf. E. H. Norman, "Mass Hysteria in Japan," *Far Eastern Survey*, Vol. 14 (1945), pp. 69-70; for the significant Sinhalese-Tamil cleavage in Ceylon which underlay the 1958 riots in that country cf. T. Vittachi, *Emergency '58: The Story of the Ceylon Race Riots* (London, 1958), pp. 11-20, 94-105; for a discussion of the Indian problem in Mexico on the eve of the 1692 riots, cf. Guthrie, "Riots in Seventeenth Century Mexico City," pp. 152-162.

[3] For the importance of economic and political divisions as backgrounds to violence, cf. Smellie, "Riot," *op. cit.*, pp. 386-387; Barnard, "Mob," *op. cit.*, p. 553; A. Ramos, *The Negro in Brazil* (Washington, D.C., 1951), pp. 38-44; for a brief characterization of the administrative conditions that precede prison riots, cf. Fox, *Violence Behind Bars*, pp. 37-42.

The Hostile Outburst

continental Europe; from abolitionism in the United States; from feminism and prohibitionism.[1] We should not contrast permanent and temporary cleavages in every respect, however. On the one hand the cleavages created by social movements may be assimilated to existing economic, religious or political divisions; on the other the cleavages resulting from a social movement—e.g., abolitionism—may form the basis for new and enduring cleavages in society.

In connection with the conduciveness of cleavages to hostility, it is important to note the degree to which several such cleavages coincide in society. In many colonial societies, for instance, the social order breaks generally into three groups: first, the Western representatives who control economic enterprises and political administration, and who frequently are allied with large local landowners; second, a large native population which—when drawn into the colonial economy—enters as tenant farmers and wage laborers; and third, a group of foreigners—Chinese, Indians, Syrians, Goans, or Lebanese—who fit "in between" the first two as traders and moneylenders.[2] The important structural feature of such a social order is that economic, political, and racial-ethnic memberships coincide. Hence *any* kind of conflict is likely to assume racial overtones and arouse a multiplicity of loyalties among the warring parties. When many cleavages coincide, moreover, a greater variety of specific situations of strain—economic, political, etc.—can open bases for *general*, and often explosive, conflict. If, on the other hand, the various lines of cleavage criss-cross, it is relatively easy to manage specific grievances peacefully.[3]

These cleavages are frequently accompanied by stereotypes and prejudices—generalized attitudes identifying the despised group and specifying the kinds of threats for which this group is responsible.[4]

---

[1] Gwynn, *Imperial Policing*, pp. 65 ff., 150-155, 172-175, 331-347, 360-365; Smellie, "Riot," *op. cit.*, pp. 387-388.

[2] R. Emerson, L. A. Mills, and V. Thompson, *Government and Nationalism in Southeast Asia* (New York, 1942), pp. 136-140; T. Hodgkin, *Nationalism in Colonial Africa* (New York, 1957), pp. 60-75. The same overlap between class and blood position in society characterized Mexico City in the seventeenth century. Guthrie, "Riots in Seventeenth Century Mexico City," pp. 1-19. The same overlap applies to the South in the Restoration, in which racial and economic competition between the rural lower-income whites and Negroes coincided. Cash, *The Mind of the South*, pp. 119-120. For an account of the multiplicity of cleavages which have entered into anti-minority outbursts in the United States, cf. Clincy, *All in the Name of God*, pp. 169-172.

[3] For a discussion of this aspect of social stability, cf. Lipset, *Political Man*, Ch. III.

[4] For examples of these stereotypes, cf. Dahlke, "Race and Minority Riots—A Study in the Typology of Violence," *op. cit.*, p. 425; Katz and Schank, *Social Psychology*, pp. 142-143; A. Davis, B. B. Gardner, and M. R. Gardner, *Deep South* (Chicago, 1941), Ch. II.

The Hostile Outburst

For example, anti-Semitic attitudes traditionally have emphasized the Jew as an unfair competitor; anti-Negro attitudes in this country center on economic competition and sexual perils; anti-Catholic attitudes have clustered around the problems of public education and the interference of the church in political affairs. Different kinds of strains in society will tend to channel hostility into different lines of cleavage, according to the existing stereotypes and prejudices.

Social cleavages, then, as well as the generalized attitudes that accompany them, form a set of structurally conducive conditions for the flow of hostility. For our analysis we take these cleavages as given. In general, cleavages take considerable time to develop.[1] They may result from a long history of interaction, competition, and conflict between two groups.[2] They may result from a social cataclysm, as in the case of the monarchist-republican and clerical-anticlerical divisions in French society which were exaggerated during the course of the French Revolution. They may be imported from one society into another, as in the case of some of the politico-economic attitudes of Irish and German laborers in the United States during the nineteenth century.[3] Whatever the origin of these cleavages, we take them as a structurally conducive starting point for the analysis of collective outbursts of hostility.

The Presence of Channels for Expressing Grievances. Now we consider the opportunities for aggrieved persons to express hostility itself—opportunities which arise because persons or agencies in positions of control are either unable or unwilling to prevent hostile outbursts. The problem of the presence of channels overlaps with the problem of social control. It is possible, however, to distinguish between the existing structure of the situation and the behavior of controlling agencies after explosive tendencies have come to the surface.

Let us first consider the situation in which agencies responsible for maintaining social order are unable to prevent hostile outbursts because they are weak or archaic. Well-documented instances of this are found in two periods of English history marked by heavy rioting —the period between 1660 and 1714, and the second decade of the nineteenth century. In both cases the machinery of authority was present but ineffective. In the late seventeenth century, for instance,

---

[1] Le Bon, *The Crowd*, pp. 80 ff.
[2] Bogardus has suggested a typical "race-relations cycle" through which the native Americans and immigrant groups proceed, and which results in a more or less permanent cleavage. E. S. Bogardus, "A Race-Relations Cycle," *American Journal of Sociology*, Vol. 35 (1929–30), pp. 612–617.
[3] Cf. Adamic, *Dynamite*, pp. 35–37; Martin, *The History of the Great Riots*, pp. 462–464; J. W. Coleman, *The Molly Maguire Riots* (Richmond, 1937), p. 27.

constables were responsible for keeping the peace, and they had the right to enlist every citizen in this task. Many of their duties were onerous and dangerous, however, and frequently the constables were unwilling to perform their duties; they were inefficient in organizing and maintaining an adequate watch and ward. Faced with a riot, these local civilian police officers were often helpless; "the accounts of the riots at Worcester in 1693, at Kendall in 1696, and at Coventry in 1705 show how rapidly the ordinary forces of the law could lose control in the small provincial towns."[1] The army and navy could be called in, but this involved delay; furthermore, the services themselves were characterized by vast desertion, mutinies, and popular suspicion.[2] This archaic machinery of order, when combined with the political and economic distresses of the day, produced one of the most explosive periods in British history.

During the second decade of the nineteenth century, a period which encompasses the violence of Luddism, the effectiveness of the agencies of control had been diminished by a number of far-reaching social changes. Parliament was able to act only after disorders had developed to an advanced stage—when emergency powers or special legislation was needed. Only the Cabinet had real authority on the national level, and it tended to neglect problems of internal disorder. Many towns, having grown to enormous size but not yet having been incorporated, lacked "any responsible authorities able to act quickly, regularly and effectively for the suppression of disturbances."[3] Police administration was archaic in the country districts. With regard to the actual wielders of force, Darvall summarizes the situation as follows:

> The authorities charged with the duty of maintaining order in Regency England had four instruments in their hands, police, voluntary defence associations, yeomanry or militia, and military. The police were almost nonexistent, the regular, professional police force of modern times originating in the next decade. Voluntary defence associations, or the old system of Watching and Warding, which was a compulsory substitute for such associations, were difficult to improvise and were at best clumsy expedients. The yeomanry and militia, the old substitute for the modern Territorial Army, were trained and intended for military rather than for civil duty, as a second line of defence for the kingdom in the event of invasion. It was inconvenient to make use of such forces in purely civil local disorders, except for a short space of time. The only efficient force,

---

[1] M. Beloff, *Public Order and Popular Disturbances 1660–1714* (London, 1938), pp. 129–133.
[2] *Ibid.*, pp. 107–128, 152–153.
[3] F. O. Darvall, *Popular Disturbances and Public Order in Regency England* (London, 1934), p. 238.

The Hostile Outburst

ready to act promptly and able to be used permanently, was the regular army, of which a considerable portion was held permanently at home even in time of war.[1]

The regular army was used most widely in preventing, detecting, and putting down disorders in this period. In one sense this aggravated the situation, however, for the weak local authorities apparently came to rely on the military more and more, and retreated from their own duties.[2] It seems no accident, therefore, that these two periods of disturbances—one at the end of the seventeenth and one at the beginning of the nineteenth century—were followed by reforms in police administration—the passage of the Riot Act in 1714, and the foundation of a modern police force during the subsequent decades in the early nineteenth century.[3]

In the United States, the president cannot take the initiative in sending federal troops into a disorderly area; he can send troops if the legislature of a state calls for them, or if the governor issues a plea when the legislature cannot be convened. At first sight this set of procedures for meeting and quelling disorders is unwieldy. As a result of precedents set by individual presidents, however, this power has been fortified in several ways. The dispatched troops remain always under federal control; the possible delays in the wording of requests for troops have been by-passed in cases of emergency; the president may respond not only to the governor's call, but also to the call of federal authorities stationed in the area; and finally, he may intervene if, in his opinion, it is necessary to guard or protect the "rights, privileges, or immunities" of citizens. Such measures have turned a potentially unwieldy instrument into a relatively effective mechanism where local authorities fail to put down disorderly outbursts of hostility.[4]

Many miscellaneous historical examples show that frequently periods characterized by hostile outbursts are preceded by evidence of an inadequate police and military control apparatus—the inadequate political organization in Baltimore on the eve of the Know Nothing disturbances in the mid-nineteenth century;[5] the weakness

---

[1] *Ibid.*, p. 250. For greater details, cf. pp. 218–273.
[2] *Ibid.*, pp. 265–273.
[3] In that period of public disorder associated with Chartism—extending from 1837 to 1848—British police reforms had been only partially institutionalized. For an attempt to demonstrate that rioting and other disorders gained their greatest foothold in those areas where archaic systems of maintaining law and order persisted, cf. F. C. Mather, *Public Order in the Age of the Chartists* (Manchester, 1959), especially Chs. III, IV, VII.
[4] B. M. Rich, *The Presidents and Civil Disorder* (Washington, D.C., 1941), especially pp. 189–211.
[5] Beals, *Brass-Knuckle Crusade*, pp. 171–172.

The Hostile Outburst

of the legal authorities and the police in Mexico during the seventeenth century;[1] the inadequacy of political and military administration maintained by many imperial powers in their colonies;[2] the absence of law and order in boom towns like those which mushroomed during the American gold rush;[3] the diminishing effectiveness of the Nazi government to prevent looting, rioting, crime, and black market activity as the fortunes of World War II turned more and more against Germany.[4]

The mere presence of adequate police and military forces to control the expression of hostility, however, is not enough to guarantee order.[5] Authorities must be willing to employ these forces; moreover, the forces must be loyal to the authorities. Hostile outbreaks may be encouraged by widespread permissiveness on the part of political authorities, the wielders of force, prestigious figures, or public opinion in general.

Frequently this permissiveness takes the form of legal discrimination. Dahlke observes that, as a background to many race riots,

> Law assigns the minority group a second or third rate role as citizen, and the group attempts to change this legal status. Violence or incipient violence (on the part of constituted authorities) is either officially approved or tacitly approved either on top levels or in some lower ranks where such sponsorship may be open and unabashed; there is a relation of hatred and suspicion between minority group and authorities, and a pattern of petty exaction, bribery and corruption; authorities do not want to assume responsibility for control of a riot or there is administrative confusion as to the control of a riot.[6]

Often this legal discrimination is reinforced by widespread public prejudice against a given minority group, as in the case of the American Negro.[7] Sometimes the ineffectiveness of the authorities

---

[1] Guthrie, "Riots in Seventeenth Century Mexico City," pp. 42–58.
[2] For a discussion of the inadequate governmental and police apparatus in Cyprus before the 1931 riots, cf. Gwynn, *Imperial Policing*, p. 334.
[3] S. A. Coblentz, *Villains and Vigilantes* (New York, 1936), pp. 22–31.
[4] United States Strategic Bombing Survey, *The Effects of Strategic Bombing on German Morale* (Washington D.C., 1947), Vol. 1, pp. 87–103.
[5] Rudé, for instance, points to the fact that before the flood of violence which persisted throughout the French Revolution, the Paris police were, from the standpoints of efficiency, centralization, and size, superior to the London police. But as Rudé indicates, the loyalty of the French forces to the government could not always be assured. G. Rudé, *The Crowd in the French Revolution* (Oxford, 1959), pp. 25–26.
[6] "Race and Minority Riots," *op. cit.*, p. 425.
[7] For instances of the supportive attitude toward race violence in the United States, cf. Cash, *The Mind of the South*, p. 132; W. Gremley, "Social Control in Cicero," *British Journal of Sociology*, Vol. 3 (1952), pp. 333–334; D. Pruden, "A Sociological Study of a Texas Lynching," *Studies in Sociology*, Vol. 1 (1936),

The Hostile Outburst

results from widespread public support of an aggrieved group and quiet public subversion of police activities.[1] Finally, a serious cleavage within the ruling classes frequently leads one faction to use hostile outbursts as a means of hindering or displacing the group in power.[2] We shall examine the importance of divided authority in more detail when we consider revolutionary movements.

Most of our examples of the availability of channels to express hostility have been drawn from the literature about outbursts involving the occurrence or threat of outright violence. The inability or unwillingness of agencies of control to act is important in cases of non-violent hostility as well. We might speculate, for instance, that both of the major anti-left hysterias which swept the United States in recent times (the Red Scare after World War I[3] and McCarthyism) reached such dizzy heights in part because of governmental participation in the scapegoating. In both cases, the government had recently passed legislation aimed at anarchists, Bolshevists, or communists, thus giving a kind of official endorsement of hostility toward such groups. Furthermore, agencies of the government itself took an active part in the scapegoating—the attorney-general's office in the Red Scare, and McCarthy's Senate subcommittee during the McCarthyite period. And finally, the single figure who might have thrown his prestige and authority into controlling the dimensions of the outburst stood by during most of the period of scapegoating—Wilson because he was incapacitated by illness,[4] and Eisenhower, who assumed, until the later days of McCarthyism, a passive attitude toward the whole affair. These observations are not meant to account for every aspect of these complex movements; they do, however, indicate some of the reasons why they reached such huge proportions.

---

pp. 5-7; Doob, *Social Psychology*, p. 292. For an example of permissiveness and support of violence by Negroes on the part of the Negro population in Harlem, cf. K. B. Clark, "Group Violence: A Preliminary Study of the Attitudinal Pattern of its Acceptance and Rejection," *Journal of Social Psychology*, S.P.S.S.I. *Bulletin*, Vol. 19 (1944), pp. 319-337.

[1] Examples of this are found in Beloff, *Public Order and Popular Disturbances 1660-1714*, pp. 107-128; Darvall, *Popular Disturbances and Public Order in Regency England*, p. 207.

[2] Cf. the role of the creole Spaniards in Mexico City on the eve of the riot of 1624 and their sympathy with the lower-class rioters. Guthrie, "Riots in Seventeenth Century Mexico City," p. 214; in the latter days of the Roman Republic a pattern of using the violence of the discontented proletariat as means for a given clique to rise to power both encouraged mob violence and led ultimately to the demise of the Republic. Heaton, "Mob Violence in the Late Roman Republic," *op. cit.*, p. 9-33, 46, 62, 89.

[3] An account of the Red Scare of 1919-20 may be found in R. K. Murray, *Red Scare* (Minneapolis, 1955).

[4] For a brief account of the consequences of Wilson's inability to function, cf. F. L. Allen, *Only Yesterday: An Informal History of the Nineteen-Twenties* (New York, 1931), p. 35.

The Hostile Outburst

Similarly, we might suggest that one reason why scapegoating reached such heights in the 1930's lay in the participation of the Roosevelt administration in heaping blame on the business community and the Republican Party for the economic depression.

So much for the conditions which encourage the choice of hostility as a response to disturbing conditions. It is also important to inquire into the possibility of expressing protest by means other than hostility. Are these other means permanently unavailable? Have they recently been shut off?[1] If so, aggrieved people are likely to be driven into hostile outbursts; under the conditions of permissiveness just reviewed, by contrast, they are "invited" to display hostility by authorities.

In considering means of protest other than hostility, it is impossible to demonstrate rigorously in every case of a hostile outburst that all other efforts must appear to have failed if hostility is to break out. In many documented instances of hostile outbursts, the necessary data are lacking. Furthermore, the character of alternative means varies from context to context in the social structure and from time to time in history.[2] The best that can be done is to illustrate in various contexts that hostile outbursts appear as a result of the gradual or sudden closing of important and legitimate channels of protest.

The prison setting offers perhaps the clearest examples of the importance of alternative means of protest in the genesis of hostile outbursts. According to Ohlin's characterization,

> The atmosphere of the prison in varying degrees is strictly authoritarian. The essential character of the relationship between the administrative staff and the inmates is one of conflict. There is a gulf of fear and distrust in most prison systems separating the authorities on the one hand from the inmate body on the other.[3]

Certain formal attempts have been made to overcome this gulf, such as inmate self-governing bodies, inmate advisory councils, group therapy, group discussion, etc. In general, however, communication between staff and inmates in American prisons is effected mainly by a rather well-defined formal and informal structure of relationships between the administrative staff and the inmates. A finely balanced system

---

[1] If the closing of certain avenues to express protest is relatively sudden, this may simultaneously be a structurally conducive condition and a precipitating factor in the development of a hostile outburst.

[2] For a classification of channels of propaganda, cf. H. D. Lasswell and D. Blumenstock, *World Revolutionary Propaganda* (New York, 1939), Chs. III–IV; for a classification of the tactics used by employers and laborers in strikes to influence the other side, cf. E. T. Hiller, *The Strike: A Study in Collective Action* (Chicago, 1928), pp. 141–155.

[3] L. E. Ohlin, *Sociology and the Field of Corrections* (New York, 1956), p. 14.

The Hostile Outburst

of interlocking expectations exists to control these relationships. The limits of this role expectation system are rather tightly drawn and are easily overstepped. . . .[1]

From time to time prison officials are subjected to pressures which impinge on this system of interlocking expectations. Among these pressures are the exigencies inherent in maintaining a custodial institution; the pressures from political parties and partisan political administrations (from which many officials and workers are appointed);[2] and the pressures from social workers and the general public for humane treatment of prisoners.[3] These cross-pressures on prison officials frequently lead them to adopt measures that close off the usual channels that prisoners use to express grievances. Ohlin summarizes the situation as follows:

> Through the media of mass communications, prisoners keep well informed of the latest developments in correctional principles and standards. Where the administration appears to be making little effort to implement the progressive measures to which they give public allegiance, a basis for widespread inmate dissatisfaction is provided. A review of the investigative reports on the riots indicates that all the riot incidents were preceded by efforts on the part of the prison administration to tighten up the security system. . . .
>
> The rioting institutions also appear to have been characterized by a harmful decentralization of authority with a breakdown of cooperation between different administrative units within the system. The various administrative units operated as self-contained and independent factions without close communication with other units. Competition among the units for administrative control also appears to have been a widespread underlying condition. The net effect of such conditions is disruption of the established expectation system which controls relations between inmates and staff. There appears to have occurred a marked disturbance and disruption of the channels normally established for the airing of grievances and distribution of rewards. The general resentment resulting from this condition was directed, mobilized, and heightened by inmate leaders. The official reaction to this unrest reflected anxious attempts to increase further the security and repressive measures.[4]

This interaction between dissatisfaction (strain) and closing off avenues of protest (structural conduciveness) produces a situation which easily gives way to violence. As one group of New Jersey inmates reported, "riots *were* necessary because by no other means

---
[1] *Ibid.*, p. 15.
[2] *Ibid.*, pp. 16–17; P. and W. McGraw, *Assignment: Prison Riots* (New York, 1954), p. 210.
[3] Ohlin, *Sociology and the Field of Corrections*, p. 17.
[4] *Ibid.*, pp. 24–25.

The Hostile Outburst

could they get their complaints before the public."[1] One of the major factors in the initiation of prison riots, therefore, is the decay of alternate means of handling dissatisfaction.[2]

Similar principles seem to apply to the occurrence of violence in the working classes of industrial societies. Recently Kerr, Dunlop, Harbison and Myers have concluded from a broad survey of industrial societies that, contrary to Marx's prognosis, "worker protest in the course of industrialization tends to peak relatively early and to decline in intensity thereafter."[3] Part of this is probably due to conditions of strain; the most radical reallocation of resources is required and the most taxing demands are made on the workers' traditional way of life relatively early in the industrialization process. Equally important, however, is the fact that as industrialization proceeds, numerous channels for expressing grievances in non-hostile ways appear:

... formal organizations of workers emerge, and ... the forms of protest become more disciplined and less spontaneous. The organizations gradually become centralized, formalized, legitimized, and viable. The industrializing élite develops its strategies and means of controlling, limiting, or directing worker protest. Protest expressions are stripped of the inchoate and volatile character of the early stages. Sporadic riots, violence, explosive outbursts are replaced by an industrial relations system for establishing and administering the rules of the work place. Spontaneous strikes give way in some industrial relations systems to the enlightened, orderly, and bureaucratic strike, almost chivalrous in its tactics and cold-blooded in its calculations.[4]

Labor history contains numerous instances of hostile outbursts which erupt shortly after the collapse or threatened collapse of an alternate method of expressing grievances. The importation of scabs to break strikes, for instance, is a frequent occasion for violence, because it threatens to undermine the strike as a mode of protest.[5]

---

[1] McGraw, *Assignment: Prison Riots*, p. 210. Of course, violence against the authorities is not the only form which hostility takes. Fox mentions harmless strikes (such as hunger or sit-down), self-slashing, and escape. *Violence Behind Bars*, pp. 14–15. Of course, as these possibilities are also ruled out, the probability of an actual violent outburst increases.

[2] Hartung and Floch mention "the destruction of semi-official, informal inmate self regulation" as conducive to collective riots in prisons. "A Socio-psychological Analysis of Prison Riots," *op. cit.*, p. 52.

[3] C. Kerr, J. T. Dunlop, F. H. Harbison, and C. A. Myers, *Industrialism and Industrial Man* (Cambridge, Mass., 1960), pp. 208–209.

[4] *Ibid.*, pp. 209–210.

[5] For examples of violence on the heels of attempted strikebreaking, cf. Smelser, *Social Change in the Industrial Revolution*, p. 229; Chicago Commission on Race Relations, *The Negro in Chicago* (Chicago, 1922), pp. 73–75; Rich, *The Presidents and Civil Disorder*, p. 154. The latter two refer to cases which occurred

The Hostile Outburst

Sometimes the breakdown of negotiations erupts in violence.[1] Lee and Humphrey, in fact, have suggested that one symptom of impending racial outbursts is the existence of "factors that clog or seriously impair the normal and accepted channels of collective bargaining so that industrial unrest has no adequate means of expression and outlet and thus may be diverted into anti-Negro excesses."[2] Finally, violence among laborers tends to flare in periods of warfare against the legitimacy, aims, and methods of the union as a channel of protest and negotiation.[3]

A final few examples of the relationship between alternate modes of protest and the outburst of hostility: The conviction that justice is not being adequately perpetrated through legal channels lies behind many instances of vigilantism, lynching, and mob activity in the history of the United States.[4] Or, again, when political or other authorities fail to respond to demands which in the past have been given a favorable hearing, hostility erupts against the authorities themselves. During the seventeenth century in Mexico City, for instance,

Several times the poor were aroused to the point where many of them went in a body to the palace, but each time they obtained satisfaction quickly and effectively with a minimum of irritation. The viceroys proved equal to the situation. That was not true in 1624 and in 1692. Thus it was that the potentially dangerous condition of society in Mexico City broke out only in two riots during the seventeenth century.[5]

The relationship between alternate means of expressing protest and hostile outbursts works in reverse as well. When hostile outbursts fail to achieve results, aggrieved groups frequently turn or return to other methods. After the Luddite riots in England, for instance,

---

when the strikebreakers were Negroes, thus adding a new dimension of structural conduciveness to the situation. Cf. also Hiller, *The Strike*, p. 103.

[1] Darvall maintains that the initiating condition for the Luddite ravages around Nottingham was the breakdown of negotiations between Nottingham hosiers and discontented framework knitters. *Popular Disturbances and Public Order in Regency England*, p. 64. In Yorkshire, Lancashire and Cheshire the violence was directed more against new machines, against which the weavers were helpless to act in other ways. *Ibid.*, p. 166; also Smelser, *Social Change in the Industrial Revolution*, pp. 227–229, 248–250.

[2] A. M. Lee and N. D. Humphrey, *Race Riot* (New York, 1943), p. 119.

[3] For the occasions in which workers were "driven" into violence and subversive activity by legal, political, and economic attacks on their attempts to organize, cf. Coleman, *The Molly Maguire Riots*, pp. 40–60; A. Bimba, *The Molly Maguires*, p. 67; Adamic, *Dynamite*, pp. 5–7, 36–37, 49–82, 85–98, 157–175, 196–253; Murray, *Red Scare*, 58–83.

[4] J. E. Coxe, "The New Orleans Mafia Incident," *Louisiana Historical Quarterly*, Vol. 20 (1937), pp. 1067–1110; Katz, "The Crowd," *op. cit.*, pp. 158–159.

[5] Guthrie, "Riots in Seventeenth Century Mexico City," p. 215.

The Hostile Outburst

The workers... reverted to other methods of securing a redress of grievances, to trades union action, to petitions to Parliament, to attempts to secure peace and parliamentary reform. They entered into such activities with greater enthusiasm because direct action had been proved in the end, and after a short period of easy success, so dangerous and so ineffective. It would be possible to show... that Luddism was merely an episode in the history upon the one hand of trades unionism, and on the other of working-class political activity, both of which had been temporarily discredited in the Luddite areas in favour of machine breaking and riot, both of which came into their own again, and absorbed the energies of former Luddites, when Luddism had been suppressed.[1]

Communication, Accessibility to Objects of Attack, and Ecology. An adequate medium of communication must be available for spreading a hostile belief and mobilizing for attack. "Persons who cannot understand one another; whose background of experiences differ greatly or who have widely different prospects upon life do not readily mold into crowds."[2] More positively, the gathering of people into an intimate setting—an audience in a public square, for instance—facilitates the formation of crowds because it permits rapid communication, common definition of the situation, and face-to-face interaction.[3] Similarly, newspapers and other media may disseminate news and rumors which go into the beliefs that accompany hostile outbursts.

Transportation, recreation, seasons, and the weather influence the timing and form of hostile outbursts. Many eruptions of mob violence begin on hot summer Sundays at beaches, recreational resorts, taverns, and public dance halls, and on the main transportation arteries. Not only are such settings likely to produce "incidents" such as a fight between persons of two races; they also provide the possibility for rapid communication of rumors and feelings through throngs of people.[4] In the Chicago riot of 1919, hot weather undoubtedly contributed to the intensity of the rioting merely by keeping "crowds on the streets and sitting on doorsteps until late at night."[5] Those who left their homes in search of excitement or violence tended to strike where they could find objects of attack—

---

[1] Darvall, *Popular Disturbances and Public Order in Regency England*, pp. 214–215. Also Smelser, *Social Change in the Industrial Revolution*, pp. 245–263.
[2] Gault, *Social Psychology*, pp. 156–157; also Lederer, *State of the Masses*, pp. 36–37.
[3] Above, pp. 75–75.
[4] J. D. Lohman, *The Police and Minority Groups* (Chicago, 1947), pp. 71–73. Shay has also suggested that lynch mobs are recruited in public places such as pool halls and beer parlors. F. Shay, *Judge Lynch: His First Hundred Years* (New York, 1938), p. 89.
[5] Chicago Commission on Race Relations, *The Negro in Chicago*, p. 11.

The Hostile Outburst

particularly at transportation exchange points, which "provide an opportunity to catch isolated individuals and attack them without fear of immediate reprisal."[1] Several days after the rioting had commenced, cool weather and rain caused a sudden abatement.[2]

Variations in the ecological distribution of hostile groups also influence the form of hostile outbursts. In Negro residential areas, violence usually takes the form of arson, bombing, other assaults on property, and attacks on persons; in Negro slums urban "pogroms" or mass racial wars tend to predominate; and so on.[3] During the Luddite riots in England in the second decade of the nineteenth century, the isolation and vulnerability of the small country workshops account in part for the fact that they were chosen for attack.[4]

STRAIN

Conditions of conduciveness are extremely general. They indicate the possibility of hostile outbursts, no matter what kind of strain confronts an aggrieved group. In considering conditions of strain that underlie hostile outbursts, we turn to the problem of which groups are most likely to take advantage of these opportunities for expressing hostility. Which groups have reason (in their own minds, at least) to attack others? What kinds of social situations drive persons to scapegoating? What, in short, are the strains that give rise to the hostile outburst?

Many strains are institutionalized; they follow the lines of ethnic, political, class, religious, and other cleavages outlined above. Examples of such strain in our society are the chronic conflicts of interest between management and labor, Democrat and Republican, etc. If such cleavages are accompanied by stereotypes that assign responsibility for evils to other groups, strains are built into the social situation and ready to be combined with other conditions that might permit hostile outbursts. Thus strain, like many other determinants of collective outbursts, is often an established feature of social life.

To introduce the problem of strain and hostile outbursts, we shall first explore the kinds of strain which lie behind most American race riots. Then we shall illustrate—in terms of the four basic components of social action (facilities, organization, norms, and values)—a few

---

[1] A. D. Grimshaw, "Urban Racial Violence in the United States: Changing Ecological Considerations," *American Journal of Sociology*, Vol. 66 (1960), p. 117.
[2] Chicago Commission on Race Relations, *The Negro in Chicago*, p. 11.
[3] Grimshaw, "Urban Racial Violence in the United States," *op. cit.*, pp. 111–116.
[4] Darvall, *Popular Disturbances and Public Order in Regency England*, p. 206.

The Hostile Outburst

of the strains that have given rise to other kinds of hostile outbursts. This discussion will overlap with Chapter III; every type of strain mentioned in that chapter could, given other conditions, constitute the basis for a hostile outburst.

In dividing the sources of strain analytically according to the components of action, we oversimplify the actual empirical build-up of hostile outbursts. In most cases a *combination* of different kinds of strain are present before an outburst. A financial panic, for instance, which scapegoating often follows, creates at least two kinds of strain—financial loss for the holders of securities[1] *and* a collapse of the contractual norms under which the securities were purchased.[2] Furthermore, one kind of grievance, during the course of its development, can be assimilated to another. In a close examination of the personnel and motivation of rioting crowds in the French Revolution, for instance, Rudé found the most consistent underlying tone to be "the compelling need of the *menu peuple* for the provision of cheap and plentiful bread and other essentials, and the necessary administrative measures to ensure it."[3] On the other hand, in these same riots, grievances were assimilated to the "slogans and ideas of the political groups contending for power both before and during the Revolution."[4] For any given outburst, therefore, a number of strains may converge and combine in different ways. Our purpose in this section is to dissect analytically the strains which may enter hostile outbursts.

What kinds of strains have accompanied the numerous race riots during the past 100 years in the United States? In the wake of the Civil War and Reconstruction, a system of occupational, political, social, educational and sexual segregation of the Negroes and whites gradually crystallized, both in the South and North. A system of discrimination relegated Negroes to an unskilled, politically disenfranchised, less literate, and socially and residentially inferior position.[5] In periods of war, demobilization after war, and rapid industrial expansion—all marked by rapid geographical and vertical mobility, labor shortages, mass racial migration, etc.—pressure on these norms accumulates.[6] Economic needs induce employers to

---

[1] This is strain in the Mobilization Series. Above, pp. 55–56.
[2] This is strain in the Normative Series. Above, pp. 60–61.
[3] Rudé, *The Crowd in the French Revolution*, pp. 196–200.
[4] *Ibid.*, p. 199.
[5] This system of segregation has been described classically in G. Myrdall, *An American Dilemma* (New York, 1944); J. Dollard, *Class and Caste in a Southern Community* (New York, 1957); Davis and Gardner, *Deep South*. Cf. also Pope, *Millhands and Preachers*, pp. 12–13.
[6] Dahlke, "Race and Minority Riots," *op. cit.*, p. 425; this is not the *only* source of pressure on the norms of discrimination. Political movements and

hire and promote Negroes; ecological pressures make for expansion of the Negro population into new residential, educational, and recreational areas. One consequence of this pressure is to increase the competition among the races for wealth, power, housing, recreational facilities, etc.[1] Such competition often brings diffuse hatreds between the races into the open; together these conflicts of interest, norms, and values may bring tensions to the boiling point.

To illustrate this general summary: Race riots have occurred during or after wars in cities which have experienced a large influx of Negroes and whites.[2] Such a setting created discomfort for both races. Whites, previously in a position unchallenged by Negroes, were threatened by economic, political, and residential competition. Such threats were heightened if the whites had traditional Southern backgrounds.[3] For Negroes, the new urban setting brought new expectations concerning wealth, status, and political power. Discrimination in such a setting was likely to be psychologically more disruptive than in the traditional South.[4]

Depending on the characteristics of the community involved, hostility tends to focus on a particular issue—housing, recreational facilities, job discrimination, etc.[5] In the anti-conscription riots during the Civil War in New York, Newark, Jersey City, Troy and Boston, one major factor was the fears of job usurpation if Negroes were emancipated.[6] In East St. Louis, in 1917, one of the country's bloodiest riots was set off when it became apparent to the workers that Negroes were being brought into the community as scabs.[7] Economic competition precipitated racial violence in Tulsa in 1921, Detroit and Mobile, Alabama, in 1943, and in Athens, Alabama, in 1946.[8]

---

governmental pressure for desegregation may also provide the focus, as is the case in the educational crisis in the South during the 1950's and 1960's.

[1] This pressure focuses on the Mobilization Component. Above, pp. 56–58.

[2] Cf. the tremendous Negro migration to various Northern cities in the period 1916-18. H. H. Donald, "The Negro Migration of 1916–18," *The Journal of Negro History*, Vol. 6 (1921), pp. 434–439; Chicago Commission on Race Relations, *The Negro in Chicago*, pp. 79–80; W. F. White, "The Eruption of Tulsa," *The Nation*, Vol. 112 (1921), p. 909. For the situation in Detroit between 1940 and 1943, J. F. Scott and G. C. Homans, "Reflections on the Wildcat Strikes," *American Sociological Review*, Vol. 12 (1947), pp. 278–279.

[3] E. Brown, *Why Race Riots?* (1944), pp. 5–6; Scott and Homans, "Reflections on the Wildcat Strikes," *op. cit.*, p. 279.

[4] Lee and Humphrey, *Race Riot*, pp. 9–10; Donald, "The Negro Migration of 1916–18," *op. cit.*, pp. 445 ff.

[5] Cf. Clark, "Group Violence," *op. cit.*, p. 319.

[6] Lofton, "Northern Labor and the Negro During the Civil War," *op. cit.*, pp. 262–272.

[7] Chicago Commission on Race Relations, *The Negro in Chicago*, pp. 73–75.

[8] *Negro Year Book, 1921–22*, p. 79; *1947*, pp. 233–234, 252, 255; Brown, *Why Race Riots?* p. 19; White, "The Eruption of Tulsa," *op. cit.*, p. 909.

The Hostile Outburst

Residentially strains develop in two directions—first, whites become resentful as Negroes begin to crowd into heretofore exclusively white neighborhoods, and second, Negroes feel pinched because their ghetto conditions are aggravated by increasing migration and their growing ability to buy and rent in better areas. Such tensions lay in the background of the Philadelphia riot in 1918, the Chicago riot of 1919, the Sojourner Truth Housing Riot in Detroit in 1942, the larger Detroit riot of 1943, the Harlem riot of 1943, and the Cicero, Illinois, riot of 1951.[1]

The political status of the Negro also changes under conditions of mass migration. By the end of World War I the Negroes' political power in Chicago had grown considerably because of their sheer increase in numbers. Shortly before the outbreak of the 1919 riot Negro politicians had played a conspicuous role in the mayoralty campaign; this activity aroused much bitterness against them.[2] The disturbance in Ocoee, Florida, in 1920 developed when Negroes attempted to exercise the franchise and whites attempted to prevent them from doing so.[3] The race riot in Houston, Texas, in August, 1917, arose from friction between city police and Negro military police.[4] Similar conflicts of jurisdiction between white civilian and Negro military authorities possibly lay behind the more than forty "instances of clashes [involving Negro soldiers, especially in the South] which took place during the [World War II] period."[5]

Pressures on recreation and transportation round out the typical background conditions to racial violence.[6] Such conditions do not always cause racial violence. They must combine with structural conduciveness, hostile beliefs, mobilization for action, and social control. Furthermore, these conditions of strain frequently overlap

---

[1] Lee and Humphrey, *Race Riot*, pp. 92–94; *Negro Year Book, 1918–19*, pp. 50–51, 232–233; Chicago Commission on Race Relations, *The Negro in Chicago*, p. 3; Brown, *Why Race Riots?* p. 3; Gremley, "Social Control in Cicero," *op. cit.*, pp. 336–337.

[2] Chicago Commission on Race Relations, *The Negro in Chicago*, p. 3.

[3] *Negro Year Book, 1921–22*, p. 74. Somerville observed in 1903 that "the localities where [lynchings] occur are, almost invariably, those in which the negro holds the balance of political power, or where his unsuppressed vote is honestly counted and ardently solicited as of value in doubtful contests between political parties or warring factions of the same party." H. M. Somerville, "Some Cooperating Causes of Negro Lynching," *North American Review*, Vol. 177 (1903), pp. 509–510.

[4] *Negro Year Book, 1918–19*, p. 51.

[5] *New Year Book, 1947*, pp. 255–256.

[6] Many ugly incidents on the beaches and in the parks of Chicago preceded the 1919 violence. Chicago Commission on Race Relations, *The Negro in Chicago*, p. 3. A riot nearly developed in Washington, D.C., at the height of the Negroes' campaign in 1943 to be employed on the Capital Transit Company's vehicles. *Negro Year Book, 1947*, p. 256.

The Hostile Outburst

with and grow out of precipitating factors. We shall illustrate this overlap presently.

To supplement the evidence for the presence of strain underlying hostile outbursts, let us illustrate, in terms of the components of action, the strains that have given rise to hostile outbursts in a number of different historical contexts.

Facilities and Strain. Lack of information gives rise to hostile outbursts if other conditions are present.[1] Nowhere is this seen more clearly than in disaster situations. Among the disruptions which a community disaster brings are "inadequate communication, partly because of the destruction of communication facilities, but more generally because of inadequate and improper use of these facilities ... ambiguity concerning what official agency has the authority for certain decisions."[2] Such failures of communication contribute to the strains that give rise to scapegoating in disasters.[3] Ignorance, too, can contribute to hostile outbursts. Thus, in early 1790 when the French peasants launched a series of attacks on chateaux throughout the country, this was caused in part

(1) by ignorance of the French language, for the peasants understood the decrees of the Assembly, when read to them, to be orders for arrest; (2) by fear that the decrees of August 4 [which contained a vast body of reforms] would not be carried out; (3) by false interpretations of those decrees; (4) by erroneous ideas implanted in the minds of peasants by those who preferred slavery and anarchy to order and liberty; and (5) by the circulation of false and forged decrees, purporting to restore the old feudal customs.[4]

Strain in Organization: Real and Threatened Deprivation. Among the most frequent forms of strain in the genesis of hostility is deprivation—real or threatened, absolute or relative. Many times this deprivation is viewed as the *consequence* of some higher-level normative change; for instance, one reason why so much rioting broke out over the system of electoral representation in the Estates-General on the eve of the French Revolution was that many citizens feared direct deprivations if their own interests were not adequately represented in

---
[1] For a discussion of the relationship between barriers to communication and hostile interaction among groups, cf. T. M. Newcomb, *Social Psychology* (New York, 1950), pp. 591–596. Newcomb views the two in interaction: hostility gives rise to reduced communication, which in turn permits the breeding of further hostility. For a general discussion of the relationship among breaks in communication and deviant behaviour, cf. S. N. Eisenstadt, "Studies in Reference Group Behaviour," *Human Relations*, Vol. III (1954), pp. 191–216. Also Turner and Killian, *Collective Behavior*, p. 36.
[2] Fritz and Williams, "The Human Being in Disasters," *op. cit.*, p. 47.
[3] Above, pp. 222–224.
[4] Stephens, *History of the French Revolution*, Vol. I, p. 476.

The Hostile Outburst

the Estates.[1] One reason why many Northern laborers opposed emancipation (a normative change) during the Civil War was that they feared that it would mean future economic competition from free Negroes.[2]

On other occasions, deprivation is real and present. Economic factors, such as abrupt food shortages, unemployment, rising prices, and falling wages are closely associated with outbursts of violence in contexts so diverse as the French Revolution, lower-class riots in seventeenth-century Mexico and in seventeenth-century England, food riots in eighteenth-century England, Luddite violence in nineteenth-century England, American labor disturbances in the nineteenth and twentieth centuries, American nativism, and peasant uprisings in Japan toward the end of the Tokugawa period.[3] The deprivations may, of course, be other than economic. The passage of unpopular political measures may set the stage of hostile outbursts.[4] In fact any frustration may constitute a strain for hostile outbursts.[5]

Strain and Norms. Many examples of normative strain have been given in Chapter III. All are appropriate background factors for collective outbursts of hostility. Normative strain may be widespread, as in periods of war, postwar demobilization, rapid institutional change, etc.[6] Or it may be localized, as in a dispute over jurisdiction in a community disaster,[7] the failure of one party to honor a promise or contractual obligation,[8] the attempt to alter the routine of work in an industrial plant.[9]

---

[1] *Ibid.*, Vol. I, pp. 19–20, 24–25, 42–43, 121.

[2] Above, p. 243. Asbury, *The Gangs of New York*, pp. 118–120.

[3] Rudé, *The Crowd in the French Revolution*, pp. 40–43, 82–83, 63–69, 114–127, 131–141, 143–146, 162–169; Guthrie, "Riots in Seventeenth Century Mexico City," pp. 20–41, 59–66, 141–151, 204, 206–211; Beloff, *Public Order and Popular Disturbances 1660–1714*, pp. 9–33, 56–75; above, pp. 55–56; R. S. Longley, "Mob Activities in Revolutionary Massachusetts," *New England Quarterly*, Vol. VI (1933), pp. 98–99; Darvall, *Popular Disturbances and Public Order in Regency England*, pp. 18–21, 53–55, 64, 106, 144, 199, 202; Adamic, *Dynamite*, pp. 25–37, 49–61; Clincy, *All in the Name of God*, p. 169; Norman, "Mass Hysteria in Japan," *op. cit.*, p. 66.

[4] Beloff, *Public Order and Popular Disturbances 1660–1714*, pp. 33–35. For a list of typical grievances which lie behind prison riots, cf. Fox, *Violence Behind Bars*, p. 306.

[5] Still another example was the scapegoating of Bolsheviks after the failure of the summer offensive against the Germans in June, 1917. Trotsky, *History of the Russian Revolution*, Vol. I, pp. 429–430.

[6] Murray, *Red Scare*, pp. 3–9; Dahlke, "Race and Minority Riots," *op. cit.*, p. 425; White, *The Forty-Niners*, pp. 53–54.

[7] van Doorn-Janssen, "A Study of Social Disorganization in a Community," *op. cit.*, pp. 200–203.

[8] For example, one of the sources of the grievances of the Egyptians against the British in 1919 was that the latter presumably did not honor a number of apparent promises made when Egyptians undertook a number of wartime sacrifices. Gwynn, *Imperial Policing*, pp. 67–68.

[9] Smelser, *Social Change in the Industrial Revolution*, Ch. IX.

The Hostile Outburst

Strain and Values. Conflicts of values are often more or less enduring features with ethnic, communal, economic, political, and other cleavages. When the cleavage is deep, a permanent state of serious strain exists in society. These cleavages can be opened, moreover, by phenomena such as mass migrations which change the relative strength of groups.[1] Specific dissatisfactions—e.g., with employment opportunities—may feed into diffuse prejudices as well. For instance, in the background to the disturbances in Ceylon in 1958 was the suspicion on the part of the educated Sinhalese that the Tamils were being given preference for jobs in the public and mercantile services.[2]

Among the most important value-conflicts which act as strains inciting to violence are those created by value-oriented movements—internal revolutions, nationalistic outbursts, charismatic religious movements, etc. Such movements establish battle-lines between important groupings—radical-reactionary, heterodox-orthodox, etc.[3]

GENERALIZED AGGRESSION, PRECIPITATING FACTORS, AND HOSTILITY

We shall now review the character of generalized hostile beliefs and the role of precipitating factors in crystallizing this belief on specific events and objects. These conditions are more determinate than the conditions of conduciveness and strain; for, once they are established, participants are ready to be mobilized into a hostile outburst.

The interplay among generalized belief, precipitating factors, and collective hostility is elegantly stated in Allport and Postman's characterization of rumor in violent outbursts:

Ordinarily four stages in the process [in the interaction between rumor and violent outburst] are discernible.

1. For a period of time before an outbreak there are murmurs of unrest. These murmurs may take the form of stories featuring discrimination, insults, or misdeeds ascribed by each group to its opponents. At this stage the rumors current do not differ from the usual run of hostile and accusatory stories. They sound like everyday gossip concerning the undesirable behavior of Negroes or Jews, or of employer greed or police brutality. But whenever the normal circulation is exceeded, or whenever the viciousness of the stories grows more acute, we may suspect a pre-riot condition. In themselves these tales will not lead to violence. They serve merely as a barometer of increasing social strain, indicating that unless the social wind

---

[1] Above, pp. 62–63. Beals, *Brass-Knuckle Crusade*, p. 174; Heaton, "Mob Violence in the late Roman Republic," *op. cit.*, p. 88.
[2] Vittachi, *Emergency '58*, p. 99.
[3] For examples of such movements, cf. Gwynn, *Imperial Policing*, pp. 89, 150.

The Hostile Outburst

shifts its direction, we may be headed for a storm. In the troubled summer of 1943, during which there were several race riots and near riots, the record shows a preceding period of intensified rumor spreading. . . .

2. Danger is indicated when the rumors assume a specifically threatening form. "Something is going to happen tonight by the river." "Be sure to come to the ball park after the game to see the fun." "They're going to catch that nigger tonight and whale the life out of him." Sometimes the stories may ascribe impending violence to the opposing camp: "The bastards have been saving up guns for a month." In the course of the Detroit disturbances in the early summer of 1943 it was rumored that carloads of armed Negroes were heading for Detroit from Chicago. . . .

3. Often, though not invariably, the spark that ignites the powder keg is itself an inflammatory rumor. The serious Harlem riot in August, 1943, followed immediately upon rumored versions of an incident between a Negro soldier and a white policeman in a Harlem hotel lobby. . . .

[The immediate occasion of the Detroit outbreak] . . . lay in wildly distorted versions of an incident on the Belle Isle beach. . . . The precipitating incident as reported in the newspapers was a fist fight between a Negro and a white man. The incident was bruited with exaggeration up and down the beach and into the city itself. Its versions followed the assimilative predilections of each rumor agent, some being tailor-made for white ears, others for black ears. One version asserted that a Negro baby had been thrown from the bridge by white sailors; another that a white baby had been thrown from the bridge by Negroes. A white woman had been attacked on the bridge by colored men; white sailors had insulted colored girls; white girls had been accosted by Negroes while swimming. . . .

4. During the heat of a riot rumors fly faster than ever, but in this frantic period their character reflects acute fanaticism. Sometimes they are hallucinatory. Tortures, rapes, murders are recounted in a frenzied manner as if to justify the violence under way and to speed up the process of vengeance.[1]

Such rumors display all the components of a hostile belief-system—anxiety, generalized aggression, and omnipotence—and the attachment, by short-circuiting, of these generalized elements to specific persons, places, situations, and events.[2]

We shall ask the following question concerning the development of hostile beliefs: What is the origin of generalized aggression? What role do precipitating factors play in fixing this aggression on specific situations? How are beliefs communicated among potential participants in hostile outbursts in order to prepare them for mobilization and action?

Generalized Aggression. Some aggression always exists in society

[1] Allport and Postman, *The Psychology of Rumor*, pp. 193-196.
[2] Above, pp. 101-109 for a full characterization of this hostile belief and its components.

The Hostile Outburst

and waits to flow into a variety of forms of hostility—griping, insult, discrimination, or, in extreme cases, violence. The study of prejudice and its relation to anxiety, projection, etc., has yielded an array of insights concerning the origins of such aggression in the individual.[1] Frequently this aggression follows lines of ethnic, religious, political, and economic cleavage.[2] Conceivably at the most generalized level aggression could be completely free-floating, i.e., available for expression on any possible pretense. Most aggression, however, has reference to a broad class of situations—e.g., criminals' aggression toward authorities, Protestants' fears and hatreds of supposed Catholic political conspiracy, Gentiles' suspicion of Jewish economic power, whites' fears of Negro contamination, etc.

Even though aggression may be institutionalized, it can be aggravated by situations in social life. Let us look at the ways in which precipitating factors tend to stir generalized aggression and focus it on definite situations.

The Role of Precipitating Factors. The precipitating factor for the hostile outburst channels generalized beliefs into specific fears, antagonisms, and hopes. In analyzing the events that precipitate hostile outbursts, it is more important to consider their *context* than to reason from their *content*.[3] This context lies in the conditions of conduciveness, strain, and generalized aggression that we have reviewed. *The precipitating factor confirms the existence, sharpens the definition, or exaggerates the effect of one of these conditions.* More particularly, a precipitating factor may operate in the following ways:

(1) A precipitating factor may confirm or justify existing generalized fears or hatreds. Many racial outbursts have originated in the report—true or false—that one of the groups in question has committed some act which is in keeping with its threatening character.

---

[1] For sample characterizations of "authoritarian" and related types of personalities, cf. Adorno, Frenkel-Brunswik, Levinson, and Sanford, *The Authoritarian Personality*; N. W. Ackerman and M. Jahoda, *Anti-Semitism and Emotional Disorder: A Psychoanalytic Interpretation* (New York, 1950). E. Frenkel-Brunswik and R. N. Sanford, "Some Personality Correlates of Anti-Semitism," *The Journal of Psychology*, Vol. 20 (1945), pp. 271–291; H. E. Krugman, "The Role of Hostility in the Appeal of Communism in the United States," *Psychiatry*, Vol. 16 (1953), pp. 253–261. For a somewhat different treatment of hostility in the personality of a Negro participant in a race riot, cf. K. B. Clark and J. Barker, "The Zoot Effect in Personality: A Race Riot Participant," *Journal of Abnormal and Social Psychology*, Vol. 40 (1945), pp. 145–148.

[2] Above, pp. 228–231.

[3] Lee and Humphrey, for instance, observe that the particular racial incident that started the Detroit race riots of 1943 was not important in itself; the important fact is that it occurred in an atmosphere of extreme tension. *Race Riot*, p. 25. For a list of events that might have but did not lead to racial fireworks in Chicago in 1917 and 1918, cf. Chicago Commission on Race Relations, *The Negro in Chicago*, pp. 53 ff. See also Lohman, *The Police and Minority Groups*, p. 80.

The Hostile Outburst

Stories of crime, sexual abuse, mischievous activity, unpatriotic displays, etc., have stirred whites into aggressive actions against Negroes.[1] Similarly, on the side of the minority group, a violent act, an arbitrary arrest of a leader, etc., may confirm the widespread fears of persecution.[2] During the various nativistic outbursts in the United States in the nineteenth century, wild stories were spread about the disrespectful acts of Catholics toward the American flag, their planned massacres, etc.[3] In the height of the Red Scare of 1919-20, all sorts of incidents which might have otherwise passed more innocently were assimilated to the generalized expectations of anarchist and Bolshevik conspiracy which was presumably at hand —strikes, isolated bombings, demonstrations, race riots, etc.[4]

(2) A precipitating factor may introduce a sharp new deprivation in the midst of generally difficult conditions. In various places we have assessed the significance of food shortages, price increases, wage cuts, etc.[5] All can act as precipitating factors in the genesis of hostility, either by aggravating existing strains or creating new strains. Such events are particularly potent if they complement existing social cleavages. For instance, in the midst of the economic crisis which lay behind the riots of 1692 in Mexico City, it appeared that the Indian groups in the population—a minority despised by many—were profiting from the famine by the sale of tortillas while non-Indians starved.[6]

(3) A precipitating factor may suddenly close off an opportunity for peaceful protest. We have reviewed a number of occasions on which alternate means of protest are closed—in the prison setting, in laborers' attempts to gain their ends through strikes and demonstrations, etc.[7] When this condition is introduced rapidly, it may trigger hostility and even violence. Other examples of closing off access to a desired objective are: the passage of an unpopular piece of legislation against which a group has been agitating;[8] the dismissal

---

[1] Chicago Commission on Race Relations, *The Negro in Chicago*, pp. 48, 58, 67, 71; *Negro Year Book*, 1921-1922, pp. 73-75, 78; Turner and Surace, "Zoot-Suiters and Mexicans," *op. cit.*, p. 16; H. C. Brearley, "The Pattern of Violence," in W. T. Couch (ed.), *Culture in the South* (Chapel Hill, 1934), pp. 680-681.
[2] Parker, *The Incredible Messiah*, pp. 54-55; United States Congress, House of Representatives, *Memphis Riots and Massacres* (Washington, D.C., 1866), pp. 6-7. For reactions in India after the arrest of Gandhi early in 1919, cf. Gwynn, *Imperial Policing*, pp. 36-43.
[3] Beals, *Brass-Knuckle Crusade*, pp. 88, 176-177; above, p. 115.
[4] Murray, *Red Scare*, pp. 64-189.
[5] Above, pp. 55-56, and 245-256.
[6] Guthrie, "Riots in Seventeenth Century Mexico City," pp. 154-155.
[7] Above, pp. 236-240.
[8] The passage of the Relief Bill of 1778 in England, which gave token benefits to Catholics, and the proposal to extend the provisions of this Bill to North

of a popular political figure who, it is felt, might relieve a distressing situation;[1] the failure of petitions to be received or to achieve tangible results.[2]

(4) A precipitating event may signalize a "failure" which demands explanation and assignment of responsibility. Some panics apparently mark a failure in leadership and set off a search for responsible parties.[3] Frequently, also, defeat in war leads to an attempt to assign responsibility to some group in the home population. Examples are the increased scapegoating of government officials, Koreans, etc., toward the end of World War II in Japan;[4] the increased incidence of riots, crime, plots, and deviance in Germany as World War II moved toward its close;[5] the scapegoating of Bolsheviks upon the failure of the Russian offensive against the Germans in 1917.[6]

(5) One hostile outburst may be a precipitating factor for further outbursts. We shall reserve full analysis of this topic until we consider the derived aspects of hostile outbursts and the problem of social control. Let us note here that the occurrence of a hostile outburst in one locale may trigger its spread to another. In the great riots of 1877, for instance, the initial riot in Baltimore, touched off by a ten per cent reduction of firemen's and brakemen's wages, spread within a few days to Pittsburgh, Reading, Chicago, and San Francisco.[7] In each locale the particular type of grievance was different. In Chicago the uprising reflected the political maneuverings of an incipient socialist movement, whereas in San Francisco, opposition to the competition from Chinese labor lay behind the workers' grievances.[8] Riots clustered at this time because one riot signaled a disruption of social control and brought other latent uprisings to the surface. In quite another context, a rash of prison riots in different

---

Britain set up a frenzy of protest and ultimately led to much of the rioting in 1780. Hibbert, *King Mob.*, pp. 37–38; J. P. de Castro, *The Gordon Riots* (London, 1926), p. 11.

[1] On the effects of the dismissal of Necker in the French Revolution, cf. Rudé, *The Crowd in the French Revolution*, pp. 48–54; Stephens, *History of the French Revolution*, Vol. I, pp. 121, 171–173. Cf. Guthrie, "Riots in Seventeenth Century Mexico City," pp. 64–103.

[2] Cf. the ignoring of the petitions of distressed unemployed in Paris by the National Assembly on the eve of the "Massacre" of the Champs de Mars during the French Revolution. Rudé, *The Crowd in the French Revolution*, pp. 82–86.

[3] Above, pp. 222–223.

[4] Leighton, *Human Relations in a Changing World* (New York, 1949), pp. 58–75.

[5] United States Strategic Bombing Survey, *The Effects of Strategic Bombing on German Morale*, Vol. I, pp. 96–103.

[6] Above, p. 246, fn.

[7] Adamic, *Dynamite*, pp. 25–35.

[8] Martin, *The Story of the Great Riots*, pp. 420–430.

The Hostile Outburst

locations is frequently set off by the news of one riot.[1] We shall explore this contagious character of hostility in detail later in the chapter.

(6) A precipitating factor may be a rumor reporting one or more of the above events. The lengthy quotation from Allport and Postman illustrates this role of rumor.[2]

Two qualifying remarks on the role of precipitating factors are in order. First, more than one precipitating event may occur in the development of any given outburst. Logically this is possible because of the large number of conditions of conduciveness and strain which have to be established before a hostile outburst can occur. One event (e.g., a gang beating) may confirm the fears of Negroes that whites are bent on intimidation; another (e.g., the brutal arrest of a Negro) may indicate to them that the usual channels of justice and law enforcement are not available to them. Second, precipitating factors overlap empirically with some of the broader background conditions of conduciveness and strain. We might consider long-term technological pressures on the labor force to be an instance of strain. Taking this as a starting-point, we would consider a sharp business crisis to be an aggravating or precipitating factor in the context of the longer-term trends.[3] Shortening our time perspective, however, we would consider the business crisis itself to be a focus of strain, and an inflammatory statement by a business official—e.g., that any enterprising workman should be able to locate work—to be the precipitating factor in the development of a hostile outburst.

The Spread of Beliefs. Above we specified the need for some mode of communication as a condition of structural conduciveness for the development of a hostile belief. The form this communication takes is variable. At one extreme we have the unrehearsed, face-to-face passing of rumor and information which gradually crystallizes into a belief on the basis of which people prepare to take action.[4] At the other extreme is the spread of information through organized propaganda and agitation.[5] Lying somewhere between these extremes is the press, which frequently passes rumors and exciting stories, many of which become part of a belief that leads to hostile outbursts. Newspapers and journals themselves differ, of course, in their

---

[1] Ohlin, *Sociology and the Field of Corrections*, p. 25.
[2] Also Katz and Schank, *Social Psychology*, p. 143.
[3] Cf. Smelser, *Social Change in the Industrial Revolution*, pp. 226–227, 248.
[4] Descriptions are to be found in L. L. Bernard, "Crowd," *Encyclopaedia of the Social Sciences*, Vol. 4, pp. 612–613; Allport, *Social Psychology*, p. 292. For an example of rumor that touched off the rioting in 1935 at the Rhodesian copper fields, cf. E. Clegg, *Race and Politics* (London, 1960), pp. 80–81.
[5] Dahlke, "Race and Minority Riots," *op. cit.*, p. 425; P. Selznick, *The Organizational Weapon* (New York, 1952), Ch. 1; Lederer, *State of the Masses*, p. 89.

The Hostile Outburst

level of involvement in wishing to create an atmosphere of hostility.[1]

Most hostile beliefs are spread by diverse means of communication. Given the general receptivity on the part of various groups in the Parisian population during the days of the French Revolution, how did the ideas which led them to violence crystallize?

It seems likely ... that the journals and pamphlets played an important part in shaping popular opinion on the main political questions of the day and, on occasion at least, in preparing such opinion directly for the great revolutionary events in the capital ... [But] with all this, a considerable—perhaps the preponderating—part in spreading ideas and moulding opinions must still have been played by the spoken word in public meeting-places, workshops, wine-shops, markets, and food-shops.[2]

MOBILIZATION FOR ACTION

The final stage of the value-added process that results in a hostile outburst is the actual mobilization and organization of action. It does not occur, however, unless the other determinants—conduciveness, strain, and a belief that has crystallized and spread—are present. Of course, some of these determinants may be created on the spot by the very leader or organization who mobilizes the participants for action.[3] In discussing mobilization we shall concentrate on three types of phenomena: (*a*) leadership; (*b*) the organization of the hostile outburst; (*c*) the "shape" of the hostility curve. Under this last heading we shall comment on two aspects of hostile outbursts which have received attention in the literature—the volatile character of the hostile crowd, and the composition of the personnel in hostile outbursts.

---

[1] For accounts of the role of the press in hostile outbursts, cf. Chicago Commission on Race Relations, *The Negro in Chicago*, pp. 521–595; Fritz and Williams, "The Human Being in Disaster," *op. cit.*, p. 50; Pruden, "A Sociological Study of a Texas Lynching," *op. cit.*, p. 6; United States Congress, House of Representatives, *Memphis Riots and Massacres*, pp. 30–31; Turner and Surace, "Zoot-Suiters and Mexicans," *op. cit.*; Lambert, "Religion, Economics, and Violence in Bengal," *op. cit.*, pp. 315–320.

[2] Rudé, *The Crowd in the French Revolution*, p. 212. Examples give, pp. 215–218.

[3] In a classic description, F. H. Allport indicates how the leader of a crowd may crystallize a belief and spur the crowd into action: "The people are brought together by a common interest preparing them for a certain type of action [strain]. The harangue of the leader, or similar stimulus common to all, increases this preparation to the point of breaking forth. The command or first movement of some individual toward the act prepared affords the stimulus for release. And finally, when act and emotion are under way, the sights and sounds of others' reactions facilitate and increase further the responses of each." *Social Psychology*, p. 292.

The Hostile Outburst

Leadership. In the literature on collective behavior much has been made of the role of the demagogue in stirring people to action.[1] Though haranguing a crowd is frequently an effective means of leading a hostile group to action, leadership may take many forms different from demagoguery. Consider the following:

(1) Action may be tripped by a model[2] who simply perpetrates a triggering act and who does not intend to lead the attack.[3] In other cases the mere occurrence of an event may provide the "leadership." Hence, in the swastika epidemic of 1959–60, the initial incident was the painting of a swastika on a synagogue in Cologne, Germany, on December 24, 1959. Though this incident may have been led, it triggered hundreds of similar, leaderless incidents throughout the Western world.[4]

(2) On some occasions a highly motivated, daring, psychopathic, etc., individual will deliberately harangue a group to action. "Many reports of [prison] riots," for instance, "attributed a central role to inmate leaders designated as psychopaths."[5] In public gatherings of enraged citizens, a leader may appear and incite the group to openly hostile expression.[6] In still other cases, instigation may be the work of leaders behind the scenes.[7] Finally, a hostile outburst may be instigated by *agents provacateurs* dispatched by the governing authorities themselves.[8]

(3) Organizations associated with a social movement may move in and assume leadership of hostile outbursts which may or may not

---

[1] E.g., Conway, *The Crowd in Peace and War*, pp. 89–98; Lederer, *State of the Masses*, pp. 38–40; Lee and Humphrey, *Race Riot*, pp. 5–6; Katz, "The Psychology of the Crowd," in Guilford (ed.), *op. cit.*, pp. 147–151. Further discussion may be found in Turner and Killian, *Collective Behavior*, pp. 112–119.

[2] Cf. the discussion of the "flight model" for the panic, above, pp. 153–154.

[3] For instance, in the great riot of 1624 in Mexico City, the stoning of the servants of a secretary of an excommunicated viceroy and their shouts of "heretic" set off the fury of a milling mob, fury which then turned into violence which brought "temporarily to an end all law and order in the City of Mexico." Guthrie, "Riots in Seventeenth Century Mexico City," pp. 97–103.

[4] D. Caplovitz and C. Rogers, "The Swastika Epidemic: A Preliminary Draft of a Report for the Anti-Defamation League" (Mimeographed, 1960), p. 1.

[5] Ohlin, *Sociology and the Field of Corrections*, p. 25. Ohlin goes on to place such leadership in proper perspective, however: "Such leaders ... are always present in the inmate population. In most instances they are powerless to effect a major disturbance unless the situation is also attended by widespread inmate dissatisfaction and resentment, which the inmate leaders can successfully mobilize to provide a collective expression of dissatisfaction." Cf. also Hartung and Floch, "A Socio-psychological Analysis of Prison Riots," *op. cit.*, p. 52.

[6] Rudé, *The Crowd in the French Revolution*, pp. 78, 218; Chicago Commission on Race Relations, *The Negro in Chicago*, pp. 59–60, 71–77; Brearley, "The Pattern of Violence," in Couch (ed.), *op. cit.*, pp. 680–681; Coxe, "The New Orleans Mafia Incident," *op. cit.*, pp. 1085–1087. Gwynn, *Imperial Policing*, p. 341.

[7] Dahlke, "Race and Minority Riots," p. 425; Lee, *Race Riot*, pp. 80–81.

[8] Darvall, *Popular Disturbances and Public Order in Regency England*, p. 208.

The Hostile Outburst

have been instigated in the movement itself. Student organizations, veterans' organizations, nativistic organizations, as well as revolutionary organizations have figured historically as engineers and mobilizers of hostility.[1]

Organization of the Hostile Outburst. The organization of the attack varies considerably. At the extreme of lack of organization we find the completely uncoordinated brawl with no evidence of a division of labor or coordination; at the extreme of organization we find the military unit with specialized roles and a high level of integration.[2] The degree of organization of any given outburst depends on the following factors:

(1) The degree of pre-existing structure. In discussing compact gatherings Hollingworth distinguishes among the following kinds of organization: the pedestrian audience, such as the gathering on the street corner; the passive audience, such as a group of spectators in an auditorium; a selected audience, such as a meeting of delegates or persons with specific grievances; a concerted audience, such as students in a classroom pursuing the solution of a problem; an organized group, such as a team or military unit.[3]

Unless this prior organization itself is disrupted by conditions of strain and precipitating factors, the organization of the hostile outburst will correspond to the degree of pre-existing organization. For instance, the casual gathering of pedestrians or bar-room customers —which exists essentially without significant leadership or division of roles—will erupt into an uncoordinated brawl if other conditions are present.[4] Purposive gatherings of enraged citizens break into a pattern of hostile expression which displays only primitive organization. Destructive mobs which emerge in race riots, for instance, show the following kinds of differential participation:

The mob in its entirety usually did not participate actively. It was one in spirit, but divided in performance into a small active nucleus and a large

---

[1] Gwynn, *Imperial Policing*, p. 69; R. C. Myers, "Anti-Communist Mob Action: A Case Study," *Public Opinion Quarterly*, Vol. 12 (1948); pp. 60–61; Beals, *Brass-Knuckle Crusade*, pp. 35–36, 85; Rudé, *The Crowd in the French Revolution*, pp. 69–71, 87–89, 122–125, 218–219; Trotsky, *History of the Russian Revolution*, Vol. III, pp. 9–23 for the movement from spontaneous uprisings among the peasants to their more or less conscious leadership. For the changing organization of hostile expression among the workers, *ibid.*, pp. 33, 42. For comments on the varying degrees to which Chartism infected the disturbances in Great Britain between 1837 and 1848, cf. Mather, *Public Order in the Age of the Chartists*, pp. 9–10.

[2] Discussion of these structural aspects of concerted action are found in Conway, *The Crowd in Peace and War*, pp. 127–135; Reuter and Hart, *Introduction to Sociology*, pp. 476–478; Bernard, "Mob," *op. cit.*, p. 552.

[3] *The Psychology of the Audience*, p. 25.

[4] LaPiere and Farnsworth, *Social Psychology*, p. 470.

proportion of spectators. The nucleus was composed of young men from sixteen to twenty-one or twenty-two years of age. Sometimes only four would be active as 150 looked on, but at times the proportion would be as great as twenty-five in 200 or fifty in 300. Fifty is the largest number reported for a mob nucleus....[1]

When hostility is directed by a highly organized revolutionary party, or when an insurrectionary movement gains control of the organized means of violence (the police, the army), the hostile behavior is very highly structured.[2] This behavior may, of course, instigate a rash of unorganized outbursts elsewhere in the society, especially if it reveals any weakness on the part of the agencies of social control.

(2) *Ecological factors*. The *form* of hostility in racial outbursts depends, as we have seen, very much on the location and accessibility of objects of attack.[3] In other outbursts as well, the sheer ecological distribution of the dissatisfied groups plays an important role in shaping the violence. If dissatisfaction is regional, the likelihood of a movement toward secession or of the raising of forces for a civil war is increased; if, on the other hand, dissatisfaction is dispersed through the geographical regions and different social layers of society, violence tends to take the form of incidents of resistance, street-fighting, attempts to subvert the police, etc. We shall discuss this important conditioning influence of ecology when we turn to types of value-oriented movements and the avenues into which they ultimately flow.[4]

(3) *The operation of agencies of social control*. As we shall see momentarily, the occurrence of one outburst of hostility excites generalized tendencies (sometimes unrelated to the original occasion for hostility) to defy authority and to vent hostilities. The entry of these new elements—some isolated individuals, some organized groups—into the outburst changes its character. The rapidity and effectiveness with which the agencies of social control counter the outburst—assuming they are able to counter it at all—affects its organization and development.

[1] Chicago Commission on Race Relations, *The Negro in Chicago*, p. 22. Further instances of the semi-organized crowd may be found in Turner and Surace, "Zoot-suiters and Mexicans," *op. cit.*, p. 16; Lee and Humphrey, *Race Riot*, p. 103. Darvall, *Popular Disturbances and Public Order in Regency England*, p. 197. Further discussion of differential participation is found in Turner and Killian, *Collective Behavior*, p. 112.
[2] For examples of the central direction of hostility, cf. Longley, "Mob Activities in Revolutionary Massachusetts," *op. cit.*, pp. 108–129; for the exercise of hostility through institutionalized governmental channels, cf. Murray, *Red Scare*, pp. 192–196.
[3] Above, pp. 240–241.
[4] Below, pp. 314–317.

The Hostile Outburst

The Spread of the Hostile Outburst. From the literature on disasters, panics, and wartime life considerable evidence has accumulated to show that a breakdown in the social order brings to the surface a number of different kinds of deviance—looting, pilfering, random assaults, sexual abuse, etc.[1] Since outbursts of hostility frequently signify a threat to the existing order, such deviance frequently accompanies eruptions of hostility. The result is a distinctive kind of "curve" for the hostile outburst. Bogardus has described such a curve for aggressive crowds:

> In mobs where anger rules, there is a mob curve. The curve rises irregularly until the objective of the mob is reached. It hovers at a dizzy height of brutal vengeance until it has wreaked its will on its victims after which it falls rapidly, almost perpendicularly. In the mob curve the effects of group contagion are evident. When the contagion bubble bursts, the mob spirit flattens out.[2]

Let us attempt to give a more definite account of this curve than can be generated with concepts such as "contagion."[3]

The history of riots and related outbursts is filled with instances of looters, gangs of delinquents, individual criminals, etc., moving in to the scene of disturbance and thereby multiplying the acts of disorder.[4] All these instances are found in qualitative accounts of individual outbursts. In a recent analysis of the swastika epidemic of 1959–60, however, Caplovitz and Rogers have compiled something approaching a quantitative account of the shape of the curve and the different kinds of hostility which produce its distinctive shape.

For the eight-week period of the epidemic, Caplovitz and Rogers plotted a time-distribution of some 559 incidents reported in the American press and compiled by the Anti-Defamation League. This

---

[1] R. Bartlett, "Anarchy in Boston," *The American Mercury*, Vol. 36 (Dec., 1935), pp. 456–464; United States Strategic Bombing Survey, *The Effects of Strategic Bombing on German Morale*, Vol. 1, pp. 87–93; C. E. Fritz and J. H. Mathewson, *Convergence Behavior in Disasters: A Problem in Social Control* (Washington, D.C., 1957), pp. 3–4, 27, 29, 89–91; Kardman and Brown, *Disaster!* pp. 40–45, 126–127. In assessing the effect of the Dutch floods of 1953, the investigators remarked that "the disaster exposed all sorts of weaknesses and tensions which in normal times might have remained latent." Ellemers, *General Conclusions. Studies in Holland Flood Disaster*, p. 58.

[2] *Social Psychology*, p. 399.

[3] For other descriptions of the mob in terms of contagion and related concepts, cf. Allport, *Social Psychology*, pp. 311–312; Katz and Schank, *Social Psychology*, p. 142; Lohman, *The Police and Minority Groups*, pp. 80–81.

[4] Chicago Commission on Race Relations, *The Negro in Chicago*, pp. 1–2, 11, 53 ff.; Parker, *The Incredible Messiah*, pp. 54–56; Rudé, *The Crowd in the French Revolution*, pp. 48–51; Guthrie, "Riots in Seventeenth Century Mexico City," pp. 128, 163–185. During the Red Scare of 1919–20, the "massacre" of Centralia, Illinois, set off a series of raids on radical meetings on the West Coast, Murray, *Red Scare*, pp. 181–189.

The Hostile Outburst

distribution—reproduced in Table 9—shows the pattern of an early, rapid peaking, then a sudden falling-off. When this distribution is broken down according to types of target—Jewish vs. non-Jewish—it is seen that the bulge of the third week consisted primarily of incidents not directed at specifically Jewish targets.[1] Table 10 shows this breakdown by type of target. It appears that toward the end of the second week of the epidemic a number of different kinds of not specifically anti-Semitic motives began to be drawn into the expression of hostility. On the basis of their data, analyzed for the whole country and for individual communities separately, Caplovitz and Rogers concluded that

the decrease in [percentage of] Jewish targets at the peak stemmed from the participation of the pure "faddists" at this stage in the life span of the epidemic, rather than the most hostile anti-Semites. Of course the ultimate test of this hypothesis would be to measure the anti-Semitic attitudes of the offenders at each stage in the life span of the fad. If this interpretation is correct, we should find that those participating at the peak are not as anti-Semitic as those participating at the beginning or the end.[2]

Though this reasoning is generally correct, the mechanism accounting for the pattern of incidents is more complicated than "faddism," or "participating to be fashionable." The initial outburst of hostility resulted from the actions of anti-Semitic individuals or groups. The triggering of an event such as the Christmas Eve incident in Cologne set off similar anti-Semitic actions. What this small and early series of incidents did was to *indicate an avenue for expressing grievances of many kinds*. Hence all kinds of latent hostilities—some specifically anti-Semitic, but many very general—were drawn toward this avenue. In fact these general incidents outnumbered those directed specifically toward Jewish targets. Then, as public concern began to rise, as offenders began to be apprehended, as public officials and others began to denounce the wave of incidents, this particular avenue of expression was made less attractive. At this time

---

[1] A methodological difficulty appears in the compilation of Tables 9 and 10. The recorded unit is "incident" not "participant." A single incident in some cases resulted from the activity of many participants. Since, however, not all participants were apprehended and recorded, it is impossible to know the number of participants, which would possibly be a better index of hostility than number of incidents.

[2] "The Swastika Epidemic," p. 9. The distinction between Jewish and non-Jewish targets is not the same as a distinction according to the character of the incident. Sometimes a swastika or similar mark was made on the non-Jewish target, and for this reason may have reflected anti-Semitic sentiments, even though not directed at a Jewish target. The distinction between Jewish and non-Jewish targets is not a completely valid indicator of the distinction between anti-Semitic incidents and generally delinquent acts. For such reasons the following discussion must be ventured with some caution.

The Hostile Outburst

the general fall-off in all kinds of hostile expressions of this sort began to appear.

Hostility, then, like the other outbursts we have analyzed, can be divided for analytic purposes into a real and a derived phase. In the initial or real phase the hostility and its expression result from the

TABLE 9[1]

THE DISTRIBUTION OF INCIDENTS OVER THE EIGHT-WEEK
LIFE-CYCLE OF THE SWASTIKA EPIDEMIC

	No. of Incidents	%
First week (Dec. 26, 1959, to Jan. 1, 1960)	14	2
Second week	130	23
Third week	204	37
Fourth week	82	15
Fifth week	68	12
Sixth week	45	8
Seventh week	10	2
Eighth week	6	1

build-up of specific conditions of strain, precipitating factors, etc. Once hostile outbursts begin, however, they become a *sign* that a fissure has opened in the social order, and that the situation is now structurally conducive for the expression of hostility. As a result, a rash of hostile actions appears, many of them motivated by hostility

TABLE 10[2]

JEWISH AND NON-JEWISH TARGETS ACCORDING TO TIME OF INCIDENT

	Week of Epidemic						
Targets	1st	2nd	3rd	4th	5th	6th	7th & 8th
Jewish Institutions, Homes, Buildings	64%	65%	38%	45%	54%	55%	50%
Non-Jewish	36%	35%	62%	55%	46%	45%	50%
Number	(14)	(130)	(204)	(82)	(68)	(45)	(16)

unrelated to the conditions giving rise to the initial outburst. This "drawing-in" effect, in which participants capitalize on the fact that an outburst has occurred, constitutes the derived phase of the hostile outburst.[3] This effect rapidly diminishes, however, as the forces of social order are mobilized to counter the expressions of hostility.

[1] Caplovitz and Rogers, "The Swastika Epidemic," p. 3.
[2] *Ibid.*, p. 7.
[3] In describing the Chartist outbreaks of the late 1830's and 1840's in England, Mather notes that "The threat to English society in the Chartist period did not in fact arise from the strength of the resistance which the rioters were capable of offering to the forces of the Crown, but from the tendency of disturbances to

The Hostile Outburst

The shape of the curve of the hostile outburst is not the same in every case. The speed of diffusion of the news of the outburst, the kinds of aggression that it taps, and the speed with which the agencies of social control nip the hostile outburst determine how closely the curve will correspond to the ideal-type shape we have outlined.[1]

This interpretation of the development of hostile outbursts accounts in part for two other aspects of the hostile crowd: (*a*) its composition; (*b*) its fickleness, or its movement from object to object. The composition of hostile mobs is diverse. Mobs have their share of those who carry the initial, specific grievances *and* those with hostilities basically independent of the initial generating conditions. Rudé's analysis of the crowds in the French Revolution, the best treatment of this subject, does in fact show such variation in the composition and motivation in most of the crowds.[2]

Le Bon has commented on the volatile character of crowds,[3] and some instances of mob behavior give evidence of this volatility. In the anti-Catholic riots in 1780 in London, for instance, the mob was observed in attacking the Lords, smashing Catholic places of worship, assaulting Irish laborers, looting, attacking prisons to release previously arrested rioters, and attacking the Bank of England.[4] This movement from object to object stems not from a kind of mystical emotional capriciousness which some have attributed to the mob, but rather from the fact that once a violent outburst has commenced, it attracts many potentially deviant and destructive

---

occur almost simultaneously in different places. This tendency was due in the first place to the widespread economic distress, which turned the manufacturing districts in times of slack trade into a veritable powder magazine, capable of being ignited by the smallest spark. Thus an outbreak in one district quickly spread to its neighbours, and the events of the summer of 1842 were to demonstrate with what rapidity a strike, beginning in a small tract of territory, situated to the south and east of Manchester, could be spread by roving bands of turnouts, until it involved the entire industrial area of the North and Midlands. The danger of concurrent outbreaks was increased by the hold which political agitation, notably that of the Chartists, had upon the masses." *Public Order in the Age of the Chartists*, pp. 21–22.

[1] For discussion of some of the factors influencing the shape of the participation curve, cf. Caplovitz and Rogers, "The Swastika Epidemic," pp. 36–37.

[2] *The Crowd in the French Revolution*, pp. 178–185. See especially his critique of historians like Taine who treated the mob as a wave of unemployed, vagabonds, criminals, and riff-raff, pp. 186–190. Cf. also Cantril, *The Psychology of Social Movements*, pp. 107–108; Pruden, "A Sociological Study of a Texas Lynching," *op. cit.*, pp. 7–8; Shay, *Judge Lynch*, pp. 86–90.

[3] *The Crowd*, pp. 36–39.

[4] Hibbert, *King Mob*, pp. 56–137; de Castro, *The Gordon Riots*, pp. 141–142. In his discussion of the incitement of the various crowds in the French Revolution, Rudé speaks of the frequency of "mutation or transformation that marks the revolutionary crowd in its most typical form." *The Crowd in the French Revolution*, p. 220.

The Hostile Outburst

persons in the population. Participants represent a diversity of motivations; the attack may shift from one object of attack to another; indeed, different parts of the mob may attack different objects simultaneously.

THE CONTROL OF HOSTILE OUTBURSTS

Once the tendency for behavior to erupt into a hostile outburst has developed to an advanced stage, what is the role of agencies of social control in determining the occurrence and extent of the outburst? This question does not, of course, exhaust the entire problem of social control.[1] Social control involves the institutionalizing of respect for law and for orderly means of expressing grievances.[2] It involves the alleviating of conditions of strain which generate dissatisfactions. It involves the softening of prejudice and discrimination which deepen social cleavages. It involves the minimizing of divisiveness among the ruling groups in society. We have already touched some of these aspects of social control in discussing structural conduciveness, strain, and generalized beliefs. Now we shall emphasize further the behavior of controlling agencies at the scene of the hostile outburst itself.

In the last analysis, the behavior of agencies of social control in the face of a hostile outburst concerns the manner in which force is exercised, though, of course, many factors other than force enter into the encouragement or discouragement of hostility. Were it only a matter of force, it is probable that all expressions of hostility could be put down easily, because of the superior power and organization of the police, military, and other official bodies employed in the control of violence. Thus, in principle, "the notion that repression cannot effectively crush revolutionary movements for long periods is a monstrous superstition."[3] Yet this *principle* of the superiority of organized wielders of force in society does not always hold in

---

[1] That is to say, the question as phrased concentrates on the organizational aspects of control. As our more extensive discussion of control in the chapter on panic shows, the problem encompasses the components of Facilities, Norms and Values as well. Above, pp. 157-168. In this chapter we shall mention chiefly the problem of facilities, but will concentrate on organization.

[2] For an excellent discussion of the historical evolution of the modes of expressing grievances, cf. E. Halevy, *A History of the English People in the Nineteenth Century*, Vol. I (London, 1949-51), pp. 148-200. For reference to some personality sources of hostility, cf. above, pp. 248-249. For discussion of the relationship between religious attitudes and attitudes toward the administration of justice on the one hand and the willingness to participate in mob action on the other, cf. Meier, Mennenga, and Stoltz, "An Experimental Approach to the Study of Mob Behavior," *op. cit.*, pp. 523-624.

[3] Hook, "Violence," *op. cit.*, p. 266. Mather, *Public Order in the Age of the Chartists*, p. 21.

The Hostile Outburst

practice. Sorel, for instance, in considering the political authorities' ability to handle hostile outbursts, remarked:

> One of the things which appear . . . to have most astonished the workers during the last few years has been the timidity of the forces of law and order in the presence of a riot; magistrates who have the right to demand the services of soldiers dare not use their power to the utmost, and officers allow themselves to be abused and struck with a patience hitherto unknown to them.[1]

Why is it, then, that those agencies who control the ultimate deterrent to hostile expression and which are in principle stronger than the perpetrators of any outburst, sometimes do not prevent hostile outbursts?

We shall examine this question on two levels—first, the behavior of the *authorities* who are responsible for deciding to control the outburst, and second, the behavior of those who *implement* these decisions on the spot, i.e., the police, military, etc. Most of our examples will be chosen from riots and other forms of violence, even though these are not the only forms of hostile outbursts. Presumably similar principles would apply in the control of scapegoating which does not involve violence. For instance, as we shall indicate below, vacillation on the part of police authorities in deciding to utilize force tends to encourage the spread of disorder. This is a general principle; it should apply to the weak executive who does not take decisive measures to apply sanctions to witch-hunters as well as the weak governor who shilly-shallies in deciding to call in the National Guard to put down a dangerous riot. Both tend to foster the further spread of overt hostility. Most of our illustrations concern riots and other manifestations of violence; this is because the examples of these in the literature are particularly clear.

With regard to the decision to employ sanctions against hostile outbursts, it is essential that authorities be both quick and decisive:

> . . . firm and timely action. Delay in the use of force, and hesitation to accept responsibility for its employment when the situation clearly demands it, will always be interpreted as weakness, encourage further disorder and eventually necessitate measures more severe than those which would suffice in the first instance. Subversive movements, or disorders of any nature, do not break out fully organized. Leaders in the early stages are apt to be more distinguished by their oratorical powers, and perhaps by capacity of political organization, than for military qualities. Given time, leaders who are men of action will assert themselves, and a know-

---

[1] *Reflections on Violence*, p. 89. On the particular cowardice of the English middle classes, *ibid.*, p. 92.

ledge of the best means of countering Government measures will be acquired.¹

In some cases of successful riots the disposition of the instruments of force is such that police or troops delay in moving to the scene of the outburst.² For instance, when the panic over the "Invasion from Mars" broadcast turned into a destructive riot in Quito, Ecuador, one reason why the violence got out of hand was that the local police had been sent to a nearby spot outside Quito where the space ship presumably had landed.³ and were absent when the mob wreaked its vengeance. On the eve of the attack on the viceroy's palace in Mexico City in June, 1692, many of the guards of the palace were away celebrating a religious festival.⁴ During many of the Luddite disturbances in Lancashire and Cheshire from 1811 to 1813, "again and again . . . it was complained that there were too few magistrates willing to act quickly and vigorously."⁵

Not all failures of the authorities to stop outbursts stem from their inability to move forces to the scene of the outburst promptly. More frequently the authorities themselves are likely to be involved directly or indirectly in the issues leading to the outburst itself. This is likely to lead to several consequences—vacillation in the enforcement of law and order, lack of impartial enforcement of justice, and even complicity in the outburst itself—all of which further the spread of the outburst.⁶ Most of the race riots in the United States in recent history have revealed this equivocal position of the authorities at hand. Let us illustrate this principle first in connection with these racial disturbances, then consider it briefly in a broader comparative context.

In the East St. Louis Race Riots of 1917,

the local authorities proved so ineffective and demoralized that the state militia was required to restore order. A Congressional Committee

¹ Gwynn, *Imperial Policing*, p. 15.
² For this reason writers on the control of riots emphasize the importance of preparedness, "getting there first," etc., in their training manuals. Bargar, *The Law and Customs of Riot Duty*, pp. 31–32, 50–51. United States War Department, War Plans Division, *The Use of Organized Bodies in the Protection and Defense of Property During Riots, Strikes, and Civil Disturbances* (Washington, D.C., 1919), pp. 29–31.
³ Britt (ed.), *Selected Readings in Social Psychology*, pp. 306–307.
⁴ Guthrie, "Riots in Seventeenth Century Mexico City," pp. 169–170. Also p. 103 for similar conditions on the eve of the riot of 1624.
⁵ Darvall, *Popular Disturbances and Public Order in Regency England*, p. 101. In this case this slowness seemed also to be related to fear of disloyalty of some of the forces. For other examples of the sheer inadequacy of forces, cf. Gwynn, *Imperial Policing*, pp. 246, 300–301, 342, 346; Kardman and Brown, *Disaster!*, p. 44.
⁶ This posture of authority is important in determining the course of value-oriented movements as well. Below, pp. 367–379.

investigated the facts of the riot and the underlying conditions, which included industrial disturbances and shameful corruption in local government. ... Both the police and the militia are severely censured by the Congressional report for gross failure to do their duty. The police, says the report, could have quelled the riot instantly, but instead they either "fled into the safety of cowardly seclusion or listlessly watched the depredations of the mob, passively and in many instances actively sharing in their work." ... [Likewise, the militia] "seemed moved by the same spirit of indifference or cowardice that marked the conduct of the police force. As a rule they fraternized with the mob, joked with them and made no serious effort to restrain them.[1]

In both the Chicago Riot of 1919 and the Detroit Riot of 1943 the local authorities vacillated for a time before calling in higher-level troops from the state even when it was clear that the local police were not handling the riot. In the Cicero, Illinois, riot of July, 1951, the local authorities seem to have been even more intimately implicated in the local racial situation. A Negro had attempted to move into a certain neighborhood and the police chief—subsequently indicted by the state on gambling charges and by the federal government for his conduct during the ensuing disturbances—actually prevented the Negro from entering the premises which he had a legal right to enter. If this is true, as Gremley points out,

then we have a subversion of the legal rights of a person by the state itself. On the surface this would seem a most complete breakdown of control as understood in terms of legal rights in American society.

Underlying it, however, is a basic conflict of roles regarding the action of the Cicero police. While on the one hand these officials have a sworn responsibility to uphold legal rights, on the other, we can assume that the Chief of Police believed he was expressing, in his actions, the sentiments of the community and acting as a mediator or even "protector" of community mores, thus crystallizing the state into an instrument to enforce mores contrary to the law of the state. The reluctance of the Cicero police to act vigorously to prevent the violence that followed also reflects this conflict of roles.[2]

In this case the authorities deserted their unambiguous commitment to the maintenance of law and order; they *entered the conflict itself*, reacting to its issues rather than treating the disturbance as a violation of social order, irrespective of the issues.[3]

---

[1] Chicago Commission on Race Relations, *The Negro in Chicago*, pp. 72, 77.
[2] "Social Control in Cicero," *op. cit.*, p. 328.
[3] Cf. below, pp. 267–268. When this kind of behavior occurs in response to a value-oriented movement, a revolutionary situation is usually at hand. Perhaps the most striking recent case of the involvement of local law-enforcement agencies in the actual issues of the racial disturbance is the Little Rock crisis of 1957. Cf. J. W. Caughey, *Their Majesties the Mob* (Chicago, 1960), pp. 196–199. For a

The Hostile Outburst

Let us now list a few instances from different historical and geographical contexts to illustrate the same principles. (*a*) In Ceylon between 1956 and 1958,

a series of strikes began all over the country. In two years Ceylon was to experience over 400 strikes. The police were under orders not to interfere with the demonstrators so that the demonstrators were able to break all the laws of peaceful picketing with impunity.... Politicians rode into police stations and demanded the immediate release of this or that suspect, held for questioning or production before a magistrate. They usually had their way.[1]

(*b*) In the face of the nationalist disturbances of March, 1919, in Egypt, some officials actually deserted their posts, which led to a further spreading of the rioting.[2] (*c*) In the French Revolution, many of the most serious riots were tacitly if not openly approved by some of the parties competing for power. In addition, the police were sometimes either afraid or unwilling to take firm and quick action to put down the impending or actual disturbance.[3] (*d*) During the Methodist movement in England in the eighteenth century, mob riots against the Methodists broke out in various parts of the country. According to Overton,

Sometimes ... these riots were instigated by the clergy; they were rarely stopped, as they ought to have been, by the magistrates. The only places where, as a rule, the Methodists could get common justice done to them were the higher secular courts and the Royal Palace.[4]

Thus when authorities are hesitant, biased, or even actively supportive of one side in a conflict, they give a green light to those bent on hostile expression.

When authorities issue firm, unyielding, and unbiased decisions in short order, the hostile outburst is dampened. Sometimes this decisive action is taken by local authorities.[5] More typically, at least

---

discussion of the passivity and vacillation of the Los Angeles authorities during the zoot-suit riots in 1943, *ibid.*, pp. 138–140. On the Tulsa riot from May 31 to June 21, 1921, cf. *Negro Year Book, 1921–1922*, p. 79. On the Springfield riot of August 14–15, 1908, cf. Chicago Commission on Race Relations, *The Negro in Chicago*, p. 68.

[1] Vittachi, *Emergency '58*, p. 104.
[2] Gwynn, *Imperial Policing*, p. 69.
[3] Stephens, *History of the French Revolution*, Vol. I, pp. 2–3, 82–83, 147–148, 266–267.
[4] J. H. Overton, *The Evangelical Revival in the Eighteenth Century* (London, 1907), p. 162.
[5] For the prevention of a riot in September, 1920, in Chicago because of the courageous and quick action of religious and police leaders, cf. Chicago Commission on Race Relations, *The Negro in Chicago*, pp. 64–66; for the prompt

The Hostile Outburst

in American history, firmness of purpose has been introduced into the situation only when state or federal authorities have been called. These authorities are generally not involved in the local issues and therefore take a more unequivocal stand in the face of outbursts than the local authorities—*a stand defined strictly in terms of the maintenance of law and order.*

In cases in which higher-level militia have been called in to handle racial outbursts, the disorder has vanished quickly.[1] Perhaps the most familiar instance is the appearance of federal troops in Little Rock in 1957. The same applies to the anarchy during the police strike in Boston in 1919, in which the state guard, when it finally came in, restored order quickly.[2] In many instances of labor violence local citizens—including the participants in the disturbances—have welcomed federal intervention because it signified the appearance of a relatively unbiased authority in a situation in which the behavior of the local officials had been blemished. In the West Virginia labor disturbances of 1921, for instance, after Harding had ordered the army to move in to take charge,

> The sending of the army brought peace, but it did little to solve the issues in dispute. The President did nothing to effect a settlement, either before or during the period of crisis. His policy was simply to preserve the peace. It was not difficult to do this since the miners had no quarrel with the federal government. Indeed, they looked upon the troops as protecting them from the operators' force of mine guards and deputy sheriffs.[3]

Such effects are not merely a function of the superior power and authority of the state or federal troops. Frequently the forces are fewer in number than those which might have been mustered at the local level. Success in quelling a disturbance depends also on the impartiality, neutrality, and firmness of the higher-level authorities, an attitude which the local officials frequently do not assume.

In addition to the action of the authorities in deciding to meet a display of hostility, we must consider how these decisions are implemented on the spot, usually by the police force.

---

action of the Fayette County officials when a lynching was impending in Lexington, Kentucky, cf. J. Jordan, "Lynchers Don't Like Lead," *Atlantic Monthly*, Vol. 177 (1946), p. 103.

[1] Chicago Commission on Race Relations, *The Negro in Chicago*, p. 77; Caughey, *Their Majesties the Mob*, pp. 139–140.

[2] Bartlett, "Anarchy in Boston," *op. cit.*, p. 463.

[3] Rich, *The Presidents and Civil Disorder*, p. 167. For similar effects, cf. pp. 121–151. For the role of federal troops in the Great Riots of 1877, cf. Martin, *The Story of the Great Riots*, pp. 434–435. For the unhealthy situation created in labor disputes by the use of private police hired by industrial establishments and usually sworn in by the local officials, cf. H. B. Davis, "Industrial Policing," *Encyclopaedia of the Social Sciences*, Vol. 12, pp. 193–194.

The Hostile Outburst

Force is not always necessary to disperse a mob. Some types of control can be exercised by changing the definition of the situation.[1] For instance, it is possible to prevent an outbreak of hostility by "[redirecting] the attention so that it is not focused collectively on one object":

> Insofar as the attention of the members is directed toward different objects, they form an aggregation of individuals instead of a crowd united by intimate rapport. Thus, to throw people into a state of panic, or to get them interested in other objects, or to get them engaged in discussion or argumentation represents different ways in which a crowd can be broken up.[2]

After a time, however, as the mob develops, this kind of control loses effectiveness. "A mob in full fury will not listen to reason; it can be stopped only by force, by tear bombs, by bayonets."[3]

What, then, constitutes an effective set of principles for troops to control a rioting mob? In general, the principles of riot control concern the determinants which operate at the later stages of the value-added process—dissemination of beliefs, and mobilization. These principles can be summarized as follows: (*a*) Prevent communication in general, so that beliefs cannot be disseminated.[4] (*b*) Prevent interaction between leaders and followers, so that mobilization is difficult.[5] (*c*) Refrain from taking a conditional attitude toward violence by bluffing or vacillating in the use of the ultimate weapons of force.[6] (4) Refrain from entering the issues and controversies that move the crowd; remain impartial, unyielding, and fixed on the principle of maintaining law and order.[7]

The history of riots yields many instances of the failure of police and military to observe these rules of handling crowds and mobs. This failure has resulted in the following kinds of situations:

---

[1] This manipulation of the definition of the situation constitutes control of Facilities. Above, pp. 157–161.

[2] Blumer, "Collective Behavior," in Lee (ed.), *op. cit.*, pp. 181–182.

[3] Bogardus, *Social Psychology*, p. 399.

[4] S. A. Wood, *Riot Control* (Harrisburg, Pa., 1952), p. 96–97. Also Bargar, *The Law and Customs of Riot Duty*, pp. 127–128; LaPiere, *Collective Behavior*, p. 544.

[5] L. C. Andrews, *Military Manpower* (New York, 1920), pp. 178, 186; United States War Department, *The Use of Organized Bodies in the Protection and Defense of Property During Riots, Strikes, and Civil Disturbances*, p. 72; Bargar, *The Law and Customs of Riot Duty*, pp. 165–169; Wood, *Riot Control*, p. 105.

[6] Andrews, *Military Manpower*, p. 178; Wood, *Riot Control*, p. 105; United States War Department, *The Use of Organized Bodies in the Protection and Defense of Property During Riots, Strikes, and Civil Disturbances*, pp. 16–17.

[7] Wood, *Riot Control*, pp. 3, 105–106. For advice concerning impartiality in race riots, cf. Chicago Commission on Race Relations, *The Negro in Chicago*, pp. 640–641; and J. D. Lohman and D. C. Reitzes, "Note on Race Relations in Mass Society," *American Journal of Sociology*, Vol. 58 (1952–53), p. 246.

The Hostile Outburst

(1) On some occasions officers are unable to enforce discipline among troops, or to train them adequately for riot duty.[1]

(2) In race riots the police frequently stand idly by and let the violence run its course.[2] In other cases justice is not enforced impartially. In the 1919 riot in Chicago, for instance, more Negroes were arrested than whites, even though more Negroes were wounded (and presumably attacked) than whites; police were concentrated in the Black Belt overwhelmingly, while rioting in other areas went unsupervised; the individual conduct of policemen was probably not as unfair as Negroes claimed, but the Chicago Commission on Race Relations later reported a number of cases of "discrimination, abuse, brutality, indifference, and neglect on the part of individuals."[3] By contrast, the outside militia displayed no cases of breach of discipline; "they were distributed more proportionately through all the riotous areas than the police, and although they reported some hostility from members of 'athletic clubs,' the rioting soon ceased."[4]

(3) In political disputes as well, inaction or sympathy with one side on the part of police officials has led to increased outbursts of hostility. One of the reasons that President Hayes decided to send troops into West Virginia during the Great Riots of 1877 was that the governor of the state maintained that two of four companies of volunteers were in sympathy with the rioters, and that only one group of 40 men could be relied upon to fight 800 rioters.[5] The success of the Amritsar anti-colonial riots in British India in 1919 seemed to stem from the "extraordinary inaction and lack of initiative of the police, who were under the command of two senior Indian officers."[6]

(4) During revolutionary periods, the disorganization of troop discipline and the indoctrination of military forces with revolutionary principles leads to passivity, fraternization, and even cooperation with revolutionary crowds.[7]

---

[1] Cf. the contrasting behavior of Washington and Adams in their use of federal troops in civil disturbances. Rich, *The Presidents and Civil Disorder*, pp. 9–16, 214.

[2] Gremley, "Social Control in Cicero," *op. cit.*, pp. 333–334; Pruden, "A Sociological Study of a Texas Lynching," *op. cit.*, p. 6; White, "The Eruption of Tulsa," *op. cit.*, p. 909.

[3] Chicago Commission on Race Relations, *The Negro in Chicago*, p. 38.

[4] *Ibid.*, p. 599; see also Lee and Humphrey, *Race Riot*, pp. 107, 118–119.

[5] Rich, *The Presidents and Civil Disorder*, p. 73.

[6] Gwynn, *Imperial Policing*, pp. 45–46.

[7] Instances of unreliability of the police, army, and navy during the French Revolution may be found in Stephens, *The History of the French Revolution*, pp. 125–126, 368–369, 386–387, 398, 400–441. For defections among Russian troops, cf. Trotsky, *History of the Russian Revolution*, Vol. 1, pp. 102 ff.; Vol. III, pp. 23, 181–182, 290–291.

The Hostile Outburst

CONCLUSIONS

We have not attempted in this chapter to account for the development of any single riot or related outburst. Rather we have attempted to outline the general determinants which must be present if any single outburst is to occur. We have organized these conditions into a sequence of increasing determinancy—structural conduciveness, strain, generalized beliefs, precipitating factors, and mobilization. Each of these has to be present for the next to assume the status of a determinant of a hostile outburst. Together the determinants constitute a sufficient condition for such an outburst.

In any particular outburst of hostility, the accumulation of the empirical events and situations which contain the determinants may be in any temporal order. For these events and situations to assume significance as determinants, however, they must occur in the context of—or be interpreted by potential participants in the context of—the logically prior necessary conditions. For instance, a racial incident between a Negro and a white may spark a race riot. But unless this incident occurs in the context of a structurally conducive atmosphere (i.e., an atmosphere in which people perceive violence to be a possible means of expression) and in an atmosphere of strain (i.e., an atmosphere in which people perceive the incident as symbolic of a troubled state of affairs), the incident will pass without becoming a determinant in a racial outburst.

In addition to this account of the positive determinants of hostile outbursts, we must assess the influence of several deterrents. How is the situation made less structurally conducive for hostility? How are conditions of strain alleviated? How are hostile beliefs dispelled? How can the aggrieved be prevented from communicating with one another? How can authorities head off mobilization to commit some sort of hostile act? The combination of all these factors—positive determinants and deterrents—yields a kind of equilibrium model of counteracting forces. Some forces push toward the outburst of hostility and some forces resist the influence of these forces. Depending on the relations among these forces at any given time, it is possible to estimate the future development of a potential outburst—whether it will wither away, be diverted into some other kind of behavior, be contained, or move toward an outburst of hostility.

CHAPTER IX

THE NORM-ORIENTED MOVEMENT

INTRODUCTION

Definition of a Norm-oriented Movement. A norm-oriented movement is an attempt to restore, protect, modify, or create norms in the name of a generalized belief.[1] Participants may be trying either to affect norms directly (e.g., efforts of a feminist group to establish a private educational system for women) or induce some constituted authority to do so (e.g., pressures from the same group on a governmental agency to support or create a public co-educational system).[2] Any kind of norm—economic, educational, political, religious—may become the subject of such movements.[3] Furthermore, norm-oriented movements may occur on any scale—for instance, agitation by a group of nations to establish an international police force; agitation by groups of businessmen for tax legislation on the federal, state, or local level; agitation by the members of a local union to federate with other unions; agitation by a minority of members of a local chapter of the Society for the Prevention of Cruelty to Animals to amend the by-laws of the chapter. Finally, the definition includes movements of all political flavors—reactionary, conservative, progressive, and radical.[4]

A normative innovation—a new law, custom, bureau, association, or segment of a political party—frequently appears as the result of a norm-oriented movement.[5] Not all normative changes, however, are

---

[1] Above, pp. 109–111.
[2] For numerous examples of both kinds of agitation, cf. R. Strachey, *Struggle. The Stirring Story of Women's Advance in England* (New York, 1930). For examples of many attempts to affect educational norms directly, cf. Bestor's account of the activities of the Chautauqua movement in the United States in the late nineteenth and early twentieth centuries. A. E. Bestor, Jr., *Chautauqua Publications* (Chautauqua, N.Y., 1934), pp. 1–12.
[3] Cf. Lasswell, Casey, and Smith, *Propaganda and Promotional Activities*, pp. xii–xvii; Gerth and Mills, *Character and Social Structure*, p. 440. For a classification of movements involving race relations, cf. C. E. Glick, "Collective Behavior in Race Relations," *American Sociological Review*, Vol. 13 (1948), pp. 288–289.
[4] Above, pp. 110–111. Turner and Killian, *Collective Behavior*, pp. 320–321.
[5] Above, p. 111 and below, pp. 305–306. Also Smelser, *Social Change in the Industrial Revolution*, and H. D. Lasswell, "Agitation," *Encyclopaedia of the*

The Norm-Oriented Movement

preceded by a movement with generalized beliefs. In fact, all normative changes could be located on a continuum from those routinely incorporated to those adopted as a result of an agitation based on a generalized belief. At one extreme of the continuum is the example of a top business manager who reorganizes the sales department of his company simply by deciding to do so; such reorganization is not preceded by a period of agitation in the name of a cause. At the other extreme are outbursts such as the Townsend Plan movement which are replete with hysteria, accusations, exaggerated claims and myths of omnipotence.[1] Between the two extremes lie many movements which achieve their ends without ever developing generalized beliefs. An example is the gradual incorporation of women into the police forces of England and the United States.[2] Later in the chapter we shall inquire into the conditions under which demands for normative change are likely to blossom into agitations based on full-blown systems of generalized beliefs.

Norm-oriented Movements and other Collective Outbursts. A norm-oriented movement involves elements of panic (flight from existing norms or impending normative change), craze (plunge to establish new means), and hostility (eradication of someone or something responsible for evils). These lower-level components appear, explicitly or implicitly, in the beliefs that accompany norm-oriented movements.[3]

Panic, craze, and hostility sometimes find open expression during the development of a norm-oriented movement.[4] The armed uprising against state authorities in Massachusetts in 1786 known as Shay's rebellion, for instance, erupted from a norm-oriented agitation to reduce the state debt and to issue paper money. Violence in the

---

Social Sciences, Vol. 1, p. 488. For a catalogue of social changes which modern American social movements have produced, see T. H. Greer, *American Social Reform Movements* (New York, 1949), pp. 281–287.

[1] Above, pp. 114–120.

[2] C. Owings, *Women Police: A Study of the Development and Status of the Women Police Movement* (New York, 1925), pp. 2–9, 97–115. For an account of a flurry of opposition among British male police, see pp. 37–38. Many agrarian reforms in Denmark during the late nineteenth and early twentieth centuries were incorporated quietly and unemotionally. F. C. Howe, "Agrarian Movements. Denmark," *Encyclopaedia of the Social Sciences*, Vol. 1, pp. 501–502.

[3] Above, pp. 111–113.

[4] For discussion of some of the specific conditions under which these lower-level outbursts appear, see above, pp. 135–157, 175–217 and 227–261. Turner and Killian treat elemental forms of collective behavior as "phases" of a social movement rather than the "whole of it." *Collective Behavior*, p. 308. On the descriptive level, norm-oriented movements are less fleeting than panics, crazes, and hostile outbursts; also they develop a more enduring *esprit de corps* among their participants than do the lower-level outbursts. Heberle, "Observations on the Sociology of Social Movements," *op. cit.*, p. 350.

The Norm-Oriented Movement

Whiskey rebellion in Pennsylvania in 1794 was a manifestation of opposition to an excise tax on spirits.[1] Personal attacks, property destruction, and other forms of hostility have accompanied suffragist and temperance movements.[2] As we shall see, the degree of overt expression of these lower-level components in norm-oriented movements depends largely on the conditions of structural conduciveness and the behavior of agencies of social control.

Many norm-oriented movements occur independently of value-oriented movements, which call for more sweeping changes. The agitation for shorter hours of labor (a norm-oriented movement) in the United States, for instance, has been limited to demands for normative change; on the whole it has not been attached to movements which challenge the values of the capitalist system.[3] In other contexts, however, the same movement may be an adjunct of a value-oriented movement. In England, continental Europe and Russia the movement for shorter hours was subordinated to socialistic aims of laboring groups in the late nineteenth century.[4]

All value-oriented movements imply a reorganization of all lower-level components, including norms.[5] For example, a movement for national independence which challenges the legitimacy of foreign rulers is in the first instance a value-oriented movement. Necessarily this movement envisions the reorganization of many political norms such as the regulation of tax-collection, the exercise of police power, etc. Frequently such nationalist movements also incorporate additional demands for normative change, e.g., agrarian reform.[6]

Other movements, although they do not explicitly challenge the legitimacy of values, in fact attempt to usurp the legitimate powers of constitutional authorities to gain their ends. The Ku Klux Klan during Reconstruction, for instance, maintained that it was upholding the values of Americanism, but it seized many governmental functions in Southern States.[7] In this chapter we shall concentrate on

---

[1] Beard, *The Rise of American Civilization*, Vol. 1, pp. 307, 357–358.
[2] Strachey, *Struggle*, pp. 288–336.
[3] S. Perlman, "Short Hours Movement," *Encyclopaedia of the Social Sciences*, Vol. 14, pp. 45–46. In the 1880's, however, the movement for shorter hours became assimilated to the doctrines of the First International and the anarchists.
[4] *Ibid.*
[5] Above, pp. 121–122.
[6] I. L. Evans, "Agrarian Movements. East Central Europe and the Balkan Countries," *Encyclopaedia of the Social Sciences*, Vol. 1, pp. 502–504; E. R. Mangel, "Agrarian Movements, Poland and Lithuania. Latvia and Estonia," *ibid.*, pp. 507–508.
[7] Coulter, *The South During Reconstruction 1867–1877*, p. 169. Another example of this borderline kind of movement is the "shirted" societies of the 1930's. C. W. Ferguson, *Fifty Million Brothers* (New York, 1937), p. 129. Above, pp. 119–120.

The Norm-Oriented Movement

movements which are not part of revolutionary and other value-oriented movements.

Norm-oriented Movements and More General Social Movements. Movements oriented to specific norms should be distinguished from those with more general programs. In general the latter possess neither sufficiently crystallized beliefs nor a sufficient degree of mobilization to fall in the category of collective outbursts.[1] Rather they provide a backdrop from which many specific norm-oriented movements emanate.

Examples of general social movements include the following: (1) The labor movement is "an organized and continuous effort on the part of wage earners to improve their standards of living over a national area."[2] From this general movement have flowed many specific agitations for normative change—shorter hours, higher wages, fringe benefits, legal protection, etc. (2) The peace movement is a general social movement which has been in existence since its beginning in England during the Revolutionary and Napoleonic Wars. During this period it has spawned many specific movements for international arbitration, codification of international law, disarmament, and finally the cessation of nuclear testing.[3] (3) The humanitarian movement, also a product of the late eighteenth and early nineteenth centuries, lay behind a vast number of more specific reforms, not only in the field of international peace, but also with regard to the status of slaves, criminals, children, animals, and the insane.[4] (4) Feminism, the general movement for women's rights, has manifested itself in numerous specific norm-oriented movements for

---

[1] Cf. Blumer's distinction between "specific social movements" and "general social movements." "Collective Behavior," in Lee (ed.), *op. cit.*, pp. 199–201. Blumer also refers to "drifts" which are even more general and less articulate than general social movements. Heberle refers to general social movements as "trends or tendencies." *Social Movements*, pp. 8–9. For similar distinctions, cf. Turner and Killian, *Collective Behavior*, pp. 344–345, and Greer, *American Social Reform Movements*, pp. 5–6.

[2] M. R. Beard, *The American Labor Movement* (New York, 1939), p. 1.

[3] A. F. C. Beales, *The History of Peace* (New York, 1936), pp. 6–14.

[4] *Ibid.*, pp. 45 ff.; R. Coupland, *The British Anti-Slavery Movement* (London, 1933), p. 36; E. G. Fairholme and W. Pain, *A Century of Work for Animals* (London, 1924), pp. 16–22; W. J. Schultz, "Animal Protection," *Encyclopaedia of the Social Sciences*, Vol. 2, pp. 62–63. Sometimes a specific organization— e.g., the Humanitarian League formed in England in 1890—appears as a kind of "bond between various lines of humane work." R. C. McCrea, *The Humane Movement* (New York, 1910), pp. 120–121. For an account of the intimate associate among anti-slavery, women's rights, and temperance in the United States in the 1830's and 1840's, cf. J. H. Tufts, "Liberal Movements in the United States—Their Methods and Aims," *The International Journal of Ethics*, Vol. 46 (1936), pp. 257–258. For an account of how these strands separated into distinct reform movements after the Civil War, cf. L. Filler, *The Crusade Against Slavery 1830–1860* (New York, 1960), pp. xv, 32–46.

The Norm-Oriented Movement

the establishment of equal rights in education, economic opportunity, political participation, etc.[1] (5) The "Country Life movement" refers to a general movement concerning "the cultural and social welfare of the rural population."[2] Within this general movement many specific problems—health, town-country relations, education, home, religion, farm youth, farm income—have come up for consideration and projected reform.[3]

In this chapter we shall not study general social movements as such, since they do not fall into our definition of a norm-oriented movement. We shall mention them from time to time, but only as they impinge on or elucidate more specific norm-oriented movements. Similarly, we shall consider broad movements of "public opinion" only insofar as they provide a background of sentiments and opinions from which collective outbursts flow and upon which their success sometimes depends.[4]

Norm-oriented Movements and Types of Organizations. Frequently agitation in a norm-oriented movement is carried out by an organization, such as a political party, a pressure group, or a club—or any combination of these. The organizations associated with a movement, moreover, influence the movement's development and its success or failure. In this chapter we shall touch only lightly on the reasons why different kinds of organizations are drawn into norm-oriented movements; we shall concentrate mainly on determinants which transcend these movements' concrete organizational differences. In this introductory section, however, we shall sketch the broad lines of variation among the kinds of organizations that become involved in norm-oriented movements.

Among these organizations a fundamental distinction is that between political parties and non-party organizations. Parties, as Heberle has shown, may be related to norm-oriented movements in various ways:

(1) "A party can be part of a broader social movement."[5] The Vegetarian Party, for instance, could join with associations such as the Seventh Day Adventists in a movement to regulate the serving of meat in army camps. (2) "[A party] may be independent from a parti-

---

[1] K. Anthony, *Feminism in Germany and Scandinavia* (New York, 1915), pp. 19–26; Strachey, *Struggle*.
[2] C. C. Taylor, "Country Life Movement," *Encyclopaedia of the Social Sciences*, Vol. 4, p. 497.
[3] *Ibid.*, p. 498.
[4] Above, p. 76. For an account of long-term developments of public opinion and its modes of expression, cf. H. Speier, "Historical Development of Public Opinion," *American Journal of Sociology*, Vol. 55 (1949–50), pp. 376–388.
[5] Heberle, "Observations on the Sociology of Social Movements," *op. cit.*, p. 352.

The Norm-Oriented Movement

cular movement and embody eventually in its membership in whole or in part several social movements; this has been the tendency in the major American parties."[1] (3) "The same movement may be represented in several different political parties."[2] The movement for federal aid to education, for instance, has found its way into the platforms of both the Democratic and Republican parties (even though the parties differ in their detailed recommendations). (4) "Finally, a social movement may reject on principle the affiliation with any political party."[3]

Non-party organizations that become involved in norm-oriented movements are also diverse. The following dimensions are relevant in classifying such organizations: (1) An organization may be *established*, i.e., in existence for some time before being drawn into a movement; or it may be a *new* group which forms as the movement develops. (2) An organization may be *formally* constituted, with title, charter, by-laws, and procedural formalities; or it may be an *informal* club or gathering of interested citizens. (3) An organization's purpose may be *general*, i.e., concerned with a range of matters much wider than the specific norm-oriented movement it joins; or it may be geared *specifically* to agitating for a single type of measure. Table 11 gives illustrations of organizations according to these dimensions;[4] each cell contains an instance of an organization (or type of organization) that has become involved in a norm-oriented movement.

The same norm-oriented movement frequently works through one organization, then changes to another. Between 1877 and 1896, for instance, the Midwestern farmers' grievances were channeled first through a large independent political association (the Farmers' Alliance), next through an independent third party (the People's Party), and finally through the Democratic Party.[5] The battle against prostitution in New York City in the late nineteenth and early twentieth centuries was fought first by transient groups of crusading citizens who disbanded after certain reforms had been effected, later

---

[1] *Ibid.* For historical instance in which major parties have taken over social movements from minor parties, cf. Haynes, *Third Party Movements Since the Civil War with Special Reference to Iowa*, p. 3; J. D. Hicks, *The Populist Revolt* (Minneapolis, 1931), pp. 340–378.

[2] Heberle, "Observations on the Sociology of Social Movements," *op. cit.*, p. 352.

[3] *Ibid.*

[4] In one sense it is incorrect to dichotomize each dimension, for each is a continuum. The entries in each cell, then—for instance, formal, new, and specific—are not to be interpreted in any absolute sense, but only relative to other organizations that become active in norm-oriented movements.

[5] Hicks, *The Populist Revolt*, Chs. 4–13.

The Norm-Oriented Movement

TABLE 11

TYPES OF ORGANIZATIONS INVOLVED IN NORM-ORIENTED MOVEMENTS

	Established		New	
	Formal	Informal	Formal	Informal
General	Southern Methodist Church in the fight for legislation on temperance[1]	Political bosses among immigrant groups[2]	Farmers' Alliance in the fight on behalf of Midwestern farmers in late nineteenth century[3]	Citizens' club interested in the general improvement of local government during periods of corruption[4]
Specific	Lobbies such as the National Association of Manufacturers[5]	Local clubs interested, e.g., in safeguarding interests of residents in neighborhood[6]	Anti-Corn Law League in the fight for tariff reduction in the 1830's and 1840's in Great Britain[7]	Local associations which spring up during a social movement or election campaign[8]

[1] For an account of how the Southern Methodist Church entered and led the fight for temperance in the Southern states between 1865 and 1900, cf. H. D. Farish, *The Circuit Rider Dismounts* (Richmond, Va., 1938), p. 324.

[2] Handlin, *The Uprooted*, p. 212.

[3] Alliancemen characterized the activities of the Alliance as "first, social; second, educational; third, financial; fourth, political." Hicks, *The Populist Revolt*, pp. 128–152.

[4] The informal gatherings of citizens before the formation of the Know Nothing Party in California in 1854 are examples; these citizens were "anxious to turn to anything which would free them from the necessity of continuing to vote for candidates nominated and controlled by thoroughly corrupt and dishonest politicians." P. Hurt, "The Rise and Fall of the 'Know Nothings' in California," *Quarterly of the California Historical Society*, Vol. IX (1930), p. 25. Later this informal agitation congealed into the Know Nothing Party, which scored successes in the elections of 1854 and 1855.

[5] For discussion of lobbies and pressure groups, cf. V. O. Key, Jr., *Politics, Parties, and Pressure Groups*, 4th ed. (New York, 1958), pp. 142–177; P. Odegard, *The American Public Mind* (New York, 1930), Ch. VII; H. Eckstein, *Pressure Group Politics: The Case of the British Medical Association* (Stanford, 1960), p. 9.

[6] The Panoramic Hill Association in Berkeley, California, is a vaguely delineated group of property-owners and other residents on Panoramic Hill, east of the campus of the University of California. It meets when the occasion demands to consider matters such as the construction of a new road, the permissibility of building apartment-houses in the vicinity, etc.

[7] H. D. Jordan, "The Political Methods of the Anti-Corn Law League," *Political Science Quarterly*, Vol. 42 (1927), pp. 58–76.

[8] Cf. the discussion of the proliferation of local reform clubs in the early and middle nineteenth century, in C. Brinton, "Clubs," *Encyclopaedia of the Social Sciences*, Vol. 3, p. 575.

The Norm-Oriented Movement

by a more enduring Committee of Fourteen, which acted as a pressure group on behalf of interested citizens.[1] Many social movements in the United States have had their beginnings in hastily convened, unstable associations and then evolved into institutionalized pressure-groups through which grievances are channeled routinely. The early Grange or Farmers' Alliance, for instance, stands in contrast with contemporary farm organizations, with their offices in Washington, their complicated lines of communication to local farm associations, and their intimate and continuous contact with Congress and the executive.[2] After such consolidation takes place, norm-oriented movements based on generalized beliefs develop only when the pressure-group has failed to gain satisfaction for its supporters through routine activity.

The Value-added Sequence of a Norm-oriented Movement. We shall analyze norm-oriented movements under the same set of categories we have already employed extensively—structural conduciveness, strain, generalized beliefs, precipitating factors, mobilization for action, and the response of agencies of social control. This treatment of the norm-oriented movement as a logical accumulation of determinants is similar to the study of the natural history of social movements.[3] In this chapter, however, we are not interested primarily in the temporal accumulation of events; we are attempting to establish the conditions under which events become significant as determinants of a norm-oriented movement.[4] The empirical succession of events may coincide with the analytic accumulation of determinants;

[1] W. C. Waterman, *Prostitution and its Repression in New York City 1900–1931* (New York, 1932), pp. 98–116.
[2] A. Leiserson, "Opinion Research and the Political Process: Farm Policy, an Example," *Public Opinion Quarterly*, Vol. 13 (1949), p. 37. For other discussions of the history of agricultural agitation in the United States, cf. Key, *Politics, Parties, and Pressure Groups*, pp. 24–46; B. B. Kendrick, "Agrarian Movements. United States," *Encyclopaedia of the Social Sciences*, Vol. 1, pp. 508–511; Greer, *American Social Reform Movements*, pp. 213–237. For parallel developments in British agricultural agitation, cf. J. L. Hammond, "Agrarian Movements. Great Britain," *Encyclopaedia of the Social Sciences*, Vol. 1, pp. 495–497. For a discussion of the evolution of Chambers of Commerce, cf. P. Studenski, "Chambers of Commerce," *Encyclopaedia of the Social Sciences*, Vol. 3, pp. 325–326.
[3] Above, pp. 18–20. For further treatments of the natural history of movements, cf. Hertzler, *Social Institutions*, pp. 80–81; Park and Burgess, *Introduction to the Science of Sociology*, p. 874; J. Davis, *Contemporary Social Movements* (New York, 1930), pp. 8–9; E. C. Lindeman, *The Community* (New York, 1921), pp. 119–137; Coleman, *Community Conflict*, pp. 9–14; J. S. Burgess, "The Study of Modern Social Movements as a Means for Clarifying the Process of Social Action," *Social Forces*, Vol. 22 (1943–44), pp. 271–275; C. W. King, *Social Movements in the United States* (New York, 1956), Ch. 3.
[4] For a distinction between the uniformities of the natural history of movements and uniformities in functional relationships, cf. P. Meadows, "An Analysis of Social Movements," *Sociology and Social Research*, Vol. 27 (1942–43), pp. 225–226.

for instance, conditions of structural conduciveness may arise first, conditions of strain next, and a generalized belief next. This coincidence need not be the case, however. A generalized belief may have lain dormant for a long time before any movement bearing its name arises; in order for this belief to become a determinant in such a movement it must be activated by conditions of conduciveness and strain. While we shall refer occasionally to temporal sequences of events, *we are not attempting to formulate generalizations about natural histories, but to generate a systematic account of the activation of events and situations as determinants.*

STRUCTURAL CONDUCIVENESS

The Structural Possibility of Demanding Normative Changes Alone. The most general condition of conduciveness concerns the possibility for demanding modifications of norms *without simultaneously appearing to demand a more fundamental modification of values.* If social arrangements permit these more limited kinds of demands, these arrangements are conducive to the development of norm-oriented movements; if social arrangements are such that all demands for normative change tend more or less immediately to generalize into conflicts over values, they are not conducive to the development of norm-oriented movements.

In specifying the kinds of social structures which meet these conditions of conduciveness we must distinguish between (1) the source of demands for normative change in the population and (2) the kind of reception that these demands receive at the political level. Gabriel Almond has made essentially the same distinction in another context in his separation of the process of *interest-articulation* from the process of *interest-aggregation*.[1] Interest-articulation refers to the structures through which interests, grievances, and desires are made explicit. Such structures include lobbies, pressure groups, armies, bureaucracies, churches, kinship, and lineage groups, ethnic groups, and status and class groups.[2] Interest-aggregation refers to the structures in which these articulated interests are combined, weighed, and forged into policy. Examples of structures for the aggregation of interests are legislatures, bureaucracies, political blocs, and coalitions.[3] Although a single organization (e.g., a political party) may engage to a degree in both articulation and aggregation of interests,

---

[1] G. A. Almond, "Introduction: A Functional Approach to Comparative Politics," in G. A. Almond and J. S. Coleman (eds.), *The Politics of the Developing Areas* (Princeton, 1960), pp. 16 ff.
[2] *Ibid.*, pp. 33–38.
[3] *Ibid.*, pp. 38–45.

The Norm-Oriented Movement

the analytic distinction between the two phases of the political process still holds.

If the expression of dissatisfaction is to be channeled into norm-oriented movements, both interest-articulation and interest-aggregation must be structurally differentiated to a high degree.[1] First, with regard to articulation, if political, economic, and ethnic cleavages coincide,[2] it is difficult to prevent specific grievances and interests from generalizing, thus giving protest a more diffuse character. For instance, many grievances of agrarian populations stem from economic conflicts between city and countryside. These specific conflicts often foster deep resentments. In addition, however,

> This hatred becomes all the more violent when racial, national, or sectional differences add weight to the socio-cultural differences of country and town. Agrarian rage against usury provided a sinister background upon which religious and political fanaticism inscribed the vengeance of Kurdish shepherd and Turkish peasant against the Armenians. Antagonism to the alien British money lender was abundantly in evidence in the inchoate agrarianism of the American South in the early decades of independence. "Eastern Capital" was a bugaboo of midwestern agrarianism of the greenback and Farmers Alliance period.[3]

In short, if the social bases for conflict of interest (e.g., position in economic or political order) are not separate from kinship, ethnic, regional, or religious groups, *any* grievance is likely to become a conflict of values.[4] If, however, the structures for articulating grievances are differentiated from one another demands tend to be formulated more in terms of specific programs for normative regulation[5] which do not excite such a wide range of conflicts.

---

[1] Eckstein makes a similar point when he suggests that the degree of centralization of pressure groups is closely associated with the degree of centralization of the government. *Pressure Group Politics*, p. 21.

[2] Above, pp. 229231–.

[3] A. Johnson, "Agrarian Movements. Introduction," *Encyclopaedia of the Social Sciences*, Vol. I, p. 491.

[4] Almond, "A Functional Approach to Comparative Politics," *op. cit.*, p. 33. Almond calls these bases "non-associational interests" which are contrasted with more specific associations such as trade unions, organizations of businessmen, ethnic associations, civic groups, etc.

[5] For a discussion of the explosive overlap between ethnic-linguistic and functional divisions in South Asia, cf. Weiner, "The Politics of South Asia," in Almond and Coleman (eds.), *op. cit.*, pp. 239–242. Note also the contrast between traditional European and American farm organizations: "The country life movements of European countries have started with quite different premises and problems than those of the United States. . . . The peasants' and farmers' organizations which multiplied so rapidly in most of the European countries during the nineteenth century concerned themselves with all aspects of living—economic, social, intellectual, and moral. Thus there was for a long time no place for a [more differentiated] country life movement such as that in the United States,

The Norm-Oriented Movement

With regard to interest-aggregation as well, a high degree of differentiation between the machinery for interest-aggregation from other kinds of social control encourages the development of more specific demands for normative change. In a society with a fusion between religious and political authority—many medieval societies could serve as examples—protests against specific normative arrangements inevitably tend to generalize into heresies.[1] Under such conditions the mechanisms for insulating specific demands from challenges to legitimacy itself are not highly developed. Similarly, in contemporary totalitarian societies, the legitimacy of the state and the political management of limited protests are relatively undifferentiated. Totalitarian ideologies generally subordinate all institutions—labor, business, education, the military—to the political and ideological concerns of the state.[2] Protest in these spheres tends to generalize into a political crisis. Deviance in many spheres tends to be treated as a political and ideological threat. This is because the claim to legitimate power is not differentiated from other kinds of social control.

By way of contrast, historical developments in parts of Western Europe and the United States have resulted in a high degree of differentiation of the claim to legitimacy from demands for institutional change. Even political leaders can be attacked severely without endangering the legitimacy of their office itself. When President Truman dismissed General MacArthur in 1951, the latter returned to the United States in great glory, rode through a ticker-tape parade in New York, mobilized all sorts of opposition to Truman, testified before Congress, and later delivered the keynote speech at the Republican National Convention. Yet through all this neither Truman's right to dismiss MacArthur, nor his right to hold the office of the Presidency, nor the sanctity of the office itself was even questioned. The question of legitimacy was separated clearly from the question of political opposition. This series of events might be contrasted with the dismissal of General Zhukov in the Soviet Union a few years later. His removal was revealed amidst a shroud of secrecy. Once dismissed, furthermore, there was no possibility that he could defend his case publicly, or initiate a movement for reform. In fact, he later confessed publicly to *ideological* errors and acknowledged that he had deserved the dismissal. Political agitation on his

---

organized for the most part by semipopular associations and teaching agencies." Taylor, "Country Life Movement," *op. cit.*, p. 498.
[1] For a characterization of the subordination of virtually all institutional spheres to moral-religious concerns, cf. Sorokin's discussion of the "ideational" mentality in *Social and Cultural Dynamics*, Vol. I, Chs. 2, 3.
[2] For a characterization of the revolutionary Nazi ideology, above, pp. 128–129.

The Norm-Oriented Movement

behalf was unthinkable because it would have constituted a threat to the legitimacy of the regime.

More broadly, the democratic countries of Northwestern Europe and North America have institutionalized—with varying degrees of finality—this principle of differentiation under formulae such as "separation of church and state," "civil control of military power," "separation of church and school," "academic freedom," "freedom of expression," etc. These formulae imply maximum autonomy for each institutional sector, and great limitations on the ability of each sector to interfere with the central political "clearing-house" for grievances in society. This high level of differentiation accounts in part for the relative predominance of norm-oriented movements as the typical mode of expressing collective grievances in these countries, and the relative absence of revolutionary movements in the same countries in recent times.[1]

The same principle applies to examples less extreme than the contrast between differentiated democratic systems and undifferentiated theocratic or totalitarian systems. When, for instance, a political party claims that it is the main instrument for guaranteeing the legitimacy of the state (as in the case of many nationalist parties in the developing nations)[2] it is difficult for competing parties or interest groups to challenge this party on bases other than the claim to legitimacy.

In short, then, for norm-oriented movements to be possible in a society, the articulation of interests and the aggregation of interests must be differentiated—both within themselves and from one another —to a high degree. This is not to say that grievances are not expressed and heard *at all* under less differentiated structural conditions;[3] it is true, however, that under such conditions grievances will be less likely to take the form of a collective outburst based on generalized norm-oriented beliefs.

The Channels of Agitation for Norm-oriented Movements. In the remaining discussion, we shall assume that the broadest conditions of conduciveness just discussed remain unchanged. Within such conditions, what kinds of channels for expressing dissatisfaction are

[1] Cf. M. Handman, "The Bureaucratic Culture Pattern and Political Revolutions," *American Journal of Sociology*, Vol. 39 (1933), pp. 301–313; J. J. Senturia, "Political Conspiracy," *Encyclopaedia of the Social Sciences*, Vol. 4, pp. 238–241.

[2] Cf. L. W. Pye, "The Politics of Southeast Asia," in Almond and Coleman (eds.), *op. cit.*, pp. 109–125. The party system of the Philippines poses an interesting contrast to most other Southeast Asian countries. P. 97.

[3] For a discussion of the structural variability in the modes of expressing grievances in different economic systems, cf. Kerr, Dunlop, Harbison, and Myers, *Industrialism and Industrial Man*, pp. 202–233.

The Norm-Oriented Movement

most conducive for the development of norm-oriented movements rather than other kinds of outbursts?

In general, the discontented must have *some* degree of access to some method of affecting the normative order. Democratic systems possess various ways of passing information, sentiments, and desires to governmental and other agencies—petitions, elections, initiatives, referenda, letters to congressmen, letters to the press, demonstrations, public opinion polls, requests for court injunctions, etc. Through such channels citizens influence authorities, who in turn are responsible for influencing the character of laws, regulations, and other kinds of norms. Under decentralized democratic systems, aroused individuals or groups may be able to by-pass such authorities altogether and thus affect the normative order directly. Examples of this direct action are movements to establish private schools for the deaf or blind, to introduce playgrounds under private auspices, to establish consumer cooperatives, or to introduce a welfare scheme into a labor union's program.[1] In such cases it is necessary to influence others privately to cooperate in building an enterprise; thus such movements have a political dimension. Still this kind of political action differs from agitating to influence governmental authorities.

For each channel available for influencing the normative order, it is possible to rely on one or more of many types of social organization—independent associations, political parties, pressure groups, clubs, political bosses, or informal gatherings.[2]

The potential availability of many different channels for affecting normative arrangements, plus the potential availability of many different kinds of organizations, presents a vast array of alternative strategies and tactics for any given movement. The development of the prohibition movement in the United States illustrates this great variety of methods. At first, the movement was carried by the Protestant churches (1810–26). Shortly thereafter, however, local organizations devoted specifically to temperance began to arise and agitate for prohibition on the local level (1826–1840's). In the late 1860's Prohibition parties began to form, and between 1880 and 1890

---

[1] Thus Schultz refers to the distinction between the "legislative" (i.e., agitating for legislation) and the "institutional" (direct creation of agency) of the animal welfare movement. "Animal Protection," *op. cit.*, pp. 62–63. The movement to establish playgrounds and related facilities has evolved over time from private philanthropic establishment to municipal support and control. C. E. Rainwater, *The Play Movement in the United States* (Chicago, 1922), p. 192; J. F. Nash, "Playgrounds," *Encyclopaedia of the Social Sciences*, Vol. 12, pp. 162–163. For examples of mixed private and public responsibility, cf. H. Best, *Blindness and the Blind in the United States* (New York, 1934) pp. 156–161, 299–308; and H. Best, *The Deaf: Their Position in Society and the Provision for their Education in the United States* (New York, 1914), pp. 129–144.

[2] Above, pp. 274–277.

The Norm-Oriented Movement

these parties attempted to secure temperance legislation at the state level. The period between 1893 and 1906 marked a reversion to non-partisan political activity at the local level. Between 1906 and 1913 non-partisan activity continued, this time at the state level. Finally, beginning in 1913, the temperance forces shifted to the national level and ultimately secured the adoption of the Eighteenth Amendment to the Constitution.[1] Later in the chapter we shall attempt to account for some of these shifts from one method to another.

Many norm-oriented movements crystallize when it appears to the discontented that *one* method of agitation has disappeared or is disappearing. Consider the following examples: (1) During the nineteenth century, labor agitation in the United States followed a rough cyclical pattern; "it... centered on economic or trade-union action during prosperity only to change abruptly to 'panaceas' and politics with the descent of depression."[2] During prosperity, when the demand for labor was high, workers could use demands for higher wages and strikes effectively; furthermore, they could afford to finance union organizations and periods of idleness in strikes. During depressions these methods for protecting their interests became ineffective. Laborers were forced to look to other channels of agitation, such as demands for protective legislation from the government, or grandiose schemes to rebuild and solidify the entire industrial structure.[3] (2) In the 1850's conflict over the slavery question had virtually paralyzed both major political parties. This temporary failure of the party system, it has been argued, accounts in part for the discontent which coalesced into the Know Nothing Movement. Later, as the parties realigned and as slavery and other issues could be better incorporated into the major party structure, this furious little nativistic movement declined as rapidly as it had arisen.[4]

[1] E. H. Cherrington, *The Evolution of Prohibition in the United States of America* (Westerville, Ohio, 1920), pp. 89–321. See also J. A. Krout, *The Origins of Prohibition* (New York, 1925, pp. 101 ff.

[2] Perlman, *A History of Trade Unionism in the United States*, pp. 141–142; for details of these fluctuations, cf. Perlman, pp. 4, 18–28, 45–58, 62–64, 68–71, 81–93; L. Symes, *Rebel America* (New York, 1937), pp. 84–85, 115, 163. With the more permanent organization of the A.F.L. in the 1880's and 1890, greater continuity came to the activity of organized labor.

[3] For a similar modification of the agitational efforts of Southern farmers in depression and prosperity, cf. T. C. McCormick, "Cotton Acreage Laws and the Agrarian Movement," *Southwestern Social Science Quarterly*, Vol. 12 (1931–32), pp. 298–299.

[4] For discussion of this interpretation of the Know-Nothing Movement, cf. Handlin, *The Uprooted*, pp. 268–269; H. J. Desmond, *The Know-Nothing Party* (Washington, 1912), pp. 57–59; Schmeckebier, *History of the Know Nothing Party in Maryland*, p. 69; Hurt, "The Rise and Fall of the 'Know Nothings' in California," *op. cit.*, pp. 17–36; G. H. Haynes, "The Causes of Know-Nothing

The Norm-Oriented Movement

When *all* avenues of agitating for normative change are perceived to be closing or closed, moreover, dissatisfaction tends to find an outlet in a value-oriented movement or in expressions of hostility.[1] All avenues of agitation cannot be closed, then, if a norm-oriented movement is to occur. Neither, however, can these avenues be completely free from obstacles. If they were, normative reorganization would occur quickly and smoothly, with no need to mobilize for action under a generalized belief.

What conditions, then, encourage the rise of generalized norm-oriented beliefs? Avenues for agitation must be open, but participants must perceive a precarious balance between their own power and the power of the opposition. Many norm-oriented movements, in fact, are driven into a flurry of excited activity when ambiguity is introduced into the battle between proponents and opponents. This ambiguity is created by an event or series of events which signifies a new chance for success in overcoming the opposition *or* a new danger of being defeated by the opposition.[2] Note the operation of this principle in the following examples: (1) The rapid growth of the short-hours movement among American workers in many states in 1871 and 1872 "can be explained by its immediate successes in New York." Labor, previously unable to reduce hours by any known means, flocked to this method when it appeared to succeed in a single instance.[3] (2) The Know Nothing Movement received a great impetus after its strong showing in the elections of 1854.[4] (3) Henry George, who had been agitating for the single tax for a number of years, ran for the mayor of New York in 1866, and came in a surprising second. This success precipitated the most vigorous period of agitation in the single tax movement's history.[5] (4) During the

---

Success in Massachusetts," *American Historical Review*, Vol. 3 (1897–98), pp. 81–81; J. P. Senning, "The Know-Nothing Movement in Illinois," *Journal of the Illinois State Historical Society*, Vol. 7 (1914), pp. 9–19. The origins of other minor parties are discussed in Key, *Politics, Parties, and Pressure Groups*, pp. 282–296.

[1] Above, pp. 231–239, and below, pp. 324–334. A borderline case between a norm-oriented movement and a revolutionary movement was the Ku Klux Klan during the Reconstruction years. "It was one of those secret organizations which spring up in disordered states of society, when the bonds of law and government are all but dissolved, and when no confidence is felt in the regular administration of justice," Horn, *The Invisible Empire*, pp. 30–31.

[2] For an account of the development of more general issues, new issues, and antagonism as opposing sides coalesce in local community conflicts, cf. Coleman, *Community Conflict*, pp. 10–14. Lasswell maintains that agitation arises "when individuals are thrown into circumstances in which their claims on society are threatened or thwarted."

[3] M. C. Cahill, *Shorter Hours* (New York, 1932), p. 146.

[4] Desmond, *The Know-Nothing Party*, pp. 63–65.

[5] A. N. Young, *The Single Tax Movement in the United States* (Princeton, 1916), pp. 89–107.

The Norm-Oriented Movement

British anti-slavery movement, a Bill to prohibit slavery in the colonies was introduced in 1791. This Bill was defeated, 163 to 88, but the strong minority showing had the effect of stirring the abolitionists into even more furious action. "[The abolitionists] at once determined to work for its reversal by the only practicable means— by mobilizing public opinion against it."[1] (5) Many conservative norm-oriented movements (e.g., anti-socialized medicine, anti-Prohibition) crystallize when it appears that an opposing group has a chance of success in pushing its program.[2] (6) After the Supreme Court decision on school integration in 1954, some twenty segregationist groups appeared throughout the South to resist implementation of this decision. One of these, the National Association for the Advancement of White People, gave the segregationist movement a temporary boost by the following series of events:

The NAAWP—the personal creation of Bryant Bowles, a Floridan— won overnight notoriety for its role in the Milford, Del., controversy. At the beginning of the 1954–55 school term, the Milford Board of Education had admitted eleven Negro students to the hitherto white high school. Bowles quickly seized the opportunity to rally resentful white people of the area and to direct them in a campaign of school boycotts and demonstrations. State authorities reacted with equivocal and confused public statements, which had the practical effect of repudiating the Milford school board. In the end, segregation was restored, the school board replaced, and Bowles elevated to a position of honor in segregationist circles.

The outcome of this local skirmish unquestionably gave encouragement and impetus to the resistance movement throughout the South.[3]

Among the conditions of structural conduciveness, then, is the presence of channels for affecting normative arrangements which are open, but within which the chances of success and the chances of failure are balanced precariously.

The Lack of Opportunities for Other Outbursts. So much for the existence of channels for attempting to effect positive normative changes by agitation. Any discussion of structural conduciveness must refer also to the lack of alternative channels for expressing dissatisfaction. If facilities conducive for (say) a craze are available for a distressed group, energy will be diverted away from norm-oriented attempts to modify existing structural arrangements. Thus the situation of American farmers in the 1880's, as one historian notes,

---
[1] Coupland, *The Anti-Slavery Movement*, pp. 93–95.
[2] Turner and Killian, *Collective Behavior*, pp. 383–384. Also Studenski, "Chambers of Commerce," *op. cit.*, p. 327. "The chambers are opposed to all social movements considered inimical to commercial interests."
[3] H. C. Fleming, "Resistance Movements and Racial Desegration," *The Annals of the American Academy of Political and Social Science*, Vol. 304 (1956), p. 45.

differed from that of farmers in the early nineteenth century with regard to such facilities:

[In the 1880's the farmers] suffered, or at least they thought they suffered, from the railroads, from the trusts and the middlemen, from the money-lenders and the bankers, and from the muddled currency. These problems were not particularly new. Always the farmer had had to struggle with the problem of transportation. He had never known a time when the price of the things he had to buy was not as much too high as the price of the things he had to sell was too low. He had had his troubles with banks and bankers. But those earlier days were the days of cheap lands, and when things went wrong the disgruntled could seek solace in a move to the West. There was a chance to make a new start. Broader acres, more fertile fields, would surely bring the desired results. And with the restless ever moving to the West, the more stable elements of society left behind made pleasing progress. Now with the lands all taken and the frontier gone, this safety valve was closed. The frontier was turned back upon itself. The restless and discontented voiced their sentiments more and fled from them less. Hence rose the veritable chorus of denunciation directed against those individuals and those corporations who considered only their own advantage without regard to the effect their actions might have upon the farmer and his interests.[1]

Other channels of expression must be perceived as unavailable as well. The forces of social control must be able to prevent the use of mob violence, *coups d'état*, etc., as channels for gaining demands.[2] Finally, if a society is gripped by an encompassing social movement which occupies the attention of large numbers of its citizens—as in the case of the slavery question in the United States at mid-nineteenth century—other norm-oriented movements are frequently muted by the overwhelming social crisis at hand.[3] In sum, structural conduciveness for norm-oriented movements requires both the accessibility to avenues for affecting normative change and the inaccessibility to other avenues.

The Possibility of Communication. Like all collective outbursts, a norm-oriented movement requires a certain ability to communicate if beliefs are to be disseminated and action is to be mobilized. In this respect political control of the media of communication is important.

---

[1] Hicks, *The Populist Revolt*, p. 95. For similar effects of the frontier on urban labor, cf. Beard, *The American Labor Movement*, pp. 2–4.

[2] For the problem of the control of hostile outbursts, cf. above, pp. 261–269. For the conditions under which value-oriented movements turn into revolutionary movements, cf. below, pp. 367–379. For a brief but excellent statement of the conditions under which *coups d'état* occur cf. H. R. Spencer, "Coup d'Etat," *Encyclopaedia of the Social Sciences*, Vol. 4, pp. 508–510.

[3] Symes, *Rebel America*, p. 86; Hopkins, *The Rise of the Social Gospel in American Protestantism*, pp. 12–13.

The Norm-Oriented Movement

So is the presence of common language and culture; diversity among natives and immigrants is no doubt partially responsible for the historical lag in the organization of American labor.[1] Finally, past movements frequently establish patterns of communications among a class of people, thus giving future movements a head start in formulating, spreading, and acting on beliefs; the Grange, for instance, undoubtedly established a degree of organization among American farmers in the 1870's which facilitated the formation of future protest movements.[2]

STRAIN

In Chapter III we discussed structural strains that underlie *all* collective outbursts, including norm-oriented movements. In Chapter V we illustrated how these strains give rise to norm-oriented beliefs in particular. In this chapter we shall continue these discussions by outlining in more detail the kinds of strain that underlie norm-oriented movements. As previously, we shall organize the discussion in terms of the four components of action—facilities, organization of motivation, norms, and values.

Strain and Facilities. Sometimes the appearance of new knowledge initiates a movement to apply this knowledge in order to eradicate a condition previously taken for granted. The increase in knowledge concerning the controls of venereal diseases was one of the main factors which stimulated the movement to disseminate this knowledge through sex education in schools.[3]

Similar conditions of strain are created when the march of events by-passes the state of knowledge. Writes Galbraith:

> ... the conventional wisdom accommodates itself not to the world it is meant to interpret, but to the audience's view of the world. Since the latter remains with the comfortable and the familiar, while the world moves on, the conventional wisdom is always in danger of obsolescence. This is not immediately fatal. The fatal blow to the conventional wisdom comes when the conventional ideas fail signally to deal with some contingency to which obsolescence has made them palpably inapplicable.[4]

Strain and Organization: Deprivation. The history of social movements abounds with agitations on the part of groups who experience a real or apparent loss of wealth, power, or prestige. For example: (1) Farmers' movements have arisen in periods of depression and

---

[1] Beard, *The American Labor Movement*, p. 4.
[2] S. J. Buck, *The Agrarian Crusade* (New Haven, 1920), pp. 43–44.
[3] M. A. Bigelow, "Sex Education and Sex Ethics," *Encyclopaedia of the Social Sciences*, Vol. 14, pp. 9–10.
[4] Galbraith, *The Affluent Society*, p. 13.

The Norm-Oriented Movement

declined in periods of prosperity.[1] (2) Dissatisfactions over land distribution have also been at the root of numerous agrarian movements.[2] (3) As we have seen, the revival of old movements and the initiation of new ones among American laborers in the nineteenth century was closely related to their changing economic fortunes.[3] (4) Movements to regulate speculation have been stimulated by the financial losses and market disorganization occasioned by financial crises.[4] (5) The movement which culminated in the rise of the Progressive Party in the early twentieth century was based in large part on the apprehension that big business was acquiring too much economic and political power.[5] (6) In the 1820's, many of the supporters of the anti-Masonry movement—among whose objectives was to prohibit Masons from holding public office—came from the ranks of ministers who felt their own religious influence waning and who resented the Masons' religious appeal.[6]

Strain and Norms. Any disharmony between normative standards and actual social conditions can provide the basis for a movement whose objective it is to modify the norms. This is particularly true when either norms or social conditions undergo rapid change in a relatively short time. An example of rapid normative change which stimulated considerable unrest is the passage in the 1920's of laws restricting foreign immigration. Italians, Germans, and Jews reacted strongly to this apparently discriminatory legislation; their resulting discontent, Handlin has argued, lay behind various social movements

---

[1] Key, *Parties, Politics, and Pressure Groups*, pp. 24–46; Buck, *The Agrarian Crusade*, pp. 19–21, 77, 99–106; Hicks, *The Populist Revolt*, pp. 77–92, 99–100, 153–154, 309–311; Lipset, *Agrarian Socialism*, p. 4–10, 89 ff., 174–178; McCormick, "Cotton Acreage Laws and the Agrarian Movement," pp. 296–299, 302–303; H. Farmer, "The Economic Background of Southern Populism," *The South Atlantic Quarterly*, Vol. 29 (1930), pp. 78–91; Greer, *American Social Reform Movements*, pp. 213–227; O. M. Kile, *The Farm Bureau Movement* (New York, 1921), pp. 30–42, 45–46; J. O. Babcock, "The Farm Revolt in Iowa," *Social Forces*, Vol. XII (1934), p. 369. Stedman suggests that farmer and labor protest through third parties in American history reaches a height when "a declining price level was combined with a business recession but before the absolute bottom was reached. When the absoluted bottom was reached, one or both of the major parties recognized the widespread character of the discontent. . . . A program of reform and action [in the major parties] was set in motion. When this happened, the vote for farmer and labor parties tended to drop off sharply." M. S. Stedman, Jr., and S. W. Stedman, *Discontent at the Polls* (New York, 1950), pp. 100–101.

[2] P. Louis, "Agrarian Movements. Classical Antiquity," *Encyclopaedia of the Social Sciences*, Vol. 1, pp. 492–495.

[3] Above, p. 283. Also Cahill, *Shorter Hours*, pp. 13, 139–140; Hoffer, *The True Believer*, p. 24.

[4] For an instance of legislation which followed the panic of 1837, cf. McGrane, *The Panic of 1837*, pp. 235–236.

[5] Greer, *American Social Reform Movements*, pp. 94–95.

[6] Myers, *History of Bigotry in the United States*, pp. 129–132.

The Norm-Oriented Movement

among them in this period.[1] Sometimes new legislation creates strains on existing normative arrangements. In the late eighteenth century, for instance, many states began to use imprisonment rather than death as punishment for criminals. The resulting conditions in the prisons—overcrowding, mixing of all ages and types of offenders, etc.—underlay various movements for prison reform.[2] Finally, norm-oriented movements themselves, which threaten to alter the normative order, stimulate counter-movements (e.g., anti-socialized medicine) among those who feel endangered by the impending change.[3]

Sometimes strain results not from changes in norms but from changing social conditions which render existing norms more offensive. Discriminatory norms concerning the employment of Negroes remained fairly stable through the late 1930's; with the onset of wartime conditions, however—which demanded patriotic sacrifices on the part of Negroes in the armed services and their labor in defense industries—many Negroes became more bitter about this discrimination and ultimately launched a movement which resulted in the establishment of the Fair Employment Practices Commission.[4] To choose another example, the recruitment of both Negroes and whites into the tenancy system after Reconstruction threatened the existence of the two-caste system; whites' resentment over these conditions lay behind not only outbursts of scapegoating but also gave a white supremacist flavor to Southern Populism.[5]

Strains and Values. The rise of new values frequently creates bases for defining certain social conditions as "evils"—social conditions which previously had passed less noticed. The twin strands of philosophical deism and evangelical piety, for instance, which consolidated in Britain in the second half of the eighteenth century, became the basis for condemning and agitating for the end of slavery, cruelty to animals, and the subordination of women. All these practices had existed for centuries without serious opposition.[6]

---

[1] *The Uprooted*, pp. 296-297. For the reactions in the South to the Supreme Court decision on educational segregation, above, p. 285.

[2] B. McKelvey, *American Prisons: A Study in American Social History Prior to 1915* (Chicago, 1936), pp. 2-17.

[3] For a survey of counter-movements in American history, cf. A. M. Schlesinger, *The American as Reformer* (Cambridge, Mass., 1950), pp. 74-81.

[4] H. Garfinkel, *When Negroes March* (Glencoe, Ill., 1959), pp. 1-61. Also H. Smythe, "Negro Masses and Leaders," *Sociology and Social Research*, Vol. 35 (1950-51), pp. 33-34. For a counter example, in which the exigencies of World War I dampened the spirit of many movements, cf. Greer, *American Social Reform Movements*, pp. 177-180.

[5] Above, p. 229, fn. Hicks, *The Populist Revolt*, pp. 36-39; Lipset, *Agrarian Socialism*, pp. 7-8.

[6] F. J. Klingberg, "Abolition," *Encyclopaedia of the Social Sciences*, Vol. 1,

The Norm-Oriented Movement

Sometimes strain on values results from changing social conditions. Catholicism, transplanted to America in the migrations of the early and middle nineteenth century, came under strong pressures to modify many of its tenets and practices in line with American religious traditions. Though the Catholic Church in America resisted such pressures successfully for almost half a century,

[in] the third quarter of the century ... a movement began to take shape within the Catholic Church giving some idea of what a purely American type of Catholicism might be. "Americanism" is the general name for this movement, though the term seems to have been used for the first time in 1884 in connection with the language controversy in the Catholic schools. It has now come to be synonymous with the nationalist and liberal movement within American Catholicism.[1]

Similarly, urbanization and industrialization in the second half of the nineteenth century undercut several traditional values of American Protestantism and stimulated the far-reaching social gospel movement within many Protestant churches.[2]

In sum, norm-oriented movements are usually fostered by strains which create "demands for readjustment in the social situation."[3] To this general formula we should add several qualifying and amplifying remarks:

First, strain need not involve "a change in objective external conditions or ... material deprivation," but may stem from alterations in *expectations* concerning social life.[4] To discuss strains in terms of discrepancies between social conditions and social expectations is preferable to the use of a concept such as "disorganization" as the basis for collective outbursts.[5] This term is too strong for some of the very delicate shifts in determinants which trigger major outbursts.

Second, strains frequently appear in periods of rapid and uneven social change—when one subsystem of society changes more rapidly than others, or, to put it the other way around, when one subsystem,

p. 369; Schultz, "Animal Protection," *op. cit.*, p. 62; Strachey, *The Struggle*, p. 12. For the early abolitionist sentiments of the Puritans and Quakers, cf., C. G. Woodson, *The Negro in Our History* (Washington, D.C., 1922), pp. 51–54.

[1] Mecklin, *The Ku Klux Klan*, p. 176. For a brief sketch of this movement within the Church, cf. Handlin, *The Uprooted*, pp. 131–138.

[2] Hopkins, *The Rise of the Social Gospel in American Protestantism 1865–1915*, pp. 14, 79–80; Abell, *The Urban Impact on American Protestantism 1865–1900*, pp. 3–4, 57.

[3] Key, *Politics, Parties, and Pressure Groups*, pp. 46–47. Key's diagnosis is restricted to political movements, but the meaning he attaches to this term is sufficiently broad to refer to norm-oriented movements in general.

[4] *Ibid.*

[5] Hoffer, *The True Believer*, p. 45.

The Norm-Oriented Movement

because of inflexibilities, resists change.[1] Rapid industrial development in England during the Industrial Revolution, for instance, by demanding new and complex skills of the labor force, brought about a crisis in education, which lagged behind these economic changes.[2] Similarly, the early institutionalization of universal suffrage in American history brought pressure to bear on popular education. In this case political change moved ahead of the ability of the society to prepare its citizens for responsible participation. This discrepancy between political and educational institutions preoccupied educational reformers in this country in the 1830's and 1840's.[3]

Third, negative stereotypes associated with cleavages frequently mean that one group is convinced that another is conspiring to create conditions of strain. If these feelings are strong, a minor change in social conditions can fire a collective outburst.[4] For instance, because a strong anti-Catholic prejudice already existed in the United States in the early nineteenth century, the economic and other kinds of competition from Catholic immigrants in the 1850's assumed magnified importance.[5] Many of the dissatisfactions which give strength to a specific situation of strain, then, may have been in existence for a long time.[6]

Fourth, any specific norm-oriented movement may be the product of many different kinds of strain. The Townsend movement, for instance, reflected simultaneously the strains resulting from long-term changes in the kinship structure which led to progressively greater isolation of the aged,[7] and the strains arising from conditions of economic deprivation of the aged in the depression of the 1930's.[8] Many social movements stem from the complex and multiple structural strains resulting from industrialization, urbanization, commercialization of agriculture, and colonial domination.[9]

[1] Hertzler, *Social Institutions*, pp. 240-255.
[2] Smelser, *Social Change in the Industrial Revolution*, pp. 286-287.
[3] Beard, *The Rise of American Civilization*, Vol. I, pp. 812-813. Part of the contemporary crisis in African education seems traceable to a similar discrepancy.
[4] For further discussion of the importance of standing cleavages, cf. above, pp. 228-231.
[5] Above, pp. 62-63. Clinchy, *All in the Name of God*, p. 73; Schmeckebier, *History of the Know Nothing Party in Maryland*, pp. 52, 69; Haynes, "The Causes of Know-Nothing Success in Massachusetts," *op. cit.*, pp. 69-78. For a discussion of the "constant" anti-Catholic sentiments in the nineteenth century, cf. Desmond, *The A.P.A. Movement*, pp. 9-11.
[6] For a discussion of the importance of generalized rural-urban cleavages in exaggerating specific grievances, cf. Johnson, "Agrarian Movements. Introduction," *op. cit.*, pp. 489-490.
[7] T. Parsons, "The Kinship System of the Contemporary United States," in *Essays in Sociological Theory*, p. 195.
[8] B. Mason, "The Townsend Movement," *Southwestern Social Science Quarterly*, Vol. 35 (1954), p. 36.
[9] For discussion of these complicated background factors, cf. H. U. Faulkner, *Politics, Reform, and Expansion 1890-1900* (New York, 1959), pp. 23-26; Beard,

The Norm-Oriented Movement

Finally, to become a determinant of a norm-oriented movement, a condition of strain must combine with appropriate conditions of structural conduciveness.[1] For example, the conditions of strain which gave rise most directly to the British anti-slavery agitation was the discrepancy between the values of evangelism and the social conditions of slavery. These values had been fomenting for many decades during the eighteenth century. The actual rise of the anti-slavery movement, however, was delayed until appropriate conditions of conduciveness were established; in this case these conditions came into existence only after the American Revolutionary War had removed much slave-holding territory from the British Empire and thus diminished the opposition to abolition.[2] (This example also shows that conditions of conduciveness need not precede conditions of strain temporally for the two to combine as determinants of a norm-oriented movement.)

THE GROWTH OF GENERALIZED BELIEFS AND THE ROLE OF PRECIPITATING FACTORS

Under the conditions of structural conduciveness and strain outlined above, generalized beliefs begin to come into play as determinants. This is not to say that beliefs are created temporally only *after* conditions of conduciveness and strain have developed. Frequently the belief—or at least some of its components—have existed for generations or centuries. In such a case the conditions of conduciveness and strain activate what has been latent, and thus draw it into the total value-added process as a determinant.

For a norm-oriented movement, the generalized belief includes a diagnosis of the forces and agents that are making for a failure of normative regulation. It also involves some sort of program—passing a law, creating a regulatory agency, scrapping an antiquated custom, etc. Those committed to the belief that adoption of this program will control, damage, or punish the responsible agent, and thus erase the source of strain.[3] The combination of all these components results in a "cause" in the name of which the aggrieved mobilize and agitate for normative change.[4]

The Rise of American Civilization, Vol. I, p. 278; Taylor, "Country Life Movement," *op. cit.*, p. 496; A. R. Desai, *Social Background of Indian Nationalism*, Revised Edition (Bombay, 1954), pp. 21–209.

[1] Both Key (*Parties, Politics, and Pressure Groups*, pp. 47–48) and Greer (*American Social Reform Movements*, p. 275) emphasize that distress alone need not produce a reform movement.

[2] Coupland, *The British Anti-Slavery Movement*, pp. 60–63.

[3] Above, pp. 111–113, for a discussion of these components of a norm-oriented belief.

[4] For discussion of the necessity of a belief in mobilizing men for action, cf.

The Norm-Oriented Movement

Generalized norm-oriented beliefs may build up in various ways. They may develop gradually over decades in a "literature";[1] they may crystallize in the mind of a single man or woman;[2] they may be hammered out in a manifesto or party platform;[3] they may be imported from one cultural setting into another, as in the case of the socialist and anarchist ideologies in middle- and late-nineteenth-century America, which came in mainly with German immigrants.[4]

The modes of disseminating beliefs varies according to the type of movement and its stage of development.[5] In the early stages of a movement, which are marked by diffuse discontent, informal methods—random verbal statements, scattered protest meetings, rumors, speculations, etc.—predominate. As the beliefs crystallize, more formal methods of pamphleteering, advertizing, publicizing, and arranging for mass lectures and demonstrations receive more emphasis.[6] Whatever the exact pattern of dissemination, many

---

Turner and Killian, *Collective Behavior*, pp. 335–337; Hoffer, *The True Believer*, p. 20; Lasswell, "Agitation," *op. cit.*, p. 488.

[1] The abolition movement in Brazil apparently was supplied with its beliefs by such an accumulation of literature. "During the eighteenth and nineteenth centuries a growing literature developed demanding the curtailment and elimination of slavery. Poets and novelists, essayists and sociologists wrote copiously on the Negro, many of their pages impregnated with a profound sympathy for the race." Ramos, *The Negro in Brazil*, pp. 66–67.

[2] Howard Scott, an engineer, was largely responsible for the ideas and ideals of Technocracy. Frederick, *For and Against Technocracy*, pp. 96–97. The word "Technocracy" itself and some of its major ideas were formulated by William Henry Smyth, another engineer. M. A. Hallgren, *Seeds of Revolt* (New York, 1933), pp. 246–247. The book, *A Vindication of the Rights of Women*, written in 1792 by Mary Wollstonecraft, was little noticed at the time of its publication, but subsequently became "the text of the [feminist] movement [in Great Britain]." Strachey, *The Struggle*, p. 12. The basic outlines of the Townsend plan were also the product of a single man's thought. Mason, "The Townsend Movement," *op. cit.*, pp. 36–37. Of course, as such ideas are incorporated into a movement, they frequently are modified because of the specific dissatisfactions of the participants, because of the personalities of leaders who mobilize these participants for action, because of the attitudes of political authorities toward the movement, etc.

[3] Buck, *The Agrarian Crusade*, pp. 121–151; Haynes, *Third Party Movements Since the Civil War with Special Reference to Iowa*, pp. 53–57.

[4] M. Hillquit, *History of Socialism in the United States* (New York, 1903), pp. 159–160; Greer, *American Social Reform Movements*, pp. 38–42; Symes, *Rebel America*, pp. 125–126; for a brief discussion of immigrants' attitudes toward their native countries—attitudes which affected American political movements—cf. Handlin, *The Uprooted*, p. 207.

[5] Lasswell, Casey, and Smith list "the channels of propaganda" as one of the ways of classifying productions of propagandists. *Propaganda and Promotional Activities*, pp. xvi, 9.

[6] Park and Burgess, *Introduction to the Science of Sociology*, p. 874. Babcock, "The Farm Revolt in Iowa," *op. cit.*, p. 370. It is likely that the orator is more important in the early stages of dissemination, the publicist more important in the later stages. For a contrast between the types of activities and the personalities of these two kinds of propagandists, cf. G. E. Swanson, "Agitation in Face-to-Face Contacts: A Study in the Personalities of Orators," *Public Opinion Quarterly*, Vol. 21 (1957), pp. 282–294.

kinds of promotional activities appear in any given movement. In the British anti-slavery agitation of 1791–92, for instance,

> Pamphlets on the horrors of the [Slave] Trade and reprints of the debates in Parliament had been widely distributed. A poem by Cowper, *The Negro's Complaint*, has been set to music and thousands of copies of it circulated. A cameo depicting a Negro in an attitude of entreaty had been designed by Wedgwood, the famous master-potter and an ardent Abolitionist, and widely adopted for decorating snuff-boxes, bracelets, and hairpins. A campaign had been launched, not unsuccessfully, to encourage the consumption of East Indian sugar instead of the slave-grown West Indian product. And the outcome of all this had been a great increase in the number of English men and women who knew the black facts of the Trade and wanted to stop it. All that was needed, therefore, was to canalize this current of public opinion and bring it to bear in full volume upon Parliament. Early in 1792, therefore, a systematic plan of action was put in operation. A new abstract of the case against the Trade was broadcasted together with a summary of the last debate. On its heels Clarkson set out on another exhaustive tour through England while Dr. Dickson was dispatched to Scotland. Corresponding Committees were set up all over the country in liaison with the London Committee....[1]

What are the roles of precipitating factors in the development of beliefs? Most important, they mark the sudden establishment or symbolization of one of the conditions of conduciveness or strain. In this way precipitating factors focus the belief on a particular person, event, or situation.[2] In addition, precipitating factors create a sense of urgency and hasten mobilization for action. Let us illustrate these general roles.

Many precipitating factors are interpreted as signs, either of the opponents' power or the proponents' chances of success. The following are instances of the power of limited setbacks to invigorate a movement: (1) The arrest of a leader. The birth control movement was given considerable impetus by the arrest of Margaret Sanger in New York in September, 1914, for distributing her pamphlet, *Family Limitation*.[3] (2) An attack on one of the protagonists for a cause. Hiller argues that "a strike may be precipitated by a simple incident, such as an attack upon the group or one of its members. But ordinarily such an event is merely a point upon which attention is fixed.

---

[1] Coupland, *The British Anti-Slavery Movement*, pp. 93–94. For an outline of the techniques of the Anti-Corn Law League a half-century later, cf. Jordon, "The Political Methods of the Anti-Corn Law League," *op. cit.*, pp. 66–67.

[2] For discussion of the process of short-circuiting, above, pp. 71–73. For the parallel role of the precipitating factors in the panic, the craze, and the hostile outburst, above, pp. 147–150, 203–205, 249–252.

[3] F. H. Hankins, "Birth Control," *Encyclopaedia of the Social Sciences*, Vol. 2, p. 562.

The Norm-Oriented Movement

It is a symbol of cumulated grievances."[1] (3) A rebuff to a movement by an authority who has the power to help in furthering its program. President Roosevelt's refusal in 1940 to push forward with racial integration in the armed forces was followed by a period of increasing bitterness in the Negro press and heightened agitation for a Negro march on Washington.[2] (4) The appointment of James Campbell, a Catholic, as Postmaster-General, set off a tremendous hysteria and flurry of agitation within the Know Nothing movement.[3] (5) The threat of success of a counter-movement.[4] (6) An illegal act, such as a crime or riot. Especially if such an act "reveals" the insidious character of an enemy, it may quicken agitation for reform. Spectacular sex crimes, for instance, apparently invigorate the pressure for passage of laws against sexual psychopaths.[5]

As we have seen, limited successes of a movement, especially unanticipated successes, often "prove" the efficacy of a given method of agitation, and stimulate more agitation of this type.

Finally, a precipitating factor may create or underline a condition of strain. Most of the explosive movements among American farmers in the past century, for instance, have been boosted by financial crises and rapidly falling farm prices.[6] In this case—as in all collective behavior—strain and precipitating factors shade into one another. Depending on the time perspective, a single event may be treated as a condition of strain or a precipitating factor, or both. This illustrates an important characteristic of collective behavior: a single empirical event or situation may be significant analytically in many ways.[7]

Any given precipitating factor may appear unexpectedly or it may be arranged by some party interested in the outcome of the movement. In the nativist, anti-Catholic A. P. A. movement of the early 1890's, for instance, a number of precipitating factors—some calculated, some not—made their appearance. Examples of the deliberate

[1] *The Strike*, p. 58.
[2] Garfinkel, *When Negroes March*, pp. 37 ff.
[3] Myers, *History of Bigotry in the United States*, p. 189.
[4] Above, p. 285.
[5] Sutherland, "The Diffusion of Sexual Psychopath Laws," *op. cit.*, pp. 146–147. For discussion of the facilitating influence of collective outbursts on racial reform, cf. Glick, "Collective Behavior in Race Relations," *op. cit.*, p. 291. For an account of the importance of the Nat Turner revolt in 1831 as a precipitating factor in the abolitionist movement, cf. Filler, *The Crusade Against Slavery 1830–1860*, pp. 52–53.
[6] Kile, *The Farm Bureau Movement*, p. 35. For the effect of sharp changes in business conditions on the labor movement, above, pp. 283 and 288. The Anti-Corn Law League's period of intensive agitation seemed to be triggered by the commercial difficulties of 1837. Jordan, "The Political Methods of the Anti-Corn Law League," *op. cit.*, p. 60.
[7] Above, pp. 50–51 and 252.

The Norm-Oriented Movement

incident were the dramatic lectures by "ex-priests" and "escaped nuns" who reported on Catholic atrocities. These were generally arranged by nativist agitators to stir up emotion. An example of the unanticipated precipitating factor was the special Catholic celebrations throughout the country in October, 1892, on the anniversary of Columbus; another was the visit, in the same year, of Msgr. Satolla, the Papal delegate, to America. Both incidents whipped up hysteria and stirred the adherents of the nativistic movement into action.[1]

MOBILIZATION OF THE MOVEMENT FOR ACTION

The final determinant in the value-added process that results in a norm-oriented movement is the mobilization of its participants for action. In certain respects the pattern of mobilization may be standardized; as Schlesinger points out,

... the humanitarians in the first half of the nineteenth century set the example [for reform activity] of creating a host of nation-wide voluntary bodies, each with its special palliative or panacea. As described by a contemporary, the first step was to choose an "imposing" designation for the organization; the second, to obtain "a list of respectable names" as "members and patrons"; the next, to hire "a secretary and an adequate corps of assistants"; then "a band of popular lecturers must be commissioned, and sent forth as agents on the wide public" and the press be "put in operation." Finally, "subsidiary societies" must be "multiplied over the length and breadth of the land." So thoroughly did these crusaders work out the pattern of reform organization and propaganda a hundred years ago that later generations have found little to add beyond taking advantage of new communication devices such as the movies and the radio.[2]

As a rule, mobilization to organize and push through a program takes a long time[3]—a longer time than is generally required for the mobilization phases of panics, crazes, and hostile outbursts.[4] For this reason the mobilization phase of a norm-oriented movement is likely to be very complicated; it has to adapt to the exigencies of maintaining an organization over long periods. Accordingly, we shall discuss the problem of mobilization under four distinct headings: (*a*) the role of leaders in organizing the movement for action; (*b*) the real and derived phases of mobilization; (*c*) the effect of the success or failure of the movement's specific strategies and tactics

---

[1] Desmond, *The A.P.A. Movement*, pp. 13, 52.
[2] *The American as Reformer*, p. 52.
[3] Greer, *American Social Reform Movements*, p. 275.
[4] This is not always the case. For instance, a single wave of revivalism—which we treat as a craze—can stretch over many years. When it does, however, it has to adjust to the exigencies of time and organization. Above, p. 212.

The Norm-Oriented Movement

on the development of the movement; (*d*) the effect of the movement's overall success or failure on its development. Each heading poses a problem of potential instability and disunity for a movement; under each heading we shall discuss this problem.

Leadership. For all collective outbursts, including norm-oriented movements, we may distinguish between two kinds of leadership—leadership in formulating the beliefs and leadership in mobilizing participants for action.[1] Sometimes the same person performs both these functions; in other cases a division of leadership roles appears within a movement.[2]

Because the organizations engaged in a movement frequently must endure over a long period, several new types of leadership appear as the movement progresses—leadership geared to the organizational exigencies of the movement rather than its ideals and goals. Roche and Sachs, for instance, note the appearance of bureaucratic types of leaders:

> The bureaucrat ... is concerned primarily with the organizational facet of the social movement, with its stability, growth, and tactics ... he concentrates on the organizational means by which the group implements and consolidates its principles. He will generally be either an officeholder in the organization or interested in holding office. While he may have strong ideological convictions, he will be preoccupied with the reconciliation of diverse elements in order to secure harmony within the organization and maximize its external appeal. He seeks communication, not excommunication.[3]

As the collectivity becomes a going concern, even more types of leaders may appear—some engaged in the pursuit of power within the collectivity itself, others engaged in maintaining the prestige of the organization or movement in the public eye.[4]

Many bases for internal conflict and fragmentation of the movement arise from this proliferation of leaders into formulators, promoters, bureaucrats, power-seekers, and prestige-seekers.[5] Each

---

[1] Above, pp. 210–211.

[2] In the Townsend movement, for instance, Dr. Francis E. Townsend was responsible for the formulation of the program, and Robert E. Clements was the chief promoter and organizer. Mason, "The Townsend Movement," *op. cit.*, pp. 36–37.

[3] J. P. Roche and S. Sachs, "The Bureaucrat and the Enthusiast: An Exploration of the Leadership of Social Movements," *Western Political Quarterly*, Vol. 8 (1955), p. 249.

[4] Turner and Killian, *Collective Behavior*, pp. 361–372, 475.

[5] Even more subtypes could be added. In the realm of beliefs, for instance, one might distinguish between the creator of ideas and propagandist. Among the propagandists, a further distinction between orators and publicists can be made. Above, p. 293, fn. For a distinction among types of leaders which overlaps with the one given here, cf. Heberle, *Social Movements*, pp. 114–115.

The Norm-Oriented Movement

type of leader develops vested interests which he seeks to safeguard. Furthermore, if a movement appears to be drifting in a direction which minimizes his own leadership role, power struggles over the course of the movement may develop.

The leader who is most important in the phase of active mobilization focuses on a set of strategies and tactics—to form a new political party; to influence existing parties; to stage a march or other kind of demonstration;[1] to influence legislatures by conventional lobbying or letter-writing; to engage in "direct action" such as boycotts, lockouts, or sit-ins;[2] to educate the public; and so on.[3] Within a single movement, conflicts may arise among leaders who differ in their emphasis on particular strategies and tactics. Later we shall investigate the occasions upon which such conflicts are likely to become intensified.

As for the recruitment of leaders into movements, no single formula accounts for the source of leadership. Leaders may be marginal or respectable;[4] they may come from "nowhere" or they may be permanently established in extremist groups which lie in wait for disturbances and then move in to assume leadership.[5] The source of leadership for any given movement, then, depends on a number of factors—the availability of the qualities of leaders among the population suffering from strain, the prior existence of organizations with similar or related dissatisfactions, and the ability of these organizations to seize power in a movement.

The Real and Derived Phases of Mobilization. The development of a norm-oriented movement may be divided into three temporal phases—the incipient phase, the phase of enthusiastic mobilization, and the period of institutionalization and organization.[6] The movement begins with slow, searching behavior; accelerates into a period

---

[1] For a catalogue of "marches" in the history of American social movements, cf. Garfinkel, *When Negroes March*, p. 41.

[2] For a historical sketch of direct-action movements in labor activities, cf. L. L. Lorwin, "Direct Action," *Encyclopaedia of the Social Sciences*, Vol. 5, pp. 155-157.

[3] For the general importance of strategy in a movement, cf. Turner and Killian, *Collective Behavior*, p. 374. For discussion of the strategy and tactics of farmer and labor parties, cf. Stedman, *Discontent at the Polls*, pp. 102-124. For conflict over strategies in the anti-Masonry movement in the 1820's and 1830's, cf. A. F. Tyler, *Freedom's Ferment: Phases of American Social History to 1860* (Minneapolis, 1944), pp. 354-358.

[4] Lipset, *Agrarian Socialism*, p. 198.

[5] For examples of the latter, cf. Selznick, *The Organizational Weapon*, pp. 113-224; Fleming, "Resistance Movements and Racial Desegregation," *op. cit.*, pp. 45-46.

[6] Hertzler has called these three phases the "period of incipient organization," the "period of efficiency," and the "period of formalism," respectively. *Social Institutions*, pp. 80-81. For similar distinctions, above, pp. 18-19.

The Norm-Oriented Movement

of supercharged activity; then settles gradually into decline or routine, day-by-day activity.[1] The enthusiastic phase displays a bulge of activity and membership which can be analyzed in terms of the real and derived aspects of a movement.[2] Let us illustrate these aspects in several movements.

If the beliefs associated with a norm-oriented movement are sufficiently inclusive to encompass a wide variety of grievances, an initial success of the movement is likely to draw in a large, heterogeneous membership. "Americanism," for instance, is a vague and inclusive symbol; it can be a receptacle for anti-Negro feelings, anti-foreign feelings, prohibitionist feelings, etc.—in short, any sentiment which can be labeled conveniently as "American." Adherents of entirely different stripes have rallied to this symbol during the past century, as the following examples show:

(1) In the Know-Nothing movement, writes Handlin,

... agitation of the slavery question and a host of reform proposals put an intolerable strain upon the existing party structure. Years of compromise had produced no durable solution; instead they had given rise to grave forebodings of the calamitous Civil War that impended.

At the point of crisis the stranger who stood in the way of attainment of some particular objective became the butt of attack. Abolitionists and reformers who found the conservative Irish arrayed against them at the polls, proslavery politicians who made much of the radicalism of some of the German leaders, and temperance advocates who regarded an alien hankering after alcohol as the main obstruction on the way to universal abstinence—such people were the backbone of the Know-Nothing Party that leaped to sudden prominence in the election of 1854.[3]

In Massachusetts agitation against the Irish was the dominating theme; but in Illinois the support of Know-Nothingism stemmed almost entirely from the splits over slavery in the major parties, and in California the enthusiasm for the movement arose from a desire to remove the corruption of California politics. Foreigners scarcely figured in the latter states.[4]

(2) The heterogeneity of those who flocked to the American Protective Association in 1891–94 was almost as great as the

---

[1] For an application of this logic to institutional innovation in general, cf. Smelser, *Social Change in the Industrial Revolution*, Chs. I, II.

[2] This bulge is similar to that in the panic, the craze, and the hostile outburst. Above, pp. 154–156, 212–215, and 257–260. The precise shape of the curve is conditioned by ecological and other factors.

[3] *The Uprooted*, p. 268.

[4] Haynes, "The Causes of Know-Nothing Success in Massachusetts," *op. cit.*, pp. 69–78; Senning, "The Know-Nothing Movement in Illinois," *op. cit.*, pp. 9–19; Hurt, "The Rise and Fall of the 'Know Nothings' in California," *op. cit.*, pp. 118–119.

membership of the Know-Nothing Movement, perhaps even greater because some Germans and Scandinavians were drawn into the movement in the Midwestern states.[1]

(3) When the Ku Klux Klan revived in 1915, its activities were restricted to certain Southern localities and directed against "alien enemies and those accused of being disloyal, the idlers and slackers, strike leaders and immoral women."[2] When its membership vaulted into the millions in the 1920's, however, the movement engulfed dozens of partially related grievances. One interpreter of the Klan movement gives this account:

> In Marion County it led the Protestant forces in an inter-religious conflict. In many middle western industrial cities and towns it has set itself the task of keeping the incoming negroes in order. There have been whippings and tar-and-feather parties. More ardent and more general, however, than any other conflict waged, has been the fight against the "bootlegger." This appears to be the main issue in Oklahoma. It has been important in Herrin County, Illinois. Among a foreign or a purely industrial population, it appears quite impossible to organize the will of the majority behind the eighteenth amendment. In such communities law enforcement is exceedingly difficult. The K.K.K. has been a club thrust into the hand of the prohibition minority. The amount of illicit liquor manufactured and sold has no doubt greatly surprised the dry forces in the small towns. With this as with so many American social problems, impatience has grown into anger, anger into law-breaking. Where two issues are blended, as at Herrin, the explosive quality of the situation is greatly multiplied. At Herrin the combined labor and liquor parties have been in political control of the county. The anti-labor and anti-liquor forces have made use of the Klan.[3]

The real and derived components can be observed in American farm movements as well. During their periods of most rapid growth, these movements have swallowed an extraordinary variety of grievances. The Northern Alliance, for instance, begun in 1877 by a number of New Yorkers, mostly Grangers, as a "political mouthpiece," was relatively inactive until the hard times of the late 1870's and early 1880's. In 1880 the effective center of the Alliance moved to Chicago, and a flood of requests for local charters began to flow. Anti-railroad themes figured most markedly in this period, but other grievances appeared as well. As conditions improved in the early eighties, interest in the organization fell off, but poor wheat prices

[1] Desmond, *The A.P.A. Movement*, pp. 45–46, 63–69.
[2] Mecklin, *The Ku Klux Klan*, pp. 5–6.
[3] F. Bohn, "The Ku Klux Klan Interpreted," *American Journal of Sociology*, Vol. 30 (1925), pp. 398–399. Also Mecklin, *The Ku Klux Klan*, pp. 38, 44–45; Clinchy, *All in the Name of God.*, pp. 95 ff.

The Norm-Oriented Movement

and the difficult winter of 1884-85 stimulated new grievances, and during the hard times of the late 1880's membership reached a peak. The Southern Alliance, started in Texas in the middle 1870's was initially an organization restricted to social and recreational affairs, but resentments concerning speculation, alien ownership, railway taxes, and paper money began to give the movement new impetus. After the appearance of a new leader, C. W. Macune, in 1886, its membership growth accelerated rapidly. During the height of the development of both Alliances (1888-90), the Southern branch annexed the organization known as the Agricultural Wheel; there were several attempts to unite the Northern and Southern Alliances, though regional differences prevented this union in the end.[1]

The accumulation of heterogeneous elements during the derived phase of phenomenal growth[2] provides the basis for internal wrangling and factionalization:

> The oddly assorted elements that entered [the Know-Nothing Party] had little in common; it took them only two years to come to know each other better, and once they did the party fell apart.... The Know-Nothing movement disappeared as rapidly as it had appeared. In that respect it traced a course later followed by similar movements that flashed across the political horizon—the A.P.A. of the 1890's and the anti-German agitation of the First World War.[3]

Norm-oriented movements with vague, inclusive symbols, then, display three central characteristics: (*a*) diversity of motivation and grievances among the participants;[4] (*b*) a period of very rapid growth and a period of equally rapid decline; (*c*) a fluid association among the strands of the same general movement, strands which continuously flow into one another, break off again, then join in some other guise.[5]

---

[1] Hicks, *The Populist Revolt*, pp. 97-127. For the heterogeneity of the anti-slavery movement after 1830, cf. Filler, *The Crusade Against Slavery 1830-1860*, p. 29.

[2] For the peaks in farm organization membership in the late eighteenth and early nineteenth centuries, cf. Kile, *The Farm Bureau Movement*, p. 35.

[3] Handlin, *The Uprooted*, pp. 268-269. For the pattern of rapid decline of the farm organizations, cf. Kile, *The Farm Bureau Movement*, p. 35.

[4] Hoffer, *The True Believer*, p. 30; Hiller, *The Strike*, pp. 18-19; Heberle, *Social Movements*, p. 93; Gerth and Mills, *Character and Social Structure*, p. 440. For the diversity of motivation in even more generalized value-oriented movements, see below, pp. 356-358.

[5] For example, cf. the proposed Third Party suggested in the 1930's, presumably to include the Townsendites, the followers of Huey Long, and the followers of Father Couglin. Whiteman and Lewis, *Glory Roads*, pp. 132-133. Between 1830 and 1843 in England several movements came temporarily together in a broader agitation—the peace movement, the Free Trade Movement, abolition and temperance. Beales, *The History of Peace*, pp. 56-65. Cf. also Brinton's remark:

The Norm-Oriented Movement

The Success or Failure of Specific Tactics. Norm-oriented movements generally have access to a *variety* of channels for agitation and a *variety* of strategies and tactics for each channel.[1] Because of this large number of alternative paths of action, several related movements frequently arise simultaneously, their major differences being in the realm of strategy and tactics. For instance, during and after World War I, the general movement by "native, Anglo-Saxon Protestant Americans" took a number of forms—the Ku Klux Klan revival, fundamentalism, agitation for prohibition, agitation for restricting immigration quotas, etc.[2]

Furthermore, the history of any given movement—its ebbs and flows, its switches, its bursts of enthusiasm—can be written in large part as a pattern of abandoning one method which appears to be losing effectiveness and adopting some new, more promising method.

This principle is seen clearly in the farmers' organization of the 1880's and 1890's. In its early days, the Farmers' Alliance concentrated on exerting pressure on both major political parties. Particularly in the northern Midwest, it managed to push through reforms which established commissions for the regulation of the railways. For a number of reasons, however, these commissions proved ineffective—they took no action, they were adjudged unconstitutional after a time, or they were dominated by the railroads.[3] Under these circumstances, a movement to establish an independent third party gained momentum:

> In the years 1889 and 1890 new members flocked into the order as never before, and with these notable accessions the plausibility of third-party action was correspondingly increased. The alliance had the strength now to enter the political field directly, and since its nonpartisan efforts had failed, what else was there left for it to do? Such a course was ably urged by professional third-party politicians—ex-Grangers, ex-Greenbackers, ex-Union Laborites—who were on hand in numbers to offer themselves as leaders of the new movement.[4]

Furthermore, "the successes scored by the farmers in the election of 1890 [election of several governors, control of legislatures in a number of states, unseating of five congressmen] greatly stimulated the agita-

---

"Many social clubs are constantly tending to become something else: political clubs, economic organizations, even religious bodies." "Clubs," *op. cit.*, p. 575.
[1] Above, pp. 281–285.
[2] Myers, *History of Bigotry in the United States*, pp. 267–329; Mecklin, *The Ku Klux Klan*, p. 99; Odegard, *Pressure Politics*, pp. 29–34; Handlin, *The Uprooted*, pp. 286–291.
[3] Hicks, *The Populist Revolt*, pp. 140–151.
[4] *Ibid.*, pp. 151–152.

The Norm-Oriented Movement

tion... for the organization of a third party along national lines."[1] A national party formed and conducted a heated campaign in the election of 1892. The results of this election disheartened party members. Only in the Far West, where the campaign was conducted on the Free Silver issue, did the Populists succeed unequivocally.[2] Between the elections of 1892 and 1894, "the silver issue tended more and more to become the chief item in the Populist creed."[3] Populists reminded themselves of the power of this issue in the 1892 election; their focus on silver was also heightened by the financial panic of 1893 and the repeal of the Sherman Silver Purchase Act. In the election of 1894, however, the Populists' performance was mediocre, even though they concentrated on the silver issue. This disappointment, plus the fact that the Democrats nominated William Jennings Bryan—a free silver man—in 1896, diverted most of the Populists' energy to yet another line of attack—to help sweep the Democrats into office and thus gain Populist ends.[4]

After each apparent failure, then, the farmers turned to an alternative that seemed more promising. At each turn, moreover, the movement suffered an internal split—some adherents arguing for continuing with the old method, some attempting to lead the movement in one new direction, some pressing for another new direction.[5]

Other movements reveal a similar pattern of shifting from method to method at critical junctures in the mobilization period:

(1) For fifty years prior to 1893, the prohibitionist movement had succeeded, by partisan political activity, in passing prohibition laws in eighteen states. In virtually all of these states, however, the laws had either been declared unconstitutional or were badly enforced. Furthermore, the national Prohibition Party had produced feeble results during its twenty-four years of organized electioneering.

In short, the partisan plan for Prohibition had failed. The Prohibition wave had receded. The moral forces were fast becoming discouraged. The situation was frequently referred to as hopeless. Reaction had indeed set in and even the religious and temperance forces of the nation had come to the point of realizing the success of the Prohibition movement depended upon the devising of some new plan which would promise more in the

---

[1] *Ibid.*, p. 207. In the South the movement to form an independent third party gained less strength, because the Southern Populists were faced with overcoming the tremendous power of the Democratic Party, which dominated Southern politics thoroughly. Pp. 207–210.
[2] *Ibid.*, pp. 264–269.
[3] *Ibid.*, p. 318.
[4] *Ibid.*, pp. 333–378.
[5] *Ibid.*, pp. 299–300.

way of uniting of the temperance forces and the solving of the liquor problem.¹

Accordingly, during the next decade the tactics of the Prohibitionists turned to non-partisan politics at the local community level.²

(2) The adherents of the English female suffrage movement were bitterly disappointed in 1870 when, after they had been agitating furiously for a long time, Gladstone came out publicly against the women's vote and ensured its defeat. A similar defeat in 1884 demoralized the suffragists even more. About this time, they began to take up electioneering as a method of agitation. Both the Conservative Party and the Liberal Party set up women's divisions. Before long, however, the Conservative Party division had split into suffragists and others, and the Liberal Party division had split into those who wished to stay in the party and those who wished to pursue independent political action. In short, in the late 1880's and the early 1890's, writes Strachey,

> ... it was roughly true that the Liberals, who professed to believe in giving the votes to women, would not do it because they thought they would lose thereby; and the Conservatives, who were expected to benefit, disliked the principle so much that they would not do it either.³

In this atmosphere of disorganization following the successive failure of several lines of agitation, extreme militancy began to grow within the movement, and seriously split the suffragists for the next two decades.⁴

(3) In the nineteenth century, as depression or prosperity rendered one method of labor agitation obsolete and made another more attractive, workingmen oscillated between direct economic action and political agitation.⁵ Even after the 1890's when the American Federation of Labor gave new continuity to the American labor movement, disputes over tactics arose, particularly when the limited economic and political methods preferred by Samuel Gompers seemed inadequate to withstand the economic pressures on organized labor.⁶

---

¹ Cherrington, *The Evolution of Prohibition in the United States of America*, p. 250.
² Above, p. 283.
³ *The Struggle*, pp. 278–284.
⁴ *Ibid.*, pp. 288–326.
⁵ Above, p. 283.
⁶ M. R. Carroll, *Labor and Politics* (Boston, 1923), pp. 27–54. For an account of the development of splits over tactics in the antislavery movement in the mid-nineteenth century, cf. Schlesinger, *The American as Reformer*, pp. 31–47; for an account of the splits in the peace movement in this country during the same period, cf. Tyler, *Freedom's Ferment*, pp. 409–423.

The Norm-Oriented Movement

The problem of settling upon methods of agitation, then, is an important source of conflict, fragmentation, and turnover of leadership in norm-oriented movements. The same kinds of instability may appear when one branch of a movement exerts pressure to agitate for a policy to use a method considered by others in the movement to be beyond the legitimate scope of the movement. For instance, when some feminists in England took up a crusade to repeal the regulations for examining and prosecuting prostitutes, this shocked the sensibilities of other feminists. The result was a split in the movement which persisted through the 1860's and 1870's.[1]

The Directions of Development after Success or Failure. Any movement which crusades under a fully developed set of generalized beliefs is bound to fail in one sense. Because its fears and hopes are likely to be exaggerated through the processes of generalization and short-circuiting,[2] even the adoption of the concrete proposals it advocates does not approach its expectations. As a result of a century of feminist agitation and success, for instance,

Women have neither attained to the general level of leadership that the pioneers of the feminist movement insisted they would attain once the legal framework was provided, nor has the female invasion of strange pastures transformed those pastures into the Promised Land. In fact, the very fervour of the pioneers has become somewhat ludicrous in modern eyes, nowhere more in evidence than among groups of so-called emancipated women. The concerted demand of women's groups for more rights and privileges mounts apace, but the belief that a brave new world was a-borning, as a specific result, has waned.[3]

Beyond this inherent tendency for even successful movements to leave a residue of disappointment, we can speak of the relative success of movements. Some movements, such as the short-ballot movement in the early twentieth century,[4] have achieved their ends almost in their entirety. Other movements, such as the Townsend movement, fail to achieve their own ends, but see the adoption of related programs. Still other movements, such as the vegetarian movement, ultimately see neither their own program nor a substitute put into effect. Generally speaking, a successful movement usually begins to focus on other, related reforms, or becomes a guardian of the

[1] Strachey, *The Struggle*, pp. 194–203; 264–269.
[2] Above, pp. 111–113.
[3] A. W. Green and E. Milnick, "What Has Happened to the Feminist Movement?" in A. W. Gouldner (ed.), *Studies in Leadership: Leadership and Democratic Action* (New York, 1950), pp. 278–279.
[4] W. B. Munro, "Short Ballot Movement," *Encyclopaedia of the Social Sciences*, Vol. 14, pp. 43–44.

The Norm-Oriented Movement

normative changes it has won;[1] correspondingly, an unsuccessful movement usually declines. In many respects, however, successful and unsuccessful movements resemble each other in their later stages. Both continue to stay alive for long periods after the phase of active agitation. Furthermore, both tend to accumulate new functions—recreation, maintenance of the organization, civic contributions, etc.—in addition to, or even in place of their original purposes.[2]

SOCIAL CONTROL

At several points in this chapter we have observed the importance of social control. First, if a political authority that receives expressions of grievances is differentiated from other aspects of social control, this makes for greater toleration of specific, norm-oriented movements.[3] Second, the success that a given agitation has in the political arena influences a movement's course of development.[4] Now we shall ask what kinds of behavior on the part of agencies of social control encourage a norm-oriented movement to retain its norm-oriented character and what kinds of behavior tend to turn this kind of movement into another kind of collective behavior.

In the first place, a *general* encouragement of a norm-oriented movement by political authorities—whether or not the authorities approve its specific proposals—usually boosts and consolidates the movement. For example: (1) The continuous existence of the Society for the Prevention of Cruelty to Animals in England was guaranteed when in 1835 it received the patronage of the Duchess of Kent and Princess Victoria.[5] (2) "Two factors which contributed to the rapid development of the playground movement were the support of the schools and [support] of agencies concerned with crime, especially juvenile delinquency."[6] (3) Agrarian movements for tariff protection

---

[1] For an account of the variety of programs pursued by the mental hygiene movement, cf. C. E. A. Winslow, "The Mental Hygiene Movement (1908–33) and Its Founder," and L. E. Woodward, "The Mental Hygiene Movement—More Recent Developments [to 1948]," in C. W. Beers, *A Mind that Found Itself* (Garden City, N.Y., 1953), pp. 303–371.

[2] For a brief discussion of the evolution of Chambers of Commerce from pressure groups for the interests of business into civic and social groups, cf. Studenski, "Chambers of Commerce," *op. cit.*, pp. 325–327. For a study of the changing emphasis of activities in declining social organizations, cf. S. L. Messinger, "Organizational Transformation: A Case Study of a Declining Social Movement," *American Sociological Review*, Vol. 20 (1955), pp. 3–10; also J. R. Gusfield, "Social Structure and Moral Reform: A Study of the Woman's Christian Temperance Union," *American Journal of Sociology*, Vol. 61 (1955–56), pp. 221–232.

[3] Above, pp. 280–281.
[4] Above, pp. 283–285 and 302–305.
[5] Fairholme and Pain, *A Century of Work for Animals*, pp. 72–73.
[6] Nash, "Playgrounds," *op. cit.*, p. 162.

The Norm-Oriented Movement

have been fortified when statesmen have included protectionism in a broader policy of national self-sufficiency.[1] (4) During the New Deal the government's generally favorable disposition toward labor occasioned an extraordinary burst of growth in union membership.[2] (5) During wartime emergencies, governments frequently adopt a supportive attitude toward various movements—e.g., labor movements, feminist movements—in order to enlist the adherents' cooperation in the war effort.[3] Conversely, when government discourages a movement, a decline in its membership follows. If, however, this discouragement means that all channels for peaceful agitation are thereby closed to the movement, this policy is likely to drive a militant minority underground, into hostile displays, or into value-oriented movements.[4]

Beyond general encouragement of a movement, what kinds of behavior on the part of authorities encourage a norm-oriented movement to retain its norm-oriented character? The agencies of social control must (*a*) permit expression of grievances but insist that this expression remain within the confines of legitimacy, and (*b*) give a hearing—as defined by institutionalized standards of "fairness"—to the complaints at hand. This does not mean that authorities must accede to the demands of the movement; rather they must leave open the possibility that these demands, along with others, will be heard, and that some responsible decision will be taken with regard to them.

In this way agencies of social control usually lift the issues from the hands of aggrieved groups and consider these issues in a setting apart from the heat of emotional commitment to generalized beliefs. A typical political response to the hysteria and scapegoating concerning sexual psychopaths is, according to Sutherland,

> ... the appointment of a committee, which in some cases has been guided by psychiatrists, which organizes existing information regarding sex crimes and the precedents for their control and presents a sexual psychopath law to the legislature and to the public as the most scientific and enlightened method of protecting society against dangerous sex criminals.[5]

Other mechanisms for controlling a fiery movement can be found in the various kinds of political machinery. An aggrieved party seeking a court injunction must carry his demands through lawyers, and

---

[1] Johnson, "Agrarian Movements. Introduction," *op. cit.*, p. 492.
[2] Key, *Politics, Parties, and Pressure Groups*, p. 56.
[3] For a discussion of the boost given the feminist movement in England during World War I, cf. Strachey, *The Struggle*, pp. 336-349.
[4] Greer, *American Social Reform Movements*, pp. 123-169; Myers, *History of Bigotry in the United States*, pp. 382 ff.
[5] "The Diffusion of Sexual Psychopath Laws," *op. cit.*, p. 147.

The Norm-Oriented Movement

lawyers have to present them to judges, who have the right to ponder and delay before coming to a decision; legislatures utilize committees and commissions for investigating serious public issues before legislating on them; and so on.[1]

Agencies of social control do not, however, always live up to these standards. They can, in effect, close off the avenues to normative change—thus encouraging alternative kinds of collective outbursts—in the following related ways:

(1) By consistently refusing to recognize one or more groups in a community:

> [one set of] consequences of unresponsive administration is the outbreak of unorganized acts of violence. In French-Canadian towns, for example, the English, who have no voice, periodically manifest such behavior.... The same behavior [is found] among the lower class in two communities rigidly dominated by an upper class. One community is in Siam; the other is a Mississippi river town. The generalization suggested is this: Whenever a pattern of control is so complete that the minority can see no way of moving to a position of power, either individually or as a group, there may exist sporadic and irrational outbursts, but not organized opposition.[2]

A slight alteration in the nature of social control in the community, however, produces a different kinds of protest:

> Dissatisfaction [grows], either as a result of specific acts of the administration or of some shifting climate of opinion; when the dissatisfied [find] no room for expression *within* the structure of authority, they [discover] a leader and [begin] attacking from the *outside*. There [is] no built-in means for expressing their influence; thus they [attempt] to make it felt by sniping or by full-scale battle. The difference between this situation and that of the English in French-Canadian towns is that these disaffected people do have a chance to make their influence felt through public controversy, with the possibility of overturning the administration.[3]

(2) By appearing to vacillate in the face of pressure from the movement. We have already observed how conflicting directives on the part of authorities in Milford, Delaware, stimulated greater aggressiveness on the part of the N.A.A.W.P. In Baltimore, by contrast, the "attempt to exploit anti-desegregation sentiment ... was thwarted by prompt and resolute action on the part of civic groups and public officials."[4] While segregation continued to be an issue in

---

[1] For extended discussion on the handling and channeling of disturbances cf. Smelser, *Social Change in the Industrial Revolution*, pp. 39–40, 81–85, 135–136, 290–292. For a theoretical discussion of some of these elements of social control —support, permissiveness, etc.—cf. Parsons, *The Social System*, pp. 299–301.

[2] Coleman, *Community Conflict*, p. 16.

[3] *Ibid.*

[4] Fleming, "Resistance Movements and Racial Desegregation," *op. cit.*, p. 45.

The Norm-Oriented Movement

Baltimore, the authorities had given strong indication that it was not going to be solved through intimidation from extremist groups.

(3) By appearing to close off the avenues for norm-oriented agitation abruptly and directly. The rise of militant nationalism in British India illustrates this principle. In the early part of the nineteenth century, the British were generally supportive of many indigenous religious and reform movements—movements for caste reform or abolition, for equal rights for women, against child marriage, against the ban on widow remarriage, against the hereditary priesthood, etc. As the result of the revolt of 1857 and subsequent minor uprisings, however, British policy tightened; their support for reform movements virtually ended, and they initiated a policy of periodic curtailment of the Indian press. As a result of such a change, Indian agitation gradually began to evolve from demands for specific reforms toward a value-oriented movement for national independence. True, the Liberals agitating for limited reforms dominated the nationalist movement until early in the nineteenth century, but

> Refusal to meet the political and economic demands by the government and its repressive measures against the growing national movement shook the faith of an increasing number of Indians in the ideology and technique of Liberal nationalism. They began to rally round the group of militant nationalists (the Extremists).[1]

In Ceylon, by contrast, where the British were consistently more responsive to reform movements and appeared always to be encouraging the goal of independence, no mass nationalist movement developed:

> In India and Burma the constitutional struggle was characterized by civil disobedience, arrests, communal riots, acts of terrorism, sabotage, fifth column activity, and collaboration with the enemy. No such acts marred Ceylon's progress towards Dominion status. The pressure was exerted chiefly by the passing of reform resolutions in the Council, discussions between Governors and leaders of majority and minority communities, the preparation and publication of memoranda and reform dispatches by Governors and ministers, agitation for the purpose of sending deputations to the Secretary of State to place Ceylon's case directly before the Imperial Government, and the introduction and discussion of bills embodying the proposed constitutional reforms.[2]

(4) By appearing openly to "take sides" in a controversy. Frequently this appears to the favored party as tacit approval for the

---

[1] Desai, *Social Background of Indian Nationalism*, pp. 272–290.
[2] S. Namasivayam, *The Legislatures of Ceylon* (London, 1951), pp. 127–128, quoted in Weiner, "The Politics of South Asia," in Almond and Coleman (eds.), *op. cit.*, pp. 202–203.

The Norm-Oriented Movement

use of extreme methods such as violence. On the other hand, the same action appears as a red flag to the underdog party, which begins to feel that it cannot rely on the forces of law and order and must resort to more extreme methods of expression.[1]

(5) By openly encouraging some other kind of collective outburst, such as mob violence[2] or revolutionary conspiracy.[3]

CONCLUSIONS

In this chapter we have outlined a model value-added process in which several determinants combine to produce a norm-oriented movement. We have illustrated each determinant by referring to a variety of movements. Empirically, of course, any given movement does not follow such a neat sequence because the several determinants continuously combine and recombine as a movement progresses, thus giving it new directions. One tactic fails, and another is taken up; the movement is infused with new energy by the occurrence of some unexpected event; an authority rebuffs a movement crudely and drives it temporarily into a violent outburst. In this chapter, we have not tried to account for the evolution of any single movement, but rather to extricate from the histories of many movements the principles which shape the development of norm-oriented movements in general.

Two final observations on the empirical unfolding of norm-oriented movements are in order. First, the events that touch off a norm-oriented movement may simultaneously give birth to other collective outbursts. The movement of a Negro family into a white neighborhood, for instance, may trigger several distinct collective outbursts: (1) panic selling by neighbors who are convinced that property values will fall drastically;[4] (2) a hostile outburst such as stoning the house or baiting the children of the new family;[5] (3) a norm-oriented movement such as an agitation to modify the zoning laws to prevent Negro families from moving into the neighborhood in the future. For all these outbursts the conditions of structural strain and the precipitating factor are identical. The different character of each movement is imparted by the way in which the participants of each perceive—correctly or incorrectly—the conditions of structural conduciveness and the agencies of social control. The

---

[1] Above, pp. 234–236.
[2] Above, pp. 262–268.
[3] Below, pp. 367–379.
[4] Ch. VI for the determinants of such an outburst.
[5] Ch. VIII for the determinants of such an outburst.

same concrete events, then, may be experienced by subgroups in different ways, and thus stimulate a rash of related but distinct outbursts.

Second, the same kinds of strain may produce different types of outbursts over time if the conditions of structural conduciveness and the behavior of authorities change. In the 1860's and early 1870's, for instance, conditions in the eastern United States were ripe for a "boom" movement of population to the West. The passage of the Homestead Act in 1862, the encouragement to Civil War Veterans to move west, the railroads' advertising campaigns and offers of credit to migrants—all contributed to a tremendous sense of promise.[1] These conditions, combined with the hard times which began with the financial panic of 1873, initiated a flow of migrants to the West. By the late 1870's and early 1880's, this flow had grown to a flood. Credit, speculation, and land values spiralled to extravagant heights; boom towns appeared overnight in Nebraska and Kansas.[2]

By 1887 the speculative boom passed its peak and collapsed into a panic; for the next decade hard times settled on the whole frontier. For many who had not yet located permanently in the West, this sustained depression produced a panicky return to the East. Migration from the West between 1888 and 1892 was substantial. This massive withdrawal seemed to reduce discontent in some Western areas:

The withdrawal of practically all the newcomers from the arid region in the extreme western part of the frontier states left there a class accustomed to the environment and not inordinately dissatisfied. The flight of the floating and speculating element from the boom towns and cities placed control in the hands of the more substantial and conservative citizens.[3]

In areas where flight to the East did not appear as a reasonable alternative, dissatisfaction moved in the direction of belligerent outbursts and crusades of reform:

... in the rural portions of the central regions, where farmers stayed and struggled with failing crops and low prices, with unyielding debts and relentless taxes, where they fought a battle, now successful, now unavailing, to retain the land they had bought and to redeem the high hopes with which they had come to the West—in this region unrest and discontent prevailed, and the grievances that later found statement in the Populist

---

[1] This condition involves the availability of facilities, which we discussed in connection with the craze. Above, pp. 188–201.
[2] Hicks, *The Populist Revolt*, pp. 4–28. For many workers in the East and farmers in the West, however, the 1870's brought bitter agitation through the Grange and the Greenback movements. Buck, *Agrarian Crusade*, pp. 77 ff.
[3] Hicks, *The Populist Revolt*, p. 35.

The Norm-Oriented Movement

creed smoldered for a season, finally to break forth in a program of open revolt.[1]

Over the period of fifteen years the same general population, suffering from the same general deprivations—economic hardships—flew first into a craze, then a panic, then a season of hostile outbursts and norm-oriented movements. It is possible to account for each outburst separately according to the determinants outlined in the past several chapters. Furthermore, each gave way to the next as a result of the appearance, disappearance, and reappearance of different conditions of conduciveness which promised a new kind of relief from the general distress.

[1] *Ibid.*, p. 35. For an analysis of the various directions which the reform movements took between 1888 and 1896, above, pp. 302–303.

CHAPTER X

THE VALUE-ORIENTED MOVEMENT

INTRODUCTION

Definition. A value-oriented movement is a collective attempt to restore, protect, modify, or create values in the name of a generalized belief.[1] Such a belief necessarily involves all the components of action; that is, it envisions a reconstitution of values, a redefinition of norms, a reorganization of the motivation of individuals, and a redefinition of situational facilities.[2]

Our definition encompasses the phenomena designated by the labels "nativistic movement," "messianic movement," "millenarian movement," "utopian movement," "sect formation," "religious revolution," "political revolution," "nationalistic movement," "charismatic movement," and many others.[3] Given the inclusive character of our definition and given the complexity of any value-oriented movement, we must specify at the outset the principal aspects of these movements which we will attempt to explain.

Major Lines of Variability among Value-oriented Movements. Value-oriented beliefs may be composed of indigenous cultural items, of items imported from outside the culture, or—perhaps most frequently—a syncretism.[4] Such beliefs may involve the restoration

---

[1] For a definition of value-oriented belief, above, pp. 120-129. Our definition of a value-oriented movement is narrower than that suggested by Ralph H. Turner, who uses the term "value-oriented social movement" to refer to "(A) social movement ... fundamentally oriented toward rendering some change in the social structure and of sufficient force to develop organization." Quoted in Messinger, "Organizational Transformation: A Case Study of a Declining Social Movement," *op. cit.*, fn., p. 3. Turner's definition apparently does not distinguish between movements oriented toward values and those oriented toward norms, though elsewhere Turner does explore the relationship between values and norms in general. Cf. his "Value Conflict in Social Disorganization," *Sociology and Social Research*, Vol. 38 (1954), pp. 301-308.

[2] Above, pp. 121-122. For discussion of the inclusiveness of value-oriented beliefs, cf. Wallace, "Revitalization Movements," *op. cit.*, pp. 264-267; Linton, "Nativistic Movements," *op. cit.*, pp. 230-231; F. W. Voget, "The American Indian in Transition: Reformation and Accommodation," *American Anthropologist*, Vol. 58 (1956), pp. 249-250. See also Durkheim, *Elementary Forms of the Religious Life*, p. 223.

[3] Wallace, "Revitalization Movements," *op. cit.*, pp. 264, 267.

[4] *Ibid.*, pp. 275-276.

The Value-Oriented Movement

of past values, the perpetuation of present values, the creation of new values for the future, or any mixture of these.[1]

We may also distinguish between religious and secular value-oriented beliefs.[2] Examples of religious beliefs are found in the following classification of the beliefs of American religious sects by E. T. Clark:

The Pessimistic Sects. These are typical groups of the disinherited, in final despair of obtaining through social processes the benefits they seek. They see no good in the world and no hope of improvement; it is rushing speedily to hell, according to the will and plan of God. The adherents of such sects magnify millenarianism and see the imminent end of the present world-order by means of a cosmic catastrophe. They have turned on the world, and they seek escape through a cataclysm which will cast down those who have been elevated and secure to the faithful important places in a new temporal kingdom as well as eternal bliss in heaven [Example: Seventh-Day Adventists]. . . .

The Perfectionist Sects. These seek holiness, personal perfection of life, or freedom from the temptations and "desires of the flesh." They are of the experimental type, realizing their hopes through strong emotional reactions [Examples: early Methodists, Holiness sects]. . . .

The Communistic Sects. These groups withdraw from "the world" into colonies where they secure the social approval which is denied them elsewhere and where they engage in economic experiments. Community of goods is the common characteristic. Some of these groups have espoused free love or community of women and their rites have run into orgiastic and antinomian excesses [Examples: Shakers, Amana Society, the House of David]. . . .

Legalistic Sects. A group of sects which stress certain rules, objective forms, observances, or "things" which can be definitely performed as essential to true religion. Frequently the distinguishing mark is the *rejection* or *denial* of some practice. These sects derive their rites or taboos from some portion of the Bible and usually look upon themselves as the "true Church" or restorers of primitive Christianity [Examples: "hook-and-eye" Mennonites, Primitive Baptists, Reformed Episcopal Church, African Orthodox Church]. . . .

Egocentric Sects. These have physical comfort, personal exhilaration, and freedom from pain, disease, and ennui as their objective [Examples: Christian Science, Divine Science, Unity School of Christianity, New Thought].

Esoteric Sects. These are devotees of the mystic. They espouse doctrines into which one needs to be initiated. They are nearly all offshoots of Hinduism and can hardly be called Christian sects. They specialize in mysteries and the occult, and their literature is scarcely understandable to

[1] Linton, "Nativistic Movements," *op. cit.*, pp. 231–234.
[2] Wallace, "Revitalization Movements," *op. cit.*, p. 277.

the ordinary man [Examples: Theosophists, Spiritualists, Vedantists, and Bahais].[1]

Secular value-oriented beliefs include nationalism, communism, socialism, anarchism, syndicalism, and so on. Many beliefs display a mixture of religious and secular elements—for example, Christian Socialism in mid-nineteenth century Britain, or *Sarekat Islam*, the nationalist movement in Indonesia in the early twentieth century.

Value-oriented movements differ according to their outcome. Religious movements, for instance, may result in the following:

(1) Religious revolution (e.g., the Protestant Reformation), in which the religious belief is the basis for challenging the legitimacy of established political authority. In any religious revolution, furthermore, the challenge may take the form of a secessionist movement (i.e., the attempt to set up a separate political unit) or internal warfare (i.e., the attempt to overthrow forcibly and assume power from a government in the same political unit). Any given revolutionary movement may be classified according to the tactics it employs— terrorism, street fighting, guerrilla warfare, *coup d'état*, etc.

(2) Formation of a more or less enduring collectivity *within a* political system, with no overt challenge to the legitimacy of existing political arrangements. Von Wiese and Becker have outlined several types of such collectivities: (*a*) the ecclesia, or the universal church into which members are born. Frequently the ecclesia is closely aligned with the state, as in the case of Catholicism, Lutheranism, and Anglicanism; (*b*) the sect, an elective body which one must join to become a member, and which emphasizes ethical demands and personal commitment; (*c*) the denomination, which is "simply (a sect) in an advanced stage of development and adjustment to (other denominations) and the secular world"; (*d*) the cult, which emphasizes the "purely personal ecstatic experience, salvation, comfort, and mental or physical healing."[2]

(3) Disappearance, whether as a result of repression by authorities, internal decay, transformation into another kind of movement, or absorption into another kind of movement.[3]

---

[1] *The Small Sects in America* (Nashville, 1937), pp. 26–29. In an overlapping classification, Wilson distinguishes among Conversionist, Adventist, Introversionist, and Gnostic sects. "An Analysis of Sect Development," *op. cit.*, pp. 5–7. See also Fauset, *Black Gods of the Metropolis*, p. 9; Knox, *Enthusiasm: A Chapter in the History of Religion*, pp. 581–582; R. J. Jones, "A Comparative Study of Religious Cult Behavior Among Negroes with Special Reference to Emotional Group Conditioning Factors," *The Howard University Studies in the Social Sciences*, Vol. II, No. 2 (Washington, 1939), pp. 1–5.

[2] *Systematic Sociology*, pp. 624–628. We shall examine the occasions when these different types tend to change into other forms below, pp. 359–361.

[3] For an account of the absorption of a primitive millenarian movement into a

The Value-Oriented Movement

Similarly, secular value-oriented movements may result in the following:

(1) Political revolution (e.g., the communist revolutions in Russia and China, the nationalist revolution in Indonesia), in which a secular belief is the basis for challenging the existing political authority. Like religious revolutions, these may be secessionist (e.g., anti-colonial revolutions, or the American Civil War), or they may be attempts to overthrow forcibly and assume power from a government (e.g., the French and Russian revolutions, or the German and Italian fascist revolutions). Finally, the political revolution, like the religious, may be classified according to the tactics employed by the revolutionary group.

(2) Formation of a more or less enduring collectivity which may remain revolutionary in principle but which is contained within the political system. Examples are the Communist parties of Britain, Holland, Belgium, and Scandinavia, and political sects, clubs, or societies like the anarchists or socialists.[1]

(3) Disappearance.

Thus many outcomes are possible for a given value-oriented movement.[2] Our task in this chapter is to ask and attempt to answer the following questions: What are the determinants of value-oriented movements in general? Why, among value-oriented movements, are some religious and others secular? Why do some value-oriented beliefs eventuate in revolutionary movements, others in peaceful sects or political parties? To answer these questions we shall rely on the variables of structural conduciveness, strain, generalized beliefs,

---

modern Marxist movement, cf. E. J. Hobsbawm, *Primitive Rebels* (Manchester, 1959), Ch. VI.

[1] R. E. Park, *Society* (Glencoe, Ill., 1955), pp. 25–27. For an account of the revolutionary cults which persisted into the terroristic phase of the French Revolution, cf. C. Brinton, *A Decade of Revolution: 1789–1799* (New York, 1934), pp. 154–158.

[2] Our subdivision of value-oriented movements according to these dimensions illustrates how value-oriented movements resemble one another and how they differ from one another. All value-oriented movements are similar in the sense that they envision the reconstitution of values. If we examine their cultural and temporal orientation, their religious-secular balance, and their ultimate fate in social action, the bases for distinguishing among them appear. For an account of the similarities and differences among religious and political revolutions, cf. Tocqueville, *The Old Regime and the Revolution*, pp. 24–27, 190; Brinton, *The Anatomy of Revolution*, 195–208; G. Le Bon, *The Psychology of Revolution* (New York, 1913), pp. 34–35; the similarities and differences among millenarianism of the late middle ages and modern communist and fascist ideologies, Cohn, *The Pursuit of the Millennium*, pp. 308–314; the similarities and differences among secular and religious movements, Wallace, "Revitalization Movements," p. 277; the similarities among nativism, revivalism, separatism, etc., Turner and Killian, *Collective Behavior*, p. 395.

The Value-Oriented Movement

precipitating factors, mobilization for action, and social control as these variables combine in a value-added process.

Our task is difficult for several reasons: (*a*) Any classification of value-oriented movements blurs empirically. Concerning his own classification of sects, for instance, Clark notes:

> An attempt has been made to group the small sects ... according to their outstanding tenets, but much overlapping has been noted. In the main features the sects are much alike. Most of them might be called Pessimistic, since they believe in the more or less imminent end of the world order and set little or no store by social processes in the realization of their ends. Both Communistic and Charismatic groups are essentially Perfectionistic. Nearly all are Legalistic in that they regard the Bible as an objective authority and insist upon observances drawn therefrom. Some sects are so nearly identical that the impartial student is unable to discover any differences, and in the case of many the differences are trivial.[1]

(*b*) Any type of value-oriented movement, such as millenarianism or messianism, changes as it is adopted in different areas of the world[2] and in different historical epochs.[3] (*c*) Value-oriented movements occur in periods of ferment which produce many other kinds of collective behavior; they must be disentangled from the general pattern of flux.[4] (*d*) One form of value-oriented movement changes into another; nationalist movements change from religious to secular, open revolts against colonial domination evolve into passive sects, etc.[5] In view of such difficulties, we must settle for the analysis of broad directional changes within empirically mixed and fluctuating movements.

---

[1] *The Small Sects in America*, p. 269. See also Wallace, "Revitalization Movements," p. 267.

[2] P. Worsley, *The Trumpet Shall Sound* (London, 1957), pp. 221 ff.; cf. also his "Millenarian Movements in Melanesia," *op. cit.*, pp. 18–19.

[3] For an account of messianism and its different manifestations, cf. H. Kohn, *Revolutions and Dictatorships* (Cambridge, Mass., 1939), pp. 26–37, and his "Messianism," *Encyclopaedia of the Social Sciences*, Vol. 10, pp. 356–357. For a summary statement of the evolution of the idea of the millennium since the Reformation, cf. E. L. Tuveson, *Millennium and Utopia* (Berkeley, 1949), pp. vi–x. For a brief comment on the changing conception of revolution over the ages, cf. S. Neumann, "The Structure and Strategy of Revolution: 1848 and 1948," *Journal of Politics*, Vol. 11 (1949), pp. 533–535. For an account of the changing character of nationalism in the West, cf. E. H. Carr, *Nationalism and After* (London, 1945), pp. 1–26.

[4] Linton, "Nativistic Movements," *op. cit.*, p. 239. For an account of the general flurry of fads, reforms, and other outbursts which characterized the period extending from the 1820's to the 1840's—a period which also produced many value-oriented movements—cf. Sears, *Days of Delusion*, pp. xviii–xix, and T. D. S. Bassett, "The Secular Utopian Socialists," in Egbert and Persons (eds.), *Socialism and American Life*, Vol. I, pp. 174–175.

[5] Barber, "Acculturation and Messianic Movements," *op. cit.*, pp. 667–668; J. S. Slotkin, *The Peyote Religion* (Glencoe, Ill., 1956), pp. 1–7; below, pp. 365–366.

The Value-Oriented Movement

Let us now clarify several frequently confused relations: the relations among value-oriented movements on the one hand, and religious change, revolutions and violence on the other.

Value-oriented Movements and Religious Change. Not all religious movements are value-oriented. We have seen that revivalism in evangelical Protestantism conforms to the typical craze process,[1] and that reform movements within the church (e.g., the Social Gospel movement) are analyzable as norm-oriented movements.[2] Furthermore, the mere diffusion of new rituals into a religion does not necessarily require a full-fledged value-oriented movement.[3] In order for a religious movement to be termed a value-oriented movement it must possess a distinctive generalized belief[4] and proceed through a definite value-added process.[5]

Value-oriented Movements and Revolution. The term "revolution" frequently refers not only to challenges to the legitimacy of a ruling power, but also to rapid social change of any sort—e.g., the Industrial Revolution, the scientific revolution, the managerial revolution.[6] Even if we restrict the meaning to Edwards' definition—"a change ... whereby one system of legality is terminated and another originated"[7]—not all revolutions fall into the category of value-oriented movements. Some, such as palace revolutions, involve a turnover in personnel and the overthrow of government as a means of gaining access to political spoils;[8] others may be based on grievances about

---

[1] Above, pp. 173-175.
[2] Above, p. 290.
[3] For examples of the incorporation of syncretic elements into American Indian religions without the occurrence of a nativistic movement, cf. A. F. C. Wallace, "New Religions among the Delaware Indians, 1600-1900," *Southwestern Journal of Anthropology*, Vol. 12 (1956), pp. 1-20; also L. Spier, "The Ghost Dance of 1870 among the Klamath of Oregon," *University of Washington Publications in Anthropology*, Vol. 2, No. 2 (Seattle, 1927), pp. 43-44.
[4] Above, pp. 120-121.
[5] Below, pp. 121-123.
[6] For an examination of different meanings of the term, cf. D. Yoder, "Current Definitions of Revolution," *American Journal of Sociology*, Vol. 32 (1926-27), p. 433; R. C. Binkley, "An Anatomy of Revolution," *The Virginia Quarterly Review*, Vol. 10 (1934), pp. 502-503; Le Bon, *The Psychology of Revolution*, pp. 25-29.
[7] *The Natural History of Revolution*, p. 2.
[8] The Latin American revolutions of the nineteenth century provide instances of these limited objectives. Cf. D. G. Munro, *The Latin American Republics* (New York, 1960), pp. 159-161; E. Lieuwen, "The Military: A Revolutionary Force," *Annals of the American Academy of Political and Social Science*, Vol. 334 (1961), p. 31. See also E. E. Kellett, *The Story of Dictatorship from the Earliest Times Till Today* (London, 1937), p. 111; H. Eckstein, "Internal Wars: A Taxonomy," Internal War Project—Memorandum No. 2 (Mimeographed, 1960), p. 10. For the limited aims of the *coup d'état* in Thailand in 1932, cf. W. M. Ball, *Nationalism and Communism in East Asia* (Melbourne, 1952), pp. 114-115; in Germany in 1918, cf. Abel, *Why Hitler Came to Power*, p. 17. On the general distinctions

The Value-Oriented Movement

specific policies, laws or customs, and hence fall into the category of "norm-oriented revolutions."[1] Examples of value-oriented revolutions are the British, French, and Russian revolutions, the fascist revolutions in Italy and Germany; the modern nationalistic revolutions directed against colonial domination, such as the Indonesian, Chinese, Indo-Chinese, and so on.

Value-oriented Movements and Violence. Because of the hostile component in the beliefs of all value-oriented movements,[2] the *potential* for violence is always present in such movements. Violence has actually accompanied revolutionary movements throughout history.[3] But not all revolutionary overthrows are violent, as when the ruling power submits without a struggle.[4] Furthermore, many non-revolutionary value-oriented movements (e.g., scattered millenarian protests) never show open hostility toward the ruling authorities, even though this hostility appears in fantasy.[5]

Much of what is written about value-oriented movements is distorted by polemics.[6] This is especially true of contemporary revolutions (e.g., in Cuba). The same is true for phenomena such as the American Civil War, which, though it occurred a century ago, still excites strong feelings in the popular mind and among scholars who analyze the events. For this reason we shall purposely minimize our reference to contemporary or controversial upheavals. However important they are for the understanding of value-oriented movements in general, they are more difficult to appraise than those movements on which we have historical and emotional perspective.

STRUCTURAL CONDUCIVENESS

What structural arrangements permit or encourage value-oriented movements rather than other kinds of outbursts? More particularly, to what degree is the value-system of a society differentiated from the other components of social action? What are the available means

---

among *coup d'état*, rebellion, insurrection, and full-fledged revolution, cf. A. Meusel, "Revolution and Counter-revolution," *Encyclopaedia of the Social Sciences*, Vol. 13, p. 367; also Trotsky, *The History of the Russian Revolution*, Vol. III, pp. 167–169.

[1] Eckstein, "Internal Wars—A Taxonomy," p. 10. For the role of the military in reform and anti-reform revolutions in recent Latin American history, cf. Lieuwen, "The Military: A Revolutionary Force," *op. cit.*, pp. 31–36.

[2] Above, pp. 122–123.

[3] Rudé, *The Crowd in the French Revolution*, pp. 233–239; C. A. Ellwood, *The Psychology of Human Society* (New York, 1925), pp. 259–260; Brooks, *American Syndicalism*, p. 158.

[4] F. Gross, *The Seizure of Political Power in a Century of Revolutions* (New York, 1958), Ch. III; Eckstein, "Internal Wars—A Taxonomy," pp. 4–5.

[5] Above, pp. 314–315, and below, pp. 365–366.

[6] Heberle, *Social Movements*, pp. 25–26.

for expressing grievances? Among the several possible kinds of value-oriented responses, does a given social structure favor one or more kinds? Finally, what are the possibilities for communicating value-oriented beliefs among those who might be receptive to them?

The Differentiation of the Value-system from Other Components of Action. In a classic article on religious sects, Gillin observed that "religious sects will arise only when religion is the dominant interest. When political interest predominates, political parties will spring up."[1] This is a simple but forceful statement of a major dimension of structural conduciveness: the degree to which a value-system is differentiated from other components of action.

When values are not differentiated from norms, breaking a norm means more than merely trespassing on property, divorcing a spouse, or failing to display proper deference; it also involves defiance of a *general value*. As Bellah points out, this fusion of values and norms is

> characterized by the comprehensiveness and specificity of ... value commitments and by ... consequent lack of flexibility. Motivation is frozen, so to speak, through commitment to a vast range of relatively specific norms governing almost every situation in life. Most of these specific norms, usually including those governing social institutions, are thoroughly integrated with a religious system which invokes ultimate sanctions for every infraction. Thus changes in economic or political institutions, not to speak of family and education, in traditional societies tend to have ultimate religious implications. Small changes will involve supernatural sanctions.[2]

Because of this lack of differentiation, specific dissatisfactions with any social arrangements eventually become religious protests, or, more generally, protests against values. For instance, if interest on loans is defined as sinful rather than merely economically unsound, controversy over interest becomes a religious conflict rather than a matter of economic policy.[3] In a theocratic setting objections against artistic and architectural styles become moral and theological matters, rather than mere matters of taste; under such conditions esthetic criticism is not differentiated from moral outrage.[4]

---

[1] J. L. Gillin, "A Contribution to the Sociology of Sects," *American Journal of Sociology*, Vol. 16 (1910–11), p. 246. Cf. Linton's remark that "a devout society will turn to (magical-revivalistic) nativism ... long before a skeptical one will." "Nativistic Movements," *op. cit.*, p. 239.

[2] R. N. Bellah, "Religious Aspects of Modernization in Turkey and Japan," *American Journal of Sociology*, Vol. 164 (1958), p. 1. Bellah treats such societies as manifesting "prescriptive" values as discussed by Becker in "Current Sacred-Secular Theory and Its Development," in H. Becker and A. Boskoff (eds.), *Modern Sociological Theory* (New York, 1957).

[3] For the long process by which the control of interest changed from the religious to the secular sphere, cf. R. H. Tawney, *Religion and the Rise of Capitalism* (New York, 1924).

[4] Above, pp. 280–281.

The Value-Oriented Movement

The political arrangements of many modern democracies present a marked contrast to these undifferentiated arrangements. In the former, Bellah observes,

... an area of flexibility (is) gained in economic, political, and social life in which specific norms may be determined in considerable part by short-term exigencies in the situation of action, or by functional requisites of the relevant social subsystems. Ultimate or religious values lay down the basic principles of social action; ... but the religious system does not attempt to regulate economic, political, and social life in great detail.... Looking at this process another way, we may say that there must be a differentiation between religion and ideology, between ultimate values and proposed ways in which these values may be put into effect. In traditional prescriptive societies there is no such discrimination. Difference of opinion on social policy is taken to imply difference as to religious commitment. The social innovator necessarily becomes a religious heretic. But in modern society there is a differentiation between the levels of religion and social ideology which makes possible greater flexibility at both levels.[1]

When the world-view is religious, then, protests against the world invariably become defined in religious terms.

The general relation between level of differentiation and type of expression of protest may be illustrated as follows:

(1) Political and religious authority were little differentiated during medieval times. As Turberville summarizes it,

The distinction which we of the modern world, as the Renaissance and Reformation have made it, are wont to make between Church and State, spiritual and temporal, was wholly foreign to mediaeval thought. There was but one society, not two parallel societies. Society had indeed two aspects—one which looked to things mundane and transient, the other which looked to things heavenly and eternal. To safeguard its earthly interests the world had its secular rulers and administrators; to aid its spiritual life it has as guides and mediators the sacred hierarchy. But the secular rulers, on the one hand, and the priesthood, on the other, were officers in the same polity.[2]

In addition, the medieval world view was dominated by the Christian version of the supernatural, and by notions of demons, witches, and

[1] "Religious Aspects of Modernization in Turkey and Japan," *op. cit.*, pp. 1–2. For discussion of the fusion of religion and politics in the nationalist churches of the West, cf. Niebuhr, *The Social Sources of Denominationalism*, pp. 106–131. For a contrast between the fusion of religious commitment and authority in Catholicism and their separation in Protestantism, cf. L. S. Cressman, "Ritual the Conserver," *American Journal of Sociology*, Vol. 35 (1929–30), p. 567. For further discussion of the implications of the level of differentiation of religion for the occurrence of voluntary conversion, cf. J. Jastrow, "Religious Conversion," *Encyclopaedia of the Social Sciences*, Vol. 4, p. 353.
[2] A. S. Turberville, *Mediaeval Heresy and the Inquisition* (London, 1920), pp. 1–2.

other magical forces.¹ Under such circumstances protests of all sorts tended to be expressed in religious terms and treated as heresies against the values of medieval Christianity.²

(2) The growth of the extreme varieties of "Holiness" movements among recent white and Negro migrants into urban centers is closely associated with the immediate "cultural heritage or tradition of the migrant. . . . The (movements seem) most prevalent in areas in which have tended to concentrate the migrant groups whose most recent heritage is that of the fundamentalist, revivalistic tradition of the southern rural areas."³

(3) In the major Western revolutions of modern times, the degree to which protests became religious depends largely on the differentiation of religious and political issues. Trotsky, in comparing the British and French revolutions, remarked:

In the middle of the seventeenth century the bourgeois revolution in England developed under the guise of a religious reformation. A struggle for the right to pray according to one's own prayer book was identified with the struggle against the king, the aristocracy, the princes of the church, and Rome. The Presbyterians and Puritans were deeply convinced that they were placing their earthly interests under the unshakable protection of the divine Providence. The goals for which the new classes were struggling commingled inseparably in their consciousness with texts from the Bible and the forms of churchly ritual. . . .

In France, which stepped across the Reformation, the Catholic Church survived as a state institution until the revolution, which found its expression and justification for the tasks of the bourgeois society, not in texts from the Bible, but in abstractions of democracy.⁴

---

[1] *Ibid.*, p. 105; Rydberg, *The Magic of the Middle Ages*.
[2] For an account of the forms of protest in medieval sects and "manias," cf. H. R. Niebuhr, "Sects," *Encyclopaedia of the Social Sciences*, Vol. 13, p. 625; Cohn, *The Pursuit of the Millennium*; B. S. Gowen, "Some Aspects of Pestilences and Other Epidemics," *American Journal of Psychology*, Vol. 18 (1907), pp. 2 22–25; Hecker, *The Dancing Mania of the Middle Ages* (1885), pp. 1–42; Hecker, *The Black Death in the Fourteenth Century*, pp. 82–98. The Protestant Reformation itself—a mixture of religious and political protest—developed on the background of undifferentiated religious and political authority. Bax, *German Society at the Close of the Middle Ages*, pp. 135–137.
[3] J. B. Holt, "Holiness Religion: Cultural Shock and Social Reorganization," *American Sociological Review*, Vol. 5 (1940), pp. 746–747. For comments on Negro "religiosity," cf. Jones, "A Comparative Study of Religious Cult Behavior Among Negroes with Special Reference to Emotional Group Conditioning Factors," *op. cit.*, p. 56; Davenport, *Primitive Traits in Religious Revivals*, pp. 47–56. For an account of the religious outlooks that foreign migrants brought to America, as well as their reactions to the American religious tradition, cf. Handlin, *The Uprooted*, pp. 24, 112–129.
[4] *History of the Russian Revolution*, Vol. I, pp. 14–15. The secular character of the French Revolution should not, however, be over-emphasized. For the strong conditioning effect which the Catholic Church had on the ideals of the eighteenth

The Value-Oriented Movement

(4) Protests in many traditional societies under colonial domination reflect the undifferentiated religious outlook of these societies. In attempting to account for the characteristics of societies that are susceptible to millenarian movements, Worsley notes that

...these societies... lack advanced technological and scientific knowledge. The people are ignorant of the findings of advanced natural science on the aetiology of diseases, on variations in soil-fertility, on the changes of the seasons, the movements of the planets, etc. They have little power either to predict the onset of natural disasters or to control or counteract them. Such ignorance in its turn is primarily determined by the low level of their technological equipment. These deficiencies in scientific knowledge and practice, especially knowledge of European society and above all of European factory production, provide ample room for the elaboration of fantastic "explanations" in animistic or other supernaturalist terms, and for the use of magic to try to solve practical problems. The primitive peasant is thus predisposed to the acceptance of supernaturalist interpretations of reality: the soil is ready tilled for the millenarian leader. As pragmatic social experience increases and as education spreads, the ground becomes less fertile for millenarism.[1]

Accordingly, a typical beginning in the development of nationalistic movements for independence in colonial areas is the growth of religious cults, sects and reform movements.[2] The religiosity of early nationalism also depends, however, on factors other than the undifferentiated world-view of such societies. Frequently the religiosity of protest is conditioned by the fact that the pressure of the colonial powers on the colonized societies is itself religious, as in missionary activity.[3] In addition, colonial powers frequently rule their colonies in such a way as to close off all means of expressing grievances other than value-oriented ones.[4]

(5) The leaders of newly established revolutionary regimes frequently define the world in undifferentiated value terms, and thus

---

century philosophers and revolutionaries, cf. Tocqueville, *The Old Regime and the Revolution*, pp. 184–186.
[1] *The Trumpet Shall Sound*, pp. 238–239.
[2] J. Guiart, "Forerunners of Melanesian Nationalism," *Oceania*, Vol. 22 (1951), pp. 81–90; Pye, "The Politics of Southeast Asia," in Almond and Coleman (eds.), *op. cit.*, p. 104. For an account of the religious reform movements in nineteenth-century India, cf. Desai, *Social Background of Indian Nationalism*, pp. 247–269. The early religious protest in Indonesia is summarized in W. F. Wertheim, *Indonesian Society in Transition* (The Hague, 1956), pp. 316–318; also G. M. Kahin, *Nationalism and Revolution in Indonesia* (Ithaca, 1952), p. 38. For discussion of the intermingling of religion and political protest in Africa, cf. J. S. Coleman, *Nigeria: Background to Nationalism* (Princeton, 1958), pp. 175–178; W. O. Brown, "Race Consciousness among South African Natives," *American Journal of Sociology*, Vol. 40 (1935), pp. 569–581.
[3] Below, p. 347.
[4] Below, pp. 326–329.

The Value-Oriented Movement

make it probable that any opposition *to the new regime* will be expressed in value-oriented terms.[1] An example of the transformation of protest into a challenge against the legitimacy of a revolutionary regime is seen in the Kronstadt Revolt of 1921 in the Soviet Union. The Petrograd workers' economic demands gradually crystallized into political opposition. The government, itself consolidating its newly gained power, took an intransigent stand against the protest and denounced it as "Menshevik" and "Socialist Revolutionary," and hence counterrevolutionary.[2] Leaders of successful value-oriented revolutionary movements, because of their undifferentiated definition of the social and political situation, have a great potential for breeding new revolutions.

The Availability of Means to Express Grievances. To summarize the above: If a social situation is defined entirely in value-oriented terms, every protest is necessarily value-oriented.[3] This kind of conduciveness, however, never exists in pure form; other conditions of conduciveness also determine in part why a value-oriented movement arises, rather than some other type of outburst. Among the most important of these conditions is the availability of means to express protest or grievances among a population suffering from any kind of strain.

Many religious sects, observed Gillin, arise among "lower classes which have been shut out from any part in the socializing process."[4] Shutting out may appear in several guises. Worsley notes three types of political situations in which millenarian movements arise:

[Millenarian movements] occur, firstly, among people living in the so-called "stateless" societies, societies which have no overall unity, which lack centralized political institutions, and which may lack specialized political institutions altogether. They have thus no suitable machinery through which they can act politically as a unified force when the occasion arises, except on a temporary, localized or *ad hoc* basis. They often have no chiefs, no courts of law other than the council of elders or of prominent or wealthy men, no policy, no army and no administrative officials....

The second major type of society in which millenarian cults develop is the agrarian, and especially feudal, State. Such societies, of course, have indeed an elaborate formal hierarchical organization unlike stateless peoples, but the cults arise among the lower orders—peasants and urban

---

[1] Bellah, "Religious Aspects of Modernization in Turkey and Japan," *op. cit.*, p. 2.

[2] R. F. Daniels, "The Kronstadt Revolt of 1921: A Study in the Dynamics of Revolution," *American Slavic and East European Review*, Vol. 10 (1951), p. 241.

[3] Cf. Bellah: "The new movement must take on a religious (i.e., value-oriented) coloration in order to meet the old system on its old terms." "Religious Aspects of Modernization in Turkey and Japan," *op. cit.*, p. 2.

[4] "A Contribution to the Sociology of Sects," *op. cit.*, p. 239.

The Value-Oriented Movement

plebians—in opposition to the official regimes. These groups, like stateless Melanesians, lack any overall political organization.

There is a third type of social situation in which activist millenarian ideas are likely to flourish. This is when a society with differentiated political institutions is fighting for its existence by quite secular military-political means, but is meeting with defeat after defeat.... Again, when the political structure of a society is smashed by war or other means, or fails to answer the needs of a people who wish to carry on the struggle, then a prophetic, often millenarian, leadership is likely to emerge.[1]

Value-oriented beliefs, then—and here we lump millenarian beliefs with all other value-oriented beliefs—arise when alternative means for reconstituting the social situation are perceived as unavailable. In terms of our scheme of analysis, this unavailability has three main aspects: (*a*) The aggrieved group in question does not possess facilities whereby they may reconstitute the social situation; such a group ranks low on wealth, power, prestige, or access to means of communication. (*b*) The aggrieved group is prevented from expressing hostility that will punish some person or group considered responsible for the disturbing state of affairs. (*c*) The aggrieved group cannot modify the normative structure, or cannot influence those who have the power to do so.[2]

This closing-off of the means of reconstituting the social order can be illustrated in the following situations in which value-oriented beliefs typically congeal: (1) among politically disinherited peoples, especially recent migrants; (2) among colonially dominated peoples; (3) among persecuted minorities; (4) in inflexible political structures; (5) in post-revolutionary situations; (6) in situations marked by the failure of government by political parties.

(1) *The politically disinherited.*[3] By this we mean especially the "lower orders" of society, including "discontented peasants" and the "jetsam of the towns and cities."[4] Niebuhr and other observers of

---

[1] *The Trumpet Shall Sound*, pp. 227–228. For a contrast between the political situation of medieval peasantry—among whom millenarian movements were conspicuously lacking—and that of the urban masses in medieval times—among whom millenarian movements flourished—cf. Cohn, *The Pursuit of the Millennium*, pp. 25–29.

[2] In terms of the table of components of action, this means that the aggrieved group feels itself powerless to reconstitute the Facilities, Mobilization, and Normative components. Under such circumstances, attention turns to the highest level, namely reconstitution of the Value component. Above, pp. 24–30.

[3] In one sense all six examples just enumerated are instances of politically disinherited peoples (e.g., natives in a colonial setting, middle classes blocked by aristocratic inflexibility, etc.). We consider the examples separately to elucidate the many different kinds of social settings in which this political condition may occur.

[4] Worsley, *The Trumpet Shall Sound*, pp. 225–226. Worsley limits the second category to the towns and cities of feudal societies, but as the following examples

religious sects have commented on the proliferation of sects among the disinherited through the ages.[1] For instance, it appears that early Christianity not only attracted predominantly the poor, simple, and low in Roman society,[2] but it also spread "with amazing rapidity and completeness" in areas like Asia Minor, where "proletarian labor ... was restive; ... its economic condition justified this unrest, and ... *it had no opportunity for redress through either political or economic action.*"[3]

Recent migrants to American cities are especially prone to join value-oriented protest movements. According to a number of studies, such migrants participate minimally in the organized political, social, and recreational activities of the city.[4] This isolation, combined with the general "cultural shock" of migration, makes for the clustering of value-oriented religious sects among recent migrants to cities.[5] Among recent Negro migrants, who suffer the same disadvantages plus the hardships of racial discrimination, the clustering of such value-oriented movements is also pronounced.[6]

(2) The colonially dominated. In colonial societies the dominant power imposes both conditions of strain and conditions of conduciveness for value-oriented movements on the native population. Thus R. Kennedy, in listing "the outstanding universal characteristics of colonialism all over the dependent areas of the world," notes the following consequences of colonialism:

the color line; political and economic subordination of the native population; poor development of social services, especially education, for natives;

---

show, the generalization applies to migrants in modern American cities as well.

[1] Niebuhr, *The Social Sources of Denominationalism*, pp. 34–49; L. Pope, *Millhands and Preachers* (New Haven, 1958), pp. 136–138; Clark, *The Small Sects in America*, pp. 269–271. Clark attempts to strengthen his observation by presenting statistics of the recruitment of the poor into small, emotional sects in recent American history.

[2] E. Troeltsch, *The Social Teaching of the Christian Churches*, Vol. I (London, 1931), pp. 45–46, 86–87.

[3] S. Dickey, "Some Economic and Social Conditions of Asia Minor Affecting the Expansion of Christianity," in S. J. Case (ed.), *Studies in Early Christianity* (New York, 1928), pp. 406, 414. Italics added.

[4] H. W. Beers and C. Heflin, "The Urban Status of Rural Migrants," *Social Forces*, Vol. 23 (1944), pp. 32–37; B. G. Zimmer, "Participants of Migrants in Urban Structures," *American Sociological Review*, Vol. 20 (1955), pp. 218–224; G. C. Leybourne, "Urban Adjustments of Migrants from the Southern Appalachian Plateaus," *Social Forces*, Vol. 16 (1937–38), pp. 238–246.

[5] Holt, "Holiness Religion: Cultural Shock and Social Reorganization," *op. cit.*, pp. 746–747.

[6] Fauset, *Black Gods of the Metropolis*, pp. 87–88, 107–108; E. D. Beynon, "The Voodoo Cult among Negro Migrants in Detroit," *American Journal of Sociology*, Vol. 43 (1937–38), pp. 897–898; H. M. Brotz, "Negro 'Jews' in the United States," *Phylon*, Vol. 13 (1952), pp. 325–326; Parker, *The Incredible Messiah*, p. 34.

The Value-Oriented Movement

and rigid social barriers between the ruling class and the subject people. These are the elements of which the colonial system is constructed.[1]

At present we consider only the inability of the native population to express their grievances.

Under conditions of colonial domination value-oriented movements such as nativism or nationalistic ideological movements do not arise immediately upon colonial contact. "[The nativistic cult] is never a primary response; it necessarily occurs late in the history of contact and invasion."[2] Generally native populations consider the possible alternatives for redress, and, finding them to be closed, turn to value-oriented beliefs. Of these alternatives we shall examine two —the possibility of expelling the foreigner by force and the possibility of inducing the foreigner to alleviate situations of strain by normative reform.

The early stages of colonial domination are marked by native resistance which is put down effectively and brutally.[3] This pacification closes the possibility of expelling the foreigner by hostile attack, and often gives rise to a value-oriented movement which promises to eliminate the foreigner and restore pre-colonial conditions or at least re-establish a native-dominated society.[4]

There are many examples of the relationship between military defeat and subsequent nativistic activity. (*a*) The Indian Shaker Church rose as the last of a number of nativistic movements following the military defeats of the Washington Indians in the mid-nineteenth century.[5] (*b*) A series of military defeats preceded the rise of the Grass Dance, the Hand Game, the Ghost Dance, and later Peyotism among the American Indians.[6] (*c*) Among the Maoris of

---

[1] R. Kennedy, "The Colonial Crisis and the Future," in R. Linton (ed.), *The Science of Man in the World Crisis* (New York, 1952), p. 311. The several colonial powers—British, French, Dutch, Americans, Belgians, Portuguese, Japanese, etc. —varied as to the extent to which they imposed these consequences. Pp. 320 ff.

[2] L. Krader, "A Nativistic Movement in Western Siberia," *American Anthropologist*, Vol. 58 (1956), p. 290.

[3] A. P. Elkin, "Native Reaction to an Invading Culture and its Bearers—with Special Reference to Australia," *Proceedings of the Seventh Pacific Science Congress of the Pacific Science Association* (Feb.–Mar., 1949), Vol. VIII (Christchurch, 1953), pp. 37–42; also Elkin, "The Reaction of Primitive Peoples to the White Man's Culture," *The Hibbert Journal*, Vol. 35 (1936–37), p. 537.

[4] J. H. Steward, "The Changing American Indian," in Linton (ed.), *op. cit.*, p. 288.

[5] J. M. Collins, "The Indian Shaker Church: A Study of Continuity and Change in Religion," *Southwestern Journal of Anthropology*, Vol. 6 (1950), pp. 399–400.

[6] For extensive illustration of the crushing defeats dealt to the American Indian tribes between 1870 and 1885—after which the nativistic movements began to proliferate, cf. Slotkin, *The Peyote Religion*, pp. 16–17. For more particular studies of individual tribes, cf. Mooney, "The Ghost-Dance Religion and the

The Value-Oriented Movement

New Zealand, "the period of despondency which followed their defeats in the eighteen-sixties saw the evolution of weird native sects that bear striking resemblances to those which evolved under Indian disillusionment in North America."[1] (*d*) In British Nigeria, outbursts of violence appeared early and sporadically among the native tribesmen, and were intermingled with religious secessionist movements.[2] (*e*) In colonial Melanesia, natives launched armed attacks on whites in those areas which were semi-controlled or uncontrolled by colonial powers; in the villages, where structural strain was more severe and where colonial control was more secure, millenarian movements tended to predominate.[3] (*f*) A significant event which preceded the rise of value-oriented Indian nationalism was the revolt of the Indian princes in 1857, which the British crushed handily. Between 1857 and 1870, small revolts met the same fate. This failure of armed resistance, coupled with growing British resistance to peaceful reform movements, set the stage for the coalescence of Indian protest into value-oriented movements.[4] (*g*) The Indonesian islands were thoroughly pacified by the Dutch before value-oriented movements began to appear.[5] In all these examples, the effect of colonial domination was to eliminate the possibility of expelling the foreigner.

Colonialism also frequently closes the possibility of reconstituting the normative order, either directly or by appeal to the colonial authorities. Examples of this can be seen in the policies of the United States government in the late nineteenth century before the outbreak of nativistic outbursts among the American Indian tribes. The federal authorities broke a number of treaties and repeatedly neglected promises made to the Indians, and thus engendered a spirit of distrust among the natives.[6] In New Zealand in the 1830's and 1840's, after a long period of vacillation in the face of demands for reform by the Maoris, the British finally introduced a constitution that

---

Sioux Outbreak of 1890," *op. cit.*, pp. 659–660, 670–676, 692–700, 708–719; G. MacGregor *et al.*, *Warriors Without Weapons* (Chicago, 1946), pp. 31–33; A. Lesser, *The Pawnee Ghost Dance Hand Game* (New York, 1933), pp. 1–4.

[1] A. G. Price, *White Settlers and Native Peoples* (Melbourne, 1949), p. 168.
[2] Coleman, *Nigeria: Background to Nationalism*, pp. 172–174.
[3] Worsley, *The Trumpet Shall Sound*, pp. 45–47.
[4] Desai, *Social Background of Indian Nationalism*, pp. 272–279.
[5] Wertheim, *Indonesian Society in Transition*, pp. 68–69. For an account of the Dutch variety of indirect rule, cf. D. Woodman, *The Republic of Indonesia* (London, 1955), pp. 147–149.
[6] Lesser, *The Pawnee Ghost Dance Hand Game*, pp. 15–45; Slotkin, *The Peyote Religion*, p. 17; Mooney, "The Ghost-Dance Religion and the Sioux Outbreak of 1890," *op. cit.*, p. 824; W. I. Thomas, *Primitive Behavior* (New York, 1937), p. 680.

The Value-Oriented Movement

handed the Maoris over to the colonists, gave them no say in the new government, and claimed from them all land excepting such as they "had been accustomed to use and enjoy, either as places of abode or tillage for the growth of crops, or otherwise for the convenience and sustenation of life, by means of labour expended thereon." This to the Maoris was a nullification of the Treaty of Waitangi, and was trickery and deception of the worst kind.[1]

Several years later the constitution was changed to follow the Treaty of Waitangi more closely. "Unfortunately [however] the New Zealand lawyers . . . discovered a means to deny the Maoris a vote. Thus the constitution and its interpretation opened a gulf between the Maori and white."[2] This sequence of events, which marked an erosion of the norms governing the relationship between natives and whites, led to the Maori wars of the 1860's. After these armed uprisings were suppressed, native sects of a value-oriented sort began to appear.

We have already shown how the British authorities' discouragement of peaceful reform movements in late-nineteenth-century India gradually drove Indian protest in the direction of a value-oriented nationalist movement. By contrast, the Ceylonese movement for national independence, never thwarted to such a degree during its reform phase, never developed a set of generalized value-oriented beliefs.[3] The Dutch system of indirect rule in Indonesia, which developed through the nineteenth century, not only permitted exploitation of the natives by Indonesian aristocrats and Chinese merchants, but also created a more authoritarian social structure than existed before the Dutch initiated this system of rule.[4] The resulting politico-economic controls ruled out much peaceful reform activity, and thus set the stage for the development of a series of value-oriented outbursts which culminated in the movement for national independence. Finally, the religious secessionist movements in South Africa also reflect the lack of political representation of the large Bantu population.[5]

(3) *Persecuted minorities.* Like colonial populations, persecuted minorities are under strain but do not have access to avenues for

---

[1] Price *White Settlers and Native Peoples*, p. 162.
[2] *Ibid.*, p. 163.
[3] Above p. 309.
[4] Kahin, *Nationalism and Revolution in Indonesia*, pp. 4–13.
[5] M. Wilson, "The Beginning of Bantu Nationalism," in A. Locke and B. J. Stern (eds.), *When Peoples Meet* (New York, 1946), pp. 516–521; also B. G. M. Sundkler, *Bantu Prophets in South Africa* (London, 1948), pp. 296–296. For similar reflections on the origin of the Mau Mau in Kenya, cf. A. Rosenstiel, "An Anthropological Approach to the Mau Mau Problem," *Political Science Quarterly*, Vol. 68 (1953), pp. 427–428.

The Value-Oriented Movement

relieving the sources of strain. Historically the Jews provide the best example of a minority which, under periods of persecution, turn to value-oriented movements of a millenarian sort.[1]

(4) *Governmental inflexibility.* Analytically similar to the strong, unresponsive colonial power is the domestic government which, through autocracy or incapacity, displays rigidity in the face of demands for reform by groups in the population. Virtually every major ideological revolution in the West has been preceded by a period of governmental inflexibility in the face of rapid social change, inflexibility "effected through manipulation of the agencies of social control, such as government, religion, and education."[2] In a classic work, Sorokin maintains that one of the major "causes" of revolution is repression of major instincts in the population.[3] Similarly, Brooks Adams observes that "most of the worst catastrophes of history have been caused by an obstinate resistance to change when resistance was no longer possible."[4]

This inflexibility may result from different kinds of institutional arrangements. It may result from the decay and loss of responsiveness of an institution, as in the case of the Catholic Church on the eve of the Reformation.[5] It may result from a prolonged deadlock

---

[1] N. Cohn, "Medieval Millenarism and its Bearing on the Comparative Study of Millenarian Movements," Paper delivered at the Conference on Religious Movements of a Millenarian Character, under the auspices of the Editorial Committee of Comparative Studies in Society and History at the University of Chicago, April 8–9, 1960 (mimeographed), pp. 2–3; J. Kastein, *The Messiah of Ismir* (New York, 1931), pp. 3–36; K. S. Pinson, "Chassidism," *Encyclopaedia of the Social Sciences,* Vol. 3, pp. 354–355. For a brief study of the revival of two Japanese cults at the Tule Lake wartime segregation center at the California-Oregon boundary, cf. M. K. Opler, "Two Japanese Religious Sects," *Southwestern Journal of Anthropology,* Vol. 6 (1950), pp. 69–78.

[2] Ellwood, *The Psychology of Human Society,* pp. 251–252, 254–256. See also Ellwood, "A Psychological Theory of Revolutions," *American Journal of Sociology,* Vol. 11 (1905–06), pp. 53–55.

[3] *The Sociology of Revolution;* the second "cause" consists of the ineptitude of the ruling classes in repressing these instincts, which we shall discuss under the heading of social control.

[4] *The Theory of Social Revolutions* (New York, 1914), p. 133; also pp. 204–206. For similar statements of the inflexibility of ruling groups before revolutionary movements, cf. Edwards, *The Natural History of Revolution,* p. 9; Trotsky, *History of the Russian Revolution,* Vol. III, pp. 173–174; Reeve, *The Natural Laws of Social Convulsion,* Vol. III, p. 502; Turner and Killian, *Collective Behavior,* pp. 503–504. Almost identical observations have been made by scholars of dictatorships—which are frequently a by-product of revolutionary convulsion. Cf. J. O. Hertzler, "The Causal and Contributory Factors of Dictatorship," *Sociology and Social Research,* Vol. 24 (1939–40), pp. 10–11; D. Spearman, *Modern Dictatorship* (New York, 1939), p. 16; A. Carr, *Juggernaut* (New York, 1939), pp. 482–484; Kellett, *The Story of Dictatorship from the Earliest Times Till To-Day,* pp. 7–8.

[5] Bax, *German Society at the Close of the Middle Ages,* pp. 95–96; Bax, *Rise and Fall of the Anabaptists* (London, 1903), pp, 118 ff. For evidence of the re-

The Value-Oriented Movement

between monarch and representatives—a deadlock which paralyzes all chances of reform—as in the period preceding the English revolution in the seventeenth century.[1] It may result from the atrophy of a once-viable system of political control, as in the case of eighteenth-century France. Through a long process of centralization, accompanied by the decay of local feudal responsibilities, the old channels of political influence had decayed. The French central government, furthermore, was erratic in its enactment and enforcement of laws.[2] Thus, with the rise of a powerful middle class, increasing discontent on the part of peasantry, and the appearance of a nascent urban proletariat, France had an all-powerful centralized government to which only few had access.[3] Similar conditions of autocratic inflexibility—though the form and content of this inflexibility varied greatly—preceded the several revolutions of 1848 and characterized Czarist Russia for many decades before the Russian revolutions of the early twentieth century.[4]

When avenues for influencing political authorities are absent, blocked, or atrophied, value-oriented beliefs begin to flourish. This is seen in Tocqueville's penetrating remarks on the shifting state of public opinion in France during the eighteenth century. The rise of the generalized ideals of liberty and a new society, he maintained, were preceded by a period of moderate agitation by the economists and physiocrats. These agitators

> conceived all the social and administrative reforms effected by the Revolution before the idea of free institutions had once flashed upon their minds. ... Their idea ... was not to destroy but to convert the absolute monarchy. ... About 1750 the nation at large cared no more for political liberty than the economists themselves. ... People sought reforms, not rights.[5]

Only *after* these demands for reform were thwarted by governmental indifference, monarchical ineffectiveness, and the destruction

---

actionary policy on the part of the church and allied groups during the period preceding the Peasants' War in the fourteenth century in England, cf. H. M. Hyndman, *The Evolution of Revolution* (London, 1921), pp. 195–196; G. G. Coulton, *The Black Death* (London, 1929), pp. 74–77.

[1] S. R. Gardiner, *The First Two Stuarts and the Puritan Revolution* (New York, 1898), p. 7; R. B. Merriman, *Six Contemporaneous Revolutions* (Oxford, 1938), pp. 30–36.

[2] Tocqueville, *The Old Regime and the Revolution*, pp. 83–94, 184–186.

[3] *Ibid.*, p. 94; H. A. Taine, *The Ancient Regime* (New York, 1931), pp. 71–72; G. Lefebvre, *The Coming of the French Revolution* (New York, 1959), p. 5.

[4] Neumann, "The Structure and Strategy of Revolution," *op. cit.*, pp. 536–538; Gross, *The Seizure of Political Power in a Century of Revolutions*, pp. 98–99; Trotsky, *History of the Russian Revolution*, Vol. I, pp. 96–97.

[5] *The Old Regime and the Revolution*, pp. 194, 196–197, 200.

of the Parliaments, did grievances begin to be defined in terms of the values—liberty, the natural state of man, etc.—which later became the basis for the French Revolution.

Three qualifications are now in order. First, we have emphasized the absence of channels of reform as structurally conducive to the rise of value-oriented beliefs. We should stress also that the government must also be able to put down hostile outbursts effectively. If a government merely refuses to listen to demands for reform without being willing or able to back this refusal by using force, the government is likely to topple through palace revolution, *coup d'etat*, insurrection, or other revolutionary movements without a value-oriented base.[1] In short, in order for value-oriented beliefs to crystallize, *all* other avenues for the expression of grievances must be unavailable. Later we shall discover that the typical combination of factors that results in a value-oriented revolutionary movement is *first* a prolonged period of inflexible *and* effective blockage of protest. This promotes the spread of value-oriented beliefs. Only *later* does the government become enfeebled in its command of the forces of repression. At this point the value-oriented belief is combined with a hostile outburst toward the government, and the result is a value-oriented revolutionary movement.

Second, not all value-oriented beliefs eventuate in revolutionary movements. As we have seen, value-oriented beliefs may disappear altogether (if the original grievances disappear, for instance), or they may give rise to a sect, political party, or club.[2]

Third, the value-oriented belief which begins to permeate the aggrieved groups when they are prevented from expressing their grievances may be centuries old, may be altogether new, or may be a mixture of old and new. The important point is that the value-oriented belief, whatever its source, begins to *spread* under the appropriate conditions.

(5) Inflexibility in new revolutionary regimes. One basis for this inflexibility lies in the tendency for newly legitimized governments to define all protest in value-oriented terms.[3] In addition, the social disorganization created by the revolutionary upheaval keeps the level of strain high. Frequently, also, the pressure to mobilize the local population is great because of revolutionary involvement in

---

[1] For historical studies of these non-value-oriented revolutions, cf. C. E. Chapman, "The Age of the Caudillos: A Chapter in Hispanic American History," *The Hispanic American Historical Review*, Vol. 12 (1932), pp. 281–300; C. E. Haring, "The Chilean Revolution of 1931," *The Hispanic American Historical Review*, Vol. 13 (1933), pp. 197–203. Above, pp. 318–319.

[2] Above, pp. 315–316.

[3] Above, pp. 323–324.

The Value-Oriented Movement

foreign and civil wars. And finally, because the machinery of social order under a new revolutionary government is uninstitutionalized, it is often applied with a heavy hand to "compensate" for its lack of established legitimacy. These several factors combine to result in a reign of terror after a revolutionary overthrow.[1] The typical effect of this terror is to freeze the channels for expressing grievances. The period of terror, itself the product of a successful value-oriented movement, frequently breeds a set of conditions that are structurally conducive for the rise of new value-oriented beliefs.

(6) The breakdown of party systems. Hertzler has characterized the pre-revolutionary party situation as follows:

... Italy, just prior to the dictatorship, had fifteen parties; Germany thirty-eight; and Poland, thirty. A multiple-party system raises unsurmountable barriers to the pursuance of a firm, consistent, stabilized executive policy. As a result of such *Zersplitterung* there is government by blocs and groupments, and even the best of coalitions, when they can be achieved, lack unity, force, and decisiveness and have difficulty in winning the support necessary to carry on public affairs in a confidence-producing manner.[2]

The failure of parties is conducive to the rise of value-oriented beliefs; it is also conducive to the transformation of these beliefs in revolutionary direction because one or more of the fragmented groups is likely to encourage illegal use of violence, or the groups are likely to deadlock so that the government cannot act forcefully.[3]

The common feature of all these examples is that a part of the population finds itself under strain and unable to find means of remedying the situation. It is without facilities for organized action on its own; it cannot attack or expel the persons or agencies considered responsible for its difficulties; and it does not have access to those who could initiate normative changes. These conditions apply whether the group be a permanently dispossessed segment of society, a colonially dominated people, a population under an inflexible system of authority, or a persecuted minority. Under such conditions—combined with other determinants—people begin to redefine the fundamental values of the entire system in which they find themselves.

Two final qualifications must be made. First, all the examples of closing off the avenues of protest given above have referred to a more

[1] Brinton, *The Anatomy of Revolution*, pp. 185–213; J. Burckhardt, *Force and Freedom* (New York, 1943), pp. 279–287.
[2] "The Causal and Contributory Factors of Dictatorship," *op. cit.*, p. 12.
[3] Cf. Roberts, *The House that Hitler Built*, pp. 35–36; Abel, *Why Hitler Came to Power*, p. 127; E. Colton, *Four Patterns of Revolution* (New York, 1935), p. 81; A. Rossi (*pseud.*) *The Rise of Italian Fascism 1918–1922* (London, 1938), pp. 21 ff.

or less centralized political structure. By using these illustrations we do not wish to imply that all repression of protest comes from centralized political authorities. Blocked protest may exist within a non-governmental organization, e.g., a church that does not satisfy the desires of its congregation.

Second, the closing off of means of protest is always relative to existing expectations. For instance, if nobles who previously had had close access to a king in his deliberations are suddenly excluded from his councils, this constitutes a closing of avenues of protest relative to their expectations. On an absolute basis, however, they may still have greater influence than other groups in the population—e.g., peasants. Because the latter do not entertain such expectations, however, their sense of exclusion is not so great.

Indeed, the means of expressing protest may be only *perceived* to be closed, perhaps because of semi-paranoid personality tendencies. The beliefs of members of the "flying saucer cults," for instance, frequently were based on the assumption that governments were helpless in the face of hostile, cosmic forces, unless they relied on the assistance of other, beneficent cosmic forces. Such beliefs defined protest to governments as useless.[1] More generally, the esoteric cult may find its recruits among persons who have developed personality characteristics because of distinctive familial experiences (e.g., a rejecting father). Such cults do not stem from an oppressive governmental apparatus; they result from the convergence of a number of like souls who perceive the world as hostile because of essentially independent personal experiences. Furthermore, even in value-oriented movements which appear to rise in the face of some specific adult deprivation (e.g., a messianic movement in an Indian tribe which has recently suffered a series of humiliating military defeats at the hands of white settlers) the differential *recruitment* into such movements results in part from personality differences in the population affected.[2]

The Insulation and Isolation[3] of Value-oriented Movements. Under certain circumstances, one means of expressing grievances is to initiate a value-oriented movement itself. The ease with which such a movement may be accommodated—either through isolation to another geographical setting or through insulation within a society—determines in part whether such value-oriented movements will arise,

---

[1] R. R. Mathison, *Faiths, Cults and Sects of America* (Indianapolis, 1960), pp. 341–344; F. Scully, *Behind the Flying Saucers* (New York, 1950), p. xi.

[2] For a discussion of the relationship between ambiguous threats and the tendency to perceive the world as ambiguous, above, pp. 143–145.

[3] For a general discussion of the importance of insulation and isolation in deviance and social control, cf. Parsons, *The Social System*, p. 309.

The Value-Oriented Movement

and what kinds of movements they will be. As Bryan Wilson has indicated,

> ... it is evident that there are different consequences for sects according to the political and moral character of the society in which they emerge. In feudal, authoritarian, or totalitarian societies, the sect is persecuted; if it persists it will do so only as a clandestine organization.... An alternative development in the past has been for the sect to migrate and seek an environment where it could live according to its own standards. The achievement of such isolation has, in itself, consequences for sect organization and promotes communistic arrangements. In such circumstances... the sect is unlikely to show marked denominational tendencies.
>
> In democratic or pluralist societies the sect is not pushed into the search for isolation, and although revolutionary type movements [for instance, Jehovah's Witnesses] may emerge, they are likely to maintain their separation from the world by other methods.[1]

Insulation and isolation overlap with the problem of the response of agencies of social control to movements, which we shall discuss later. At present let us indicate some historical examples of insulation and isolation as modes of accommodating value-oriented movements.

Two outstanding examples of accommodating movements through insulation are (1) The monastic order which is contained within the church. This has been a dominant method of accommodation in the Catholic Church.[2] (2) Denominationalism, which is the dominant method of accommodation in American and British Protestantism.[3] When imported into a colonial area through missionary activity, denominationalism frequently produces a rash of secessionist sects and cults. This effect is very marked among the South African Bantu, in which the Protestant pattern of denominationalism has combined with the indigenous tradition of Bantu kraal-splitting.[4] The effects of institutionalizing denominationalism can also be seen in contemporary Japan. The postwar Japanese constitution—which guaranteed greater religious freedom than before—has permitted the emergence of many pre-war schismatic bodies as independent sects. Before 1945

---

[1] "An Analysis of Sect Development," p. 8. The isolation and insulation of sects corresponds to Wirth's discussion of secessionist and pluralistic minorities. L. Wirth, "The Problem of Minority Groups," in Linton (ed.), *op. cit.*, pp. 354–361.

[2] Cutten, *The Psychological Phenomena of Christianity*, pp. 148–150; P. Meadows, "Movements of Social Withdrawal," *Sociology and Social Research*, Vol. 29 (1944–45), pp. 47–50.

[3] For commentary on American denominationalism, particularly as experienced by immigrant groups, cf. Niebuhr, *The Social Sources of Denominationalism*, pp. 201–210, and Handlin, *The Uprooted*, pp. 110–116. For a brief account of a period of vigorous sect-formation within this setting during the first half of the nineteenth century, cf. Sears, *Days of Delusion*, pp. xviii–xix.

[4] Sundkler, *Bantu Prophets in South Africa*, pp. 170, 295.

"those bodies which were not branches of established religions existed precariously . . . and were harassed by the police if their policies were believed to be in opposition to State Shintō and acknowledged standards of patriotism."[1] A final example of insulation: The spread of Christianity in its first centuries depended in part on "the religious policy of Rome, which furthered the interchange of religions by its toleration, hardly presenting any obstacles to their natural increase or transformation or decay, although it would not stand any practical expression of contempt for the ceremonial of the State-religion."[2] The institutionalized insulation of value-oriented movements constitutes, then, a set of conditions which is conducive to the rise of value-oriented movements.

One way of safeguarding the political integrity of the constituted authorities of any system is to permit the insulated development of value-oriented movements. One of the consequences of denominational pluralism in the Anglo-Saxon tradition is to permit a value-oriented movement (religious schism) to develop without challenging the legitimacy of the political constitution. In this way religious conflict is segregated from political conflict, and value-conflict at lower political levels (i.e., the political organization of the churches) is segregated from value-conflict at higher political levels (i.e., state and federal government).[3]

Even if insulation is not possible, a sect may sometimes withdraw to an area which is more tolerant of its peculiarities. North America, with its wide open spaces and its tradition of religious toleration, has been the haven for groups which found a hostile reception in their countries of origin. The English Puritans, the Doukhobors, and the Amana settlers are but a few of the groups which have sought isolation in North America.[4] Even within this country religious

[1] L. C. May, "The Dancing Religion: A Japanese Messianic Sect," *Southwestern Journal of Anthropology*, Vol. 10 (1954), p. 119.

[2] A. Harnack, *The Expansion of Christianity in the First Three Centuries*, Vol. I (New York, 1904), p. 22.

[3] The institutionalization of this system of denominational pluralism also accounts for various areas of "touchiness" in the American political scene. The Catholic Church, for instance, is likely to be regarded as suspect first because as an organization it does not draw the line between religion and politics to nearly the degree to which it is drawn in the dominant religious tradition of the country, and second, because it does not permit denominationalism within its own ranks. On these two grounds the Catholic Church is likely to be regarded as out of keeping with the American religious tradition. Another instance of touchiness concerns the famous court case of the constitutionality of the refusal of the Jehovah's Witnesses to salute the American flag. While in itself the issue does not seem enormous, it assumed great significance in the American setting because it marked a symbolic crossing of the line which separates value-oriented movements in the religious sphere from their possible political implications.

[4] W. B. Selbie, *Nonconformity: Its Origin and Progress* (London, 1912), pp.

The Value-Oriented Movement

groups under attack (e.g., the Mormons) have been able to withdraw to distant geographical areas.[1] Finally, the possibility of emigrating to set up expatriate communities in other lands is yet another way of removing potential value-oriented challenges to the legitimacy of a political system.[2]

Possibilities of Communication. As in all collective behavior, the spread of a value-oriented movement depends on the possibility of disseminating a generalized belief. One of the "essential preliminary conditions" for revolutions, for instance, is "a high development of traffic and a widespread similarity of thought."[3] The actual method by which communication is carried—mouth to mouth, the press, etc.—varies from situation to situation,[4] but *some* channels of communication must be available. Consider the following examples:

(1) In addition to the spread of Judaism, which anticipated and prepared the way for Christianity, the latter was facilitated by the following historical developments, according to Harnack:

(*a*) The *Hellenizing* of the East and (in part also) of the West, which had gone on steadily since Alexander the Great: or, the *comparative unity of language and ideas which this Hellenizing had produced.* ...

(*b*) The *world-empire of Rome* and *the political unity* it secured for the nations bordering on the Mediterranean. ...

(*c*) The exceptional facilities, growth, and security of *international traffic* [roads, trade, etc.] ...[5]

(2) Colonial powers often consolidate communication patterns in colonial areas which foster the spread of value-oriented beliefs such as nationalism. This consolidation is facilitated by establishing countrywide trading and communication patterns, imposing a common language, centralizing a colonial area politically, using mass media, and attempting to convert the population to a common religion.[6]

43–44; H. B. Hawthorn (ed.), *The Doukhobors of British Columbia* (Vancouver, 1955), p. 23; B. M. H. Shambaugh, *Amana That Was and Amana That Is* (Iowa City, 1932), pp. 41–5, 63. For a brief description of the appropriateness of the American social setting for the Owenite experiments in the first half of the nineteenth century, cf. Bassett, "The Secular Utopian Socialists," in Egbert and Persons (eds.), *op. cit.*, p. 167.

[1] T. F. O'Dea, *The Mormons* (Chicago, 1957), pp. 41–75.
[2] The American political expatriate communities in cities like Paris, London, and Rome are functionally equivalent to sects which have been effectively isolated from the possibility of challenging the legitimacy of the political authority.
[3] Burckhardt, *Force and Freedom*, pp. 268–269.
[4] For a contrast between the communication patterns of the mid-seventeenth and mid-nineteenth centuries, and their implications for the development of revolutions in those periods, cf. Merriman, *Six Contemporaneous Revolutions*, p. 211.
[5] *The Expansion of Christianity in the First Three Centuries*, pp. 19–21.
[6] Kahin, *Nationalism and Revolution in Indonesia*, pp. 37–41; Coleman, *Nigeria;*

The Value-Oriented Movement

(3) A high rate of internal migration usually occasions widespread strain in a society, as we shall see. In addition, however, it facilitates the development of collective movements. In India, for instance, rapid urbanization creates conditions whereby

... large numbers of rootless, crowded, and often unmarried urban workers are easily provoked to violence and readily organized by political groups. [In addition,] the continued ties between the urban worker and the rural area to which he returns for births, weddings, and funerals, and in which he settles when he has sufficient income, serve to bring urban political ideas and organization to the rural areas.[1]

STRAIN

The conditions of structural conduciveness are a framework within which the remaining conditions rise to significance as determinants of the value-oriented movement. Without conditions of conduciveness, that is, the conditions of strain (which we shall now outline) may be determinants of some other kind of outburst (e.g., a norm-oriented movement, a craze) but not determinants of a value-oriented movement.

Strain and Facilities. Inadequacy of knowledge or techniques to grapple with new situations sets the stage for value-oriented movements. Worsley, in summarizing the conditions which breed millenarian movements, includes the lack of "advanced technological and scientific knowledge."[2] Value-oriented beliefs are not a simple function of superstition or lack of knowledge; the inadequacy of facilities to explain unusual events or cope with situational problems does, however, contribute to the rise of these, rather than other types of movements.

Background to Nationalism, pp. 63–65. Coleman also points out (p. 413) that the British emphasis on "freedom of speech, of press, of assembly, and of movement, including the freedom to study abroad" has facilitated the development of nationalism in the Gold Coast and Nigeria. For an analysis of the ways in which the Japanese occupation during World War II fostered cultural unity, especially in Indonesia, cf. W. H. Elsbree, *Japan's Role in Southeast Asian Nationalist Movements 1940 to 1945* (Cambridge, Mass., 1953), pp. 120, 165–167. Among the factors which encouraged the spread of Peyotism and other nativistic movements among the American Indians in the late nineteenth and early twentieth centuries were the development of intertribal councils, the juxtaposition of reservations, the ease of travel, the use of English rather than sign language for intertribal communication, and the use of the white media of communication, especially the mails. Slotkin, *The Peyote Religion*, pp. 18–19.

[1] Weiner, "The Politics of South Asia, in Almond and Coleman (eds.), *op. cit.*, p. 174.

[2] Above, p. 323; also "Millenarian Movements in Melanesia," *op. cit.*, p. 25. Davenport attributed the rise of "emotional movements" in part to "difficulty of communication and a great amount of ignorance in a population." *Primitive Traits in Religious Revivals*, p. 8.

The Value-Oriented Movement

Strain and Organization. Many studies reveal that value-oriented beliefs arise under conditions of severe physical deprivation, e.g., hunger or disease.[1] In addition, economic hardship (which may or may not involve physical deprivation) has been found to be closely associated with the spread of early Christianity,[2] millenarian movements in the late Middle Ages,[3] Chassidism,[4] American fundamentalism,[5] American Holiness sects,[6] Harlem sects such as the Father Divine Movement,[7] nationalistic movements in underdeveloped areas,[8] the French Revolution,[9] the revolutions of 1848,[10] the Russian Revolution of 1917,[11] and the fascist revolutions in Italy[12] and Germany.[13] Other forms of deprivation and frustration—the failure of a government in the conduct of war,[14] the removal of tribes

[1] Mooney, "The Ghost-Dance Religion and the Sioux Outbreak of 1890," *op. cit.*, pp. 189–824; Thomas, *Primitive Behavior*, p. 680; MacGregor, *Warriors Without Weapons*, pp. 37–41; Price, *White Settlers and Native Peoples*, pp. 37, 158–163, 196–197; Gowen, "Some Aspects of Pestilences and Other Epidemics," *op. cit.*, p. 2; Coulton, *The Black Death*, pp. 70–71; Barber, "Acculturation and Messianic Movements," *op. cit.*, pp. 664–666.

[2] Troeltsch, *The Social Teaching of the Christian Churches*, Vol. 1, pp. 45–46; Dickey, "Some Economic and Social Conditions of Asia Minor Affecting the Expansion of Christianity," in Case (ed.), *op. cit.*, pp. 406–410.

[3] Cohn, *The Pursuit of the Millennium*, pp. 22–30, 314–315.

[4] Pinson, "Chassidism," *op. cit.*, pp. 353–355.

[5] H. R. Niebuhr, "Fundamentalism," *Encyclopaedia of the Social Sciences*, Vol. 6, p. 527.

[6] Pope, *Millhands and Preachers*, pp. 133 ff.; A. T. Boisen, "Economic Distress and Religious Experience: A Study of the Holy Rollers," *Psychiatry*, Vol. 2 (1939), p. 194.

[7] Parker, *The Incredible Messiah*, pp. 35 ff.; Cantril, *The Psychology of Social Movements*, pp. 139–140.

[8] Coleman, *Nigeria: Background to Nationalism*, pp. 178–180; Kahin, *Nationalism and Revolution in Indonesia*, pp. 7–28.

[9] Binkley, "An Anatomy of Revolution," *op. cit.*, p. 511. For a collection of reflections and controversies on the precise influence of economic factors, especially among the peasants, in the genesis of the French Revolution, cf. R. W. Greenlaw (ed.), *The Economic Origins of the French Revolution: Poverty or Prosperity?* (Boston, 1958).

[10] Neumann, "The Structure and Strategy of Revolution," *op. cit.*, pp. 536, 538.

[11] Trotsky, *History of the Russian Revolution*, Vol. I, pp. 62, 406, 411–412; Vol. II, pp. 1, 344–345; M. T. Florinsky, *The End of the Russian Empire* (New Haven, 1931), Chs. VI–VIII.

[12] Rossi, *The Rise of Italian Fascism 1918–1922*, pp. 6–19; M. T. Florinsky, *Fascism and National Socialism* (New York, 1938), pp. 1–6.

[13] For an account of economic discontent in pre-Nazi Germany, cf. Abel, *Why Hitler Came to Power*, p. 121; Heiden, *A History of National Socialism*, pp. 96–97, 124–125; Schuman, *The Nazi Dictatorship* (New York, 1935), pp. 101 ff. For a study of the same phenomena through the composition of the Nazi party and through electoral support, cf. H. H. Gerth, "The Nazi Party: Its Leadership and Composition," in Merton, Gray, Hockey and Selvin, *Reader in Bureaucracy*, pp. 100–113; C. P. Loomis and J. A. Beegle, "The Spread of German Naziism in Rural Areas," *American Sociological Review*, Vol. 11 (1946), pp. 724–734. For general importance of the economic element in the build up of revolutions, cf. Edwards, *The Natural History of Revolution*, pp. 69–70.

[14] For the importance of military defeat in the rise of the revolutionary situation

The Value-Oriented Movement

from their traditional lands,[1] an intensification of religious or political persecution,[2] etc.—have also been uncovered as bases for value-oriented movements.

Such deprivations are relative to expectations. By an absolute measure, groups which are drawn into value-oriented movements may be improving. This seems to be the case in connection with the major Western revolutions; "they took place in societies economically progressive," and they drew in part upon those classes which were advancing most rapidly.[3] Again, in many colonial countries it is those people who have recently received higher education—i.e., have "improved" fastest culturally—that lead and join militant nationalist movements.[4] In both cases this improvement on absolute grounds involves deprivation on relative grounds; for the same groups, with their new gains in one sphere (e.g., economic, cultural) often are held back in another (e.g., political).

Strain and Norms. The normative disorganization that war occasions accounts in part for the frequent rise of revolutionary movements during and after wars.[5] As background factors to the Cargo Cults in Melanesia, Guiart has mentioned the "lack of balance in actual native society, the traditional frame having been undermined or destroyed, and the newly organized one being the result of a more or less open and direct interference in local native affairs."[6] Behind the same movements Worsley has isolated normative changes in work practices, enforced through "blackbirding" and indenturing

---

in 1921 in Germany, cf. R. T. Clark, *The Fall of the German Republic* (London, 1935), pp. 23 ff.

[1] Mooney, "The Ghost-Dance Religion and the Sioux Outbreak of 1890," *op. cit.*, pp. 663 ff., 670 ff., and 692 ff.; Lesser, *The Pawnee Ghost Dance Hand Game*, pp. 5–23; G. Goodwin and C. Kaut, "A Native Religious Movement among the White Mountain and Cibecue Apache," *Southwestern Journal of Anthropology*, Vol. 10 (1954), p. 387.

[2] Above, pp. 329–330. Note here that persecution is relevant as *two* determinants of a value-oriented movement—first, structural conduciveness, or the closing off of avenues for the expression of grievances, and second, the intensification of the grievances themselves. The same might be said of the social conditions which produce "disinherited" peoples. Niebuhr, *The Social Sources of Denominationalism*, pp. 34–72; Clark, *The Small Sects in America*, pp. 273–274; Worsley, *The Trumpet Shall Sound*, pp. 225–226; Shils, "Ideology and Civility," *op. cit.*, pp. 463–464; also above, pp. 325–329.

[3] Brinton, *The Anatomy of Revolution*, pp. 30–33; see also Reeve, *The Natural Laws of Social Convulsion*, pp. 142–143, 178.

[4] Wertheim, *Indonesian Society in Transition*, pp. 44–51; Pye, "The Politics of Southeast Asia," and Weiner, "The Politics of South Asia," in Almond and Coleman (eds.), *op. cit.*, pp. 132–134, 176–177, 228–229.

[5] Kornhauser, *The Politics of Mass Society*, pp. 168–172; R. Hunter, *Revolution: Why, How, When?* (New York, 1940), pp. 35–37.

[6] "Forerunners of Melanesian Nationalism," *op. cit.*, p. 89; also his " 'Cargo Cults' and Political Evolution in Melanesia," *South Pacific*, Vol. 5 (1951), p. 129.

The Value-Oriented Movement

laborers.[1] Farquhar has cited the destruction of traditional Indian marital, religious, and other norms under British rule between 1800 and 1895, a period which produced a number of religious and nationalistic movements.[2] Institutional anomalies and anachronisms also characterized French and Russian societies on the eve of their great revolutions.[3] We shall return to the subject of normative strain presently when we consider the empirical combinations of different types of strain.

Strain and Values. In his essay on the rise of religious movements, Gillin wrote that one fundamental factor is the "heterogeneity of the population of any social group," or its "social unlikeness" which results from the "imperfect assimilation of population elements suddenly brought together."[4] Such cultural conflict may take many forms—different generations of immigrants come into conflict because of their different degrees of assimilation;[5] immigrants experience "culture shock" as they mix with established residents;[6] value-conflict on a sectional basis—as in America in pre-Civil War days—may give rise to splits within churches;[7] racial schism may give rise to religious schism.[8] Sometimes two or more of these may combine, as in the case of the Negro immigrant, who experiences the tribulations of both the racial minority and the recent migrant.[9]

The spread of value-oriented movements in colonial areas is frequently associated with the degree of value-deterioration. In

---

[1] *The Trumpet Shall Sound*, pp. 32, 236–237; for an account of the importance of agricultural changes for social developments, including nativistic movements, in the Solomon Islands, cf. C. S. Belshaw, "Trends in Motives and Organization in Solomon Island Agriculture," *Proceedings of the Seventh Pacific Science Congress of the Pacific Science Association*, Vol. VIII (Feb.–Mar., 1949), pp. 171–189.

[2] J. N. Farquhar, *Modern Religious Movements in India* (New York, 1915), pp. 17–27.

[3] Tocqueville, *The Old Regime and the Revolution*, pp. 79–100, 123, 150; Taine, *The Ancient Regime*, especially pp. 25–26; Kohn, *Revolutions and Dictatorships*, pp. 91–92.

[4] "A Contribution to the Sociology of Sects," *op. cit.*, pp. 240–241, 244.

[5] Niebuhr, *The Social Sources of Denominationalism*, pp. 213–235; Handlin, *The Uprooted*, pp. 138–141.

[6] For a characterization of the fluidity of the population in upstate New York in the early nineteenth century—a period which saw the rise of Mormonism, Millerism, Universalism, Fourierism, Swedenborgianism, Mesmerism, the Finneyite movement, and the Oneida experiment in sexual communism in this region—cf. O'Dea, *The Mormons*, pp. 7–13. On the problem of culture shock generally, cf. Holt, "Holiness Religion: Cultural Shock and Social Reorganization," *op. cit.*, pp. 742–747.

[7] Niebuhr, *The Social Sources of Denominationalism*, pp. 135 ff.

[8] W. E. B. du Bois (ed.), *The Negro Church* (Atlanta, 1903), pp. 41, 44, 45, 48, 111, 123–124; C. G. Woodson, *The History of the Negro Church* (Washington, 1921), pp. 72–99; Niebuhr, *The Social Sources of Denominationalism*, pp. 255–262; Sundkler, *Bantu Prophets in South Africa*, pp. 32–36.

[9] Fauset, *Black Gods of the Metropolis*, pp. 8–9, 80–81.

The Value-Oriented Movement

connection with the spread of the Ghost Dance among the American Indians in the late nineteenth century, for instance, Lesser points out that

> Those tribes who accepted the doctrine at once were, like the Pawnee ... at a cultural impasse. Those tribes who rejected the doctrine were either in an aboriginal state in which the values of their old life still to a certain extent functioned, or they were under the influence of specific religions brought to them by missionaries, or, as in the case of the Navaho and Osage, they were well off materially and did not feel the need of the new doctrine.[1]

Clarifications and Qualifications. We have reviewed a sample of the strains which, given an appropriate combination with other determinants, underlie value-oriented movements. Empirically, of course, the strains do not fall into the neat categories we have outlined. Strains occur in different clusters; they accumulate in different sequences; they vary in strength and significance. By way of qualifying our oversimplified and schematic list, then, let us comment on the historical appearance of strain.

For any value-oriented movement, strains are multiple and complex.[2] Troeltsch was able to give the following "brief enumeration" of religious strains alone which lay behind the rise of Christianity:

> ... the destruction of national religions, which was a natural result of the loss of national independence; the mingling of races, which led naturally to the mingling of various cults; the rise of mystery-religions, with their exclusive emphasis upon the inward life, and their independence of questions of nationality and birth; the fusion of various fragments of religion which had broken away from their national foundation; the philosophical religion of culture with its various forms of assimilation to the popular religions; the need of a world empire for a world religion, a need which was only partially satisfied by the worship of the Emperor; the amazing deepening and spiritualizing of ethical thought during a

---

[1] *The Pawnee Ghost Dance Hand Game*, p. 58; for similar reasoning in connection with the spread of a Ghost Dance movement in 1870, cf. A. L. Kroeber, *Handbook of the Indians of California* (Washington, D.C., 1925), p. 869, and du Bois, *The 1870 Ghost Dance*, pp. v, 136–138. Strain on the values of colonially dominated peoples has been assigned importance in the following sample of studies: Rosenstiel, "An Anthropological Approach to the Mau Mau Problem," *op. cit.*, p. 422; C. S. Belshaw, "The Significance of Modern Cults in Melanesian Development," *The Australian Outlook*, Vol. 4 (1950), pp. 123–124; Worsley, *The Trumpet Shall Sound*, pp. 17 ff., 28 ff., 144 ff., 205; F. Hawley, "The Keresan Holy Rollers: An Adaptation to American Individualism," *Social Forces*, Vol. 26 (1948), pp. 272–280; V. Petrullo, *The Diabolic Root* (Philadelphia, 1934), pp. 24–25; Farquhar, *Modern Religious Movements in India*, pp. 1–6.

[2] For a classification of the kinds of psychological situations that give rise to ideological changes, cf. H. H. Toch, "Crisis Situations and Ideological Revaluation," *Public Opinion Quarterly*, Vol. 19 (1955), pp. 53–56.

The Value-Oriented Movement

period of intellectual development which covered four hundred years of unexampled richness and in criticism and intensive growth; and, finally, the decline of polytheism (which was connected with all these factors) both in its *Mythus* and its form of worship, and the desire for a final form of religion which would offer external values to mankind.[1]

Modern nationalist movements have emerged from that vast complex of changes described frequently as "modernization" or "development," which includes colonialization, agricultural commercialization, industrialization, and urbanization, each complicated in its own right.[2] Not only are these changes complex; they build up in different ways from sources external and internal to the society,[3] they unfold at different speeds, and they develop unevenly in all cases.[4]

The same multiplicity of strains lay behind the French Revolution. The partial decline of the feudal order and its partial replacement with the commercial-urban order had brought severe structural strains down upon the major social groupings in eighteenth-century France. Large parts of the nobility were left without traditional local political responsibilities because of the extraordinary centralization of government in Paris; they were further threatened by the rising cost of living in the eighteenth century, by the increasing wealth of the bourgeoisie, and by the growing tendency for the King to sell titles of nobility. Because the decay of the aristocracy was not complete, however, their continuing privileges and demands rankled with several other classes in France at the time. The middle classes, though

---

[1] *The Social Teaching of the Christian Churches*, Vol. I, p. 43.

[2] For general statements of the complexity of social change in the movement from traditional to modern society, cf. B. Malinowski, *The Dynamics of Culture Change* (New Haven, 1945), pp. 64–83; Wilson and Wilson, *The Analysis of Social Change*, pp. 2–23; R. Firth, "Money, Work and Social Change in Indo-Pacific Economic Systems," *International Social Science Bulletin*, Vol. VI (1954), pp. 400–410; F. M. Keesing, "Cultural Dynamics and Administration," *Proceedings of the Seventh Pacific Science Congress of the Pacific Science Association* (Feb.–Mar., 1949), Vol. VIII, pp. 109–115. For case studies of the complexity of such changes which underlie nationalistic movements, cf. C. du Bois, *Social Forces in Southeast Asia* (Minneapolis, 1949), pp. 25–51; W. Watson, *Tribal Cohesion in a Money Economy* (Manchester, 1958), especially, pp. 190–219; Desai, *Social Background of Indian Nationalism*, pp. 21–209; Coleman, *Nigeria: Background to Nationalism*, pp. 63–166; Wertheim, *Indonesian Society in Transition*, pp. 90–273; and J. M. van der Kroef, "Social Movements and Economic Development in Indonesia," *American Journal of Economics and Sociology*, Vol. 14 (1954–55), pp. 123–138.

[3] Weiner, "The Politics of South Asia," in Almond and Coleman (eds.), *op. cit.*, p. 182.

[4] Eisenstadt, "Sociological Aspects of Political Development in Underdeveloped Countries," *op. cit.*, p. 298; P. T. Bauer and B. S. Yamey, *The Economics of Underdeveloped Countries* (Chicago, 1957), p. 64. For a brief discussion of the unevenness of social change which characterized modern Germany, cf. Parsons, "Some Sociological Aspects of the Fascists Movements," *op. cit.*, pp. 135–136.

The Value-Oriented Movement

improving with regard to wealth and education, found themselves excluded from certain occupations, privileges, and entrance into high society. The peasants, though generally improving from the standpoint of land ownership, found themselves burdened with demands, duties, and taxes from the feudal masters who had, from the standpoint of the exercise of responsible authority, deserted them. Such strains spilled over into the military, in which the privileges of military rank were still tied to aristocracy, and the possibilities of advancement for the lesser born were minimal. The troops themselves had suffered from the rising prices, since they were required to buy subsistence with their own pay. The clergy as a whole found its authority growing weaker; and within the church, the same obstacles to advancement on the part of commoners led to increasing dissatisfaction at the lower levels. Meanwhile, in the towns, independent craftsmen were beginning to feel the pinch of competition from manufactories, and an increasing population of indigent rural origin was beginning to take refuge in the urban centers.[1]

These strains, even in outline, are very diverse. Yet at different times before and during the Revolution of 1789, all these classes were capable of being moved by the doctrines of the Revolution. These doctrines, by emphasizing generalized beliefs, such as freedom, individualism, reason, simplicity, etc.,[2] could harbor many diverse dissatisfactions. The aristocracy appear to have taken up the eighteenth-century doctrines first; thence the doctrines spread to the middle classes, by which time they had become the dominant mode of public opinion[3]. During the course of the Revolution itself, many mobs were brought into action by the slogans and ideas of the dominant ideology,[4] and the sympathy of the military with the revolutionary ideals frequently led to fraternization, refusal to fire on crowds, or outright cooperation with the rebellious groups.[5]

Having noted that many types of strain may find their way into the same general movement, we should now recall that the same strains may result in different movements.[6] As we have seen, if

---

[1] This thumbnail sketch of the types of structural strain in eighteenth-century France was gleaned primarily from the following sources: Tocqueville, *The Old Regime and the Revolution*; Taine, *The Ancient Regime*; Lefebvre, *The Coming of the French Revolution*; and E. G. Barber, *The Bourgeoisie in 18th Century France* (Princeton, 1955), Chs. VI, VII.

[2] For an account of the main lines of the doctrine which was to become the foundation of many of the revolutionary developments, cf. Taine, *The Ancient Regime*, pp. 173–246.

[3] *Ibid.*, pp. 297, 399.

[4] Above, pp. 252–253.

[5] Stephens, *History of the French Revolution*, Vol. I, pp. 396–403. Below, pp. 376–379.

[6] For example, Linton has observed that "very frequently societies are [not]

The Value-Oriented Movement

economic deprivations or institutional anachronisms combine with one set of structurally conducive conditions, a hostile outburst may occur;[1] if the same strains combine with another set of structurally conducive conditions, a norm-oriented movement may result;[2] or, indeed, the strains may be alleviated without recourse to any collective outburst at all.

A final illustration of the indeterminate relations between type of strain and type of value-oriented movement may be found in the followings of the "bizarre cults," e.g., those which cluster in Southern California,[3] and of the "wandering messiahs" who appear from time to time through the ages.[4] These little movements, though they are value-oriented, usually do not result from a single type of strain weighing upon a single economic or social class. These movements tend to draw people from a variety of backgrounds. Whatever strains exist among their members may stem from early childhood experiences. Particularly if an area becomes known as the haven for cranks, quacks and agitators, it may draw people selectively from many regions and walks of life.[5] Or alternatively, if the messianic leader is peripatetic, he may accumulate a few faithful in each locale through which he passes.

These illustrations indicate that we should expect relatively low correlations between a specific type of strain and a specific type of value-oriented movement, though sometimes strong correlations may appear to exist. Let us take the apparent association between culture contact and nativistic movements. The spread of the Ghost Dance movement, both in 1870 and 1890, appears to be related to the intensity of disorganization caused by culture contact.[6] Belshaw

---

homogeneous and [do not] react as wholes to contact situations, especially... societies which have a well developed class organization. In such societies nativistic tendencies will be strongest in those classes or individuals who occupy a favored position and who feel this position threatened by culture change. This factor may produce a split in the society." "Nativistic Movements," *op. cit.*, p. 239.

[1] Above, pp. 227–247.
[2] Above, pp. 278–292.
[3] For instance, C. Lindsay, *The Natives are Restless* (Philadelphia, 1960), pp. 83–93; H. T. Dohrman, *California Cult* (Boston, 1958), pp. 96–102; C. W. Ferguson, *The Confusion of Tongues* (London, 1929), pp. 4–109. For similar cults in London, cf. E. O'Donnell, *Strange Cults and Secret Societies of Modern London* (London, 1934).
[4] R. Matthews, *English Messiahs* (London, 1936); G. Seldes, *The Stammering Century* (New York, 1938), pp. 117–131.
[5] At New Harmony, Indiana, during the spring of 1825, there appeared "scores of cranks with curious hobbies, many persons impelled by curiosity and many others attracted by the prospect of life without labor. The heterogeneous mass would have afforded Charles Dickens an unlimited supply of character studies, for eccentricity ran riot in a hundred directions." G. B. Lockwood, *The New Harmony Movement* (New York, 1907), p. 82.
[6] Above, pp. 327–328.

The Value-Oriented Movement

maintains that Cargo Cults in Melanesia arise in communities that stand halfway between their traditional culture and European culture:

> These people ... have all been in contact with thriving European communities, but none of them have been able to participate in vigorous activity leading to a higher standard of life. I think it is most significant that the two extremes of Melanesian life do not appear so far to have succumbed to these cults, though they have problems of their own. On the one hand, we have the thriving native settlements in or near such towns as Port Moresby, Rabaul, Vila and in New Caledonia, and areas of intensive missionary industrial work. Here the people are in the grip of modern life—and have little time or inclination to organize into cults. On the other hand, we have areas such as the interior of New Guinea and Malekula, where cults continue in their native form, unmodified by European intrusion.[1]

Such formulations apparently have considerable explanatory strength. When pushed too far, however, they run into embarrassing cases. Stanner observes, for instance.

> The known disturbances [have occurred] in long settled areas (Ule Island), well-pacified areas (Madang) and areas of recent influence (Vailala, the New Guinea Highlands). The correlations, if any, with the duration, intensity or specific local character of European settlement were not sufficiently obvious to attract observers' attention at the time.[2]

In at least two known cases, Cargo Cult phenomena have occurred with little or no cultural contact, but rather as responses to internal strains in specific New Guinea populations.[3]

---

[1] "The significance of Modern Cults in Melanesian Development," *op. cit.*, p. 123.

[2] W. E. H. Stanner, *The South Seas in Transition* (Sydney, 1953), p. 62. See also Guiart, " 'Cargo Cults' and Political Evolution in Melanesia," *op. cit.*, p. 128.

[3] R. M. Berndt, "A Cargo Movement in the Eastern Central Highlands of New Guinea," *Oceania*, Vol. XXIII (1952), pp. 51 ff. The sight of European airplanes in the 1930's and a few Europeans in the 1940's had set up considerable speculation, but this ended in positive attitude toward the Europeans. Before the Japanese war a few materials had begun to appear in the villages, and people felt that these were some sort of blessing or gifts. In some cases the natives felt antagonism because the goods were not coming faster. The actual cargo cult began either during or just after the war, and was based on the feelings that the Europeans had "cheated" the natives by withholding the supplies of goods. See also pp. 141–142. For a similar case, which may not even have been a value-oriented movement at all, cf. R. F. Salisbury, "An 'Indigenous' New Guinea Cult," *The Kroeber Anthropology Society Papers*, No. 18, Spring, 1958, pp. 67–78. Also in connection with the Cargo Cults, Worsley has noted that "there is evidently no close correlation between economic fluctuations and specific cult outbreaks." *The Trumpet Shall Sound*, p. 36. For controversy over the correlation between outbursts among American Indians and deprivation, cf. M. J. Herskovits, *Acculturation* (Gloucester, Mass., 1958), pp. 76–82; D. F. Aberle, "The Prophet Dance and Reactions to White Contact," *Southwestern Journal of Anthropology*.

The Value-Oriented Movement

Any correlation between any type of deprivation and any type of value-oriented movement, then, must be assessed as part of a *system* of operating variables. This system is represented in our approach as the value-added process of accumulating determinants. Finally, the same event or series of events may be significant as *several* determinants. The U.S. government policy toward the Indians in the last quarter of the nineteenth century assigned the Indians to reservations, destroyed inter-tribal warfare as the basis of prestige among the tribes, destroyed tribal religious celebrations and political organization, and restricted nomadism.[1] This policy was significant both as a source of strain (in the sense that old cultural patterns were deteriorating) and as a source of structural conduciveness (in the sense that the autonomous Indian political structure was being destroyed, that the American government was, on the whole, unresponsive to Indian petitions, and that the government was able effectively to put down hostile outbursts on the part of the Indians).[2]

Similarly, the activities of missionaries may have significance as many determinants in the rise of a value-oriented movement. In the first place, these activities are a source of strain because they are a conscious attempt to modify existing traditional values.[3] In addition, because the point of incidence of strain is on values, missionary activities create structurally conducive conditions. Particularly if missionary work is supplemented by effective governmental repression of hostile outbursts, it has the effect of declaring all other responses except value-responses out of bounds. Frequently the result is a value-oriented movement, though it does not always evolve in the directions desired by the missionaries. These observations apply also to cases of cultural colonialism (such as the French pattern) which attempts to assimilate native culture to the culture of the dominant power.[4]

Vol. 15 (1959), pp. 74–83; and L. Spier, W. Suttles and M. J. Herskovits, "Comment on Aberle's Thesis of Deprivation," *Southwestern Journal of Anthropology*, Vol. 15 (1959), pp. 84–88.

[1] Slotkin, *The Peyote Religion*, pp. 13–14.

[2] For further discussion of the multiple effects of colonial administration, cf. G. H. L. F. Pitt-Rivers, *The Clash of Culture and the Contact of Races* (London, 1927), pp. 58–60, 62–65; W. Middendorp, "The Administration of the Outer Provinces of the Netherlands Indies," in B. Shrieke (ed.) *The Effect of Western Influence on Native Civilisations in the Malay Archipelago* (Batavia, Java, 1929), pp. 50–61.

[3] Sundkler, *Bantu Prophets in South Africa*, pp. 25–32; G. Balandier, "Messianismes et Nationalismes en Afrique Noire," *Cahiers Internationaux de Sociologie*, Vol. 14 (1953), pp. 61–62; H. Kuper, *The Uniform of Colour* (Johannesburg, 1947), pp. 107–128; Price, *White Settlers and Native Peoples*, pp. 193–196.

[4] For an account of the French policies in colonial countries, cf. L. P. Mair, *Native Policies in Africa* (London, 1936), Ch. IV; J. Gillespie, *Algeria: Rebellion*

The Value-Oriented Movement

THE CRYSTALLIZATION OF VALUE-ORIENTED BELIEFS

Under the conditions of conduciveness and strain outlined above, value-oriented beliefs begin to crystallize. Such beliefs "explain" the conditions of strain which give rise to it. One of the functions of the Leninist ideology, for instance, is

[to] go behind appearances to the realities, defined always in terms of the class struggle. [The Leninist propagandist] must not deviate from his principles or sink into false or superficial explanations. A war, a strike, or a political scandal furnish him opportunities; but more often the propagandist will work from more trivial and concrete facts in order to connect what appeared to be only an accident to a general political explanation, which is, of course, that of the Communist party. Thus does the French Communist Party go about demonstrating the "evils of the Marshall Plan"—from a small scarcity, from the closing of a factory, from a reduction of the water supply in a rural community.[1]

Value-oriented beliefs also focus attention on concrete situations,[2] bring a number of different grievances together under a single cause or myth.[3]

Value-oriented Beliefs as Interpretations and Solutions. As we have seen, the common, underlying features of all value-oriented beliefs can be stated in terms of the components of action. Such beliefs concentrate on a source of evil which overshadows all of life. As such, this evil is a threat to the very foundations of the social order (Values) and by implication, to the normative arrangements, and to organized social life in general. In the same belief a positive set of values is put forth. A new social order is envisioned; institutional chaos will give way to harmony and stability; the evil will be eradicated, and human happiness will result.[4]

What this belief interprets and solves is a function largely of the conditions of conduciveness and strain which give rise to it. This is seen in the following examples:

(1) The Negro cults, such as that of Father Divine, promise to

---

and Revolution (New York, 1960), pp. 1–5; Ball, *Nationalism and Communism in East Asia*, pp. 62–84.

[1] J. M. Domenach, "Leninist Propaganda," *Public Opinion Quarterly*, Vol. 15 (1951), pp. 266–267. For a further account of the "explanatory" character of generalized beliefs, above, pp. 81–82. For the "explanatory" functions of religious beliefs in periods of unemployment, cf. E. W. Bakke, *Citizens Without Work* (New Haven, 1940), pp. 19–26.

[2] T. Abel, "The Pattern of a Successful Political Movement," *American Sociological Review*, Vol. 2 (1937), p. 349.

[3] Edwards, *The Natural History of Revolution*, pp. 90–91; Sorel, *Reflections on Violence*, pp. 142–143.

[4] Above, pp. 121–123.

The Value-Oriented Movement

erase a multitude of economic and racial problems through rebirth, a change in identity, and the pursuit of a new moral life.[1] These themes are closely related to the kinds of deprivations which are most acute for the American Negro in northern urban centers.[2]

(2) The ideology of the French eighteenth-century enlightenment was related directly to the institutional anachronisms which fettered the major classes in France. Tocqueville remarked that

> all [the philosophic writers] concurred in one central point, from which their particular notions diverged. They all started with the principle that it was necessary to substitute simple and elementary rules, based on reason and natural law, for the complicated and traditional customs which regulated society in their time.[3]

Then, for their individual and specific reasons, each class seized upon these doctrines and interpreted its own particular situation in terms of them. The aristocracy, for instance, invoked the rights of man and citizenship to protect its members from royal impingement and to obtain or retain its share of power.[4] The middle classes and clergy interpreted their own particular woes in terms of this language and these ideals. The result, according to Tocqueville, was this:

> There were ... two social bodies: society proper, resting on a framework of tradition, confused and irregular in its organization, with a host of contradictory laws, well-defined distinctions of rank and station, and unequal rights; and above this, an imaginary society, in which every thing was simple, harmonious, equitable, uniform, and reasonable.
>
> The minds of the people gradually withdrew from the former to take refuge in the latter. Men became indifferent to the real by dint of dwelling on the ideal, and established a mental domicile in the imaginary city which the authors had built.[5]

(3) The themes of nationalistic movements in underdeveloped

---

[1] Above, pp. 123-125. For similar reasoning with regard to the Negro Jewish cults, cf. Brotz, "Negro 'Jews' in the United States," *op. cit.*, pp. 324–325; with regard to the "back-to-Africa" movement of Marcus Garvey, cf. E. F. Frazier, "The Garvey Movement," *Opportunity*, Vol. IV (1926), pp. 346–348.

[2] For similar reasoning with respect to the rise of early Christianity, cf. Dickey "Some Economic and Social Conditions of Asia Minor Affecting the Expansion of Christianity," in Case (ed.), *op. cit.*, pp. 406–409, 414–416.

[3] *The Old Regime and the Revolution*, p. 171.

[4] Lefebvre, *The Coming of the French Revolution*, p. 27. Above, p. 343.

[5] *The Old Regime and the Revolution*, pp. 178–179; also, pp. 131, 139, 142, 146. See also Taine, *The Ancient Regime*, pp. 223–231. Abel comments that "an ideology, in order to function as the basis of a successful movement, must link up the goal with the issue. This can best be accomplished by setting forth a plan in which the items are the opposite of that which is regarded as the cause of the problem-experiences." "The Pattern of a Successful Political Movement," *op. cit.*, p. 350.

areas—independence, unification, and improvement[1]—also reflect the character of conduciveness and strain affecting colonially dominated societies. Independence means removing all sorts of strains by expelling the foreigner; it also means ending a political situation which appears to close all means of protest to the native population. Nationalism as an ideology of unity provides an attempt to overcome the strains of colonial and post-colonial conditions:

National strength or prestige becomes the supreme goal. . . . The costs, inconveniences, sacrifices, and loss of traditional values can be justified in terms of this transcending, collective ambition. The new collective entity, the nation-state . . . draws directly the allegiance of every citizen, organizing the population as one community; it controls the passage of persons, goods, and news across the borders; it regulates economic and social life in detail.[2]

In the face of strain, disunity, and conflict, then, the nationalist solution is to provide a basis for integration at a level higher than the traditional local bases for unity.

(4) Ulam has argued that "at the crucial point of transition from a pre-industrial society to a modern, at least partly industrialized state, Marxism becomes in a sense the natural ideology of that society and the most alluring solution to its problems."[3] Marxism is "natural" because it gives a synthetic explanation for the major strains in societies moving through the industrial transition; it combines "the stability and simplicity of the past with unavoidable technological improvement."[4] This theme appeals to parts of the population that feel the pull between the traditional rural or village setting and the modern industrial urban setting.[5]

A value-oriented belief defines evil and envisions regeneration in terms of the conditions of strain and conduciveness giving rise to the belief. How adherents view the coming regeneration depends above all on conduciveness and social control. If the adherents see the avenues for reconstituting the social order to be irrevocably closed, the belief tends to drift toward passive resignation and reliance on

---

[1] Ball, *Nationalism and Communism in East Asia*, p. 1; Farquhar, *Modern Religious Movements in India*, pp. 354–355.
[2] K. Davis, "Social and Demographic Aspects of Economic Development in India," in S. Kuznets, W. E. Moore and J. J. Spengler (eds.), *Economic Growth: Brazil, India, Japan* (Durham, 1955), p. 294.
[3] A. B. Ulam, *The Unfinished Revolution* (New York, 1960), p. 10; see also J. R. Fiszman, "The Appeal of Maoism in Pre-industrial Semicolonial Political Cultures," *Political Science Quarterly*, Vol. 74 (1959), pp. 71–88.
[4] *Ibid.*, p. 62.
[5] For an account of how many nationalist ideologies maximize both the traditional and modern, the indigenous and "Western," etc., above, pp. 127–128.

The Value-Oriented Movement

the intervention of supernatural forces to bring the regeneration. If adherents see the possibility of remaking the current social order themselves, the belief drifts toward activism.

Since the themes of passivity or activity of a belief depend so much on the response of agencies of social control, we shall reserve full discussion of these themes until later. At present we shall indicate, on a scale from passivity to activity, the kinds of regeneration that characterize value-oriented beliefs.[1] At the passive extreme is complete withdrawal from social reconstruction, and reliance on intoxication or ritual for regeneration.[2] Moving toward the active, we find reliance on the hope for some intervening force, a messiah or culture hero perhaps, whose arrival will destroy the unregenerate and usher in the millennium.[3] Next we find value-oriented beliefs which emphasize regeneration by individual rebirth through conversion or change of identity, or both.[4] Even more active are some of the pietistic withdrawal beliefs, which envision geographical separation from the parent society, but once this is done, active work to construct a utopian world in the new setting.[5] Veering more toward the active side is the belief that regeneration will take place by converting or proselytizing others.[6] Finally, the most activist kind of belief calls for the outright destruction of the old order; this characterizes certain anarchist, syndicalist, and communist beliefs.

This schematic characterization of modes of regeneration is simplified and static; for we maintain that *any* value-oriented movement can become very passive or very active. In particular, as agencies of social control modify their stance toward a given value-oriented movement, it frequently changes in beliefs with regard to mode of regeneration.[7]

Syncretism and Value-oriented Beliefs. A salient characteristic of value-oriented beliefs is that they combine ideas from inside and outside the culture, and from many levels of cultural and social

---

[1] For a brief discussion of the activity-passivity dimension in connection with millenarian movements, cf. Hobsbawn, *Primitive Rebels*, pp. 58–65.

[2] Petrullo, *The Diabolic Root*, pp. 5–6, 140–151; Sundker, *Bantu Prophets in South Africa*, pp. 180–233; Harnack, *The Expansion of Christianity in the First Three Centuries*, Vol. 1, pp. 148–161.

[3] For an account of the "return of the culture hero" as a theme in messianic movements, cf. W. D. Wallis, *Messiahs: Their Role in Civilization* (Washington, 1943), pp. 155–160. On messianism in general, cf. Kohn, "Messianism," *op. cit.*, pp. 356–357, and Shils, "Ideology and Civility," *op. cit.*, pp. 463–464. For a study of Jehovah's Witnesses, a messianic sect, cf. H. H. Stroup, *The Jehovah's Witnesses* (New York, 1945), pp. 123–146, and Braden, *These Also Believe*, pp. 370–384.

[4] Parker, *The Incredible Messiah*, p. 157.

[5] Wilson, "An Analysis of Sect Development," *op. cit.*, p. 6.

[6] *Ibid.*, pp. 5–6.

[7] Below, pp. 364–379.

The Value-Oriented Movement

organization.[1] This syncretism has been observed in connection with the formation of religious cults and sects,[2] modern nationalistic movements,[3] and modern totalitarian movements.[4] The reasons for this syncretism are as follows: (*a*) Strains have rendered the older values inadequate as bases for the institutionalization of social life; these values are reconstituted by invention, importation, and elaboration. (*b*) The various groups under pressure who take up value-oriented beliefs accommodate them to their own particular problems. (*c*) The formulators of new value-oriented beliefs draw from distinctive and limited experiences.

Dissemination of Beliefs. Value-oriented beliefs, like all beliefs associated with collective behavior, can be communicated by diverse means—word-of-mouth rumor, propagation by clubs and societies, mass meetings, propaganda, etc.[5] In the spread of any single value-oriented belief, many methods of dissemination invariably come into play.

THE ROLE OF PRECIPITATING FACTORS IN VALUE-ORIENTED MOVEMENTS

A precipitating factor is an event that creates, sharpens, or exaggerates a condition of strain or conduciveness. It provides adherents of a belief with more evidence of the workings of evil forces, or greater promise of success. A precipitating factor, then, links the generalized belief to concrete situations, and thus brings the movement closer to actualization. For the present discussion, it

---

[1] Wallace, "Revitalization Movements," *op. cit.*, pp. 275–276; Festinger, Riecken and Schachter, *When Prophecy Fails*, pp. 54–55.

[2] Harnack, *The Expansion of Christianity in the First Three Centuries*, Vol. 1, pp. 33–39, 301–302, 391; D. Obolensky, *The Bogomils* (Cambridge, 1948), p. 111; O'Dea, *The Mormons*, pp. 26–35; Fauset, *Black Gods in the Metropolis*, pp. 73–75; Braden, *These Also Believe*, pp. 71–76; Sundkler, *Bantu Prophets in South Africa*, pp. 262–263, 297; Petrullo, *The Diabolic Root*, pp. 172–174; Lesser, *The Pawnee Ghost Dance Hand Game*, pp. 105–106, 116–123, 320–321; P. Radin, "A Sketch of the Peyote Cult of the Winnebago: A Study in Borrowing," *Journal of Religious Psychology*, Vol. 7 (1914), pp. 6–22; Stanner, *The South Seas in Transition*, pp. 65–66; Worsley, *The Trumpet Shall Sound*, pp. 101–103; Krader, "A Nativistic Movement in Western Siberia," *op. cit.*, pp. 289–290; W. A. Hinds, *American Communities* (Oneida, N.Y., 1878), pp. 88–89; J. H. Noyes, *History of American Socialisms* (Philadelphia, 1870), pp. 164–166.

[3] Du Bois, *Social Forces in Southeast Asia*, pp. 42–48; Woodman, *The Republic of Indonesia*, Ch. VIII.

[4] Parsons, "Some Sociological Aspects of the Fascist Movements," *op. cit.*, pp. 134–135.

[5] Edwards, *The Natural History of Revolution*, pp. 45–54; Domenach, "Leninist Propaganda," *op. cit.*, pp. 271–272; Neumann, "The Rule of the Demagogue," *op. cit.*, pp. 494–497; Heiden, *A History of National Socialism*, pp. 124–125; du Bois, *The 1870 Ghost Dance*, pp. 136–138.

The Value-Oriented Movement

does not matter whether the precipitating event occurs spontaneously or is arranged by someone interested in the fate of the movement.[1]

Precipitating Factors and Strains. Sudden economic deprivation—e.g., inflation or unemployment—crystallizes many value-oriented movements.[2] A political failure—such as failure in war, perpetration of an unpopular treaty—may also enliven a nascent value-oriented movement.[3] Finally, to choose a mixed political-economic example, numerous revolutionary movements have crystallized around the refusal of citizens to acquiesce in a tax imposition by the government.[4]

Precipitating Factors and Conduciveness. Any event or situation which changes the definition of structural conduciveness can facilitate or obstruct the appearance of a value-oriented movement. One kind of facilitation is found in the development of a situation that opens the possibility of communicating among different aggrieved groups. The Japanese occupation in Indonesia, for instance, not only increased the use of the Indonesian language, but also helped weaken regional and class differences, as well as "break down the isolation of the villages from the central authority."[5] In this way the Japanese occupation hastened the crystallization and spread of the nationalist movement.

Another kind of facilitation concerns a change in the definition of the impregnability of the governing authorities. Whereas before World War II, many colonial governments in Southeast Asia had been able to resist native demands effectively, their quick defeat at the hands of the Japanese destroyed the natives' impression of their invulnerability. This, combined with the fact that the Japanese sometimes armed native populations and permitted more native political participation, not only hastened the crystallization of nationalist aspirations, but also pushed these aspirations in a revolutionary direction.[6]

---

[1] Above, pp. 295–296.

[2] Trotsky, *History of the Russian Revolution*, Vol. I, pp. 42–43, 411–412; Brinton, *The Anatomy of Revolution*, pp. 31–34; Rossi, *The Rise of Italian Fascism, 1918–1922*, pp. 17–20; Meusel, "Revolution and Counter-Revolution," *op. cit.*, pp. 370–371; P. Robertson, *Revolutions of 1848* (New York, 1960), p. 18; Cohn, *The Pursuit of the Millennium*, p. 315; Bax, *Rise and Fall of the Anabaptists*, p. 118.

[3] For the importance of the annexationist issue in Italy just after World War I, cf. Rossi, *The Rise of Italian Fascism 1918–1922*, pp. 30–51; the Decembrist movement in Russia in the 1820's apparently crystallized around an incident in which the Czar refused to discipline a psychopathic commander for cruel treatment of soldiers. Gross, *The Seizure of Political Power in a Century of Revolutions*, pp. 66–67.

[4] Merriman, *Six Contemporaneous Revolutions*, p. 89; Brinton, *The Anatomy of Revolution*, p. 82.

[5] Elsbree, *Japan's Role in Southeast Asian Nationalist Movements 1940 to 1945*, pp. 120, 167.

[6] W. L. Holland, "Introduction," in Holland (ed.), *Asian Nationalism and the*

The Value-Oriented Movement

Finally, a value-oriented movement, like a norm-oriented movement, is, or is perceived by the faithful to be, engaged in a cause and locked in combat against forces which it must overcome.[1] One of the most important kinds of precipitating factors—which often heighten enthusiasm and participation in the movement—is any event which gives evidence of a sudden change in the movement's fortune. Whether this change in fortune is "good" or "bad" for the movement seems to matter less than the fact that the event introduces a new bit of evidence for the adherents and thus excites new activities.

To illustrate: One of the events which added interest and excitement to the Millerite predictions of the end of the world in 1843 was the appearance of an apparently new comet:

> No astronomer's forecast of its arrival had prepared the public for the arresting spectacle. In a day when men were more given to reading a meaning into unusual events, the appearance of such an object in the skies could hardly fail to arouse comment, questioning, and, in some instances, fear. But this was no ordinary time and this no ordinary comet. Nature herself seemed to be conspiring with the Millerites to turn men's eyes toward the skies.[2]

On the other hand, a sudden *dis*confirmation of a prediction also seems to heighten the activity of the faithful.[3]

The importance of a sudden change in fortune is seen in connection with religious cults, nationalistic, and revolutionary movements. "It often happens," Fauset reports, "that the individual is directed unexpectedly to [a] cult by some dramatic experience, as when an ill person is suddenly and miraculously healed. Such a person will date his advent into the cult from that moment."[4] Nationalist movements in one country are given impetus by nationalist stirrings elsewhere, for they indicate that at least somewhere the purposes of the movement show signs of being realized.[5] The same holds for revolutionary movements. Frenchmen, for instance, were given inspiration by the American Revolution, which showed evidence that the ideals of the eighteenth-century enlightenment were coming to fruition somewhere, if not currently in France.[6]

West (New York, 1953), p. 4; Elsbree, *Japan's Role in Southeast Asian Nationalist Movements 1940 to 1945*, pp. 84–85.

[1] Above, pp. 122–124.
[2] F. D. Nichol, *The Midnight Cry* (Tacoma Park, Washington, D.C., 1944), p. 135.
[3] Festinger, Riecken, and Schachter, *When Prophecy Fails*, pp. 3–28.
[4] *Black Gods of the Metropolis*, p. 76.
[5] Coleman, *Nigeria: Background to Nationalism*, pp. 187–196.
[6] Lefebvre, *The Coming of the French Revolution*, p. v; for the importance of the French revolutionary outburst of February, 1848, in fomenting other outbursts throughout Europe, cf. Robertson, *Revolutions of 1848*, pp. vii, 115, 168.

The Value-Oriented Movement

Frequently a new chance of success appears with the advent of a leader, who not only formulates a belief around which the faithful may unite, but also promises to swing the movement into action. In this case there is a telescoping of several determinants of the value-added process—crystallization of belief, precipitating factor, and mobilization—into a single empirical phenomenon, leadership.

MOBILIZATION FOR ACTION

Though analytically separable, the determinant of mobilization is linked closely to the determinant of social control. Whether a value-oriented movement becomes a passive cult, a sect, an isolated community experiment, or a revolutionary movement, depends largely on the conditions of conduciveness and on the way the parent society receives the movement once it has arisen. Therefore the analyses of mobilization and social control should be read together for a full picture of the determinants influencing movements during their later stages. Under mobilization we shall consider the same four topics covered in the last chapter—leadership, the real and derived aspects of value-oriented movements, the effect on a success or failure, and the institutionalization of the movement. We shall also trace the implication of each of these topics for the internal unity and stability of the value-oriented movement.

Leadership. Weber characterized charismatic leadership as follows:

> The term "charisma" will be applied to a certain quality of an individual personality by virtue of which he is set apart from ordinary men and treated as endowed with supernatural, superhuman, or at least specifically exceptional powers or qualities. These are such as are not accessible to the ordinary person, but are regarded as of divine origin or as exemplary and on the basis of them the individual concerned is treated as a leader....[1]

This type of leadership characterizes value-oriented movements. Specific manifestations of charismatic leaders are the dreamer or prophet of the cult,[2] the nationalist crusader,[3] and the totalitarian demagogue.[4] The major reason why leadership takes this particular

---

[1] *Theory of Social and Economic Organization*, pp. 358–359.
[2] For examples, cf. Stanner, *The South Seas in Transition*, p. 63; Lesser, *The Pawnee Ghost Dance Hand Game*, pp. 56–62; Parker, *The Incredible Messiah*, pp. 15–16; Fauset, *Black Gods of the Metropolis*, pp. 23, 107–108; Beynon, "The Voodoo Cult among Negro Migrants in Detroit," *op. cit.*, p. 896; Sears, *Days of Delusion*, pp. 50–51, 82.
[3] For example, Gandhi, Jinnah, Ataturk, Nasser, Soekarno, Nkruhmah, and Castro.
[4] Abel, *Why Hitler Came to Power*, p. 166; Heiden, *A History of National Socialism*, pp. 44–45, 124–125; Gerth, "The Nazi Party: Its Leadership and Composition," in Merton, Gray, Hockey, and Selvin (eds.), *op. cit.*, pp. 100–103.

form in the value-oriented movement lies in the character of the movement itself. Because it is oriented toward values, the movement involves an envisioned reconstruction of an entire social order, from top to bottom.[1] To follow the leadership of one man in such an adventure involves a diffuse, total kind of commitment on the part of the followers. Charismatic leadership is, in short, the most generalized form of leadership, for in such a leader is placed the hopes for a collective reconstitution of values.

Despite the diffuse character of the commitment to a charismatic leader in a value-oriented movement, we should not exaggerate its importance. Insofar as a value-oriented movement receives material aid from outside sources, and insofar as it inherits an organizational structure, the need for charismatic leadership lessens.[2] Furthermore, a charismatic leader—like all other leaders in collective outbursts—occupies a place in a value-added process. He cannot become a leader until the prior stages are established. Sometimes he contributes partially to establishing some of these prior stages. The aspiring leader, for example, can argue that because of persecution the only recourse of an aggrieved group is to reconstitute the values of society; he can formulate a generalized belief and thus assume significance at this stage as well. We should not, however, extrapolate from these occasions and create a "great man" or "conspiratorial" theory of value-oriented movements. The number of determinants for which a single charismatic leader is responsible—and the degree to which he is responsible for them—is always an open question.

Real and Derived Aspects of Value-oriented Movements. Once a value-oriented movement gives evidence of the possibility of success, it shows a burst of activity, and begins to gain numerous adherents who join for reasons perhaps unrelated to the original objectives of the movement. A few scattered studies have indicated that in the communitarian experiments in the United States during the nineteenth century, the early idealistic impetus has resulted in the recruitment of others to the experiments who were, to use Noyes' colorful language,

the conceited, the crotchety, the selfish, the headstrong, the pugnacious, the unappreciated, the played-out, the idle, the good-for-nothing generally;

---

[1] Above, pp. 122–124 and 129–140 for an account of the comprehensiveness of value-oriented movements.

[2] For an instance of outside intervention in a revolution, cf. Merriman, *Six Contemporaneous Revolutions*, pp. 1–10, 114 ff. For the importance of pre-existing organization—factories, villages, associations, clubs, etc.—in revolutionary movements, cf. Meusel, "Revolution and Counter-Revolution," *op. cit.*, pp. 369–370; Harnack, *The Expansion of Christianity in the First Three Centuries*, Vol. 1, p. 22; Stephens, *History of the French Revolution*, Vol. I, pp. 111–113.

The Value-Oriented Movement

who, finding themselves utterly out of place and at a discount in the world as it is, rashly concluded that they are exactly fitted for the world as it ought to be.[1]

Further evidence for the derived aspect of value-oriented movements is found in the millenarian movements of medieval and Renaissance times. Inquiring into the occasions on which these movements showed greatest vitality, Cohn observed:

> It was always in the midst of some great revolt or revolution that the revolutionary millenarian group first emerged into daylight. This is equally the case with John Ball and his followers in the English peasants' revolt of 1381; the extreme Taborites during the early stages of the Hussite revolution in Bohemia, 1419–1421; Thomas Müntzer and his "League of the Elect" in the German peasants' revolt of 1525; and the Radical Anabaptists who, in the midst of a wave of revolts in the capitals of the ecclesiastical states in north-west Germany, established the "New Jerusalem" at Münster in 1534–1535. What is seldom realized... is how little these groups had in common with the mass uprisings which they tried to exploit.[2]

Usually the prophet who headed the millenarian movement which fused with these revolts had been "obsessed by apocalyptic fantasies for years before it occurred to him, in the midst of some social upheaval, to address himself to the poor as possible followers."[3] From his examples Cohn concluded:

> It has sometimes been argued that a revolutionary millenarian group fulfills the function of preparing the way for more realistic social movements. This was not the case with [the movements above], for each of these appeared only when an organized insurrection of a decidedly realistic kind was already under way. The spectacle which presents itself is, rather, of a band of a few hundred dedicated enthusiasts struggling to master, in the interests of its own apocalyptic fantasy, a vast popular movement numbering tens or hundreds of thousands. And if the millenarian group differed vastly from the mass movement around it in aim and outlook and strategy, it differed just as much in social composition. The prophet himself was not

---

[1] *History of American Socialisms*, p. 653. For recruitment at New Harmony in particular, cf. Hillquit, *History of Socialism in the United States*, pp. 62–63. Regarding the failure of the Brook Farm experiment, Swift concluded that the application of standards for recruitment in advance of forming the community would have made its persistence more probable. L. Swift, *Brook Farm* (New York, 1900), pp. 112–113. In connection with the Italian fascist movement, Rossi remarked that by the beginning of 1922, the movement was sufficiently successful to provide various advantages to members—"uniform, arms, expeditions, subsidies, loot, flattery, and all the other advantages reserved to fascists." Such attractions presumably would attract members on bases other than ideological commitment. *The Rise of Italian Fascism 1918–1922*, p. 180.

[2] "Medieval Millenariam and its Bearing on the Comparative Study of Millenarian Movements," p. 8; also *The Pursuit of the Millennium*, p. 317.

[3] "Medieval Millenarism and its Bearing on the Comparative Study of Millenarian Movements," p. 9.

The Value-Oriented Movement

normally, any more than in other millenarian movements, a manual worker or even a former manual worker, but an intellectual or half-intellectual. . . . As for [the] following—it is significant that all these [millenarian] movements flourished in areas where there existed a population which had no institutionalized means of defending or furthering its interests.[1]

This speculative fusion of medieval and Renaissance millenarian movements with any kind of protest developed more or less spontaneously. In modern times certain revolutionary movements—especially international communism—have *institutionalized* the principle of joining and attempting to draw to themselves many kinds of generalized protest.[2]

The Success or Failure of Specific Tactics. Value-oriented movements display the same regularity as norm-oriented movements: Changes of direction and bursts of enthusiasm occur as one set of tactics appears to be losing its effectiveness and another appears to show more promise.

For any given value-oriented movement, e.g., a nationalist movement, a variety of potential lines of attack are open—to revive ancient religions or other cultural patterns, to agitate for normative reform, to engage in terrorist activity, and so on.[3] At any given time, however, one line of attack seems to adherents to be more promising than another. This relative promise may result from recent evidence of failure of one method or success of another. We may trace any movement by its swings from one line of attack to another. Thus, the Indian nationalist movement over a period of 150 years went through phases of religious and social reform, violent revolt, quiet liberal reform movements, militant aggressiveness (which included a variety of sub-tactics such as the boycott, general strike, and terrorism), non-cooperation, and civil disobedience.[4] At present nationalism in the Melanesian island chain is in the transition from nativistic cults to more politically oriented nationalism.[5] The success of revolu-

---

[1] *Ibid.*, p. 9.

[2] Selznick, *The Organizational Weapon*, pp. 2–6, 72–73, 171–172. For an account of many groups' efforts to exploit the Voodoo cult in Detroit, cf. Beynon, "The Voodoo Cult among Negro Migrants in Detroit," *op. cit.*, pp. 904–905. For a brief account of the role of secret societies in the Revolution of 1848, cf. Robertson, *Revolutions of 1848*, pp. 21–23.

[3] For a catalogue of the various directions of the Indian nationalist movement around the turn of the century, cf. Farquhar, *Modern Religious Movements in India*, pp. 363–386.

[4] Desai, *Social Background of Indian Nationalism*, pp. 271–335; also R. B. Gregg, *Gandhism and Socialism* (Triplicane, 1931), pp. 28–30.

[5] Worsley, *The Trumpet Shall Sound*, pp. 192–193; Guiart, "Forerunners of Melanesian Nationalism," *op. cit.*, and " 'Cargo Cults' and Political Evolution in Melanesia," *op. cit.*

tionary movements—e.g., the Bolshevik movement in Russia and the Nazi movement in Germany—depends largely on the choice of appropriate tactics at the right times by the leaders.[1]

We should qualify the last two paragraphs in several ways: (a) Changes in strategy and tactics are not always part of a large master plan. Sometimes they evolve by trial-and-error methods. (b) Which strategies and tactics fail and which succeed depends largely upon the actions of political authorities and other agencies of social control. (c) Changes in strategy and tactics are frequently made at a cost to the movement. Such changes constitute one of the major bases for internal splits in a movement—splits between leaders or factions advocating one line of attack and those advocating another.

Institutionalization of Value-oriented Movements. As any value-oriented movement develops—whether it becomes a sect, a communitarian experiment, or a successful revolutionary party—it must adapt to exigencies which arise with permanent existence.[2] The movement must generate new types of leadership to sustain the organization of the movement itself; it must seek permanent bases of financing; it must accommodate new and more specialized activities within the movement; it must routinize its modes of recruitment.

The sect-to-denomination or sect-to-church formula has been discussed widely as the typical process of routinization for religious movement. According to Wilson, the sect, which represents the new, enthusiastic stage of a value-oriented movement, possesses the following features:

it is a voluntary association; membership is by proof to sect authorities of some claim to personal merit—such as knowledge of doctrine, affirmation of a conversion experience, or recommendation of members in good standing; exclusiveness is emphasized, and expulsion exercised against those who contravene doctrinal, moral, or organizational precepts; its self-conception is of an elect, a gathered remnant, possessing special enlightenment; personal perfection is the expected standard of aspiration, in whatever terms this is judged; it accepts, at least as an ideal, the priesthood of all believers; there is a high level of lay participation; there is opportunity for the member spontaneously to express his commitment; the sect is hostile or indifferent to the secular society and to the state.[3]

---

[1] On the changes in strategy and tactics which Lenin made during the course of the Bolshevik revolution, cf. Trotsky, *History of the Russian Revolution*, Vol. I, pp. 318-319; Vol. II, pp. 68-69, 312 ff.; Vol. III, pp. 83-86, 127-128, 277-278. On the importance of the strategic decisions made by Hitler in his rise to power, cf. A. Bullock, *Hitler: A Study in Tyranny* (New York, 1958), pp. 79-108.

[2] Weber's discussion of the "routinization of charisma" takes account of such exigencies. *Theory of Social and Economic Organization*, pp. 363 ff.

[3] "An Analysis of Sect Development," *op. cit.*, p. 4.

The Value-Oriented Movement

As the sect begins to face the exigencies of sustaining itself over long periods, it evolves gradually toward the denomination, which displays the following characteristics:

it is formally a voluntary association; it accepts adherents without imposition of traditional prerequisites of entry, and employs purely formalized procedures of admission; breadth and tolerance are emphasized; since membership is laxly enrolled, expulsion is not a common device for dealing with the apathetic and the wayward; its self-conception is unclear and its doctrinal position unstressed; it is content to be one movement among others, all of which are thought to be acceptable in the sight of God; it accepts the standards and values of the prevailing culture and conventional morality; there is a trained professional ministry; lay participation occurs but is typically restricted to particular areas of activity; services are formalized and spontaneity is absent; education of the young is of greater concern than the evangelism of the outsider; additional activities are largely non-religious in character; individual commitment is not very intense; the denomination accepts the values of the secular society and the state; members are drawn from any section of the community, but within one church, or any one religion, membership will tend to limit itself to those who are socially compatible.[1]

Such a formula is central in the literature of religious change;[2] furthermore, it has been applied to a great number of empirical cases.[3] The universal applicability of the sect-to-denomination process has been challenged, however, on several grounds: (*a*) It is too limited a statement of the possible adaptations of religious groups, even within Christianity. (*b*) It is limited to particular countries such as the United States. (*c*) It does not take account of the distinctive influence of the sect's original values, its initial level of insulation or isolation from the parent society, and so on.[4]

---

[1] *Ibid.*, pp. 4–5.
[2] Troeltsch, *The Social Teaching of the Christian Churches*, Vol. 1, pp. 331–343; Niebuhr, *The Social Sources of Denominationalism*, pp. 17 ff.; Pope, *Millhands and Preachers*, pp. 118–140; Clark, *The Small Sects in America*, p. 279. For a related distinction between enthusiasm and institutionalization, cf. Knox, *Enthusiasm*, p. 590.
[3] Brewer, "Sect and Church in Methodism," *op. cit.*, pp. 400–408; O. R. Whitley, "The Sect-to-Denomination Process in an American Religious Movement: The Disciples of Christ," *Southwestern Social Science Quarterly*, Vol. 36 (1955), pp. 275–281; V. A. Daniel, "Ritual and Stratification in Chicago Negro Churches," *American Sociological Review*, Vol. 7 (1942), pp. 352–361; Sundkler, *Bantu Prophets in South Africa;* G. Shepperson, "The Politics of African Church Separatist Movements in British Central Africa, 1892–1916," *Africa*, Vol. 24 (1954), pp. 233–246; Beynon, "The Voodoo Cult among Negro Migrants in Detroit," *op. cit.*, pp. 905–906.
[4] B. Johnson, "A Critical Appraisal of the Church-Sect Typology," *American Sociological Review*, Vol. 22 (1957), pp. 88–92; H. W. Pfautz, "The Sociology of Secularization: Religious Groups," *American Journal of Sociology*, Vol. 61 (1955–56), pp. 121–128; Wilson, "An Analysis of Sect Development," *op. cit.*;

The Value-Oriented Movement

Even though such limitations on the sect-to-denomination process are justified, we should not lose sight of the fact that no matter what the origin of a value-oriented movement—whether it be sect, community experiment, political revolutionary party—it must adapt to practical and organizational exigencies. In the communitarian experiments of the early nineteenth century in the United States, persistence or lack of persistence depended largely on how effectively these communities adapted to the exigencies of economic management, political regulation, recruitment, and education of the young.[1]

In the political sphere, a revolutionary movement which seizes power must undergo a similar process of routinization. Because it is now responsible for the political integration of a society—rather than the overthrow of a political system—it must be accommodated to a multitude of exigencies.[2] This fundamental phenomenon of adjustment has led some to claim that revolutions change very little if anything in society;[3] this claim, though exaggerated,[4] reminds us that revolutionary movements, like all value-oriented movements, must undergo a process of routinization if they are to persist.

The Bases of Disunity and Instability in Value-oriented Movements. On the basis of our account of mobilization, we may enumerate several bases of internal disunity and instability for value-oriented movements:

(1) The appearance of different types of leaders as the movement develops—the formulator, the propagandist, the agitator, the

---

also his "The Pentecostalist Minister: Role Conflicts and Status Contradictions," *American Journal of Sociology*, Vol. 64 (1959), p. 496.

[1] C. Nordhoff, *The Communistic Societies of the United States* (New York, 1875), pp. 385, 399–405; Shambaugh, *Amana That Was and Amana That Is*, pp. 17–18, 61–62, 94, 109–110, 120–122, 126, 337–339, 342–347, 416; G. E. Chaffee, "The Isolated Religious Sect as an Object for Social Research," *American Journal of Sociology*, Vol. 35 (1929–30), pp. 623–625; Hinds, *American Communities*, pp. 11, 37, 39–41, 55–56; M. Holloway, *Heavens on Earth* (London, 1951), pp. 89–91, 95 ff.; Noyes, *History of American Socialisms*, pp. 124–126;. A. Ballou, *History of the Hopedale Community* (Lowell, Mass., 1897), pp. 1, 134–136.

[2] Parsons, *The Social System*, pp. 525–533; Hopper, "The Revolutionary Process," op. cit., p. 277; C. Brinton, "The Manipulation of Economic Unrest," *The Tasks of Economic History*, Supplement VIII (1948), p. 28. For the use of the political rally in establishing a new political regime, cf. T. Sinclair, "The Nazi Party Rally at Nuremberg," *Public Opinion Quarterly*, Vol. 2 (1938), pp. 570–583; for the use of art as propaganda for similar purposes, cf. D. L. Dowd, "Art as National Propaganda in the French Revolution," *Public Opinion Quarterly*, Vol. 15 (1951), pp. 532, 542–543.

[3] Ellwood, *The Psychology of Human Society*, pp. 262–263; Le Bon, *The Psychology of Revolution*, pp. 31–32, 59; Burckhardt, *Force and Freedom*, pp. 280–281; Sorel, *Reflections on Violence*, pp. 108–109.

[4] For an analysis of what does change and what does not change in revolutions, cf. Brinton, *The Anatomy of Revolution*, Ch. 8; his *A Decade of Revolution*, pp. 274 ff.; Trotsky, *History of the Russian Revolution*, Vol. I, p. 237.

organizer, etc.[1] Invariably these different leaders—whose objectives differ—come into conflict with one another.[2]

(2) The heterogeneity of the movement which results in part from the real and derived phases of development. Frequently this forms the basis for splits in a movement.[3] In any case the value-oriented movement, as it becomes established, must accommodate the interests of divergent groups which swept it into existence.[4] Frequently the divisions within a value-oriented movement appear only after it has overcome—or sees the chance of overcoming—a common adversary. The appearance of tribalism and regionalism in nationalist movements after independence has been achieved or is in sight illustrates this generalization.[5]

(3) Changes in strategy and tactics. As a value-oriented movement unfolds, conflict develops each time a major reorientation in strategy and tactics takes place. If the shift is toward militancy, the moderates protest. Sometimes, in fact, what has at one time been a successful line of attack in a movement hinders the future development of the movement because advocates of this line of attack resist some new strategy or tactic. In the unfolding of the Indian nationalist movement, for instance, Desai observes that:

(The) religio-reform movements in the earlier phases of Indian nationalism ... were the forms in which the national awakening found expression and even further developed for some time. In the phases, however, when new classes and communities came into existence or developed national, class, or group consciousness, and, further when the national movement

---

[1] Brinton, "The Manipulation of Economic Unrest," *op. cit.*, pp. 25-26.

[2] For the development of similar tendencies in norm-oriented movements, above, pp. 296–306.

[3] For a discussion of the relationship between heterogeneity of membership and conflict in New Harmony, cf. Holloway, *Heavens on Earth*, pp. 110-111.

[4] Collins has attributed the continuity of the Indian Shaker Church in part to the fact that it has "allowed scope both to those who wished to emphasize the aboriginal basis of religion and those who wanted to imitate the Whites." "The Indian Shaker Church," *op. cit.*, p. 411.

[5] "The main reason for the widening of the rift (within the Indian nationalist movement in the 1920's)", writes Lumby, "was the growing antagonism between Hindus and Muslims which anticipated and accompanied the gradual handing over to Indians of some of the political power hitherto in British hands. A symptom of this was the increase in the number and severity of communal riots during the twenties." E. W. R. Lumby, *The Transfer of Power in India* (London, 1954), p. 17. An analysis of the intensification of regional, linguistic, and caste divisions within India after independence is found is S. E. Harrison, *India: The Most Dangerous Decades* (Princeton, 1960). For the appearance of centrifugal forces in two African nationalist movements, cf. Coleman, *Nigeria: Background to Nationalism*, pp. 332 ff., 413; B. Rivlin, "Unity and Nationalism in Libya," *Middle East Journal*, Vol. III (1949), pp. 31-44. For brief discussion of Lenin's awareness of similar centrifugal forces in Bolshevik Russia, cf. Trotsky, *History of the Russian Revolution*, Vol. III, p. 38. See also Worsley, *The Trumpet Shall Sound*, pp. 236-237.

The Value-Oriented Movement

acquired a broader multi-class and multi-communal basis, most of these very religio-reform movements, instead of becoming forms of development and expression of the national consciousness, became fetters on its development. Some of them even became anti-national disruptive forces retarding the process of a united national movement for freedom. The reversal of their role was mainly due to their transformation from national religio-reform movements into religio-communal movements. This became particularly manifest from 1918 onwards.[1]

(4) Institutionalization. The divisive effects of institutional accommodation of a movement and the exigencies of prolonged existence are best seen in the American communitarian experiments in the nineteenth century. As these exigencies became more and more pressing, one of two reactions occurred: (*a*) The idealists began to feel that the ideals of the movement could not be realized and sooner or later lost hope for the movement.[2] (*b*) Certain committed individuals or groups in the community began to feel that the practical compromises represented backsliding and degeneration of the movement.[3] This is a typical occasion for secession. It has played a large role in the history of religious schism in general.[4] In such cases conflict is likely to be explosive because the movement is attempting to consolidate a system of legitimacy; all conflicts tend to become value-conflicts, for which solutions short of dissolution or secession are difficult to find. Consider the fate of the communitarian experiments: Most of these were extremely short-lived; furthermore, they ended amidst vitriolic conflict over legitimacy.[5] Those that persisted were, by and large, ethnically homogeneous communities which had existed as religious groups prior to their communitarian phase—e.g., the Rappites, the Zoarites, the Inspirationists of Amana, etc.[6] In the

---

[1] *Social Background of Indian Nationalism*, p. 281. Above, pp. 309 and 329. For an account of the brief conflict between Lenin and the Bolsheviks regarding Lenin's change of tactics as recommended in the *Theses of April 4*, cf. Trotsky, *History of the Russian Revolution*, Vol. I, p. 300.

[2] Noyes, *History of American Socialisms*, p. 173; Hillquit, *History of Socialism in the United States*, pp. 140-141; Ballou, *History of the Hopedale Community*, pp. 99-100.

[3] Noyes, *History of American Socialisms*, pp. 64-65; Ballou, *History of the Hopedale Community*, pp. 362-364; Holloway, *Heavens on Earth*, pp. 218-219.

[4] Clark, *The Small Sects in America*, pp. 21-22; Sundker, *Bantu Prophets in South Africa*, p. 170; for a similar account of the formation of the Anabaptist community in the early sixteenth century, cf. C. H. Smith, *The Story of the Mennonites* (Berne, Indiana, 1941), p. 10.

[5] Noyes, *History of American Socialisms*, pp. 646-652; Swift, *Brook Farm*, p. 14; Lockwood, *The New Harmony Movement*, pp. 112-113, 145-146; Bassett, "The Secular Utopian Socialists," in Egbert and Persons (eds.), *op. cit.*, p. 165; Ballou, *History of the Hopedale Community*, pp. 348-350.

[6] Holloway, *Heavens on Earth*, pp. 159-160; Noyes, *History of American Socialisms*, pp. 654-655; Hillquit, *History of Socialism in the United States*, pp. 139-140; Nordhoff, *The Communistic Societies*, p. 387.

The Value-Oriented Movement

experiments that persisted the legitimacy of values had been better established than in the communities that did not persist; hence the compromises of institutionalization could be effected without flaring so easily into conflicts over values.

SOCIAL CONTROL

Although social control refers to the minimization of the effects of *any* of the stages of value-added, we shall discuss control in the following special sense. A value-oriented belief, once crystallized, has a potential for moving in many directions—it may come to naught; it may form into a cult, a sect, or eventually a denomination; it may become an underground conspiracy; it may secede from the parent body that spawned it; it may grow into a revolutionary attempt to overthrow constitutional authorities.[1] Even at an advanced stage of the development of a value-oriented belief, then, considerable indeterminacy remains as to the direction in which the movement may turn. A major determinant of the course of the movement lies in the behavior of agencies of social control in response to the movement.

A Model for Containing Value-oriented Movements. A value-oriented belief arises when the conditions of conduciveness and strain combine in particular ways.[2] What happens to these beliefs once they have arisen is still an open question. To analyze the fortunes of value-oriented movements further, we shall create a model statement of how such a movement can be peacefully contained within a system. This containment involves the selective closing of certain behavioral alternatives and the selective opening of others. It involves four kinds of behavior on the part of authorities:

(1) Ruling out uninstitutionalized expression of hostility. This means applying social controls of the sort discussed in Chapter VIII.[3]

(2) Ruling out direct challenges to legitimacy. This involves drawing a definite circle around those governmental activities which are constitutionally inviolable. Any change in the definition of legitimacy must be carefully restricted and governed by defined procedures—such as the procedures of constitutional amendment.

In the following discussion we shall refer to the successful ruling out of these two behavioral alternatives as "political effectiveness" on the part of the authorities.

(3) Opening channels for peaceful agitation for normative change,

[1] Above, pp. 315–316.
[2] Above, pp. 319–347.
[3] Above, pp. 261–268.

The Value-Oriented Movement

and permitting a patient and thorough hearing for the aggrieved groups. We shall refer to this practice as "flexibility" on the part of the authorities.

(4) Attempting to reduce the sources of strain that initiated the value-oriented movement. We shall refer to such behavior as "responsiveness" on the part of the authorities.

If authorities behave in these ways, we should expect the value-oriented movement either to disappear, to change into some other, less threatening kind of movement (e.g., a norm-oriented movement) or to assume a value-oriented form which is containable within the system (e.g., an institutionalized cult, sect, or denomination). This model of containment is not always followed by political authorities, however; correspondingly, a value-oriented movement may take other directions. We shall examine the effects of two frequent ideal-type deviations from the model: (*a*) the effects of permanent political effectiveness, unresponsiveness and inflexibility—or, stated more simply, the effects of permanent repression; (*b*) the effects of a period of repression followed by a weakening of effectiveness. The first tends to drive the movement underground and then into passivity; the second tends to drive the movement underground, or at least into an extreme value-oriented position, and then permits it to rise as a full-scale, and frequently bloody value-oriented revolutionary movement.

The Effects of Permanent Repression. Toward the last third of the nineteenth century the white encroachments on Indian lands had reached an apex, and a multiplicity of strains had been imposed on many Indian tribes.[1] The major wars to resist this encroachment had been put down effectively in the mid-1870's. Furthermore, the United States government permitted the continued deterioration of Indian life and failed to respond to the entreaties, petitions, and delegations of the Indians.[2] The whites were pursuing policies, in short, which were effective, inflexible, and unresponsive from the Indians' standpoint.

From the late 1870's onward, Indian protest began to assume a new guise. Active warfare against the whites was by and large limited to guerrilla outbursts; even those were more or less completely repressed by the early 1880's. The Plains Indians, "finding naturalistic forms of readjustment inadequate, . . . turned increasingly to new religions."[3] Many of these were tribal and localized religions; others, notably the Grass Dance and the Hand Game, spread widely.

---
[1] Above, pp. 339–342.
[2] Slotkin, *The Peyote Religion*, pp. 9–17.
[3] *Ibid.*, p. 17.

The Value-Oriented Movement

In the 1880's the strongest value-oriented religion was the Ghost Dance, which by and large was millenarian. The ideology of the Ghost Dance limited itself to fantasy destruction of the whites on the whole; on occasion, however, it gave way to violent outbreaks.[1] Also in the late nineteenth century the Peyote religion appeared. This cult was based on a belief envisioning the return of native ways; its ritual centered on the consumption of a powerful drug made from the Peyote cactus.

After the critical turning point of the early 1890's, during which the whites not only effectively crushed the sporadic outbursts associated with the Ghost Dance, but actively discouraged it, the Peyote religion gradually came to represent the dominant Indian mode of adjustment. Slotkin accounts for this evolution as follows:

The Ghost Dance was not only nativistic but also militant, providing a supernatural means for overthrowing the domination-subordination relation between Whites and Indians. Its central doctrine was the imminent renovation in the world (including the destruction of White society and culture) as a solution for the problems confronting the Indians. The Ghost Dance succumbed to three circumstances. First, the anticipated world renovation did not take place. And there was no reinterpretation of the doctrine to make it viable. . . . Second, the Ghost Dance was involved in the Sioux Disturbance of 1890-91; therefore the rite was prohibited by White officials in order to maintain the domination-subordination relation between Whites and Indians. Third, after the Sioux Disturbance was ferociously suppressed by the U. S. Army, the Indians became resigned to subordination; consequently they required a program of accommodation rather than the Ghost Dance program of opposition.

The Peyote Religion was nativistic but not militant. Culturally, it permitted the Indians to achieve a cultural organization in which they took pride. Socially, it provided a supernatural means of accommodation to the existing domination-subordination relation.[2]

To sum up, a value-oriented movement under conditions of continuous repression tends to become moribund. It evolves progressively toward the most passive and least politically threatening form of organization, even though the destruction of the oppressors is secretly envisioned. In extreme cases the organization of the movement disappears altogether.[3]

---

[1] The most notable occasion is the Ghost Dance outbreak of violence among the Sioux in 1890-91. Cf. Mooney, "The Ghost-Dance Religion and the Sioux Outbreak of 1890," *op. cit.*, pp. 819-828; also pp. 706-724 for other instances of outbreaks. See also MacGregor, *Warriors Without Weapons*, pp. 32-33, and Lesser, *The Pawnee Ghost Dance Hand Game*, pp. 53-67.

[2] *The Peyote Religion*, p. 21. See also B. Barber, "A Socio-Cultural Interpretation of the Peyote Cult," *American Anthropologist*, Vol. 43 (1941), pp. 673-674; Petrullo, *The Diabolic Root*, pp. 26-27.

[3] For an example of the organizational collapse of a native movement under

The Value-Oriented Movement

The Effects of Repression Followed by a Weakening of Effectiveness. Technically defined, a value-oriented revolution is a combination of a value-oriented belief with a hostile outburst. Hence the social control of hostility is very important for the control of revolutionary movements. In ideal-typical sequence, the value-oriented revolutionary movement unfolds in the following way: The society experiences a period of strain and dissatisfaction which is met by a posture of effectiveness, inflexibility, and unresponsiveness on the part of the agencies of social control. Thus the sequence starts in a way identical to that considered under the heading of permanent repression. After a period, however, when a value-oriented belief has developed, the agencies of social control change their posture; they begin to display inconsistency, vacillation or weakness. At this time the movement begins to evolve toward a value-oriented revolutionary movement. In this model summary of the build-up of the value-oriented revolutionary movement, we are not attempting to account for all revolutionary outbursts. If authorities are ineffective *from the very beginning* of the development of the period of strain, grievances do not smoulder and build into a value-oriented belief. The aggrieved simply overthrow the authorities quickly, as in a *coup d'état* or a palace revolution.[1]

The nationalist revolutions under colonial domination correspond roughly to this ideal-type sequence of repression followed by relaxation. The first phase of colonial domination is pacification, or closing off the possibility of hostile outbursts and challenges to the legitimacy of the colonial power. As strains builds up in the colonial situation, value-oriented beliefs begin to crystallize; these remain passive, however, because of the effective repression on the part of the colonial power. The beliefs become revolutionary only when repression relaxes, i.e., when the colonial power changes its policies or weakens to the point of being unable to contain the movement.

We may illustrate this sequence by referring to the development of Indonesian nationalism. By the late nineteenth century, the islands had been thoroughly pacified by the Dutch and the colonial economic and political system had begun to work its deteriorating effects on the traditional East Indian cultures. The dominant initial response to this situation was a fantasy "flight from the West," which culminated in the Samin movement at the end of the nineteenth and beginning of the twentieth centuries. This movement was a traditionally nativistic type:

---

the arrest of its leader, cf. Krader, "A Nativistic Movement in Western Siberia," *op. cit.*, p. 288.
[1] Above, pp. 318–319.

The Value-Oriented Movement

Samin, a farmer in Blora (Central Java), became the leader of a peasants' movement, which opposed economic capitalism and preached a return to rustic simplicity of the pre-capitalistic society in which one might only procure food and clothes by one's own labour. Some supporters of this movement even went as far as to deny the legality of all authority, to regard access to arable land and woods as free from government restrictions and to refuse to pay taxes or render services.[1]

Though relying on passive resistance on the whole, the movement gave rise to several armed outbreaks in the early twentieth century, and to the use of armed forces and the arrest of the leader by the Dutch.[2]

The rise of the Samin movement, as well as other movements which stressed education and the Moslem religion, justify Kahin's conclusion that "before 1912 the emphasis of Indonesian nationalism except for its Pan-Islamic and incipient Modernist Islamic currents was cultural rather than political, though political overtones were often present."[3] In 1912, however, the movement took a decidedly political turn, partly because of the increasing accumulation of grievances, and partly because the absence of a full-scale repressive apparatus—which the Dutch had not yet developed—permitted some political activity. The political turn in 1912 is reflected in the appearance of the famous organization of *Sarekat Islam*, which called for Indonesian self-government. The organization had outwardly a religious emphasis, but gradually this emphasis "yielded place to a political one," which in some cases called for complete independence, "to be attained by force if necessary."[4]

The history of the Indonesian nationalist movement for the three decades before the outbreak of World War II is a history of the contrapuntal relationship between nationalist exploration of new lines of attack and Dutch repression. Initially the repressive activity of the Dutch (as well as the example of success of the Bolshevik Revolution) drove the nationalists toward the extreme left and resulted, in 1921, in a formal split between the communists and the central authorities of *Sarekat Islam*. After a period of active competition with the moderates, the communist organization was effectively crushed after the abortive 1926–27 rebellions, in which the communist leadership played an important role. At this juncture, many Moslem nationalists—as a result of "the bitter struggle between *Sarekat Islam* and the communists and the sharp reaction by

---

[1] Wertheim, *Indonesian Society in Transition*, p. 318.
[2] Kahin, *Nationalism and Revolution in Indonesia*, pp. 43–44.
[3] *Ibid.*, p. 64.
[4] *Ibid.*, pp. 65–66, 69.

the government to the communist rebellion"—became convinced "that work towards their socio-religious and national ideals could be better carried on through nonpolitical channels."[1] For a time this moderate approach overshadowed the militant, but in 1936 it was jolted by the Dutch rejection of a moderate proposal for the evolutionary development of an independent Indonesia over a ten-year period. As the nationalist movement shifted from method to method in this interwar period, it accumulated numerous splits, even though, in the last two years before the outbreak of World War II, the movement was becoming increasingly unified.[2]

Up to World War II the Dutch had been *effective*, on the whole, in their use of force to prevent hostile outbursts and challenges to legitimacy, relatively *inflexible* (though not completely so) in permitting normative agitation and relatively *unresponsive* (though not completely so) in meeting demands for normative change. The war and the Japanese occupation undermined Dutch effectiveness in keeping down the nationalist movement. First, the weak Dutch stand before the Japanese discredited the myth of their invulnerability; second, the increased political participation and supply of arms to the Indonesians during the Japanese occupation increased their striking power; finally, the power hiatus after the Japanese evacuation, plus the unwillingness of many Western nations to go along with Dutch aspirations to re-establish the colonial status, allowed the nationalist movement to come into the open as a war of independence.[3] The history of the Indonesian nationalist movement, then, reflects the posture of the political authorities with which the movement continuously came into contact.

A trend from nativistic cults toward secular nationalism seems to be evolving in the Melanesian chain, home of the Cargo Cults. Furthermore, the pattern of this evolution is closely related to the behavior of the colonial authorities. In general, the more passive millenarian cults begin to become less vital *either* when they are repressed by the colonial authorities *or* when the authorities permit other types of protest such as trade unions, political parties, etc.[4]

[1] *Ibid.*, p. 87.
[2] *Ibid.*, pp. 94–100.
[3] *Ibid.*, pp. 101–105; Elsbree, *Japan's Role in Southeast Asian Nationalist Movements 1940 to 1945*, pp. 41, 52–53, 84–85, 96–97, 145–146; also Pye, "The Politics of Southeast Asia," in Almond and Coleman (eds.), *op. cit.*, p. 107.
[4] Worsley, *The Trumpet Shall Sound*, pp. 192–193, 231, 254–256; see also J. W. Davidson, "The Changing Political Role of Pacific Islands' Peoples," *South Pacific*, Vol. 6 (1952), p. 381; L. P. Mair, *Australia in New Guinea* (London, 1948), pp. 64–68. For specific instances of the effects of repression, cf. *The Trumpet Shall Sound*, pp. 17–21, 74, 98–99, 101–103, 218–219; Belshaw, "The Significance of Modern Cults in Melanesian Development," *op. cit.*; Guiart,

The Value-Oriented Movement

Not all value-oriented movements necessarily culminate in revolutionary outbursts. If the colonial government can, before the value-oriented battlelines are drawn irrevocably, introduce a degree of responsiveness to their demands, *while simultaneously maintaining effective control over hostile outbursts*, the movement can transform into a peaceful agitation which culminates in orderly establishment of a nation-state. This response to nationalism lies behind the relatively smooth transition to independence in the British colonies of Ceylon, Ghana, Nigeria, and to a lesser extent, India.[1] In some colonial situations, however, a point of no return is reached. Battlelines become so fixed that compromise or flexibility on the part of the colonial power is viewed by natives as deceit, trickery, or weakness. Under such conditions the only solution is a colonial war which erupts when the military potential of the rebels begins to match that of the colonial power. This situation has developed in some French colonies, such as Indo-China and Algeria.[2] At another level, the racial, semi-colonial situation in South Africa seems to have reached such an extreme degree of rigidity and repression that the only way out in the long run is geographical partition of the races or racial revolution.

The build-up of the major Western ideological revolutions also conforms to the model of repression followed by a lessening of effectiveness. As the discussion of conduciveness and strain suggests,[3] these revolutions have been preceded by a long period of inflexibility, unresponsiveness, and political effectiveness in repressing outbursts. In this atmosphere value-oriented beliefs begin to develop. At this point, moreover, the authorities, facing the rising movement, stand in a position to contain it or divert it in a revolutionary direction. Thus, as Burckhardt summarizes the balance,

---

"Culture Contact and the 'John Frum' Movement on Tanna, New Hebrides," *Southwestern Journal of Anthropology*, Vol. 12 (1956), pp. 105–116. "Paliau Movement in Manus," *South Pacific*, Vol. 4 (1950), pp. 207–208; Berndt, "A Cargo Movement in the Eastern Central Highlands of New Guinea," *op. cit.*, p. 150; C. H. Allan, "Marching Rule: A Nativistic Cult of the British Solomon Islands," *South Pacific*, Vol. 5 (1951), pp. 79–85; C. S. Belshaw, "Recent History of Medeo Society," *Oceania*, Vol. 22 (1951), pp. 6–9.

[1] Coleman, Nigeria: *Background to Nationalism*, Ch. 18; D. E. Apter, *The Gold Coast in Transition* (Princeton, 1955) especially Ch. 7; V. P. Menon, *The Transfer of Power in India* (Princeton, 1957); above, p. 309. Malaya is an exception to the rule, for even though the British have been taking, at a slow pace, the general steps toward independence, a sizeable Communist movement has developed. The situation in Malaya is complicated, however, by the fact that a great number of the Communist guerrillas are Chinese migrants, and that they utilize the jungle terrain, where effective repression is extremely difficult. Ball, *Nationalism and Communism in East Asia*, pp. 135–137.

[2] For the hardening of lines in Algeria, especially after 1945, cf. Gillespie, *Algeria: Rebellion and Revolution*, pp. 46–96.

[3] Above, pp. 330–332 and 343–344.

The Value-Oriented Movement

According to its nature... the suppressed power can either lose or enhance its resilience.... Indeed, the national spirit in the finest sense of the word may become aware of itself by having suffered oppression. In the latter case, something breaks out, subverting the public order. Either it is suppressed, whereupon the ruling power, if it is a wise one, will find some remedy, or unexpectedly to most people, a crisis in the whole state of things is produced, involving whole epochs and all or many peoples of the same civilization.... The historical process is suddenly accelerated in terrifying fashion. Developments which otherwise take centuries seem to flit by like phantoms in months or weeks, and are fulfilled.[1]

The response of the authorities to a value-oriented protest, then, is extremely important in determining which direction the movement proceeds. Again, to quote Burckhardt,

... the Reformation could have been considerably checked and the French Revolution largely mitigated.

In the Reformation, a reform of the clergy and a moderate reduction of Church property carried out by the ruling classes, and by them alone, would have sufficed. Henry VIII and the Counter-Reformation after him show what could really have been done. There was in men's minds a profound discontent, but no general, clear ideal of a new Church.

It would have been much more difficult to avert an eruption in 1789, because the educated classes were inspired by a Utopia and the masses by an accumulated store of hatred and revenge.[2]

Burckhardt's last comment reveals the hardening of positions that results if the government remains inflexible and unresponsive for a long period. If this occurs, the battle-lines are formed, and the critical issue becomes the authorities' political effectiveness. If the authorities continue to be effective, the movement tends to go underground, withdraw into cults, or to seek emigration. The moment, however, that the authorities' effectiveness weakens, the value-oriented movement moves in a revolutionary direction. This, as we shall see presently, has been the developmental pattern for the major Western internal revolutions.

How do we identify the authorities' declining effectiveness?[3] Some writers answer this with a vague reference to the feebleness of the

---

[1] *Force and Freedom*, p. 267.
[2] *Ibid.*, pp. 267–268.
[3] In the discussion that follows, we shall consider only the initial revolutionary overthrow. Many revolutions have passed through a "moderate" phase which has given way to a second revolutionary seizure of power. Though we shall not consider this problem, presumably the same ineffectiveness that characterized the old regime can be shown to characterize the moderate phase. On the behavior of the moderates, cf. Edwards, *The Natural History of Revolution*, pp. 118–129; Brinton, *The Anatomy of Revolution*, p. 129; Meusel, "Revolution and Counter-Revolution," *op. cit.*, pp. 374–375; Hopper, "The Revolutionary Process," *op. cit.*, pp. 275–276.

The Value-Oriented Movement

ruling classes.[1] More identifiable signs of this ineffectiveness are the "multiplication of factions and parties," which paralyze the government and its ability to use force to put down disturbances;[2] the vacillation of the government in passing reforms and its unwillingness to live up to the reforms it passes;[3] the bankruptcy of a government which forces it to turn for help to those subjects toward whom it simultaneously maintains an inflexible and unresponsive posture;[4] and a major cleavage among the ruling classes.[5]

Ultimately ineffectiveness of the authorities reveals itself in their failure to display force in the face of hostile outbursts. "It is obvious," observed Le Bon, "that revolutions have never taken place, and will never take place, save with the aid of an important faction of the army."[6] This aid may originate from the failure of the ruling classes to call out the troops; from the failure of the officers to obey the orders; from the refusal of the troops to fight the revolutionaries, either by standing idly by, by fraternizing with the revolutionaries, or by actively assisting the revolutionaries.[7]

The appropriate combination of the variables of flexibility, responsiveness and effectiveness can be seen in the Italian fascist revolution which brought Mussolini to power after World War I. Following the war, Italy floundered under the woes of demobilization, the frustrations of political settlements, and severe economic deprivations of unemployment and a rising cost of living.[8] "To no other country did demobilization bring such difficult problems."[9] Throughout this postwar period, moreover, the government and political parties were frozen in deadlock, both within themselves and among one another. Any political leader had insurmountable opposition from several of the many parties, and this created a situation of political paralysis.[10]

In such an atmosphere the fascist movement, which had been

[1] Le Bon, *The Psychology of Revolution*, p. 49; Sorokin, *The Sociology of Revolution*.
[2] J. O. Hertzler, "Crises and Dictatorships," *American Sociological Review*, Vol. 5 (1945), p. 161. Hertzler is referring here to the rise of dictatorships, not revolutionary movements, but he notes the "close relationship between revolution and dictatorship."
[3] Brinton, *The Anatomy of Revolution*, pp. 40–41; Trotsky, *History of the Russian Revolution*, Vol. I, pp. 96–97.
[4] Brinton, *The Anatomy of Revolution*, pp. 37–40; Hunter, *Revolution*, pp. 302 ff.
[5] Brinton, *An Anatomy of Revolution*, pp. 52–59.
[6] *The Psychology of Revolution*, p. 29.
[7] Brinton, *The Anatomy of Revolution*, p. 55; Colton, *Four Patterns of Revolution*, p. 81; R. N. Baldwin, "Political Police," *Encyclopaedia of the Social Sciences*, Vol. 12, pp. 203–207; Trotsky, *History of the Russian Revolution*, Vol. I, pp. 120–121; Robertson, *Revolutions of 1848*, pp. 29–30; Gillespie, *Algeria: Rebellion and Revolution*, pp. 187–189.
[8] Above, pp. 339, 353.
[9] Rossi, *The Rise of Italian Fascism 1918–1922*, p. 9.
[10] *Ibid.*, pp. 52–65.

The Value-Oriented Movement

"feeble and almost nonexistent before September 1920," began to expand rapidly in late 1920 and in the first half of 1921. The greatest advance came in the Po Valley, and in Apulia in Southern Italy, where the landlords were attempting to smash workers' organizations and hence were willing to give strong support to lawless fascist gangs bent on terrorizing communists, socialists, and public officials. In all places where the fascists succeeded in occupying the territory, "the police and the military intervened to help the fascists' maneuvers and defend them against reprisals, and the struggle quickly became one-sided."[1] The central government adopted a permissive attitude toward the fascists as well. Giolitti, the premier, wishing to weaken both the socialists and the Populari, would take no action to stop the fascists, even though the socialists were insisting that he put down the violence. Later in 1921, the government did issue "fresh regulations on the 'disarmament of citizens,' ordering searches to be made and arms seized." But the enforcement of such regulations, left almost entirely in the hands of local authorities, brought only token searches of fascist establishments and genuine searches of the headquarters of socialist syndicates. In a moment of desperation the government, realizing the uselessness of such regulations, contemplated abolishing the fascist squads by decree, but in the end the government leaders merely "issued more and more regulations, which everybody ignored."[2]

Under this governmental ineffectiveness, fascism flourished as a revolutionary movement. In addition, the economic crisis worsened steadily from the end of 1920 (when there were about 100,000 unemployed) to the beginning of 1922 (when the figure had risen to more than 600,000). This also fed many recruits into the ranks of the fascists. The actual March on Rome in autumn, 1922, which meant the rise of Mussolini to power, was in certain respects an anti-climax; for all the forces necessary for his success had been in existence for some time.[3]

Germany after World War I offers both contrasts and parallels with Italy. Immediately after the war, the Ebert regime—facing the shock of military defeat, the strains of demobilization, and the presence of many possibly revolutionary groups—guaranteed its short-term survival by aligning itself with the military. As Clark summarizes the situation in 1918,

> It was only afterwards that the details of the bargain (between Ebert and the military) became known and the real role of Ebert as the sabotager-in-

[1] *Ibid.*, pp. 118, 121.
[2] *Ibid.*, pp. 158–170.
[3] *Ibid.*, pp. 332–333; see also Spearman, *Modern Dictatorship*, pp. 44–48.

The Value-Oriented Movement

chief of revolution was understood. The army was the key to the situation. It was not, as in the Russian revolution, in full dissolution. On the contrary, despite the chaos in the rear and the formation of soldiers' councils even at Imperial headquarters, there was a solid, well-disciplined coherent force, well armed and well officered, which could very easily dispose of armed resistance. . . . That army was now coming home. To the extremists it was the main danger, for it represented precisely that power which Kerensky had lacked. Had the Majority leaders been for a moment sincere in their desire for something so comparatively modest as a Socialist revolution, their obvious course was to have closed the Socialist ranks and flung on the army the onus of creating civil war. Instead, Ebert made his bargain. If Hindenburg and the officers' corps stayed at their posts during the demobilization period—the danger period—and supported him and his colleagues in the maintenance of order, they on their side would deal firmly with Bolshevism . . . (Thus) while three-quarters of the army was quietly demobilizing itself, while excited crowds still thronged the streets, while in every big town soldiers, sailors, and civilians went about armed, normal life was being resumed.[1]

The Revolution of 1918, then, which consisted in its most active phase of a general revolutionary strike called by the Independents and the Spartacists (two political groupings on the left) was crushed handily by the alliance between the army command and the Ebert government.[2] An alliance between constitutional authority and military also lay behind the easy defeat of the Communist Insurrection of 1920 as well.[3]

In 1923 the German situation was more complicated. The central government was being defied by the state government in Bavaria.[4] One major bone of contention was Bavaria's refusal to put down rightist movements, including the national socialist, in its own territory. After a season of inactivity, the central government ordered the local military commander to suppress the *Völkische Beobachter*, the Nazi organ. The Commissioner of Bavaria and the local army commander refused to obey this order. Only after a week's delay and repeated representations was the newspaper suspended (on October 4, 1923). "From that time down to the Beer Hall Putsch of Nov. 8, there was little pretense of respecting the authority of the Reich within the territorial limits of Bavaria."[5]

In this setting of "protracted success in the defiance of legitimate authority" the Beer Hall *Putsch* materialized. The domestic situation

---
[1] *The Fall of the German Republic*, pp. 47–48.
[2] *Ibid.*, pp. 52–55.
[3] F. M. Watkins, *The Failure of Constitutional Emergency Powers under the German Republic* (Cambridge, Mass., 1939), pp. 25–34.
[4] *Ibid.*, pp. 37–38.
[5] *Ibid.*, p. 41.

had worsened in the summer of 1923 with uncontrolled monetary inflation. The situation seemed ripe for an extremist group such as Hitler's to move into the vacuum of power and capitalize on the Bavarian defiance of the central government. "In the hour of final decision," however, as Watkins summarizes it,

the various right radical factions proved incapable of arriving at a common plan of action. Commissioner von Kahr (of Bavaria) and his supporters were interested mainly in restoring the Bavarian monarchy, while Adolf Hitler's loyalties were almost entirely directed toward the person of Adolf Hitler. On the eve of the Beer Hall *Putsch* the National Socialist leader tried to remedy this situation with a characteristic touch of melodrama. By the simple device of holding a pistol at the head of the state commissioner, he forced that startled official to make a public declaration of his adherence to the movement. But this dramatic episode ... served no other purpose than to demonstrate the moral insignificance of enforced consent. Once he had regained his freedom of movement, Commissioner von Kahr proceeded to wire frantic declarations of loyalty to the Berlin government. The sincerity of these protestations was demonstrated on the very next day, when he and von Lossow joined forces to crush the insurrection. The victory march of National Socialism was dissipated in a hail of bullets, and before many hours had passed its supporters were in full flight. In the final reckoning, no emergency regime could have served more effectively than the Bavarian state commission to safeguard the interests of the Weimar Constitution.[1]

Between 1924 and 1929 the German political situation was stabilized both by an improving economic situation and by the policies of Streseman. "Anti-republican movements which had long thriven on sentiments of misery and despair were forced increasingly into the background."[2] With the crash of 1929, however, a new balance of forces emerged in Germany. The extremist parties, greatly swollen by the ranks of unemployed and others, entered the political party scene, and their obstructiveness, combined with the weakness of the Social Democrats, created a situation of political paralysis reminiscent of the situation in Italy immediately after World War I. Under such circumstances the extremist groups—although unable to venture a frontal attack on the military or the constitutional parties—were able to marshal private armies to perpetrate illegal violence on mass meetings of other extremist groups, to bully vendors of newspapers and party publications, and to engage in street brawls with opposing parties.[3] The government's response to this outlawry and brigandry—which it permitted with increasing laxness between

[1] *Ibid.*, p. 46.
[2] *Ibid.*, p. 52.
[3] *Ibid.*, pp. 55–57.

The Value-Oriented Movement

1930 and 1932—displayed an ineffectiveness that contributed greatly to the growth of revolutionary movements.[1]

The response of the agencies of social control in the Russian Revolution of 1917 displays a similar pattern. During earlier periods of potential revolution—in the Decembrist period of the early nineteenth century, in the terrorist period of the late nineteenth century, and in the two decades leading up to the explosion of 1905—the military forces had remained loyal to the Tsars.[2] In 1917, however, the army and bureaucracy itself were disorganized and unable to contain the protest. The contrast between 1917 and 1905 is especially instructive, since many of the social forces in operation were similar. At both times Russia was experiencing the pains of the early stages of industrialization.[3] In both 1905 and 1917 Russia had been fighting in a foreign war for a substantial period, though the Japanese War was not nearly so exhausting as World War I. The same political parties were struggling for power in 1905 and 1917.[4] The difference between the two periods lay primarily in the degree to which the wielders of force permitted or joined in the revolutionary activity. As Gross notes,

... the revolution of 1905 was to an extent a microcosm of 1917. The Japanese War and defeat was of much smaller dimensions. The workers and peasants revolted, but the army and bureaucracy was still intact. Here and there soldiers and sailors rebelled, it is true. But, in 1905 the whole bureaucratic system and the army apparatus were still in operation. *In 1917 the pillars of the tsarist system—the bureaucracy and the army—were disintegrating even before the workers and the people of St. Petersburg revolted.* When the February days came the workers struck, and there were no organized social forces strong enough to support the regime. The workers struck, the population rebelled, the army regiments disintegrated and joined the revolution.[5]

What the Tsarist regime lacked before the February revolution Kerensky also lacked between the February and October revolutions.

[1] *Ibid.*, p. 59.
[2] Gross, *The Seizure of Power in a Century of Revolutions*, pp. 63–79, 125–130, 151–186.
[3] Kohn, *Revolutions and Dictatorships*, pp. 91–92.
[4] Gross, *The Seizure of Power in a Century of Revolutions*, p. 183; L. Gottschalk, "Causes of Revolution," *American Journal of Sociology*, Vol. 50 (July, 1944), p. 7.
[5] *The Seizure of Power in a Century of Revolutions*, p. 194. One further difference between 1905 and 1917 was that in the former the Tsar made an "ersatz" capitulation to popular demands and created a parliamentary or advisory body which was soon to lose any effectiveness which was originally promised. Pp. 182–193. For further evidence on the disorder in the Tsarist regime, cf. Florinsky, *The End of the Russian Empire*, Chs. IV, IX; N. N. Golovine, *The Russian Army in the World War* (New Haven, 1931), Chs. X, XI; Trotsky, *History of the Russian Revolution*, Vol. I, pp. 16–32, 76–79.

The Value-Oriented Movement

Faced with mounting inflation and military defeat, unable to introduce reforms of any sort,[1] erratic in its use of force,[2] and unable to command the loyalty or discipline of the military forces,[3] the Kerensky government was snarled in the trap of unresponsiveness, inflexibility and ineffectiveness which made it a target for revolutionary overthrow.

The French Revolution, finally, poses difficult problems of interpretation. For, as Lefebvre has observed, it was not one but several revolutions under a single name.[4] If we restrict our attention to the days of 1789, however, it is possible to observe the interplay of unresponsiveness, inflexibility, and ineffectiveness in this case, too. It should be noted that upon the date of convening the Estates-General in the spring of 1789 no significant body of opinion felt that a political revolution was imminent, even though the utopian ideology of the Enlightenment—in the name of which the Revolution was ultimately perpetrated—was already highly developed.[5] Most of the delegates who convened hoped for certain reforms to be granted in return for financial support of the government. Many preconditions for revolution had, however, been long in the making. These included the definition of opposition to the regime in value-oriented terms;[6] the decay of feudal patterns of authority, with consequent divisions among the traditional ruling classes;[7] widespread strain which affected adversely the nobility, the middle class, the clergy, the peasants, and the workmen;[8] and finally, the crystallization of a set of generalized beliefs of a value-oriented character. What was required for a revolution was a setting in which these conditions could be combined with a successful defiance of authority. The convocation of the Estates-General and the events of the next several months provided the occasion for a succession of such defiances. Actually, these defiances did not always involve a display of violence; sometimes the revolution was accomplished when the King failed to utilize his forces.

The first major governmental capitulation in the face of defiance appeared in connection with the Oath of the Tennis Court on June

[1] Trotsky, *History of the Russian Revolution*, Vol. I, pp. 183, 203–204, 224, 271, 376; Vol. II, pp. 140–331.
[2] *Ibid.*, Vol. II, pp. 50, 223.
[3] *Ibid.*, Vol. I, pp. 248–266, 373, 389; Vol. II, pp. 283, 346; Vol. III, pp. 69, 187, 288.
[4] *The Coming of the French Revolution*, p. 5.
[5] *Ibid.*, p. 179; Tocqueville, *The Old Regime and the French Revolution*, p. 15; Stephens, *History of the French Revolution*, Vol. I, pp. 9–10.
[6] Above, pp. 331–332.
[7] Above, p. 331.
[8] Above, pp. 343–344.

The Value-Oriented Movement

20, 1789. Having declared themselves on June 15, in defiance of the King, to be the National Assembly of France, the Third Estate had been ordered suspended until a royal session of June 22. Refusing to suspend operations, the delegates nevertheless found themselves blocked from the usual meeting hall. Thereupon they retired to the tennis court, where they swore they would never separate until a constitution was formed. After a brief period of confusion, the King capitulated without any use of violence on either side and ordered the nobles to join the assembly for further deliberations. This was, in effect, a partial revolution, for there had been a successful defiance of authority and a partial transfer of power.

A second shift in power occurred in the series of riots beginning on July 12, 1789. Necker, the finance minister in whom the Third Estate placed many of its hoped for reforms, was dismissed by the King on July 12. On this day, and the several days following (including July 14, the day of the attack on the Bastille), mobs roamed the streets of Paris, generally unquelled by the King's troops, who were either unable or unwilling to put down the crowds. After these outbursts the King submitted further to the demands of the assembly. He promised to recall Necker; he paid a visit to Paris on July 17; he appointed Lafayette head of the new National Guard and went along with the election of Bailly as Mayor of Paris. Much of the violence in the riots of July 12 and the few days thereafter did not have as a *direct* objective the revolutionary overthrow of the monarchy; indeed the National Assembly wished not to be held responsible for the violence. But the display of violence, and, more important, the inability and unwillingness of the King's troops to put it down forthwith, led to a further capitulation of the King and to another partial revolution.[1]

A third phase of the revolution also involved a show of violence and an equivocal attitude on the part of the authorities. On October 5, a large gathering of starving women marched on Versailles; the next day they attacked the palace. Under the pressure of such events, and under the urging of Lafayette, the King agreed to move to Paris (where he would be under more direct threat and control of the people), and also agreed finally to accepting the Declaration of the Rights of Man.[2]

By such stages the revolution proceeded to run its course, changes of power gradually shifting as it became apparent that the forces of order were inadequate to control the displays of violence. Sometimes

---
[1] The accounts of the last two paragraphs are taken from Stephens, *History of the French Revolution*, Vol. I, pp. 60–155.
[2] *Ibid.*, pp. 221–228.

The Value-Oriented Movement

this violence arose for reasons such as hunger, price changes, etc.[1] In each case, however, the disturbance revealed the fundamental weakness of the constituted authorities.

These examples from revolutions in underdeveloped areas and from the West illustrate the importance of agencies of social control in the later stages of value-oriented movements. Other examples could be given.[2] To summarize: If a value-oriented movement is to assume a revolutionary cast, authorities *at some level*—perhaps at the top level, perhaps at some regional level, perhaps at the middle-officer level, perhaps at the level of the troops themselves—must appear to be unable or unwilling to enforce their authority. Since force is an ultimate sanction in political control, the *possibility* of its use always is present when a movement turns in a revolutionary direction. This is not to say that violence always appears in a value-oriented revolution. Perhaps the authority capitulates without a show of force if he considers himself sufficiently at a disadvantage. Perhaps adherents of the movement itself will not engage in a show of force if they appear unlikely to succeed. Sometimes the appearance of force will not involve a frontal attack on the authorities by a revolutionary group itself, but will be the occurrence of violence *somewhere else* in the system which the authority is unable to handle. The revolutionary opposition may capitalize on this incapacity, even though the revolutionary group did not perpetrate the violence. Thus, when a movement becomes revolutionary, violence is always a possibility; whether it becomes an actuality, and how it becomes an actuality are open questions.

CONCLUSIONS

In this long chapter we have organized the determinants of the value-oriented movement as a value-added process. The logic is identical to the logic we used for all other kinds of collective behavior. The value-added process can be represented as a tree, which, at each point of branching, presents a number of alternative branches. The "trunk" of the tree is represented by the conditions of conduciveness, without which the value-oriented movement cannot proceed to any of the branches. In characterizing conduciveness we ask: Is the definition of the situation couched in value terms or are values

---

[1] Above, pp. 245–246.
[2] For an account of the questionable loyalties of the British troops in the Puritan revolution of 1640, cf. Gardiner, *The First Two Stuarts and the Puritan Revolution*, p. 122; for instances of weakening loyalty and fraternization during the Hungarian and Polish Revolutions of 1956, cf. Gross, *The Seizure of Power in a Century of Revolutions*, pp. 316–323.

The Value-Oriented Movement

differentiated from other aspects of social life? What are the possibilities of expressing grievances in the system? Is it possible for the aggrieved groups to communicate their dissatisfactions to one another? By considering such questions we set up the conditions which make a value-oriented movement possible.

These conditions of conduciveness, however, do not guarantee the appearance of a value-oriented movement. A number of other conditions must be established within the limits of conduciveness. The first of these conditions is strain. If the social structure is free from strain, even conditions of conduciveness will not create a value-oriented movement. When serious conditions of strain—the major types of which we attempted to outline—bear on the system, then behavior tends to branch toward the value-oriented movement rather than some other kind of behavior.

An important branching involves the growth of a value-oriented belief. Does there exist a set of value-oriented beliefs within which all the foci of strain can be interpreted conveniently? Does a leader appear to symbolize or formulate such a set of beliefs? If value-oriented beliefs do not crystallize, the response to strain cannot be collective, because the aggrieved groups do not share a common definition of the situation. In the absence of generalized beliefs we would expect segmented protests, but not a coordinated, collective value-oriented movement. In connection with generalized beliefs, we assessed the special role of precipitating factors, which fix the value-oriented beliefs on concrete events and situations, and thus ready the adherents for collective action.

Finally, though people widely accept a value-oriented belief, a value-oriented movement will not eventuate unless the adherents are mobilized for action. Leadership is extremely important in this stage of mobilization. Because of the character of value-oriented commitment, the possibility of internal instability and disunity of value-oriented movements is very great.

Even though all these determinants are present, it is still possible for a single value-oriented movement to branch out to one of several outcomes. This depends largely on the response of agencies of social control to the movement. Social control, considered in its broadest sense, operates throughout the development of a movement; by changing the conditions of conduciveness, by reducing strain, by discrediting opposing value-oriented beliefs, the agencies of social control may defeat or deflect a movement. In our discussion of social control, however, we concentrated on the response of agencies of social control to value-oriented movement which was already mobilized for action. According to the behavior of these agencies on

The Value-Oriented Movement

three counts—flexibility, responsiveness, and effectiveness[1]—the value-oriented movement may move in the direction of an underground conspiracy, a sect or denomination, a passive cult, or a revolutionary party.

This formulation of a movement in value-added terms has two important methodological implications:

(1) In analyzing value-oriented movements we should not search for concrete historical items—tax measures, assassinations, economic deprivations, ideologies, weak police systems, etc.—as typical determinants. Such phenomena do frequently enter the unfolding process and assume the status of determinants. No inherent quality of the phenomena themselves, however, makes them determinants. They may act as determinants in other movements, or as determinants of nothing at all. They must occur in the context of the value-added sequence as a whole if they are to assume significance as determinants of value-added movements.

(2) In considering the causes of value-oriented movements, or the role of various factors—repression, strain, ideas, or weakness and vacillation of authority—we should not represent these variables as a simple list, but must view them as an organized body of determinants, each of which comes into play only after certain patterns of the other determinants have been established. It is fruitless to seek an abstract role of some factor without considering the pattern of the outburst as a whole.

Finally, we must stress that the temporal unfolding of any given value-oriented movement does not necessarily correspond to the logical priority of determinants in the value-added process. Beliefs that are potentially revolutionary may exist temporally long before strain arises to activate these beliefs as determinants of a value-oriented movement; revolutionary organizations may lie in wait for conditions of conduciveness and strain, upon which they then capitalize. The tactics of communist groups in underdeveloped countries, for instance, are to capitalize on whatever conditions of conduciveness (e.g., repression by authorities) or strain (e.g., economic crisis) may be present. This qualification does not affect the logical status of the value-added process itself. Even though a revolutionary organization may exist well before strains arise upon which it attempts to ride to power, the same logical relations hold between strain and mobilization. Strain is a necessary condition—whether long in existence or created on the spot—for mobilization to appear as a determinant of a value-oriented movement.

---

[1] These concepts are defined technically in terms of the channels for expressing dissatisfaction above, pp. 364-365.

CHAPTER XI

CONCLUDING REMARKS

SUMMARY

In Chapter I we presented the issues that must be confronted in any systematic attempt to account for collective behavior. We tentatively defined collective behavior, identified its major types, and specified its general determinants. In Chapter II we outlined a conceptual framework for analyzing collective behavior. We isolated the components of social action (*viz.*, values, norms, mobilization of motivation, and facilities), explored the relations among the components, and examined the composition of each component. In Chapter III we sketched, in terms of the components of action, the major structural strains that give rise to collective behavior. In Chapter IV we specified—again in the same terms—the general character of collective behavior. We defined it as an uninstitutionalized mobilization to reconstitute a component of social action on the basis of a generalized belief—hysterical, wish-fulfillment, hostile, norm-oriented, and value-oriented. Finally, in Chapters VI-X we examined the determinants of each form of collective behavior—the panic, the craze, the hostile outburst, the norm-oriented movement, and the value-oriented movement. The major determinants are structural conduciveness, strain, crystallization of a generalized belief, precipitating factors, mobilization for action, and social control.

We conceive the operation of these determinants as a value-added process. Each determinant is a necessary condition for the next to operate as a determinant in an episode of collective behavior. As the necessary conditions accumulate, the explanation of the episode becomes more determinate. Together the necessary conditions constitute the sufficient condition for the episode. It should be stressed, moreover, that we view the accumulation of necessary conditions as an analytic, not a temporal process.

Because our analysis has become so detailed and our illustrations so numerous, we have perhaps on occasion obscured some of the relations among our explanatory concepts. In this final chapter we shall give an overview of these relations.

Concluding Remarks

THE ISSUES THAT ARISE IN EXPLAINING COLLECTIVE BEHAVIOR

The range of relevant data to be explained is that class of phenomena known as collective behavior. The initial issue is to specify the defining characteristic of these phenomena. We chose—in contrast to many others who analyze collective behavior—to make the defining characteristic *the kind of belief under which behavior is mobilized*. Collective behavior is action based on a generalized belief, which we analyzed in detail in Chapters IV and V. We also decided that though collective behavior often displays distinctive psychological states (e.g., the loss of personal identity), distinctive patterns of communication (e.g., the rumor) and distinctive patterns of mobilization (e.g., the demagogue and his following), these are not necessary defining characteristics of such behavior.

The next issue in marking out an area for study is to identify its characteristic types. The major types of collective behavior, we noted, are the panic, the craze, the hostile outburst, the norm-oriented movement, and the value-oriented movement. Having done this, we turn to the two major issues of explanation itself: the *general* determinants of collective behavior (Why does collective behavior occur at all?), and the *unique combination* of determinants for any collective episode (Why one rather than another form of collective behavior)? To these issues all our theoretical constructs are oriented.

TWO SETS OF ORGANIZING CONSTRUCTS

Our analysis of collective behavior is built on two sets of organizing constructs: the components of social action, and the value-added process. The first is a language for describing and classifying action. It is a "flow chart" for tracing the course of action, and not a direct source of explanatory hypotheses. The value-added process, on the other hand, is a means for organizing determinants into explanatory models.[1]

The two sets of organizing constructs supplement one another in the following ways:

(1) Structural conduciveness, the first stage of value-added, refers

---

[1] Formally, the "components of action" and "value-added" have a dimension of generality-specificity in common. The components of action—values, norms, mobilization, and facilities—are organized into a hierarchy of increasing specificity. Each component can be organized into a number of increasingly specific levels. Above, pp. 32–34 and 35–45. The value-added process also involves a series of transitions from general to specific. The early stages (e.g., conduciveness) are conceived as general conditions, by contrast with the later stages (e.g., mobilization), which are more specific in their determination of an episode of collective behavior.

Concluding Remarks

to the degree to which any structure permits a given type of collective behavior, e.g., a hostile outburst. To assess this conduciveness, we ask two questions: Do the existing structural arrangements directly encourage overt hostility? Do these arrangements prohibit other kinds of protest? In the first question we ask to what degree the existing structure "invites" people to choose overt hostility; in the second we ask to what degree the existing structure "drives" them into hostile outbursts.

If we are to discuss conduciveness in a determinate way, we must identify the possible means of reconstituting the existing structure. Here the basic components of action become relevant. They provide a basis for classifying the several avenues for reconstituting social action—*viz.*, to redefine the situational facilities, to attack individual agents who are responsible, to reorganize norms, or to redefine the values of the system. Thus the two organizing constructs—"value-added" and the "basic components"—supplement one another. Conduciveness (a part of the value-added scheme) indicates the most general necessary condition for a collective outburst; the basic components of action indicate the major types of conduciveness.

(2) Strain refers to the impairment of the relations among parts of a system and the consequent malfunctioning of the system. In the value-added process strain is a necessary condition for any collective outburst. It can assume significance as a determinant, however, only within the scope established by the prior conditions of conduciveness. To classify the major *types* of strain, we again turn to the basic components of action; strain may affect facilities, organized role behavior, norms, or values.

(3) The crystallization of a generalized belief marks the attempt of persons under strain to assess their situation. They "explain" this situation by creating or assembling a generalized belief. Again, the major *types* of belief, and their relations to one another, are derived from the components of action.

(4) Once an episode of collective behavior has appeared, its duration and severity are determined by the response of the agencies of social control. To classify the major responses of these agencies, we turn to the components of action. We ask, for instance, what avenues of behavior—e.g., hostile expression, norm-oriented protest —these agencies attempt to close off or leave open.

GENERATING PROPOSITIONS ABOUT COLLECTIVE BEHAVIOR

In creating propositions about collective behavior we start with a master proposition and proceed, by several steps, to generate more

Concluding Remarks

specific propositions and to establish the conditions under which these propositions hold.

The master proposition is found in Chapter IV: People under strain mobilize to reconstitute the social order in the name of a generalized belief. Stated so generally, this proposition is not very helpful in interpreting the actual data of collective outbursts. How do we make it more specific?

Initially we identify a number of different kinds of generalized belief—hysterical, wish-fulfillment, hostile, etc. Next we ask, for each belief, under what conditions people will develop such a belief and act on it? Take panic, for instance. Under what conditions of *conduciveness* do people develop and act on a hysterical belief? In reply we discuss the character of the escape situation, among other things. The condition of maximum conduciveness is limited and closing exits. Completely open or completely closed exits are not conducive to panic. By this operation we ask under what conditions of conduciveness the master proposition—specified for panic—will hold. In this way we generate increasingly more specific conditions for establishing the propositions. By introducing even more conditions—those of strain, precipitating factors, social control, etc.—we apply even more restrictions on the applicability of the proposition. Or, to put it the other way around, we successively rule out the situations in which the proposition will *not* hold.[1] In Chapters VI through X we performed this kind of restricting operation each time we considered a new determinant for each kind of collective behavior.

ACCEPTING OR REJECTING PROPOSITIONS ABOUT COLLECTIVE BEHAVIOR

Having introduced a number of restricting conditions on the master proposition, we arrive at statements such as the following: "Panic will occur if the appropriate conditions of conduciveness are present *and* if the appropriate conditions of strain are present *and* if a hysterical belief develops, *and* if mobilization occurs, *and* if social controls fail to operate."

How do we decide whether to accept or reject such a statement? What kinds of data do we examine? How do we handle apparently contradictory evidence, e.g., the presence of strain but no panic, conduciveness but no panic, etc.?

The ideal procedure to be followed in establishing scientific propositions is to create a laboratory situation in which all the relevant variables except one are held constant, then to manipulate this one

[1] Above, pp. 13–14.

Concluding Remarks

variable systematically. In the case of the complex statement about panic, for instance, we would vary conduciveness systematically in one set of experiments, vary strain in another set, and so on, and determine whether each condition is necessary for panic. Furthermore, we could determine what combination of the conditions has to be present to produce a panic. Experimentation, however, is virtually impossible in the study of collective behavior. Ethical prohibitions prevent investigators from literally creating a panic, and practical difficulties in establishing a genuine panic in a laboratory setting are almost overwhelming.[1]

An approximation to the laboratory situation can frequently be achieved by using statistical techniques, by which we can hold many variables constant and estimate the combined effect of several variables. As the illustrations in this volume indicate, however, existing data in the field of collective behavior seldom permit elegant statistical manipulation. In most cases our confidence in the propositions we generate must rest on another approximation to controlled experimentation. What is this approximation?

We have relied mainly on *systematic comparative illustration* from the available literature on collective behavior. This method takes two forms, positive and negative. (*a*) We have attempted to identify the common characteristics of situations that produce episodes of collective behavior. For instance, we have attempted to locate an actual or perceived condition of limited and closing exits in all panic situations. (*b*) We have examined those situations in which a collective outburst has nearly occurred to discover which determinants were absent. In connection with riots, for instance, we studied the ways in which agencies of social control prevent the actual mobilization for attack; in this way the agencies of control prevent a determinant of a hostile outburst from operating. Sometimes we have combined these positive and negative methods of systematic comparative illustration by examining those occasions on which one form of collective behavior (e.g., a panic) turns into another (e.g., a hostile outburst). In so doing we asked which significant determinants disappear and which determinants appear, thus changing the character of the episode.

A critical issue to be posed for any proposition before it can be called a *scientific* proposition is: Can we find evidence that would lead us to reject the proposition? In connection with our analysis two types of negative evidence can be found: (*a*) Situations in which one or more necessary conditions (e.g., strain) are absent, but in

---

[1] See, however, above, pp. 4, 137.

Concluding Remarks

which a collective outburst occurs. This would indicate that the condition heretofore considered necessary for the collective episode is in fact not essential. (*b*) Situations in which one or more necessary conditions are present but in which the collective outburst does not occur. Such situations do not, however, always constitute negative evidence. In discussing the indeterminacy of strain, we insisted that not all situations of strain need produce any particular kind of collective episode, indeed any collective episode at all.[1] Strain, we argued, must *combine* with the other appropriate necessary conditions (conduciveness, mobilization, etc.) to be operative as a determinant. For those situations in which we find strain but no collective outburst, then, we must ask if other necessary conditions are absent. If one or more of them is absent, the presence of strain without a collective episode does not constitute negative evidence. If, however, strain *and* all the other necessary conditions are present, but no outburst occurs, this is negative evidence.

COLLECTIVE BEHAVIOR AND OTHER FORMS OF BEHAVIOR

In this volume we excluded many other kinds of behavior, such as crime, suicide, drug addiction, ceremonial behavior, etc., from the field of collective behavior.[2] Having excluded them, we then erected an analytic framework for explaining collective outbursts and collective movements. May we conclude by suggesting that this analytic framework, relaxed in appropriate ways, can be brought to bear on many of these other forms of behavior. Suicide, for instance, arises from some of the same kinds of social malintegration that underlie many collective outbursts. For suicide, then, we might ask: Given a certain type of strain, what conditions determine whether suicide or some other kind of behavior arises? To answer this question we would have to extend our consideration of variables such as conduciveness, the operation of social and individual controls, etc., beyond the scope employed in this volume. By such an extension, however, it should be possible to incorporate many related kinds of behavior into the same theoretical framework that we have used to analyze collective behavior alone.

[1] Above, pp. 48–49.
[2] Above pp. 73–78.

BIBLIOGRAPHY

General Works

Adorno, T. W., Frenkel-Brunswik, E., Levinson, D. J., and Sanford, R. N., *The Authoritarian Personality* (New York: Harper & Brothers, 1950)

Allen, F. L., *Only Yesterday: An Informal History of the Nineteen-Twenties* (New York: Blue Ribbon Books, 1931)

Allier, R., *The Mind of the Savage* (translated by Fred Rothwell) (New York: Harcourt, Brace & Co., 1930)

Allport, F. H., *Social Psychology* (Boston: Houghton Mifflin, 1924)

Allport, G. W., "The Historical Background of Modern Social Psychology," in Lindzey, G. (ed.), *Handbook of Social Psychology* (Cambridge, Mass.: Addison-Wesley, 1954), Vol. I, pp. 3–56.

———, and Postman, L., *The Psychology of Rumor* (New York: Henry Holt, 1947)

Bakke, E. W., *Citizens Without Work* (New Haven: Yale University Press, 1940)

Bales, R. F., "How People Interact in Conferences," *Scientific American*, Vol. 192 (1955), pp. 31–35.

Barnard, C. I., "The Functions and Pathology of Status Systems in Formal Organizations," in Whyte, W. F. (ed.), *Industry and Society* (New York: McGraw-Hill, 1946)

Barnhart, J. D., "Rainfall and the Populist Party in Nebraska," *American Political Science Review*, Vol. 19 (1925), pp. 527–540.

Basowitz, H., Persky, H., Korchin, S. J., and Grinker, R. R., *Anxiety and Stress: An Interdisciplinary Study of a Life Situation* (New York: McGraw-Hill [Blakiston Division], 1955)

Bassett, T. D. S., "The Secular Utopian Socialists," in Egbert, D. D., and Persons, S. (eds.), *Socialism and American Life* (Princeton: Princeton University Press, 1952)

Bauer, P. T., and Yamey, B. S., *The Economics of Under-developed Countries* (Chicago: University of Chicago Press, 1957)

Bauer, R. A., Inkeles, A., and Kluckhohn, C., *How the Soviet System Works* (Cambridge, Mass.: Harvard University Press, 1957)

Bax, E. B., *German Society at the Close of the Middle Ages* (London: Swan Sonnenschein, 1894)

Bean, L., *How to Predict Elections* (New York: Alfred A. Knopf, 1948)

Beard, C. A., and Beard, M. R., *The Rise of American Civilization* (New York: Macmillan, 1946)

Beers, H. W., and Heflin, C., "The Urban Status of Rural Migrants," *Social Forces*, Vol. 23 (1944), pp. 32–37.

Bibliography

Bendix, R., *Max Weber: An Intellectual Portrait* (Garden City, N.Y.: Doubleday, 1959)

Benedict, R., "Continuities and Discontinuities in Cultural Conditioning," *Psychiatry*, Vol. I (1938), pp. 161–167.

———, "Magic," *Encyclopaedia of the Social Sciences*, Vol. 10, pp. 39–44.

Berle, A. A., Jr., and Means, G. C., *The Modern Corporation and Private Property* (New York: Macmillan, 1935)

Bernard, L. L., "Crowd," *Encyclopaedia of the Social Sciences*, Vol. 4, pp. 612–613.

Bloch, H. A., and Niederhoffer, A., *The Gang: A Study in Adolescent Behavior* (New York: Philosophical Library, 1958)

Blumer, H., "Collective Behavior," in Gittler, J. B. (ed.), *Review of Sociology: Analysis of a Decade* (New York: John Wiley & Sons, 1957), pp. 127–158.

———, "Collective Behavior," in Lee, A. M. (ed.), *New Outline of the Principles of Sociology* (New York: Barnes & Noble, 1951), pp. 166–222.

———, "Social Disorganization and Individual Disorganization," *American Journal of Sociology*, Vol. 42 (1936–37), pp. 871–877.

Bogardus, E. A., *Fundamentals of Social Psychology* (third edition) (New York: D. Appleton-Century Co., 1942)

Brinton, C., "Clubs," *Encyclopaedia of the Social Sciences*, Vol. 3, pp. 573–577.

———, "The Manipulation of Economic Unrest," *The Tasks of Economic History*, Supplement VIII (1948), pp. 21–31.

Britt, S. H. (ed.), *Selected Readings in Social Psychology* (New York: Rinehart & Co., 1950)

———, *Social Psychology of Modern Life* (revised edition) (New York: Rinehart & Co., 1950)

Brown, R. W., "Mass Phenomena," in Lindzey, G. (ed.), *Handbook of Social Psychology* (Cambridge, Mass.: Addison-Wesley, 1954), Vol. II, pp. 833–876.

Burris, E. E., *Taboo, Magic, Spirits: A Study of Primitive Elements in Roman Religion* (New York: The Macmillan Company, 1931)

Cantril, H., *The Psychology of Social Movements* (New York: John Wiley & Sons, 1941)

Cash, W., *The Mind of the South* (Garden City, N.Y.: Doubleday, n.d.)

Chorus, A., "The Basic Law of Rumor," *Journal of Abnormal and Social Psychology*, Vol. 48 (1953), pp. 313–314.

Christensen, A., *Politics and Crowd-Morality: A Study in the Philosophy of Politics* (London: Williams & Norgate, 1915)

Clodd, E., *Magic in Names and in Other Things* (London: Chapman & Hall, 1920)

Coleman, J. S., *Community Conflict* (Glencoe, Ill.: The Free Press, 1957)

Conway, M., *The Crowd in Peace and War* (New York: Longmans, Green & Co., 1915)

Bibliography

Cornelius, W. J. J., *Science, Religion and Man* (London: Williams & Norgate, 1934)

Coulter, E. M., *The South During Reconstruction 1865-1877* (Baton Rouge: Louisiana State University Press, 1947)

Coulton, G. G., *The Black Death* (London: Ernest Benn, 1929)

Crankshaw, E., "Big Business in Russia," *Atlantic*, Vol. 202, No. 5 (Dec., 1958), pp. 35-41.

Cressman, L. S., "Ritual the Conserver," *American Journal of Sociology*, Vol. 35 (1929-30), pp. 564-572.

Cuber, J. F., "The Measurement and Significance of Institutional Disorganization," *American Journal of Sociology*, Vol. 44 (1938-39), pp. 408-414.

Cutten, G. B., *Three Thousand Years of Mental Healing* (New York: Charles Scribner's Sons, 1911)

Daniel, V. A., "Ritual and Stratification in Chicago Negro Churches," *American Sociological Review*, Vol. 7 (1942), pp. 352-361.

Davis, A., Gardner, B. B., and Gardner, M. R., *Deep South: A Social Anthropological Study of Caste and Class* (Chicago: University of Chicago Press, 1941)

Davis, J., and Barnes, H. E., *An Introduction to Sociology* (Boston: D. C. Heath & Company, 1927)

Davis, K., "Social and Demographic Aspects of Economic Development in India," in Kuznets, S., Moore, W. E., and Spengler, J. J. (eds.), *Economic Growth: Brazil, India, Japan* (Durham: Duke University Press, 1955)

Dawson, C. A., and Gettys, W. E., *An Introduction to Sociology* (New York: The Ronald Press, 1929)

Deutsch, M., "The Directions of Behavior: A Field-Theoretical Approach to the Understanding of Inconsistencies," in Chein, I., Deutsch, M., Hyman, H., and Jahoda, M. (eds.), "Consistency and Inconsistency in Intergroup Relations," *Journal of Social Issues*, Vol. V (1949), pp. 43-51.

Dollard, J., *Class and Caste in a Southern Community* (Garden City, N.Y.: Doubleday, 1957)

Domenach, J.-M., "Leninist Propaganda," *Public Opinion Quarterly*, Vol. 15 (1951), pp. 265-273.

Donald, H. H., "The Negro Migration of 1916-18," *The Journal of Negro History*, Vol. 6 (1921), pp. 383-498.

Doob, L. W., *Propaganda: Its Psychology and Technique* (New York: Henry Holt, 1935)

——, *Social Psychology* (New York: Henry Holt, 1952)

Douglass, H. P., *The Church in the Changing City* (New York: George H. Doran, 1927)

——, and Brunner, E. de S., *The Protestant Church as a Social Institution* (New York: Harper & Brothers, 1935)

Douglass, J. H., "The Funeral of 'Sister President,'" *Journal of Abnormal and Social Psychology*, Vol. 39 (1944), pp. 217-223. Reprinted in Newcomb, T. M., and Hartley, E. L. (eds.), *Readings in Social Psychology* (New York: Henry Holt, 1947), pp. 650-654.

Bibliography

Downs, A., *An Economic Theory of Democracy* (New York: Harper, 1957)

Durkheim, E., *The Division of Labor in Society* (Glencoe, Ill.: The Free Press, 1949)

———, *The Elementary Forms of the Religious Life* (Glencoe, Ill.: The Free Press, 1954)

———, *Suicide* (Glencoe, Ill.: The Free Press, 1951)

Eisenstadt, S. N., "Studies in Reference Group Behaviour," *Human Relations*, Vol. VII (1954), pp. 191–216.

Evans-Pritchard, E. E., "The Morphology and Function of Magic: A Comparative Study of Trobriand and Zande Ritual and Spells," *American Anthropologist*, Vol. 31 (1929), pp. 619–641.

Farago, L. (ed.), *German Psychological Warfare* (New York: G. P. Putnam's Sons, 1942)

Faris, R. E. L., *Social Disorganization* (New York: The Ronald Press, 1948)

Ferguson, C. W., *Fifty Million Brothers: A Panorama of American Lodges and Clubs* (New York: Farrar & Rinehart, 1937)

Festinger, L., et al., "A Study of Rumor: Its Origin and Spread," *Human Relations*, Vol. 1 (1948), pp. 464–486.

———, Pepitone, A., and Newcomb, T., "Some Consequences of De-Individuation in a Group," *Journal of Abnormal and Social Psychology*, Vol. 47 (1952), pp. 382–389.

Firth, R., "Money, Work and Social Change in Indo-Pacific Economic Systems," *International Social Science Bulletin*, Vol. VI (1954), pp. 400–410.

———, *Primitive Polynesian Economy* (London: George Routledge & Sons, 1939)

———, "Rumor in a Primitive Society," *Journal of Abnormal and Social Psychology*, Vol. 53 (1956), pp. 122–132.

———, "The Analysis of *Mana*: An Empirical Approach," *The Journal of the Polynesian Society*, Vol. 49 (1940), pp. 483–510.

———, "The Sociology of 'Magic' in Tikopia," *Sociologus*, Vol. 4 (1954), pp. 97–116.

Fowler, W. W., *The Roman Festivals of the Period of the Republic* (London: Macmillan, 1899)

Fox, R. C., "Training for Uncertainty," in Merton, R. K., Reader, G. C., and Kendall, P. L. (eds.), *The Student Physician* (Cambridge, Mass.: Harvard University Press, 1957), pp. 207–241.

Frazer, Sir J. G., *The New Golden Bough* (edited, and with notes and forward by Gaster, T. H. (New York: Criterion Books, 1959)

French, J. R. P., "Organized and Unorganized Groups under Fear and Frustration," in *Authority and Frustration*, University of Iowa Studies: Studies in Child Welfare, Vol. XX (Iowa City: University of Iowa Press, 1944), pp. 231–308.

———, "The Disruption and Cohesion of Groups," *Journal of Abnormal and Social Psychology*, Vol. 36 (1941), pp. 361–377.

Bibliography

Freud, S., *Group Psychology and the Analysis of the Ego*, in Strachey, J., et al. (eds.), *The Standard Edition of the Complete Psychological Works of Sigmund Freud* (London: The Hogarth Press, 1955), Vol. XVIII, pp. 65–143.

Fülöp-Miller, R., *Leaders, Dreamers, and Rebels* (translated by Eden and Cedar Paul) (New York: The Viking Press, 1935)

Galbraith, J. K., *The Affluent Society* (Boston: Houghton Mifflin, 1958)

Gardner, B. B., and Moore, D. G., *Human Relations in Industry* (Homewood, Ill.: R. D. Irwin, 1955)

Gault, R. H., *Social Psychology* (New York: Henry Holt, 1923)

Gayer, A. D., Rostow, W. W., and Schwartz, A. J., *The Growth and Fluctuation of the British Economy 1790–1850* (Oxford: at the Clarendon Press, 1953)

Gerth, H., and Mills, C. W., *Character and Social Structure: The Psychology of Social Institutions* (New York: Harcourt, Brace & Co., 1953)

Ginsberg, M., "Social Change," *British Journal of Sociology*, Vol. 9 (1958), pp. 205–229.

Glick, C. E., "Collective Behavior in Race Relations," *American Sociological Review*, Vol. 13 (1948), pp. 287–294.

Gluckman, M., *Rituals of Rebellion in South-east Africa* (Manchester: Manchester University Press, 1954)

Goffman, E., "Embarrassment and Social Organization," *American Journal of Sociology*, Vol. 62 (1956–57), pp. 264–271.

Goode, W. J., "A Theory of Role Strain," *American Sociological Review*, Vol. 25 (1960), pp. 483–496.

Gowen, B. S., "Some Aspects of Pestilences and other Epidemics," *American Journal of Psychology*, Vol. 18 (1907), pp. 1–60.

Gregg, R. B., *Gandhism and Socialism: A Study and Comparison* (Triplicane, Madras: S. Ganesan, 1931)

Grosser, D., Polansky, N., and Lippitt, R., "A Laboratory Study of Behavioral Contagion," *Human Relations*, Vol. 4 (1951), pp. 115–142.

Haddon, A. C., *Magic and Fetishism* (London: Archibald Constable & Co., 1906)

Halevy, E., *A History of the English People in the Nineteenth Century* (London: Ernest Benn, 1949–51)

Hallgren, M. A., *Seeds of Revolt* (New York: Alfred A. Knopf, 1933)

Hallowell, A. I., *The Role of Conjuring in Saulteaux Society* (Philadelphia: University of Pennsylvania Press, 1942)

Handlin, O., *The Uprooted: The Epic Story of the Great Migrations that made the American People* (New York: Grosset & Dunlap, no date—copyright 1951)

Handman, M., "The Bureaucratic Culture Pattern and Political Revolutions," *American Journal of Sociology*, Vol. 39 (1933), pp. 301–313.

Hardy, C. O., *Risk and Risk-bearing* (Chicago: University of Chicago Press, 1923)

Haynes, J., "Risk as an Economic Factor," *Quarterly Journal of Economics*, Vol. 9 (1895), pp. 409–441.

Bibliography

Hecker, J. F. K., *The Black Death in the Fourteenth Century* (translated by Babington, B. G.) (London: A. Schloss, 1833)

———, *The Dancing Mania of the Middle Ages* (translated by Babington, B. G.) (New York: J. Fitzgerald, 1885)

Hertzler, J. O., *Social Institutions* (Lincoln: University of Nebraska Press, 1946)

Hobsbawm, E. J., "Economic Fluctuations and Some Social Movements since 1800," *Economic History Review*, Second Series, Vol. V (1952), pp. 1–25.

Hoffer, E., *The True Believer* (New York: New American Library, 1958)

Hollingworth, H. L., *The Psychology of the Audience* (New York: American Book Company, 1935)

Homans, G. C., *The Human Group* (New York: Harcourt, Brace & Co., 1950)

Hurry, J. B., *Vicious Circles in Sociology and their Treatment* (London: J. & A. Churchill, 1915)

Inkeles, A., and Rossi, P. H., "National Comparisons of Occupational Prestige," *American Journal of Sociology*, Vol. 61 (1956), pp. 329–339.

Jacobson, D. J., *The Affairs of Dame Rumor* (New York: Rinehart, 1948)

Jahoda, M., "The Problem," in Chein, I., Deutsch, M., Hyman, H., and Jahoda, M. (eds.), "Consistency and Inconsistency in Intergroup Relations," *Journal of Social Issues*, Vol. V (1949), pp. 4–11.

Jastrow, J., "Conversion, Religious," *Encyclopaedia of the Social Sciences*, Vol. 4, pp. 353–355.

Katona, G., *Psychological Analysis of Economic Behavior* (New York: McGraw-Hill, 1951)

Katz, D., "The Psychology of the Crowd," in Guilford, J. P. (ed.), *Fields of Psychology* (New York: D. Van Nostrand Company, 1940), pp. 145–162.

———, and Schanck, R. L., *Social Psychology* (New York: John Wiley & Sons, 1938)

Katz, E., and Lazarsfeld, P. F., *Personal Influence: The Part Played by People in the Flow of Mass Communications* (Glencoe, Ill.: The Free Press, 1955)

Kerr, C., Dunlop, J. T., Harbison, F. H., and Myers, C. A., *Industrialism and Industrial Man* (Cambridge, Mass.: Harvard University Press, 1960)

Knapp, R. H., "A Psychology of Rumor," *Public Opinion Quarterly*, Vol. 8 (1944), pp. 22–37.

Knight, F. H., "Risk," *Encyclopaedia of the Social Sciences*, Vol. 13, pp. 392–394.

———, *Risk, Uncertainty and Profit* (Boston: Houghton Mifflin, 1921)

Kornhauser, W., *The Politics of Mass Society* (Glencoe, Ill.: The Free Press, 1959)

Kriesberg, M., "Cross-Pressures and Attitudes: A Study of Conflicting Propaganda on Opinions Regarding American-Soviet Relations," *Public Opinion Quarterly*, Vol. 13 (1949), pp. 5–16.

Bibliography

Kroeber, A. L., *Anthropology* (New York: Harcourt, Brace & Co., 1948)

——, *Configurations of Culture Growth* (Berkeley and Los Angeles: University of California Press, 1944)

Lang, K., and Lang, G. E., *Collective Dynamics* (New York: Thomas Y. Crowell, 1961)

LaPiere, R. T., *Collective Behavior* (New York: McGraw-Hill, 1938)

——, and Farnsworth, P. R., *Social Psychology* (New York: McGraw-Hill, 1936)

Larsen, O. N., "Rumors in a Disaster," *Journal of Communication*, Vol. IV (1954), pp. 111–123.

Lasswell, H. D., "Agitation," *Encyclopaedia of the Social Sciences*, Vol. 1, pp. 487–488.

——, and Blumenstock, D., *World Revolutionary Propaganda: A Chicago Study* (New York: Alfred A. Knopf, 1939)

Lazarsfeld, P. F., Berelson, B., and Gaudet, H., *The People's Choice: How the Voter Makes up his Mind in a Presidential Campaign* (New York: Columbia University Press, 1952)

Le Bon, G., *The Crowd* (London: Ernest Benn, 1952)

Lee, A. M., and Lee, E. B., *The Fine Art of Propaganda* (New York: Harcourt, Brace & Co., 1939)

Leighton, A. H., *Human Relations in a Changing World* (New York: E. P. Dutton, 1949)

Lewis, W. A., *Economic Survey 1919–1939* (London: George Allen & Unwin, 1949)

Leybourne, G. C., "Urban Adjustments of Migrants from the Southern Appalachian Plateaus," *Social Forces*, Vol. 16 (1937–38), pp. 238–246.

Lindesmith, A. R., and Strauss, A. L., *Social Psychology* (revised edition) (New York: The Dryden Press, 1957)

Lipset, S. M., *Political Man: The Social Bases of Politics* (Garden City, N.Y.: Doubleday, 1960)

——, and Bendix, R., *Social Mobility in Industrial Society* (Los Angeles and Berkeley: University of California Press, 1959)

——, Lazarsfeld, P. F., Barton, A. H., and Linz, J., "The Psychology of Voting: An Analysis of Political Behavior," in Lindzey, G. (ed.), *Handbook of Social Psychology* (Cambridge, Mass.: Addison-Wesley, 1954), Vol. II, pp. 1124–1175.

Lofton, W. H., "Northern Labor and the Negro During the Civil War," *The Journal of Negro History*, Vol. 34 (1949), pp. 251–273.

Lohman, J. D., and Reitzes, D. C., "Note on Race Relations in Mass Society," *American Journal of Sociology*, Vol. 58 (1952–53), pp. 240–246.

Loomis, C. G., *White Magic: An Introduction to the Folklore of Christian Legend* (Cambridge, Mass.: The Medieval Academy of America, 1948)

MacCurdy, J. T., *The Structure of Morale* (Cambridge: University Press, 1943)

McDougall, W., *Introduction to Social Psychology* (London: Methuen, 1908)

Bibliography

McDougall, W., *The Group Mind* (New York: G. P. Putnam's Sons, 1920)

MacIver, R. M., *Social Causation* (Boston: Ginn & Co., 1942)

Malinowski, B., *Coral Gardens and Their Magic* (New York: American Book Company, 1935)

——, *Magic, Science and Religion and Other Essays* (Garden City, N.Y.: Doubleday, 1955)

——, *The Dynamics of Culture Change: An Inquiry into Race Relations in Africa* (New Haven: Yale University Press, 1945)

Marett, R. H., "Mana," *Encyclopaedia of Religion and Ethics*, Vol. VIII, pp. 375–380.

Marshall, R., "Precipitation and Presidents," *The Nation*, Vol. 124 (1927), pp. 315–316.

Martin, E. D., *The Behavior of Crowds* (New York: Harper & Brothers, 1920)

——, *The Conflict of the Individual and the Mass in the Modern World* (New York: Henry Holt, 1932)

——, "Some Mechanisms which Distinguish the Crowd from Other Forms of Social Behavior," *Journal of Abnormal and Social Psychology*, Vol. 18 (1923), pp. 187–203.

Mauss, M., *The Gift* (translated by Ian Cunnison) (Glencoe, Ill.: The Free Press, 1954)

Maxwell, W. N., *A Psychological Retrospect of the Great War* (London: George Allen & Unwin, 1923)

May, R., *The Meaning of Anxiety* (New York: The Ronald Press, 1950)

Mead, M., *Male and Female* (New York: William Morrow & Co., 1949)

Meadows, P., "Movements of Social Withdrawal," *Sociology and Social Research*, Vol. 29 (1944–45), pp. 46–50.

Meerloo, A. M., *Aftermath of Peace* (New York: International Universities Press, 1946)

——, *Delusion and Mass-delusion* (New York: Nervous and Mental Disease Monographs, 1949)

Merton, R. K., *Social Theory and Social Structure* (revised and enlarged edition) (Glencoe, Ill.: The Free Press, 1957)

——, "The Role Set: Problems in Sociological Theory," *British Journal of Sociology*, Vol. 8 (1957), pp. 106–120.

——, Gray, A. P., Hockey, B., and Selvin, H. C. (eds.), *Reader in Bureaucracy* (Glencoe, Ill.: The Free Press, 1952)

Meyer, J. R., and Conrad, A. H., "Economic Theory, Statistical Inference, and Economic History," *Journal of Economic History*, Vol. 17 (1957) pp. 524–544.

Mintz, A., "The Failure of a Propaganda Campaign Attempting to Influence the Behavior of Consumers in the National Interest by Predominantly Selfish Appeals," *Journal of Social Psychology*, Vol. 38 (1953), pp. 49–62.

Moore, W. E., and Feldman, A. S., *Labor Commitment and Social Change in Developing Areas* (New York: Social Science Research Council, 1960)

Bibliography

Munro, D. G., *The Latin American Republics: A History* (Third Edition) (New York: Appleton-Century-Crofts, 1960)

Munthe, A., *The Story of San Michele* (London: John Murray, 1930)

Myrdall, G., *An American Dilemma* (New York: Harper & Brothers, 1944)

Newcomb, T. M., *Social Psychology* (New York: The Dryden Press, 1950)

Odegard, P., *The American Public Mind* (New York: Columbia University Press, 1930)

Odier, C., *Anxiety and Magic Thinking* (translated by Marie-Louise Schoelly and Mary Jane Sherfey) (New York: International Universities Press, 1956)

Overton, J. H., *The Evangelical Revival in the Eighteenth Century* (London: Longmans, Green, & Co., 1907)

Park, R. E., *Society: Collective Behavior, News and Opinion, Sociology and Modern Society* (Glencoe, Ill.: The Free Press, 1955)

——, and Burgess, E. W., *Introduction to the Science of Sociology* (Chicago: University of Chicago Press, 1924)

Parsons, T., *Essays in Sociological Theory* (Revised Edition) (Glencoe, Ill.: The Free Press, 1954)

——, *Structure and Process in Modern Societies* (Glencoe, Ill.: The Free Press, 1960)

——, *The Social System* (Glencoe, Ill.: The Free Press, 1951)

——, " 'Voting' and the Equilibrium of the American Political System," in Burdick, E., and Brodbeck, A., *American Voting Behavior* (Glencoe, Ill.: The Free Press, 1959), pp. 80–120.

——, Bales, R. F., et al., *Family, Socialization and Interaction Process* (Glencoe, Ill.: The Free Press, 1955)

——, Bales, R. F., and Shils, E. A., *Working Papers in the Theory of Action* (Glencoe, Ill.: The Free Press, 1953)

——, and Shils, E. A., *Toward a General Theory of Action* (Cambridge, Mass.: Harvard University Press, 1951)

——, and Smelser, N. J., *Economy and Society* (Glencoe, Ill.: The Free Press, 1956)

Penrose, L. S., *On the Objective Study of Crowd Behaviour* (London: H. K. Lewis & Co., 1952)

Persons, S., "Christian Communitarianism in America," in Egbert, D. and Persons (eds.), *Socialism and American Life* (Princeton: Princeton University Press, 1952)

Peterson, W., and Gist, N., "Rumor and Public Opinion," *American Journal of Sociology*, Vol. 57 (1951–52), pp. 159–167.

Polansky, N., Lippitt, R., and Redl, F., "An Investigation of Behavioral Contagion in Groups," *Human Relations*, Vol. 3 (1950), pp. 319–348.

Polanyi, K., Arensberg, C. M., and Pearson, H. W., (eds.), *Trade and Market in the Early Empires* (Glencoe, Ill.: The Free Press and the Falcon's Wing Press, 1957)

Bibliography

Prasad, J., "The Psychology of Rumour: A Study Relating to the Great Indian Earthquake of 1934," *British Journal of Psychology*, Vol. 26 (1935), pp. 1–15.

Pratt, J. B., *The Religious Consciousness: A Psychological Study* (New York: Macmillan, 1920)

Reuter, E. B., and Hart, C. W., *Introduction to Sociology* (New York: McGraw-Hill, 1933)

Reynolds, L. G., *Labor Economics and Labor Relations* (second edition) (New York: Prentice-Hall, 1954)

Roethlisberger, F. J., "The Foreman: Master and Victim of Double Talk," *Harvard Business Review*, Vol. 23 (1945), pp. 282–298.

———, and Dickson, W. F., *Management and the Worker* (Cambridge, Mass.: Harvard University Press, 1953)

Rose, A. M., "Rumor in the Stock Market," *Public Opinion Quarterly*, Vol. 15 (1951), pp. 461–486.

Ross, E. A., *Social Psychology* (New York: Macmillan, 1916)

Rostow, W. W., *British Economy of the Nineteenth Century* (Oxford: at the Clarendon Press, 1949)

Roth, J. A., "Ritual and Magic in the Control of Contagion," *American Sociological Review*, Vol. 22 (1957), pp. 310–314.

Roy, D., "Efficiency and 'The Fix': Informal Intergroup Relations in a Piecework Machine Shop," *American Journal of Sociology*, Vol. 60 1954–55), pp. 255–266.

Rydberg, V., *The Magic of the Middle Ages* (translated by Edgren, A. H.) (New York: Henry Holt, 1879)

Samuelson, P. A., *Economics: An Introductory Analysis* (fourth edition) (New York: McGraw-Hill, 1958)

Schlesinger, A. M., "Tides of American Politics," *Yale Review*, Vol. 29 (Winter, 1940), pp. 217–230.

Schneider, L., and Dornbush, S. M., *Popular Religion: Inspirational Books in America* (Chicago: University of Chicago Press, 1958)

Scott, W. D., *The Psychology of Public Speaking* (New York: Noble and Noble, 1926)

Seldes, G., *The Stammering Century* (New York: The John Day Company, 1928)

Selye, H., *The Story of the Adaptation Syndrome* (Montreal: Acta, Inc., 1952)

Selznick, P., *Leadership in Administration: A Sociological Interpretation* (Evanston, Ill.: Row, Peterson & Co., 1957)

Sherif, M., *An Outline of Social Psychology* (New York: Harper & Brothers, 1948)

———, "The Concept of Reference Groups in Human Relations," in Sherif, M., and Wilson, M. O. (eds.), *Group Relations at the Crossroads* (New York: Harper & Brothers, 1953), pp. 203–231.

———, and Harvey, O. J., "A Study in Ego Functioning: Elimination of Stable Anchorages in Individual and Group Situations," *Sociometry*, Vol. 15 (1952), pp. 272–305.

Bibliography

Shibutani, T., "The Circulation of Rumors as a Form of Collective Behavior," Unpublished Ph.D. Dissertation, University of Chicago, 1948.

Shils, E. A., and Janowitz, M., "Cohesion and Disintegration in the Wehrmacht," in Lerner, D. (ed.), *Propaganda in War and Crisis* (New York: George W. Stewart, 1951)

———, and Young, M., "The Meaning of the Coronation," *Sociological Review*, New Series, Vol. 1 (1953), pp. 63-81.

Sidis, B., *The Psychology of Suggestion* (New York: D. Appleton and Company, 1916)

Smelser, N., J., "A Comparative View of Exchange Systems," *Economic Development and Cultural Change*, Vol. VII (1959), pp. 173-182.

———, *Social Change in the Industrial Revolution* (Chicago: University of Chicago Press, 1959)

Sorel, G., *Reflections on Violence* (translated by Hulme, T. E., and Roth, J) (Glencoe, Ill.: The Free Press, 1950)

Sorokin, P. A., *Social and Cultural Dynamics* (New York: American Book Company, 1937)

Speier, H., "Historical Development of Public Opinion," *American Journal of Sociology*, Vol. 55 (1949-50), pp. 376-388.

Spencer, H., *The Principles of Sociology* (New York: D. Appleton and Company, 1897), Vol. II-1.

Stanner, W. E. H., *The South Seas in Transition* (Sydney: Australasian Publishing Company, 1953)

Storms, G., *Anglo-Saxon Magic* (The Hague: Martinus Nijhoff, 1948)

Stouffer, S. A., et al., *Studies in Social Psychology in World War II. Volume II: The American Soldier: Combat and Its Aftermath* (Princeton: Princeton University Press, 1949)

Strauss, A., "Research in Collective Behavior: Neglect and Need," *American Sociological Review*, Vol. 12 (1947), pp. 352-354.

Strecker, E. A., *Beyond the Clinical Frontiers* (New York: W. W. Norton, 1940)

Strodtbeck, F. L., "The Family as a Three-Person Group," *American Sociological Review*, Vol. 19 (1954), pp. 23-29.

Stryker, P., "How to Fire Executives," in Editors of Fortune, *The Executive Life* (Garden City, N.Y.: Doubleday, 1956), pp. 179-194.

Swanson, G. E., "Agitation in Face-to-Face Contacts: A Study of the Personalities of Orators," *Public Opinion Quarterly*, Vol. 21 (1957), pp. 288-294.

———, "A Preliminary Laboratory Study of the Acting Crowd," *American Sociological Review*, Vol. 18 (1953), pp. 522-533.

———, *The Birth of the Gods: The Origin of Primitive Beliefs* (Ann Arbor: University of Michigan Press, 1960)

———, "Social Change in the Urban Society," in Freedman, R., Hawley, A. H., Landecker, W. S., and Miner, H. M., *Principles of Sociology* (New York: Henry Holt, 1952), pp. 554-584.

Symes, L., *Rebel America* (New York: Harper & Brothers, 1934)

Bibliography

Tayler, J. L., *Social Life and the Crowd* (Boston: Small, Maynard & Co., 1907)

Thomas, W. I., *Primitive Behavior: An Introduction to the Social Sciences* (New York: McGraw-Hill, 1937)

Thompson, J. W., "The Aftermath of the Black Death and the Aftermath of the Great War," *American Journal of Sociology*, Vol. 26 (1920–21), pp. 565–572.

Tinker, F. T., and Tinker, E. L., *Old New Orleans: Mardi Gras Masks* (New York: D. Appleton, 1931)

Toch, H. H., "Crisis Situations and Ideological Revaluation," *Public Opinion Quarterly*, Vol. 19 (1955), pp. 53–67.

Trotter, W., *Instincts of the Herd in Peace and War* (London: T. Fisher Unwin, 1922)

Turner, M. E., and Stevens, C. D., "The Regression Analysis of Causal Paths," *Biometrics*, Vol. 15 (1959), pp. 236–258.

Turner, R. H., "Value-Conflict in Social Disorganization," *Sociology and Social Research*, Vol. 38 (1953–54), pp. 301–308.

——, and Killian, L. M., *Collective Behavior* (Englewood Cliffs, N. J.: Prentice-Hall, 1957)

Veblen, T., *The Theory of the Leisure Class* (New York: The Modern Library, 1934)

Vogel, E., "The Marital Relationship of Parents and the Emotionally Disturbed Child," Ph.D. Dissertation, Harvard University, 1958.

Vogt, E. Z., and Hyman, R., *Water Witching U.S.A.* (Chicago: University of Chicago Press, 1959)

von Wiese, L., *Systematic Sociology: On the Basis of* Beziehungslehre *and* Gebildelehre (adapted and amplified by Howard Becker) (New York: John Wiley & Sons, 1932)

Waller, W., *The Family: A Dynamic Interpretation* (revised by Reuben Hill) (New York: The Dryden Press, 1951)

Watson, W., *Tribal Cohesion in a Money Economy: A Study of the Mambwe People of Northern Rhodesia* (Manchester: Manchester University Press, 1958)

Weber, M., *The Methodology of the Social Sciences* (translated and edited by Shils, E. A. and Finch, H. A.) (Glencoe, Ill.: The Free Press, 1949)

——, *The Theory of Social and Economic Organization* (translated by Parsons, T., and Henderson, A. M.) (Glencoe, Ill.: The Free Press, 1947)

Webster, H., *Magic: A Sociological Study* (Stanford: Stanford University Press, 1948)

Whiteman, L., and Lewis, S. L., *Glory Roads: The Psychological State of California* (New York: Thomas Y. Crowell, 1936)

Whyte, W. F., and Gardner, B. B., "The Position and Problems of the Foreman," *Applied Anthropology*, Vol. IV (1945), pp. 17–28.

Wilson, G., and Wilson, M., *The Analysis of Social Change: Based on Observations in Central Africa* (Cambridge: at the University Press, 1954)

Bibliography

Wirth, L., "Ideological Aspects of Social Disorganization," *American Sociological Review*, Vol. 5 (1940), pp. 472–482.

———, "The Problem of Minority Groups," in Linton, R. (ed.), *The Science of Man in the World Crisis* (New York: Columbia University Press, 1952), pp. 346–372.

Woodson, C. G., *The Negro in Our History* (Washington, D.C.: The Associated Publishers, 1922)

Wray, D. E., "Marginal Men of Industry: The Foremen," *American Journal of Sociology*, Vol. 54 (1948–49), pp. 298–301.

Young, K., *Social Psychology* (New York: F. S. Crofts & Co., 1945)

———, *Source Book for Social Psychology* (New York: Alfred A. Knopf, 1927)

Zimmer, B. G., "Participation of Migrants in Urban Structures," *American Sociological Review*, Vol. 20 (1955), pp. 218–224.

Works Relating to the Panic

Argent, A., "Characteristics of Panic Behavior," in Daughtery, W. E., in collaboration with Janowitz, M., *A Psychological Warfare Casebook*, published for Operations Research Office (Baltimore: The Johns Hopkins Press, 1958), pp. 666–668.

Aveling, F., "Notes on the Emotion of Fear as Observed in Conditions of Warfare," *British Journal of Psychology*, Vol. 20 (1929), pp. 137–144.

Bagehot, W., *Lombard Street: A Description of the Money Market* (London: John Murray, 1931)

Bernert, E. H., and Iklé, F. C., "Evacuation and the Cohesion of Urban Groups," *American Journal of Sociology*, Vol. 58 (1952), pp. 133–138.

Boring, E., *Psychology for the Armed Forces* (Washington, D.C., The Infantry Journal, 1945)

Blum, R. H., and Klass, B., *A Study of Public Response to Disaster Warnings* (Menlo Park, Calif.: Stanford Research Institute, 1956)

Brucker, H., "Press Communication in Relation to Morale and Panic," in *Panic and Morale*, conference transactions of the New York Academy of Medicine and the Josiah Macy Jr. Foundation (New York: International Universities Press, 1958), pp. 67–73.

Bull, N., "The Dual Character of Fear," *Journal of Psychology*, Vol. V (1938), pp. 209–218.

Cantril, H., with the assistance of Gaudet, H., and Herzog, H., *The Invasion from Mars* (Princeton: Princeton University Press, 1947)

Carr, L. J., "Disaster and the Sequence-Pattern Concept of Social Change," *American Journal of Sociology*, Vol. 38 (1932–33), pp. 207–218.

Clifford, R. A., *The Rio Grande Flood: A Comparative Study of Border Communities in Disaster*. Disaster Study Number 7 of the Committee on Disaster Studies of the Division of Anthropology and Psychology (Washington, D.C.: National Academy of Science—National Research Council, 1956)

Bibliography

Collman, C. A., *Our Mysterious Panics 1830-1930* (New York: William & Company, 1931)

Conant, C. A., *A History of Modern Banks of Issue* (New York: G. P. Putnam's Sons, 1915)

Danzig, E. R., Thayer, P. W., and Galanter, L. R., *The Effects of a Threatening Rumor on a Disaster Stricken Community*. Disaster Study Number 10 of the Division of Anthropology and Psychology of the Committee on Disaster Studies (Washington, D.C.: National Academy of Science—National Research Council, 1958)

Demerath, N. J., "Some General Propositions: An Interpretative Summary," *Human Organization*, Vol. 16 (1957), pp. 28-29.

Denny-Brown, D., "Effects of Modern Warfare on Civil Population," *Journal of Laboratory and Clinical Medicine*, Vol. 28 (1942-43), pp. 641-645.

Ellemers, J. E., *General Conclusions. Studies in Holland Flood Disaster Volume IV* (Amsterdam: Instituut voor Sociaal Onderzoek van het Nederlandse Volk and Washington, D.C.: Committee on Disaster Studies of the National Academy of Sciences—National Research Council, 1955)

———, and Henny M. in 't Veld-Langeveld, "A Study of the Destruction of a Community," in *Community Studies. Studies in Holland Flood Disaster 1953 Volume III* (Amsterdam: Instituut voor Sociaal Onderzoek van het Nederlandse Volk and Washington, D.C.: Committee on Disaster Studies of the National Academy of Sciences—National Research Council, 1955), pp. 73-156.

Etlinge, L., *Psychology of War* (Fort Leavenworth: Army Service Schools Press, 1917)

Fisher, I., *Booms and Depressions: Some First Principles* (New York: Adelphi Company, 1932)

Foreman, P. B., "Panic Theory," *Sociology and Social Research*, Vol. 37 (1952-53), pp. 295-304.

Form, W. H., and Nosow, S., with Stone, G. P., and Westie, C. M., *Community in Disaster* (New York: Harper & Brothers, 1958)

———, and Loomis, C. P., et al., "The Persistence and Emergence of Social and Cultural Systems in Disasters," *American Sociological Review*, Vol. 21 (1956), pp. 180-185.

Foy, E., and Harlow, A. F., *Clowning Through Life* (New York: E. P. Dutton, 1928)

Fritz, C. E., "Disasters Compared in Six American Communities," *Human Organization*, Vol. 16 (1957), pp. 6-9.

———, and Marks, E. S., "The NORC Studies of Human Behavior in Disaster," *Journal of Social Issues*, Vol. 10 (1954), pp. 12-25.

———, and Mathewson, J. H., *Convergence Behavior in Disasters: A Problem in Social Control*. Disaster Study Number 9 of the Division of Anthropology and Psychology of the Committee on Disaster Studies. (Washington, D.C.: National Academy of Science—National Research Council, 1957)

Bibliography

Fritz, C. E., and Williams, H. B., "The Human Being in Disasters: A Research Perspective," *The Annals of the American Academy of Political and Social Science*, Vol. 309 (Jan., 1957), pp. 42–51.

Galbraith, J. K., *The Great Crash: 1929* (Boston: Houghton Mifflin, 1955)

Gilbert, G. M., "Social Causes Contributing to Panic," in *Panic and Morale*, conference transactions of the New York Academy of Medicine and the Josiah Macy Jr. Foundation (New York: International Universities Press, 1958), pp. 152–161.

Grinker, R. J., and Spiegel, J. P., *Men Under Stress* (Philadelphia: Blakiston, 1945)

Hirshleifer, J., "Some Thoughts on the Social Structure after a Bombing Disaster," *World Politics*, Vol. VIII (1956), pp. 206–227.

Hirst, F. W., *The Six Panics and Other Essays* (London: Methuen, 1913)

Hocking, W. E., *Morale and Its Enemies* (New Haven: Yale University Press, 1918)

Homans, G. C., "Anxiety and Ritual," *American Anthropologist*, Vol. 43 (1941), pp. 164–172. Reprinted in Lessa, W. A., and Vogt, E. Z. (eds.), *Reader in Comparative Religion* (Evanston, Ill.: Row, Peterson and Co., 1958), pp. 112–118.

Hudson, B. B., "Anxiety in Response to the Unfamiliar," *Journal of Social Issues*, Vol. 10 (1954), pp. 53–60.

Iklé, F. C., and Kincaid, H. V., *Social Aspects of Wartime Evacuation of American Cities*. Disaster Study Number 4 of the Committee on Disaster Studies of the Division of Anthropology and Psychology (Washington, D.C.: National Academy of Science—National Research Council, 1956)

Janis, I. L., *Air War and Emotional Distress* (New York: McGraw-Hill, 1951)

———, "Problems of Theory in the Analysis of Stress Behavior," *Journal of Social Issues*, Vol. 10 (1954), pp. 12–25.

Johnson, D. M., "The 'Phantom Anesthetist' of Mattoon: A Field Study of Mass Hysteria," *Journal of Abnormal and Social Psychology*, Vol. 40 (1945), pp. 175–186. Reprinted in Newcomb, T., and Hartley, E. L. (eds.), *Readings in Social Psychology* (New York: Henry Holt, 1947), pp. 639–650.

Jones, E. D., *Economic Crises* (New York: Macmillan, 1900)

Kardiner, A., "The Traumatic Neuroses of War," *Psychosomatic Medicine Monograph II-III* (Washington, D.C.: Committee on Problems of Neurotic Behavior, Division of Anthropology and Psychology, National Research Council, 1941)

Kartman, B., and Brown, L. (eds.), *Disaster!* (New York: Pellegrini & Cudahy, 1948)

Killian, L. M., *A Study of Response to the Houston, Texas, Fireworks Explosion*. Disaster Study Number 2 of the Committee on Disaster Studies of the Division of Anthropology and Psychology (Washington, D.C.: National Academy of Science—National Research Council, 1956)

———, "Some Accomplishments and Some Needs in Disaster Study," *Journal of Social Issues*, Vol. 10 (1954), pp. 66–72.

Bibliography

Killian, L. M., "The Significance of Multiple-Group Membership in Disaster," *American Journal of Sociology*, Vol. 57 (1951–52), pp. 309–314.

Kilpatrick, F. P., "Problems of Perception in Extreme Situations," *Human Organization*, Vol. 16 (1957), pp. 20–22.

Kris, E., "Danger and Morale," *American Journal of Orthopsychiatry*, Vol. 14 (1944), pp. 147–155.

Lanham, C. T., "Panic," in Greene, J. I. (ed.), *The Infantry Journal Reader* (Garden City, N.Y.: Doubleday, Doran & Co., 1943), pp. 274–289.

Linebarger, P. M. A., *Psychological Warfare* (second edition) (Washington, D.C.: Combat Forces Press, 1954)

Loewenberg, R. D., "Rumors of Mass Poisoning in Times of Crisis," *Journal of Criminal Psychopathology*, Vol. V (1943), pp. 131–142.

McGrane, R. C., *The Panic of 1837: Some Financial Problems of the Jacksonian Era* (Chicago: University of Chicago Press, 1924)

Marshall, S. L. A., *Men Against Fire* (Washington, D.C.: The Infantry Journal and New York: William Morrow & Company, 1947)

Medalia, N. Z., and Larsen, O. N., "Diffusion and Belief in a Collective Delusion: The Seattle Windshield Pitting Epidemic," *American Sociological Review*, Vol. 23 (1958), pp. 180–186.

Meerloo, J. A. M., *Patterns of Panic* (New York: International Universities Press, 1950)

——, "Peoples' Reaction to Danger," in *Panic and Morale*, conference transactions of the New York Academy of Medicine and the Josiah Macy Jr. Foundation (New York: International Universities Press, 1958), pp. 174–178.

Menzel, D. H., *Flying Saucers* (Cambridge, Mass.: Harvard University Press, 1953)

Michael, D. N., "Civilian Behavior under Atomic Bombardment," *Bulletin of the Atomic Scientists*, Vol. XI (1955), pp. 173–177.

Mintz, A., "Non-Adaptive Group Behavior," *Journal of Abnormal and Social Psychology*, Vol. 46 (1951), pp. 150–159.

Moore, H. E., *Tornadoes over Texas* (Austin: University of Texas Press, 1958)

Moscow, A., *Collision Course: The Andrea Doria and The Stockholm* (New York: G. P. Putnam's Sons, 1959)

National Research Council, "Fear: Ally or Traitor," in Greene, J. I. (ed.), *The Infantry Journal Reader* (Garden City, N.Y.: Doubleday, Doran & Co., 1943), pp. 266–272.

Norman, E. H., "Mass Hysteria in Japan," *Far Eastern Survey*, Vol. 14 (1945), pp. 65–70.

Quarantelli, E. L., "The Nature and Conditions of Panic," *American Journal of Sociology*, Vol. 60 (1954–55), pp. 267–275.

Pennington, L. A., Hough, R. B., Jr., and Case, H. W., *The Psychology of Military Leadership* (New York: Prentice-Hall, Inc., 1943)

Pepitone, A., Diggory, J. C., and Wallace, W. H., "Some Reactions to a Hypothetical Disaster," *Journal of Abnormal and Social Psychology*, Vol. 51 (1955), pp. 706–708.

Bibliography

Perkins, D. W., *Wall Street Panics 1813-1930* (Waterville, N.Y.: D. W. Perkins, 1931)

Prince, S. H., *Catastrophe and Social Change* (New York: Columbia University Studies in History, Economics, and Public Law, 1920)

Rickman, J., "Panic and Air-raid Precautions," *The Lancet*, Vol. 234 (1938), pp. 1291-1294.

Robinson, D., *The Face of Disaster* (Garden City, N.Y.: Doubleday, 1959)

Ruppelt, E. J., *The Report on Unidentified Flying Objects* (Garden City, N.Y.: Doubleday, 1956)

Ryner, I., "On the Crises of 1837, 1847, and 1857, in England, France, and the United States," *University Studies* (published by the University of Nebraska), Vol. V (1905), pp. 143-189.

Schmideberg, W., "The Treatment of Panic in Casualty Area and Clearing Station," *Life and Letters Today*, Vol. 23 (1939), pp. 162-169.

Schneider, D. M., "Typhoons on Yap," *Human Organization*, Vol. 16 (1957), pp. 10-15.

Schuler, E. A., and Parenton, V. J., "A Recent Epidemic of Hysteria in a Louisiana High School," *Journal of Social Psychology*, Vol. 17 (1943), pp. 221-235.

Schwartz, S., and Winograd, B., "Preparation of Soldiers for Atomic Maneuvers," *Journal of Social Issues*, Vol. 10 (1954), pp. 42-52.

Spiegel, J. P., "The English Flood of 1953," *Human Organization*, Vol. 16 (1957), pp. 3-5.

Spiegel, H. X., "Psychiatric Observations in the Tunisian Campaign," *American Journal of Orthopsychiatry*, Vol. 14 (1944), pp. 381-385.

Strauss, A. L., "The Literature on Panic," *Journal of Abnormal and Social Psychology*, Vol. 39 (1944), pp. 317-328.

Titmuss, R. M., *Problems of Social Policy* (London: His Majesty's Stationery Office and Longmans, Green & Co., 1950)

Torrance, E. P., "The Behavior of Small Groups under the Stress Conditions of 'Survival,'" *American Sociological Review*, Vol. 19 (1954), pp. 751-755.

Tyhurst, J. S., "Individual Reactions to Community Disaster: The Natural History of Psychiatric Phenomena," *American Journal of Psychiatry*, Vol. 107, No. 10 (1951), pp. 764-769.

United States Strategic Bombing Survey, *The Effects of Strategic Bombing on German Morale*, Vol. 1 (Washington, D.C.: United States Government Printing Office, 1947)

van Doorn-Janssen, M. Jeanne, "A Study of Social Disorganization in a Community," in *Community Studies. Studies in Holland Flood Disaster 1953 Volume III* (Amsterdam: Instituut voor Sociaal Onderzoek van het Nederlandse Volk, and Washington, D.C.: Committee on Disaster Studies of the National Academy of Sciences —National Research Council, 1955), pp. 157-213.

van Langenhove, F., *The Growth of a Legend* (New York: G. P. Putnam's Sons, 1916)

Bibliography

Vaught, E., "The Release and Heightening of Individual Reactions in Crowds," *Journal of Abnormal and Social Psychology*, Vol. 22 (1928), pp. 404–405.

Wallace, A. F. C., *Human Behavior in Extreme Situations: A Survey of the Literature and Suggestions for Further Research*. Disaster Study Number 1 of the Committee on Disaster Studies of the Division of Anthropology and Psychology (Washington, D.C.: National Academy of Science—National Research Council, 1956)

——, "Mazeway Disintegration: The Individual's Perception of Socio-Cultural Disorganization," *Human Organization*, Vol. 16 (1957), pp. 23–27.

Williams, H. B., "Some Functions of Communication in Crisis Behavior," *Human Organization*, Vol. 16 (1957), pp. 15–19.

Wolfenstein, M., *Disaster: A Psychological Essay* (Glencoe, Ill.: The Free Press and The Falcon's Wing Press, 1957)

Young, M., "The Role of the Extended Family in a Disaster," *Human Relations*, Vol. VII (1954), pp. 383–391.

Works Relating to the Craze

Allen, W. W., and Avery, R. B., *California Gold Book* (San Francisco: Donohue & Henneberry, 1893)

Bain, R. C., *Convention Decisions and Voting Records* (Washington, D.C.: The Brookings Institution, 1960)

Bancroft, H. H., *History of California* (San Francisco: The History Company, 1888), Vol. VI.

Barber, B., and Lobel, L. S., "'Fashion' in Women's Clothes and the American Social System," *Social Forces*, Vol. 31 (1952), pp. 124–131.

Bell, Q., *On Human Finery* (London: The Hogarth Press, 1947)

Bergler, E., *Fashion and the Unconscious* (New York: Robert Brunner, 1953)

Bishop, J. B., *Our Political Drama: Conventions, Campaigns, Candidates* (New York: Scott-Thaw Co., 1904)

Burns, J. M., *John Kennedy: A Political Profile* (New York: Harcourt, Brace, 1960)

Clerget, P., "The Economic and Social Role of Fashion," *Annual Report of the Smithsonian Institution, 1913* (Washington, D.C.: Government Printing Office, 1914), pp. 755–765.

Cleveland, C. C., *The Great Revival in the West 1797–1805* (Chicago: University of Chicago Press, 1916)

Cobliner, W. G., "Feminine Fashion as an Aspect of Group Psychology: Analysis of Written Replies Received by Means of a Questionnaire," *Journal of Social Psychology*, Vol. 31 (1950), pp. 283–289.

Cole, A. H., "Agricultural Crazes: A Neglected Chapter in American Economic History," *American Economic Review*, Vol. 16 (1926), pp. 622–639.

Davenport, F. M., *Primitive Traits in Religious Revivals* (New York: Macmillan, 1910)

Bibliography

David, P. T., Goldman, R. M., and Bain, R. C., *The Politics of National Party Conventions* (Washington, D.C.: The Brookings Institution, 1960)

Davies, P. J., *Real Estate in American History* (Washington, D.C.: Public Affairs Press, 1958)

Dewey, D. R., "Wildcat Banks," *Encyclopaedia of the Social Sciences,* Vol. 2, pp. 454–456.

Dice, C. A., *The Stock Market* (New York: McGraw-Hill, 1926)

Duguid, C., *The Story of the Stock Exchange* (London: Grant Richards, 1901)

Emery, H. C., *Speculation on the Stock and Produce Exchanges of the United States*. Columbia University Studies in History, Economics, and Public Law, Vol. VII (New York: Columbia University, 1896)

Fallers, L. A., "A Note on the 'Trickle Effect,' " *Public Opinion Quarterly,* Vol. 18 (1954), pp. 314–321.

Farish, H. D., *The Circuit Rider Dismounts: A Social History of Southern Methodism 1865–1900* (Richmond, Va.: The Dietz Press, 1938)

Flugel, J. C., *The Psychology of Clothes* (London: Hogarth Press, 1930)

Gewehr, W. M., *The Great Awakening in Virginia, 1740–1790* (Durham: Duke University Press, 1930)

Gibson, T., *The Cycles of Speculation* (New York: The Moody Magazine and Book Co., 1917)

Goffman, E., "Symbols of Class Status," *British Journal of Sociology,* Vol. 2 (1951), pp. 294–304.

Gray, L. C., "Land Speculation," *Encyclopaedia of the Social Sciences,* Vol. 9, pp. 64–70.

Haberler, G., *Prosperity and Depression: A Theoretical Analysis of Cyclical Movements* (Lake Success, N.Y.: United Nations, 1946)

Handman, M., "Boom," *Encyclopaedia of the Social Sciences,* Vol. 2, pp. 638–641.

Hayes, S. P., "An Historical Study of the Edwardean Revivals," *American Journal of Psychology,* Vol. 13 (1902), pp. 550–574.

Hickernell, W. F., *Financial and Business Forecasting* (Bureau of Business Conditions: A Division of Alexander Hamilton Institute, 1928)

Hurlock, E. B., "Motivation in Fashion," *Archives of Psychology,* Vol. 17, No. 111 (1929–30), pp. 3–71.

——, *The Psychology of Dress: An Analysis of Fashion and its Motive* (New York: The Ronald Press, 1929)

Jack, N. K., and Schiffer, B., "The Limits of Fashion Control," *American Sociological Review,* Vol. 13 (1948), pp. 730–738.

Janney, J. E., "Fad and Fashion Leadership among Undergraduate Women," *Journal of Abnormal and Social Psychology,* Vol. 36 (1941), pp. 275–278.

Johnstone, J., and Katz, E., "Youth and Popular Music: A Study in the Sociology of Taste," *American Journal of Sociology,* Vol. 62 (1956–57), pp. 563–568.

Bibliography

Keller, C. R., *The Second Great Awakening in Connecticut* (New Haven: Yale University Press, 1942)

Kellett, E. E., *Fashion in Literature: A Study in Changing Taste* (London: George Routledge & Sons, 1931)

Kroeber, A. L., "On the Principle of Order in Civilization as Exemplified by Changes of Fashion," *American Anthropologist*, Vol. 21 (1919), pp. 235–263.

Loud, G. C., *Evangelized America* (New York: The Dial Press, 1928)

Mackay, C., *Extraordinary Popular Delusions and the Madness of Crowds* (Boston: L. C. Page & Company, 1932)

McLoughlin, W. G., Jr., *Modern Revivalism: Charles Grandison Finney to Billy Graham* (New York: Ronald Press, 1959)

Melville, L., *The South Sea Bubble* (London: Daniel O'Connor, 1921)

Meyersohn, R., and Katz, E., "Notes on a Natural History of Fads," *American Journal of Sociology*, Vol. 62 (1956–57), pp. 594–601.

Mindell, J., *The Stock Market: Basic Guide for Investors* (New York: B. C. Forbes & Sons, 1948)

Moos, M., and Hess, S., *Hats in the Ring* (New York: Random House, 1960)

Mottram, R. H., *A History of Financial Speculation* (London: Chatto & Windus, 1929)

Nystrom, P. H., *Economics of Fashion* (New York: Ronald Press, 1928)

Posthumus, N. W., "The Tulip Mania in Holland in the Years 1636 and 1637," *Journal of Economic and Business History*, Vol. 1 (1928–29), pp. 434–466.

Richardson, J., and Kroeber, A. L., "Three Centuries of Women's Dress Fashions: A Quantitative Analysis," *Anthropological Records*, Vol. 5, No. 2 (Berkeley: University of California Press, 1947), pp. 111–153.

Sakolski, A. M., *The Great American Land Bubble* (New York: Harper & Brothers, 1932)

Sapir, E., "Fashion," *Encyclopaedia of the Social Sciences*, Vol. 6, pp. 139–144.

Schnieder, H. W., "Religious Revivals," *Encyclopaedia of the Social Sciences*, Vol. 13, pp. 363–367.

Simmel, G., "Fashion," *International Quarterly*, Vol. 10 (1904–1905), pp. 130–155.

Stoddard, H. L., *Presidential Sweepstakes: The Story of Political Conventions and Campaigns* (New York: G. P. Putnam's Sons, 1948)

Sweet, W. W., *Religion in the Development of American Culture 1765–1840* (New York: Scribner, 1952)

———, *Revivalism in America: Its Origin, Growth and Decline* (New York: Charles Scribner's Sons, 1944)

———, *The Rise of Methodism in the West* (Nashville: Smith & Lamar, 1920)

Swinney, J. B., *Merchandising of Fashions* (New York: Ronald Press, 1942)

Bibliography

Taylor, B., *Eldorado; or, Adventures in the Path of Empire* (New York: G. P. Putnam & Sons, 1871)

Thiers, A., *The Mississippi Bubble: A Memoir of John Law* (New York: W. A. Townsend & Company, 1859)

Thorp, W. L., "Speculative Bubbles," *Encyclopaedia of the Social Sciences*, Vol. 3, pp. 24-27.

Tracy, J., *The Great Awakening: A History of the Revival of Religion in the time of Edwards and Whitefield* (Boston: Tappan & Dennet, 1842)

Vanderblue, H. B., "The Florida Land Boom," *The Journal of Land and Public Utility Economics*, Vol. III (1927), pp. 113-131 and 252-269.

Weigall, T. H., *Boom in Paradise* (New York: Alfred H. King, 1932)

Weisberger, B. A., *They Gathered at the River* (Boston: Little, Brown & Company, 1958)

White, S. E., *The Forty-Niners: A Chronicle of the California Trail and El Dorado* (New Haven: Yale University Press, 1921)

Williams, C. R., "The Welsh Revival, 1904-5," *British Journal of Sociology*, Vol. 3 (1952), pp. 242-259.

Wilson, N. C., *Silver Stampede; The Career of Death Valley's Hell Camp, Old Panamint* (New York: Macmillan, 1937)

Winslow, O. A., *Jonathan Edwards, 1703-1758* (New York: Macmillan, 1940)

Wiston-Glynn, A. W., *John Law of Lauriston* (Edinburgh: E. Saunders & Co., 1907)

Young, A. B., *Recurring Cycles of Fashion 1760-1937* (New York: Harper & Brothers, 1937)

WORKS RELATING TO THE HOSTILE OUTBURST

Ackerman, N. W., and Jahoda, M., *Anti-Semitism and Emotional Disorder: A Psychoanalytic Interpretation* (New York: Harper & Brothers, 1950)

Adamic, L., *Dynamite: The Story of Class Violence in America* (New York: The Viking Press, 1934)

Andrews, L. C., *Military Manpower* (New York: E. P. Dutton & Company, 1920)

Asbury, H., *The Gangs of New York: An Informal History of the Underworld* (Garden City, N.Y.: Garden City Publishing Co., 1928)

Baldwin, R. N., "Political Police," *Encyclopaedia of the Social Sciences*, Vol. 12, pp. 203-207.

Bartlett, R., "Anarchy in Boston," *The American Mercury*, Vol. 36 (1935), pp. 456-464.

Bargar, B. L., *The Law and Customs of Riot Duty* (Columbus, O.: Published by the Author, 1907)

Beloff, M., *Public Order and Popular Disturbances 1660-1714* (London: Oxford University Press, 1938)

Bernard, L. L., "Mob," *Encyclopaedia of the Social Sciences*, Vol. 10, pp. 552-554.

Bimba, A., *The Molly Maguires* (London: Martin Lawrence, 1932)

Bibliography

Bogardus, E. S., "A Race-Relations Cycle," *American Journal of Sociology*, Vol. 35 (1929-30), pp. 612-617.

Brearley, H. C., "The Pattern of Violence," in Couch W. T. (ed.), *Culture in the South* (Chapel Hill: University of North Carolina Press, 1934), pp. 678-692.

Brown, E., *Why Race Riots? Lessons from Detroit* (Public Affairs Pamphlet No. 87, 1944)

Bucher, R., "Blame and Hostility in Disaster," *American Journal of Sociology*, Vol. 62 (1956-57), pp. 467-475.

Caplovitz, D., and Rogers, C., "The Swastika Epidemic: A Preliminary Draft of a Report for the Anti-Defamation League," (Mimeographed, 1960)

Caughey, J. W., *Their Majesties the Mob* (Chicago: University of Chicago Press, 1960)

Chicago Commission on Race Relations, *The Negro in Chicago* (Chicago: University of Chicago Press, 1922)

Clark, K. B., "Group Violence: A Preliminary Study of the Attitudinal Pattern of its Acceptance and Rejection: a Study of the 1943 Harlem Riot," *Journal of Social Psychology*, S.P.S.S.I. Bulletin, Vol. 19 (1944), pp. 319-337.

——, and Barker, J., "The Zoot Effect in Personality: A Race Riot Participant," *Journal of Abnormal and Social Psychology*, Vol. 40 (1945), pp. 145-148.

Clinchy, E. R., *All in the Name of God* (New York: John Day, 1934)

Coleman, J. W., *The Molly Maguire Riots* (Richmond: Garrett & Massie, 1936)

Commission on Interracial Cooperation, *The Mob Still Rides. A Review of the Lynching Record, 1931-1935* (Atlanta: Commission on Interracial Cooperation, 1935)

Coxe, J. E., "The New Oreleans Mafia Incident," *Louisiana Historical Quarterly*, Vol. 20 (1937), pp. 1067-1110.

Cutler, J. E., *Lynch-law* (New York: Longmans, Green & Co., 1905)

Dahlke, H. O., "Race and Minority Riots—A Study in the Typology of Violence," *Social Forces*, Vol. 30 (1951-52), pp. 419-425.

Darvall, F. O., *Popular Disturbances and Public Order in Regency England* (London: Oxford University Press, 1934)

Davies, R. T., *Four Centuries of Witch-Beliefs* (London: Methuen, 1947)

Davies, H. B., "Industrial Policing," *Encyclopaedia of the Social Sciences*, Vol. 12, pp. 193-196.

de Castro, J. P., *The Gordon Riots* (London: Oxford University Press, 1926)

Dollard, J., Miller, N. E., Doob, L. W., Mowrer, O. H., and Sears, R.R., *Frustration and Aggression* (New Haven: Yale University Press, 1939)

Evans-Pritchard, E. E., *Witchcraft, Oracles and Magic among the Azande* (Oxford: at the Clarendon Press, 1958)

Fox, V., *Violence Behind Bars: An Explosive Report on Prison Riots in the United States* (New York: Vantage Press, 1956)

Bibliography

Frenkel-Brunswik, E., and Sanford, R. N., "Some Personality Correlates of Anti-Semitism," *The Journal of Psychology*, Vol. 20 (1945), pp. 271–291.

Gremley, W., "Social Control in Cicero," *British Journal of Sociology*, Vol. 3 (1952), pp. 322–338.

Grimshaw, A. D., "Urban Racial Violence in the United States: Changing Ecological Considerations," *American Journal of Sociology*, Vol. 66 (1960), pp. 109–119.

Guthrie, C. L., "Riots in Seventeenth Century Mexico City: A Study in Social History with Special Emphasis upon the Lower Classes," Ph.D. Dissertation, University of California, Berkeley, 1937.

Guzman, J. P., *Negro Year Book, 1947* (Tuskegee: Tuskegee Institute Department of Records and Research, 1947)

Gwynn, C. W., *Imperial Policing* (London: Macmillan, 1934)

Hartung, F. E., and Floch, M., "A Socio-psychological Analysis of Prison Riots: An Hypothesis," *Journal of Criminal Law, Criminology, and Police Science*, Vol. 47 (1956–57), pp. 51–57.

Heaton, J. W., "Mob Violence in the Late Roman Republic," *Illinois University Studies in the Social Sciences*, Vol. 23 (1938–39) (Urbana, Ill.: University of Illinois Press, 1939)

Hibbert, C., *King Mob: The Story of Lord George Gordon and the London Riots of 1780* (Cleveland: The World Publishing Company, 1958)

Hiller, E. T., *The Strike: A Study in Collective Action* (Chicago: University of Chicago Press, 1928)

Honigmann, J. J., "Witch-Fear in Post-Contact Kaska Society," *American Anthropologist*, Vol. 49 (1947), pp. 222–243.

Hook, S., "Violence," *Encyclopaedia of the Social Sciences*, Vol. 15, pp. 264–267.

Hovland, C. I., and Sears, R.R., "Minor Studies of Aggression: VI. Correlation of Lynchings with Economic Indices," *The Journal of Psychology*, Vol. 9 (1940), pp. 301–310.

Jordan, J., "Lynchers Don't Like Lead," *Atlantic Monthly*, Vol. 177 (Feb., 1946), pp. 103–108.

Kluckhohn, C., *Navaho Witchcraft* (Papers of the Peabody Museum of American Archaeology and Ethnology, Harvard University) (Cambridge, Mass.: The Museum, 1944), Vol. XXII—No. 2.

Knowles, K. G. J. C., " 'Strike-Proneness' and its Determinants," *American Journal of Sociology*, Vol. 60 (1954–55), pp. 213–229.

——, *Strikes—A Study in Industrial Conflict: With Special Reference to British Experience between 1911 and 1947* (Oxford: Basil Blackwell, 1952)

Krige, J. D., "The Social Function of Witchcraft," *Theoria: A Journal of the Arts Faculty, Natal University College*, Vol. I (1947), pp. 8–21. Reprinted in Lessa, W. A., and Vogt, E. Z. (eds.), *Reader in Comparative Religion* (Evanston, Ill.: Row, Peterson & Co., 1958), pp. 282–291.

Krugman, H. E., "The Role of Hostility in the Appeal of Communism in the United States," *Psychiatry*, Vol. 16 (1953), pp. 253–261.

Bibliography

Lambert, R. D., "Religion, Economics, and Violence in Bengal," *Middle East Journal*, Vol. IV (1950), pp. 307–328.

Lee, A. M., and Humphrey, N. D., *Race Riot* (New York: The Dryden Press, 1943)

Levinger, L. J., *Anti-Semitism Yesterday and Tomorrow* (New York: Macmillan, 1936)

Lohman, J. D., *The Police and Minority Groups* (Chicago: Chicago Park District, 1947)

Longley, R. S., "Mob Activities in Revolutionary Massachusetts," *New England Quarterly*, Vol. VI (1933), pp. 98–130.

Lowenthal, L., and Guterman, N., *Prophets of Deceit: A Study of the Techniques of the American Agitator* (New York: Harper & Brothers, 1949)

McGraw, P., and McGraw, W., *Assignment: Prison Riots* (New York: Henry Holt, 1954)

Martin, E. W., *The History of the Great Riots* (Philadelphia: National Publishing Company, 1877)

Mather, F. C., *Public Order in the Age of the Chartists* (Manchester: Manchester University Press, 1959)

Meier, N. C., Mennenga, G. H., and Stoltz, H. Z., "An Experimental Approach to the Study of Mob Behavior," *Journal of Abnormal and Social Psychology*, Vol. 36 (1941), pp. 506–524.

Mintz, A., "A Re-examination of Correlations between Lynchings and Economic Indices," *Journal of Abnormal and Social Psychology*, Vol. 41 (1946), pp. 154–160.

Murray, R. K., *Red Scare: A Study in National Hysteria 1919–1920* (Minneapolis: University of Minnesota Press, 1955)

Myers, G., *History of Bigotry in the United States* (New York: Random House, 1942)

Myers, R. C., "Anti-Communist Mob Action: A Case Study," *Public Opinion Quarterly*, Vol. 12 (1948), pp. 57–67.

Nadel, S. F., "Witchcraft in Four African Societies: An Essay in Comparison," *American Anthropologist*, Vol. 54 (1952), pp. 18–29.

Norton, W. J., "The Detroit Riots—and After," *Survey Graphic*, Vol. 32 (Aug., 1943), pp. 317–318.

Notch, F. K., *King Mob* (New York: Harcourt, Brace, & Co., 1930)

Ohlin, L. E., *Sociology and the Field of Corrections* (New York: Russell Sage Foundation, 1956)

Plummer, A., "The General Strike During One Hundred Years," *Economic Journal (Economic History Supplement)*, Vol. I (1926–29), pp. 184–204.

Pruden, D., "A Sociological Study of a Texas Lynching," *Studies in Sociology*, Vol. 1 (1936), pp. 3–9.

Raper, A. F., *The Tragedy of Lynching* (Chapel Hill: University of North Carolina Press, 1933)

Rich, B. M., *The Presidents and Civil Disorder* (Washington, D.C.: The Brookings Institution, 1941)

Bibliography

Rudé, G., *The Crowd in the French Revolution* (Oxford: at the Clarendon Press, 1959)

Saul, L. J., *The Hostile Mind: The Sources and Consequences of Rage and Hate* (New York: Random House, 1956)

Scott, J. F., and Homans, G. C., "Reflections on the Wildcat Strikes," *American Sociological Review*, Vol. 12 (1947), pp. 278-287.

Shay, F., *Judge Lynch: His First Hundred Years* (New York: Ives Washburn, 1938)

Smellie, K., "Riot," *Encyclopaedia of the Social Sciences*, Vol. 13, pp. 386-388.

Somerville, H. M., "Some Cooperating Causes of Negro Lynching," *North American Review*, Vol. 177 (1903), pp. 506-512.

Starkey, M. L., *The Devil in Massachusetts: A Modern Inquiry into the Salem Witch Trials* (New York: Alfred A. Knopf, 1949)

Turner, R. H., and Surace, S. J., "Zoot-Suiters and Mexicans: Symbols in Crowd Behavior," *American Journal of Sociology*, Vol. 62 (1956-57), pp. 14-20.

United States Congress. House of Representatives, *Memphis Riots and Massacres*, Report No. 101, 39th Congress, 1st Session, Ordered to be Printed, July 25, 1866.

United States War Department, War Plans Division, *Military Protection. United States Guards. The Use of Organized Bodies in the Protection and Defense of Property During Riots, Strikes, and Civil Disturbances* (Washington: Government Printing Office, 1919)

Veltford, H. R., and Lee, S. E., "The Cocoanut Grove Fire: A Study in Scapegoating," *Journal of Abnormal and Social Psychology*, Vol. 38 (1943), pp. 138-154 (Clinical Supplement).

Vittachi, T., *Emergency '58: The Story of the Ceylon Race Riots* (London: Andre Deutsch, 1958)

White, W. F., "The Eruption of Tulsa," *The Nation*, Vol. 112 (1921), pp. 909-910.

Wilson, M. H., "Witch Beliefs and Social Structure," *American Journal of Sociology*, Vol. 56 (1951), pp. 307-313.

Wood, S. A., *Riot Control* (Harrisburg, Pa.: The Military Service Publishing Company, 1952)

Work, M. N., *Negro Year Book, 1916-1917* (Tuskegee: The Negro Year Book Publishing Co., 1917)

——, *Negro Year Book, 1918-1919* (Tuskegee: The Negro Year Book Publishing Co., 1919)

——, *Negro Year Book, 1921-1922* (Tuskegee: The Negro Year Book Publishing Co., 1922)

WORKS RELATING TO THE NORM-ORIENTED MOVEMENT

Abell, A. I., *The Urban Impact on American Protestantism 1865-1900* (Cambridge, Mass.: Harvard University Press, 1943)

Anthony, K., *Feminism in Germany and Scandinavia* (New York: Henry Holt, 1915)

Bibliography

Arkwright, F., *The ABC of Technocracy* (New York: Harper & Brothers, 1933)

Babcock, J. O., "The Farm Revolt in Iowa," *Social Forces*, Vol. 12 (1934), pp. 369-373.

Beales, A. C. F., *The History of Peace: A Short Account of the Organised Movements for International Peace* (New York: The Dial Press, 1936)

Beals, C., *Brass-Knuckle Crusade: The Great Know-Nothing Conspiracy: 1820-1860* (New York: Hastings House, 1960)

Beard, M. R., *The American Labor Movement: A Short History* (New York: Macmillan, 1939)

Best, H., *Blindness and the Blind in the United States* (New York: Macmillan, 1934)

——, *The Deaf: Their Position in Society and the Provision for their Education in the United States* (New York: Thomas Y. Crowell, 1914)

Bestor, A. E., Jr., *Chautauqua Publications: An Historical and Bibliographical Guide* (Chautauqua, N.Y.: Chautauqua Press, 1934)

Bigelow, M. A., "Sex Education and Sex Ethics," *Encyclopaedia of the Social Sciences*, Vol. 14, pp. 8-13.

Bohn, F., "The Ku Klux Klan Interpreted," *American Journal of Sociology*, Vol. 30 (1925), pp. 385-407.

Buck, S. J., *The Agrarian Crusade: A Chronicle of the Farmer in Politics* (New Haven: Yale University Press, 1920)

Burgess, J. S., "The Study of Modern Social Movements as a Means for Clarifying the Process of Social Action," *Social Forces*, Vol. 22 (1943-44), pp. 271-275.

Cahill, M. C., *Shorter Hours: A Study of the Movement Since the Civil War*. Columbia University Studies in History, Economics, and Public Law, No. 380 (New York: Columbia University Press, 1932)

Carroll, M. R., *Labor and Politics: The Attitude of the American Federation of Labor toward Legislation and Politics* (Boston: Houghton Mifflin, 1923)

Chase, S., *Technocracy: An Interpretation* (New York: John Day Company and the Rider Press, 1933)

Cherrington, E. H., *The Evolution of Prohibition in the United States of America* (Westerville, Ohio: The American Issue Press, 1920)

Coupland, R., *The British Anti-Slavery Movement* (London: Thornton Butterworth, 1933)

Darrow, C., and Yarros, V. S., *The Prohibition Mania* (New York: Boni and Livewright, 1927)

Davis, J., *Contemporary Social Movements* (New York: The Century Co., 1930)

Desmond, H. J., *The A.P.A. Movement* (Washington: The New Century Press, 1912)

——, *The Know-Nothing Party* (Washington: The New Century Press, 1904)

Eckstein, H., *Pressure Group Politics: The Case of the British Medical Association* (Stanford: Stanford University Press, 1960)

Bibliography

Evans, I. L., "Agrarian Movements. V. Eastern Europe. East Central Europe and the Balkan Countries," *Encyclopaedia of the Social Sciences*, Vol. 1, pp. 502–504.

Fairholme, E. G., and Pain, W., *A Century of Work for Animals: The History of the R.S.P.C.A., 1824–1924* (London: John Murray, 1924)

Farmer, H., "The Economic Background of Southern Populism," *The South Atlantic Quarterly*, Vol. 29 (1930), pp. 77–91.

Faulkner, H. U., *Politics, Reform and Expansion 1890–1900* (New York: Harper & Brothers, 1959)

Filler, L., *The Crusade Against Slavery 1830–1860* (New York: Harper & Brothers, 1960)

Fleming, H. C., "Resistance Movements and Racial Desegregation," *The Annals of the American Academy of Political and Social Science*, Vol. 304 (1956), pp. 44–52.

Frederick, J. G. (ed.), *For and Against Technocracy: A Symposium* (New York: Business Bourse, 1933)

Garfinkel, H., *When Negroes March: The March on Washington Movement in the Organizational Politics for FEPC* (Glencoe, Ill.: The Free Press, 1959)

Green, A. W., and Milnick, E. "What Has Happened to the Feminist Movement?" in A. W. Gouldner (ed.), *Studies in Leadership: Leadership and Democratic Action* (New York: Harper & Brothers, 1950)

Greer, T. H., *American Social Reform Movements: Their Pattern Since 1865* (New York: Prentice-Hall, 1949)

Gusfield, J. R., "Social Structure and Moral Reform: A Study of the Woman's Christian Temperance Union," *American Journal of Sociology*, Vol. 61 (1955–56), pp. 221–232.

Hammond, J. L., "Agrarian Movements. III. Great Britain," *Encyclopaedia of the Social Sciences*, Vol. 1, pp. 495–497.

Hankins, F. H., "Birth Control," *Encyclopaedia of the Social Sciences*, Vol. 2, pp. 559–565.

Haynes, F. E., *Third Party Movements Since the Civil War with Special Reference to Iowa* (Iowa City: The State Historical Society of Iowa, 1916)

Haynes, G. H., "The Causes of Know-Nothing Success in Massachusetts," *American Historical Review*, Vol. 3 (1897–1898), pp. 67–82.

Heberle, R., "Observations on the Sociology of Social Movements," *American Sociological Review*, Vol. 14 (1949), pp. 346–357.

———, *Social Movements: An Introduction to Political Sociology* (New York: Appleton-Century-Crofts, 1951)

Hicks, J. D., *The Populist Revolt: A History of the Farmers' Alliance* (Minneapolis: The University of Minnesota Press, 1931)

Hopkins, C. H., *The Rise of the Social Gospel in American Protestantism 1865–1915* (New Haven: Yale University Press, 1940)

Horn, S. F., *Invisible Empire: The Story of the Ku Klux Klan 1866–1871* (Boston: Houghton Mifflin, 1939)

Howe, F. C., "Agrarian Movements. IV. Western Europe. Denmark," *Encyclopaedia of the Social Sciences*, Vol. 1, pp. 501–502.

Bibliography

Hurt, P., "The Rise and Fall of the 'Know Nothings' in California," *Quarterly of the California Historical Society*, Vol. IX (1930), pp. 16–49, 99–128.

Johnson, A., "Agrarian Movements. I. Introduction," *Encyclopaedia of the Social Sciences*, Vol. 1, pp. 489–492.

Jordan, H. D., "The Political Methods of the Anti-Corn Law League," *Political Science Quarterly*, Vol. 42 (1927), pp. 58–76.

Kendrick, B. B., "Agrarian Movements. VI. United States," *Encyclopaedia of the Social Sciences*, Vol. 1, pp. 508–511.

Key, V. O., Jr., *Politics, Parties, and Pressure Groups* (fourth edition) (New York: Thomas Y. Crowell, 1958)

Kile, O. M., *The Farm Bureau Movement* (New York: Macmillan, 1921)

King, C. W., *Social Movements in the United States* (New York: Random House, 1956)

Klingberg, F. J., "Abolition," *Encyclopaedia of the Social Sciences*, Vol. 1, pp. 369–372.

Krout, J. A., *The Origins of Prohibition* (New York: Alfred A. Knopf, 1925)

Lasswell, H. D., Casey, R. D., and Smith, B. L., *Propaganda and Promotional Activities: An Annotated Bibliography* (Minneapolis: University of Minnesota Press, 1935)

Lee, A. M., "Techniques of Social Reform: An Analysis of the New Prohibition Drive," *American Sociological Review*, Vol. 9 (1944), pp. 65–77.

Leiserson, A., "Opinion Research and the Political Process: Farm Policy an Example," *Public Opinion Quarterly*, Vol. 13 (1949), pp. 31–38.

Lemmon, S. M., "The Ideology of the 'Dixiecrat' Movement," *Social Forces*, Vol. 30 (1951–52), pp. 162–171.

Lewinson, P., *Race, Class, & Party: A History of Negro Suffrage and White Politics in the South* (London: Oxford University Press, 1932)

Lewis, R., "Americanization," *Encyclopaedia of the Social Sciences*, Vol. 2, pp. 33–34.

Lindeman, E. C., *The Community: An Introduction to the Study of Community Leadership and Organization* (New York: Association Press, 1921)

Lipset, S. M., *Agrarian Socialism: The Coöperative Commonwealth Federation in Saskatchewan* (Berkeley and Los Angeles: University of California Press, 1950)

Louis, P., "Agrarian Movements. II. Classical Antiquity," *Encyclopaedia of the Social Sciences*, Vol. 1, pp. 492–495.

McCormick, T. C., "Cotton Acreage Laws and the Agrarian Movement," *Southwestern Social Science Quarterly*, Vol. 12 (1931–32), pp. 296–304.

McCrea, R. C., *The Humane Movement: A Descriptive Survey* (New York: Columbia University Press, 1910)

McKelvey, B., *American Prisons: A Study in American Social History Prior to 1915* (Chicago: University of Chicago Press, 1936)

Bibliography

Maier, N. R. F., "The Role of Frustration in Social Movements," *Psychological Review*, Vol. 49 (1942), pp. 586–599.

Mangel, E. R., "Agrarian Movements. V. Eastern Europe. Poland and Lithuania. Latvia and Esthonia," *Encyclopaedia of the Social Sciences*, Vol. 1, pp. 507–508.

Mason, B., "The Townsend Movement," *Southwestern Social Science Quarterly*, Vol. 35 (1954), pp. 36–47.

Meadows, P., "An Analysis of Social Movements," *Sociology and Social Research*, Vol. 27 (1942–43), pp. 223–228.

Mecklin, J. M., *The Ku Klux Klan: A Study of the American Mind* (New York: Harcourt, Brace and Company, 1924)

Messinger, S. L., "Organizational Transformation: A Case Study of a Declining Social Movement," *American Sociological Review*, Vol. 20 (1955), pp. 3–10.

Munro, W. B., "Short Ballot Movement," *Encyclopaedia of the Social Sciences*, Vol. 14, pp. 43–44.

Nash, J. F., "Playgrounds," *Encyclopaedia of the Social Sciences*, Vol. 12, pp. 161–163.

Neuberger, R. L., and Low, K., "The Old People's Crusade," *Harper's Magazine*, Mar., 1936, pp. 426–438.

Odegard, P. H., *Pressure Politics: The Story of the Anti-Saloon League* (New York: Columbia University Press, 1928)

Owings, C., *Women Police: A Study of the Development and Status of the Women Police Movement* (New York: Frederick H. Hitchcock, 1925)

Perlman, S., *A History of Trade Unionism in the United States* (New York: Macmillan, 1937)

———, "Short Hours Movement," *Encyclopaedia of the Social Sciences*, Vol. 14, pp. 44–46.

Podmore, F., *Robert Owen* (London: Hutchinson, 1906)

Rainwater, C. E., *The Play Movement in the United States: A Study of Community Recreation* (Chicago: University of Chicago Press, 1922)

Roche, J. P., and Sachs, S., "The Bureaucrat and the Enthusiast: An Exploration of the Leadership of Social Movements," *Western Political Quarterly*, Vol. 8 (1955), pp. 248–261.

Schlesinger, A. M., *The American as Reformer* (Cambridge: Harvard University Press, 1950)

Schmeckebier, L. F., *History of the Know Nothing Party in Maryland* (Baltimore: The Johns Hopkins Press, 1899)

Schultz, W. J., "Animal Protection," *Encyclopaedia of the Social Sciences*, Vol. 2, pp. 61–63.

Senning, J. P., "The Know-Nothing Movement in Illinois," *Journal of the Illinois State Historical Society*, Vol. 7 (1914), pp. 7–26.

Stedman, M. S., Jr., and Stedman, S. W. *Discontent at the Polls: A Study of Farmer and Labor Parties 1827–1948* (New York: Columbia University Press, 1950)

Strachey, R., *Struggle: The Stirring Story of Woman's Advance in England* (New York: Duffield, 1930)

Bibliography

Studenski, P., "Chambers of Commerce," *Encyclopaedia of the Social Sciences*, Vol. 3, pp. 325-329.

Sutherland, E. H., "The Diffusion of Sexual Psychopath Laws," *American Journal of Sociology*, Vol. 56 (1950-51), pp. 142-148.

Taylor, C. C., "Country Life Movement," *Encyclopaedia of the Social Sciences*, Vol. 4, pp. 497-499.

Tufts, J. H., "Liberal Movements in the United States—Their Methods and Aims," *The International Journal of Ethics*, Vol. 46 (1936), pp. 253-275.

Tyler, A. F., *Freedom's Ferment: Phases of American Social History to 1860* (Minneapolis: University of Minnesota Press, 1944)

van der Kroef, J. M., "Social Movements and Economic Development in Indonesia," *American Journal of Economics and Sociology*, Vol. 14 (1954-55), pp. 123-138.

Ware, N. J., *The Labor Movement in the United States 1860-1895* (New York: D. Appleton & Company, 1929)

Waterman, W. C., *Prostitution and its Repression in New York City 1900-1931* (New York: Columbia University Press, 1932)

Winslow, C. E. A., "The Mental Hygiene Movement (1908-33) and Its Founder," Supplement to Beers, C. W., *A Mind that Found Itself* (Garden City, N.Y.: Doubleday, 1953), pp. 303-322.

Woodward, L. E., "The Supplement to Mental Hygiene Movement—More Recent Developments [to 1948]", Supplement to Beers, C. W., *A Mind that Found Itself* (Garden City, N.Y.: Doubleday, 1953), pp. 323-371

Young, A. N., *The Single Tax Movement in the United States* (Princeton: Princeton University Press, 1916)

WORKS RELATING TO THE VALUE-ORIENTED MOVEMENT

Abel, T., "The Pattern of a Successful Political Movement," *American Sociological Review*, Vol. 2 (1937), pp. 347-352.

———, *Why Hitler Came to Power* (New York: Prentice-Hall, 1938)

Aberle, D. F., "The Prophet Dance and Reactions to White Contact," *Southwestern Journal of Anthropology*, Vol. 15 (1959), pp. 74-83.

Adams, B., *The Theory of Social Revolutions* (New York: Macmillan, 1914)

Allan, C. H., "Marching Rule: A Nativistic Cult of the British Solomon Islands," *South Pacific*, Vol. 5 (1951), pp. 79-85.

Almond, G. A., "Introduction: A Functional Approach to Comparative Politics," in Almond, G. A., and Coleman, J. S. (eds.), *The Politics of the Developing Areas* (Princeton: Princeton University Press, 1960)

Apter, D. E., *The Gold Coast in Transition* (Princeton: Princeton University Press, 1955)

Arendt, H., *The Origins of Totalitarianism* (New York: Meridian Books, 1958)

Bibliography

Atkins, G. G., *Modern Religious Cults and Movements* (New York: Fleming H. Revell, 1923)

Balandier, G., "Messianismes et Nationalismes en Afrique Noire," *Cahiers Internationaux de Sociologie*, Vol. 14 (1953), pp. 41-65.

Ball, W. M., *Nationalism and Communism in East Asia* (Melbourne: Melbourne University Press, 1952)

Ballou, A., *History of the Hopedale Community* (Lowell, Mass.: The Vox Populi Press, 1897)

Barber, B., "Acculturation and Messianic Movements," *American Sociological Review*, Vol. 6 (1941), pp. 663-669.

——, "A Socio-cultural Interpretation of the Peyote Cult," *American Anthropologist*, Vol. 43 (1941), pp. 673-675.

Barber, E. G., *The Bourgeoisie in 18th Century France* (Princeton: Princeton University Press, 1955)

Bax, E. G., *Rise and Fall of the Anabaptists* (London: Swan Sonnenschein & Co., 1903)

Becker, H., "Current Sacred-Secular Theory and Its Development,'" in Becker, H., and Boskoff, A. (eds.), *Modern Sociological Theory in Continuity and Change* (New York: The Dryden Press, 1957)

Bellah, R. N., "Religious Aspects of Modernization in Turkey and Japan," *American Journal of Sociology*, Vol. 64 (1958), pp. 1-5.

Belshaw, C. S., "Recent History of Medeo Society," *Oceania*, Vol. 22 (1951), pp. 1-23.

——, "The Significance of Modern Cults in Melanesian Development," *The Australian Outlook*, Vol 4 (1950), pp. 116-125.

Berndt, R. M., "A Cargo Movement in the Eastern Central Highlands of New Guinea," *Oceania*, Vol. XXIII (1952-53), pp. 40-65, 137-158, 202-234.

Beynon, E. D., "The Voodoo Cult among Negro Migrants in Detroit," *American Journal of Sociology*, Vol. 43 (1937-38), pp. 894-907.

Binkley, R. C., "An Anatomy of Revolution," *The Virginia Quarterly Review*, Vol. 10 (1934), pp. 502-514.

Boisen, A. T., "Economic Distress and Religious Experience: A Study of the Holy Rollers," *Psychiatry*, Vol. 2 (1939), pp. 185-194.

Braden, C. S., *These Also Believe: A Study of Modern American Cults and Minority Religious Movements* (New York: Macmillan, 1956)

Brewer, E. D. C., "Sect and Church in Methodism," *Social Forces*, Vol. 30 (1951-52), pp. 400-408.

Brinton, C., *A Decade of Revolution: 1789-1799* (New York: Harper & Brothers, 1934)

——, *The Anatomy of Revolution* (New York: Vintage Books, 1958)

Brooks, J. G., *American Syndicalism: The I.W.W.* (New York: Macmillan, 1913)

Brotz, H. M., "Negro 'Jews' in the United States," *Phylon*, Vol. 13 (1952), pp. 324-337.

Brown, W. O., "Race Consciousness among South African Natives," *American Journal of Sociology*, Vol. 40 (1935), pp. 569-581.

Bibliography

Bullock, A., *Hitler: A Study in Tyranny* (New York: Bantam Books, 1958)

Burckhardt, J., *Force and Freedom: Reflections on History* (New York: Pantheon Books, 1943)

Carr, A., *Juggernaut: The Path of Dictatorship* (New York: The Viking Press, 1939)

Carr, E. H., *Nationalism and After* (London: Macmillan, 1945)

Chaffee, G. E., "The Isolated Religious Sect as an Object for Social Research," *American Journal of Sociology*, Vol. 35 (1929–30), pp. 618–630.

Chapman, C. E., "The Age of the Caudillos: A Chapter in Hispanic American History," *The Hispanic American Historical Review*, Vol. 12 (1932), pp. 281–300.

Clark, E. T., *The Small Sects in America* (Nashville: Cokesbury Press, 1937)

Clark, R. T., *The Fall of the German Republic* (London: George Allen & Unwin, 1935)

Clegg, E., *Race and Politics: Partnership in the Federation of Rhodesia and Nyasaland* (London: Oxford University Press, 1960)

Cohn, N., "Medieval Millenarism and its Bearing on the Comparative Study of Millenarian Movements," paper delivered at the Conference on Religious Movements of a Millenarian Character, under the auspices of the Editorial Committee of Comparative Studies in Society and History at the University of Chicago, April 8–9, 1960 (mimeographed).

——, *The Pursuit of the Millennium* (New York: Harper & Brothers, 1961)

Coleman, J. S., *Nigeria: Background to Nationalism* (Berkeley and Los Angeles: University of California Press, 1958)

Collins, J. M., "The Indian Shaker Church: A Study of Continuity and Change in Religion," *Southwestern Journal of Anthropology*, Vol. 6 (1950), pp. 399–411.

Colton, E., *Four Patterns of Revolution* (New York: Association Press, 1935)

Crook, W. H., *Communism and the General Strike* (Hamden, Conn.: The Shoe String Press, 1960)

Cutten, G. B., *The Psychological Phenomenon of Christianity* (New York: Charles Scribner's Sons, 1908)

——, *Speaking with Tongues* (New Haven: Yale University Press, 1927)

Daniels, R. F., "The Kronstadt Revolt of 1921: A Study in the Dynamics of Revolution," *American Slavic and East European Review*, Vol. 10 (1951), pp. 241–254.

Davidson, J. W., "The Changing Political Role of Pacific Islands' Peoples," *South Pacific*, Vol. 6 (1952), pp. 380–385.

Desai, A. R., *Social Background of Indian Nationalism* (Bombay: Popular Book Depot, 1954)

Dickey, S., "Some Economic and Social Conditions of Asia Minor Affecting the Expansion of Christianity," in Case, S. J. (ed.), *Studies in Early Christianity* (New York: Century, 1928), pp. 393–416.

Bibliography

Dohrman, H. T., *California Cult: The Story of "Mankind United"* (Boston: Beacon Press, 1958)

Dowd, D. L., "Art as National Propaganda in the French Revolution," *Public Opinion Quarterly*, Vol. 15 (1951), pp. 532–546.

du Bois, C., *Social Forces in Southeast Asia* (Minneapolis: University of Minnesota Press, 1949)

——, *The 1870 Ghost Dance* (Berkeley: University of California Press, 1939)

du Bois, W. E. B. (ed.), *The Negro Church*, Atlanta University Publication No. 8 (Atlanta, Ga.: The Atlanta University Press, 1903)

Eckstein, H., "Internal Wars: A Taxonomy," Internal War Project—Memorandum No. 2 (Mimeographed, 1960)

Edwards, L. P., *The Natural History of Revolution* (Chicago: University of Chicago Press, 1927)

Eisenstadt, S. N., "Sociological Aspects of Political Development in Underdeveloped Countries," *Economic Development and Cultural Change*, Vol. V (1957), pp. 289–307.

Elkin, A. P., "Native Reaction to an Invading Culture and its Bearers—with Special Reference to Australia," *Proceedings of the Seventh Pacific Science Congress of the Pacific Science Association* (Feb.–Mar., 1949) (Christchurch: The Pegasus Press, 1953), Vol. VIII, pp. 37–42.

——, "The Reaction of Primitive Races to the White Man's Culture: A Study in Culture-Contact," *The Hibbert Journal*, Vol. 35 (1936–37), pp. 537–545.

Ellwood, C. A., *The Psychology of Human Society* (New York: D. Appleton & Co., 1925)

——, "A Psychological Theory of Revolutions," *American Journal of Sociology*, Vol. 11 (1905–1906), pp. 49–59.

Elsbree, W. H., *Japan's Role in Southeast Asian Nationalist Movements 1940 to 1945* (Cambridge, Mass.: Harvard University Press, 1953)

Emerson, R., Mills, L. A., and Thompson, V., *Government and Nationalism in Southeast Asia* (New York: Institute of Pacific Relations, 1942)

Farquhar, J. N., *Modern Religious Movements in India* (New York: Macmillan, 1915)

Fauset, A. H., *Black Gods of the Metropolis* (Philadelphia: Publications of the Philadelphia Anthropological Society, 1944)

Ferguson, C. W., *The Confusion of Tongues: A Review of Modern Isms* (London: William Heinemann, 1929)

Festinger, L., Riecken, H. W., and Schachter, S., *When Prophecy Fails* (Minneapolis University of Minnesota Press, 1956)

Fiszman, J. R., "The Appeal of Maoism in Pre-industrial, Semicolonial Political Cultures," *Political Science Quarterly*, Vol. 74 (1959), pp. 71–88.

Florinsky, M. T., *The End of the Russian Empire* (New Haven: Yale University Press, 1931)

——, *Fascism and National Socialism* (New York: Macmillan, 1938)

Frazier, E. F., "The Garvey Movement," *Opportunity*, Vol. IV (1926), pp. 346–348.

Bibliography

Gardiner, S. R., *The First Two Stuarts and the Puritan Revolution* (New York: Charles Scribner's Sons, 1898)

Gerth, H. H., "The Nazi Party: Its Leadership and Composition," in Merton, R. K., Gray, A. P., Hockey, B., and Selvin, H. C. (eds.), *Reader in Bureaucracy* (Glencoe, Ill.: The Free Press, 1952), pp. 100–113.

Gillespie, J., *Algeria: Rebellion and Revolution* (New York: Frederick A. Praeger, 1960)

Gillin, J. L., "A Contribution to the Sociology of Sects," *American Journal of Sociology*, Vol. 16 (1910–11), pp. 236–252.

Golovine, N. N., *The Russian Army in the World War* (New Haven: Yale University Press, 1931)

Goodwin, G., and Kaut, C., "A Native Religious Movement among the White Mountain and Cibicue Apache," *Southwestern Journal of Anthropology*, Vol. 10 (1954), pp. 385–404.

Gottschalk, L., "Causes of Revolution," *American Journal of Sociology*, Vol. 50 (1944), pp. 1–8.

Greenlaw, R. W. (ed.), *The Economic Origins of the French Revolution: Poverty or Prosperity?* (Boston: D.C. Heath, 1958)

Gross, F., *The Seizure of Political Power in a Century of Revolutions* (New York: Philosophical Library, 1958)

Guiart, J., " 'Cargo Cults' and Political Evolution in Melanesia," *South Pacific*, Vol. 5 (1951), pp. 128–129.

———, "Culture Contact and the 'John Frum' Movement on Tanna, New Hebrides," *Southwestern Journal of Anthropology*, Vol. 12 (1956), pp. 105–116.

———, "Forerunners of Melanesian Nationalism," *Oceania*, Vol. 22 (1951), pp. 81–90.

Haring, C. E., "The Chilean Revolution of 1931," *The Hispanic American Historical Review*, Vol. 13 (1933), pp. 197–203.

Harnack, A., *The Expansion of Christianity in the First Three Centuries* (translated and edited by James Moffatt) (New York: G. P. Putnam's Sons, 1904)

Harrison, S. E., *India: The Most Dangerous Decades* (Princeton: Princeton University Press, 1960)

Hawley, F., "The Keresan Holy Rollers: An Adaptation to American Individualism," *Social Forces*, Vol. 26 (1948), pp. 272–280.

Hawthorn, H. B. (ed.), *The Doukhobors of British Columbia* (Vancouver: The University of British Columbia and J. M. Dent & Sons, 1955)

Heiden, K., *A History of National Socialism* (New York: Alfred A. Knopf, 1935)

Herskovits, M. J., *Acculturation: The Study of Culture Contact* (Gloucester, Mass.: Peter Smith, 1958)

Hertzler, J. O., "The Causal and Contributory Factors of Dictatorship," *Sociology and Social Research*, Vol. 24 (1939–40), pp. 3–21.

———, "Crises and Dictatorships," *American Sociological Review*, Vol. 5 (1940), pp. 157–169.

Bibliography

Hillquit, M., *History of Socialism in the United States* (New York: Funk & Wagnalls Co., 1903)

Hinds, W. A., *American Communities* (Oneida, N.Y.: Office of the American Socialist, 1878)

Hobsbawm, E. J., *Primitive Rebels: Studies in Archaic Forms of Social Movement in the 19th and 20th Centuries* (Manchester: Manchester University Press, 1959)

Hodgkin, T., *Nationalism in Colonial Africa* (New York: New York University Press, 1957)

Holland, W. L. (ed.), *Asian Nationalism and the West: A Symposium Based on Documents and Reports of the Eleventh Conference Institute of Pacific Relations* (New York: Macmillan, 1953)

Holloway, M., *Heavens on Earth: Utopian Communities in America 1680-1880* (London: Turnstile Press, 1951)

Holt, J. B., "Holiness Religion: Cultural Shock and Social Reorganization," *American Sociological Review*, Vol. 5 (1940), pp. 740-747.

Hopper, R. D., "The Revolutionary Process: A Frame of Reference for the Study of Revolutionary Movements," *Social Forces*, Vol. 28 (1950), pp. 270-279.

Hoover, C. B., *Germany Enters the Third Reich* (New York: Macmillan, 1933)

Hoshor, J., *God in a Rolls-Royce* (New York: Hillman-Curl, 1936)

Hunter, R., *Revolution: Why, How, When?* (New York: Harper & Brothers, 1940)

Hyndman, H. M., *The Evolution of Revolution* (New York: Boni and Liveright, 1921)

Johnson, B., "A Critical Appraisal of the Church-Sect Typology," *American Sociological Review*, Vol. 22 (1957), pp. 88-92.

Jones, R. J., "A Comparative Study of Religious Cult Behavior Among Negroes with Special Reference to Emotional Group Conditioning Factors," *The Howard University Studies in the Social Sciences*, Vol. II, No. 2 (Washington, D.C.: The Graduate School for the Division of the Social Sciences, Howard University, 1939)

Kahin, G. McT., *Nationalism and Revolution in Indonesia* (Ithaca: Cornell University Press, 1952)

Kastein, J., *The Messiah of Ismir* (New York: The Viking Press, 1931)

Keesing, F. M., "Cultural Dynamics and Administration," *Proceedings of the Seventh Pacific Congress of the Pacific Science Association* (Feb.-Mar., 1949) (Christchurch: The Pegasus Press, 1953), Vol. VIII, pp. 102-117.

Kellett, E. E., *The Story of Dictatorship from the Earliest Times Till To-day* (London: Ivor Nicholson & Watson, 1937)

Kennedy, R., "The Colonial Crisis and the Future," in R. Linton (ed.), *The Science of Man in the World Crisis* (New York: Columbia University Press, 1952), pp. 306-346.

Knox, R. A., *Enthusiasm: A Chapter in the History of Religion* (New York: Oxford University Press, 1950)

Bibliography

Kohn, H., "Messianism," *Encyclopaedia of the Social Sciences*, Vol. 10, pp. 356–363.

——, *Revolutions and Dictatorships* (Cambridge, Mass.: Harvard University Press, 1939)

Krader, L., "A Nativistic Movement in Western Siberia," *American Anthropologist*, Vol. 58 (1956), pp. 282–292.

Kroeber, A. L., *Handbook of the Indians of California* (Washington: Government Printing Office, 1925)

Kuper, H., *The Uniform of Colour: A Study of White-Black Relationships in Swaziland* (Johannesburg: Witwatersrand University Press, 1947)

Le Bon, G., *The Psychology of Revolution* (New York: G. P. Putnam's Sons, 1913)

Lederer, E., *State of the Masses: The Threat of the Classless Society* (New York: W. W. Norton, 1940)

Lefebvre, G., *The Coming of the French Revolution* (New York: Vintage Books, 1959)

Lesser, A., *The Pawnee Ghost Dance Hand Game: A Study of Cultural Change* (New York: Columbia University Press, 1933)

Lieuwen, E., "The Military: A Revolutionary Force," *Annals of the American Academy of Political and Social Science*, Vol. 334 (1961), pp. 30–40.

Lindsay, C., *The Natives are Restless* (Philadelphia: J. B. Lippincott, 1960)

Linton, R., "Nativistic Movements," *American Anthropologist*, Vol. 45 (1943), pp. 230–240.

Lockwood, G. B., *The New Harmony Movement* (New York: D. Appleton & Company, 1907)

Loomis, C. P., and Beegle, J. A., "The Spread of German Nazism in Rural Areas," *American Sociological Review*, Vol. 11 (1946), pp. 724–734.

Lorwin, L. L., "Direct Action," *Encyclopaedia of the Social Sciences*, Vol. 5, pp. 155–158.

Lumby, E. W. R., *The Transfer of Power in India 1945–7* (London: George Allen & Unwin, 1954)

MacGregor, G., with the collaboration of Hassrick, R. B., and Henry, W. E., *Warriors Without Weapons: A Study of the Society and Personality Development of the Pine Ridge Sioux* (Chicago: University of Chicago Press, 1946)

Mair, L. P., *Australia in New Guinea* (London: Christophers, 1948)

——, *Native Policies in Africa* (London: George Routledge & Sons, 1936)

Mannheim, K., *Man and Society in an Age of Reconstruction* (London: Kegan Paul, 1940)

Mathison, R. R., *Faiths, Cults and Sects of America: From Atheism to Zen* (Indianapolis: Bobbs-Merrill, 1960)

Matossian, M., "Ideologies of Delayed Industrialization," *Economic Development and Cultural Change*, Vol. VI (1958), pp. 217–228.

Matthews, R., *English Messiahs: Studies of Six English Religious Pretenders 1656–1927* (London: Methuen, 1936)

Bibliography

May, L. C., "The Dancing Religion: A Japanese Messianic Sect," *Southwestern Journal of Anthropology*, Vol. 10 (1954), pp. 119-137.

Merriman, R. B., *Six Contemporaneous Revolutions* (Oxford: at the Clarendon Press, 1938)

Menon, V. P., *The Transfer of Power in India* (Princeton: Princeton University Press, 1957)

Meusel, A., "Revolution and Counter-revolution," *Encyclopaedia of the Social Sciences*, Vol. 13, pp. 367-376.

Middendorp, W., "The Administration of the Outer Provinces of the Netherlands Indies," in Schrieke, B. (ed.), *The Effect of Western Influence on Native Civilizations in the Malay Archipelago* (Batavia, Java: G. Kolff & Co., 1929), pp. 34-70.

Mooney, J., "The Ghost-Dance Religion and the Sioux Outbreak of 1890," *Fourteenth Annual Report of the Bureau of Ethnology*, Part 2 (Washington: Government Printing Office, 1896)

Munch, P. A., "The Peasant Movement in Norway," *British Journal of Sociology*, Vol. 5 (1954), pp. 63-77.

Neumann, S., "The Rule of the Demagogue," *American Sociological Review*, Vol. 13 (1948), pp. 487-498.

——, "The Structure and Strategy of Revolution: 1848 and 1948," *Journal of Politics*, Vol. 11 (1949), pp. 532-544.

Nichol, F. D., *The Midnight Cry* (Takoma Park, Washington, D.C.: Review and Herald Publishing Association, 1944)

Niebuhr, H. R., "Fundamentalism," *Encyclopaedia of the Social Sciences*, Vol. 6, pp. 526-527.

——, "Sects," *Encyclopaedia of the Social Sciences*, Vol. 13, pp. 624-631.

——, *The Social Sources of Denominationalism* (Hamden, Conn.: The Shoe String Press, 1954)

Nordhoff, C., *The Communistic Societies of the United States* (New York: Harper & Brothers, 1875)

Noyes, J. H., *History of American Socialisms* (Philadelphia: J. B. Lippincott & Co., 1870)

Obolensky, D., *The Bogomils: A Study in Balkan Neo-Manichaeism* (Cambridge: University Press, 1948)

O'Dea, T. F., *The Mormons* (Chicago: University of Chicago Press, 1957)

O'Donnell, E., *Strange Cults and Secret Societies of Modern London* (London: Philip Allan, 1934)

Opler, M. K., "Two Japanese Religious Sects," *Southwestern Journal of Anthropology*, Vol. 6 (1950), pp. 69-78.

Ortega y Gasset, J., *The Revolt of the Masses* (New York: W. W. Norton, 1932)

"Paliau Movement in Manus" (Extract from the Report of the United Nations Visiting Mission to Trust Territories in the Pacific on New Guinea, Aug. 15, 1950), *South Pacific*, Vol. 4 (1950), pp. 207-208.

Parker, R. A., *The Incredible Messiah* (Boston: Little, Brown, 1937)

Petrullo, V., *The Diabolic Root: A Study of Peyotism, the New Indian Religion, among the Delawares* (Philadelphia: University of Pennsylvania Press, 1934)

Bibliography

Pfautz, H. W., "The Sociology of Secularization: Religious Groups," *American Journal of Sociology*, Vol. 61 (1955-56), pp. 121-128.

Pinson, K. S., "Chassidism," *Encyclopaedia of the Social Sciences*, Vol. 3, pp. 354-357.

Pitt-Rivers, G. H. L.-F., *The Clash of Culture and the Contact of Races* (London: George Routledge & Sons, 1927)

Pope, L., *Millhands and Preachers: A Study of Gastonia* (New Haven: Yale University Press, 1958)

Price, A. G., *White Settlers and Native Peoples* (Melbourne: Georgian House and Cambridge: University Press, 1949)

Pye, L. W., "The Politics of Southeast Asia," in Almond, G. A., and Coleman, J. S. (eds.), *The Politics of the Developing Areas* (Princeton: Princeton University Press, 1960), pp. 65-152.

Radin, P., "A Sketch of the Peyote Cult of the Winnebago: A Study in Borrowing," *Journal of Religious Psychology*, Vol. 7 (1914), pp. 1-22.

Ramos, A., *The Negro in Brazil* (translated by R. Pattee) (Washington: The Associated Publishers, 1951)

Reeve, B., and Reeve, H., *Flying Saucer Pilgrimage* (Amherst, Wisc.: Amherst Press, 1957)

Reeve, S. A., *The Natural Laws of Social Convulsion* (New York: E. P. Dutton & Co., 1933)

Rivlin, B., "Unity and Nationalism in Libya," *Middle East Journal*, Vol. III (1949), pp. 31-44.

Roberts, S. H., *The House that Hitler Built* (London: Methuen, 1939)

Robertson, P., *Revolutions of 1848: A Social History* (New York: Harper & Brothers, 1960)

Rossi, A. [*pseud.*], *The Rise of Italian Fascism 1918-1922* (translated by Peter and Dorothy Wait) (London: Methuen, 1938)

Rosenstiel, A., "An Anthropological Approach to the Mau Mau Problem," *Political Science Quarterly*, Vol. 68 (1953), pp. 419-432.

Salisbury, R. F., "An 'Indigenous' New Guinea Cult," *The Kroeber Anthropology Society Papers*, No. 18, Spring, 1958, pp. 67-78.

Schuman, F. L., *The Nazi Dictatorship* (New York: Alfred A. Knopf, 1935)

Scully, F., *Behind the Flying Saucers* (New York: Henry Holt, 1950)

Sears, C. E., *Days of Delusion* (Boston: Houghton Mifflin, 1924)

Selbie, W. B., *Nonconformity: Its Origin and Progress* (London: Williams and Norgate, 1912)

Selznick, P., *The Organizational Weapon: A Study of Bolshevik Strategy and Tactics* (New York: McGraw-Hill, 1952)

Senturia, J. J., "Political Conspiracy," *Encyclopaedia of the Social Sciences*, Vol. 4, pp. 238-241.

Shambaugh, B. M. H., *Amana That Was and Amana That Is* (Iowa City: The State Historical Society of Iowa, 1932)

Shepperson, G., "The Politics of African Church Separatist Movements in British Central Africa, 1892-1916," *Africa*, Vol. XXIV, No. 3 (1954), pp. 233-246.

Bibliography

Shils, E., "Ideology and Civility: On the Politics of the Intellectual," *The Sewanee Review*, Vol. LXVI, No. 3 (Summer, 1958), pp. 450–480.

Sinclair, T., "The Nazi Party Rally at Nuremberg," *Public Opinion Quarterly*, Vol. 2 (1938), pp. 570–583.

Slotkin, J. S., *The Peyote Religion: A Study in Indian-White Relations* (Glencoe, Ill.: The Free Press, 1956)

Smith, C. H., *The Story of the Mennonites* (Berne, Indiana: Mennonite Book Concern, 1941)

Sorokin, P. A., *The Sociology of Revolution* (Philadelphia: J. B. Lippincott, 1925)

Spearman, D., *Modern Dictatorship* (New York: Columbia University Press, 1939)

Spencer, H. R., "Coup d'Etat," *Encyclopaedia of the Social Sciences*, Vol. 4, pp. 508–510.

Spier, L., "The Ghost Dance of 1870 among the Klamath of Oregon," *University of Washington Publications in Anthropology*, Vol. 2, No. 2, pp. 39–56, Nov., 1927 (Seattle: University of Washington Press, 1927)

———, L., Suttles, W., and Herskovits, M. J., "Comment on Aberle's Thesis of Deprivation," *Southwestern Journal of Anthropology*, Vol 15 (1959), pp. 84–88.

Stephens, H. M., *A History of the French Revolution* (New York: Charles Scribner's Sons, 1886)

Steward, J. H., "The Changing American Indian," in Linton, R. (ed.), *The Science of Man in the World Crisis* (New York: Columbia University Press, 1952), pp. 282–305.

Stroup, H. H., *The Jehovah's Witnesses* (New York: Columbia University Press, 1945)

Sundkler, B. G. M., *Bantu Prophets in South Africa* (London: Lutterworth Press, 1948)

Swift, L., *Brook Farm: Its Members, Scholars, and Visitors* (New York: Macmillan, 1900)

Taine, H. A., *The Ancient Regime* (New York: Peter Smith, 1931)

Tawney, R. H., *Religion and the Rise of Capitalism* (New York: New American Library, 1954)

Tocqueville, A. de., *The Old Regime and the Revolution* (translated by John Bonner) (New York: Harper & Brothers, 1856)

Troeltsch, E., *The Social Teaching of the Christian Churches* (translated by Olive Wyon) (London: George Allen & Unwin, 1931)

Trotsky, L., *The History of the Russian Revolution* (translated by Max Eastman) (Ann Arbor: University of Michigan Press, 1957)

Turberville, A. S., *Medieval Heresy and the Inquisition* (London: Crosby Lockwood and Son, 1920)

Tuveson, E. L., *Millennium and Utopia: A Study in the Background of the Idea of Progress* (Berkeley: University of California Press, 1949)

Ulam, A. B., *The Unfinished Revolution: An Essay on the Sources of Influence of Marxism and Communism* (New York: Random House, 1960)

Bibliography

Voget, F. W., "The American Indian in Transition: Reformation and Accommodation," *American Anthropologist*, Vol. 58 (1956), pp. 249-263.

Wallace, A. F. C., "New Religions among the Delaware Indians, 1600-1900," *Southwestern Journal of Anthropology*, Vol. 12 (1956), pp. 1-20.

———, "Revitalization Movements," *American Anthropologist*, Vol. 58 (1956), pp. 264-281.

Wallis, W. D., *Messiahs: Their Role in Civilization* (Washington: American Council on Public Affairs, 1943)

Watkins, F. M., *The Failure of Constitutional Emergency Powers under the German Republic* (Cambridge, Mass.: Harvard University Press, 1939)

Weiner, M., "The Politics of South Asia," in Almond, G. A., and Coleman, J. S. (eds.), *The Politics of the Developing Areas* (Princeton: Princeton University Press, 1960), pp. 153-246.

Wertheim, W. F., *Indonesian Society in Transition* (The Hague: W. van Hoeve, 1956)

Whitley, O. R., "The Sect-to-Denomination Process in an American Religious Movement: The Disciples of Christ," *Southwestern Social Science Quarterly*, Vol. 36 (1955), pp. 275-281.

Wilson, B. R., "An Analysis of Sect Development," *American Sociological Review*, Vol. 24 (1959), pp. 3-15.

———, "The Pentecostalist Minister: Role Conflicts and Status Contradictions," *American Journal of Sociology*, Vol. 64 (1959), pp. 494-504.

Woodman, D., *The Republic of Indonesia* (London: The Cresset Press, 1955)

Woodson, C. G., *The History of the Negro Church* (Washington: Associated Publishers, 1921)

Worsley, P. M., "Millenarian Movements in Melanesia," *The Rhodes-Livingstone Journal. Human Problems in British Central Africa*. No. XXI (March, 1957), pp. 18-31.

———, *The Trumpet Shall Sound: A Study of 'Cargo' Cults in Melanesia* (London: MacGibbon & Kee, 1957)

Yoder, D., "Current Definitions of Revolution," *American Journal of Sociology*, Vol. 32 (1926-27), pp. 433-441.

INDEX

Abel, T., 128
action, defined, 24
Adams, B., 330
agricultural crazes, 189, 191, 192
Allport, F. A., 107 fn., 253 fn.
Allport, G. W., and Postman, 10–11, 81 fn., 247–248
Almond, G., 278
ambiguity, 92, 135 fn.
  control of, 88–89
  structured and unstructured, 86–89
American Land Bubble, 190
American Protective Assn., 63, 115–116, 119, 295, 299–300
analytic vs temporal priority, 19–20, 134, 147 ff., 168–169, 277–278
anti-left hysteria, 235–236
Anti-Semitism, 104, 106, 108, 116, 257–259
anxiety, 89–92
  defined, 89
  and panic, 146–147
  structuring of, 90–91
  in terms of components of action 89–90
audience, 75–76, 255

Bagehot, W., 138, 159, 167, 178, 212
Bales, R. F., 23
bandwagon, 170, 172, 180 ff., 192–196, 202 ff., 213 ff. (*see* craze)
Barber, B., 13
battlefield, with relation to panic, 136, 139, 141, 153–154, 160, 161, 165, 168
Bell, Q., 21
Bellah, R. N., 320–321
Beloff, M., 232
Belshaw, C. S., 345–346
Benedict, R., 97, 99
Bernard, L. L., 48
Berndt, R. M., 346 fn.
Bishop, J. B., 182
Blumer, H., 2 fn., 6–8, 9, 73 fn., 267
Bogardus, E. A., 171, 231 fn., 257, 267

Bohn, F., 300
boom, 15, 170–171, 176, 179–180, 189–192, 202 ff., 212–213 ff., 218–219, 311 (*see* craze)
Brinton, C., 18, 79, 340
British Revolution, 322
Brown, R., 2, 5–6, 9, 155 fn.
bubble, 171, 206, 213 (*see* craze)
Bucher, R., 107 fn., 224, 228
Bull, N., 91 fn.
Burckhardt, J., 337, 370–371

Cantril, H., 138, 142, 144, 146 fn., 160, 166, 223
Caplovitz, D. and Rogers, C., 257 ff.
Cargo cults, 340, 346
Carr, L. J., 10
ceremonials, 73–75, 107
charismatic authority, 180 ff.,
  charismatic leadership, 355–356
Chase, S., 114
Cherrington, E. H., 303–304
Chicago Commission on Race Relations, 255–356, 263–264, 268
Chicago riot of 1919, 240–241
Christensen, A., 104–105
Clark, E. T., 314–315, 317, 373
cleavage, 20, 229–231, 241, 247 ff., 279, 291
Cohn, N., 330, 357–358
Cole, A. H., 189, 191, 192
Coleman, J. S., 308
collective behavior, the nature of, 67–68
  accepting or rejecting propositions about, 385–387
  bases for classifying, 5–12
  compared with other types of behavior, 23, 73–78
  and components of action 45–46, 67 ff.
  defined, 8–9, 71, 73
  determinants, 12–18
  difficulties in analyzing, 3–4
  elementary forms, 7

Index

as generalized behavior, 71–73
generalized beliefs, 71 ff.
generating propositions about, 384–385
hysterical beliefs, 71 ff.
and other forms of behavior, 387
relation to components of action, 45–46, 73
relation to social change, 73
short-circuiting, 71 ff.
social control, 73
state of research on, 3–4
and strain, 48–49 ff.
synonyms for, 2–3
two sets of organizing constructs, 383–384
types, 2
types of beliefs, 83
wish-fulfillment beliefs, 71 ff.
communitarian experiments, 356–357, 363–364
components of social action, 9, 23–46, 90–94, 129–130, 383 ff.
and concrete social action, 31–32
generalization of, 69–71
hierarchical relations among, 32–34, 49 ff.
illustrations of, 30–31
individual attitudes toward, 29–30
internal organization of each, 34–40
mobilization of motivation, 24, 27–28
norms, 24, 26–27
reconstitution of, 67–71
situational facilities, 24, 28
strain, 49–51 ff.
structure of, 42–45
usage in study of collective behavior, 45–46
values, 24–26
Conrad, A. H., 14 fn.
contagion, 7
in hostile outburst, 257
in panic, 155 ff.
Country Life Movement, 274, 279–280
Coupland, R., 294
craze, 2, 72, 101, 170–221
agricultural, 189 ff.
bandwagon, 171–172, 180 ff., 192–196, 202 ff., 213 ff.
boom, 170, 179–180, 189–192, 202 ff., 213 ff.
charismatic authority, 180 ff.
comparison with panic, 218–219
control of the boom, 218–219
control of other crazes, 219–220
control through leadership, 218–219
crystallization and spread of specific belief, 205–210
defined, 170–171
economic sphere, 171–172, 176–180, 206, 211 ff., 215 ff.
expressive sphere, 172–173
fad, 172–173, 197
fashion, 172–173, 184–187, 207–208, 211, 214
fashion cycle, 196–198, 202 ff., 217
leadership, 210–212
mobilization for action, 210–221
occurrence, 171–175
political sphere, 171–172, 180–184, 206–207, 211 ff.
precipitating factors, 203–205
"real" and "derived" phases, 173, 212 ff.
religious sphere, 173–175, 187–188
revivalism, 173–175, 198–201, 202–203 ff.
social control, 218–220
speculative phase, 212–215
structural conduciveness, 175–188
structural strain, 188–201
symbolization of status, 184–187, 196 ff.
turning point, 215–220
value-added process, 175 ff.
wish-fulfillment fantasy, 201–203
crime, 77
crowd, 108, 170–171, 260 ff.
aggressive, 257
French Revolution, 260, 344
types, 7
(*see* hostile outburst)
cult, 123–125, 334, 340, 345, 348–349, 345

Dahlke, O., 19, 234
Danzig, E. R., *et al.*, 160
Darvall, F. O., 232–233, 239 fn., 240, 263
David, P. T., *et al.*, 193 fn., 194 fn.
Davis, K., 350
Dawson, C. A., 18
Demerath, N. J., 140–141
denominational pluralism, 336
depression of 1929, 162–164

429

Index

Desai, A. R., 309, 362-363
Desmond, H. J., 115, 119
Detroit race riots, 81
Dickey, S., 326
disaster
  and ambiguity, 86
  hostile outburst, 223-224, 228, 245
  natural history, 18-19
  and panic, 136, 139, 160
  premonitions of, 84
  types, 10 fn.
Dixicrat movement, 110, 114, 119
Dollard, J., et al., 107 fn.
Durkheim, E., 48, 91

Edwards, L. P., 318, 348
Eisenstadt, S., 122 fn., 127
Etlinge, L., 141, 161

fad, 172-173, 197
  natural history, 19, 197 (see craze)
Farago, L. (ed.), 158
Faris, R. E. L., 214
Farmers' Alliance, 76, 110, 275 ff., 302
Farquhar, J. N., 341
Fascism, Italian, 372-373
fashion, 15, 172-173, 207-208, 211, 214 (see craze)
fashion cycle, 172-173, 184 ff., 196-198, 202 ff., 217 (see craze)
Father Divine Peace Mission, 123-125, 348-349
Fauset, A. H., 354
Feminist Movement, 273-274, 305
Festinger, L., et al., 100 fn.
Fleming, H. C., 285, 308
Flugel, J. C., 185, 198
flying saucer cult, 334
flying saucer scare, 142, 150, 159, 160-161
Foreman, P. B., 86, 141, 151-152, 156
Form, W. H., and Nosow, S., et al., 165, 166
French Revolution, 242, 245-246, 253, 260, 265, 322, 331, 343-344, 349, 354, 377-378
Fritz, C. E., and Williams, H. B., 136, 245
Fülöp-Miller, R., 143-144

Galbraith, J. K., 107, 163, 191, 213, 218, 219, 287

Gaster, T. H., 107
Gault, R. H., 240
Gayer, A. D., et al., 191
generalized beliefs, 16, 79 ff, 202 ff., 384 ff.
  and collective behavior, 79-80
  defined, 8
  hostile, 100-109
  and hostility, 83, 85, 107-108
  hysterical, 71-72, 83, 84-95
  norm-oriented, 83, 109-120
  and norm-oriented movement, 109-111, 292-294
  and panic, 133
  and preparation for action, 82 ff.
  and reduction of ambiguity, 81-82
  and short-circuiting process, 71-73, 82, 90, 92, 101 ff.
  and strain, 81
  transmissibility, 84
  types, 83 ff.
  value-added, 83 ff., 111 ff.
  value-oriented, 83, 120-130
  wish-fulfillment, 71-72, 83, 85, 94-100, 108
Gerth, H., and Mills, C. W., 73
Gettys, W. E., 18
Ghost Dance, 125-126, 327, 342, 345, 366
Gibson, T., 147
Gillin, J. L., 320, 324, 341
Ginsberg, M., 15 fn.
Gray, L. C., 177-178, 179
Green, A. W., and Milnick, E., 305
Greenback movement, 110, 119
Gremley, W., 264
Grimshaw, A. D., 241
Grinker, R. J., and Spiegel, J. P., 142, 168
Gross, F., 276
Guiart, J., 340
Guthrie, C. L., 239
Gwynn, C. W., 262-263, 268

Handlin, O., 288-289, 299, 301
Handman, M., 179, 211, 215
Hardy, C. O., 87
Harnack, A., 336-337
Harvey, O. J., 85
Heberle, R., 110, 274-275
Henry George's single tax movement, 110, 284
Hertzler, J. O., 50 fn., 333

Index

Hicks, J. D., 286, 302–303, 311–312
Hiller, E. T., 294–295
Hocking, W. E., 165
Hollingworth, H. L., 255
Holt, J. B., 322
Hook, S., 261
hostile beliefs, 101–109
  ambiguity, 104
  anxiety, 104–105
  assignment of responsibility to agents, 105–106
  characteristics of, 101
  hostility, 107–108
  scapegoating, 107
  short-circuiting, 101–102 ff., 107
  and value-added, 101 ff.
  wedge-driving rumor, 101
  wish-fulfillment, 108
hostile outbursts, 222–269
  as adjuncts of larger-scale social movements, 226–227
  communication, accessibility to objects of attack, and ecology, 240–241
  and components of action, 241–247
  curve, 257–261
  defined, 226
  difference among terms, 227
  disaster, 223–224, 228, 245
  generalized aggression, 248–249
  hostile beliefs, 247–248, 252–253
  leadership, 254–255
  lynching, 75
  mobilization for action, 253–261
  mobs, 255 ff.
  organization, 255–257
  precipitating factors, 249–252
  presence of channels for expressing grievances, 231–240
  race riots, 234, 241–247, 255–256, 263–264, 268
  "real" and "derived" phase, 259–261
  salient issues, 224–227
  scapegoating, 223, 235 ff.
  social control, 261–269
  spread, 257–261
  structural conduciveness, 224, 227–241
  structural strain, 224 ff., 241–247
  structure of responsibility, 228–231
  value-added process, 253 ff.
hostility, 83
Humanitarian movement, 273

hysterical beliefs, 71–72, 83, 84–95, 100–101, 150
  ambiguity, 85, 86–89, 92
  anxiety, 85, 89–92
  "bogey rumor," 90
  components of, 85
  defined, 84
  examples of, 84–85
  fear, 150–153
  and panic, 133
  redefinition of situation, 85
  value-added process, 85, 91 ff.

ideology, 8–81
Iklé, F. C., and Kincaid, H. V., 136
individual deviance, 78
Indonesian nationalism, 367–369
Institute for Propaganda analysis, 76
interaction
  and collective behavior, 10
  in panic, 153–157
internal revolution
  Naziism, 128–129, 373–376
Invasion from Mars broadcast, 137–138, 142, 160, 166, 223, 263

Janis, I. L., 224
Janney, J. E., 197
Johnson, A., 279

Kahin, G. McT., 268
Kartman, B., and Brown, L., (eds.), 167 fn.
Katz, D., and Lazarsfeld, P., 207
Kennedy, R., 326–327
Kerr, C., et al., 238
Key, V. O., Jr., 290
Killian, L. M., 140
Kluckhohn, C., 25–26
Knapp, R. H., 80
Knight, F. H., 85 fn., 87
Know-nothingism, 63, 116, 283 ff., 295, 299 ff.
Krader, L., 327
Kris, E., 86
Kronstadt Revolt of 1921, 324
Ku Klux Klan, 116, 272, 284 fn., 300

Labor movement, 273, 383 ff., 304
Lang, K., and Lang, G., 2
LaPiere, R. T., 2 fn., 74 fn., 132, 133 fn., 140, 151 fn., 164, 170, 202
  and Farnsworth, P. R., 108

Index

leadership, 253
  in craze, 210–212
  in hostile outburst, 254–255
  in norm-oriented movement, 297–298
  in panic, 161–164
  in value-oriented movement, 355–356
LeBon, G., 79–80, 260, 372
Lee, A. M., and Humphrey, N. D., 239, 249 fn.
Lefebvre, G., 377
Lesser, A., 342
Linebarger, P. M. A., 141
Loomis, C. G., 97
Lowenthal, L., and Guterman, N., 104, 106, 108
Luddite riots, 239–249, 263
lynching, 75, 106, 108

MacDougall, W., 20
Mackay, C., 96–97, 216
Malinowski, B., 95, 97
mania, 170 (*see* craze)
Marett, R. H., 98 fn.
Marshall, S. L. A., 136, 139, 153–154, 160, 162
Martin, E. D., 20
Marxism–Leninism, 348, 350
mass movement, 170 (*see* norm-oriented and value-oriented movements)
Mather, F. C., 259–260 fn.
Matossian, M., 217
May, L. C., 336
McDougall, W., 152–153
McLoughlin, W. G., Jr., 174, 201, 209
Mecklin, J. M., 63 fn., 290
Meerloo, A. M., 79, 132, 141
Melville, 222 fn.
Menzel, D. H., 159
Messianic movements, 13, 170, 345
Meyer, J. R., 14 fn.
Meyersohn, R., and Katz., D., 19, 197
millenarian movements, 122, 323–325, 330, 338, 357–358, 366, 367
Mintz, A., 137 fn.
Mississippi Bubble, 99, 190–192, 216, 218, 222–223
mob, 7, 48, 108, 226, 240 ff., 260 ff.
  French Revolution, 344
  lynching, 106
  race riot, 255–256
  (*see* hostile outburst)

mobilization for action, 17
  in craze, 210–221
  for flight, 133, 153–157
  in hostile outburst, 253–261
  in norm-oriented movement, 296–306
  in value-oriented movement, 355–364
mobilization of motivation
  as component of social action, 24, 27–28
  seven levels of specificity, 39–40
Mooney, J., 126
Moore, W. E., 146
Moos, M., and Hess, S., 196 fn.
Mottram, R. H., 178 fn.

Namasivayam, S., 309
nationalist movements, 122 fn., 127–128, 272, 309, 323, 326–329, 343, 349–350, 354, 358–359, 362–363, 367 ff.
native Americanism, 116–117
nativistic movements, 125–127, 283, 338 fn.
natural history, 18–20
Naziism, 128–129, 158
Nichol, F. D., 354
Niebuhr, H. R., 325–326
normative strain
  synonyms for, 59
norm-oriented beliefs, 83, 109–120
  ambiguity arising from strain, 112
  anxiety and identification of responsible agents, 112–115
  magic and omnipotence, 117–119
  and social movements, 109–111
  value-added, 111–112
  vision of "cure" through normative reconstitution, 115–117
norm-oriented movement, 270–312
  channels of agitation, 281, 285
  components of action, 287–292
  defined, 270
  directions of development after success or failure, 305–306
  growth of generalized beliefs, 292–294
  lack of opportunities for other outbursts, 285–286
  leadership, 297–298
  mobilization for action, 296–306

Index

and more general social movements, 273-274
and other collective outbursts, 271-273
possibility of communication, 286-287
precipitating factors, 294-296
"real" and "derived" phases, 298-301
social control, 306-310
structural conduciveness, 278-287
structural possibility of demanding normative changes alone, 278-281
structural strain, 287-292
success or failure of specific tactics, 302
types of organizations, 274-277
value-added sequence, 277-278 ff.
norms
as components of social action, 24, 26-27
defined, 27
seven levels of specificity, 37-38
Norton, W. J., 82 fn.
Noyes, J. H., 356-357
Nystrom, P. H., 20-21, 173, 205 fn.

Ohlin, L. E., 236-237, 254
Overton, J. H., 265

panic, 9, 15, 101, 131-169
anxiety, 146-147 ff.
beliefs, 143-144
clarifications, 134-135
components of action, 158 ff.
contagion, 153-157
cultural and individual differences in definition of panic situations, 143-146
curve of reactions, 155-156
defined, 131, 132, 154
determinants, 12-13
facilities and control, 158-161
fear, 150-153
hysterical belief, 133, 143-144
interaction patterns, 153-157
leadership, 161-164
miscellaneous factors, 145-146
mobilization for flight, 133, 153-157
morale, 145
norms and control, 164-167
organization and control, 161-163
personality variables, 144-145

physical condition, 145
precipitating factors, 133-134, 147-150, 160-161
prevention and control, 157-168
"real" and "derived" phases, 154 ff.
social control, 133-134
structural conduciveness, 133-134, 135-143, 159
structural strain, 133, 140-143, 159-160
suggestion, 152-153
termination and aftermath, 156-157
value-added process, 132 ff., 157 ff., 168 ff.
values and control, 167-168
Park, R. E., 2 fn.
and Burgess, E. W., 142-143 fn.
Parsons, T., 23, 24, 35 fn. 334 fn.
parties, 274 ff., 282-283, 333
peace movement, 273
Penrose, L. S., 84, 210
Perkins, D. W., 147
Perlman, S., 283
Peyote religion, 78, 327, 366
Phantom Anesthetist of Mattoon, Ill., 156-157
physical contours of collective behavior, 9-10
Populist movement, 76, 286, 302 ff., 311-312
Prasad, J., 81-82
precipitating factors, 16-17
in craze, 203-205
in hostile outburst, 249-252
in norm-oriented movement, 294-296
in panic, 133-134, 147-150, 160-161
in value-oriented movement, 352-355
Price, A. G., 328, 329
Prince, S. H., 78
prohibition, 114-115, 282, 283, 303-304
propaganda, 76-77
anti-Semitic, 106 ff.
psychological analysis of collective behavior, 11-12, 20-21
public, 7
public opinion, 76

Quarantelli, E. L., 89-91, 131, 136-137, 140, 147-148 fn.

Index

Raper, A. F., 106
"real" and "derived" phases, 154 ff.
   craze, 212–215
   hostile outburst, 257–261
   norm-oriented movement, 298–301
   panic, 154 ff.
   value-oriented movement, 356–357
Reformation, 187, 315, 330, 371
reform movement, 15 (*see* norm-oriented movement)
   and norm-oriented beliefs, 109 ff.
revival, religious, 173–175, 198–201, 202 ff., 208–210, 212, 214–215, 217 ff.
revolutionary movement, 15–16, 354 (*see* value-oriented movement)
   natural history, 18
Rich, B. M., 266
Rickman, J., 143
riot, 16, 17, 72, 234 ff., 239 ff., 251 ff., 263 ff.
   French revolution, 242
   natural history, 19
   prison, 236–237 ff., 251–252
   race, 81–82, 234, 240–245, 254–256, 263–264, 268
   zoot-suit, 105–106
   (*see* hostile outburst)
risks, 86–88
Roche, J. P., and Sachs, S., 297
Ross, E. A., 171
Rudé, G., 242, 253, 260
rumor, 80–83, 108
   "bogey", 84, 90–91
   distortions of, 100 fn.
   "pipe-dream", 94, 98–99
   in violent outbursts, 247–248
   wedge-driving, 101
Russian revolution, 376–377

Sakolski, A. M., 190
Schlesinger, A. M., 57, 296
Schneider, H. W., 173–174
Schuler, E. A., and Parenton, V. J., 143 fn.
Scott, W. D., 76 fn.
sects, 200, 314–315, 317 ff., 324 ff., 335 ff., 359–360
Sherif, M., 85
Shils, E. A., 23–24, 122
Simmel, G., 196
situational facilities
   as components of social action, 24, 28
   generalization of, 69–71
   seven levels of specificity, 40–42
Slotkin, J. S., 327 fn., 366
social control, 17, 73, 384
   and craze, 218–220
   hostile outbursts, 261–269
   norm-oriented movement, 306–310
   panic, 133
   value-oriented movement, 364–379
social gospel movement, 112, 119, 209 fn., 290
social movement, 7–8, 74–75, 277, 286 ff.
   and hostile outbursts, 227
   natural history, 18
   and norm-oriented beliefs, 109 ff.
   types, 8
   (*see* norm-oriented and value-oriented movements)
social system, 24
Sorel, G., 262
Sorokin, P., 330
South Sea Bubble, 206, 216–217, 218, 222
Spiegel, J. P., 138 fn.
Stanner, W. E. H., 346
Stephens, H. M., 245
Stoddard, H. L., 172, 194
Storms, G., 98
Strachey, R., 304
Strauss, A., 12–13, 145 fn.
Strecker, E. A., 108
structural conduciveness, 15, 383 ff.
   as condition for panic, 133, 135–143
   in craze, 175–188
   in hostile outbursts, 224, 227–241
   indeterminancy, 133
   in norm-oriented movement, 278–287
   possibility of communication, 139–140
   possibility of strain, 135–136
   possibility of withdrawal from danger, 136–139
   in value-oriented movement, 319–338
structural reorganization
   general nature, 67–71
structural strain, 15–16, 47–66, 69–71, 384

Index

and collective behaviour, 48–49, 65–66
and components of social action, 49–51, 64–66
and craze, 188, 201
defined, 47
as determinant of social action, 47
hostile outburst, 48–49, 241–247
and mobilization of motivation, 54–59
and norm-oriented movement, 287–292
and norms, 59–62
and panic, 133, 140 ff.
and situational facilities, 51–54
synonyms for, 47–48
and types of beliefs, 83
and values, 62–64
and value-oriented movement, 338–347
suffrage movement, 304
suggestion
  in panic, 152–153
superstition, 80–81
Sutherland, E. H., 114, 307

Tannenbaum, F., 75
Taylor, C. C., 274, 279–280 fn.
technocracy, 110, 114, 116, 118–120, 293 fn.
temporal characteristics of collective behavior, 9–10
Tocqueville, A. de, 61, 331, 349
Torrance, E. P., 161
Townsend Movement, 110, 114, 117–118, 271, 291, 293 fn., 305
Troeltsch, E., 342–343
Trotsky, L., 322
tulip mania, 191, 216
Turberville, A. S., 321
Turner, R. H., 312 fn.
  and Killian, L. M., 2 fn., 74, 82 fn., 170–171
  and Surace, S. J., 101, 105–106

Ulam, A. B., 350

value-added process, 80, 82, 84, 85, 92 ff., 111–112, 121–123, 382 ff.
and craze, 175 ff.
example from economics, 13–14
and explanation, 14
in hostile outburst, 253 ff.
and natural history, 18–20
in norm-oriented movement, 277–278 ff.
and panic, 32 ff., 157 ff.
in value-oriented movement, 316 ff.
value-oriented beliefs, 83, 120–130
crystallization of, 348–352
distinction between religious and secular, 314 ff.
examples of, 120–121
illustration of themes in value-oriented movements, 123–129
value-added, 121–123 ff.
value-oriented movement, 313–381
availability of means to express grievances, 324–334
bases of disunity and instability, 361–364
breakdown of party systems, 333–334
among colonially dominated, 326–329, 367 ff.
and components of action, 338 ff.
crystallization of value-oriented beliefs, 348–352
definition, 313
differentiation of value-system from other components of action, 320–324, 338 ff.
dissemination of beliefs, 352
effects of permanent repression, 365–367
effects of repression followed by weakening of effectiveness, 367–379
governmental inflexibility, 330–332
inclusiveness, 313
inflexibility in new revolutionary regimes, 332–333
institutionalization of, 359–361
insulation and isolation, 334–337
leadership, 355–356
major lines of variability among, 313–318
mobilization for action, 355–364 380
model for containment, 364–365
among persecuted minorities, 329–330
among politically disinherited, 325–326
possible results of, 315–316
possibilities of communication, 337–338

Index

value-oriented movements (*cont.*)
  precipitating factors, 352–355
  "real" and "derived" aspects, 356–357
  relation to revolution, 318–319
  relation to violence, 319
  similarities and differences among, 316 fn.
  social control, 364, 379, 380
  structural conduciveness, 319–338, 347, 379–380
  structural strain, 338–347, 380
  success or failure of specific tactics, 358–359
  syncretism, 351–352
  themes in, 123–129
  value-added process, 316 ff.
values
  as components of social action, 24, 25–26
  defined, 25
  seven levels of specificity, 35–37
  and strain, 62–64
Van Doorn-Janssen, M. J., 139
Vaught, E., 155
Veltford, H. R., and Lee, S. E., 223–224
Vittachi, T., 265
Von Wiese, L., and Becker, H., 315

Wallace, A. F. C., 132 fn.
Watkins, F. M., 374–376
Weber, M., 28 fn., 180–182, 355
Weiner, M., 338
Wertheim, W. F., 368
White, S. E., 190
Whiteman, L., and Lewis, S. L., 117–118
Wilson, B., 200, 335, 359–360
wish-fulfillment beliefs, 71–72, 83, 94–100, 201–203
  ambiguity, 94, 96–97
  anxiety, 95, 97
  characteristics of, 94–96
  generalized, 97–100
  magic, 94–100
  pipe dream rumors, 94
  rumor, 98–99
  short-circuiting, 95–98
  value-added process, 94 ff.
Wiston-Glynn, A. W., 99, 222–223
Wolfenstein, M., 131, 145
worker-socialist movements, 74–75
Worsley, P. M., 323 ff., 338, 340–341

Young, K., 172, 210–211

zoot suit riots, 105–106